SAINTS and SALVATION

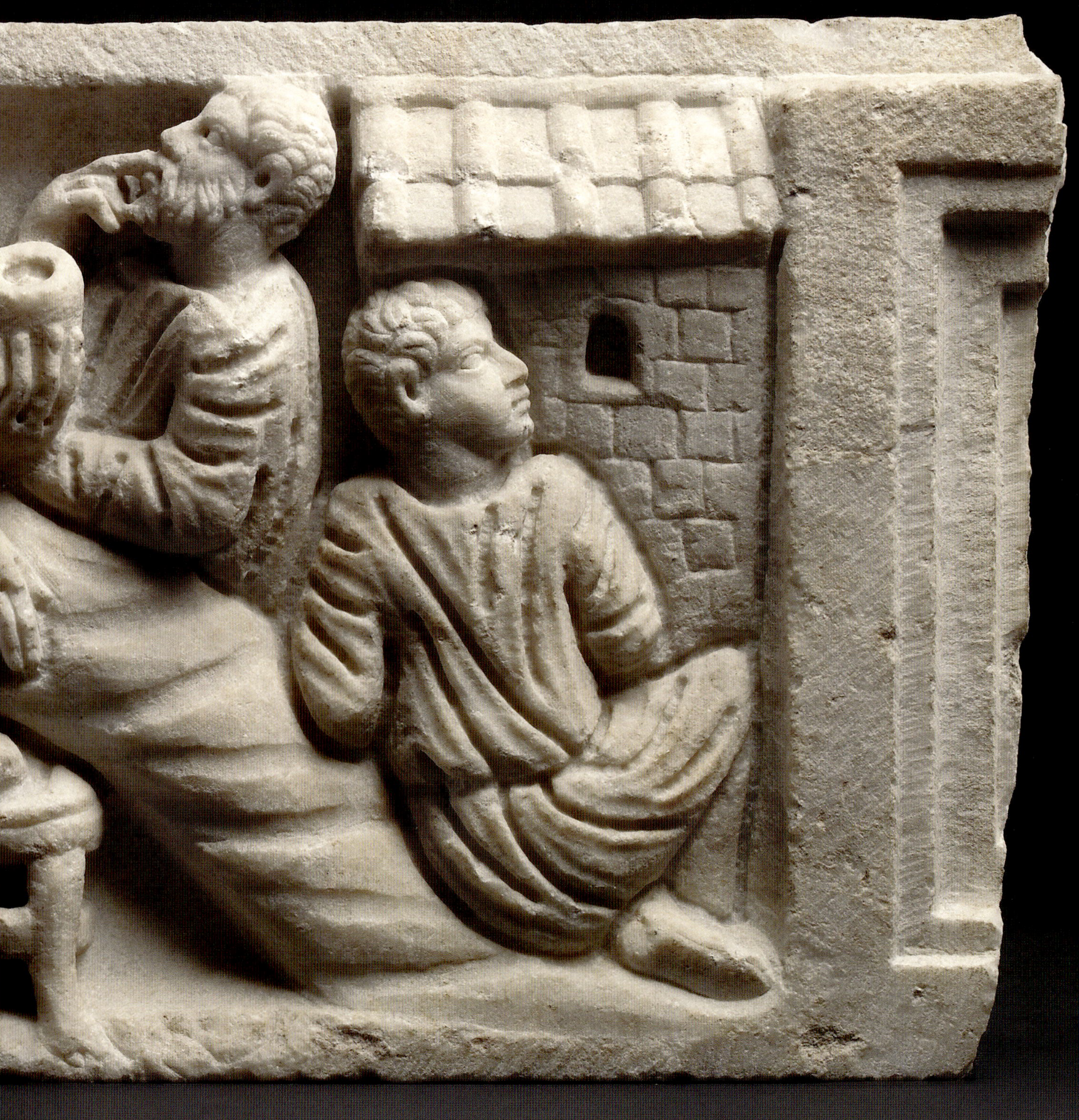

Ashmolean Museum
University of Oxford

Saints and Salvation

The Wilshere Collection of gold-glass, sarcophagi and inscriptions from Rome and Southern Italy

Edited by
Susan Walker

with contributions by
Sean V. Leatherbury and David Rini

Scientific analysis by
Annelore Blomme, Patrick Degryse, Peter Ditchfield, Kelly Domoney, Julian Henderson, Graham Morgan and Andrew Shortland

Saints and Salvation: The Wilshere Collection of gold-glass, sarcophagi and inscriptions from Rome and Southern Italy

Susan Walker, David Rini, Sean Leatherbury, Patrick Degryse, Annelore Blomme, Andrew Shortland, Kelly Domoney, Julian Henderson, Peter Ditchfield and Graham Morgan have asserted their moral rights to be identified as the authors of this work.

British Library Cataloguing in Publications Data

A catalogue record for this book is available from the British Library

EAN 13: 978-1-85442-90-2

Published by the Ashmolean Museum, University of Oxford

Designed and typeset in Arno and Clarendon URW by Adrian Hunt
Printed and bound in Belgium by Albe de Coker

PRECEDING PAGE: A youth is diverted from a funerary banquet. Detail of cat. **39**

For further details of Ashmolean titles please visit: www.ashmolean.org/shop

ASHMOLEAN

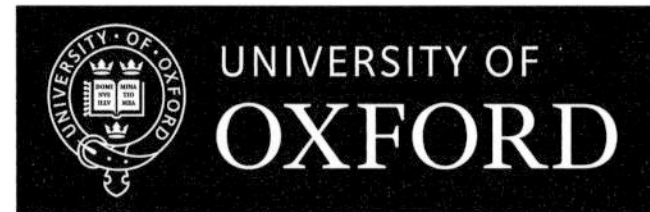

List of Contents

Preface

Alexander Sturgis

Saints and Salvation tells the story of a remarkable collector, Charles Wilshere (1814?–1906), and his passion for the English Catholic church. From newly studied archival sources we learn how Wilshere achieved his personal mission of introducing museum visitors to the then brand-new subject of early Christian art and archaeology.

Research for this book has been drawn from a wide range of disciplines. There has been ground-breaking use of scientific examination of late Roman gold-glass, improving our understanding of how it was made and for whom it was commissioned. The results have been used to create a full catalogue of the Ashmolean's collection, the third largest in the world.

The research team was led by Dr Susan Walker, from 2004–2014 Keeper of Antiquities at the Ashmolean, and responsible for securing the purchase of the Wilshere Collection for the museum. Major contributors include Dr Sean Leatherbury, who became engaged with the project while completing a DPhil at Oxford University, and David Rini, who had published a scholarly study of one of the Wilshere gold-glasses as a student of the University of Pisa.

The research effort has engaged several departments within the Ashmolean Museum: Antiquities, Conservation, Photography, Development and Publications. Within the University, the research team has worked with the Oxford Centre for Late Antiquity, the Research Institute for Art and Archaeology, Pusey House, Keble College, Wolfson College and the Bodleian Library. Many institutions in the UK and abroad have provided invaluable support, most notably the University of Cranfield, Hertfordshire Archives and Local Studies, the British Museum, the British School at Rome and the Vatican Library and Museum.

This book could not have been published without the generous support of Christian Levett, in so many ways a major benefactor of the Ashmolean, to whom we, once again, offer our sincere thanks. The scientific research was enabled by a generous grant from the Thriplow Trust. Susan Walker's research in Rome, Naples and Salerno was fully supported by a Hugh Last Fellowship at the British School at Rome.

As a private landowner Wilshere has remained unknown, his outstanding collection unstudied. The scope of this book, using the materiality of the objects and archival research to bring Wilshere and his collection into focus, reflects both the Ashmolean's historic identity as a collection of collections and its modern role as a hub of object-based scientific research.

Acknowledgements

Susan Walker

A project of the complexity of *Saints and Salvation* requires the support of a large number of people and institutions. Without the financial support of Christian Levett and the Thriplow Trust, and the academic support of the British School at Rome, where Susan Walker held a Hugh Last Fellowship from January–March 2013, the research programme and current publication could not have been completed. Susan Walker would especially like to thank her contributing authors Sean V. Leatherbury and David Rini for their sustained energy, persistence and patience.

In the Ashmolean Museum, Susan Walker thanks the former Director Christopher Brown and his successor Alexander Sturgis; all colleagues within the Department of Antiquities, especially Clare Burton, Paul Collins, Helen Hovey, Ilaria Perzia, Alison Roberts, Paul Roberts and Michael Vickers; in the Department of Conservation Daniel Bone, Nicky Lobaton, Mark Norman, Dana Norris, Jevon Thistlewood and Stephanie Ward; in the Development Department Helen Duncan; in the Photographic Studio David Gowers, Annie Holly and Alice Howard; in the Publications Office Declan McCarthy and Marie Hale, Catherine Bradley (copy-editing), Adrian Hunt (design) and Elaine Taylor (indexing).

Within the University of Oxford, Alison Cooley, Centre for the Study of Ancient Documents, Faculty of Classics, and the University of Warwick; Martin Goodman, Faculty of Oriental Studies; Jonathan Prag, Faculty of Classics; Jas' Elsner, Faculty of Classics and Corpus Christi College; Peter Ditchfield, Research Laboratory for Art and Archaeology; Hermione Lee, retiring President of Wolfson College; Marlia Mango, School of Archaeology and St John's College; Bryan Ward-Perkins, Trinity College and Euthymios Rizos, Oxford Centre for Late Antiquity; Anna James, St Cross College, Librarian of Pusey House.

For input and support from individuals and other institutions, Andrew Shortland and Kelly Domoney, University of Cranfield; Julian Henderson, University of Nottingham; Elspeth Morgan; Graham Morgan, formerly of the University of Leicester; Chris Entwistle, Department of Prehistory and Europe, and Andrew Meek, Department of Scientific Research, British Museum; Jennifer Price, University of Durham; Yvonne Beadnell, Hilary Cool and Mike Baxter; Tony Rook, Gordon Longmead (Welwyn); Claire Ramsey and colleagues, Hertfordshire Archives and Local Services.

Patrick Degryse and Annelore Blomme, University of Leuven; Guntram Koch, University of Marburg; Doris Bielefeld; Christopher Smith, Director of the British School at Rome; all BSR staff, especially Alexandra Giovenco (BSR Appointments

Manager, 2013)and Gill Clark (Registrar); Umberto Utro and Claudia Lega, Museo Sacro Cristiano, Vatican Museums; Fr Antonio Orazzo and Maria Cristina de Ruggiero, Pontificia Facoltà Teologica dell'Italia Meridionale, Sezione San Luigi-Biblioteca; Rita Carbonaro, Biblioteche reunite civica e Ursino-Recupero, Catania; Chiara Lambert and Francesca dell'Acqua, University of Salerno.

For access to key archives, Susan Walker and David Rini thank the staff of the Biblioteca Apostolica Vaticana, Sezione Archivi, especially its Director, Marco Buonocore and Paolo Vian, Director, Biblioteca Apostolica Vaticana, Sala Manoscritti; the staff of the State Archive of Rome; Valerie Scott, Beatrice Gelosia and Alexandra Giovenco, British School at Rome Library and Archive.

For advice and further access to significant collections of archives, David Rini thanks Paolo Liverani of the Università degli Studi di Firenze, Dipartimento di Storia, Archeologia, Geografia, Arte e Spettacolo, Lucina Vattuone of the Vatican Museum, Ufficio Stampa; the staff of the Bibliotheca Hertziana di Roma (Max-Planck-Institut für Kunstgeschichte) and the Biblioteca di Archeologia e Storia dell'Arte, Rome.

A final draft of the essays was read by Lindsay Smith and by John Wilkes, to whom an especial debt of gratitude is due. Any remaining errors and omissions remain the responsibility of the editor.

Dedication

N.A.W.W., D.I.G., H.N.C.

SEMPER IN PACE VIVATIS
PIE ZESES

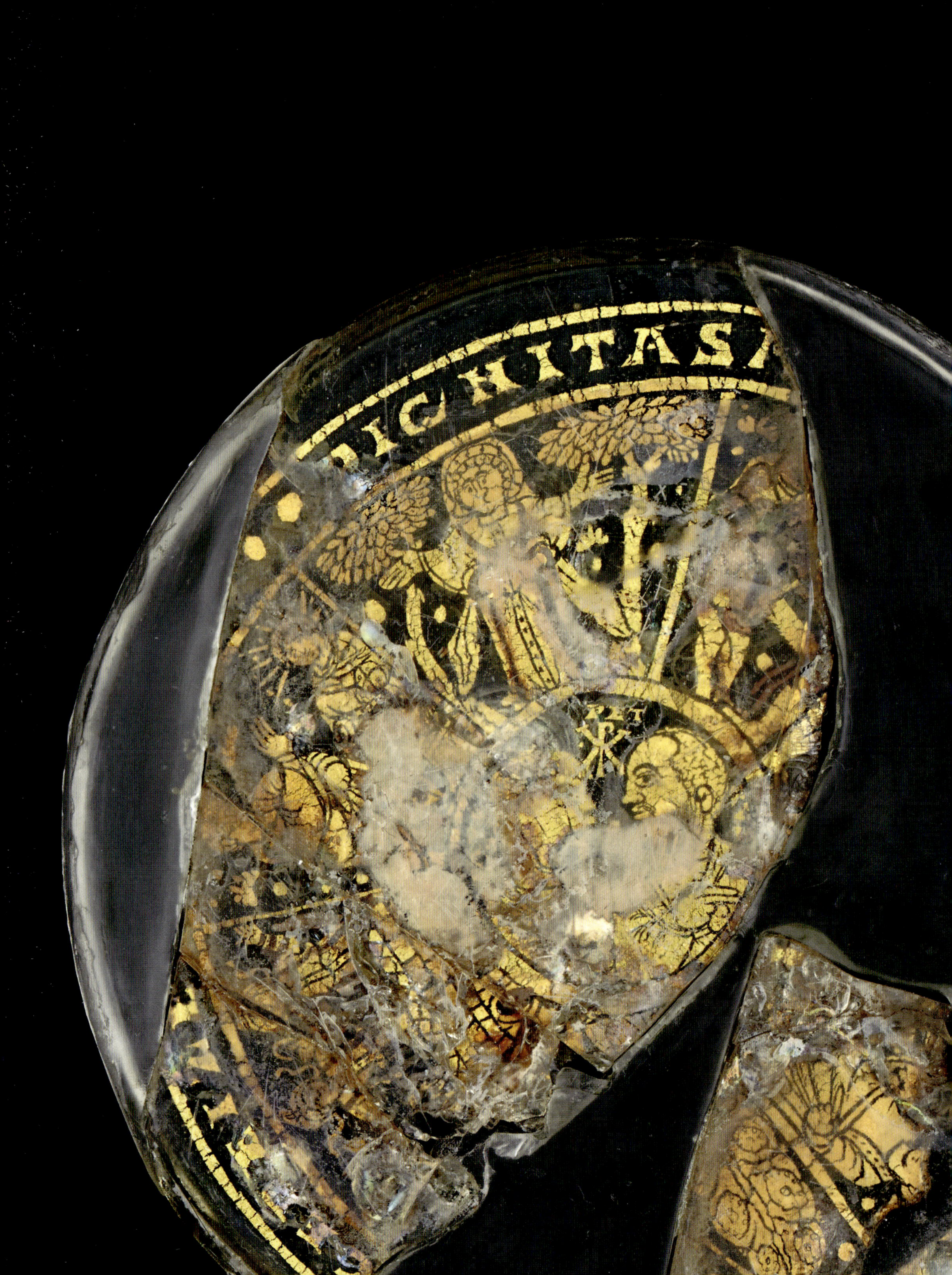

Introduction

In the 1860s Charles Wilshere, a wealthy landowner and passionate supporter of the English Catholic Oxford Movement, set about forming a collection of late antique objects from Rome and southern Italy that illustrated his profound interest in the history and cults of the early church: gold-glass (glass vessels and other products with enclosed gold leaf decoration), marble gravestones and sarcophagi, and finger-rings and amulets bearing personal affirmations of faith. Wilshere's carefully selected collection was always intended to introduce students and the wider public in Britain to early Christian art and archaeology. This was then a brand-new field of study dominated by the Vatican, with its investigation almost entirely restricted to Roman Catholic scholars. To fulfil his aims in 1865 Wilshere sent his most important gold-glass vessels on loan for 29 years to the recently founded South Kensington Museum, since 1899 known as the Victoria and Albert Museum. During this time he stated his intention to form a museum of inscriptions on stone and small objects at his home in Welwyn, Hertfordshire. In 1895 Wilshere drew up a Declaration of Trust promising to bequeath the collection for teaching purposes to Pusey House, Oxford, which remains the centre for Anglo-Catholic worship in the city today.

Nineteenth-century study and publication of the Wilshere Collection

In the course of the nineteenth and twentieth centuries elements of Wilshere's collection have been published piecemeal. Thus the major gold-glass items in Wilshere's collection were quickly published with drawings by the indefatigable Jesuit scholar Father Raffaele Garrucci, both before and after Wilshere's acquisition of them.[1] Major finds in stone were reported by the distinguished Vatican archaeologist Giovanni Battista de Rossi, and were published by Garrucci and others.[2] The English translators and editors of de Rossi's major work also noted major items of gold-glass in the collection.[3] Wilshere's gold-glass also featured, some of it for the first time, in a remarkably forward-looking study of gold-glass by the German scholar Hermann Vopel.[4]

Unfortunately, however, the collection as such was not fully catalogued in Wilshere's lifetime, and some objects remain obstinately elusive, the collection

St Peter and St Paul surrounded by biblical scenes of salvation. Detail of Cat. **23**

apparently doomed never to be fully captured.[5] Thus Appendix 1, a concordance of lists reconstructing what we know of the collection, is based upon the most complete surviving inventory, compiled at Pusey House by T. B. L. Webster in 1925–9. This and Appendix 2, which includes Wilshere's inventory of loans to the exhibition of 1868, reveal numerous lacunae. The current work, then, remains a progress report on the collection and its formation.

The Wilshere Collection in Oxford

By the time that the Declaration of Trust was written in 1895, the gold-glass and other small objects from the Wilshere Collection were already housed in Keble College, Oxford. Wilshere died aged 92 in 1906, but the stone objects did not move to Oxford until 1925, when the collection was reunited at Pusey House. The young scholar T. B. L. Webster – later, as Professor T. B. L. Webster of University College London, to be distinguished for his studies of ancient representations of classical Greek drama – was commissioned to write a catalogue. In this work he published for the first time photographs of four of the most significant gold-glasses, a list of the 13 most important vessels in the collection and the eight Jewish inscriptions.[6] In the 1950s the gold-glass was photographed for an international corpus, and most of the gold-glass and an engraved silver spoon were moved from Pusey House to the neighbouring Ashmolean Museum, where they remained on long-term loan.[7] Sadly eight antiquities of no religious interest were apparently stolen from the cloister of Pusey House in 1976.[8] Following the publication of the Jewish texts by the American scholar A. T. Kraabel in 1979, the remaining stone objects followed the glass on long-term loan to the Ashmolean in 1984. The curators of the Department of Antiquities, notably Michael Vickers, displayed many of the inscriptions and the gold-glass, and made objects kept in reserve available for study. Thus the loans to the Ashmolean enabled the terms of Wilshere's bequest to be realised. Financial support for the display of the Jewish inscriptions was supplied by Professor Kraabel's then institution, Luther College, Decorah, Iowa, USA, in recognition of Professor O. W. Qualley (1897–1988).

In 2007 the Ashmolean was able to purchase the collection, with help from the Art Fund, the Victoria and Albert Museum's Purchase Grant Fund, the Friends of the Ashmolean and private donors. Regrettably some small objects not individually recorded in the Deed of Trust and kept in Pusey House even after the sale of the collection to the Ashmolean in 2007 were sold on the art market in 2008. This took place without the knowledge of the Ashmolean curators, at that time located off-site and much engaged with the final stages of a major programme of redevelopment.[9] After the museum reopened in 2009 the gold-glass and Jewish inscriptions were redisplayed in the permanent gallery of the Mediterranean World from AD 300 and the gallery of Reading, Writing and Counting. In 2015 the display of the Jewish inscriptions, all of them in Greek, was replaced by the Christian inscriptions from Aeclanum, Cumae and Rome, and the Jewish memorial to Alexander, all in Latin, as part of the AHRC- funded Ashmolean Museum Latin Inscriptions (ASHLi) project.

Some minor objects from the collection remain in Pusey House. With the most helpful collaboration of Anna James, librarian and archivist of Pusey House, and dealers in London and Brussels, strenuous efforts are now being made to trace the objects apparently stolen in 1976 and to recover the objects sold in 2008. The aim is to reunite the Wilshere Collection, enabling its original purpose to be fulfilled at the Ashmolean Museum.

Twentieth-century study and publication of the Wilshere Collection

Though lacking a catalogue, over the course of the twentieth century most of the major objects in the Wilshere Collection were included in corpora of gold-glass, Jewish and Early Christian inscriptions and late Roman sarcophagi. Thus, using T. B. L. Webster's article of 1929, the Jewish inscriptions were included in a well-illustrated corpus published in 1936.[10] Nearly all the gold-glass appeared in C. R. Morey's posthumously published catalogue of gold-glass in the Vatican Museums and other collections in 1959.[11] A. T. Kraabel explored the unpublished Jewish material in 1979, with access to papers in Pusey House documenting some of the collection's history.[12] In the 1980s much work was undertaken by Marlia Mango and Julian Henderson to record the gold-glass and sample selected items to understand their origins; however, this research, supported by the Getty Foundation, has remained unpublished. In the 1990s the sarcophagi were briefly described from photographs in a new corpus of early Christian sarcophagi.[13] A corpus of early Christian inscriptions from the south Italian region of the Hirpini was published in 1993; this included small-scale reproductions of transcriptions made by Wilshere for de Rossi of the three texts from Aeclanum in the Wilshere Collection.[14] Here the inscriptions were recorded as 'lost since their removal to London in 1880', but recent archival research indicates that they were actually moved to Welwyn in 1868 and, as stated above, to Oxford in 1925.

For the purposes of this catalogue, the focus will be on the early Christian and Jewish material in the Ashmolean collections. However, all known and some uncertain objects from the Wilshere Collection are listed in Appendix 1, together with a historical concordance of all known numbers. Additional objects of currently unknown location appear in Wilshere's 1868 list, transcribed in Appendix 2. Those objects falling outside the narrative of this catalogue will be published online as part of the Ashmolean's current digitisation project.

The current project

In the last 20 years significant advances have been made in our understanding of the chemistry of ancient glass. That new knowledge is applied in this catalogue to explore the origins of the raw glass used in the manufacture of gold-glass in late antique Rome, a line of research first proposed over a century ago by Hermann Vopel.[15] Marlia Mango and Julian Henderson have kindly contributed their data to the current programme of analysis by Andrew Shortland and Patrick Degryse (Appendices 4a and 4b); Marlia Mango's acute observation of the glass, shared with the principal author, has also been used as the starting point of many of the catalogue entries. As part of the research process, the glass has been re-examined and photographed beneath a microscope and with back-lighting by Dana Norris, formerly objects conservator at the Ashmolean Museum with a special interest in ancient glass. She has also contributed a section on the process of making gold-glass as revealed by XRF analysis (pp.97–99). New photographs were taken for the catalogue by David Gowers, Head of the Ashmolean's Photographic Department. These are individually credited and dated within the catalogue entries, as a record of the state of the objects at the time. Some of the marble inscriptions have been removed from their slate frames by specialist stone conservator Elspeth Morgan; these offer interesting information about the recycling of stone in late antiquity, and the range of marbles available for earlier use. To this end isotopic analysis of some of the pieces was undertaken by Peter Ditchfield of the University of Oxford's Research Laboratory for Art History and Archaeology

(Appendix 5), and Graham Morgan, formerly of the University of Leicester, reported on mortar samples (Appendix 6).

Despite the inclusion of all the key items in the Wilshere Collection within twentieth-century corpora of Jewish and Christian inscriptions, gold-glass and late Roman sarcophagi, this is the first time that the collection has been studied as a near-whole. The rewards of such an approach are significant, not least for the history of the collection and its sources. Two key collections of the southern Italian enlightenment contributed to its formation; both experienced similar histories, collapsing in the aftermath of the overthrow of the Bourbon monarchy in Naples in 1860. Mismanagement of holy relics in late eighteenth-century Rome, and a fateful under-evaluation of the significance of a Jewish catacomb in the nineteenth century, led to significant objects falling from state to private ownership. David Rini's contribution illuminates a key archival resource from the Vatican Library for understanding these developments. He has also contributed substantial amounts of information held at the State Archive of Rome.

Another advantage of studying the entire collection is that it offers a microcosm of Rome in the fourth-century AD. It is possible, and instructive, to compare the decoration of early Christian and Jewish glass and stone, and to see how both relate to decoration in other media. Dr Sean Leatherbury's contribution explores these relationships; he has also contributed significant iconographic discussion and associated bibliography to the catalogue entries. More broadly, the Wilshere Collection offers an interesting glimpse of the growing discomfort of the Church Fathers, known from surviving texts, with the persistence of pagan burial practices in an increasingly Christian city. In the decoration of glass and sarcophagi we see evidence of a move from the illustration of private prayers and expressed wishes for the commendation of an individual soul to the veneration of the early Christian martyrs.

Last but not least, Wilshere's own story is affecting. As his family died out, his long and industrious life is poorly documented; yet from letters to Giovanni Battista de Rossi and Raffaele Garrucci held in the Vatican Library and the San Luigi Library in Posilippo we obtain glimpses of a kindly, if forceful and ambitious man. Grave disappointments were borne with Christian fortitude, but a key to understanding the collector is that a profound faith provided not only spiritual but also intellectual nourishment to an energetic man with the financial resources to realise his dreams.

St Peter (?) with a female figure, perhaps a personification of the Church. Detail of cat. **58**

Notes

1. Garrucci 1858, 1864, 1872–81.
2. De Rossi 1866, 1868, 1872.
3. Northcote and Brownlow 1869, 1879.
4. Vopel 1899.
5. Sotomayor 1963: 223 sounds a note of fatal compromise.
6. Webster 1929. The ms list of 105 objects is kept at the Department of Antiquities, Ashmolean Museum.
7. Morey 1959. Letters recording the publication and the loan agreement are kept in the archives of the Department of Antiquities at the Ashmolean Museum.
8. The apparent theft is only known from a manuscript note made by Kraabel while visiting Pusey House to research the Jewish inscriptions published in Kraabel 1979. See below, p.44.
9. Christie's Antiquities sale, London, King Street, 13 October 2008, Lot 55. Kraabel 1979: 50, no.4 was among the objects sold.
10. Frey 1936.
11. Morey 1959.
12. Kraabel 1979.
13. Dresken-Weiland 1991.
14. Felle 1993.
15. Vopel 1899; see further below, p.95.

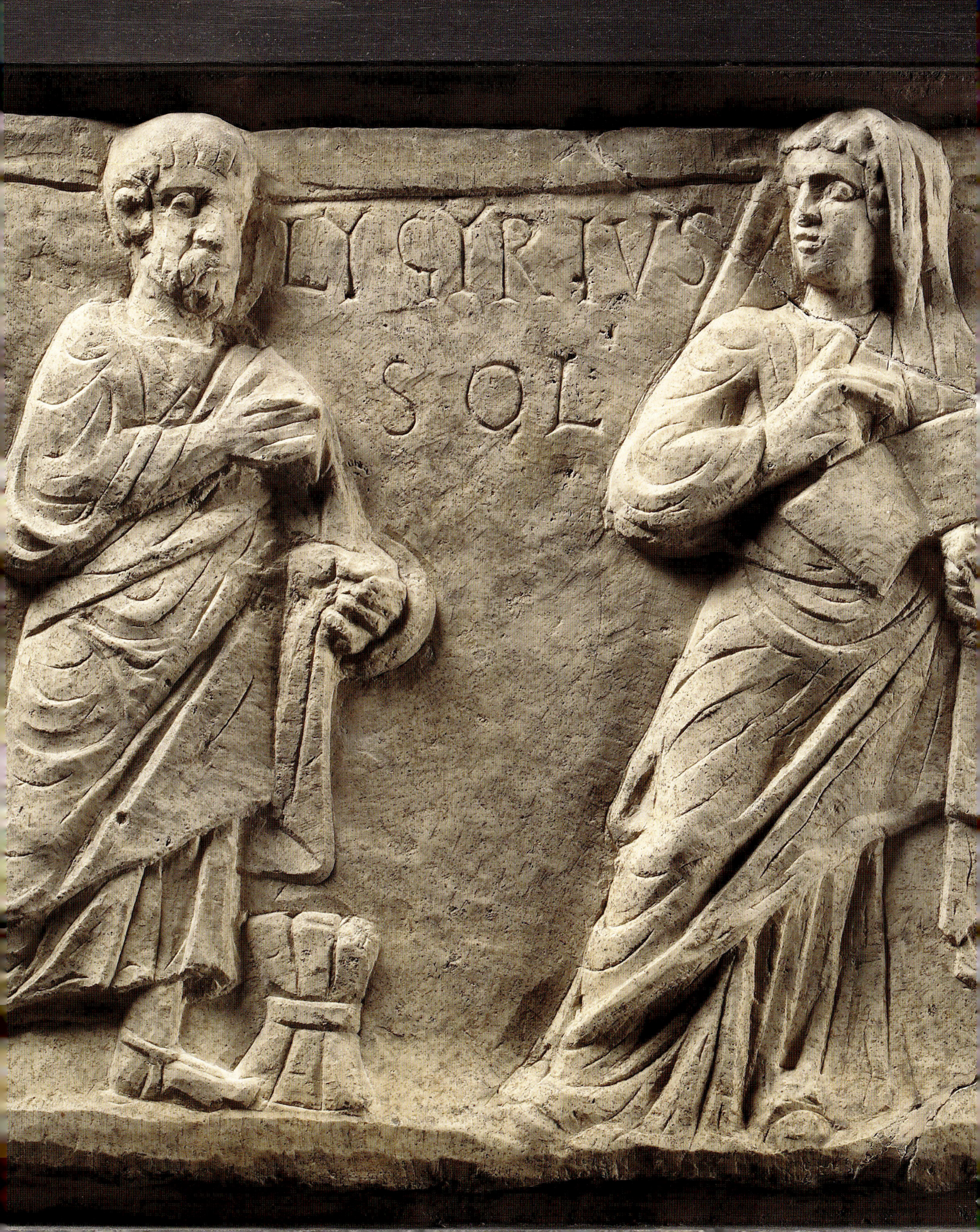
SOL

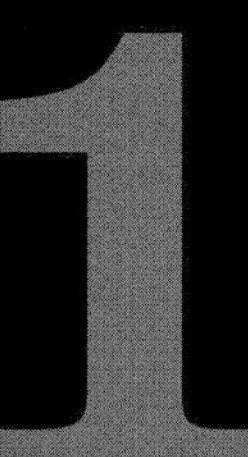

Daniel brings the prisoned cake.
Detail of cat. 33

The formation of the Wilshere Collection

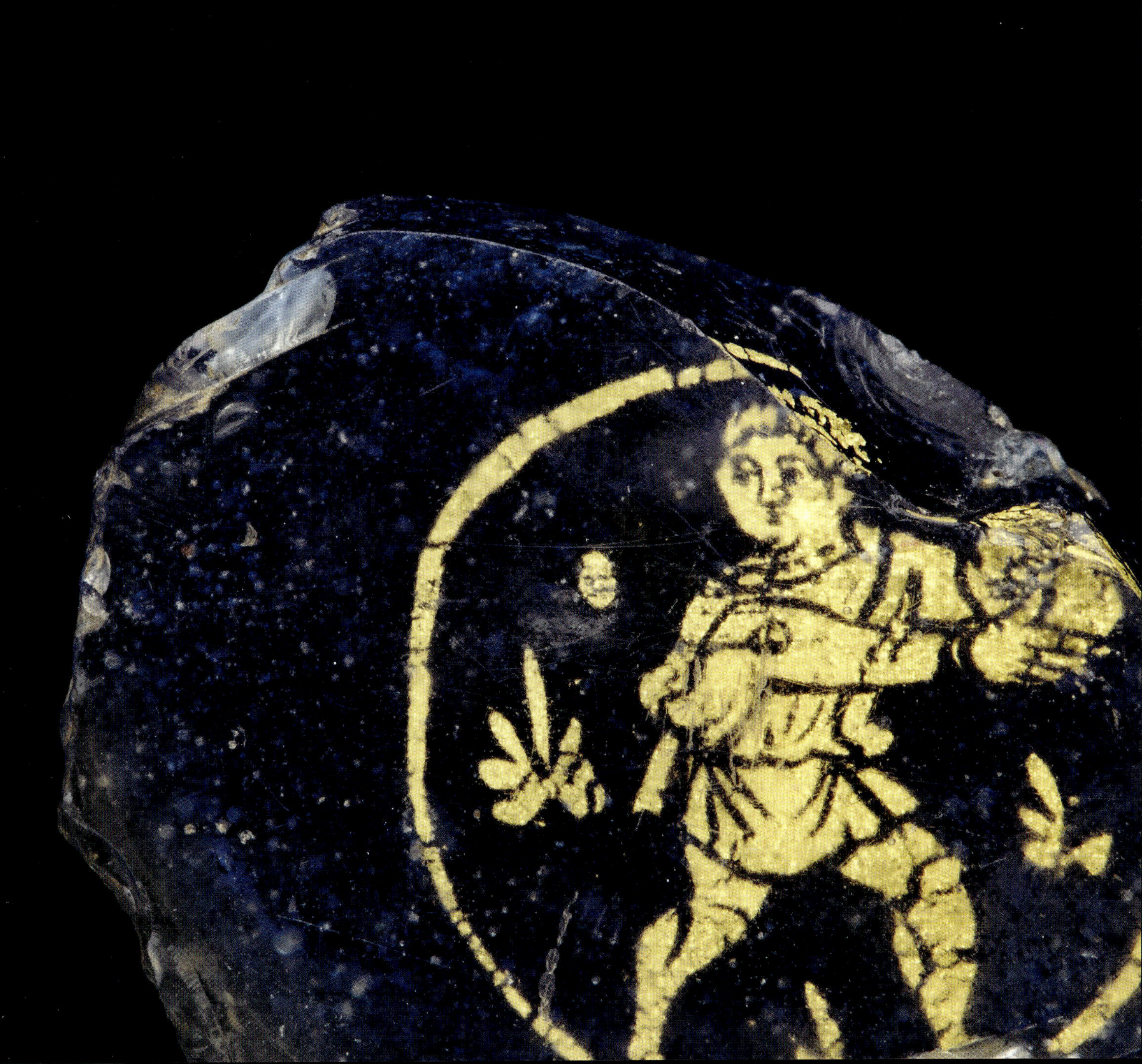

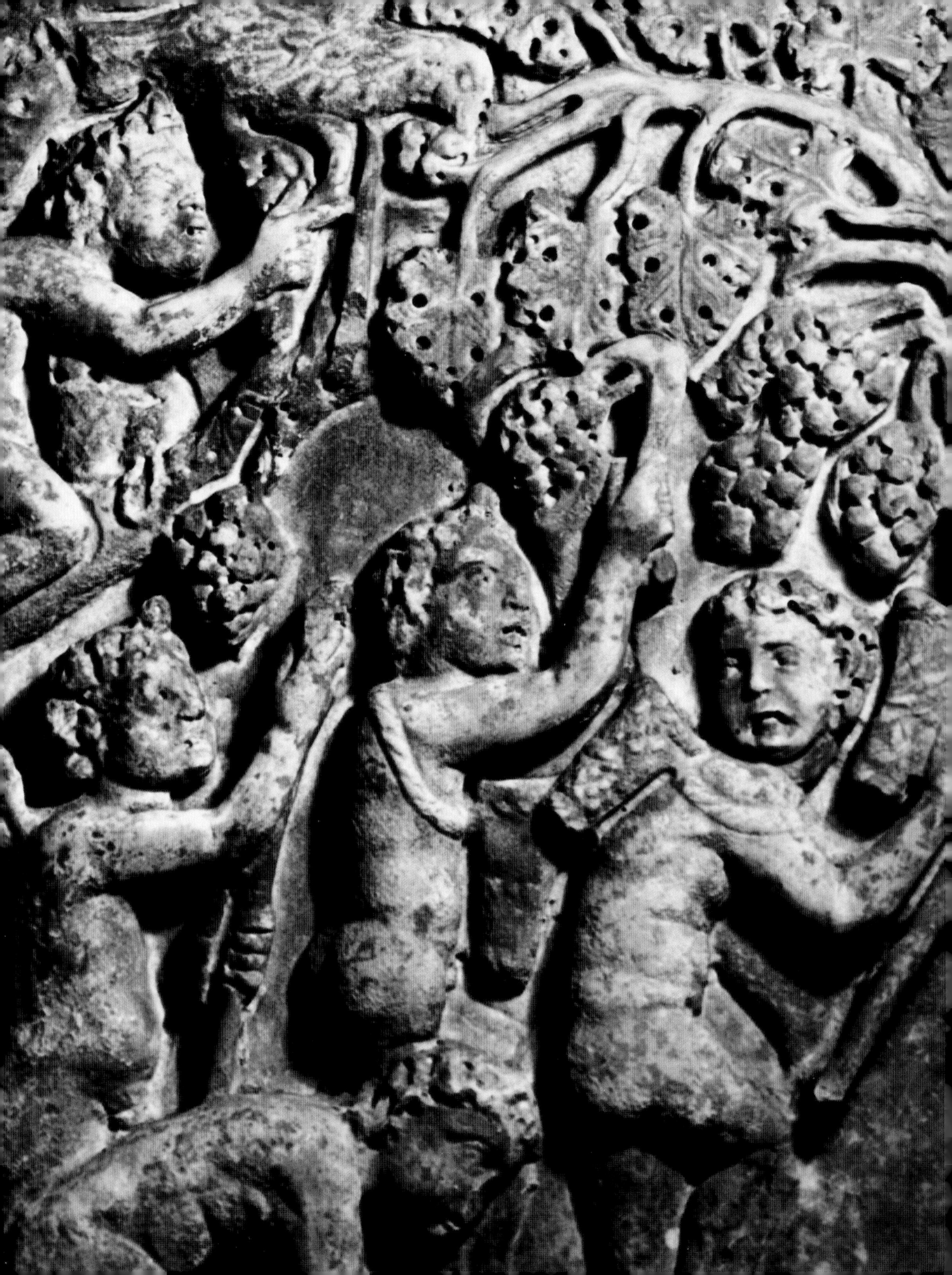

Chapter 1

The collector and his collection

Charles Willes Wilshere, a Hertfordshire gentleman

The Wilshere Collection of late Roman gold-glass, sarcophagi and inscriptions was formed by a landowner from Welwyn, Hertfordshire. Born a Georgian at Hitchin, Hertfordshire on 20 February 1814, Charles Willes Wilshere died an Edwardian at Welwyn on 29 September 1906, having shown, according to one local obituarist, 'wonderful vitality, being confined to his bed for only three weeks'.[1] An informal photograph taken in the late 1890s (Fig. 1) shows a robust and apparently contented elderly man with patriarchal beard, standing in the splendid gardens of the family estate at The Frythe, Welwyn.

As a second son, Charles Wilshere did not expect to inherit The Frythe. He was well-educated: a degree from Trinity College, Cambridge was followed by legal training at Lincoln's Inn, London. He was cosmopolitan, marrying in Munich and travelling frequently in France, Germany and Italy. The family estate at Welwyn came to him on the unexpected death in Paris on 10 November 1868 of his unmarried elder brother William. For ten years, from 1837–47, William Wilshere had served as Whig M.P. for Great Yarmouth on the Norfolk coast; he was later appointed Deputy Lieutenant and, in 1858, High Sheriff of Hertfordshire.[2] The considerable extra burden of local management and public roles, including service as Justice of the Peace and Deputy Lieutenant of Hertfordshire, was assumed by Charles Wilshere with great energy and sense of purpose. Yet it hardly inhibited his activities as a traveller, a collector of antiquities and a fervent supporter of the Anglo-Catholic Oxford Movement. The robust judgement of his obituarist was entirely typical of Charles Wilshere's long and extremely active life.

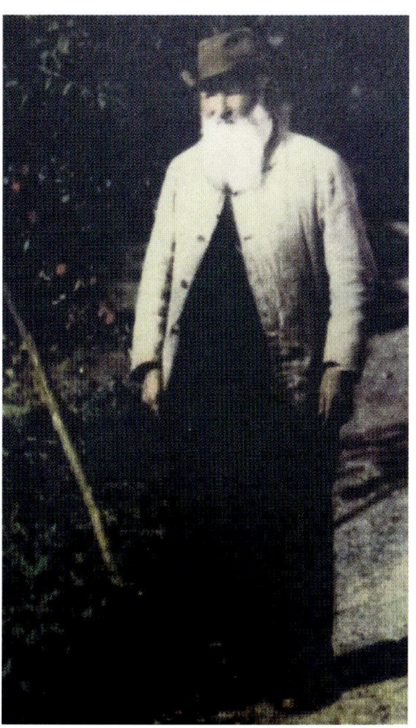

Fig. 1 (above) Photograph of Charles Wilshere in the garden of The Frythe, 1899. After Gordon Longmead, 2006

(Opposite) Detail of Fig. 19, a sarcophagus relief once in the Wilshere Collection, now lost

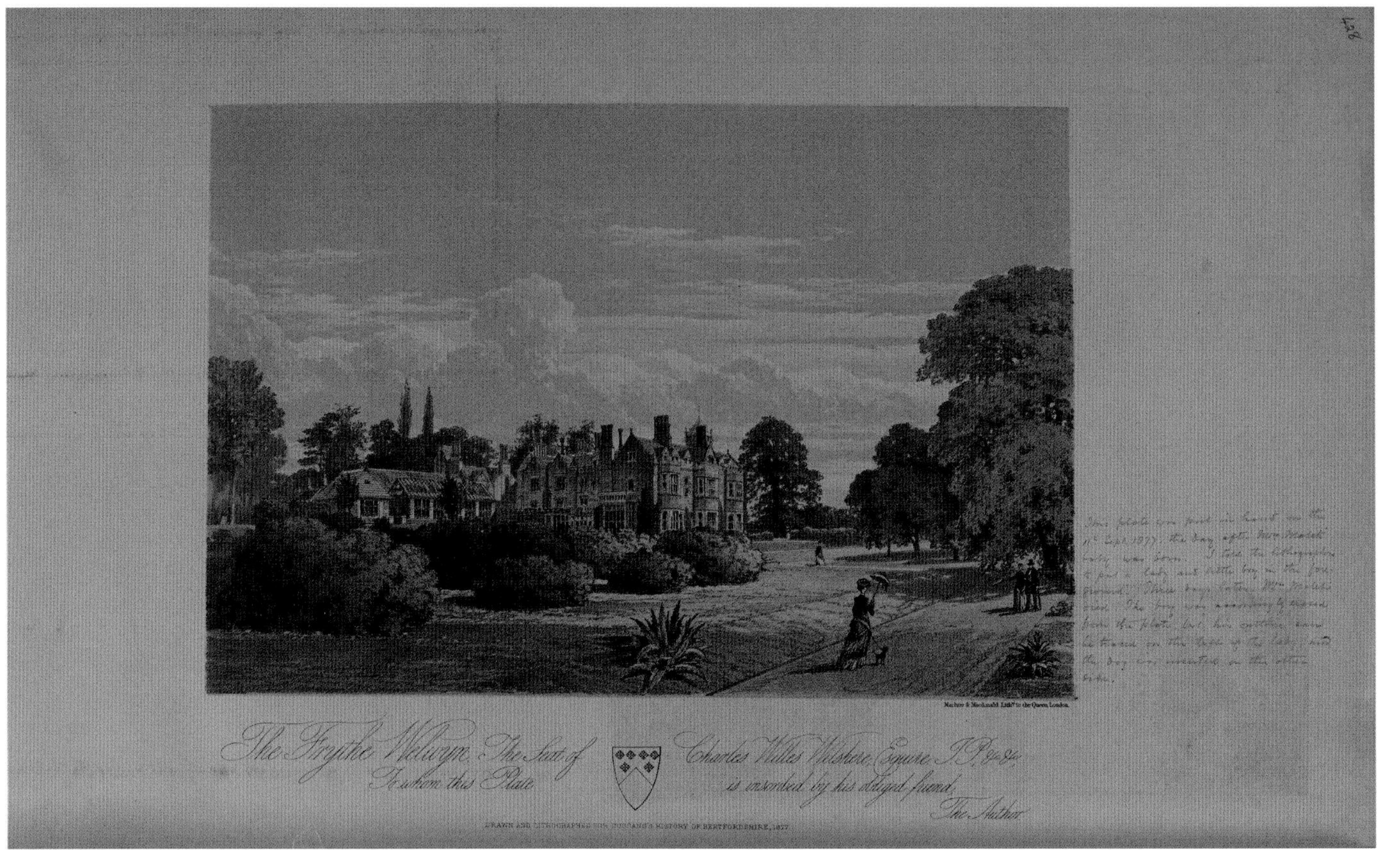

Fig. 2 *The Frythe, Welwyn, seat of Charles Willes Wilshere, J.P., to whom this plate is inscribed by his obliged friend, The Author.* J. E. Cussans, *History of Hertfordshire (1877),* annotated edition, p.428. HALS

A family tragedy

Despite high levels of activity sustained in various areas of religious, cultural, agricultural and public life for the better part of a century, detailed information about Charles Wilshere is surprisingly sparse, particularly in archives held in the United Kingdom. The lack of documentation may be a long-term effect of the tragedy that befell the Wilshere family in the 1870s. In September 1877 Florence Malet, the third of Wilshere's four daughters and the only one to marry,[3] died of puerperal fever, aged 29; her son Sydney survived her for only two years. With the passing of Florence and Sydney all hope of succession to the family name and The Frythe at Welwyn was lost – a grave blow as the estate had been leased and then owned by the Wilshere family since 20 September 1533.[4]

An engraving of The Frythe commissioned in 1877 by John Edwin Cussans for his book, *The History of Hertfordshire* (Fig. 2), perfectly captures the disastrous turn in the family's fortune. A young woman accompanied by a dog briskly walks along a path before the elegantly landscaped gardens and imposing, Gothic-style house, built only 30 years previously. A note pencilled by Cussans at the right side of the engraving in the annotated publication, now kept in the Hertfordshire Archives and Local Studies Office, explains that, on Charles Wilshere's instruction, the dog had replaced a boy, whose shadow can still be made out to the left of the woman. The original plate, begun by the royal lithographers Maclure and Macdonald on 11 September 1877, had been intended to congratulate Wilshere on his grandson's birth the previous day.

Cussans observed that Wilshere's profound Christian faith helped him through this bitter experience, endowing him with a remarkable equanimity captured in the photograph of him in his mid-eighties (Fig. 1).

Wilshere and the Oxford Movement

Wilshere was an enthusiastic supporter of the Oxford Movement, also known as the Tractarians, led first by John Henry Newman until his conversion to Catholicism in 1846, and later by Edward Bouverie Pusey. His name was given to Pusey House in Oxford, the 'house of sacred learning' and eventual beneficiary of Wilshere's passion for early Christian archaeology. Pusey House is still the centre of Anglo-Catholic worship and scholarship in Oxford today (Fig. 3).[5]

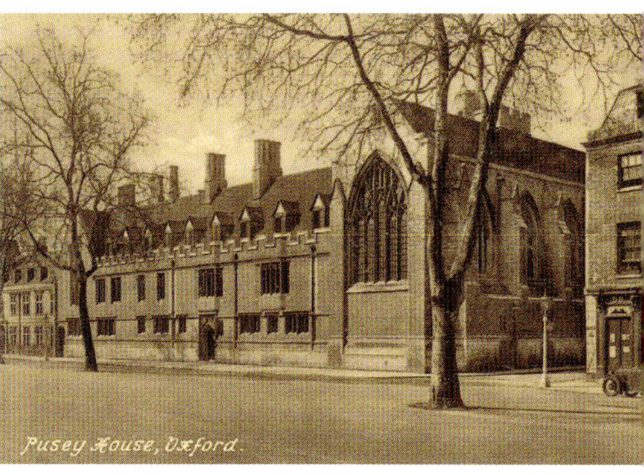

Fig. 3 Postcard of Pusey House, St Giles, Oxford, showing the chapel and the seminary in about 1925, the time of the installation of Wilshere's collection and its cataloguing by T. B. L. Webster, published in 1929. www.oxfordhistory.org.uk/stgiles/tour/west/60_61_pusey_house.html

Wilshere's commitment to the Oxford Movement was undertaken in an extremely sensitive political climate. In September 1850 Pope Pius IX ordered by letter the establishment of a Roman Catholic episcopal hierarchy in England for the first time since the sixteenth-century Protestant Reformation.[6] Nicholas Wiseman, newly named Archbishop of Westminster, prepared the papal rescript and a pastoral letter to the people of England entitled 'Out of the Flaminian Gate', in which he announced that the counties of England were now under the governance of the Roman Catholic Church and England had been returned to her proper ecclesiastical orbit around the papal sun.[7] This correspondence, widely known as the Papal Aggressions, was strongly opposed by the Prime Minister, Lord John Russell, and by Queen Victoria, whose regal authority was directly challenged. Nor were they alone: 1,673 petitions bearing 260,078 signatures against the Papal Aggressions and Tractarianism had been received from parishes in England and Wales, and 6,000 members of the legal profession had characterised 'Out of the Flaminian Gate' as a violation of English law.[8] Like so many of her parishioners, the Queen herself was opposed to Tractarianism, seeing the Oxford Movement as a papal subterfuge in which Roman Catholic ritual was introduced to the Anglican Church and state interference in the church's governance and practice was resisted.[9] In 1851 the Ecclesiastical Titles Act was passed: no religious titles based upon the name of any place in the United Kingdom were to be permitted without royal assent, and no priest with an illegal title could receive gifts of property.[10]

Wilshere joined the Oxford Movement's lay society, the English Church Union, on its formation in 1859.[11] His legal training would have made him well-suited to a prominent role in the Union, which was principally concerned with defending the status of priests conducting rites now deemed illegal in the eyes of the established Church of England. However, his name does not appear among those who held high office within it. Nonetheless, under the name 'Fidelis' (the faithful one) Wilshere published a number of highly polemical tracts defending an English version of Catholic doctrine.[12] One of these, an almanac for English Catholics drawn from the *Sarum Portiforium* of 1541, might have been occasioned by the first parliamentary reconsideration of the Ecclesiastical Titles Act, regarded as discriminatory by the Liberal and High Anglican Prime Minister William Gladstone.[13] Another was first presented in June 1876 to the St Albans, Hatfield and Welwyn branch of the English Church Union.[14] In the latter paper Wilshere assembled the evidence of arrangements for worship in the catacombs and in early basilicas to argue for a position for the officiating priest behind the altar. Two pamphlets published in the late 1870s and 1880s used legal arguments against government interference in church appointments and patronage, and in the affairs of convocation. This was a pressing concern of the Oxford Movement's members, the more so following the passing of another controversial law, the Public Worship Regulation Act of 1874, secured against the growing Oxford Movement by the Archbishop of Canterbury Archibald Campbell Tait with the support of the Prime Minister Benjamin Disraeli.[15] Another paper by Wilshere on Anglican Orders was published in 1872 in Rome as well as

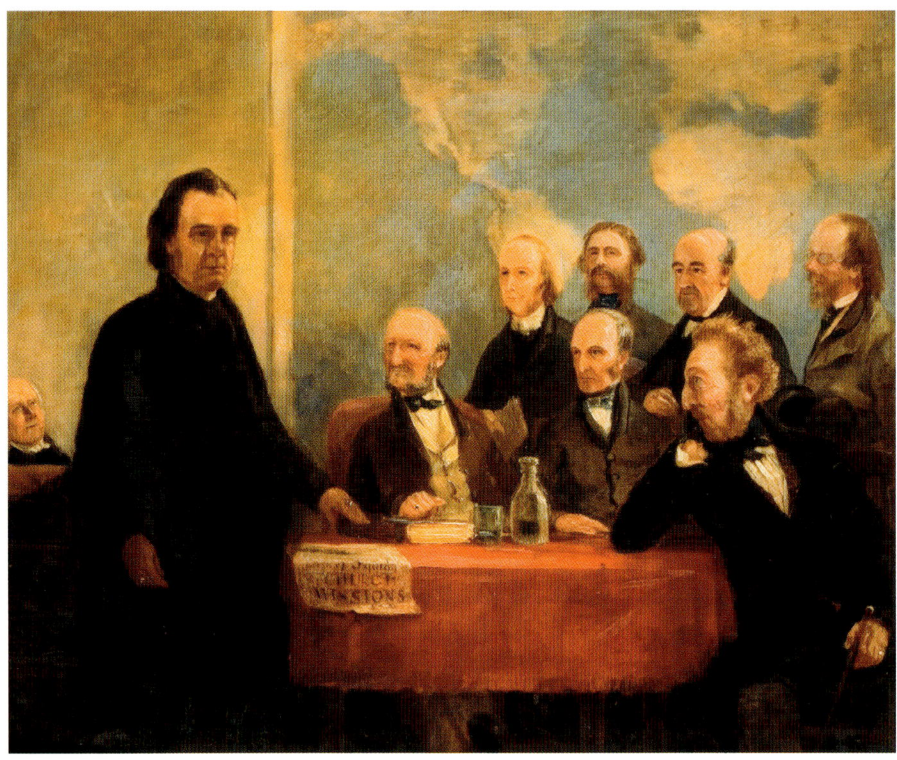

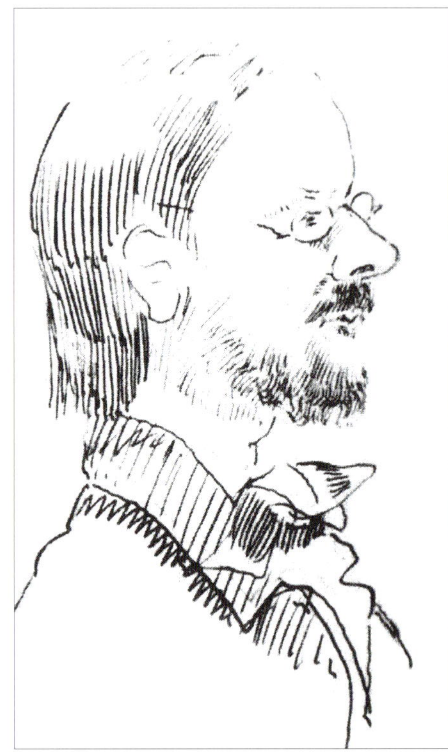

Fig. 4 Samuel Lucas, *A Missionary Meeting at Hitchin*, oil on canvas, about 1845. Hitchin Museum and Art Gallery HITHIM 330

Fig. 5 Drawing of Charles Wilshere by Samuel Lucas. After Gordon Longmead (ms of part of 2006 publication, HALS). *An uncropped version identifies Wilshere as the sitter and dates the drawing to 1857, but the painting was certainly completed in 1845.*[18]

Oxford and London.[16] In this Wilshere absolved himself of any errors, declaring that, having been in Rome at the time, he had not been able to check the proofs of the English publication.

Wilshere's last paper, published in his 87th year, ran to more than 20 pages of Latin with scholarly appendices.[17] Indeed he outlived all the Oxford Movement's founders. His socially active religious commitment goes back much earlier: a painting (Fig. 4) by the Quaker brewer Samuel Lucas of Hitchin, Hertfordshire, where the adult Wilshere had his principal residence before inheriting The Frythe in 1868, shows the bearded and balding 31- year-old at the right of the back row of men planning a missionary project, led by the Baptist minister standing in the foreground. The identification is based on a drawing of Wilshere made by the same artist (Fig. 5).

Wilshere's travels

Charles Wilshere travelled in Europe throughout his adult life. Through his marriage he acquired a family in Bavaria: his wedding to Elizabeth Marie, daughter of Mr W. M. Farmer, of Nonesuch, Surrey, the M.P. for Huntingdon, took place in Munich on 25 August 1840. A letter written to the Jesuit scholar Father Raffaele Garrucci on 7 July 1870, reporting progress on the cataloguing of the drawings of the catacombs, was sent from the same city.[19] In July 1871 Wilshere told de Rossi of his forthcoming visit to Oberammergau which, despite the unmentioned exigencies of the Franco-Prussian War, had become a regular summer holiday destination for the collector. Here the famous Passion Play had been performed according to its ten-year cycle in 1870; it would thus also have been performed in 1840, the year of Wilshere's marriage in nearby Munich.[20] A letter written in December 1892 to de Rossi opens with a joke about Wilshere's alleged lack of ability to speak German, for which he was teased by his nephews; his mother-in-law Frances Farmer had been born into a British family resident in Danzig, Prussia, and his sister-in-law Evarilda married the Baron Johann Peter Friedrich Gustav von Ascheberg in Munich earlier in 1840. The couple had two children, but Evarilda died in 1843; Wilshere and Elizabeth named their second daughter after her.[21]

In 1866 Wilshere reported that he had visited Cologne, correctly understanding that gold-glass had been imported to the city from Rome in the fourth century AD. Here he had tried to buy a shallow dish (*patera*) decorated with blue and green gold-glass medallions from the wealthy collector and hotel-owner Karl Disch, but to no avail. The dish was eventually sold on 16 May 1881 to Augustus Wollaston Franks, who presented it to the British Museum.[22]

Looking over the surviving letters written by Wilshere, the correspondence with Garrucci was sent from Rome, Munich, London and Welwyn; a letter to the English collector C. D. E. Fortnum was dispatched from Florence in 1865, and letters from Wilshere to the Vatican's archaeologist Commendatore Giovanni Battista de Rossi came from Welwyn, Oxford, London and Rome. One letter reported a visit with the family to Sicily, where the epitaph cat. **56** was purchased in Syracuse in 1885.[23] Wilshere's unfortunate third daughter was named, like the distinguished nurse Florence Nightingale, for the Italian city in which she was born in 1848.[24]

Building for the future and recording the past: Wilshere as architect

When not travelling to enhance his knowledge of early Christianity, Charles Wilshere was extremely active in and around Welwyn. He was a Justice of the Peace, and also owned several substantial estates, extending from Hertfordshire into Bedfordshire and Cambridgeshire. There is much evidence in and around Welwyn for Wilshere's active interest in architecture: in 1853 he designed the porch and faceless clock tower at The Frythe as an addition to the house recently commissioned by his elder brother William, the MP for Great Yarmouth (Fig. 6).

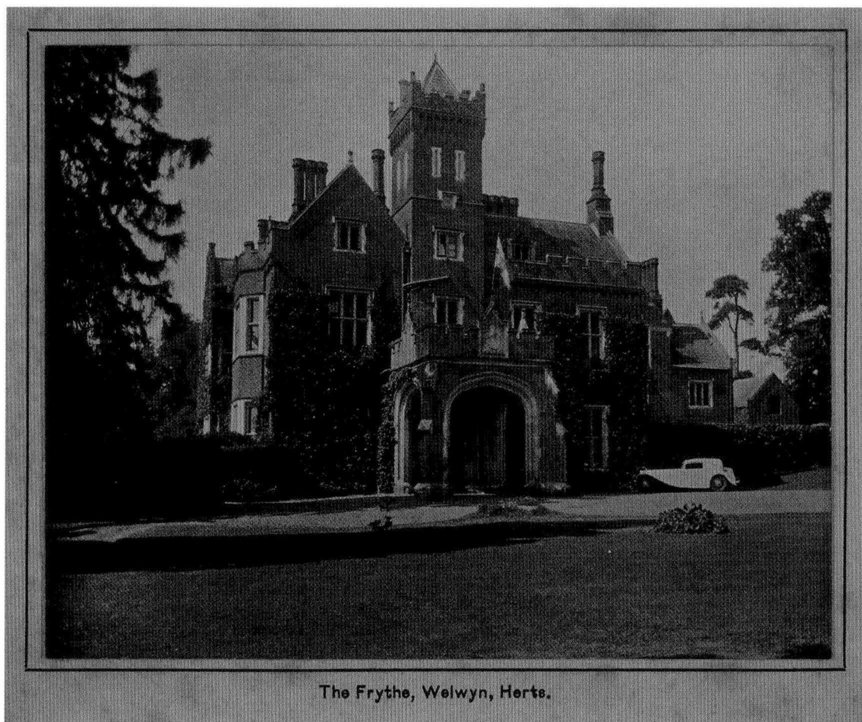

Fig. 6 The Frythe as a hotel, showing Wilshere's porch and the faceless clock tower. Photograph taken about 1938. HALS DE/WS/C8

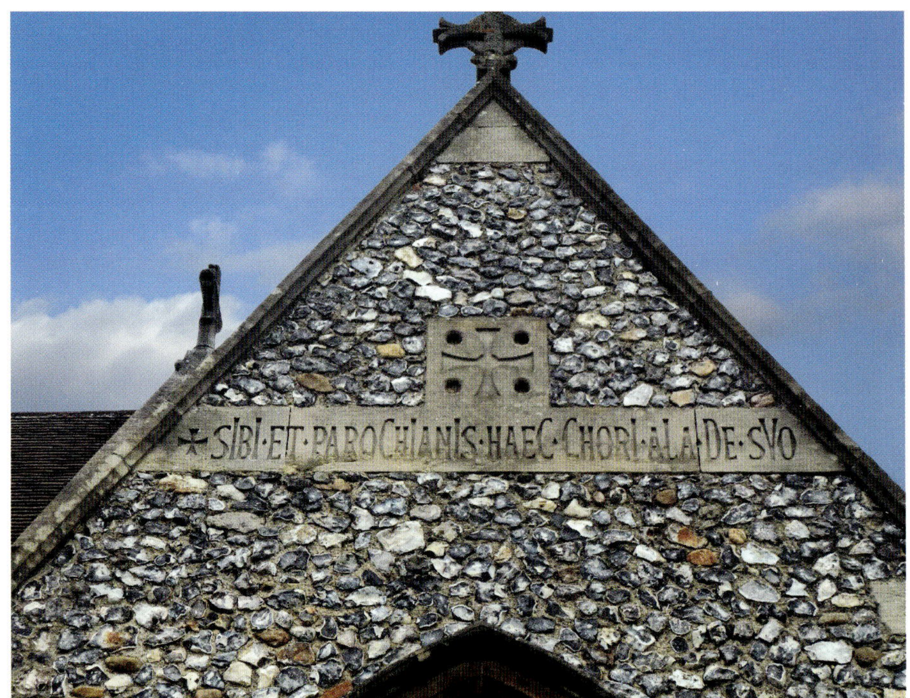

Fig. 7 Chronogram set in stone above the gable end of St Nicholas's Chapel, St Mary's Church, Welwyn. The inscription reads:

SIBI.ET PAROCHIANIS. HAEC. CHORI.ALA. DE. SVO (CVRA. CAROLI. WILLES. WILSHERE. CONDITA EST)

'This choir aisle was built for himself and the parishioners at his own expense (and as a token of his care by Charles Willes Wilshere).' Adding up the larger letters as the Roman numerals I=1, V=5, L=50, C=100, D=500 gives a date of 1869. Photograph by David Gowers.[29]

Wilshere also constructed a private chapel at The Frythe, perhaps as a convenience for his frail brother William. A new door at The Frythe was typically commemorated in a Latin chronogram recording a visit by Queen Victoria in 1866, probably to Welwyn rather than the house itself.[25] Latin chronograms also marked Charles Wilshere's construction of a family chapel with a private entrance at the parish church of St Mary's in Welwyn (Fig. 7), as well as on the extension of the church and the endowment of a new bell at Ayot St Peter's. The latter was convenient for travel from The Frythe, but the move also reflected considerable tension with the vicar at Welwyn, who objected to Wilshere's grandiose extension to St Mary's and his attempts to influence the parishioners towards Anglo-Catholicism.[26]

Wilshere's taste for chronograms, in which apparently random capital letters marked a sequence of Latin numbers whose sum revealed the date of the building, gave rise to some playful and witty teasing of 'the Squire's' Roman tendencies in the local press.[27] Chronograms puzzled the cataloguer, if not the recipient of Wilshere's letters. A chronogram was sent to de Rossi with New Year greetings for 1878; bearing no other postmark or date, it was catalogued with the letters of 1890.[28]

Two chronograms on buildings commissioned by Wilshere in Welwyn in 1874 and 1878 record his displeasure at being denied by the vicar of St Mary's opportunities to extend the parish church or to hold meetings of the English Church Union at the church school.[30] On Homerswood Cottage, Digswell Hill, he wrote that 'the proposed extension of the Parish Church was to the liking of neither the Rector nor the people', while on Becket Hall, London Road, Wilshere commented that 'Since the use of the Church School has been denied to those defending the church, another one is now taking shape, bigger and more richly adorned'.

The chronograms giving the exact dates of construction allow us to link Wilshere's frustration with the passing of the Public Worship Regulation Act of 1874 (see above, p.21) and its aftermath. The act was very much directed against the growing influence of the Oxford Movement, and the vicar may well have regarded Wilshere's projects as illegal.

Less controversial architectural projects included the construction of workers' cottages on the estate. Their pleasant and functional design by Wilshere anticipated the architecture of the Garden City Movement by some 40 years. He also directed the recording of the Early English domestic chapel at Almshoebury in anticipation of its demolition in 1865. The drawings were displayed at the Oxford Architectural Society, where they were said to have aroused considerable interest; the project was later recalled by Wilshere in a letter to the historian Cussans.[31]

The Frythe in the twentieth and twenty-first centuries

After Wilshere's death in 1906, his wife Elizabeth having died before him, The Frythe passed to his surviving unmarried daughters Edith, Everilda and Alice. When Alice, the last survivor, died in 1934 the estate passed to a great-nephew of Elizabeth Wilshere, Captain Gerald Maunsell Gamul Farmer, who was obliged by the terms of the bequest to change his name to Wilshere.[32] Having seen distinguished service in the First World War, Captain Wilshere re-launched The Frythe as a residential hotel for retired officers and the gentry (Fig. 6). Their numbers were apparently insufficient to fill the house, so tennis and other recreational pleasures were added to the offer. However, the good life was not destined to last long: in August 1939 The Frythe was requisitioned by a section of Military Intelligence, who

> showed up on the doorstep with no prior notice and informed staff and residents of the hotel that The Frythe, effective immediately, was seized for the war effort. The proprietor, himself a veteran of World War I, who had been severely wounded and a POW, naturally objected but was told that, with a war on the verge of eruption, the nation needed the estate.[33]

The Frythe became a secret centre for researching and developing, first, sabotage operations and then, after the formation of the Special Operations Executive in the summer of 1940, deadly weapons and military vehicles used for clandestine

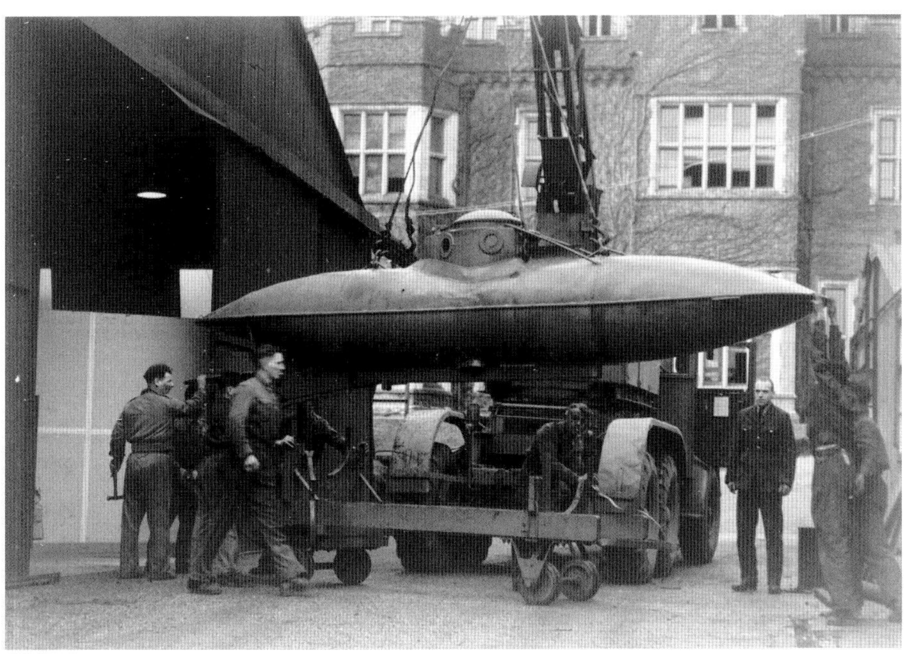

Fig. 8 The Welman submarine at The Frythe during the Second World War. Imperial War Museum IWM HU.56768

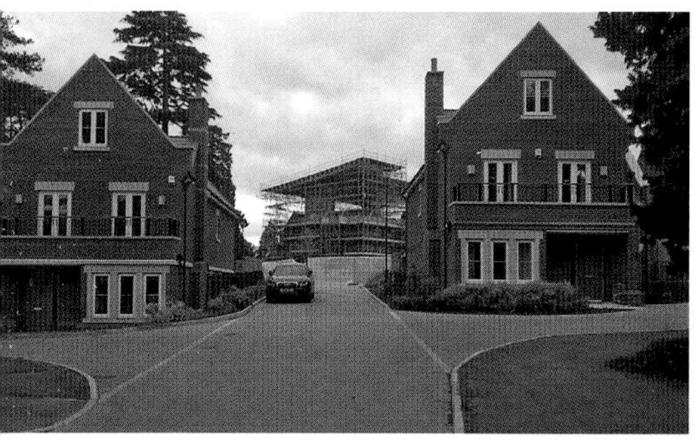

Fig. 9 New homes in Wilshere Park, with The Frythe in the background, May 2017.

transportation of troops and agents. These were inventions of the sort later made famous by Ian Fleming in his James Bond novels (Fig. 8).[34] The garden terraces near the house were occupied by huts and tanks used to conduct the experiments.

Captain Wilshere lived in Welwyn village during the war years. A post-war letting of the estate to Imperial Chemical Industries, and the subsequent sale of the estate in 1962 to Unilever Ltd, allowed him and his wife to emigrate to Bermuda. After his wife died Captain Wilshere returned, presumably as a tax exile, to the Isle of Man, where he died in 1972. Five years later The Frythe was purchased by Smith, Kline and French, who continued to develop the research facilities.

The current state of The Frythe offers a telling reflection of our times. In 2008 the estate was sold for £15,000,000 to the offshore company Lands Improvement with a view to redevelopment; the research laboratories were accordingly demolished and the land sold to Linden Homes for £40,000,000 in 2013. Wilshere Park, as the estate is now known, comprises 196 houses on a 47-acre site, while the grand residence built by William Wilshere and embellished by his brother Charles has been turned into 14 luxury apartments (Fig. 9).[35] It is to be hoped that some, at least, of the exotic trees from the splendid Victorian gardens have survived this latest turn in their fortunes.

Collecting and believing

Wilshere's Italian network

Wilshere's tightly focused archaeological collection was overwhelmingly concerned with Christian and Jewish material from the catacombs of Rome. To acquire such objects, then hardly known in England, Wilshere built strong relationships with leading Vatican and Jesuit authorities on early Christian archaeology and art; these lasting friendships were facilitated by a network of English scholar-priests who had converted to Catholicism and frequently travelled to Rome. Sixty-nine unpublished letters from Wilshere to the Papal Commissioner for Christian Archaeology, Cavaliere, later Commendatore Giovanni Battista de Rossi are preserved in the archives of the Biblioteca Apostolica Vaticana in Rome, while eleven to the Jesuit archaeologist Father Raffaele Garrucci are in the archive of the Biblioteca San Luigi in Posilippo.[36] Unfortunately, none of the correspondence from de Rossi and Garrucci to Wilshere seems to have survived, perhaps because of Wilshere's private status; equally, the value of the Italian correspondence may not have been recognised by Wilshere's heirs.

Nonetheless, the surviving letters to his Italian correspondents offer valuable insights into Wilshere's ability to negotiate with other collectors and museum directors in Italy and England, and no less into his remarkable knowledge of early Christian art and archaeology and the philosophy behind his collection. Wilshere was able to correspond in excellent French and (less grammatical, but nonetheless fluent and clear) Italian as well as English, the content of his letters also demonstrating his knowledge of Latin, ancient Greek and cuneiform script. The tone of the correspondence reveals a warm, confident, optimistic and energetic personality, characteristics also noted by Cussans. And though no letters have survived from de Rossi to Wilshere, references to the English collector made in de Rossi's *Bullettino di Archeologia Cristiana* (to which Wilshere was an enthusiastic subscriber) capture Wilshere's passion for his subject and his courtesy to others:

In questi medesimi giorni due ne ho veduti acquistati in Roma di caldi amatori dei cristiani cimeli, il sig. Wilshere e il sig. Federico Harford… ('In these very days I have seen two purchases made in Rome by passionate amateurs of Christian antiquities, Mr Wilshere and Mr Frederick Harford…').

Un singolare marmo votivo cristiano scritto e figurato, il più singolare marmo votivo Cristiano fino ad oggi a me noto … e stato acquistato in Roma pel suo museo e trasferito in Inghilterra dal sig. Wilshere, il cuoi nome più volte con onore ho ricordato. Debbo alla cortese liberalità ed amicizia del nobile gentiluomo la fotografia del marmo, dalla quale è tratto il mio disegno… ('A unique Christian marble votive, inscribed and figured, the most unusual Christian marble votive yet known to me was purchased in Rome for his museum and transferred to England by Mr Wilshere, whose name I have mentioned with honour many times. I owe to the courteous generosity and friendship of the noble gentleman the photograph of the marble, from which my drawing was made').[37]

Wilshere's English network

Through his engagement with the Oxford Movement, Wilshere had come to know other British scholars who were active in bringing early Christian art and archaeology to the attention of the English-speaking public. His friend James Spencer Northcote (1821–1907) was one of a network of correspondents of de Rossi and Garrucci. Northcote converted to Catholicism and trained as a priest at the Collegio Pio, Rome after his wife died in 1853. He became the leading figure of a small group of English Catholic priests trained in Rome who wrote scholarly but admirably accessible works on early Christian art: in 1869 Northcote jointly edited with William Robert Brownlow (later Bishop of Clifton) an English version of de Rossi's great work *Roma Sotterranea* ['*Subterranean Rome*'].[38] The highly ambitious English edition, for which the Italian title was retained, reflected not only the authors' respect for de Rossi's remarkable industry and scholarship, but also their own didactic purpose:

Two courses were open to us; either to bring out a translation from the Italian original, or to embody in a work of our own the most interesting and important facts which these volumes contain. The first would have been incomparably the easier, and in some respects the more satisfactory course. But the size and cost of such a work would have put it entirely beyond the reach of many, whom we were most anxious to benefit. We therefore decided on the plan adopted in this volume which we now introduce to our readers, and which, we believe, will be found to contain as fair a summary as its dimensions would allow – not only of de Rossi's two volumes of *Roma Sotterranea*, published in 1864 and 1867, but also of many articles in his bi-monthly *Bullettino di Archeologia Cristiana*, of papers read by him before learned societies in Rome and elsewhere, and of his occasional contributions to works published by others…

The task which we have undertaken is now accomplished. We have placed within the reach of English readers as complete an account of the Roman Catacombs and their contents, more especially of the Catacomb of St Callixtus, as we have been able to collect from the works of Commendatore de Rossi. The present Part treats of ancient Christian art, on which it gives far more abundant information than has ever before appeared in the English language.[39]

Northcote and Brownlow's work was sufficiently esteemed to merit translations into French and German, as well as the compilation of a revised and enlarged edition, published in 1879; in the same year a three-volume version was published with an account of de Rossi's recent discoveries at the catacomb of St Callixtus.[40] Stung by criticisms of confusion of authorship, in the latest version Northcote and Brownlow included marginal notes and in their preface quoted a letter from de Rossi, who praised their efforts – not least the translations, given that the climate for research was so inauspicious in 'the convulsions of [the Franco-Prussian] war in France and Germany, and disasters which have convulsed Europe and the Church'. Such an observation captured a dark geopolitical reality entirely absent from Wilshere's letters.[41]

Editing and updating the work of the late William Palmer with similar skill and sensitivity, Northcote and Brownlow went on to publish an introduction to Early Christian symbolism. They used wall paintings, sarcophagi and gold-glass, among other media, to introduce an English readership to the early Christian narration of key stories from the Bible and the formation of the early Church in Rome.[42] Among the excellent illustrations is Wilshere's gold-glass cat. **3**, for which a helpful footnote by Northcote and Brownlow informs the reader that 'several good specimens of these glasses, and among them C1b [cat. **3**], may be seen in the South Kensington Museum, lent by Mr Wilshere.'[43]

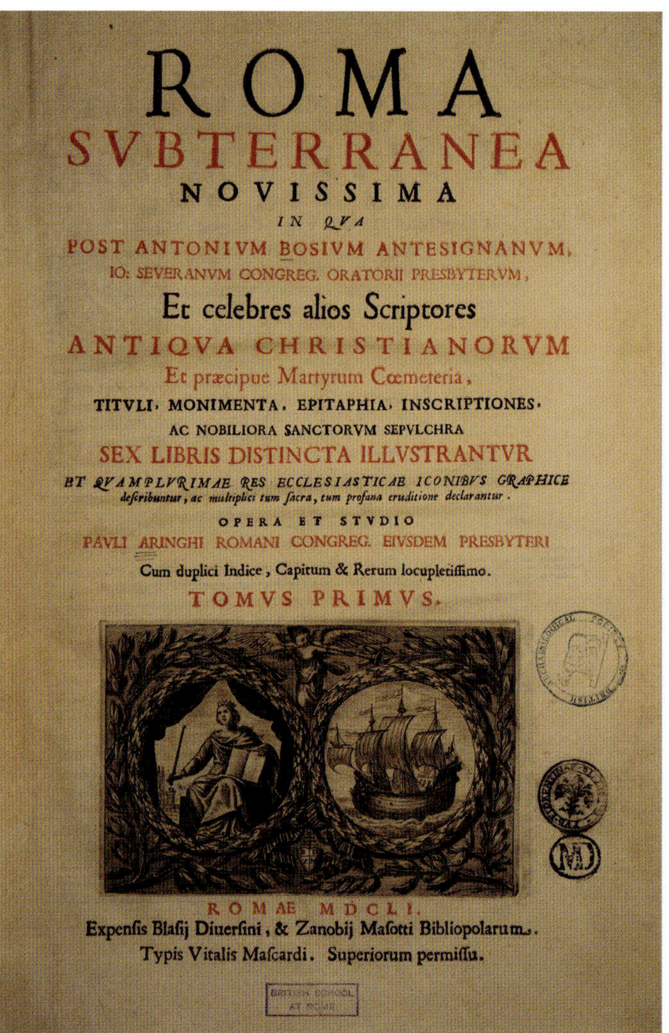

ROMA
SVBTERRANEA
NOVISSIMA
IN QVA
POST ANTONIVM BOSIVM ANTESIGNANVM,
IO: SEVERANVM CONGREG. ORATORII PRESBYTERVM,
Et celebres alios Scriptores
ANTIQVA CHRISTIANORVM
Et præcipue Martyrum Cœmeteria,
TITVLI, MONIMENTA, EPITAPHIA, INSCRIPTIONES,
AC NOBILIORA SANCTORVM SEPVLCHRA
SEX LIBRIS DISTINCTA ILLVSTRANTVR
ET QVAMPLVRIMAE RES ECCLESIASTICAE ICONIBVS GRAPHICE
describuntur, ac multiplici tum sacra, tum profana eruditione declarantur.
OPERA ET STVDIO
PAVLI ARINGHI ROMANI CONGREG. EIVSDEM PRESBYTERI
Cum duplici Indice, Capitum & Rerum locupletissimo.
TOMVS PRIMVS.

ROMAE MDCLI.
Expensis Blasij Diuersini, & Zanobij Masotti Bibliopolarum.
Typis Vitalis Mascardi. Superiorum permissu.

Fig. 10 Title page of Antonio Bosio, *Roma Sotteranea*, edited by Gaetano Severano. British School at Rome Library

Indeed the same glass had been illustrated in Brownlow's chapter on gilded glass found in the catacombs in *Roma Sotterranea*, with the observation:

> Among private collections, Mr C. W. Wilshere's in this country is probably one of the best; it contains about twenty specimens, the more important of which are at present in the Loan Collection of the South Kensington Museum.[44]

Further encouragement to the reader to visit the display of Wilshere's gold-glass in the South Kensington (later the Victoria and Albert) Museum appears in the same volume in the detailed discussion of the biblical scenes on cats **3** and **23**.[45]

Northcote was later entrusted with a major task of great sensitivity and personal significance to Wilshere: the preparation of a reply in Latin to Pope Leo XIII on the occasion of the announcement of the award of a papal medal to him in 1893.[46]

Another trusted friend of Wilshere was the younger Enrico Stevenson. This brilliant Anglo-Italian scholar of epigraphy, topography and numismatics is still regarded today, notwithstanding his early death, as a towering figure in the early Christian archaeology of Italy.[47] All these individuals, among other, less well-known intermediaries, are mentioned in Wilshere's letters; on visits to Rome, each acted as a courier, informal negotiator and postman for his colleagues and for their Italian mentors.[48] Stevenson, indeed, was entrusted with the return of the gold-glass of Genesius to the Vatican in a suitably inscribed box (see below, p.36).[49] Often the correspondence and errands flowed from Italy to England, some of them via Wilshere, who did not always prove a reliable conduit: in 1871 he temporarily lost a letter from de Rossi to Mr Nesbit, later discovered in a roll of paper.[50] It is probable that Wilshere saw himself as complementing the roles of his English friends in archaeological exploration and publication, by purchasing, exporting to England and putting in the public domain early Christian art and artefacts that could be appreciated by museum visitors and students.

The exploration of the catacombs of Rome

Though Wilshere never wrote more than learned papers on early Christian art and archaeology for a very restricted readership, it is evident from his published tracts that he had detailed knowledge of the history of the rediscovery of the catacombs in the early seventeenth century. Re-entry to the catacombs after many centuries of neglect had been inspired by the private devotion of the sixteenth-century saint Philip Neri to the early Christian martyrs.[51] The original *Roma Sotterranea* was the work of the Maltese antiquary Antonio Bosio, the first systematic explorer of the catacombs. After Bosio's premature death, more than a thousand of his note-cards were edited for publication in 1632–4 by Gaetano Severano, a member of the Oratory of St Philip Neri in San Severino (Fig. 10).

As a youth of 18 Bosio had been introduced to the catacombs, and most probably also to the Oratory and its excellent library, by Pompeo Ugonio, a penitent of Filippo Neri.[52] Wilshere's personal familiarity with Bosio's work is revealed in correspondence of the early 1870s, when he spent much time and effort trying to sell drawings of the Roman catacombs on behalf of Raffaele Garrucci; the Jesuit scholar had fallen on hard times in the radical aftermath of the collapse of the Bourbon monarchy in Naples and the Papal State in Rome.[53] Despite Wilshere's persistent efforts to persuade Garrucci to provide a list identifying the subjects of the drawings, Garrucci apparently insisted that Wilshere should write the captions himself, using

Bosio as a source. As the drawings had apparently been copied or cut from Arringhi's Latin edition of Bosio's work, this seems a reasonable instruction.[54] Wilshere reported his progress to Garrucci; he appears to have needed confirmation of only one of the 65 drawings.

Wilshere's identifications formed the basis of a list which Henry Cole, then Director of the South Kensington Museum, could submit to his Board of Trustees, with a view to purchase. In the event the purchase was not concluded; worse, some of the drawings were damaged in transit and through careless handling at the museum, after which the correspondence between Wilshere and Garrucci ceased. The last letter from Wilshere to Garrucci in the S. Luigi archive, reporting the damage to the drawings, is dated 8 February 1872. One can only imagine Garrucci's reaction to its somewhat insouciant tone, though Wilshere clearly hoped to placate him with an offer of giving him the full price agreed and partly paid in advance.

> *... Mi spiace di dirla che i disegni sono un poco guasti: in modo che se vuol ritenergli, la pregherò di ritinere anche la moneta che già tiene sul conto; questo in ogni caso.*
>
> *Ella deciderà dunque se preferisce aver i disegni tali quali; o la rimanente del prezzo combinato. Il guasto proviene da due cose: principalmente dal fregamento (non so se questa sia la parola) soferto nel viaggio: taluni fogli della carta di China vitrapasti non erano morbidi assai, ed hanno ammaccato il lapis (spero che me capirà). Secondo: nel museo hanno scritti al'angolo di ciascuno, in richiastro, la papira dell'Arringhi dove si trova gli originali disegni.*
>
> *Ora mi scriva risposto.*
>
> *Ella in ogni caso non ritornerà i denari gia pagati: preferisce di aver i disegni, o i bilanci?*
>
> *Pregho una risposta al più presto, e resto suo servo ed amico devot.mo [devot(issi)mo]*
>
> *C. W. Wilshere*

> (I'm sorry to tell you that the drawings are a little spoiled: in the event that you want to keep them, I pray you to keep also the money that you already hold on account: this in any case.
>
> You will then decide if you prefer to have the drawings however they are; or the remaining amount of the full price.
>
> The damage comes from two things: principally from rubbing (I don't know if this is the word) suffered in transit: some glazed sheets of China paper were not damp enough, and have smudged the pencil (I hope that you will understand me). Second: in the museum they wrote on the corner of each one, as a reference, the manuscript of Arringhi, where one finds the original drawings.
>
> Now you'll write me a reply.
>
> In any case you will not return the money already paid: do you prefer to have the drawings, or the balances?
>
> I beg you to send a response as soon as possible, and remain your servant and devoted friend
>
> C. W. Wilshere)[55]

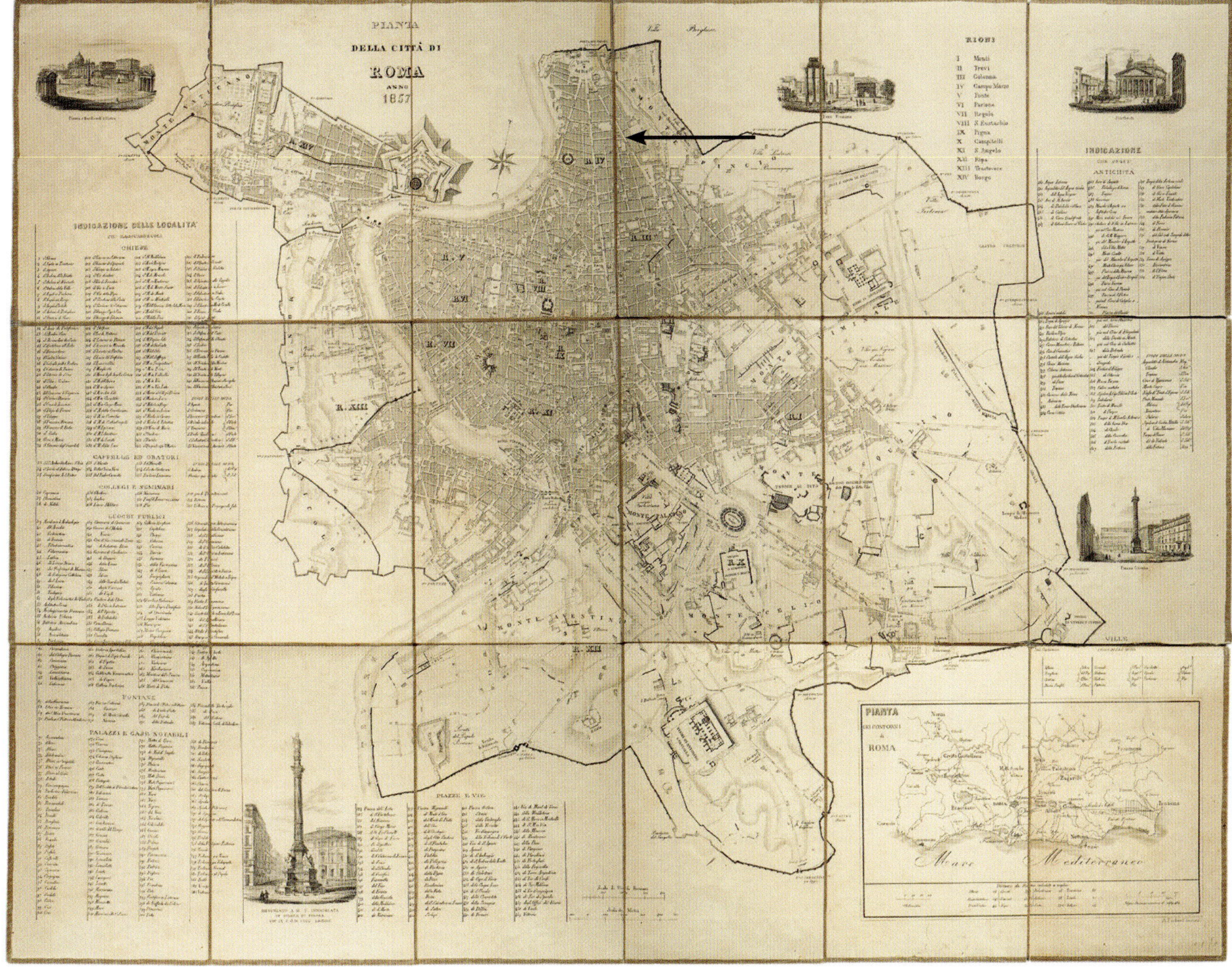

Wilshere and the Roman art market

Fig. 11 Map of Rome engraved in 1857 by Achille Pariboni. The approximate position of Tommaso Capobianchi's shop is marked with an arrow. British School at Rome Archive 609.2.85.4

Buying and selling antiquities in Rome in the 1860s

It is possible that Wilshere began to collect antiquities in Italy as a younger man, but no record survives earlier than his acquisition of the gold-glass from the Museo Recupero and other Roman sources. This purchase, from the Roman antiquarian Tommaso Capobianchi, whose shop was located at Via del Babuino 152 A and B (Fig. 11), took place in 1864–5. Today the Via del Babuino retains hints of its nineteenth-century role in the art and antiquities trade in the re-creation of the sculptors' workshop of Luigi Canova and the Tadolini family; however, no.152, like so many of its neighbours, is at the time of writing an up-market clothes shop. The archive of letters sent to Garrucci shows that the Capobianchi family were themselves frequent travellers, operating in London and Paris, and sometimes moving too quickly for the collectors' convenience.[56] Their shop was so well known to English visitors to Rome that Tommaso Capobianchi earned a personal citation in John Murray's guide to the city.[57]

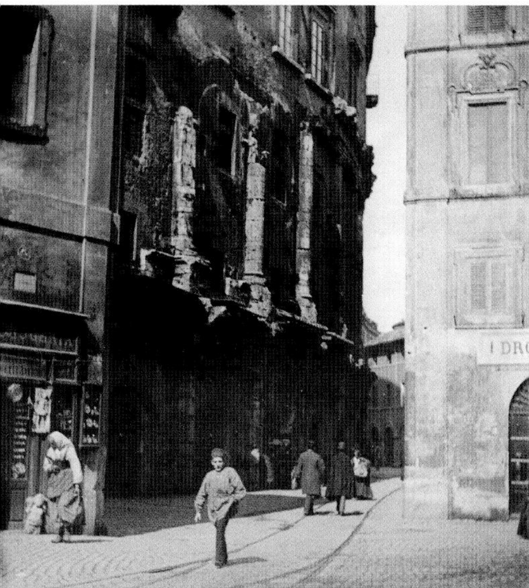

Fig. 12 A seventeenth-century house forms a backdrop to Piazza Montanara, the picturesque square that disappeared in 1934 for the opening of the Via del Mare. On the left is the Theatre of Marcellus. Unknown photographer, end of the nineteenth century. Periodici Locali Newton/ www.romasparita.eu/foto-roma-sparita/48378/ piazza-montanara-8

An evocative picture of collecting in Rome in the 1860s is offered by the Polish collector Count Michel Tyskiewicz:

> The Rome of that day [1865] was indeed a Paradise for lovers and buyers of antiquities. Under Pius IX there still hung about the Eternal City an atmosphere that was almost patriarchal, or even provincial. In many respects you might fancy yourself back in the eighteenth century…The calm that reigned there, the liberty enjoyed by all who did not meddle with politics, the kind and cordial reception given to strangers by cardinals, nobles and people alike, the quiet and simple life led by everyone, the numberless interests of the place, and its artistic and scientific surroundings – these and other reasons attracted a vast influx of rich foreigners, *savants*, nobles and sovereigns, who came to pass the winters in the Papal capital. And out of all of them the worthy Romans managed to extract a profit.
>
> The worship of antiquities was held in great honour in such a society, presided over by the fostering care of Baron Pier Ercole Visconti, Director of Excavations and of the Papal Museums, and dispenser of permits to dig, to sell and to export. Under his paternal administration everything was easy, and done with the best grace in the world. As may be imagined, the dealers in antiquities were numerous and much frequented. Rome at this time was full of gardens, huge villas, unoccupied sites, and vineyards. Outside the walls, more vineyards, market gardens and pastures; while the cultivation of fields and gardens, as well as the buildings now rising in Rome itself, provided abundantly for the daily wants of both seller and buyer.[58]

According to Tyskiewicz's lively account, the city was a significant market for small antiquities such as coins, medals and gems:

> During the short period of the palmy days of the Piazza Montanara (Fig. 12) – the place where peasants sold their finds on Saturday evenings to dealers, who promptly auctioned them in their shops, where for the rest of the week they sold tobacco or other goods – no bronze statues of any size, nor marbles of any sort, were sold there. These were seldom met with save at Ostia or such places, where the excavations were undertaken by the papal government. There was little building going on in Rome, and the few constructions undertaken by the State – such as tobacco factories or the railway station – exposed to light a great many small objects of antiquity, but no large sculptures.[59]

Gold-glass medallions from the catacombs may be counted as exceptional pieces among the small antiquities then characteristic of the Roman art market. Thus Wilshere's purchase of the Recupero Collection of gold-glass from Tommaso and Vincenzo Capobianchi was still remembered in the 1890s, but Wilshere himself was not mentioned, though the collector visited the Vatican in 1893, aged 81, and corresponded with de Rossi until the latter's death in 1894:

> In the Via del Babuino lived old Capobianchi. He never had a large number of works of art at once, but all were good, and therefore sold rapidly. One day, while travelling in Sicily, he had the good fortune to acquire a quantity of glass cups of the early Christian era, ornamented between two thicknesses of glass with gilded subjects and inscriptions. The description of these glasses was published by Father Garrucci [a friend of Tyskiewicz] and sent to England,

where, considering the period, they fetched a good price. Today, glasses so rare and beautiful would have realised thrice the sum, and few museums possess more than a few scattered specimens…[60]

In this account Tyskiewicz implies that the sale of gold-glass from the Recupero Collection was actually made in England on the strength of Garrucci's well-illustrated catalogue, commissioned by the Capobianchi family in an attempt to sell the collection to the Italian state.[61] Though Capobianchi certainly travelled to England from time to time to offer antiquities for sale, and it is possible that Wilshere saw Garrucci's catalogue in England before making the acquisition, it is clear from Wilshere's letters to de Rossi and to Fortnum that the sale of the Recupero gold-glass was actually concluded in Rome. The objects were then sent by diplomatic bag directly from the British Embassy in Florence to London for delivery to the South Kensington Museum (p.36–7).

Vincenzo Capobianchi, artist and dealer

The sale of the gold-glass in Catania in 1862 was actually made to Tommaso Capobianchi's son Vincenzo, a figure of considerable significance to the later nineteenth-century art and antiquities market. The younger Capobianchi's long career offers valuable insights into the close links between dealers, collectors, archaeologists and museum officials in Rome, elevated after 1870 to be the capital of the new nation of Italy.[62] Born to Tommaso Capobianchi and Elisa Lorini in 1836, Vincenzo studied drawing in the Vatican with Tommaso Minardi (1787–1871), thereby acquiring a profound knowledge of classical art. He became a painter of orientalist and Neo-Pompeian scenes, genres that became increasingly popular as Rome became progressively secularised after the collapse of the Papal States in the 1870s. Capobianchi was one of a number of artists employed under contract to the French dealer Adolphe Goupil; other notable figures included the Catalan painter Mariano Fortuny y Marsal, father of the famous fashion designer of the same name, and Attilio Simonetti.[63]

In order to meet the demands of a new and growing market with a romantic interest in archaeology, Goupil imposed stylistic and narrative requirements on the painters, who furnished their studios with elaborate props. Inevitably some artists found the sale of the props more immediately lucrative than that of their paintings, and consequently developed galleries selling antiquities. Vincenzo Capobianchi went into partnership with Giuseppe Giacomini. Like Alessandro Recupero a century earlier, the younger Capobianchi was especially well known for his expertise in numismatics. However, his knowledge of art was evidently very broad; he wrote sales catalogues of the Simonetti, Ruspoli, Borghese and Stroganoff Collections of antiquities and works of art. On 24 February 1888 Capobianchi directed the auction in Rome of the collection of Giuseppe Scalambrini, from whom Wilshere had bought a gilded fragment of a sarcophagus lid three years before.[64]

Vincenzo Capobianchi's interests extended to current archaeology. In the summer of 1862 he offered with Achille Stocchi to detach at their own expense (and presumably for sale) a series of paintings from a Roman nymphaeum found on the Monte della Giustizia, Rome, in which the Ministry of Justice had no interest. However, the concession had already been awarded to the Prussian legation.[65] In the early 1870s Capobianchi was commissioned by de Rossi to illustrate for the *Bullettino di Archeologia Cristiana* a new discovery from a private collection.[66] In 1885 he was elected to the *Deputazione Romana di Storia Patria*, a Roman committee on the

The Frythe
Welwyn

16 March 1869

Dear Father Garrucci

In answer to your kind letter I have to reply that I value my Christian Glass so highly that it is likely to remain in my possession a very long while. Being unique in some of its specimens, and being also the only collection in private hands and there being positively no specimens of value at all approaching mine in any national collection out of Italy, except at the British Museum, where as you know, there

when I last wrote that I had been to the British Museum and seen the codex of the 4th (or 5th) century of the Septuagint in greek; regarding which you asked me to make enquiries, and especially to ask about having some copies made of the illustrations.

It is almost in the condition of a papyrus of Herculaneum. Only half a dozen of the designs are distinctly to be made out: the whole is black, only the letters and designs are of a deeper black.

There are engravings of all the designs which can be at all well traced, in one of the first volumes of engravings in the Archaeologia of the London

Society of Antiquaries, published early in the last century.

Believe me I remain dear Father Garrucci with the greatest esteem and respect

Yours

C. Wilshere

is nothing nearly so fine; I feel sure that as Christian antiquities (thanks to yourself and to Cav: de Rossi and one or two other writers) are daily more appreciated, I shall, some time or other, be able to make my own terms with the French, Prussian, or Russian Government, if not with our own. I do not refuse to sell to private individuals, and indeed should not regard the quarter from

which an offer came, so much as its amount.

I may say that the managers of the Leeds Exhibition, to whom I lent my glass last year gave me a guaranty in writing of £1200 in case of loss or destruction; and that in reply to an enquiry five weeks ago on behalf of the South Kensington Museum I stated that fact, and added that I would not part with it to the Director for that sum.

I forget whether I told you

history of the motherland reporting to Rodolfo Lanciani.[67] Vincenzo Capobianchi lived to the age of 90, suffering in his last years a form of dementia, from which he died in 1926.

Wilshere as negotiator

Wilshere's motives for collecting and making his collection available to the public were primarily driven by religious zeal, but correspondence with Garrucci shows that he was also shrewd and a tough negotiator. A letter written in 1869 clearly states his pride in his collection of Christian gold-glass, and his acute awareness of its monetary value (Fig. 13).[68] It may be surmised (no letter from him survives) that Garrucci had made Wilshere too low an offer for the collection. This letter, written on 16 March 1869 in English (Wilshere reserved his native language for significant communications where he was anxious to avoid misunderstandings arising from his own grammatical errors in Italian or French), contains an important statement of Wilshere's principles:

> Dear Father Garrucci,
> In answer to your kind letter I have to reply that I value my Christian glass so highly that it is likely to remain in my possession a very long while. Being unique in some of its specimens, and being also the only collection in private hands, and there being positively no specimens of value at all approaching mine in any national collections out of Italy except at the British Museum, where, as you know, there is nothing nearly so fine; I feel sure that as Christian antiquities (thanks to yourself and to Cav[aliere]. de Rossi and one or two other writers) are daily more appreciated, I shall some time or other, be able to make my own terms with the French, Prussian or Russian government, if not with our own. I do not refuse to sell to private individuals, and indeed should not regard the quarter from which an offer came, so much as the amount.
>
> I may say that the managers of the Leeds exhibition, to whom I lent my glass last year, gave me a guarantee in writing of £1200 in case of loss or destruction; and that in reply to an enquiry five weeks ago, on behalf of the South Kensington Museum, I stated that fact, and added that I would not part with it to the director for that sum....
>
> Believe me to remain, dear Father Garrucci, with the greatest esteem and respect,
> Yours
> C. W. Wilshere

The surviving correspondence, notably to de Rossi, with whom Wilshere corresponded for nearly 30 years, provides confirmation of Wilshere's long-lasting relationships with his Italian academic and papal contacts. That with Garrucci may have been broken by the careless handling of the drawings of the catacombs (see above, p.30), but in 11 extant letters, written from 1868 to 1872, we see Wilshere going to extraordinary lengths to broker sales of objects to London museums on Garrucci's behalf.[69] In the 1890s Wilshere was awarded a medal by Pope Leo XIII 'for his generosity in giving the top of a triumphal arch which he had rescued from some mason's yard and a piece of ancient Christian glass, both now in the Vatican.'[70]

The 'top of the triumphal arch' surely refers to an inscription from the city of Aeclanum – namely the significant republican text *CIL* IX 1140, recording the building

Fig. 13 Part of Wilshere's letter to Garrucci of 16 March 1869, explaining the value of his glass collection. Biblioteca San Luigi, Posilippo, Letters to R. Garrucci, R 14/1869. by courtesy of the Pontificia Facoltà Teologica dell'Italia Meridionale Sezione San Luigi – Biblioteca

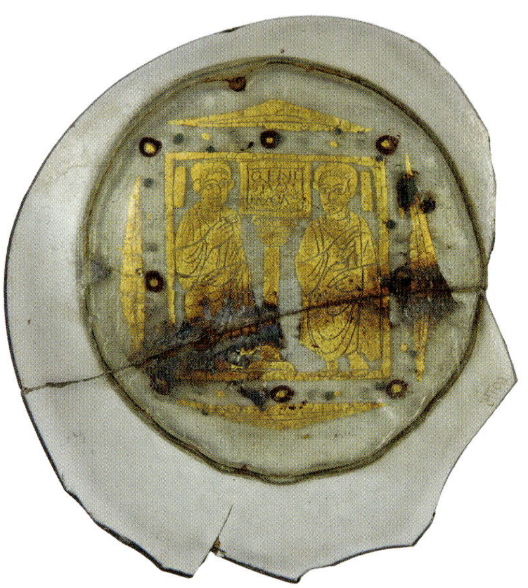

Fig. 14 Gold-glass of Genesius and Luke, formerly in the collection of Baron Alessio Recupero, acquired by Wilshere in 1865 and returned to the Vatican in 1893. Photo: Vatican Museums, Museo Sacro Cristiano, Inv. 60775

of the walls of the city. This monumental text had been the subject of fruitless negotiations by Wilshere, undertaken in the early 1870s in hope of an exchange of the monumental text for early Christian objects of equal value. The deal was to have been negotiated with Giuseppe Fiorelli, the distinguished director of the Archaeological Museum of Naples; there followed equally wearisome negotiations in the 1890s with de Rossi's colleague at the Vatican, Commendatore C. L. Visconti. Eventually Wilshere gave the inscription to de Rossi in thanks for the latter's apparent recovery from a stroke, but the actual transaction must have happened after de Rossi's death later in 1894.[71]

The other returned object mentioned in the citation was the gold-glass representing the martyr Genesius with Saint Luke (Fig. 14), published by Garrucci on multiple occasions and in the twentieth century by Morey and others.[72] Morey noted that the gold-glass was kept in the Vatican Library, Museo Sacro, within a plush-lined leather case inscribed in gilded letters: LEONI.XIII/P.M./HVMILLIME OFFERT/C.W.WILSHERE/M.D.CCC.XCIII ('To Leo XIII, most high priest, C. W. Wilshere humbly offers [this], 1893').[73]

The glass (but not the presentation case) is now on public display. Wilshere's letters to de Rossi of 1892–3 set out the details of this transaction at some length. De Rossi's half-English disciple Enrico Stevenson (see above, p.29) was charged with carrying the glass to Rome and commissioning the inscribed case. Wilshere was especially pleased with the blessing he and his family received from Pope Leo XIII.[74]

The letter to de Rossi forming the plan for the return of the gold-glass of Genesius also provides significant information about the formation of the collection. At the time of acquisition in 1865, de Rossi had asked Wilshere to leave this particular glass in Rome, as Genesius was regarded as a local saint in the city, and the glass was the only known material record of him.[75] Genesius was an actor from Arles who declared his own conversion to Christianity following a mock Christian baptism performed to amuse the emperor Diocletian, an act which cost him his life; his relics are still kept in a chapel in the church of Santa Susanna on the Quirinal.[76] However, as Wilshere recalled much later in 1894, the glass had already been sent to England – to de Rossi's amazement, for it had only been purchased five days earlier. At the time de Rossi had joked that Wilshere must have built a private underground railway from Rome to London to move it so quickly, but in the letter of 1894 Wilshere admitted that he had taken the glass to the British Embassy in Florence, where the ambassador had kindly arranged for it to be sent to London 'in the royal post', i.e. the diplomatic bag. Evidently the matter had been on Wilshere's conscience ever since, and the anniversary of Leo XIII's election offered an opportunity to make good the restitution of the glass of the martyred Genesius. This letter also shows that Wilshere knew that the Recupero Collection (see further below, p.51) was the source of the glass.[77]

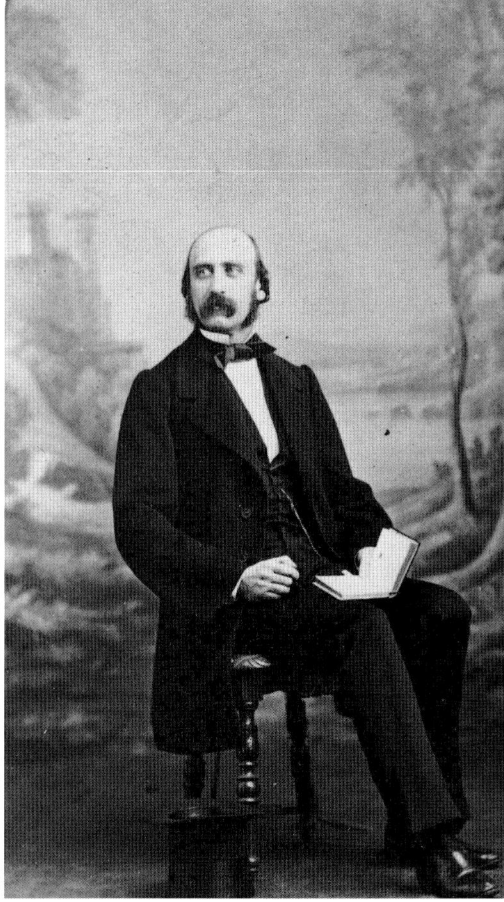

Fig. 15 Full-length studio portrait of de Rossi, signed 1866, Fratelli d'Alessandri, Rome. Library of Congress LC-USZ62-122565, Lot 6633, p.5

Wilshere's letters to de Rossi: evidence for other purchases, academic interests and personal affection

Correspondence between Wilshere and de Rossi, which began in 1865 and continued until the latter's death in 1894, includes reports of other purchases, notably the rare base of a gold-glass chalice made for Heraclides (cat. **1**), purchased in Rome (the exact source is not given) in 1870.[78] Wilshere is known to have made purchases from the numismatist and dealer Luigi Depoletti: these included a blue glass medallion from the wall of a glass dish, said to come from a cemetery on the Via Portuense (cat. **30**), and the pagan cinerary urn of Cornelia (cat. **32**). Wilshere also asked de Rossi to look out for him small items of no interest to the Vatican; after visiting Cologne and failing to buy a vessel from the wealthy hotel owner Karl Disch, who refused to sell, he was especially interested in acquiring examples of the blue glass medallions set into the walls of vessels.[79] There can then be little doubt that de Rossi himself was advising Wilshere on purchases, and indeed facilitating their sale; he was holding antiquities for Wilshere prior to export from Italy and negotiating exchanges of objects with museum directors on Wilshere's behalf.[80] Equally, Wilshere negotiated on de Rossi's behalf to sell a model of the *duomo* (cathedral) of Siena to the South Kensington Museum; the eventually fruitless negotiations are preserved in the correspondence files of de Rossi and in the museum's archives.[81]

Other letters from Wilshere to de Rossi record the purchase of an inscription from Syracuse, Sicily, cat. **56**, which Wilshere mistakenly believed to be Christian, and the gilded fragment of sarcophagus lid, cat. **38**, which he, again mistakenly, believed to represent the meal at Tiberias.[82] De Rossi was asked to comment on the text and Greek script of the Syracusan inscription, and to negotiate a lower price from the Roman antiquities dealer Scalambrini for the gilded sarcophagus lid. However, he evidently declined to do so, since Wilshere stated in a subsequent letter that de Rossi might buy the piece on his behalf at the full asking price of 300 lire.[83]

Virtually every letter includes references to matters of academic interest, whether it be subscriptions to de Rossi's *Bullettino*, advice sought from de Rossi on early Christian antiquities for exhibit at the Society of Antiquaries of London, or his opinion of newly reported archaeological discoveries. Wilshere also acted as an intermediary between de Rossi and Canon James Spencer Northcote, who was to publish an expanded English version of De Rossi's *Roma Sotterranea* in 1869 and 1879.[84]

Many postcards with Christmas, New Year and birthday greetings from Wilshere to de Rossi's family were also kept; these were affectionately written in Italian or Latin transliterated into Greek, as they had no envelope and Wilshere did not want them read by others. Similar greetings sent by sealed letter are in Italian. Wilshere also used Greek script on a postcard to de Rossi reporting his progress in tracking a codex edition of the poems of Pope Damasus, held by the Bodleian Library in Oxford.[85]

The direct participation of de Rossi, a prominent and highly respected papal official, in sales to and various other dealings with a private collector was by no means unusual at the time, nor was it a novelty in the history of the church's administration of antiquities. Nor was Wilshere an ordinary collector. Alhough the export of early Christian antiquities, especially to non-Catholic lands, was much lamented in Italy, Wilshere's stated mission to spread knowledge of early Christian art in England surely fell upon sympathetic ears in Catholic Rome and Naples. This must have been especially true during a time of major conflict in Europe and personal hardship for officers of the church.

Official reaction to Wilshere's purchases

Despite the affectionate cordiality of the correspondence, the export to England of the Recupero Collection had caused alarm on the part of the Papal authorities. It may then be the case that Garrucci's offer to Wilshere,[86] though apparently private, had been made on behalf of de Rossi. In the previous month de Rossi had applied to the Ministry of Public Works, Commerce, Fine Arts, Industry and Agriculture for additional funds to buy back gold-glasses sold from the Vatican collections in the eighteenth century to private collectors based in Italy and Sicily; these had then been resold in the chaos of the Risorgimento years to English collectors and museums:[87]

> *gli oggetti che dovrebbero per ogni titolo entrare nella Biblioteca Vaticana vanno ora ad arricchire gli stranieri musei, specialmente quello di Londra. Negli ultimi anni abbiamo deplorato la partenza da Roma dei vetri cristiani ornati di figure in oro, i quali nello scorso secolo dalle romane catacombe erano andati in Sicilia. Nelle ultime vicende politiche erano stati comprati da un antiquario romano ed ora stanno in Inghilterra. Cosi la raccolta di vetri cristiani della Vaticana è ora quasi ecclissata dai bellissimi che ora le mancano, e stanno per entrare nel museo Bretannico… Ciò avviene per mancanza di un assegno destinato a quest'uopo dal fondo degli acquisti per i musei. Talché il museo che in Roma dovrebbe essere il più privilegiato è il meno provvisto. Se sul fondo del Ministero dei Lavori Pubblici ogni anno fosse assegnata una quota di scudi duecento all'accrescimento del Museo Sacro del Vaticano, pare che ciò potrebbe bastare.*
>
> ('The objects that should by every title enter within the Vatican Library now go to enrich foreign museums, especially that of London. In recent years we have deplored the departure from Rome of Christian glasses decorated with figures in gold, which in the last [i.e. eighteenth] century travelled from the Roman catacombs to Sicily. In the recent political turbulence they were bought by a Roman antiquarian [Tommaso and Vincenzo Capobianchi] and now they are in England. In this way the Vatican's collection of Christian glasses is almost eclipsed by the very fine pieces that are now lost, that are now destined to enter the collections of the British Museum… Such things happen for lack of an assigned [sum] destined for this purpose within the acquisition funds for museums. Thus the museum that ought to be the most privileged in Rome is the least provided for. If within the fund of the Ministry of Public Works 200 *scudi* were assigned each year for the development of the Sacred Museum of the Vatican, it appears that such a sum could suffice.)[88]

In fact, at the time of their purchase of the gold-glass from the Recupero Collection in 1862, Tommaso and Vincenzo Capobianchi had written to Count Bandini, Minister of Commerce and Public Works, to offer the collection to the then Papal State.[89]

Tommaso e Vincenzo Capobianchi
Negozianti Via del Babuino, no.
152, A,B

Eccellenza Illustrissima,
Tommaso e Vincenzo Capobianchi Negozianti di oggetti antichi e di belle arti, avendo comprato in Catania e recato in Roma la collezione di vetri cimiteriali cristiani che facevano parte del Museo del fù Barone Recupero, si fecero un dovere di presentarli alla Eccellenza Vostra affine di darle spontaneamente la preferenza di acquisto pel Museo Cristiano Vaticano.

Gli esponenti, affine di agevolare le trattative si presero la cura di inciderne in litografia i disegni fedelissimi, e di farne stendere da persona idonea [Raffaele Garrucci] una illustrazione per dare così il commodo di meglio considerarli evalutarne il merito.

Sperando gli esponenti che l'Eccellenza V(ostra) sarà per gradire le premure loro, e non permetterà che oggetti tanto interessanti per l'archeologia Cristiana vadano ad arricchire qualche museo estero forse anche di nazione non Cattolica.

F(irma)to
12 luglio 1862
Alla sezione V per tenere
M.C.L.P.

A Sua Eccellenza Illustrissima
Il. Sig(nor) Conte Bandini
Ministro del Commercio e
di Lavori Pubblici
('Tommaso and Vincenzo Capobianchi
Traders, Via del Babuino, no.152, A,B

Illustrious Excellency,
('Tommaso and Vincenzo Capobianchi, Sellers of antiques and fine art, having bought in Catania and shipped to Rome the collection of funerary Christian glass that formed part of the Museum of the late Baron Recupero, obliged themselves to present the collection to Your Excellency with the aim of spontaneously offering first refusal of the collection to the Vatican's Christian Museum.

The applicants, in order to facilitate the negotiations, took it upon themselves to engrave in lithographs the most accurate drawings, and to set out under the direction of an appropriate person [Raffaele Garrucci] an illustration of the glasses to give in this way the convenience of a better consideration and evaluation of their value.

The applicants hope that Your Excellency will accept their kindness and will not permit objects of such great interest for Christian archaeology to go to enrich some foreign museum, even one in a non-Catholic nation.

Signed
Tommaso and Vincenzo Capobianchi

12 July 1862
To Section V for retention

To His Most Illustrious Excellency
Signor Count Bandini
Minister of Commerce and
Public Works')

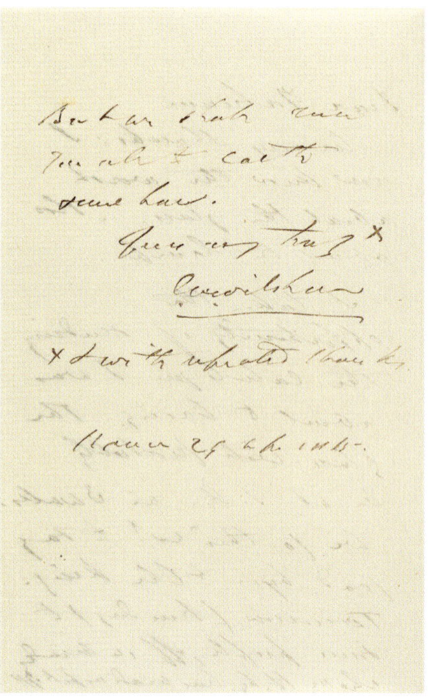

Fig. 16 Letter from Charles Wilshere to C. D. E. Fortnum, thanking him for his advice on valuation of the gold-glass and detailing the shipment of the Recupero glass from Florence to London. Sackler Library, now Department of Antiquities, Ashmolean Museum

Understanding its rarity and significance, and appealing to the Papal State Minister's sense of Catholic patriotism, the Capobianchi family had evidently commissioned Raffaele Garrucci to publish the glass with illustrations. Garrucci's publication of 1862–3, then, was effectively a sales catalogue.[90] When the proposed sale to the Vatican's Christian Museum failed, the publication served to tempt museum curators overseas, as well as private collectors such as Wilshere. The negative results of the Capobianchis' appeal to the Minister demonstrate that financial constraints on the Vatican Museums had continued throughout the 1860s, a period of great political and economic instability at the climax of the Risorgimento, when many noble collections were being sold (see further below, p.50).

In addition to the papers cited above, an earlier appeal by de Rossi for the consideration of eight glasses from an unnamed source – also for sale by the Capobianchi brothers, but not in this case illustrated by a catalogue – had been lodged in 1861.[91] The source of these glasses is not specified in the documents; they may have comprised other glasses eventually bought by Wilshere from the Capobianchi's shop that were not part of the Recupero Collection, or they might possibly have formed part of the Matarozzi Collection of 17 gold-glasses purchased by the British Museum in 1863.[92] De Rossi states in his petition that the glasses were of interest to an unnamed London institution.

Notwithstanding the existential threat to the Papal States in the 1860s, the tone and content of de Rossi's plea will be familiar to any curator working today in a publicly funded museum and attempting to stem the flow of locally significant antiquities abroad. De Rossi wrongly stated that the glasses were destined for the British Museum, not the South Kensington Museum. He also implied that the gold-glasses had been sold to the Sicilian collector Recupero directly from the catacombs, although it is clear from the records made for Gaetano Marini that in the late eighteenth century four of the five glasses sold to Recupero were still in the care of the Vatican curator Abbate Severini (see below, p.61). However, de Rossi states elsewhere that Severini found the gold-glass of Genesius in the catacombs, so there may have been little delay between the discovery and the sale:

> *monumento singolare rinvinuto nella fine dello secolo scorso dall'Abbate Severini custode de' sacri cemetery di Roma, il cui disegno serbato nei manuscritti del Marini nella Vaticana ho communicato at ch.p. Garrucci per l'edizione dei vetri cemeteriali.*
>
> ('A singular monument found at the end of the last century by Abbot Severini, custodian of the sacred cemeteries of Rome, of which the drawing is preserved in the manuscripts of Marini in the Vatican. I alerted Father Garrucci of this for his publication of the funerary glasses.')[93]

The extravagant claim for the quality of the Recupero pieces was intended to invoke financial support for future acquisitions of antiquities threatened with export to collectors and museums in non-Catholic countries. However, the Vatican still maintains an uncontested supremacy today in the quality and quantity of its late Roman gold-glass.

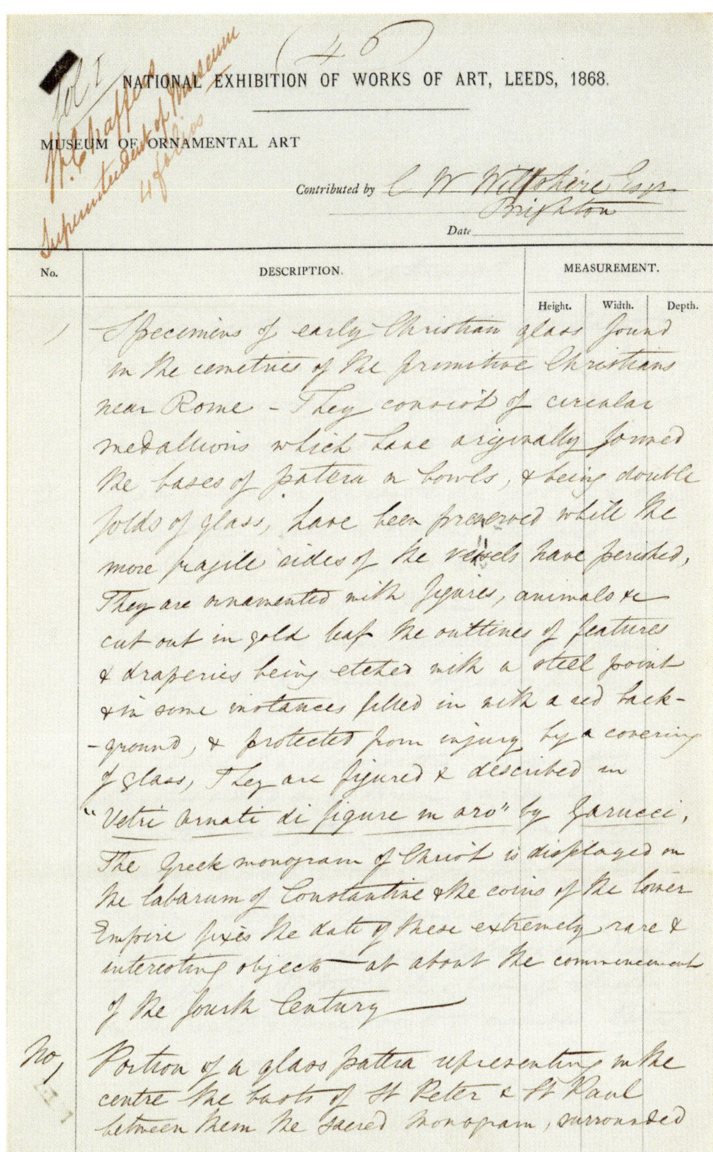

(46)

NATIONAL EXHIBITION OF WORKS OF ART, LEEDS, 1868.

MUSEUM OF ORNAMENTAL ART

W. Chaffers Superintendent of Museum 4 folios

Contributed by C. W. Wilshere Esqr. Brighton

Date

No.	DESCRIPTION.	MEASUREMENT. Height.	Width.	Depth.
1	Specimens of early Christian glass found in the cemetries of the primitive Christians near Rome – They consist of circular medallions which have originally formed the bases of patera or bowls, & being double folds of glass, have been preserved while the more fragile sides of the vessels have perished, They are ornamented with figures, animals &c cut out in gold leaf the outlines of features & draperies being etched with a steel point & in some instances filled in with a red back-ground, & protected from injury by a covering of glass, They are figured & described in "Vetri Ornati di figure in oro" by Garucci, The Greek monogram of Christ is displayed on the labarum of Constantine & the coins of the lower Empire fixes the date of these extremely rare & interesting objects — at about the commencement of the fourth Century —			
No 1	Portion of a glass patera representing in the centre the busts of St Peter & St Paul between them the sacred monogram, surrounded			

Fig. 17 Cover page of the inventory of loans of Wilshere's gold-glass and embroideries to the National Exhibition of Art in England, Leeds 1868. Ashmolean Museum, Department of Antiquities

Displaying Wilshere's Collection

Nineteenth-century displays in South Kensington, Leeds and Welwyn

As noted above, Wilshere's intention in buying Christian and Jewish antiquities in Italy and shipping them to England was to instruct museum visitors in the art and archaeology of early Christianity and its Hebrew roots. To this end the pieces from the Recupero Collection were shipped directly in 1865 from Florence to the South Kensington Museum (later the Victoria and Albert Museum), London, where they remained on loan until 1894. The move was reported in a hastily scrawled, and hence only partially legible, letter from Wilshere, written on the eve of departure from Florence on 25 April 1865 to the well-known English collector C. D. E. Fortnum, who evidently advised Wilshere on prices.

In 1868, only two years after the loan commenced, Wilshere demanded that the gold-glass be included in a major exhibition in Leeds of the finest works of art held in England; the loan register was compiled by a curator representing the exhibition (Fig. 17 and Appendix 2).

The gold-glass was limited to the 13 pieces acquired from the Recupero sale of 1862; it was accompanied by two ecclesiastical embroideries which were apparently returned to The Frythe, whence they had most likely come, for 'two pieces of needlework framed' are listed as kept in a water-closet adjoining the office in an inventory of the house compiled for Charles Wilshere by his late brother William's executors in 1867.[94] This does not necessarily mean that William had acquired or inherited them, as the inventory also lists in the same locations two sarcophagi, not further described, which may have been among Charles Wilshere's early acquisitions; both locations appear more suited to storage than display. The embroideries were sold on behalf of Gerald Wilshere at Sotheby's in October 1942, where they apparently fetched only £22 against an estimate of £100.[95] After the Leeds exhibition the gold-glasses were returned to display at the South Kensington Museum.[96]

Given his own religious affiliation, his knowledge of the history of exploration of the catacombs in which the gold-glass had been found and his good relations with Henry Cole, it may be no coincidence that Wilshere's principal collection of gold-glass was loaned to the new South Kensington Museum. Inspired by the Great Exhibition of 1851, the museum had been opened by Queen Victoria on 22 June 1857 on the site of Brompton Park House, which boasted the first-ever museum refreshment rooms.[97] Brompton Park House was located next to the London Oratory, which had only moved to its present site on the Brompton Road in 1854, during a nineteenth-century revival of interest in St Philip Neri, his life and work.[98]

The devotional aspect of the display in Leeds was further enhanced by the two fifteenth-century English ecclesiastical embroideries, respectively depicting St Lawrence, holding the gridiron on which he was martyred, and St Augustine, founder of the English Church. They were complemented by the display in South Kensington of an early German enamelled crucifix, loaned by Wilshere from 24 January 1866 until 1 May 1879, and a chalice with detached enamelwork on pierced silver, loaned from 6 February 1869 until 28 August 1897.[99] Effectively Wilshere's collection of gold-glass might be said to have evoked the devotional motive of the early explorers of the catacombs, and its public display so near the London Oratory exemplified the educational role of the lay community of the Oratorians.

In contrast, Wilshere kept his collection of inscriptions and sarcophagi at home in Welwyn; on 28 August 1871 he wrote from The Frythe to Garrucci that he intended to set up a small museum there once the building works on the house had been completed:

> *finora il bassorilievo resta imballato con molti altri oggetti che aspettano che i lavori alla mia casa siano terminati: allora mio piccolo museo cristiano sarà disposto in ordine.*
>
> ('up to now the relief remains boxed up with many other objects that await an end to work on my house: then my little Christian museum will be set out in order.')[100]

No record survives in the letters to Garrucci and de Rossi of a museum at The Frythe, or indeed of any visitors to see the inscriptions and sarcophagi. However, Wilshere's obituarist noted a collection of significance at The Frythe, and he did record in a late letter to de Rossi details of his negotiations with Pusey House concerning the deed of gift of '*mia piccola collezione di cimeli cristiani che formano il nucleo di un museo d'antichità cristiana fino al 800'* ('my small collection of Christian relics which form the nucleus of a museum of Christian antiquity up to [AD] 800'.)[101]

Indeed the Declaration of Trust clearly stated that 'the inscribed stones and bas-reliefs [sarcophagi]', all of which were individually listed in the schedule, were 'at present at The Frythe Welwyn in charge of the said Charles Willes Wilshere'.

The stone objects presented formidable difficulties of weight, size, display and interpretation, and it may have been the case that the London museum directors were unwilling to take them on loan. The glass, by contrast, was portable and visually attractive, though even today its display presents problems of lighting.

Twentieth- and twenty-first-century displays in Oxford

In old age, Wilshere had made provision for the educational potential of the collection to last long after his death. The Declaration of Trust consigning his collection to the care of the Trustees of Pusey House, Oxford included an explicit statement of Wilshere's intention that the collection 'should be open for the inspection and examination of students at Pusey House … and of such other persons as the Trustees [of Pusey House, signatories to the Declaration] think fit…'[102] An earlier will handwritten by Wilshere in front of witnesses in April 1885, apparently during a bout of serious illness, suggests a valuation of £2,250 for the pictures and antiquities at The Frythe; it is unlikely that this estimate included the gold-glass on loan to the South Kensington Museum.[103] The estimate appears in a tender letter explaining the division of Wilshere's estate between his surviving daughters, expressing too the hope that he and his elderly wife would be reunited with their late daughter Florence and her son Sydney; on the same sheet a breathtaking list of debts of £10,500 run up by Wilshere's eldest 'darling' daughter Edith is itemised and she was suitably fined in the will.[104]

The history of the Wilshere Collection in the century following his death in 1906 may be followed at least in part through compilations of partial inventories and a sales catalogue, each document of varying quality (Appendix 1). Unfortunately the gold-glass and small objects contained within the wooden box mentioned in the Declaration of Trust were, unlike the inscriptions and sarcophagi, not listed individually, the box having been sent to Keble College, Oxford in advance of the Declaration. However, 12 of the gold-glasses that had *not* been loaned to the South Kensington Museum were described, along with 14 gems, cameos and finger-rings, in an inventory of 4 September 1893 (Appendix 1). This was most likely commissioned or even dictated, the Latin texts corrected and the document dated by Wilshere himself, but the full manuscript is not in his hand; possibly the task was assigned to one of his daughters.

After the stone inscriptions and sarcophagi were moved to Pusey House in 1925, a list of objects was compiled by T. B. L. Webster (1905–74), then a student of the university and later distinguished for his work on ancient Greek comedy and the iconography of the Greek theatre on Greek vases.[105] This is the most detailed list extant today (Appendix 1). However, no title page or heading has survived, so it is not clear whether the 105 entries represent all antiquities then at Pusey House, or simply those that Webster understood to comprise the entire Wilshere Collection. Nor is it clear whether this untitled and undated typescript was actually compiled by Webster or by a typist when the collection was inventoried, or whether the typescript was made later, following Webster's notes, which have not survived; the typescript font was in use through the mid-twentieth century. Even this list

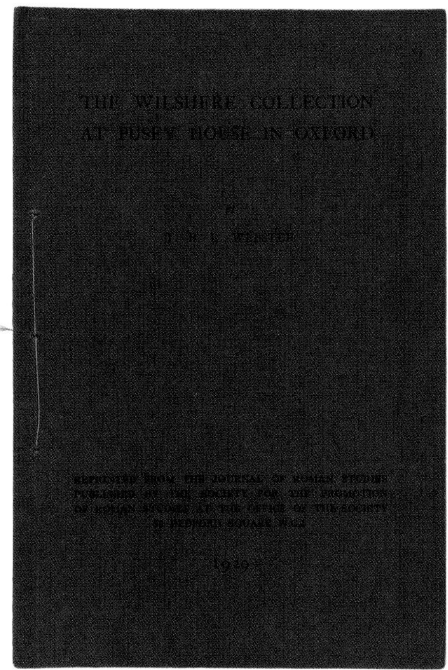

Fig. 18 Cover of an offprint of T. B. L. Webster's partial publication of the Wilshere collection in the Journal of Roman Studies, 1929

has unexpected omissions and uncertain inclusions: some gold-glass known to have belonged to Wilshere is missing (cats **1**, **7** and **35**), and the list includes several antiquities that lie beyond Wilshere's recorded interests or geographical area of collecting. However, the introduction to Webster's partial publication of the list (Fig. 18) implies that all the objects he had listed *were* bequeathed to Pusey House by Wilshere, whose collection he describes as

> miscellaneous objects of very varying date and provenance, though mostly of the early Christian period ... formed by purchases made at various times and places, though chiefly in Rome....[106]

Thus, though the ancient secular objects are not recorded in surviving nineteenth-century lists or correspondence, it is possible, even probable, that Wilshere's daughters sent to Oxford not only the stone objects listed in the Declaration of Trust of 1895, but also all antiquities still at The Frythe in the 1920s, regardless of their relevance to the interests of Pusey House. The objects selected for publication by Webster included a funerary inscription from Syracuse that he (and Wilshere) believed to be Byzantine, but is in fact pagan and of early imperial date (cat. **56**), 13 of the most important gold-glasses, of which four were illustrated with photographs for the first time (cats **3**, **13**, **22** and **23**), and the texts of all but one of the Jewish inscriptions (cats **43–46** and **48–50**), the earlier publication of which Webster was unaware.[107]

The principal objects sent to Oxford in the wooden box were the gold-glasses. Of these, the items formerly placed on loan to the South Kensington Museum were set in cases lined with blue velvet; the cases were still with the collection when much of it was moved on loan to the Ashmolean in 1957, but at the time of writing are apparently no longer extant. The wooden box also contained rings and seals, objects described by Tyskiewicz as characteristic of the Roman art market of the 1860s (see above, p.32). Although correspondence from 1958 in the Ashmolean Museum files indicates that two fragments of engraved glass and one fragment of gold-glass from this group of objects were separately transferred to the museum on loan, these were evidently returned to Pusey House. No record of the return survives, but these glass fragments were among the objects sold by the then Principal and Governors of Pusey House at Christie's, King Street, London in October 2008. The sale also included at least six of the gems, cameos and rings described in Wilshere's partial inventory of 1893, and at least one of the Jewish objects published by Kraabel in 1979. The description of the lot in the auction catalogue described the objects as 'The Property of Pusey House, Oxford. Various early 20th-century donors.'[108]

A third group of eight objects was also at Pusey House by the mid-1920s. With one exception, a relief from a Roman sarcophagus showing vintaging *putti* (wingless cupids: Declaration of Trust no.6, Webster no.24), these objects are not mentioned in the Declaration of Trust of 1895 or in the manuscript of 1893, and seven of them may not have belonged to Wilshere. However, all were numbered and described in variable detail, alas without dimensions, in Webster's draft catalogue, and they were briefly mentioned, along with their location in the cloister of Pusey House, in the publication.[109] Sadly an unpublished research note made by Kraabel in the late 1970s indicates that all eight, including the sarcophagus relief, were stolen from the cloister of Pusey House in 1976.[110] The theft was not disclosed to the Ashmolean curators when the stone objects from the Wilshere Collection were transferred to the Museum on loan in 1984; indeed, later correspondence concerning the whereabouts of the sarcophagus relief suggests that the incident may not even have been recorded within Pusey House.[111] None of the antiquities in this group has any Christian or Jewish significance. They have not yet been traced.

The missing sarcophagus relief is listed in the Declaration of Trust as 'No. 6. Bas-relief. Vintage. 20" x 17"', and is the only item listed by Wilshere with no obvious Christian connotations. What was the collector's purpose in acquiring it? Similar scenes appear between three figures of the Good Shepherd on the front of a sarcophagus in the Vatican Museum, photographed in the 1870s for John Henry Parker:

> Among the sarcophagi photographed by Simelli and reproduced by Mr Parker (Plate XVII, no.2) is one representing a vine, from which a number of putti are gathering grapes and treading them out in the press below, others are tending and milking sheep. But in the centre and at each end of the sarcophagus is a large figure of the Good Shepherd standing on a pedestal, with a sheep on his shoulders and a pastoral crook in his hand.[112]

This may have been the inspiration for Wilshere's purchase. In 1997 the German scholar Doris Bielefeld suggested that the missing relief may have been one of a pair, the other panel having been immured since the seventeenth century in a wall facing the garden of Palazzo Mattei in Rome.[113]

The stone objects listed in the Declaration of Trust and the major group of gold-glass thus have a more visible history. Some, if not all, of the objects that do not fit within the core early Christian and Jewish categories may have been earlier or later acquisitions, if indeed they had ever belonged to Wilshere. In the following chapter the Italian sources of Wilshere's collection, where they are known, are explored in greater detail to give an historical context to the collection.

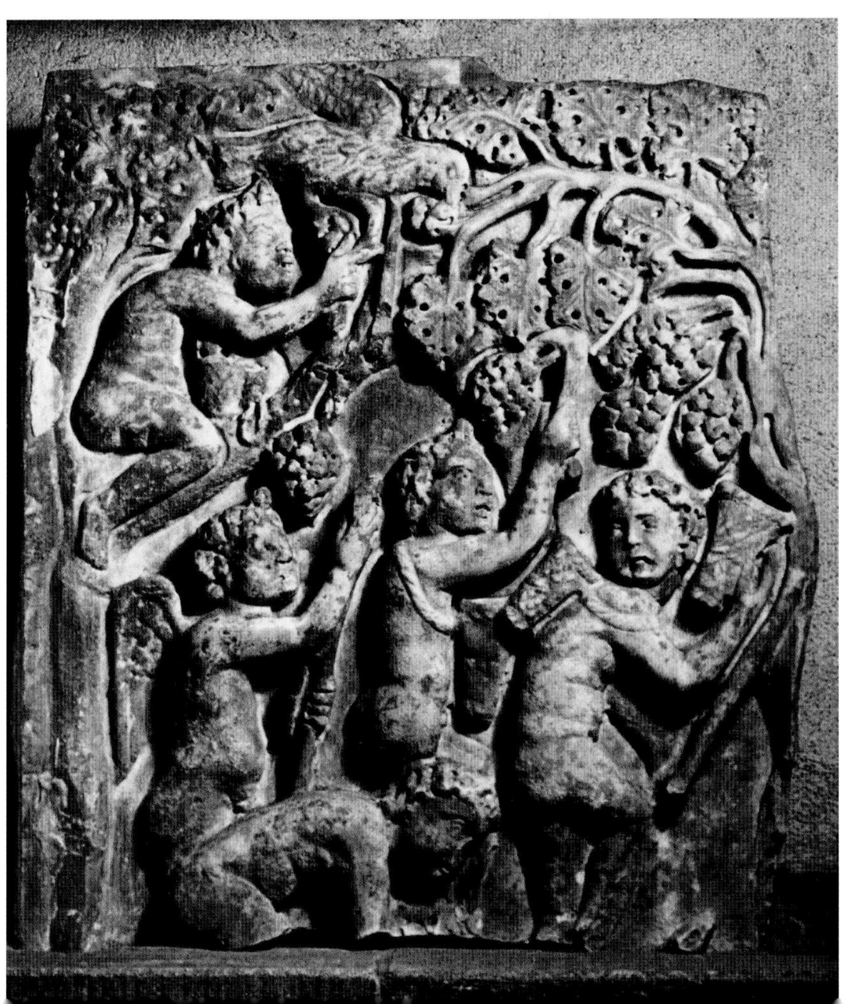

Fig. 19 Relief from a Roman sarcophagus showing *putti* harvesting grapes, as displayed in the cloister at Pusey House before 1976. Department of Antiquities, Ashmolean Museum

Notes

1. Hertfordshire Archives and Local Studies (hereafter HALS), Gerish Box 82/The House/ The Frythe/undated and unsourced newspaper obituary of Charles Willes Wilshere, October 1906.
2. Burke's Landed Gentry[12] 1914, 2041: Wilshere of The Frythe.
3. A valentine made in London between 1850 and 1875, addressed to Miss Eva Wilshere, England, suggests that Florence's elder sister Everilda did not lack admirers, but for whatever reason she did not marry. V & A E.790–1959.
4. HALS, ref. II–II 59227–8.
5. www.puseyhouse.org. The standard history of the Oxford Movement, using original correspondence, remains Liddon 1893. See recently Strong and Herringer 2012 and Brown and Nockles 2012.
6. Wallis 1993: 53.
7. The date of the letter is 7 October 1850. See Wallis 1993: 55–6.
8. Wallis 1993: 57–60.
9. Wallis 1993: 57.
10. Wallis 1993: 55, 68.
11. See obituary cited in n.1.
12. Kraabel 1979: 42; Hugh 1961.
13. *The Portuary Kalendar for the Year of Our Lord 1867, Oxford and London.* On the repeal of the act in 1871, see Wallis 1993: 78–9.
14. '*The North Side of the Table with a digression on the 'Basilican Position'. A paper read before the members of the English Church Union at a meeting of the St Albans, Hatfield and Welwyn branch held at Welwyn, June 22nd, 1876. London.*
15. *Leave Convocation Alone, London 1879, second edition September 1882; Leave Church Patronage Alone, second edition Oxford and London, 1886.*
16. *Are not Anglican Orders a fact in history? A reply to a pamphlet entitled 'Are Anglican Clergy real Priests?', sold for two pence or four soldi. Rome, L. Piale. Oxford and London, James Parker and Co., 1872.*
17. Kraabel 1979: 42 with n.7.
18. Hertfordshire Archives and Local Studies Acc 4493.
19. For the marriage, see the obituary of Charles Wilshere (n.1 above); for the letter to Garrucci, Biblioteca S. Luigi, Posilippo, R 45/1870.
20. 'Je pars lundi pour Oberammergau', letter of 23 June 1871 from Wilshere to de Rossi, Vatican City, Biblioteca Apostolica Vaticana, Vat.lat. 14247, 1871.152.
21. Biblioteca Apostolica Vaticana Vat.lat. 14292, 1892.1183.
22. Biblioteca Apostolica Vaticana, Vat.lat. 14245, 322–3, undated,1866. BM PE 1881.6–24.1, Howells 2015: 15–16; 90–101, no.16.
23. Biblioteca Apostolica Vaticana Vat.lat. 14273, 1885/339.
24. Obituary of Florence Malet, unnamed and undated newspaper cutting pasted into the annotated edition of Cussans 1877: 431.
25. Frank E. Ballin, 'Welwyn and the Frythe', *Hertfordshire Countryside, vol.12, no.48 (Spring 1958).*
26. Ballin 1973; Rook and Rook 1996:14.
27. Cussans 1877: 429 (annotated edition, Hertfordshire County Record Office). Wilshere's daughters also referred to him, playfully or otherwise, as 'The Squire'.
28. Biblioteca Apostolica Vaticana Vat.lat. 14284/1890.3.
29. On chronograms and a full explanation of this and other texts by Wilshere, see Rook and Rook 1996: 26–7.
30. Rook and Rook 1996: 1; the chronograms are elucidated, pp 26–77.
31. Cussans 1877: vol.II. The letter is dated Christmas 1880 and refers to work undertaken by Wilshere before 1865.
32. See http://homepage.ntlworld.com/jeffery.knaggs/Frythe.html for a detailed and evocative twentieth-century history of the house; see also Longmead 2006 for excellent photographs.
33. www.timelapse.dk/soe.php.
34. Kemp 1996:164 offers a scathing indictment of the Welman as 'the result of a situation where enthusiasm for unorthodox and unusual means of attacking the enemy lost touch with the realities of making war'.
35. Dave Burke, '£40 million' Welwyn site sale paves way for 200 homes, *Welwyn and Hatfield Times, September 2013.*
36. A transcript of all the letters in both collections was made by the present author in 2013. They are cited in part or in full here to support the narrative, with translations by the present author, but no full publication is attempted in this catalogue.
37. De Rossi, 1870: 81; 1872: 36. Federico Harford is to be identified as the Reverend Frederick Kill Harford (1832–91), a prebendary of Westminster Abbey. He was a pioneer of music therapy for the sick and a friend of the artist Gustave Doré. The marble votive is cat. **58**.
38. Northcote and Brownlow 1869.
39. Northcote and Brownlow 1879a: prefaces to volume I and volume II, the former quoting Northcote and Brownlow 1869.
40. Northcote and Brownlow 1869, 1879, 1879a.
41. Northcote and Brownlow 1879a: vii. The letter from de Rossi was written on 25 May 1872.
42. Palmer, Northcote and Brownlow 1885.
43. Palmer, Northcote and Brownlow 1885: 10.
44. Northcote and Brownlow 1879a: 298.
45. Northcote and Brownlow 1879a: 302–4.
46. The reply is reported to de Rossi with a full transcript of Northcote's Latin text in a letter from Wilshere of 29 May 1893:Biblioteca Apostolica Vaticana Vat.lat 14294. 1893.291.
47. On Stevenson see Fiocchi Nicolai 1998, Nieddu 1998 and Ramieri 1998.
48. Other correspondents included Mr Wynne-Finch (1866: possibly Lieutenant-Colonel Charles Arthur Wynne-Finch, 1841–1903); Mr Albert Pearson (1868) and the Reverend C. F. Lowden (1878).
49. Biblioteca Apostolica Vaticana Vat.lat 14292/1892.1183, dated 20 December 1892
50. Profuse apologies were offered in French on 23 June 23 1871: Biblioteca Apostolica Vaticana Vat.lat 14250.1871.152.
51. See G. Finocchiaro in Tellini-Manodoro 1995: 189.
52. On Bosio see Parisi 1971; for Pompeo Ugonio see Finocchiaro in Tellini-Manodoro 1995: 190–1.
53. Biblioteca S. Luigi, Posilippo, letters R 30, 39, 45, 54, all dating to 1870; R 14, 18, 29 from 1871.
54. Arringhi 1651. For the letter to Garrucci revealing the origin of the drawings, see below.
55. Biblioteca San Luigi R 11/1872, sent from The Frythe, Welwyn on 8 February.
56. Biblioteca San Luigi R 29/1871, dated 28 August on return to Welwyn from Oberammergau. In letter R 23/1871, dated 11 July, Tommaso Capobianchi explains the movements of his brother Vincenzo and of money due to Garrucci following the successful sale of a silver vase in London.
57. Murray 1867: xxvii.
58. Tyskiewicz 1898, 37–8. Tyskiewicz's memoirs were published in instalments in *Revue Archéologique* from 1895 until his death aged 69 in November 1897. His friend Salomon Reinach subsequently published them as a pamphlet, translated into English in the same year by Mrs Andrew Lang, Leonora Blanche Alleyne Lang – who was variously credited (or not) as author, collaborator and translator of her husband's enormously successful publications of fairy tales. I am grateful to David Rini for alerting me to this valuable source.
59. Tyskiewicz 1898, 54–5.
60. Tyskiewicz 1898, 40-1. Howells 2015: 15 mistakenly speculates that this passage refers to the Matarozzi Collection. I am grateful to David Rini for this observation.
61. Garrucci 1862-3 (often wrongly cited as 1864).
62. De Calletaÿ 2016.
63. Spinazzò 2010.
64. See cat. **38**. Wilshere asked de Rossi for help in brokering the deal.
65. Lanciani, Malvezzi Campeggi and Buzzetti 2000: 371.

66. De Rossi 1872: 8.
67. Lanciani, Malvezzi Campeggi and Buzzetti 2000: 371.
68. Biblioteca S. Luigi, Posilippo: letter R 14, 1869.
69. Summary lists of correspondence, but not the correspondence itself, between Charles Wilshere and various officers of the South Kensington Museum, later the Victoria and Albert Museum, survive in the museum's Correspondence Abstract Registers. These summarise negotiations on the sale of the series of (eventually) 71 pencil drawings owned by Raffaele Garrucci. Apparently the potential purchase was not concluded.
70. For the Papal honour see Kraabel 1979: 42 with n.6, citing Pusey House records. A handwritten label survives from the 1920s display, now kept in the archive of the Department of Antiquities, Ashmolean Museum. The occasion for the return was the fifteenth anniversary of Leo's accession, but the gift was made when Wilshere was planning the long-term future of his collection.
71. For the negotiations of the 1870s see (for correspondence with de Rossi) Biblioteca Apostolica Vaticana Vat.lat. 14250, 1871.103, 106; (for correspondence with Garrucci) Biblioteca S. Luigi R18, R29/1871. For the gift to the Vatican see Biblioteca Apostolica Vaticana Vat.lat. 14295, 1894.124.
72. Garrucci 1858: pl.XIX, no.4; Garrucci 1862: no.6; Garrucci 1864: no.4; Garrucci 1876: pl.CLXXXVIII, no.5; Vopel 1899, no.418; Leclerq 1923, no.281, col.1842; Morey 1959: 19, no.79; Vattuone 2000: 134, no.79.
73. The source of Morey's information is surely the inventory of the Vatican Library's Museo Sacro: Biblioteca Apostolica Vaticana Arch. Bibl.66B, p.17. I am grateful to David Rini for this reference.
74. Biblioteca Apostolica Vaticana Vat.lat. 14292, 1892.1183; 14293, 1893.112, 1893.156; 14294, 1893.291.
75. Biblioteca Apostolica Vaticana Vat.lat. 14292, 1892.1183.
76. Webb 2010: 84.
77. Biblioteca Apostolica Vaticana Vat.Lat. 14292, 1892.1183.
78. Biblioteca Apostolica Vaticana, Vat. lat. 14247 1870/357. The document is unheaded and undated, but from the content appears to have been written in Rome during the winter of 1870–1.
79. Biblioteca Apostolica Vaticana, Vat. lat. 14245, 1965/7, dated 10 January 1865. For Karl Disch's vessel see above, p.00.
80. Biblioteca Apostolica Vaticana, Vat. lat. 14247, 1870/163, written from Welwyn on 24 May (inscriptions from Vigna Randanini); 1871/106, written from England on 13 May (inscriptions from Aeclanum).
81. Biblioteca Apostolica Vaticana, Vat. lat. 14273, 1885/509 and 1885/535, written on 13 and 28 August 1885.
82. Biblioteca Apostolica Vaticana, Vat. lat. 14273, 1885/339, 20 May 1885 (sarcophagus lid); 1885/509 13 August 1885 (inscription).
83. Biblioteca Apostolica Vaticana, Vat. lat. 14273, 1885.509, 13 August 1885.
84. Northcote 1879. See also pp.27–28 above.
85. For example Biblioteca Apostolica Vaticana, Vat. lat. 14257, 1876/428, 30 December ; 14261, 1878/634, 23 December; Vat. lat. 14263, 1880/2, 1 January; 1882/645, 30 December. Progress at the Bodleian: Vat. lat. 14273, 1885/528, written on 21 August.
86. See above, p.35 and Fig. 13 for Wilshere's reply.
87. Archivio di Stato, Roma: 3/4/1869. Sulla vendita ed estrazione dei vetri cristiani. Approvazione di un fondo. 6581/68 Numeri del Ministero, 2600. Ministero del Commercio e dei Lavori Publicci. Provincia di Roma, Sez. 5, Tit.1, Fasc.5, Letter no.1, 3/4/1869, a bifolio of four pages in cursive Italian. The letter is signed by G. B. de Rossi. The signature to Ministerial Protocol 2600 is illegible. I am grateful to David Rini for a transcript of this letter.
88. The English translation of this and other documents held by the Archivio di Stato is by the present author.
89. Protocol no.4737, filed 12 July 1862, Archivio di Stato Sezione 5, Titolo 1, Fascicolo 5. I am grateful to David Rini for locating and transcribing the document.
90. Garrucci 1862–3, often misdated as 1864. The publication was commissioned by the Capobianchis in the summer of 1862 and was filed in the Ministry of Commerce and Public Works by 1863.
91. Protocol 8280, Archivio di Stato, 19 December 1861. In Protocol number 156 of the preceding day, de Rossi was ordered to investigate the glasses further in an attempt to reduce their price of 2000 *scudi*, regarded by the Papal authorities as exorbitant. A file note of 9 February 1862 records the unchanged price as too high. I am grateful to David Rini for locating, photographing and transcribing the document.
92. Howells 2015: 14–15 discussed the acquisition of the Matarozzi Collection, but was unaware of this document.
93. De Rossi 1864: 46; Garrucci 1864: 115.
94. HALS DE/WSF3.
95. HALS DE/WS/E36; DE/WS/C4 for the valuations of the collection and items of furniture. Seventeen old master paintings were also sold; they were of the Flemish, German and Italian schools, among which a painting of a woman and child by Lucas Cranach fetched £500.
96. The movements are recorded in Victoria and Albert Museum, Art Museum Loan Index B, MA/1/31/2.
97. Physick 1982.
98. The London Oratory was constructed in Brompton Road by 1856; at the same time, the South Kensington Museum was being built on a site immediately to the west.
99. The current location of these objects, if they are still extant, is unknown. They are not identifiable in any late nineteenth- or twentieth-century inventory of Wilshere's collection.
100. Biblioteca San Luigi, Posilippo: R 29, 1871.
101. Biblioteca Apostolica Vaticana Vat.lat. 14292, 1892.1183.
102. See Appendix 3 for a full transcript. The Declaration of Trust is now held by the Department of Antiquities, Ashmolean Museum, Oxford.
103. HALS DE/HA/B1771.
104. HALS DE/HA/B1771/2.
105. Handley 2003.
106. Webster 1929: 150.
107. Webster 1929; Kraabel 1979: 43.
108. Christie's sale of 13 October 2008, Lot 55. Some of the objects have now been traced.
109. Webster 1929: 152.
110. Kraabel's sketches, until 2008 held at Pusey House, and the correspondence about the sarcophagus are kept in the archive of the Department of Antiquities, Ashmolean Museum.
111. The relief was published without dimensions or known location by Bielefeld 1998:113, no.73, pl.77.3.
112. Northcote and Brownlow 1879a: 358.
113. Bielefeld 1997:45. The relief in the Palazzo Mattei is published by Guerrini 1982: no.100, pl.71.

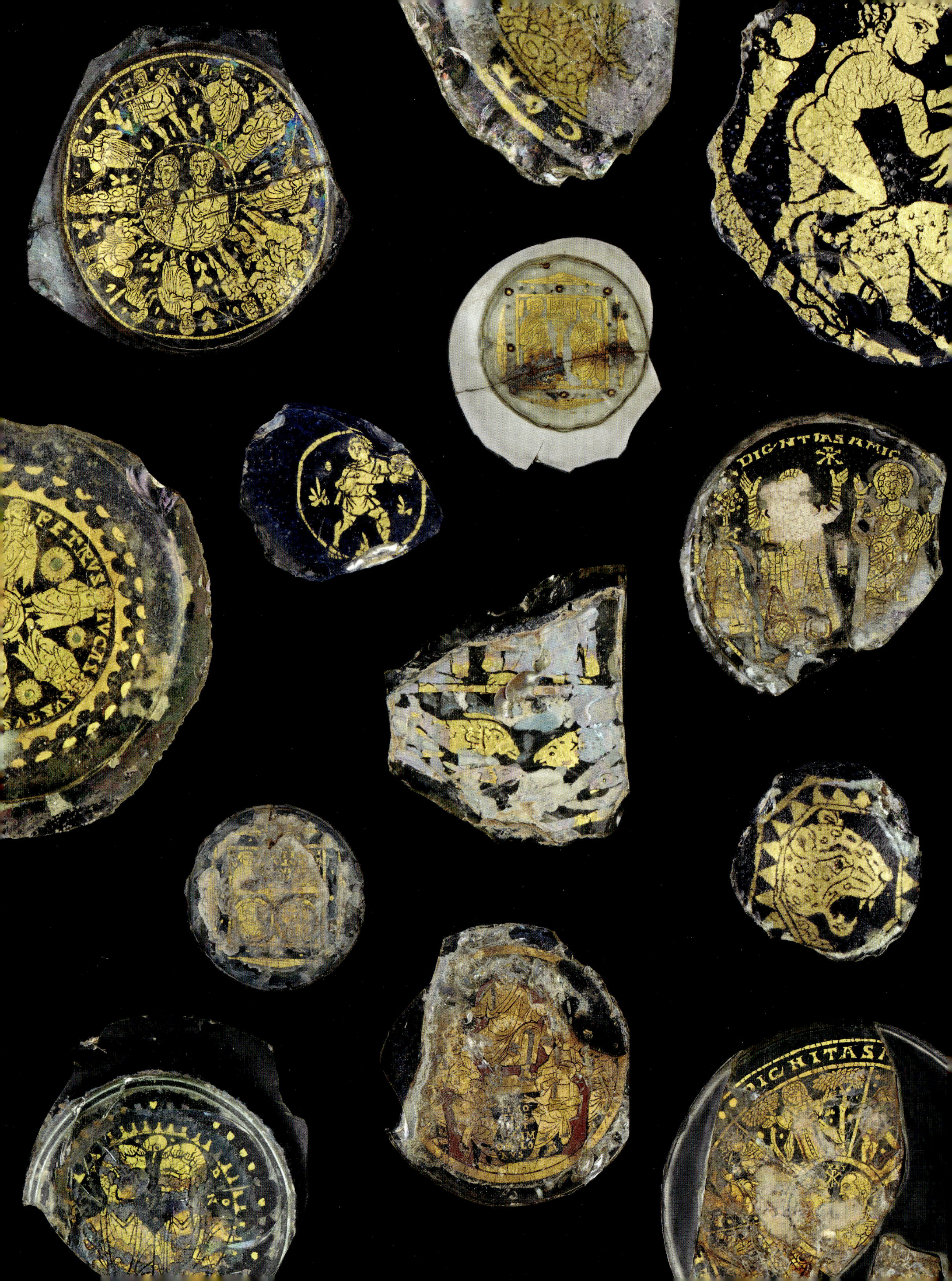
DIGNTIAS AMIC
PETRVS

Chapter 2

The sources of Charles Wilshere's collection

In this chapter the focus on Wilshere's collecting activities, introduced in the first chapter, is broadened to consider the economic and social circumstances of the collectors whose antiquities he acquired. The earliest surviving records of Wilshere's most significant gold-glasses are reviewed by David Rini in a section that includes a brief review of the history of recording texts.

The sources of gold-glass vessels and a silver spoon in the Wilshere Collection

Both de Rossi, in his plea for funds of 1869, and Tyskiewicz, in his memoirs written 25 years later, mention the acquisition of an historic collection of ancient gold-glass by Wilshere's principal suppliers, the Roman dealers Tommaso and Vincenzo Capobianchi (Fig. 20). The sale to Vincenzo Capobianchi occurred in 1862 in Catania, Sicily, where the gold-glass had formed part of a much larger collection of the Recupero family, the history of which can be traced back to the era of the European Enlightenment.[1]

In broad terms, the history of the Museo Recupero is matched by many other Italian private collections. The objects were acquired in the eighteenth century by an individual collector, in this case Baron Alessandro Recupero of Alminusa, also known as Alessio Motta (1745–1803; see further below, p.51). Recupero, like many of his peers, had international contacts, and combined a passionate personal commitment to his subject with a broad, increasingly didactic, intellectual outlook.[2] For his immediate heirs, the collection became a focus of wider interest, both for visitors to the family home and for specialist scholars compiling corpora. However, for subsequent generations, there was a loss of focus and memory, combined with increasing socio-economic difficulty during the convulsions of the final period of

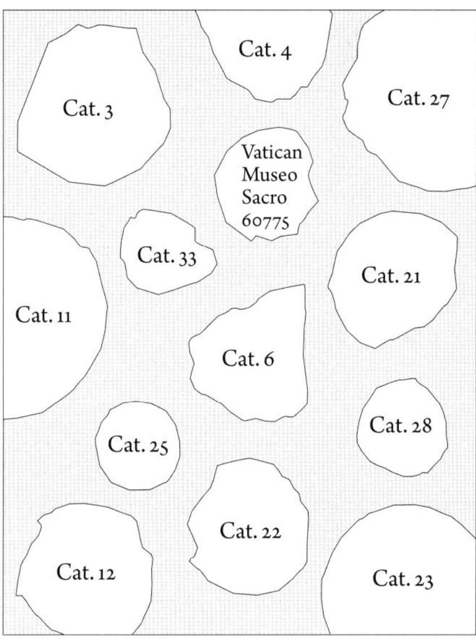

Fig. 20 Gold-glass sold to Wilshere from the Museo Recupero, Catania

the Risorgimento and the unification of Italy in the 1860s. This resulted in pressure to disperse and/or sell the collection, even as southern Italy was undergoing a brutal transition from aristocratic and church patronage of contemporary artists to a free market. The situation was volatile, changing 'quasi di un giorno all'altro' ('almost from one day to the next')following the overthrow of the Bourbon monarchy in 1861.[3]

Besides the Recupero Collection, other gold-glasses (including cat. **20**) were purchased by Wilshere from the Capobianchi family – most significantly the single Jewish gold-glass (cat. **13**) that was in the collection of Tommaso Capobianchi's son Vincenzo. No earlier history has survived for these pieces. Vincenzo Capobianchi evidently had a significant interest in gold-glass.[4]

Another Roman supplier to Wilshere of at least one gold-glass (cat. **30**) and a marble cinerary urn (cat. **42**) was the dealer Luigi Depoletti, also known to Tyskiewicz:

> ... Another man much sought after was old Depoletti, whose shop was always full of recently discovered antiquities including gems and Roman coins ... Specimens of all sorts were to be found at Depoletti's, even of forgeries, for Depoletti was no expert in matters artistic; he would often ask a large price for some piece of rubbish, and sell something really good for almost nothing at all. But he was the most honest man in the world, and only deceived others because he was deceived himself ...[5]

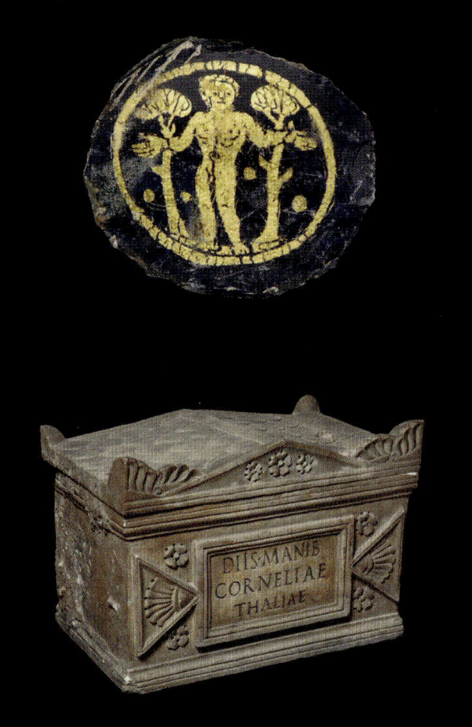

Fig. 21 Objects sold to Wilshere by Luigi Depoletti, cats **30** (top) and **42** (bottom)

On the inside of the lid of the ornate cardboard box in which the silver spoon (cat. **59**) was kept is a pencilled note in Wilshere's hand that reads 'Porto [Portus] / Ostia', the possible provenance of the object.[6] The Roman vendor is unknown: de Rossi recorded the spoon as 'acquistato testè in Roma dal sig. Wilshere' ('acquired just recently in Rome by Mr Wilshere'), which implies that the date of purchase was 1868. The provenance was recorded by de Rossi as 'dai dintorni di Roma' ('from the area surrounding Rome'). Indeed, de Rossi's article on nine early Christian spoons from Portus and other areas near Rome may have inspired Wilshere's note.[7]

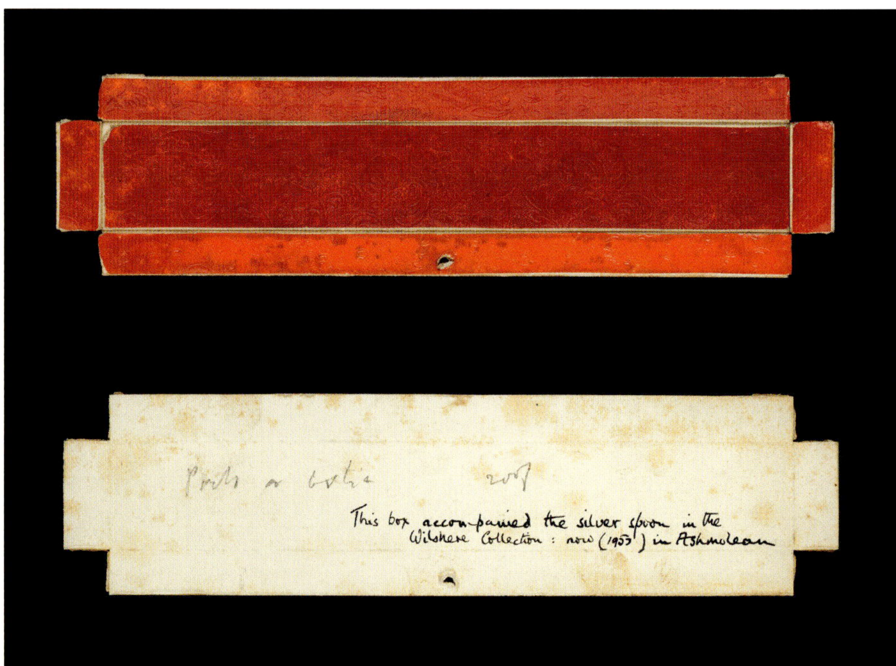

Fig. 22 The box in which the silver spoon (cat. **59**) was kept, with a pencilled note of the alleged provenance in Wilshere's hand on the inside of the lid.

Other instances of purchases from unnamed Roman vendors may be found in Garrucci's published descriptions. The second of these describes a glass apparently not now in the Wilshere Collection; either Wilshere sold or exchanged pieces, or he kept this piece in Rome for a while and decided against purchase.[8]

The Museo Recupero

Though it lies beyond the scope of this catalogue to investigate in detail the circumstances of the Museo Recupero,[9] it is worth considering at greater length the history of this remarkable collection. It is our principal source for tracing the collection history of Wilshere's gold-glass, along with that of the Vigna Randanini texts and the inscriptions from ancient Aeclanum.

Including the glass representing Genesius and Luke returned to the Vatican in 1893 (see p.36, Fig. 14), the Museo Recupero provided 13 of the most significant gold-glasses within Wilshere's collection. They had been in the Recupero family since the late eighteenth century when the collection was formed, largely in Rome, by Baron Alessandro Recupero, then also known as Alessio Motta.[10] Alessandro Recupero was born on 30 September 1745. Evidently a boy of considerable intelligence, he was educated by his uncle Giuseppe Recupero, a noted geologist and Canon of Catania Cathedral, whose work on the natural history of Etna was published posthumously by Agatino Recupero, another nephew (Fig. 23).[11]

In 1766 Alessandro's elder brother Gerolamo renounced his title of Baron of Alminusa. The 21-year-old Alessandro was sent to Palermo to manage the family's estates in his place, succeeding to the barony and with it feudal rights over Alminusa. Unfortunately in 1770 the young baron became the subject of what is described in publications of family members in the nineteenth century as an '*atroce calumnia*' ('atrocious calumny').[12] Obliged to leave his native Sicily, Alessandro travelled in Italy, eventually settling in Rome. Whatever his alleged misdeed, he lost touch neither with his family nor with the church. In the course of his travels the young man became passionately interested in art and archaeology. In Rome he began collecting and gained a reputation as a knowledgeable and able connoisseur,

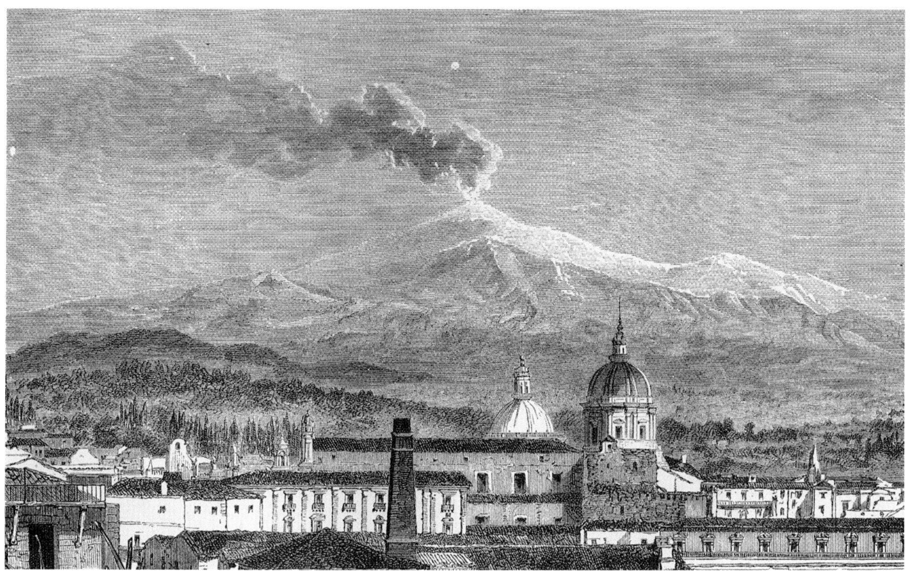

Fig. 23 View of Mount Etna from Catania. Engraving, German School, nineteenth century, from Herman J. Klein and Dr Thome, *God's Glorious Creation of the Mighty Marvels of Earth, Sea and Sky*. Bridgeman Art Library FEH 328996

the author of learned papers (*memorie* and *dissertazioni*)[13] and the giver of trusted opinions on the authenticity or otherwise of objects that other collectors were considering for purchase or already regretting.

Alessandro Recupero was elected to various learned societies: the Accademia degli Aborigeni in Rome in 1779, the Società letteraria de' Volsci of Velletri in 1784 and the Accademia Etrusca of Cortona in 1786. He was most noted for his cabinet of ancient coins and medals. In a published letter, of interest as much for its Jacobin political context as its scholarship, the distinguished art historian Ennio Quirino Visconti fulsomely praised 'Citizen Alessandro Recupero' for his rich collection, assembled with scholarship and consisting of not only more than 500 ancient coins and medals, but also very numerous lead medallions and inscribed gems, categories of object hitherto not greatly esteemed by collectors.[14] Gaetano Marini (on whom see further below, p.53) regarded Recupero's collection of medals as 'very rare, even unique'.[15] Recupero was celebrated not least for his unrivalled knowledge of the history of Rome as reflected in its coinage: in 1797 he published 'Lettere su le collezioni di medaglie' in the *Magazzino Enciclopedico*.[16]

Like his uncle's work, Alessandro Recupero's study of Rome's history was published posthumously. It was edited by his younger brother and heir Giuseppe, for Alessandro died after a short illness in 1803. Aged only 58, he was unmarried and had no known children.[17] The collection passed to his younger brother Giuseppe, like his uncle a noted expert on volcanology and natural history. It moved from Rome to Catania, where overseas visitors enjoyed seeing the cabinets in the family palazzo, having been treated by Giuseppe to a tour of nearby Mount Etna. Among others, Giuseppe Recupero's hospitality was enjoyed by Abbate Paolo Balsamo and Thomas Wright Vaughan, George Russell, Captain John Hansen with Lieutenant-General Sir Miles Nightingall, KCB., and Richard Duppa.[18] Giuseppe Recupero saw to the completion of his brother's manuscript catalogue of his collection of Roman coins, published by Filippo Barravecchia in Palermo in 1808.[19] The Greek coins had already been sold to the Danish royal cabinet in 1805.[20]

When Giuseppe died in 1826, the surviving collection was still intact, but his will ensured its division within the family.[21] Thirty-one Latin inscriptions are known to have been acquired for the Museo Recupero.[22] Like the gold-glass, most of these had been purchased in Rome: one, known since the sixteenth century, had been seen in the later eighteenth century by Gaetano Marini at an antiquities dealer's shop.[23] Indeed, several texts were purchased by Recupero from noble Roman collections such as the Mattei,[24] Casali and Colonna, and had thus been recorded, the records later collected by Mommsen for publication in *CIL* VI.[25] After Recupero's death, some of these texts were sold to other collectors in Catania and Taormina; four are now in the archaeological museum of Catania.[26] None was sold to Wilshere on his visit to Sicily in 1885.

Giuseppe's son Giacinto published a eulogistic biography of his uncle Alessandro in 1834; in the same year his brother Giacomo called for the establishment of a department of archaeology within Catania University.[27] However, the dispersal of the collection within the family eventually led to the sale of the collection in Catania in 1862, in the aftermath of the collapse of the Bourbon monarchy in 1861.

Tracking the history of Alessandro Recupero's gold-glass: drawings from Gaetano Marini's Inscriptiones Christianae

David Rini

Some of Alessandro Recupero's glasses are illustrated in a remarkable corpus of Christian inscriptions compiled in the later eighteenth century. The Vatican Library holds the corpus in question: drawings and scholarly annotations with transcriptions of Latin and Greek inscriptions – mostly of Roman date – collected by Abbot Gaetano Luigi Marini (1742–1815),[28] an Italian palaeographer, librarian and antiquarian who held the positions of Keeper of the Papal Archives in Castel Sant'Angelo from 1782 to 1800 and Head of the Vatican Library from 1800 to 1808.[29] The corpus bears the title of '*Inscriptiones Christianae Latinae et Graecae aevi milliarii*' and is dedicated to Pope Pius VI (1775–99).[30] The work was completed under the aegis of the Jesuit fathers Gaspare Oderico, Francescantonio Zaccaria and Giuseppe Raggi. It was never published.

Marini was born in Santarcangelo di Romagna (Italy) on 18 December 1742, the son of Filippo Marini and the Countess Francesca Baldini. He completed his first studies in the seminary in Rimini (*Seminario Arcivescovile*). While there, he studied under the supervision of the medievalist, doctor, naturalist and archaeologist Giovanni Bianchi (Lat. '*Janus Plancus*'/It. 'Iano' or 'Giano Planco', 1693–1755), a widely published author,[31] and founder of the Accademia dei Lincei. In Santarcangelo Marini furthered his studies with Giovanni Paolo Giovenardi (1708–89).[32] In 1762 Marini graduated in *utroque jure* (civil and canon law) in Ravenna under the auspices of the Bolognese Cardinal Giovanni Fantuzzi[33] (1718–99), a local biographer and connoisseur, who eventually invited him to move to Rome. Marini arrived in Rome in December 1764 and lived there until his departure for Paris in 1808. He died in Paris in 1815.[34]

Marini's intent was to prepare a comprehensive edition of Latin and Greek inscriptions for the whole of the first millennium AD – an arduous and virtually impracticable research endeavour which he never accomplished. Nonetheless, Marini's work is still uniquely valuable to modern scholarship because of the great wealth of information preserved on numerous surviving drawings and cards. In this vein, Marini's *Inscriptiones* are witness to the provenance of numerous artefacts from early Christianity and shed light on the study of antiquity in early modern Rome.

Antiquity, with its material legacy, had been at the centre of attention for centuries before Marini's time. More than two centuries after the invention of printing, when Marini was working in Rome, he collected a total of 9,775 epigraphic texts, made available for study through the meticulous collection of manuscript annotations and transcriptions of inscriptions, as well as through the ordering of drawings of their supports.[35] The first half of the eighteenth century, indeed, had witnessed the publication of the *Antiquae inscriptiones* by Maruqard Gude (1635–89),[36] a major collaborative work published thanks to the co-operation of James Kool (Joannes Koolio), Franz Hessel (Francisco Hesselio, born *c.* 1730) and Johan Georg Graevius (Joannis Georgii Graevii), who issued the book in Leuven in 1731. However, the most relevant, and influential, work on Latin epigraphy published in Italy during the course of the eighteenth century was undoubtedly the *Novus thesaurus veterum inscriptionum* by Lodovico Antonio Muratori, a book published in four volumes in Milan between 1739 and 1742.[37]

Other relevant works were published by Marquis Scipione Maffei (1675–1755) and Stefano Morcelli (1737–1821). The *Museum Veronese* by Maffei was published in Verona in 1749. The same author completed another study in 1749, eventually published posthumously in Lucca in 1765: the *Ars critica lapidaria*,[38] a comprehensive treatise on epigraphy. The last work mentioned here is that by Morcelli: *De stilo inscriptionum Latinarum*,[39] which appeared in three volumes in Padua in 1781. Even after the discovery of printing, the tradition of preparing epigraphic manuscripts did not die out. Handwritten collections of inscriptions, including monuments from individual cities or notes on local history and archaeology, continued to be produced.[40]

Marini's *Inscriptiones Christianae*

Marini's epigraphic manuscripts, a monumental series of four volumes, continued the long scholarly tradition briefly summarised above. Nonetheless, Marini shifted the goal of his research to an ambitiously scoped, distinct new direction: the history of early Christianity. The very title of the *Inscriptiones Christianae* specifies 'Christian' inscriptions: in reading it one realises that Marini was actually looking for non-literary evidence for the study of Christian religion and history. Indeed, in Marini's *Inscriptiones Christianae* objects are assumed to be reliable conveyors of information on past Christian beliefs and liturgical practices. This idea is confirmed by Marini himself on multiple occasions: he refers to his decision to restart his research on the *Inscriptiones* in 1795:

> [...] *torna al diletto lavoro della raccolta di tutte le iscrizioni cristiane greche e latine de' primi dieci secoli, condotto già a buon porto, e ricco a quest'ora di forse più di 12 mila monumenti scritti in differenti materie. Spera che una tal'opera debba poter essere di grandissima importanza, lustro, ed utilità della nostra santa Religione, e di tutta la Storia ecclesiastica*
>
> (...back to the beloved work of collecting all Christian inscriptions in Greek and Latin from the first ten centuries, now rich with perhaps more than 12,000 inscribed monuments in different materials. He hopes that such a work should have the capacity to be of the greatest importance, prestige and usefulness for our holy Religion, and for the whole History of the Church)[41]

In sum, Marini was interested in writing a new history of Christian tradition based on monuments and inscriptions. He believed that relics of the Christian past were worthy to be the subject of proper history, especially for the period from the third century AD through to the year 1000.

Marini did not work alone. He asked numerous Italian and international connoisseurs and amateurs to send him letters with transcriptions of inscriptions, along with drawings of their material supports. Unfortunately no significant information about the authors of the drawings or the names of Marini's correspondents has survived.[42] Drawings were collected primarily as documents for the study of what they represented rather than for who had drawn them. However, even though there is no clear evidence of who actually drew the five pictures discussed here, we can now better describe the time and intellectual context of their production.

On only two occasions have the *Inscriptiones Christianae* been seriously studied by two Vatican librarians who published them in parts after the death of Marini: Cardinal Angelo Mai (1782–1854), prefect of the Vatican Library, who published a few chapters from the *Inscriptiones* in the first section of volume five of his *Scriptorum veterum nova collectio e vaticanis codicibus edita* (Rome, 1831),[43] and the archaeologist

Giovanni Battista de Rossi (1822–94), who extensively used annotations from Latin inscriptions for his *Inscriptiones Christianae Urbis Romae* (Rome, after 1857).[44] Beyond these efforts, the *Inscriptiones* of Marini have been almost completely neglected by modern archaeologists and art historians and were studied only in haphazard fashion[45] until 2015, when they were discussed in a multi-authored scholarly publication edited by Vatican librarian Marco Buonocore.[46]

The *Inscriptiones* contain drawings and annotations of inscriptions categorised as *Tituli* (inscriptions or writings on various supports containing the ancient names of offices and posts) and are divided into two parts and 32 chapters (Part I: chapters I–XV; Part II: chapters XVI–XXXII). The indexes at the end of the work are also split into two sections.[47] The list of names comprises 11 columns at the end of the fourth volume.[48] Other drawings and annotations collected by Marini during his research and not included in the four volumes of the *Inscriptiones* are also extant, and are now bound in 35 miscellaneous volumes.[49]

Figured and inscribed gold-glass is a very well-represented category of small objects from the catacombs in the *Inscriptiones;* Marini included a total of 233 cards, prints and drawings in the twelfth chapter of the *Inscriptiones*. Some repetitions occur because Marini confused his sources. Some glasses therefore appear more than once in different parts of the page or sections of the chapter (eight instances of this occur). The adjusted total of glasses whose reproductions appear in the twelfth chapter thus comes to 225 items; the reproductions were mounted in groups of related iconography on 17 consecutive pages. The chapter where they are reproduced is titled *Caput XII. Tituli Minores in Vitro:* Chapter 12. Minor Inscriptions recorded on Glass.[50] All drawings, presumably first-hand reproductions, copy glasses at actual size; they often appear to be the work of different unknown hands, using diverse drawing instruments – both pen and pencil are used - and inks, mostly dark brown and black. There is no use of colour anywhere, except for one watercolour.[51] Overall, the twelfth chapter of the *Inscriptiones* contains 19 Indian ink drawings, one watercolour, a sketch and 19 pencil drawings. Other drawings represent unpublished glasses whose current location is unknown.[52] All prints and drawings are on numbered white cards, about ten per page, glued to the main page in an average of about four to six superimposed sequences of rows.

The twelfth chapter includes drawings and annotations of figured and inscribed gold-glass on five cards that copy objects which eventually became part of the Wilshere Collection.[53] Four glasses are now kept at the Ashmolean Museum's Department of Antiquities[54] and a fifth glass, copied in a card on page 112, was returned by Wilshere to the collection of the Vatican Museum.[55] Together the drawings, along with the annotations regarding the provenance of these objects, are invaluable to modern scholars and conservators because they represent the earliest documentation of the historical existence of four gold-glasses in the Wilshere Collection.

All drawings copy the glasses at actual size and, with one exception,[56] appear to be the work of a single hand, using dark brown ink, with no colour; there is therefore no attempt to reproduce additional enamel decoration of the gold leaf nor, given limited miniaturist skill, to reproduce the originals with a degree of fidelity. The drawings represent the glasses' features sketchily, with evident simplifications – especially in the reproductions of details in the gold leaf. In addition to this, in one case the Latin inscriptions on one glass are incorrectly transcribed,[57] while in another they are copied in an incomplete fashion.[58]

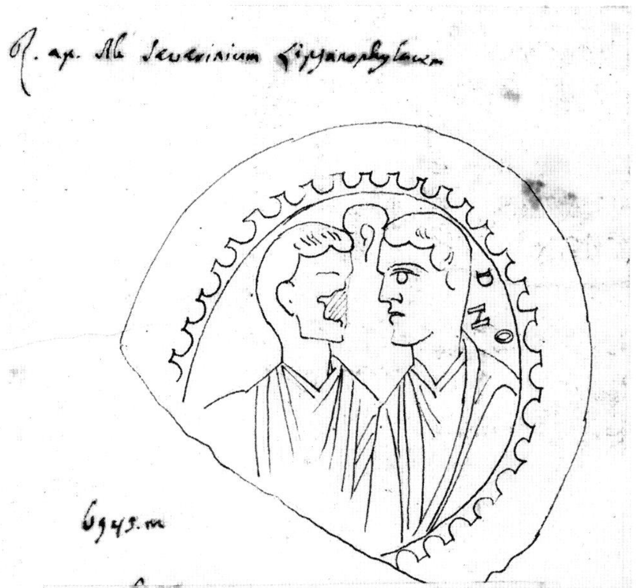

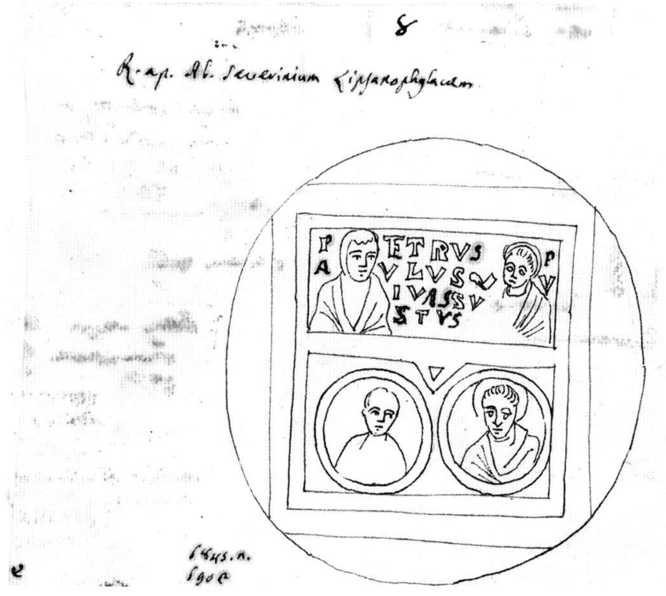

Fig. 24 (left) Drawing of cat. 12, from Gaetano Marini's papers. Biblioteca Apostolica Vaticana, Vat. lat. 9071, p.220, no.9

Fig. 25 (right) Drawing of cat. 25, from Gaetano Marini's papers. Biblioteca Apostolica Vaticana, Vat. lat. 9071, p.209, no.8

Marini's records of gold-glasses in the Wilshere Collection

CAT. 12 = MOREY, NO.358

The drawing on card number nine on page 220 (Fig. 24) features a very sluggishly outlined shape, even though it accurately shows a break on the lower left as it now appears on the actual gold-glass.[59] The width of the vessel wall remaining above the actual glass disc (2.0 cm) was not copied. The remains of the figured gold leaf with the two busts of Ursus and Dionysius at the centre of the glass have been copied scrupulously: the two beardless male busts are represented with full hair, frontal, with their heads in profile and facing each other toward the centre of the disc. They are dressed with a tunic and a mantle (*pallium*) of the small, hooded (*omophorion*) type. Between the two heads a very simplified outline of a wreath with one remaining ribbon (*lemniscus*) is also copied. Human anatomy and drapery are both very simplified. They have been reduced to simple lines marked with very straight strokes. There is no trace of shading.

The circular Latin inscription on the gold-glass, in thickened letters, has been copied only partially.[60] The busts are enclosed within two circular borders in the actual glass, while in the drawing they appear with one border. The dotted border on the outer edge on the gold-glass was not copied. The draughtsman also tended to draw the letters in outline only, leaving the body of the letter blank – an orthographical feature shared by all transcribed texts in the drawings of this group.

CAT. 25 = MOREY, NO.360

The drawing on card number eight on page 209 (Fig. 25) shows a very much simplified copy of the glass now in the Wilshere Collection, one of the better preserved pieces in the whole set. This drawing is by the same hand as that of the image discussed above. The glass is copied fairly carefully, though with some lack of concern. It appears somewhat unfinished. The outer border is reproduced as it is now. There is no trace of any of the 12 dots present around the external border of the actual disc.

The figures are copied with some care, even though the drawing seems to be incomplete on the lower margin, where the contours of the male bust in the left *clipeus* (medallion) are not finished. The drawing copies the disc's decoration in gold leaf featuring a square-shaped architectural outline. The square is divided into two superimposed registers enclosing four *imagines clipeatae* (portraits mounted as if on shields). Four male busts are represented: the two above are those of the apostles Peter and Paul. The lower level features the busts of two other males: Justus and Sixtus. The horizontal Latin inscription on the upper register, in thickened lettering, is correctly transcribed in full. The division of the original text in four superimposed lines is also reproduced with great care.[61]

CAT. 23 = MOREY, NO.388

The drawing on card number one on page 218 (Fig. 26) is probably the most interesting of those discussed here.[62] Indeed, it is the only drawing of gold-glass in Marini's archives that has already attracted the interest of modern scholarship. Raffaele Garrucci mentions this card (reproducing the drawing with some minor emendations in a couple of his publications),[63] and it had been already discussed by the undersigned in a previous publication.[64] This drawing certainly features distinctive details: it represents the gold-glass in a better preserved state than the object now in the Wilshere Collection. In addition, the figured decoration of the gold leaf represents episodes from the Old Testament and a scene of martyrdom from the Apocrypha.

The artist is most likely the same author of the drawings studied above. The figures are simplified to an outline of the gold leaf incisions and the rendering of the inscriptions features the same oversimplification described for the other drawings above. In addition, the Latin annotation on this card,[65] and the information published by Garrucci,[66] both carry a great deal of information on the origin and date of this drawing and those by the same hand in this set.

The drawing copies scenes on the actual disc, now in the Wilshere Collection, with busts of the apostles Peter and Paul in tunic and mantle (*pallium*) set in the central, shield-shaped medallion (*clipeus*). Both busts are presented frontally with

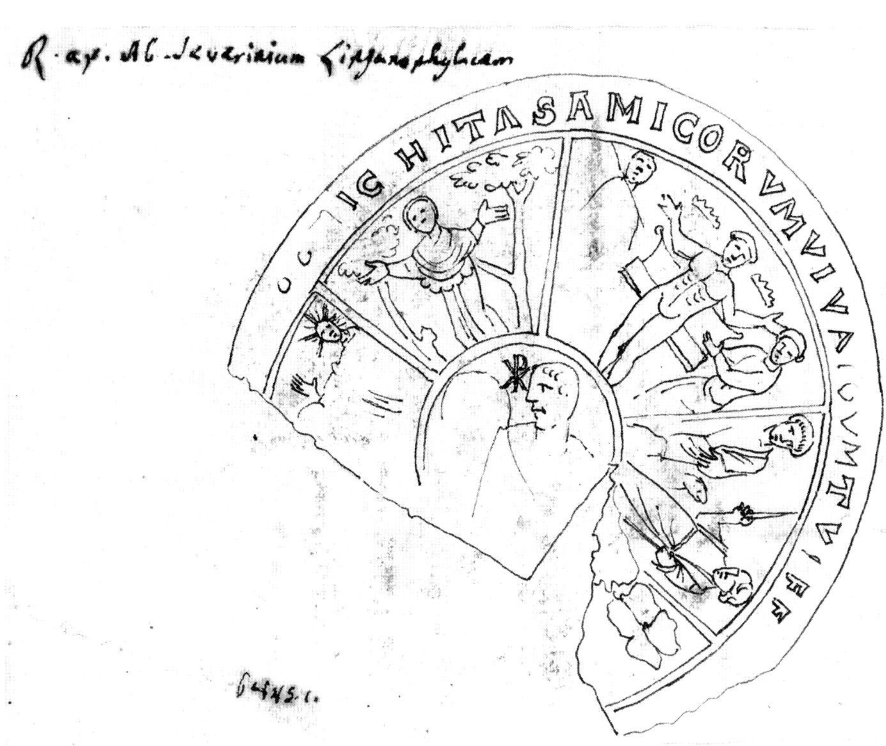

Fig. 26 Drawing of cat. 23, from Gaetano Marini's papers. Biblioteca Apostolica Vaticana, Vat. lat. 9071, p.218, no.1

heads in profile facing each other; the left bust is beardless with full hair while the right bust is half bald, with curving pointed beard. Between the two heads is the Christogram XP. Six trapezoidal panels radiate from the central *clipeus* (medallion), three of which are still extant in the gold-glass. From left to tight a haloed female figure, possibly Susannah standing at prayer with arms raised, is depicted between two trees. The woman wears a tunic decorated with long stripes, her hair curling around the forehead. Other sections copied in the drawing that are now mostly lost feature the martyrdom of prophet Isaiah. He is represented as a young man in the nude, shown standing frontally, his arms raised while he is being bisected by very sketchily copied figures of two male executioners at his sides. They wear short girdled tunics. On the glass itself, blood dripping from Isaiah's wounds was represented with drops of red enamel paint. As noted above, no details of the ancient decoration in added enamel colour are reproduced in the drawing, though in later publications Garrucci showed them as shaded.[67]

The following panel contains Moses slaying the serpent. Unfortunately this section is almost completely lost in the actual glass. According to the drawing the glass decoration featured a beardless male figure, standing frontally and dressed in tunic and *pallium*, the latter held up by the left arm. A rearing, coiled serpent was also present in the middle of the panel next to this figure. On the other side of this panel is another standing male figure, also dressed in a tunic and *pallium*; he holds a wand in his right hand, extending it to the centre.

The following panel, broken through one side, shows Moses striking a rocky cliff from which a vertical stream flows. The section with the stream is the only remaining feature in the actual glass. The next panel (redrawn on multiple occasions by Garrucci and absent in Marini's drawing)[68] is still extant in the actual object, and representss the episode of the three Hebrews in the furnace. They are depicted in a frontal pose at prayer. The furnace is shown as a masonry structure surmounting a series of three arcades. The three Hebrews were depicted wearing girdled tunics buttoned at the front and with striped sleeves. They all wear Persian caps with flying strings.

The last section is a representation of the king Ezekias. It has been only partially reproduced in the drawing, as part of the left section was already lost at the time when the drawing was made. The glass is broken diagonally. Only one hand of a right arm is preserved from the figure of a male standing, three-quarters right. A radiate bust of the sun is also represented on the top right-hand corner.

The Latin inscription on the gold-glass has been partially copied in the drawing.[69] The inscription has been also copied without the outer continuous edge as it appears in the actual object. The outer edge of the glass was not copied and is missing in the drawing. A closer look at the drawing in the Marini archives shows that the glass drawn featured a very special figuration from the Apocrypha – an image now almost completely lost to the glass in its current state because of the loss of the glass section.

This drawing indeed represents the earliest iconography of the prophet Isaiah's martyrdom, a scene extremely rare at this time and unknown in Rome.[70] This almost unique iconography links this glass with the narration of the story of Isaiah's martyrdom as told in the life of Isaiah – then recounted in turn in the *Lives of Prophets* (*Vitae Prophetarum*),[71] a Jewish apocryphon of the Apostolic age, and in the well-known *Ascension of Isaiah* (*Ascensio Isaiae*),[72] a Jewish-Christian apocryphon of the same period, and its probable Judeo-Christian origin in Syria.[73] Evidently these non-canonical texts were known in fourth-century Rome; the family commissioning this gold-glass figuration may have therefore requested this unique iconography.[74] The style of this drawing is comparable to those discussed above and is very likely by the same hand. Human features and drapery are here reduced to simple lines marked with very straight strokes. The outer border of the glass is simply drawn on a circular outline, with no regard for the unique features of the actual glass. The ancient object is broken in three sections; it has cracks on both surfaces and many spots of yellowish film that have not been copied here.

MOREY NO.79 = VATICAN MUSEUM, INV. 60775

On card number 11 on page 212 (Fig. 27),[75] the drawing copies the upper part of a gold-glass returned to the Vatican Library by Wilshere in 1893. Though the glass is complete today (Fig. 14), for reasons that are now unclear the glass represented in the drawing is broken, with the entire lower part missing. The outer border of the glass is represented with a continuous line in the drawing.

The draughtsman, also responsible for the other drawings, simply outlined the two standing figures of Genesius and Lucas (Luke), copying the representation on the glass carefully but with no special interest in detail. No attempt to present the three dimensions of the object is visible anywhere, nor is there any shading. The Latin inscription on the tablet on top of the column at the centre is copied with some care,[76] while the card features a Latin annotation on the top-hand corner recalling the provenance of the object.[77] This glass was in the repository of relics of Abbot Giovanni Severini at the Lateran.

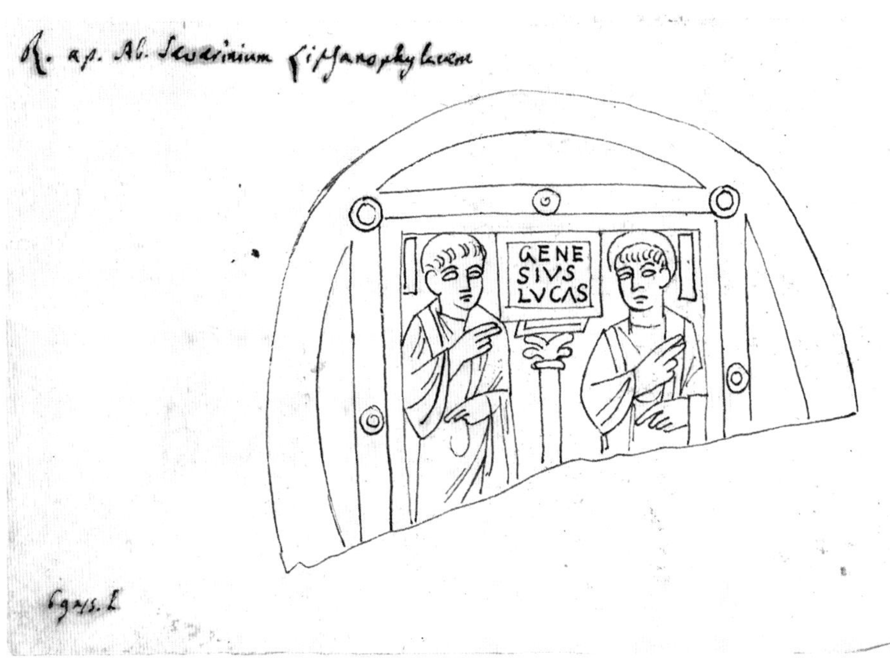

Fig. 27 Drawing of Vatican Inv. 60775, from Gaetano Marini's papers. Biblioteca Apostolica Vaticana, Vat. lat. 9071, p.212, no.11

CAT. 22 = MOREY NO.364

The drawing on card number seven on page 206,[78] (Fig. 28) greatly differs from those on the other cards discussed above, both in style and attention to detail; it was very probably made by another hand. The drawing is a detailed copy of the gold-glass now in the Wilshere Collection and was executed by a skilled, unknown draughtsman. This card also shows evidence of both the material consistency and provenance of the gold-glass. In contrast to the drawings discussed above, the location of this glass is noted as already in Rome in the collection of the Sicilian antiquarian Alessio Recupero.[79] At the time of drawing in the later eighteenth century, the glass was in the same condition as it is today.

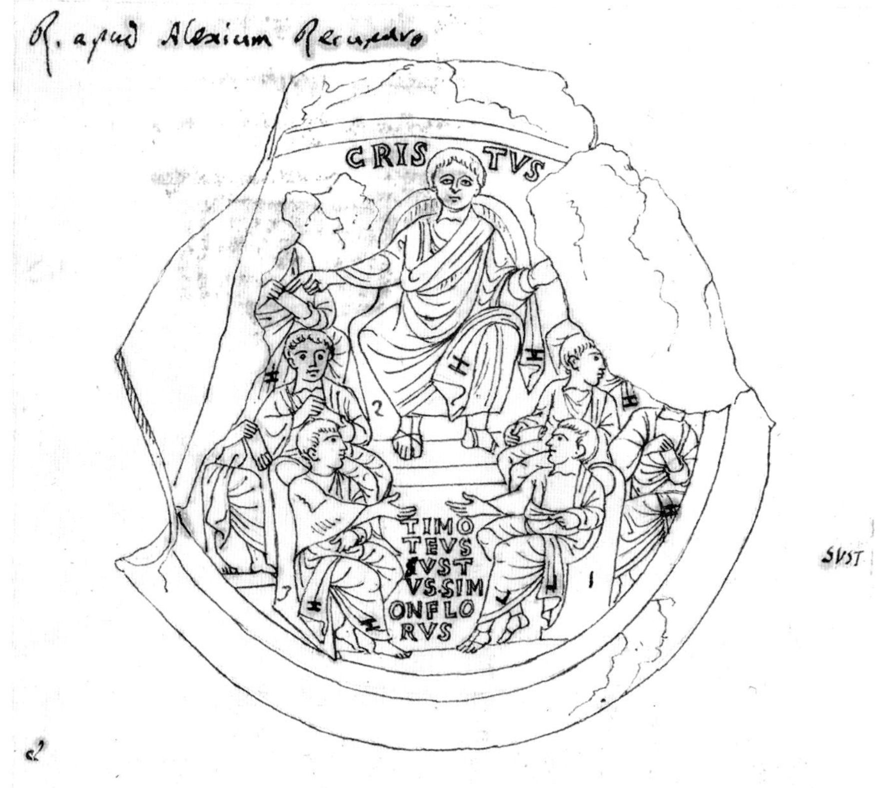

Fig. 28 Drawing of cat. 22, from Gaetano Marini's papers. Biblioteca Apostolica Vaticana, Vat. lat. 9071, p.206, no.7

The drawing shows the glass broken away at upper left and right and cut back on the left to the disc. Worth noticing are the dotted lines drawn on the copy (left margin and top right-hand corner of the disc) which reveal the draughtsman's interest in the rendering of the physical status of the gold-glass, including minor cracks. The circular band border on the glass is also drawn with great attention and fidelity. The figures copied in the drawing include Christ, beardless, seated on a tall chair, in the position of a teacher. Here Christ is represented frontally and surrounded by other seated male figures of apostles holding scrolls. Christ wears long twisted locks on his shoulders, and is dressed in a Roman tunic with a stripe (*clavus*) visible on the right. Woven decoration often resembling letters of the Greek alphabet (*gammadia*), here in the form of the letter 'I', is present on both the skirt and on the *clavus* descending between the legs from the left knee. Christ, like all the other figures in the scene, wears tied sandals. The figure of Christ is extending his right hand in a speaking gesture and touches a rolled scroll (*rotulus*) that a seated figure, possibly Peter, is holding with both hands to left. The drawing shows this figure only partially because of the loss of part of the glass.

The seated figure to the right of Christ, possibly Paul, is almost completely missing from the drawing, except for a small segment on the lower right where an 'I' is still visible on a fold of the *pallium* hanging down from the left leg. All the figures around Christ are in similar posture and costume. The two central figures, wearing *pallium* and wide-sleeved tunics with *clavus* on their shoulders, are extending their hands in a speaking gesture. Both are seated with crossed legs and wear tied sandals. The inscription on the glass has been carefully transcribed; word order and alignment are carefully observed throughout the entire drawing.[80] On the glass itself certain features of the clothing, the *gammadia* and sandals are rendered in red or black enamelled paint; these colours are not distinguished on the drawing.

To sum up, Marini's drawings represent the earliest documentation of the material existence of five gold-glasses in Wilshere's collection and carry relevant information about their historical status. In addition, the presence of annotations that confirm information published by Garrucci in 1858 helps us to understand their date and origin. In this vein, one can argue that four of the five drawings were made during the fourth quarter of the eighteenth century in Rome, and were commissioned by Abbot Giovanni Severini when he was keeper of the Lipsanophylacum del Vicariato at the Lateran. He then made them available to Marini for research and use as illustrations in the *Inscriptiones*. The fifth drawing, of superior quality, was probably commissioned by Alessio Recupero, perhaps at Marini's request; it must have been made between 1770 and 1800.

The *Lipsanophylacum* and *Lipsanoteca*

As noted above, four of the gold-glasses drawn for Marini, apparently by the same artist, are described as being '*R[omae] ap[ud] Ab[atem] Severinium Lipsanophylacum*' (literally 'at Rome in the repository of relics of Abbot Severini').[81] This scholarly comment by Gaetano Marini is to be understood as a reference to the office of the *Custode delle ss. Reliquie e dei cimiteri* (literally 'Keeper of the most holy Relics and cemeteries'). This had been created in 1672 by Pope Clement X to manage the *corpi santi* and their effects – that is, the removal from the catacombs of the bodies or body parts of saints and martyrs, which were sometimes offered for unauthorised resale as holy relics, along with any objects associated with them.[82] Some of the office holders were immensely distinguished, and did much to promote the understanding of the objects in their care.[83] Giacomo Severini was charged with their management in the later eighteenth century, when the relics were still kept in the private homes of the two custodians (the homes in question were, however, undoubtedly church property).[84] With reference to the gold-glass of Genesius, returned by Wilshere to the Vatican in 1893 (Morey no.79 = Vatican Museum 66175; see above, p.36 and Fig. 14), de Rossi implies that Abbot Severini himself had discovered the object:

> *monumento singolare rinvenuto nella fine dello scorso secolo dall'abbate Severini custode de sacri cemeteri di Roma, il cui disegno serbato nei manoscritti del Marini nella Vaticana ho communicato al ch.(iarissimo) p.(adre) Garrucci per l'edizione dei vetri cemeteriali.*[85]
>
> ('A unique monument found at the end of the last century by Abbot Severini, Keeper of the holy cemeteries of Rome, the drawing of which, conserved in the manuscripts of Marini in the Vatican, I sent to the renowned Father Garrucci for the publication of funerary glasses.')

This text suggests that Severini may have found the other gold-glasses recorded by Marini as being in his care.

Severini died in 1800. There followed a scandal in which his heir, his brother Andrea, apparently thought and surely claimed that he had inherited, along with his brother's house and chattels, the sacred objects under Giacomo's custody. He proceeded to sell these to individual collectors.[86] It is therefore likely that these four glasses were acquired by Alessandro Recupero after Giacomo Severini's death.

As Recupero himself died unexpectedly in 1803, the recent acquisition of some of the gold-glasses would explain why they had such a low profile within his own researches, and why they did not feature among the list of the objects in the collection individually recorded in 1826 on the death of his heir Giuseppe Recupero.[87]

In the nineteenth century the Latinised Greek term *Lipsanophylacum* was renamed in Italianised Latin the *Lipsanoteca*, and the sacred objects were brought within the physical custody of the office of the Cardinal Vicar of Rome to avoid any further unauthorised sales.[88] Within the catacombs, all excavations were licensed by the Pontifical Commission for Sacred Archaeology, founded in 1851 by Pope Pius IX with the Cardinal Vicar of Rome as President and de Rossi, already a distinguished archaeologist, as its secretary. De Rossi's brother Michele, a geologist who worked with de Rossi on the re-exploration of the catacombs, was also a member.[89] The relics were kept not only in the chapel of the office of the Cardinal Vicar of Rome, but also in *lipsanotecae* in the Lateran and the Vatican.[90] Some relics continued to be available for loan to churches with a special interest in their display, and the central *lipsanoteca* at the Lateran was opened for the display of relics on the Thursday before Easter.[91] The practice was briefly abandoned after the collapse of the papal state in 1870, but revived in 1881 by the zealous Cardinal Parocchi, Vicar of Rome. Fierce regulations were proposed by a board of management, including:

> *16. Se venisse a notizia del Custode che una o più persone di qualsivoglia condizione e stato, presumessero di farsi distributrici di Sacre Reliquie senza la necessaria autorizzazione, ovvero di farne sacrilegamente commercio e di spacciarne delle dubbie o delle false, sarà suo stretto dovere di rendercene prontamente informati, affinché possiamo con ogni sollecitudine ed efficacia metter freno a cotali deplorevoli e scandalosi disordini.*
>
> ('16. If it comes to the notice of the custodian that one or more persons of whatever condition or state are presumed to be managing the distribution of sacred relics without the necessary authorisation, or defaming them with sacrilegious commercial activities or selling dubious or fake relics, it will be his duty to inform us immediately, so that we may with all due care and efficiency put a stop to such deplorable and scandalous disorders.')[92]

At the same time, the chapel in the Lateran in which the relics were displayed was redecorated and furnished under Pope Pius IX (reg. 1846–78) to resemble a catacomb, complete with paintings of the biblical scenes and texts familiar from their walls and ceilings. The relics, now in elaborate boxes of various precious materials, were placed upon an altar lit with candles set in gilded candelabra, later donated by the Pope Leo XIII (reg. 1878–1903).[93] The theatrical display, no doubt inspired by de Rossi's recent discoveries at the catacombs of Domitilla, attracted considerable public interest and requests for further information, leading Minoccheri to compile his brief history, which was published in 1894.

The sources of Jewish and Christian inscriptions in the Wilshere Collection

Another group of acquisitions by Wilshere, comprising the eight inscriptions from the Jewish catacomb at Vigna Randanini (Rome), has a different history. Here we see a vacuum of (then papal) state management of a private excavation begun on 1 May 1859.[94] The fluid situation was exploited both by Raffaele Garrucci and Giuseppe

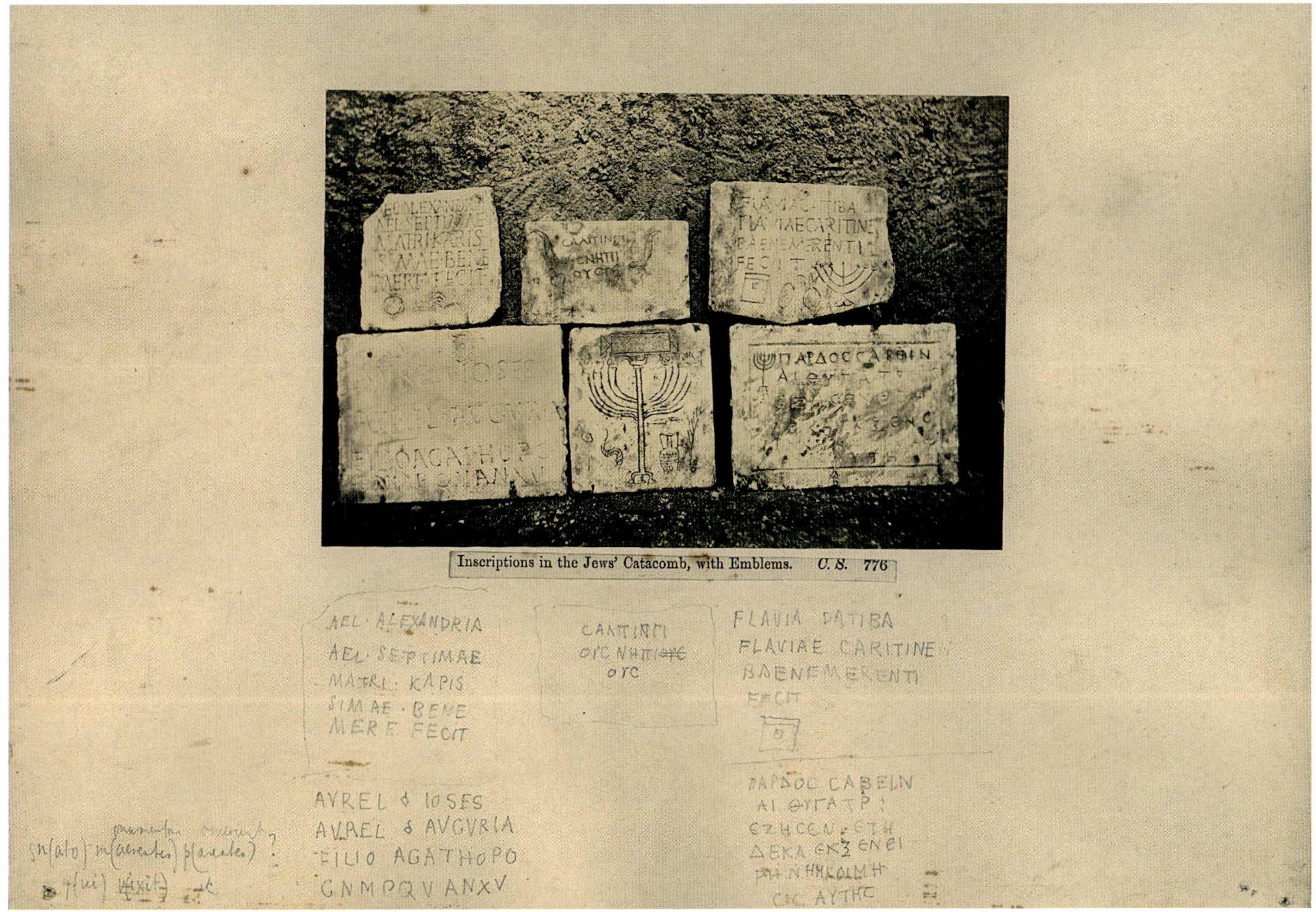

Fig. 29 The display of inscriptions at the Vigna Randanini, photographed for J. H. Parker in 1864–9. Cat. **45** is at the right end of the lower row. Ashmolean Museum, J. H. Parker archive, no.776

Randanini, the latter being the proprietor of the land on which the excavation took place. Wilshere was one of a number of private collectors who profited from this sorry state of affairs. However, we see him both astutely avoiding a lawsuit and, at the same time, aiding papal officials in their research for publication of the material by providing them with careful transcriptions of the texts. This is also true of the inscriptions from ancient Aeclanum (southeast of Beneventum, on the Via Appia), which offers an interesting example of Wilshere both aiding papal research and, after much fruitless negotiation for an exchange with Christian objects of equal value, returning the significant pagan inscription (*CIL* IX 1140) – not to the Museum of Naples, but to the Vatican.[95] Though de Rossi was able to track down and inspect inscriptions from the catacomb of Vigna Randanini sold to Italian collectors, the current location of these and other texts looted from the catacomb in later years is now unknown, with a few exceptions. Of the buyers, only Wilshere saw himself as a curator.[96]

Wilshere's acquisition of the Jewish inscriptions from the Vigna Randanini catacomb and their history in Italy and in England

In 1870 Charles Wilshere purchased eight funerary inscriptions that he had personally selected, found between 1859 and 1865 in the Jewish catacomb of the Vigna Randanini, located opposite San Sebastiano at the junction of the Via Appia

Antica and the Via Appia Pignatelli.[97] The vendor was Ignace Randanini, son of the proprietor Giuseppe Randanini. The elder Randanini had received permission to excavate the site after de Rossi had advised the Papal Commission for Sacred Archaeology not to assume formal control of excavations in the vineyard.[98] The subsequent lack of clear management of the private excavation and its finds provided opportunities for Raffaele Garrucci, perceived in the Vatican as a rival to de Rossi, to advise Randanini to make records of the site, and as early as 1862 to publish his own account of the cemetery. The site thus became an attraction for visiting collectors and scholars.[99]

Concerned about the growing significance of the finds, and Garrucci's threat to de Rossi's plan for a new, archaeological edition of Bosio's *Roma Sotterranea*, on 29 May 1862 the papal authorities sent de Rossi and Carlo Visconti to inspect the site and record the inscriptions.[100] However, the same papal authorities several times refused to buy the finds or (despite the recommendations of both de Rossi and Visconti) to compensate the Randanini family for their efforts to conserve the site and display the inscriptions. By May 1870 the younger Randanini thus felt free to sell them, and not only to Wilshere.

On 4 June 1870 an official noted that Wilshere had congratulated the papal government on its vigilance in preventing him from adding to his own order an unidentified sarcophagus. This was possibly the painted and gilded fragment of a strigillated chest decorated with two lateral panels featuring a harpist directed by the muse Urania a seated man holding a scroll, a standing bearded man in philosophical dress and a sundial between them. This sarcophagus was noted by Herzog in 1861, described by Garrucci in 1862 and photographed for Parker; it was then presumed lost until recognised, parts of it still in the catacomb, by Leonard Rutgers in the 1980s.[101] The astute Wilshere had no doubt seen the danger of an impending lawsuit: indeed, on 6 July 1870 a lawsuit was filed against Ignace Randanini by the papal state.[102]

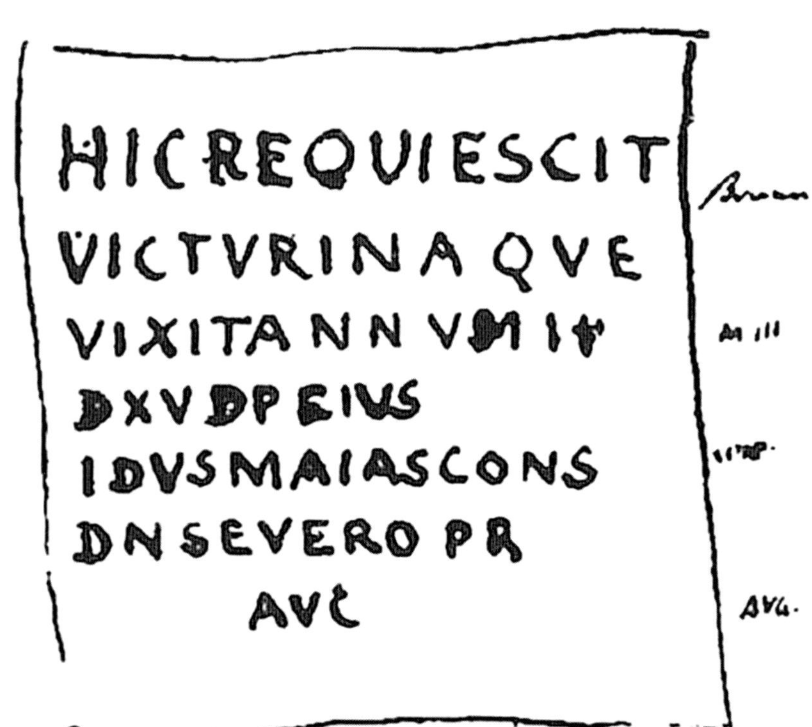

Fig. 30 Wilshere's copy of the text of cat. 53. Downloaded with permission from EDCS–12400877

Wilshere owned one fragmentary gold-glass depicting a menorah (cat. **13**). This too has been assumed to come from the Vigna Randanini,[103] though nineteenth-century records show that it was in the collection of the orientalist painter Vincenzo Capobianchi, son of Wilshere's principal dealer Tommaso Capobianchi.[104] Moreover, Garrucci reported finding only imprints and fragments of glass in the Randanini catacombs,[105] so its archaeological provenance remains uncertain; Capobianchi may have acquired it from another collector.

Despite the legal difficulties surrounding the excavation of the Vigna Randanini, relations between Wilshere and the papal authorities remained cordial. Wilshere supplied de Rossi with his own copy of the text of the most significant monument he had purchased from the Vigna Randanini, the sarcophagus lid commemorating the archon Zotikos (cat. **44**) and among others, the tombstone of Victurina (Fig. 30, cat. **53**).[106]

The flurry of legal activity over the fate of Jewish inscriptions and other funerary objects from the catacomb of Vigna Randanini, formerly regarded as unworthy of interest to the papal authorities, may reflect not only the growing weakness and eventual demise of the papal state in 1870, but also the marked improvement in the situation of the Jewish community of Rome following the inclusion of the city within the unified Italian state. After this date Jews were no longer obliged to live in the ghetto and were further relieved of various economic, social and religious restrictions formerly imposed upon them by the papal authorities.

Christian inscriptions: the tombstone of Sapis from Cumae

On 3 November 1868 Wilshere sent de Rossi some corrections for an unspecified destination, either de Rossi's personal files or a note intended for publication in *Bullettino d'Archeologia Cristiana.*

> *Una piccola rettificazione nella provenienza delle iscrizioni: le tre che Ella ha ricevute per la posta vengono tutti da Mirabella (Aeclanum) vicino a Benevento. L'ultima sola (coll'acclamazione 'QUI LEGIS ORA PRO ME' [ME is erased and ILLO substituted] (non mi ricordo bene le parole) ho comprato a Puzzoli [sic: Pozzuoli]: è stata trovata in Cuma, ove formava il soglio di una porta (illa in Londina).*
>
> ('A small correction to the provenience of the inscriptions: the three which you received in the post all come from Mirabella (Aeclanum) near Benevento. The last alone (with the acclamation "QUI LEGIS ORA PRO ME" [ME is erased and ILLO substituted] (I don't remember the words well) I bought at Pozzuoli: it was found at Cumae, where it formed the threshold of a door (that one is in London…')[107]

Wilshere thus acquired the monument to Sapis (cat. 52) in Pozzuoli in 1868, most probably on the same journey that took him to Naples, where he bought the texts from Aeclanum (see further below). The Pozzuolan vendor was Abbot Giuseppe di Criscio (1826–1911), a remarkable parish priest who was widely respected for his knowledge of epigraphy and numismatics; he published 12 monographs and 21 articles on his own collection and on the ancient monuments of the Campi Flegrei on the northern coast of the Bay of Naples.[108] In the 1890s di Criscio, by then in advanced years and anxious about the fate of his collection after his death, sold the bulk of it to the University of Michigan, where it is now kept in the Kelsey Museum of Art and Archaeology.[109] However, he was clearly already selling items of interest to other collectors in the 1860s, when, as we have seen, unstable political and economic conditions obliged families and, especially towards the end of the decade, Catholic priests to sell their collections. Wilshere seems to have been especially impressed by the personal call to prayer addressed to ancient viewers of Sapis's monument.

Christian inscriptions from ancient Aeclanum

Wilshere owned three Christian funerary inscriptions from ancient Aeclanum, a town of the Irpinia region (cats **53–5**). Aec(u)lanum was located in the Calore Valley at the crossing of the Via Herdonitana with the Via Appia, 22 km southeast of Beneventum. Fortified after the Social War in the first century BC, in the second century AD it became a Roman colony. In late antiquity it was also known as Ad Quintumdecimum, after the milestone recording the distance from ancient Aeclanum to Beneventum. The town was destroyed by the Byzantine emperor Constans II in AD 662. The ancient city boasted walls of *opus paene reticulatum* with small towers at intervals of 20m and three gates. Urban amenities included a theatre, an amphitheatre, a market (*macellum*), large baths, a cistern and an aqueduct. There was also an early Christian basilica and baptistery.[110]

The city became prominent in the fifth century AD as the seat of a bishop (first Memor, then his son the heretic Julian, deposed by Zosimus in 418), and as the home town of the legendary Greek martyr Marcianus. It is thought that an earthquake in AD 369 prompted church building. The cemetery at Mirabella Eclano yielded 55 early Christian tombstones, 39 of which (an unusually high proportion) are dated by consular years to the fifth and sixth centuries AD. Many of these were collected by Romualdo Maria Cassitto, grandson and homonym of Romualdo Cassitto di Alberona, who in 1750 had been appointed director of excavations at Aeclanum by the Bourbon king Charles III. In the early nineteenth century the Museo Cassittiano at Bonito was much visited; the German scholar Theodor Mommsen, instigator and principal compiler of the *Corpus of Inscriptorium Latinarum*, was hosted by the family in 1845. However, after the collapse of the Bourbon kingdom of Naples and the Two Sicilies in 1861 some of the collection was dispersed; other texts passed to descendants whose families still reside in Bonito.[111]

A letter written to de Rossi in November 1868 reveals that Wilshere obtained the inscriptions from Aeclanum during a visit to Naples earlier in the same year; he had sent de Rossi transcriptions of the Christian texts in the post.[112] During this visit he also acquired in Pozzuoli the funerary text from Cumae (cat. 52) which, he reported to de Rossi in the same letter, had been found in use as a door threshold (see above, p.25). There is no record of a visit to Bonito in the letters to de Rossi and Garrucci, and it is therefore probable that the inscriptions from Aeclanum were already available in 1868 for purchase in Naples. Here too Wilshere purchased the important republican text (*CIL* IX 1140) recording the building of the walls and eastern city gate of Aeclanum after the Social War in the first century BC by a patron of the city, C. Quinctius Valgius. In *CIL* the location of the text is recorded as the Museo Cassittiano,[113] but, as suggested above, it is more likely that Wilshere purchased the stone in Naples. In a letter to Garrucci written in 1871 he discussed a disc with Assyrian text that he purchased in Naples, and explains '*era tra la roba petrina che ho portato da Napoli*' ('it was in the midst of the stone stuff that I brought from Naples'). In a letter to de Rossi discussing the value of the text he states that Giuseppe Fiorelli, Director of Naples Museum, had already offered to buy it.[114]

A record of a medal given to Wilshere in the 1890s by Pope Leo XIII following the eventual gift of this text to the Vatican notes that Wilshere had rescued the text from a stonemason's yard (see above, p.35).[115] However, the Cassitti were still prominent in local government in the 1860s and it seems improbable that such a key text, already recorded for his corpus by Mommsen, would have met such a fate. Wherever its location at the time of sale to Wilshere, the export of the text to England evidently caused a protest. Two letters to Garrucci, kept in the Biblioteca S. Luigi and written on 13 May and 28 August 1871, and one to de Rossi, also written in 1871, refer to a proposed deal with Giuseppe Fiorelli. In this Wilshere agreed to return the inscription (*CIL* IX 1140) in return for a Christian object in any material of equal value (estimated by Charles Newton of the British Museum at 1500 francs: Wilshere notes here that Fiorelli had earlier offered the Cassitti family 500 *scudi* for the inscription). De Rossi was asked to expedite the deal on Wilshere's behalf.[116] The republican text, in four perfectly joining pieces, had been shipped to Welwyn by early 1871, where it remained boxed pending the resolution of the exchange.[117]

The proposed exchange evidently did not happen, however, and eventually Wilshere presented the stone to the Vatican as an act of thanks to God for the apparent recovery of de Rossi from a stroke. Sadly, by the time the inscription arrived in Rome, the gift had become a posthumous homage to the great archaeologist, who died on 20 September 1894.[118]

Notes

1. The relevant texts of de Rossi and Tyskiewicz are cited in detail above, pp.38–9, 32–3.
2. De Benedictis 1991: 141: 'Il collezionismo privato appare dunque nel Settecento orientarsi progressivamente verso una generalizzata prospettiva scientifico-didattica.' On the effect of European Enlightenment thought upon Catania, seat of the Recupero family, see Agnello 1957: 142–3; see also Policastro 1950.
3. Fusco 1981: 157; see also Haskell 1981.
4. On Vincenzo Capobianchi see above, p.33 and De Calletaÿ 2016.
5. Tyskiewicz 1898: 39.
6. The box was transferred to the Department of Antiquities at the Ashmolean from Pusey House in 2008.
7. De Rossi 1868: 81 (date of acquisition); 79 (provenance).
8. For example Garrucci 1876: 114, nos 4 (see below, cat. **26**) and 5, described as 'Avuto in Roma dal medisimo signor Wilshere' ('held in Rome by the same Mr Wilshere').
9. The Recupero family is listed among several Sicilian noble collectors by Agnello 1957: 158.
10. Olivier-Poli 1825: 201–2.
11. Recupero, G. 1815; Recupero, A. 1815. On Giuseppe Recupero, 'il filosofo della montagna' in the cultural context of eighteenth-century Catania, see Musummarra 1958–9: 71. On Alessandro's thorough education see Olivier-Poli 1825: 201–2.
12. Recupero G. 1834: 158–63.
13. Olivier-Poli 1825: 201–202.
14. Visconti 1798: 6–7 with n.10. I owe this and the following reference to David Rini. The praise is repeated in Recupero, G. 1808. On the political context of Visconti's letter, see Pepe 1996.
15. Marini 1795: 825, with reference to a small base in Recupero's collection dedicated to the goddess Fortuna Tutela.
16. Recupero A. 1797: 340–63; Olivier-Poli: 1825: 201; Recupero, G. 1834; Capone 1963.
17. Recupero G. 1808.
18. Balsamo and Wright Vaughan 1810; Russell 1819: 207–8; Hansen 1820: 206–7; Duppa 1829: 418, recording tour in 1822–3; Brydone 1840: 21ff.
19. Giuseppe Recupero, *Monumenti antichi inediti della collezione Recuperiana*, Palermo, 1808.
20. *The Gentleman's Magazine*, vol.100 (July 1806), col.652.
21. An inventory of the estate of Giuseppe Recupero is kept in the Bibliotheche Riunite Civica e Ursino Recupero in Catania: 41133 U-R Mss C.59, *Inventario dell'eredità del Barone Giuseppe Recupero, copia legale del 18 dicembre 1826, authenticate per atti del notaro Gerolamo Macarone, del fu Alessandro, in Catania.*
22. Ferrara 1829: 508–9; Korhonen 2001: 94–7.
23. *CIL* VI, 10781.
24. *CIL* VI, 21917 from the Mattei Collection was purchased by Recupero from the sculptor and dealer Bartolomeo Cavaceppi.
25. *CIL* VI, 8688, 10134, 11945 were sold to the

Reina Collection; *CIL* VI, 15585 (a modern copy), 21917, 22648 and *CIL* X, 7103 are in the archaeological museum of Catania.
26. Korhonen 2001: 96–7.
27. Giacinto Recupero 1834; Giacomo Recupero, *Per lo stabilmento di un Istituto archeologico nella R. Università degli Studi di Catania* (Palermo 1834); see also Musumarra 1958: 83.
28. Buonocore 1997: 58–60; Buonocore 2001: 45–71; Buonocore 2007: 203–9; Buonocore 2015; Mazzoleni 2015.
29. M. Marini 1822; Mecenate 1823; de Rossi 1861: XXXI–XXXIV; Leclerq 1932: 2145–63; Ferretto 1942: 296–7; Bignami Odier 1973: 185–90; Boutry 2002: 583–5; Rocciolo 2008: 451–4; Heid 2012: 868–70.
30. 'Christian Latin and Greek Inscriptions of the First Millennium' (full title: *Inscriptiones Christianae Latinae et Grecae aevi miliarii conlegit digessit adnotationibus auxit Caietanus Marinus a Bibliotheca Vaticana item a scriniis Sedis Apostolicae*), Vatican City, Biblioteca Apostolica Vaticana, Vat. lat. 9071–4).
31. Fantuzzi 1789: vol. VII, 94–6; Tognini 1884: Vol. II, 231–85; Cardi 1909: 52–64.
32. Donato 2001: Vol. 56; Gasperoni 1942: Vol. 16, 329–36.
33. Giacomelli 1994.
34. Buonocore 2001: 45–71; see also Buonocore 2007: 203–9.
35. Marini's texts: Vatican City, Biblioteca Apostolica Vaticana Vat.lat.9071=1146, Vat.lat.9072=2631, Vat.lat.9073=3191, Vat. lat.9074=2257 + 500 *carmina*, giving a total of 9775.
36. Gude, Leuven, 1731.
37. Muratori, 1739–42.
38. Maffei, 1765.
39. Morcelli, 1765.
40. *Corpus Inscriptionum Latinarum* (Supplementa Italica).
41. Vatican City, Biblioteca Apostolica Vaticana, Vat. lat. 9106, f.1.
42. Marini's correspondence has been only partially published and is now kept at the Vatican Library and in many other European libraries (Vatican City, Biblioteca Apostolica Vaticana, Vat. lat. 9042–60); see Carusi 1916–40 (III): 109–112; Gasperoni 1942: 329–36; Gasperoni 1942b: 78–90; Buonocore 1989: 107–20; Buonocore 1991: 215–34; Polverini Fosi 1992: 181–213; Rini 2015.
43. Mai 1831 published caps. I–VI, pars I (Vatican City, Biblioteca Apostolica Vaticana, Vat. lat. 9071, pp.1–152) and chapter XVI, pars II (Vatican City, Biblioteca Apostolica Vaticana, Vat. lat. 9072, pp.273–336); and the *additamenta* (Vatican City, Biblioteca Apostolica Vaticana, Vat. lat. 9074 pp.1011, 1014, 1016, 1023).
44. De Rossi 1857–61, 1888, 1915.
45. Bertini Calosso 1907: 189–241; see also Mazzoleni 2011: 923–44.
46. Buonocore 2015.
47. Vatican City, Biblioteca Apostolica Vaticana, Vat. lat. 9071, f. III; Buonocore 1999: 80–1; Buonocore 2000: 213–38; see also Poddi 2015; Maiani 2015; Ilardi 2015; Negroni 2015.
48. Vatican City, Biblioteca Apostolica Vaticana, Vat. lat. 9074: 1033–77.
49. The volumes were bound by Angelo Mai between 1833 and 1835; Vatican City, Biblioteca Apostolica Vaticana, Vat. lat. 9075–109; Manuscript Vat. lat. 9107 contains drawings and annotations from works in glass, lead, counterfeit copies and mosaics.
50. Lega 2015; 'Chapter 12: minor inscriptions in glass': Vatican City, Biblioteca Apostolica Vaticana, Vat. lat. 9071 (Caput XII, *Tituli minores in vitro*), pp.206-223.
51. Vatican City, Biblioteca Apostolica Vaticana, Vat. lat. 9071, p.218, no.7.
52. Vatican City, Biblioteca Apostolica Vaticana, Vat. lat. 9071 (p.207, no.3, p.209, no.2, p.216, no.5, p.217, no.9, p.219, no.1, p.223, no.5, p.223, no.9).
53. Vatican City, Biblioteca Apostolica Vaticana, Vat. lat. 9071, Morey, no.79 = p.212, drawing no.11; cat. **12** = Morey, no.358 = p.220, drawing no.9; cat. **25** = Morey, no.360 = p.209, drawing no.8; cat. **22** = Morey, no.364 = p.206, drawing no.7; cat. **23** = Morey, no.388 = p.218, drawing no.1.
54. Ashmolean Museum, Department of Antiquities, AN2007.5, AN2007.7, AN2007.11, AN2007.35 (cats.**12**, **25**, **22** and **23**).
55. (inv. 60775 = Morey, no.79); Vatican City, Biblioteca Apostolica Vaticana, Vat. lat. 9071, p.212, no.11. See p.00 for an account of the return.
56. Cat. 22, Vatican City, Biblioteca Apostolica Vaticana, Vat. lat. 9071, p.206, no.7.
57. Cat. 23, Vatican City, Biblioteca Apostolica Vaticana, Vat. lat. 9071, p. 218, no.1; the inscription on the glass, between two lines, says DIGNITAS A[MICORVM VIVATIS FELIC]ITE[R IN PA]CE DEI ZE[SES]. The inscription in the drawing reads [D] IGNITAS AMICORVM VIVA[TIS], which is not transcribed in full; the rest of the inscription is missing.
58. Cat. **25**, the inscriptions on the glass, to the left of the left bust and to the right of the right bust, read VRSV/S and DIO/ N[YSIVS]. The inscription on the drawing reads D[I]ON[YSIVS] on the right of the right bust. The inscription on the left of the left bust is missing.
59. Vatican City, Biblioteca Apostolica Vaticana, Vat. lat. 9071, p. 220 (card no.9).
60. Inscription on the drawing: D[I] ON[YSIVS].
61. Inscription on the drawing: P ETRVS P / A VLVS I V / [L]IVS SV / STVS.
62. Vatican City, Biblioteca Apostolica Vaticana, Vat. lat. 9071, p. 218 (card no.1). This drawing was probably executed by Seroux d'Agincourt (Vatican City, Biblioteca Apostolica Vaticana, Vat. lat. 9104, f.46r) and was used by the French art historian for an illustration in his *Histoire de l'art par les monuments* (Seroux d'Agincourt 1823, Pl.XII, no.27). Marini catalogued this gold-glass twice, adding a description on a different card (Vatican City, Biblioteca Apostolica Vaticana, Vat. lat. 9071, p.211, card no.3).
63. Garrucci also mentions that he was given access to this drawing by Giovanni Battista de Rossi and that it had been commissioned by Abbot Giacomo Severini; Garrucci: 1858: 1, no.2, Pl.I, no.2; see also Garrucci 1861: 692–703; Garrucci 1862 a and b, p.4, no.1.
64. Rini 2006.
65. 'R[omae] ap[pud] Ab[batem] Severinium Lipsanophylacum' (trans. 'at Rome in the repository of relics of Abbot Severini'): see pp.00–00.
66. ('[...] Fra le schede del Marini no.218, che n'ebbe il disegno dall'ab. Severani (for Severini) custode delle reliquie.'); Garrucci remembers that this drawing was given to Marini by Abbot Severini (Giacomo Severini), keeper of relics at the Lipsanoteca del Vicariato. Garrucci 1858: 1; for a history of the Lipsanoteca see Minoccheri 1894.
67. Garrucci, 1861: Pl.1; Garrucci 1864: Pl.1, no.3; Garrucci 1876: Pl.CLXXI, no.3.
68. Garrucci 1858: Pl.I, 2; Garrucci 1861: 692–703; Garrucci 1864: Pl.I, 1; Garrucci 1864b: Pl I, 3.
69. Inscription on the drawing [D]IGNITAS AMICORVM VIVA[TIS]: ('the dignity of friends, may you (pl.) live'); the rest of the inscription on the outer edge is misinterpreted. The inscription within the central *clipeus* reads: PAV/LVS PET RVS, ('Paul, Peter').
70. Bernheimer 1952: 19–34; Hollander 1970: 354–9; Bisconti 1983, cols. 2152–4 (with bibliography); Bisconti 1992: 78–85; Provoost, 1995: 234–45.
71. Schermann 1907; Schermann 1907b; Torrey 1946.
72. Tisserant 1909; Charles 1919.
73. On *The Ascension of Isaiah* see also Acerbi 1989; Bettiolo and Norelli 1995.
74. For a possible representation of Isaiah alone, tied to two trees, on a small blue-glass medallion in the Wilshere Collection, see cat. **30**, Fig. 21, p.50. This reading of the iconography is uncertain but, if correct, may be dated some decades earlier than cat.**23**, which from its use of recycled decolourant dates to the later fourth century.
75. (inv. 60775) Vatican City, Biblioteca Apostolica Vaticana, Vat. lat. 9071, p.212 (card no.11).
76. Inscription on the drawing: GENE / SIVS / LVCAS.
77. 'R[omae] ap[ud] Ab[batem] Severinium Lipsanophylacum' ('at Rome in the repository of relics of Abbot Severini').
78. Vatican City, Biblioteca Apostolica Vaticana, Vat. lat. 9071, p.206 (card no.7).
79. 'R[omae] apud Alexium Recupero' ('at Rome in the collection of Alessio Recupero'): Vatican City, Biblioteca Apostolica Vaticana, Vat. lat. 9071, p. 206, (card no.7).

80. Inscription on the drawing: CRISTVS / PETRUS / [PAV]LV[S] / TIMO /TEVS / IVST / VSSIM / ON FLO / RVS ('Christ/ Peter/Paul/Timotheus/Justus [a misreading of Systus, i.e. Sixtus], Sim/on, Flo/rus').
81. Du Fresne 1885: 119.
82. Minoccheri 1894: 14; I am grateful to David Rini for alerting me to this valuable source. See also Ferretto 1942: 201–5.
83. For example Canon Marco Antonio Boldetti, who published a fundamental work on the catacombs (Boldetti 1720): Minoccheri 14, 16.
84. Minoccheri 1894: 15.
85. De Rossi 1864: 47.
86. Ferretto 1942: 205.
87. The inventory now in the Biblioteche Riunite Civica e Ursino Recupero at Catania mentions only '*vetri*', ('glasses or glass [objects]').
88. Minoccheri 1894: 15 with n.1, a rescript of Nicolaus Finocchi, secretary to the Cardinal Vicar of Rome, dated 1801.
89. Minoccheri 1894: 13.
90. Minoccheri 1894: 13–14.
91. Minoccheri 1894: 5.
92. Minoccheri 1894: 26.
93. Minoccheri 1894: 8.
94. Dello Russo 2011: 1–24.
95. Letters to de Rossi re the negotiation for an exchange with Naples: Vatican City, Biblioteca Apostolica Vaticana, Vat. lat. 14247, 1868.270; Vat. lat. 14250, 1871.103; 1871.106. Letters to Garrucci: Biblioteca S. Luigi, R18 and R29/1871. For the eventual return as a gift see Vat. lat. 14295, 1894.124.
96. Noy 1995: 274 no.327, seen by de Rossi at the house of A. Reda in Bergamo. For later depredations that have resurfaced see 234–5, no. 268; 247–8, nos. 284–5.
97. Dello Russo 2011 for the nineteenth-century history of the excavation; for the twentieth century, see the photographs in Frey 1936, taken in 1935, and Noy 1995: 173–81. The papers in the State Archive of Rome, ASR Min LLPP., Ind., Agr., Comm., Belle Arti sez.5, tit.1, art.5c b420/429, state that only five (unspecified) inscriptions were sold to Wilshere, but another three may be securely attributed to the tomb from contemporary records and subsequent publications.
98. ASR, Min. LL. PP., Agr., Comm., Belle Arti, sez.5, tit.1, art.5c, b420/29, f.4538.
99. Garrucci 1862.
100. PIAC, de Rossi archive 3325/16229-16330. On the conflict between de Rossi and Garrucci see Nestori 1998.
101. ASR, Min. LL. PP., Ind., Agr., Comm., Belle Arti, sez.5, tit.1, art.5c, b420/429, f.4188: dello Russo 2011: 20, n.101 implies the sarcophagus has Jewish symbols on it, but the archive report does not mention such details. Herzog 1861: 98; Garrucci 1862: 19–21; Parker photograph 563; Rutgers 1988; Noy 1995: 179. The sarcophagus was not visible on a visit to the site in February 2013.
102. ASR, Min. LL. PP., Ind., Agr., Comm., Belle Arti, sez.5, tit.1, art. 5c, b 420/29 f. 4538: dello Russo 2011: 20 n.101.
103. Kraabel 1979: 49 for the supposed origin of the gold-glass.
104. For Vincenzo Capobianchi see above, pp 00–00 and de Callataÿ 2016.
105. Garrucci 1862: 8; Noy 1995: 176.
106. PIAC, de Rossi archive 3325/16282.
107. Biblioteca Apostolica Vaticana Vat. lat. 14247. 1868.270 for Zotikos.
108. Tuck 2005: 4; D'Ambrosio and Giammellini 2001: 8–10.
109. Tuck 2005.
110. Martiniello 1996; for the early Christian epigraphy see Felle 1993, with corrections and additions by Lambert 2008. Ancient Aeclanum is at the time of writing the subject of a major programme of survey and excavation: http://www.apollineproject.org/aec.html. I am grateful to Dr Ben Russell of Edinburgh University, a co-director of the project, for this information.
111. Lambert 2008: 118.
112. Vatican City, Biblioteca Apostolica Vaticana, Vat. lat. 14247, 1868.270.
113. *CIL* IX (1883) 1140.
114. Biblioteca S. Luigi, Letters to Raffaele Garrucci, R 18/1871; Vatican City, Biblioteca Apostolica Vaticana, Vat. lat. 14250, 1871.106.
115. Kraabel 1979:42, n.6, based on a note kept at Pusey House, Oxford, to which the medal was given by his daughters.
116. Biblioteca S.Luigi, Letters to Raffaele Garrucci, R 18 and R 29/1871.
117. Vatican City, Biblioteca Apostolica Vaticana, Vat. lat. 14250, 1871.103.
118. The gift was proposed to de Rossi in a letter of 26 April 1894: Biblioteca Apostolica Vaticana, Vat. lat. 14295, 1894.124.

2

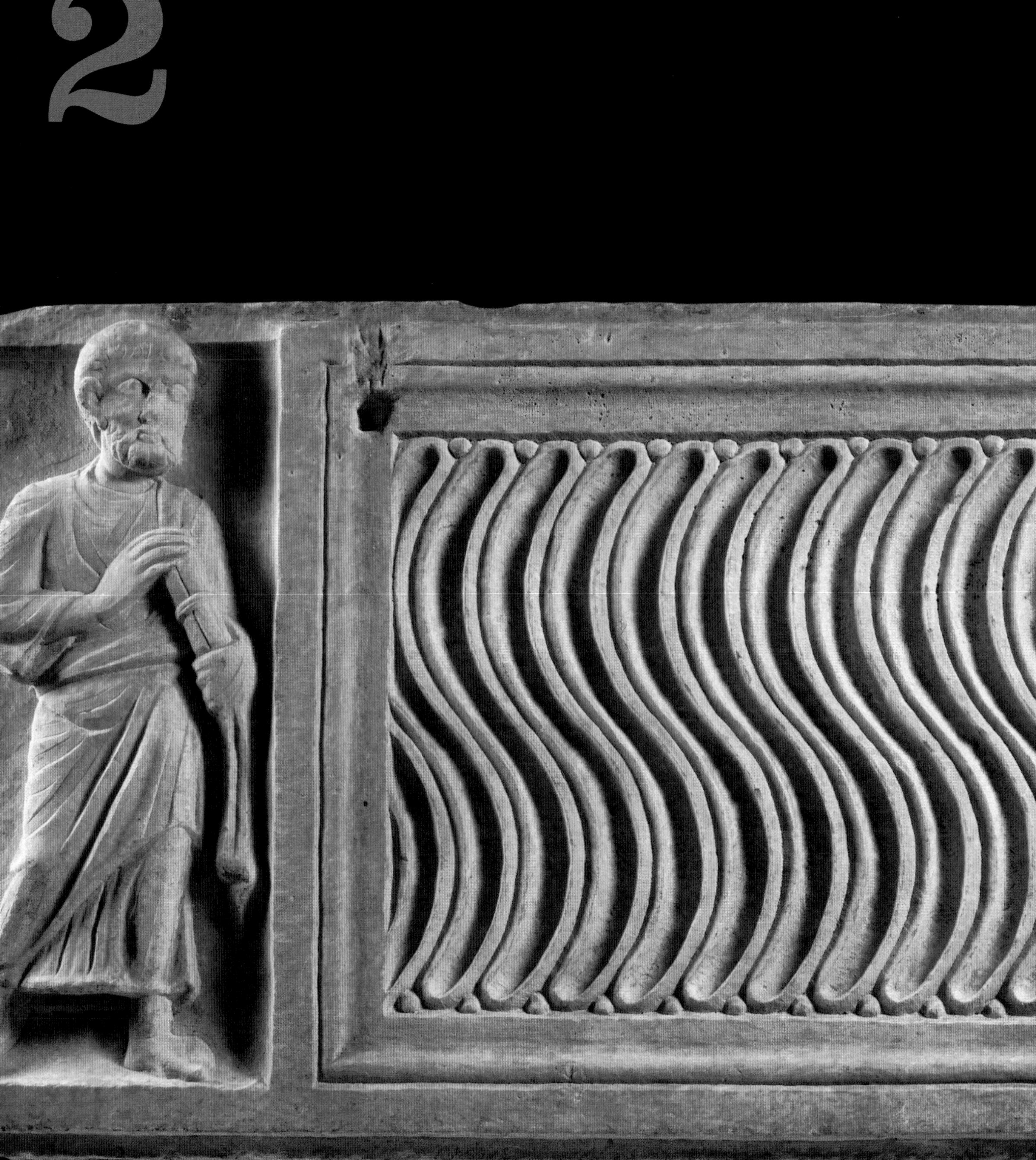

The Wilshere Collection in context

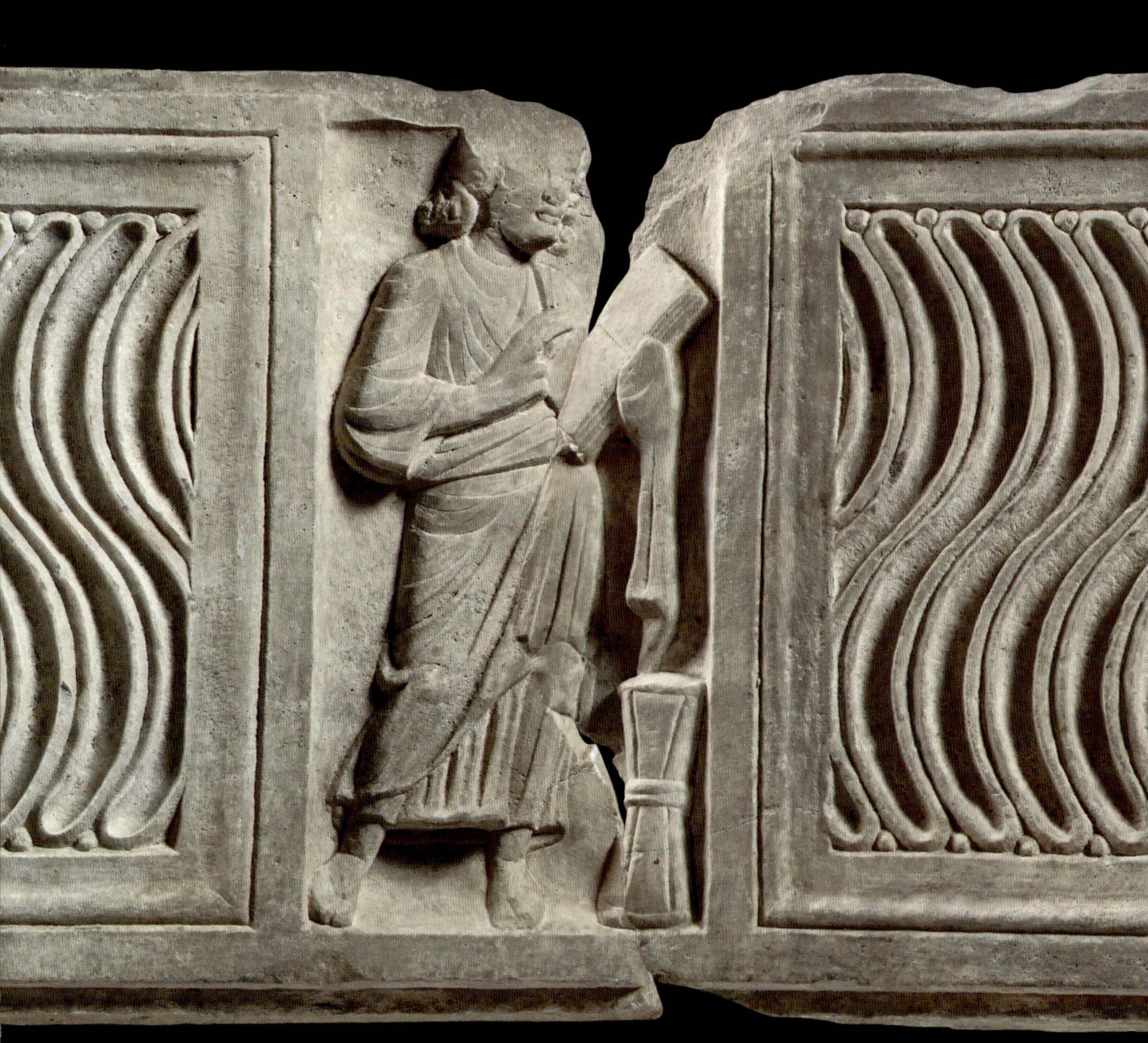

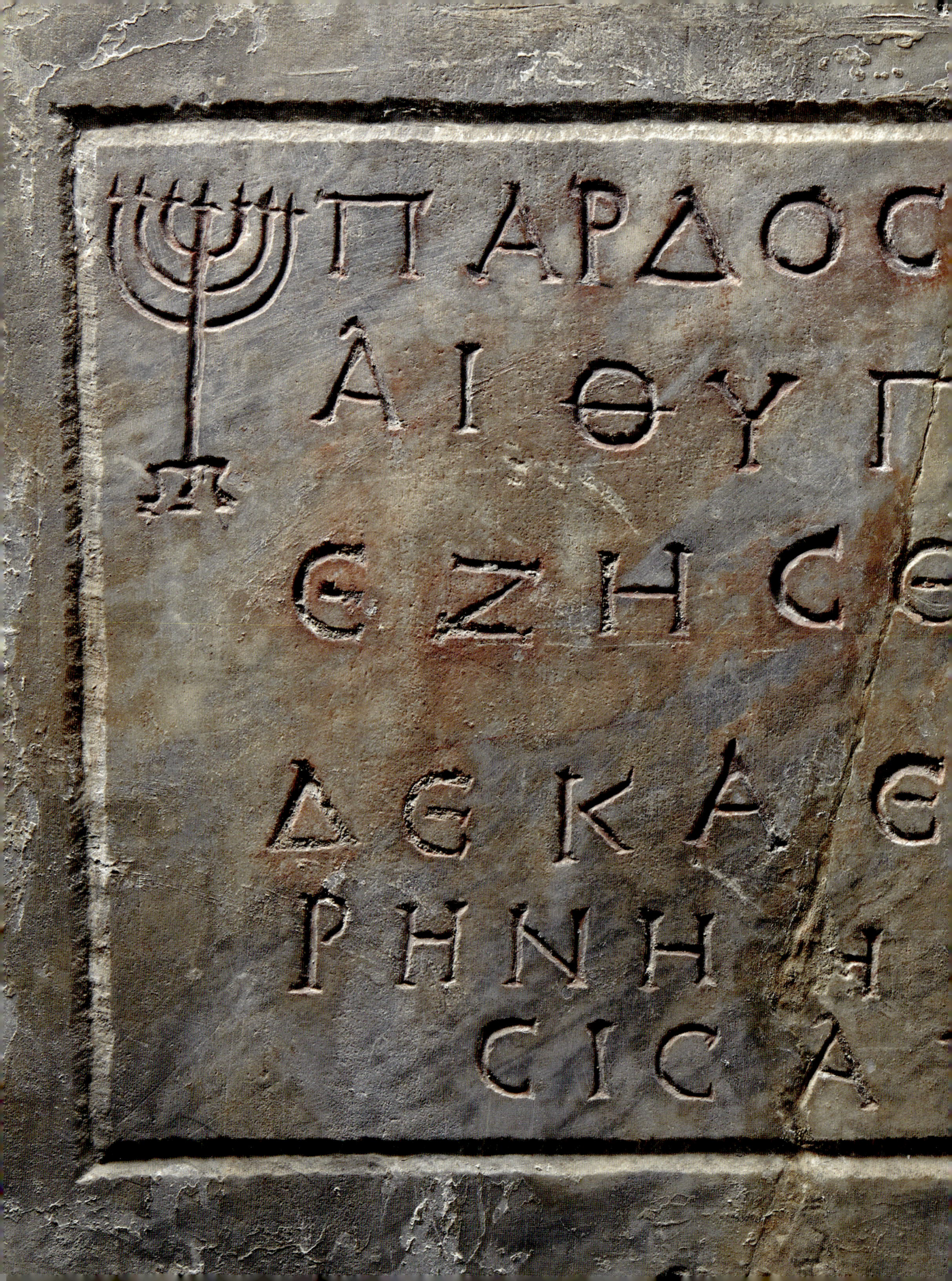

ΠΑΡΔΟC
ΑΙΘΥΠ
ΕΖΗCΕ
ΔΕΚΑΕ
ΡΗΝΗΗ
CICA

Chapter 3

Honouring the dead in late antique Rome

For centuries the Romans had honoured their dead with feasts at the tomb and gifts at the grave.[1] After the legalisation of Christianity in the early fourth century AD, these ancient, pagan funerary rituals were adapted to fit a new social order in which Christian, Jewish and continuing pagan affiliations could be publicly expressed and celebrated in or near the catacombs on the outskirts of Rome, where many were buried.

At the same time, the Roman *suburbia* saw an extraordinary investment in vast Christian basilicas. Several were endowed by the imperial family, mostly on their land, while other churches were developed, also in some areas of the inner city, by increasingly influential bishops.[2] Individual bishops held sway only in certain districts of Rome, leading in the 350s and 360s to locally based sectarian conflict. After a bitter battle the victor, Pope Damasus (AD 366–84), constructed a holy ring of shrines to the early Christian martyrs around the outer reaches of Rome, employing distinguished artists to embellish its monuments.[3] The pope promoted the patron saints of Rome, Peter and Paul, specifically as citizens of Rome to boost the solidarity of the faithful; the campaign of *Concordia Apostolorum* is prominently represented in gold-glass.[4] Damasus's Christianisation of the territory beyond the walls of Rome appears to have deliberately referenced the story of Christianity within the city, the pope creating a sense of historical and geographical continuity with his chain of shrines.[5]

The catacombs and the management of burial

The word catacomb derives from the Greek κατὰ κύμπας, literally meaning 'down in the hollows'. The term refers to the quarries around the margins of Rome, originally cut to extract tufa and sand for urban construction and to channel water from cisterns, resources that were exhausted by the third century AD. The networks of water channels offered for reuse ready-made galleries cut in single geological

(previous spread) St Peter (left) and Christ (right) on the front of a sarcophagus. Detail of cat. **41**

(opposite) Menorah flanks the text of Sabeina's tombstone. Detail of cat. **45**

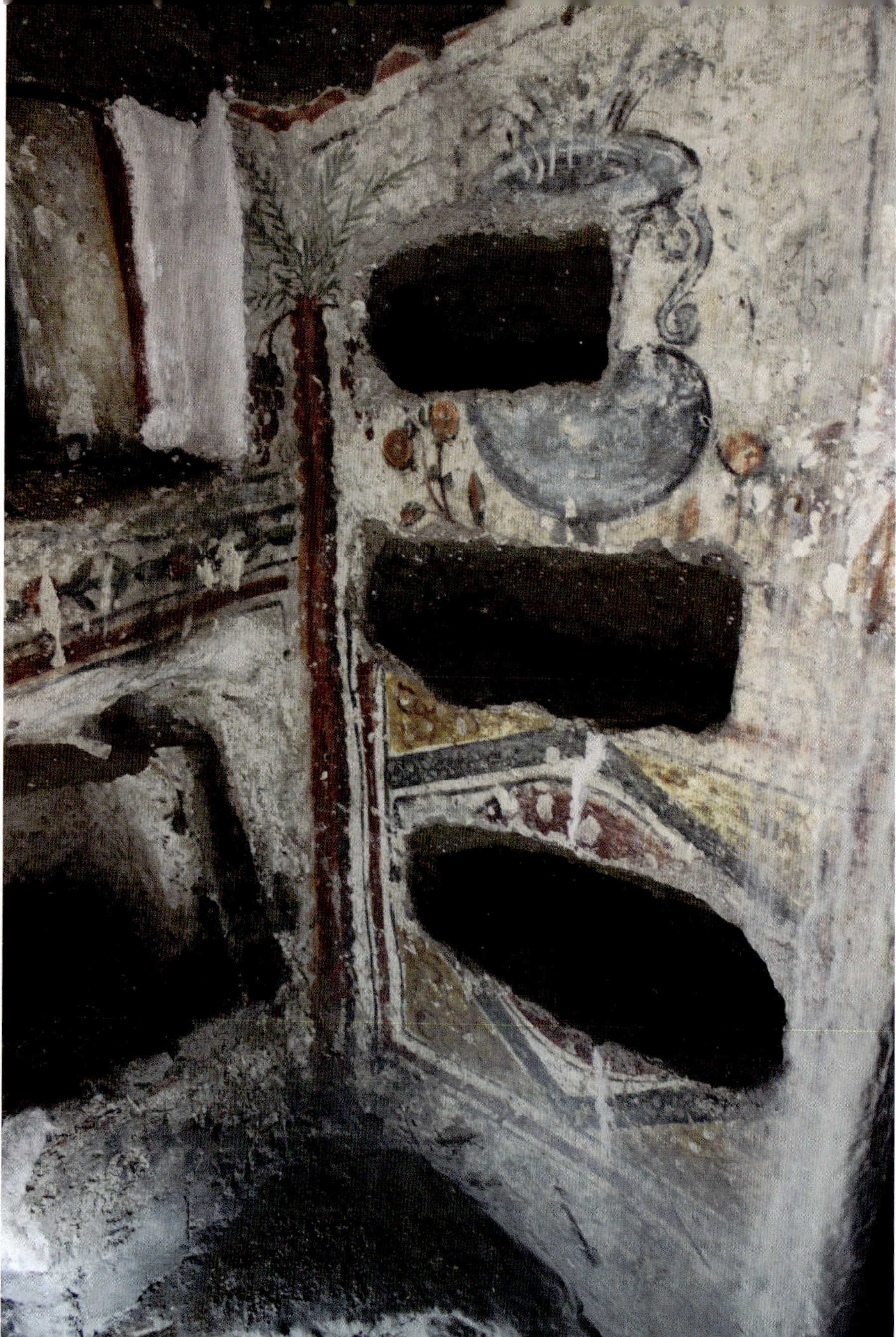

Fig. 31 The Jewish catacomb of Vigna Randanini, Via Appia, Rome: detail showing *loculi* cut into the walls of an earlier and grander painted *cubiculum*. Photo: Sean Leatherbury.

strata in fishbone shape.[6] Until late antiquity the open, but by then disused quarries were tunnelled to create economical burial sites for the inhabitants of the densely populated city.[7]

By this time, for reasons that are still poorly understood, the custom of inhumation had replaced cremation as the preferred funerary rite for pagans, Jews and Christians alike. This revival of an earlier practice served to put considerable pressure on the limited available suburban space for burial.[8] It is popularly believed that the network of tunnels and interconnecting chambers within the catacombs sheltered the early Christians from their pagan persecutors. However, there is no surviving evidence that the catacombs were ever used in this way, nor does it seem likely that the burial of private individuals in the catacombs was controlled by the Church: study of the Latin word *coemeterium*, transliterated from the Greek κοιμητήριον, suggests that, in the fourth century AD, the term was mostly used to refer to the graves of martyrs and associated shrines managed by the nascent church authorities.[9] Thus in the fourth century AD families remained largely in control of the burial of private individuals, which may help to explain why the pagan custom of feasting at the tomb continued in the face of opposition from the church, as well as why some catacombs appear to have housed a mixture of Jewish, Christian and/or pagan burials.[10] Evidently it was possible to buy from the *fossores* – skilled excavators whose ancestors had worked the rock beds of the catacombs when they were still used as quarries – any size of available and affordable space within a catacomb. Options for purchase varied from a *loculus*, literally a small space, used in the context of a catacomb to mean a slot cut in the wall of a corridor or chamber, which might itself house multiple bodies, to a *cubiculum,* a small room sometimes furnished with *arcosolia,* arched alcoves for burial cut into the wall.[11]

Nonetheless the regular plans of some tunnel networks, arranged on a grid, or in a comb or fishbone pattern, suggest a degree of centralised management of at least some sectors of the catacombs, possibly on behalf of the poorer members of the community, by burial clubs, professional *collegia* or the church. In the fourth century the church was given official responsibility for burying the poor, Christian or not, by the emperor in exchange for tax exemptions.[12] Some catacombs were developed on land owned by members of the imperial family, among them Flavia Domitilla. Granddaughter of Vespasian and niece of Domitian, her husband Titus Flavius Clemens, a nephew of Vespasian, was executed in AD 95 on Domitian's orders 'for atheism and Jewish practices'.[13] The site seems to have remained imperial property, housing the burials of many imperial slaves and freedmen. Though several catacombs were developed on imperial land, some landowners belonged to the old aristocracy. Priscilla, for instance, a member of the ancient, consular Acilii Glabriones family, gave her name to a large catacomb on the Via Salaria; it was probably used by a mixture of communities, among whom Christians were prominent.[14] These donors gave their names to networks of catacombs, even as others such as Sabina or Pudentianus gave their names to churches built on their land. In cases of a later association with venerated saints, the donors' names still remain in use today.

Feasting and gifts to the dead

In operation from the second century AD, the catacombs reached their peak of use in the fourth century. Many of the more spacious *cubicula* still bear traces of benches, seats, thrones, wells and tables furnished with marble or ceramic plates to accommodate feasting, a practice particularly widespread in the 330s, the closing years of Constantine's reign.[15] Some catacombs, notably one built on land named after Pamphilus, but probably in imperial ownership,[16] still preserve evidence for the placement of gifts to the dead, either within the *loculus* or set into its closing wall of plaster.[17] Among the latter gifts and markers were the bases of gold-glass vessels.[18] Northcote and Brownlow, drawing upon the work of de Rossi, noted that 'even the bottoms of these glass cups have frequently perished in the attempt to detach them from the plaster, and the impression left in the cement is all that remains'.[19]

The role of gold-glass in funerary ritual

The presence of gold-glass medallions broken from vessels among other domestic offerings to the dead in fourth-century tombs, such as lamps, dolls and ceramic vessels, has led some scholars to conclude that this was the end use of gold-glass plate – originally commissioned for domestic use or to mark significant family events, such as a marriage or the birth or growth to maturity of children, or even as a gift made at a public festival, such as New Year.[20] Domestic offerings in this context have been understood as representing important moments in the rapport between the living and the dead, and in the journey of the deceased to the afterlife.[21]

However, the primary purpose of gold-glass for domestic use has been challenged in the past quarter-century. It has been suggested that the function of gold-glass was funerary, and the specific purpose of permanently immuring the inscribed gold-glass base in the sealing of the *loculus* was to serve as a form of epitaph. This thus engaged mourners to remember individuals as part of a community, whether through marriage or through the unity of the church.[22]

Indeed, the iconography of much gold-glass used for feasting and drinking is strongly associated with prayers for the dead (see Chapter 5, pp.113–115);[23] the manufacture of the glass is unwaveringly consistent (see Chapter 4, pp.94–96 and Appendices 4a and 4b) and the obligations on relatives to remember the dead were pressingly frequent.[24] It therefore seems preferable to regard chalices inscribed with toasts to individuals and dishes with clear glass walls and gold-leaf medallions sandwiched into their bases (in this catalogue forming most of the content of Gold-Glass Groups 1–3) as commissioned expressly for the *refrigerium*, or feast at the graveside. Alternatively, these may have been used for feasts offered in memory of the deceased on fixed days of the month, for significant personal anniversaries or for public festivals commemorating the dead.[25] The practice of burial of the vessels varied, probably according to family custom and status.

So in the early seventeenth century Bosio reported finding bases of vessels (*tondi*) decorated with gold leaf, and small blue glass medallions still set in the mortar sealing the graves.[26] A century later Boldetti reported finding two or three complete vessels. However, his published illustration shows a shallow dish with handles, a form not known elsewhere in the gold-glass repertoire and one that, according to recent experiment, would have been technically near-impossible to produce (see below, p.93).[27] It is probable, then, that in many cases the complete vessel was commissioned for use at the funeral feast, either to serve food or, in the case of chalices, to toast the deceased. After use it was deliberately smashed, the relatives of the deceased retaining the gold-glass base, which was cemented into the plaster seal of the tomb.[28] There has been much scholarly discussion of whether the breakages were deliberate or accidental. The latter seems unlikely, as the jagged broken walls of the vessel were sometimes inserted into the plaster with the intact base-ring facing out.[29]

In the northern city of Cologne, itself a significant Roman centre for glass manufacture located on the Rhine frontier in Lower Germany, gold-glass imported from Rome has been found in fourth-century AD cemeteries. The shallow bowls of clear glass were decorated with small medallions; coloured glass outer layers bore gold leaf images but no text (featured here as gold-glass group 4). In Cologne the entire vessel was placed in the tomb as a gift to the dead.[30] It is possible that the same type of vessel was similarly treated in Rome: de Rossi saw the impression of large plates of this description, which had probably perished in the attempt to detach them from the cement.[31] Unfortunately the small-scale medallions surviving from Rome have mostly been reset as collectors' items, so it is difficult to reconstruct the ancient use of the vessels from which they were taken.

In Cologne plaques decorated with elaborate gold leaf scenes were placed on the corpse within the grave. An analysed example now in the collections of the British Museum was made of glass decoloured with antimony only.[32] Having no protective outer layer of glass, such plaques were evidently designed specifically for burial. So surely was a blue glass bowl decorated with unprotected, gold leaf medallion portraits of boys, set against a background of peacock feathers, each boy gazing at a biblical story of salvation below him.[33] Similar plaques lacking any archaeological context have survived from Rome; one, in the collections of the British Museum by 1838, is decoloured with antimony only and shows a boy named Fortunatus receiving the *toga virilis* from his father to mark his coming of age.[34] The use of antimony to decolour unprotected glass plaques suggests that, like the blue glass medallion portraits, these objects should be dated early within the sequence established for late Roman gold-glass (see further below, p.103–4).

Gift or grave marker?

The evidence from Cologne and the catacombs of Rome shows that fourth-century gold-glass medallions forming the base of vessels were sometimes used not as tomb markers, but as gifts to the deceased. All gold-glass vessels were designed to be read from the interior. In Rome the surviving fragment was sometimes inserted into the tomb with the base-ring of the vessel protruding outward, perhaps with the intention of allowing the dead to 'read' the image and the text cut into the gold leaf.[35] The practice is evidenced for pagan, secular and Christian gold-glass (Fig. 32).[36] At the same time, visitors to the grave could see the image and text, at least in reverse, and were protected from jagged broken glass; moreover, the vessel wall had a good anchorage in the plaster closing the tomb.

Nonetheless the circular form of the medallion, whether attached to the vessel wall or cut from its base, recalled the form of gold-glass portrait medallions of the third century AD. Significantly, these earlier gold-glasses are only known from Rome, where the discovery of two still in their original location, facing outwards, indicates that they were used as grave markers.[37] Several surviving medallions commemorate individuals, many of them named. Some were shown in military dress, while others were portrayed with objects indicating a role of, for example, musician (see Fig. 53) or scribe. The resemblance of the gold-glass portrait medallions to the painted *tondo* portraying the Severan imperial family and to contemporary frontal portraits in other media has been noted.[38]

Given the nature of the third-century burials in the Roman catacombs, many of which were located on imperial property, it is possible that the subjects of the gold-glass portraits, like those with inscribed memorials, were members of the imperial *familia* – high-ranking freed slaves and their descendants. These subjects celebrated in gold-glass their roles in life, just as they might otherwise have chosen to be represented on a sarcophagus or stone funerary relief – and indeed as they might have appeared with the emperor on public monuments celebrating imperial events.[39] The glass medallions are flat on the front and concave at the back, with bevelled edges. This suggests that they were designed to be set in a mount, which was probably made of metal and not retained for the tomb. However, there is no surviving evidence that the medallions were ever worn as pendant jewellery, though at 4–5 cm diameter their size is compatible with such use.[40]

The tradition did not completely die out in the fourth century: the Theodosian portrait fragment cat. **19**, for example, apparently belonged to a medallion of high quality. Moreover, some later fourth-century gold-glass vessel bases celebrating the memory of named martyrs might also have been used as grave markers; certain vessels were carefully grozed (regularly chipped) to form medallions which could

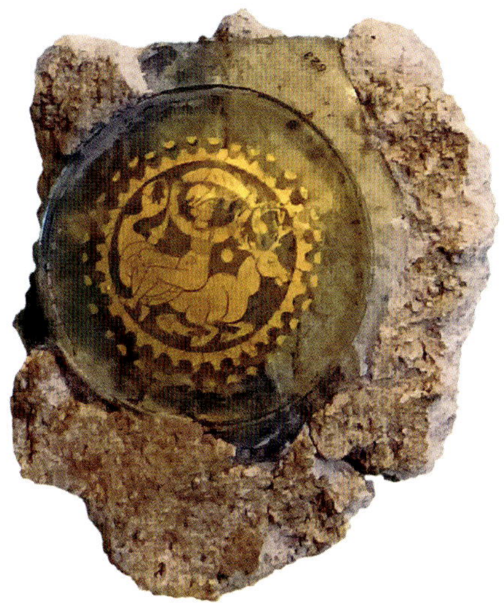

Fig. 32 Gold-glass from the catacombs with plaster still attached, displayed in the Vatican Museum. The shape of the surviving vessel wall shows that the remains of the glass vessel faced into the tomb. Photo: the author

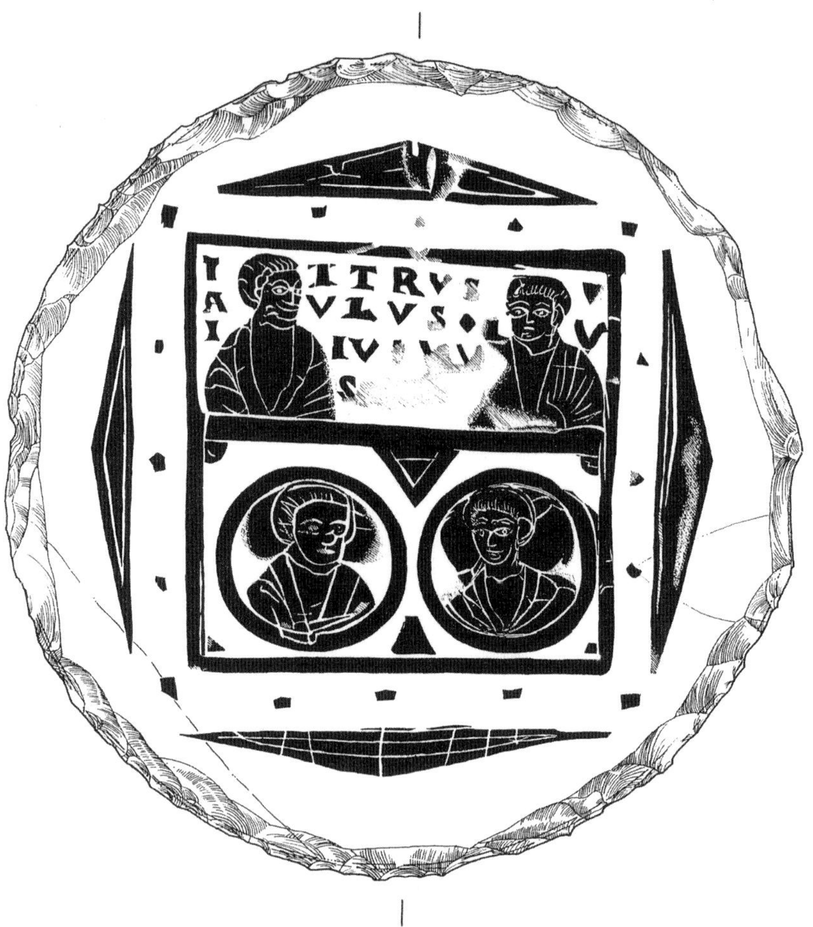

Fig. 33 Drawing by Rupert Cook of cat. 25, a gold-glass vessel cut back, or grozed, to form a medallion. The image, now much obscured, portrays Saints Peter and Paul watching over the martyred popes Julius and Sixtus, both shown in tondo portraits recalling the form of third-century gold-glass medallions.

have been used in this way. In some cases tondo images of papal martyrs, made from cut gold leaf, recalled the form of the third-century portraits (Fig. 33). These men were the senior servants of Christ, just as the subjects of the third-century portraits may have been senior servants of the emperor. The grozed bases could be placed facing out of the tomb wall to be read from the inside of the vessel by approaching pilgrims. However, much grozing took place after the gold-glass had been removed from the catacombs, so the date of formation of the later medallions is not clear.[41]

The Church's attitude to funeral feasts

The enduring importance of funerary feasts in fourth-century Rome, and indeed elsewhere in the Mediterranean world, is amply evidenced – not only by furnishings within the catacombs and other cemeteries, but also by surviving texts of speeches made by the Church Fathers. The latter strongly disapproved of feasting to honour the dead, regarding funerary banquets as an unnecessary extravagance; the resources expended upon them could have been better used to help the poor.[42] Moreover it did not behove the faithful dead to be celebrated with the kind of ceremony and ritual vessels more suited to commemorating martyrs, as truly exceptional witnesses to the Christian faith.[43]

Not the least of the Fathers' concerns was that behaviour at funerary feasts was notoriously louche: many participants got drunk and women were prey to debauchery.[44] Indeed it has been observed that the representation of outdoor funerary feasts at a *stibadium* (literally bundles of foliage wrapped in cloth to make a curved, bolster-style support for diners around a table bearing food) lost favour in the decoration of Roman marble sarcophagi after the early fourth century AD.[45] The gradual disappearance of scenes of feasting from the personalised lids of sarcophagi may reflect the growing disapproval with which funerary feasts were viewed by the authorities.[46] Nonetheless such feasts are shown in catacomb paintings, where we also see references to socially inclusive biblical meals such as the miracle of the loaves and fishes, perhaps in pious response to the criticism that funerary feasts were wasteful and an exclusive rite for the rich: the paintings have been variously interpreted as eucharists or celestial *convivia*.[47] Occasionally the *stibadium* and laden table are shown on Jewish gold-glasses, where the diners themselves are omitted.[48]

Despite the move to communal feasting managed by the Church, it is clear from the surviving literature that such celebrations were themselves the occasion for unseemly behaviour: at the festival of the Apostles' triumph, Jerome and Augustine lamented 'the saints, whom drunkards now persecute with their cups, as much as furious pagans used to pursue them with stones'. Wine-bibbing caused a scandal in the Basilica of Saint Peter, where Christian *agapai* were celebrated in the portico for the benefit of the hungry poor.[49] Visiting the tombs of the Christian saints were recently converted peasants, 'who before embracing the faith of Christ had long been the slaves of profane usages … They joyously stain with odiferous wine the tombs of the Saints. They sing in the midst of their cups …' Paulinus, Bishop of Nola, went on to explain the art of fresco wall-painting as a didactic diversion delaying the feast.[50]

Ecclesiastical alternatives

In view of the Church's concerns, Christians were encouraged to transfer their attentions away from remembering their own dead to commemorating the sanctity of the tortured martyrs. To this end six martyr churches were built in the suburbs by the imperial family. The vast buildings recalled in shape the Roman circus, where many martyrdoms had taken place.[51] The new churches and their ancillary buildings and courtyards could accommodate hundreds of worshippers, allowing the private funeral meal to become a communal feast. The churches were built at the tombs of Peter, Paul, Peter and Marcellinus, Lawrence and Agnes, and at the joint cult of Peter and Paul established in the mid-third-century AD *catacumbas* – beneath the later church of San Sebastiano on the Via Appia. A further two churches celebrating unidentified saints were built in the Via Praenestina and the Via Ardeatina by Pope Marcus in 336. All these churches were linked to existing catacombs, and vast cemeteries were constructed beside them to house thousands of tombs. This major development encouraged the burial of private individuals close to the saint, who offered protection to the faithful.

The martyrs' tombs were themselves much embellished by Pope Damasus (AD 368–83).[52] Damasus celebrated the virtues and suffering of the martyrs in more than 70 metrical verses he composed himself; the extravagantly lengthy texts, 'signed' in stone, were carved with great elegance and refinement by the distinguished engraver Furius Dionysius Philocalus. The newly monumentalised martyrs' tombs were thus turned into sites of 'celebrity' pilgrimage linked by steps and designated paths; tours were arranged for visitors on Sundays.[53]

The managed move away from the commemoration of deceased individuals to the communal celebration of martyrs may be traced in the development of later fourth-century gold-glass. It displays a rise in (on the whole) gold leaf engraving of inferior quality. The glass itself contained a mixture of decolorants that suggests the recycling of earlier gold-glass products, apparently as the long-distance trade in raw glass diminished in the later fourth century. The quality of the gold leaf set into recycled glass (catalogue group 3) is varied: in many cases it was crudely cut with images and names of the martyrs. Significantly, scenes of their martyrdom did not feature. Whether honouring a martyr or a deceased relative, fourth-century funerary iconography is relentlessly positive, looking forward to the afterlife and celebrating the peace of eternal rest.[54]

Individual popes, probably including Damasus (whose name is invariably abbreviated to Damas), also appear on gold-glass, under the protection of Saints Peter and Paul (for example Popes Julius and Sixtus, Fig. 33).[55]

In terms of glass shape, beakers, much seen in images of feasts on early fourth-century sarcophagi, and chalices for wine were replaced by heavy, flatter dishes used for serving food (for example Fig. 33). Shallow bowls continued in use (Fig. 34), and there are some instances of martyrs being invoked as intercessors for personal salvation (Fig. 35). The rise of Peter and Paul as the leading saints of Rome is well documented in gold-glass. Their dominance in gold leaf images is restricted to the group using recycled raw glass, the latest in the chronological sequence (catalogue group 3, Fig. 35, see further below, p.104).

In marble sarcophagi, too, we see a move away from complex narrative scenes of feasting at the grave and stories of salvation taken from the Bible to single figures of Christ with Peter and Paul, the two patron saints of Rome, each separated from the other by a panel carved with curved channels resembling the strigil used by the Romans to scrape oil from the body (Fig. 36).

Despite the apparently successful change of commemorative focus, the ecclesiastical authorities did not entirely manage to change behaviour at funeral and anniversary feasts (see above, p.79). In the AD 380s, Augustine found it necessary to

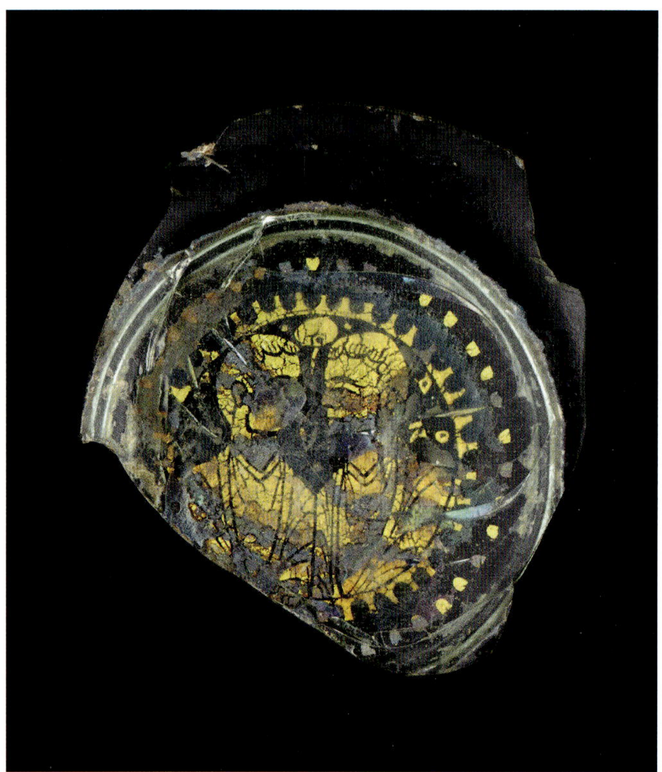

Fig. 34 Base of cat. **12**, a shallow glass bowl with gold leaf images probably representing the third-century martyrs Ursus and Dion[ysius]; a stylised crown is set between their heads

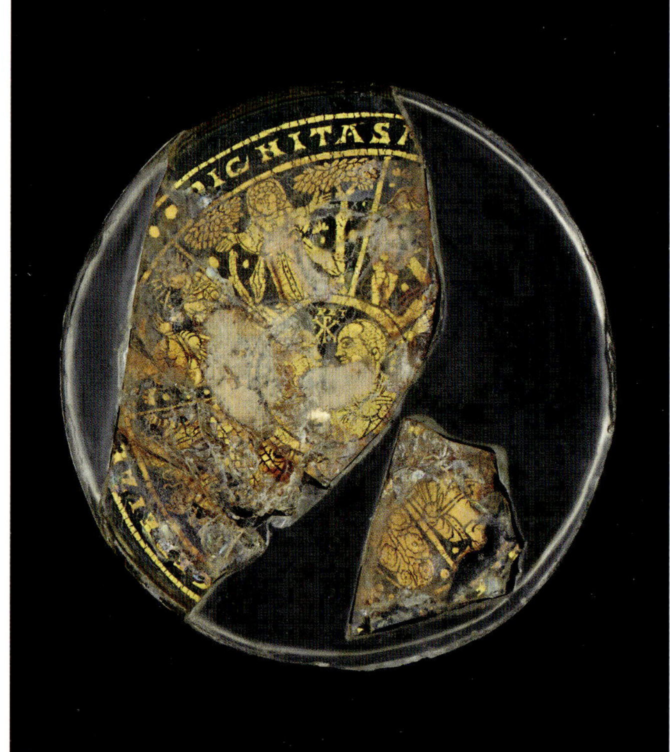

Fig. 35 Saints Peter and Paul appear at the centre of a series of biblical scenes evoking personal salvation on the base of a gold-glass dish from Rome (cat. **23**)

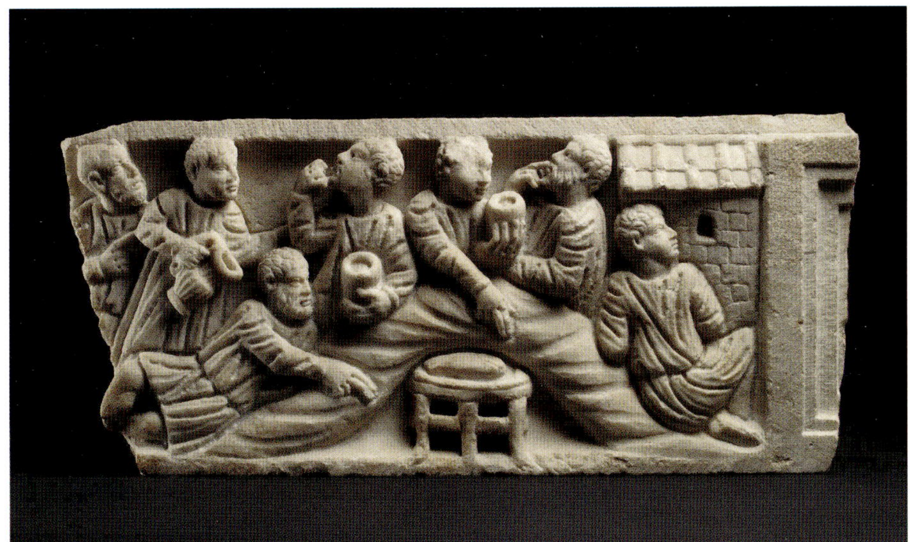

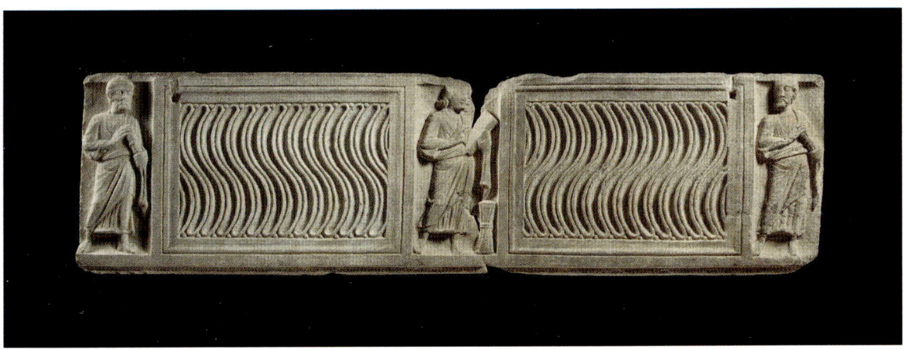

Fig. 36 (above) The left end of a sarcophagus lid, with scenes of feasting beside the built tomb of the youth shown at the right, about AD 300–30 (cat. **39**); (below) Saints Peter and Paul appear at the ends of a sarcophagus chest featuring Christ at the centre, *c.*AD 390 (cat. **41**)

report his mother Monica's attendance at the anniversary feast of a Christian martyr in minimalist, almost apologetic tones. She only sipped a little lukewarm wine as a courtesy to other participants, and it had already been heavily diluted with water.[56]

Changing burial customs in late antiquity

Gradually the customs of feasting and offering gifts to the dead died out, along with the use of the catacombs. With the establishment of parish churches in the centre of Rome from the fifth century, there arose a demand for relics of the saint for whom the church was named to be moved from suburban catacomb to city church. From the middle of the sixth century, a period of insecurity in the Roman Campagna, burial within the walls of the city was permitted and customs radically changed.[57] Grave goods fell from fashion, and the wealthy had long been encouraged to rid themselves of the burden of money by giving it to the church and adopting an ascetic lifestyle.

The invasion of Alaric in AD 410 also had the effect of dispersing wealth from the city of Rome.[58] The dead in the catacombs were slowly forgotten and the tombs themselves became prey to robbers, notably during the Goth and Vandal invasions of the sixth century AD. Nonetheless repairs were subsequently made to the martyrs' shrines, and burials continued to be made near them as late as the seventh century. However, the eighth-century Lombard and ninth-century Saracen attacks left all but a few shrines of Christian martyrs abandoned and the catacombs forgotten, until the revival of interest in the late sixteenth century.[59]

Memorials to members of the Jewish diaspora in Rome

Seven of the eight inscriptions collected by Wilshere from the Jewish catacomb in the Vigna Randanini were decorated with incised images of objects used in Jewish ritual. These slabs were most likely selected by Wilshere for their interesting appearance, and perhaps also for their relative rarity: less than half of the hundreds of surviving Jewish funerary texts from Rome are decorated with symbols of faith.[60] A count of the inscriptions with symbols, which are most conveniently recorded by Leon,[61] shows that such symbols predominantly appear on the tombs of officials within the community and their immediate family: the *archisynagogus*, leader of the synagogue; the *gerousiarchos*, leader of the community of elders; the *archon*, elder of the council, elected annually and eligible for re-election and honorary life-election; the *grammateus*, secretary to the council of elders. It is evident from the layout of these texts that the symbols took precedence and were incised, or, in the case of the *archon* Zotikos (cat. **44**) painted first; the text was subsequently cut around them and both were then coloured in red. The predominance of the symbols forbade the use of guidelines, with a consequent fall in the quality of the engraving of the text.

Among the individuals featuring in the Wilshere texts, Alexander (cat. **48**) is the sole member of the community to have a Latin memorial. The unusual use of Latin perhaps reflected relative personal wealth, and it enabled him to have his profession recorded as *bubularus, bucular[i]us* or *butularus in macello*, best translated as 'meat-seller in the market'.[62] The irregular orthography of the text prevents certainty: did Alexander supply live animals from the market for ritual slaughter, or was he himself the butcher? Given the fact that all other named officers had roles within the synagogue, it is likely that Alexander also performed a service for the community. The formula appearing at the end of the text, referring to 'the just', may actually refer to a group of pious people within the community, who commissioned Alexander to supply their fine, ritually pure meat.[63]

Symbols were also used for memorials to children and young adults, and to pious women. All these groups were critical to the formation and governance of the Jewish communities of ancient Rome. However, not every official, child or pious woman had a decorated tombstone, as is shown by the undecorated memorial (cat. **43**) of Justus the secretary, son of Maron, a re-elected archon; nor were symbols entirely restricted to these groups. Though in a Jewish context evidently referring to the management of the synagogue, the terms used to describe the officials are very similar to those used in the governance of the Greek communities of the Roman empire. Indeed, many of the Jewish diaspora in imperial Rome came from the eastern Mediterranean region, where Greek was the *lingua franca*; the use of Hebrew became widespread, and perhaps compulsory in the western diaspora only from about AD 400.[64]

All but one of Wilshere's Jewish memorial texts are written in Greek, with the exception betraying a greater familiarity with Greek than Latin.[65] The host language was gradually adopted first for personal names, especially of girls, and then more generally as the language of the Jewish diaspora community. Indeed, where parents and children are named in the same text, the Wilshere Collection reveals consistent adoption of Latin names for the children, while the parents' names were Greek. The more widespread use of Latin in the Vigna Randanini catacomb may suggest a greater degree of individual prosperity, arising from integration within the wider community of Rome. It may also show that burials continued for longer than in the Jewish catacombs at Monteverde and Villa Torlonia, the latter accommodating poorer Jews, often in shared graves.[66] The use of symbols occurs across both languages, and also in conjunction with Hebrew and Aramaic texts.[67]

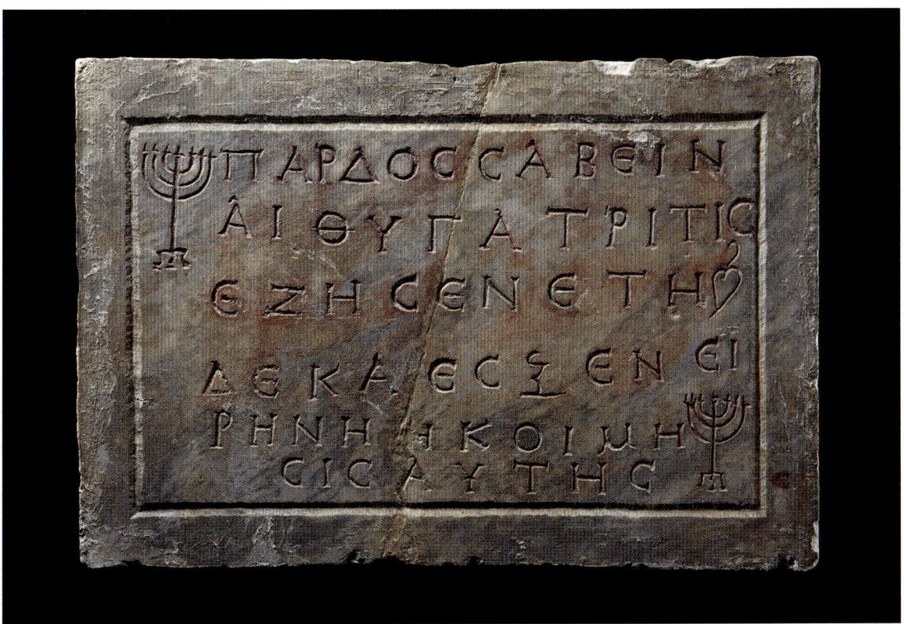

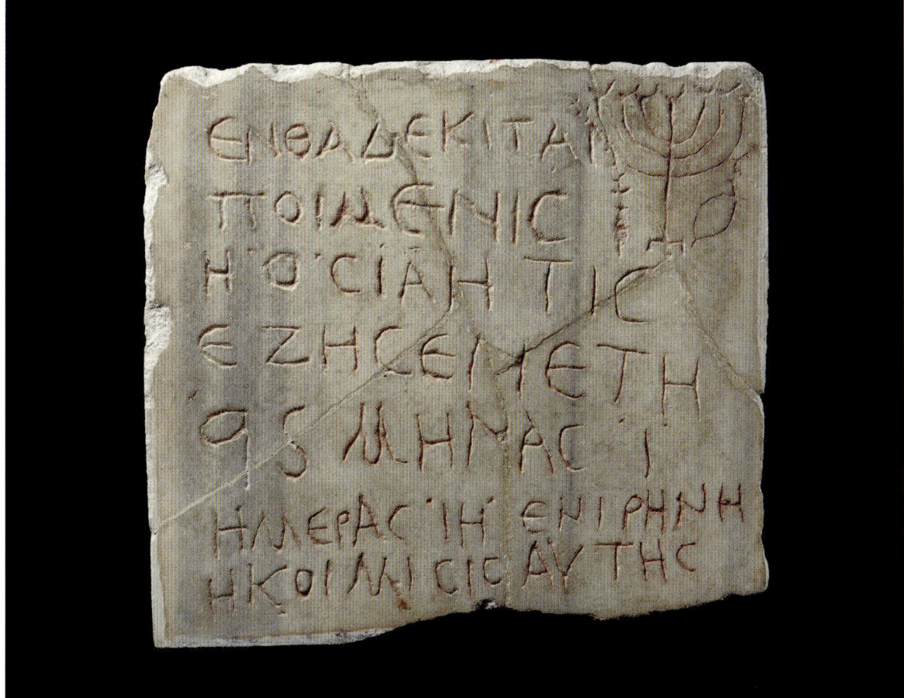

The most common symbol depicted on the tombstones is the menorah. It appears alone on the memorials to Alexander and Venerosa, and twice, marking the beginning and end of the text, on the memorial to Sabina (Fig. 37). The interpretation of the menorah as a marker of Jewish identity has been questioned, but seems here beyond dispute, both in the archaeological context of the Vigna Randanini catacomb and considering the precedence of symbols over text described above.[68]

A more complex array of symbols appears on the tombstone of Poimenis, perhaps because she lived to the exceptional age of 96. The menorah is shown between the *lulab*, bound branches of myrtle, palm and willow used in the autumnal festival of the *sukkoth*, along with the *ethrog*, a citron fruit (Fig. 38).

Fig. 37 Tombstone of Sabina, daughter of Pardos (cat. 45)

Fig. 38 Tombstone of Poimenis (cat. 50)

The infant Numenis (cat. **49**) was commemorated with the tree-like menorah also used to mark the graves of Alexander (cat. **48**) and Venerosa (cat. **47**), and also with a jar used to anoint his body with oil.[69] Melition, who died aged 29, received an ornate memorial from her daughter Dulcitia (cat. **57**). Here each syllable and each digit are separated by a triangular mark, and the central menorah is balanced by two elongated *hederae* (carved ivy leaves, often used to decorate pagan inscriptions); their elongated form probably reflects the mason's exuberance and Garrucci was surely wrong to see them as *ethrogin*. However, on one tombstone from the Vigna Randanini the *hedera* bears a *lulab*.[70] Sabina's memorial was also marked with a *hedera* at the end of the third line of text (cat. **45**, see Fig. 37). Indeed, even the monumental slab commemorating the archon Zotikos (cat. **44**), no doubt intended to cover his burial in an *arcosolium*, was decorated with *hederae*, one of which was inverted, and a centrally placed *cantharus*, a drinking cup surely commemorating the funeral feast. The *hederae*, too, may have evoked festive drinking, as a wreath of ivy leaves was traditionally worn by Bacchus, the pagan god of wine. However, a menorah and *lulab* mark the end of the text commemorating Zotikos.

On the gold-glass fragment in Wilshere's collection (cat. **13**), the menorah is decorated with polychrome fruits recalling the biblical description of the menorah in the second temple (Fig. 47).[71] Two horizontal lines above its lamps mark a central division of the decoration; unfortunately the upper part of the glass, which might have shown the ark of the Torah scrolls, is missing.

As noted above, the more prevalent use of Latin in the catacombs of the Vigna Randanini suggests that these were used for longer than other Jewish catacombs within the city of Rome. Unlike the Christian community, Jewish owners of catacomb plots had no religious motive to request burial near a saint or martyr. However, the Vigna Randanini is located directly opposite the cemeteries of Saints Callixtus and Sebastianus on the Via Appia, and must in consequence have been vulnerable to the same problems of insecurity from the sixth century onwards. There are no texts that could be dated later than the fifth–sixth centuries, and the cemetery was clearly looted and the *loculus* closure slabs smashed long before its excavation in the 1850s and 1860s.

The social status of the deceased

The social status of owners of gold-glass has been a matter of some scholarly discussion, with gold-glass widely and surely reasonably regarded as a less refined, and hence less expensive, craft than, say, the commissioning of ivory diptychs or silver dining services.[72] However, in terms of glass production the making of decoloured vessels decorated with a sandwich layer of gold leaf, the latter cut and engraved with text and pictures, and sometimes enhanced with enamel colouring, is very much at the top end of the craft: 'costly, but not automatically aristocratic', in Howells' judgement.[73] As suggested above (p.77), it is possible that third-century gold-glass portraits, none of which are held within the Wilshere Collection, represented senior servants of the emperor.

Within the repertoire of portraits on fourth-century gold-glass vessels, individuals are richly dressed, the women often wearing heavy jewelled collars and mantles decorated with embroidery. Colour is often added to their jewels and clothes, and hairstyles are often elaborate. This suggests that the persons commemorated in the gold leaf were indeed wealthy. In contrast to the earlier gold-glass portraits, no skills or professions are represented. The only hint we have of exceptional social status

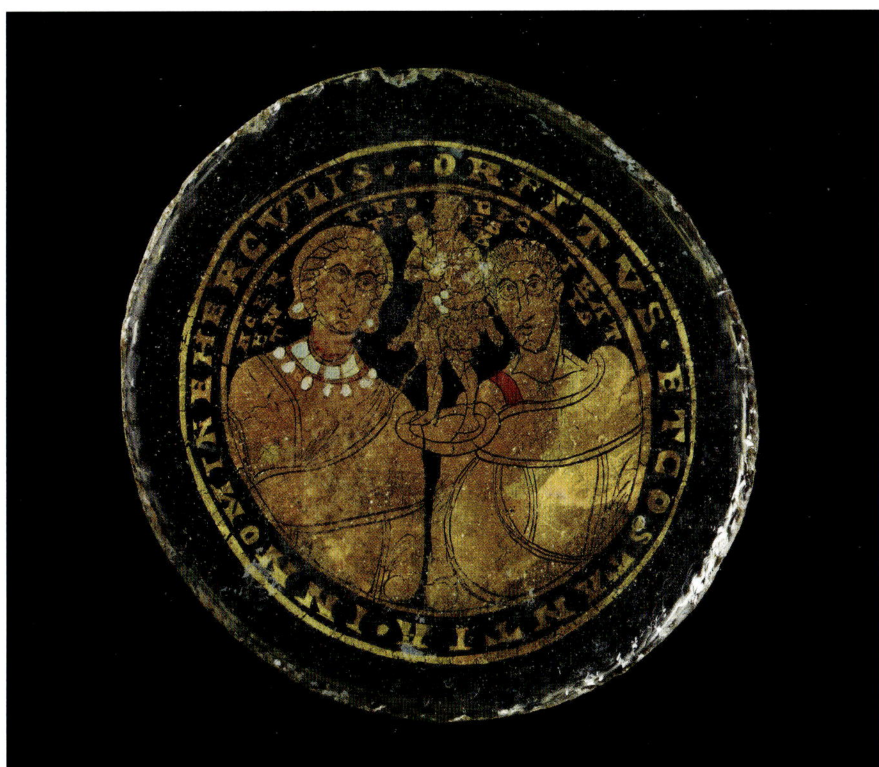

Fig. 39 Orfitus and Constantia on a gold-glass base in the British Museum. © Trustees of the British Museum

appears in one large gold-glass vessel base, acquired by the British Museum from the collection of Count Matarozzi in 1863, which features portraits of a couple named Orfitus and Constantia (Fig. 39). They are most likely to be identified with the pagan Prefect of Rome, who held office each year from 354 until 359, with the exception of AD 357, and his wife, sister of the emperor Constantius.

The unique content of the text has caused much comment. In an outer ring the couple are named 'ORFITUS. ET CONSTANTIA. IN NOMINE HERCULIS, 'Orfitus and Constantia. In the name of Hercules''. Squeezed around their heads and the figure of Hercules is the remainder, which reads 'ACERENT/ IN. FELICES BIBATIS'.[74] The couple are set beside one another, with the figure of Hercules before them; he is standing on a flexible, semi-transparent base and, perhaps significantly, turned toward Constantia. Dressed in a lion skin, the hero bears his club and the three apples of Hesperides. The *clavus* (coloured stripe, in Rome denoting social status) on Orfitus's tunic is painted deep red, while Constantia wears white jewellery, also the colour of the apples. The interpretation of the text depends on the restoration of the missing case ending of *acerentin*. Was the word intended as an epithet of Hercules as conqueror of the underworld, thereby referring to the death of (probably) Constantia, or does it signal another possibility?

Alan Cameron proposed that the population of the small town of Acerentia, located in southern Italy on the borders of Lucania and Apulia, commissioned the gold-glass dish as a gift to its wealthy patron Orfitus.[75] The text may then be translated as 'Orfitus and Constantia in the name of Hercules, [the people of] Acerentina [give this]. Live happy!' An alternative version reads: 'Orfitus and Constantia in the name of Hercules, Conqueror of the Underworld, Live happy!' In the latter sense, the injunction to live happily could imply 'for eternity', a meaning more frequently conveyed in a Christian context. The use of the term '*felix*' is often reserved in Latin address for people distant from the speaker, indeed usually deceased.[76] Moreover, a similar text appears on a non-extant gold-glass vessel base, preserved only in a line drawing. This shows Hercules wearing the lion skin and grasping the wrist of Minerva, with the text 'TICI ABEAS HERCULE ATENENTINO [*sic*] PROPITE', translated as '[uncertain word]may you have by [or from] Hercules, Conqueror of the Underworld, may you prosper!'[77]

Notwithstanding the contested interpretation of this text, it is a reasonable inference that portraits on fourth-century gold-glass vessel bases were not necessarily commissioned by people of the same social status as the subjects of the portraits. If the principal purpose of these vessels was to serve food at the funeral feast, then the glass was most likely commissioned by those arranging and attending the event. They may have been members of the extended family, including former slaves and others not enjoying the same social status as the subjects of the portraits. However, third-century gold-glass portraiture was most likely commissioned by individuals close to the subject of the portrait and of equivalent social status, if not by the subjects themselves. Social parity may account for the more direct gaze of the subjects of third-century medallion portraits, hence for the engagement of the viewer.[78] The form of portraits on fourth-century gold-glass should consequently be regarded as beyond the control of their subjects. Strictly speaking, they may not be considered as examples of self-representation, even when the subjects are named.

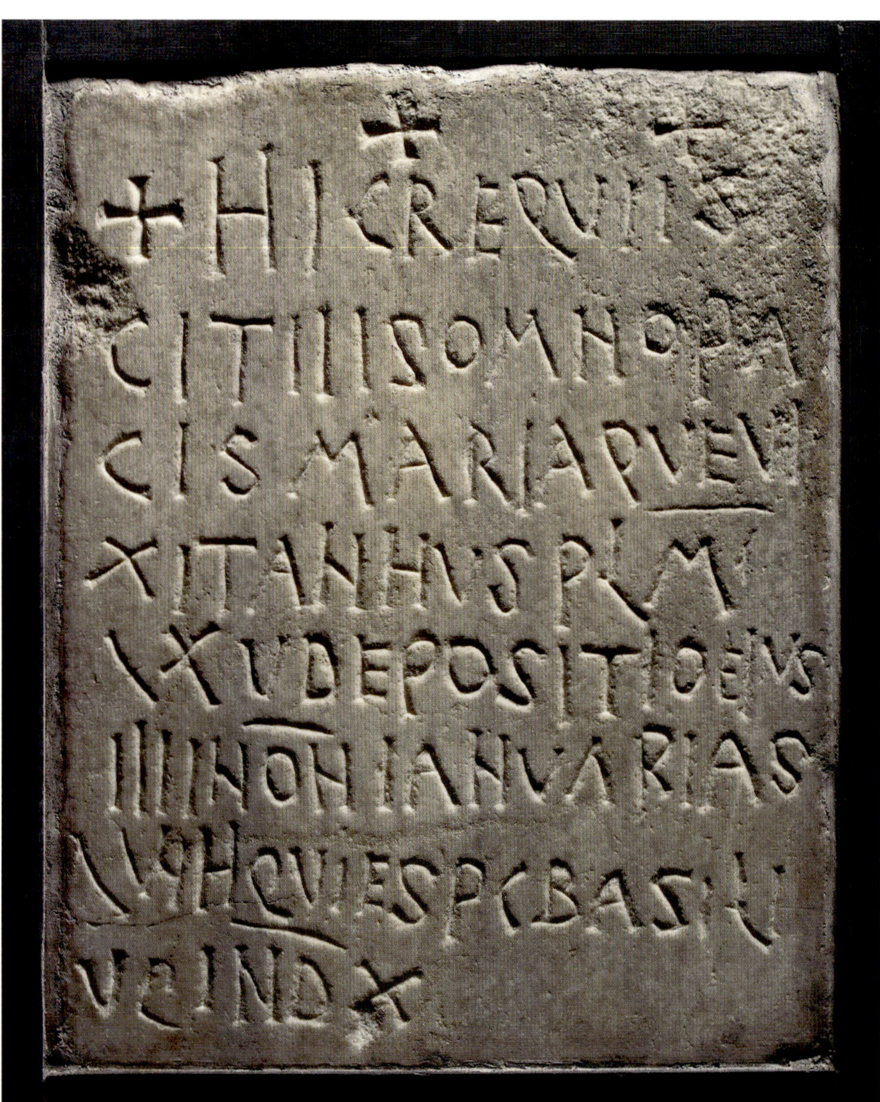

Fig. 40 Cat. 55: Funerary inscription from Aeclanum, dated 6 January AD 546: 'Maria rests here in peaceful sleep.'

The status of individuals buried with gold-glass vessels in Cologne warrants further investigation. So do the contexts of the very similar Latinised Greek toasts found in the Cologne/Trier region on other types of vessel, including engraved glass bowls, *diatreta* (carved openwork glass cups, also heavily clustered in this area) and more modest painted ceramic drinking cups.[79] The presence of gold-glass and the use of Latinised Greek suggest a strong link between this region and Rome. The most likely reason for these unusual coincidences is the presence of the imperial court at Trier. The evidence of burials published to date suggests the use of gold-glass and Latinised Greek toasts by individuals of relatively high social status compared with the local population. They may have been members of families serving the emperor in a military or civilian capacity, who had moved to the Rhineland from Rome.

In contrast to the subjects of pagan and Christian gold-glass portraits, the Jews commemorated in the catacombs of the Vigna Randanini were not apparently wealthy, with the possible exception of Alexander (see above, p.82). Less than half of the memorial stones had images of Jewish liturgical objects, which may have been reserved for people of particular importance to the community – be they officials in the synagogue, individuals celebrated for their piety or those of either gender who had lived exceptionally long or unusually short lives. The strong focus on a sense of community is especially striking in this group of memorials. There is much evidence for untimely death; in contrast, there are very few representations of or references to children in fourth-century gold-glass. When these do appear, as in third-century medallions used as grave markers, children are invariably shown with other members of the family.

Memorials to Christian women in Aeclanum

The fifth- and sixth-century funerary inscriptions collected by Wilshere honour elite women, who were members of a Christian community living within a bishopric providing a structured, ecclesiastical authority.[80] The cemetery at Mirabella Eclano has yielded to date 54 Christian tombstones, of which 33 (an unusually high proportion) bear consular dates as a formal record of the burial of individuals, thus offering a precise date for the commissioning of the memorial.[81] Consular dates were only used in a Christian context; in addition to providing a formal record of burial, the term *depositio* also bore the sense of entrusting the body temporarily to the earth until the time came for personal resurrection, and it provided surviving relatives with the date on which anniversary rituals were to be observed.[82]

From the balanced spread of fifth- and sixth-century dates it is clear that the practice of incising the text on recycled stone taken from buildings no longer in use is comparable to that of the Christian memorial to Sapis from Cuma and the Jewish burials of the Vigna Randanini, which are widely regarded as being of fourth-century date (see further below, p.108). Moreover the use of formulae expressing personal loss and a hope for peace for the dead remained consistent with earlier practice across all faith communities.[83]

Conclusion

Any precise archaeological context has long been lost from the funerary material in the Wilshere Collection. However, the objects reviewed here may be seen to fit into much broader patterns of known funerary practice across the Jewish and

Christian communities of Rome and southern Italy in late antiquity. In particular the gold-glass documents a striking social change from pagan, individual commissions of superior artistic quality to the provision of larger bowls and plates of lesser artistic distinction, apparently used for serving food to Christian and Jewish groups. Within the Christian serving vessels we see evidence for a gradual move away from the commemoration of individuals to the remembrance of saints and martyrs, a development encouraged by the increasingly dominant church. In Jewish stone memorials we see a consistent focus on the community and its most valued members.

In the design of these modest epitaphs, greater weight was given to the representation of liturgical objects, where used, than to the alignment of text. These trends, along with assessments of the evidence for such practices as recycling, will be further examined from a material point of view in the next chapter.

Notes

1. Toynbee 1971, Hopkins 1983 and Morris 1992 offer wide perspectives of the archaeological and documentary evidence. Bodel 2008 is particularly useful on this period and the problems of interpreting the evidence. On feasting see specifically Jensen 2008. On third-century tombs and the development of the catacombs see Borg 2013.
2. See Curran 2002 (2010), especially Chapter 4: The Christianization of the Topography of Rome.
3. See recently Thunø 2015: 172–87, and below, p.116.
4. Huskinson 1982; Thunø 2015: 70, fig. 41.
5. Thunø 2015: 181, 205.
6. Borg 2013: 118
7. Bodel 2008: 197–9 with n.39
8. Bodel 2008: 181 with n.8, quoting Morris 1992: 31.
9. Rébillard 2009, 4–7; Bodel 2008: 202–3 with n.49.
10. Rébillard 2009: 14, 34–6.
11. On the *fossores* see Guyon 1974.
12. See Fiocchi Nicolai in Fiocchi Nicolai, Bisconti and Mazzoleni 2009: 15–17 for centralised management of Christian catacombs; Borg 2013: 121 on the role of the Church.
13. Borg 2013: 79
14. The associations are problematic. See Osiek 2008: 252–3 and Borg 2013: 98–105 for a discussion of the difficulties.
15. Fiocchi Nicolai, Bisconti and Mazzoleni 2009: 44–6.
16. Borg 2013: 97.
17. Fiocchi Nicolai, Bisconti and Mazzoleni 2009: 83, fig. 93 shows coins cemented into the sealing plaster of a *loculus* in the catacomb of Pamphilus. See also Meredith 2015.
18. Fiocchi Nicolai 2001: 63, 72.
19. Northcote and Brownlow 1879: 299.
20. Smith 2000: 179.
21. Smith 2000: 191, drawing on De Santis 1994: 31.
22. Deichmann 1993: 153; Borg 2013: 262–3; Meredith 2015: 221–3.
23. Compare that of late antique glass pendants principally found in graves in the Roman province of Syria-Palestina: Entwistle and Finney 2013.
24. Rébillard 2009: 140–75.
25. Howells 2013: 118 notes the impracticality of the design for functional tableware and suggests that the plates were intended for display, like large silver plate. See Cooley 2012: 110 for similar toasts on engraved glass vessels from Pozzuoli, all from graves where the context is known.
26. Bosio 1632: 197 (Catacomb of Callistus); 508 (Catacomb of Priscilla).
27. Boldetti 1720: 191–2. See also Northcote and Brownlow 1879: 299, and Howells 2015: 24–5 with pl.10.
28. Bisconti in Fiocchi Nicolai, Bisconti and Mazzoleni 2009: 80.
29. Painter in Harden 1987: 266.
30. Painter in Harden 1987: 263–4 gives a summary of the evidence from the Rhineland.
31. De Rossi 1864: 89–91, reported by Northcote and Brownlow 1879: 321.
32. Howells 2015: 99–101, no.16.
33. British Museum BEP 1881, 0624.1 for the bowl and S 317 for the plaque and its burial context, on which see also Meek 2013: 129, Table 6; Howells 2015: 26–7, plates 12 a–b, 14; 99–101, no.16; 101–3, no. 17. Meredith 2015: 220, n.3 suggests that the lack of any protective layer on the cup is due to the use of cobalt blue glass, which would have obscured the gold leaf. In practice, cobalt blue or other highly coloured glass was always used as a base, not a covering layer.

The unprotected gold leaf decoration on plaques was usually mounted on transparent glass.

34. BM OA 887: Howells 2015: 137, no. 43 dates it to the late fourth century. However, the decolouration with antimony only suggests an earlier date.
35. Eighteen gold-glasses published by Morey retain some of their plaster setting; four of these (nos 42, 68, 103 and 122) were certainly facing inwards. The distinction between inward- and outward-facing gold-glass vessel bases is not made by Meredith 2015: 221, who assumes that all faced outward, to be read by visitors to the tomb.
36. Morey 1959: nos 103 (pagan/secular), 42, 68, 122 (Christian). The 14 glasses facing outwards divide equally between pagan/secular and Christian content.
37. Howells 2015: 55.
38. Meredith 2015: 226 with nn.31–4.
39. Borg 2013: 72–112 for the catacombs. Meredith 2015: 226 makes a significant distinction between the strongly detailed individualism of third-century portraits in gold-glass compared with the sketchy presentation of individuals in fourth-century gold-glass vessel bases.
40. Howells 2015: 115–16, no.30 demonstrates that the medallions were made of blown, not cast glass as asserted by Harden 1987: 277, no.153. Meredith 2015: 226 sometimes identifies the medallions as pendants, but offers no evidence that they were ever suspended for wear as such.
41. Howells 2015: 24.
42. Augustine, *Ep.* 22, 2–6; Jensen 2008: 141. See Borg and Witschel 2001: 114 on the ceremonial display attending a *stibadium* meal.
43. Zeno, *Tractatus*, 1.25; Ambrose, *De Helia et ieiuno* 17, 62; Rébillard 2009: 144–6.
44. Zeno, *Tractatus*, 1.25. On the banning of women from visiting tombs at night by the council of Elvira (Spain) see Rébillard 2009: 144 with n.18.
45. Koch 2000: 25.
46. Rébillard 2009: 142–53.
47. Fiocchi Nicolai, Bisconti and Mazzoleni 2009: 110–13 for a discussion of the many possible meanings of banquet scenes on catacomb paintings.
48. For example Morey, no.458.
49. Jerome, *Ep*.31, *ad Eustochium*. Augustine, *Enarratio* in *Psalmum*.lix; *Ep.* xxix, *ad Alypium* §10, quoted by Northcote and Brownlow 1879: 306.
50. Paulinus of Nola, *Poema* xxvi, quoted by Northcote and Brownlow 1879: 307.
51. See Fiocchi Nicolai 2001: 53 for the new churches, their locations and their role.
52. Fiocchi Nicolai 2001: 79–80.
53. Carletti and Ferrua 1985.
54. Bisconti in Fiocchi Nicolai, Bisconti and Mazzoleni 2009: 118–25.
55. Morey, nos 106, 107, 250 and 340; Grig 2004.
56. Augustine, *Confessions* 6, 2, 2; Rébillard 2009: 147.
57. Fiocchi Nicolai 2001: 90–1.
58. Brown 2012.
59. Fiocchi Nicolai in Fiocchi Nicolai, Bisconti and Mazzoleni 2009: 65–6. See also p.00.
60. Leon 1960: 198–9. Painted images have largely disappeared.
61. Leon 1960: 263-346, Appendix of Inscriptions.
62. The market is not specified. For the text see most recently Cooley 2017: 2959, no.161.
63. Williams 2004: 131.
64. Reynolds and Tannenbaum 1987: 22.
65. Nonetheless the Randanini catacomb shows a greater use of Latin than in the other Jewish catacombs of Rome. See Leon 1960: 75–7 and Rutgers 1995: 180.
66. Leon 1960: 112 (girls' names); Rutgers 1995: 180 (date of the tombs and social class of the deceased); Cooley 2017.
67. Rutgers 1995:182–3.
68. Elsner 2003: 117 questions the menorah as a marker of Jewish identity in late antiquity.
69. Noy 1995: 292 suggests this type of menorah incorporates a *lulab*.
70. Garrucci 1862: 58–9; Noy 1995: 291 Goodenough (1953) iii: 769 for the *lulab*.
71. Exodus 25: 33–6 and 37: 20–1; Hachlili 2000: 30–1.
72. Cameron 1996: 298; Howells 2015: 52.
73. Howells 2015: 52.
74. Howells 2013: 118.
75. Cameron 1996: 299–300.
76. Meredith 2015: 231; Tomlin 2005.
77. Garrucci 1858: pl.XXXV.8; Smith 2000: 132.
78. Meredith 2015a: 228.
79. Adams 2003: 407 with n.186. For the gold-glass see Nüsse 2008 and Ristow 2007. On *diatreta* see recently Meredith 2015b. The present author intends to undertake further research in this area.
80. See above, p.00 and Martiniello 1996.
81. Felle 1993: 84; Lambert 2005, 295, n.25. Further archaeological survey and excavation is currently being undertaken at Aeclanum by Ben Russell of the University of Edinburgh, who reports (pers. comm.) that more funerary inscriptions have been discovered.
82. Cooley 2017: 299–301, no.162 = cat. **53**; 301–3, no.163 = cat. **55**.
83. Lambert 2005: 291, nn.6–7.

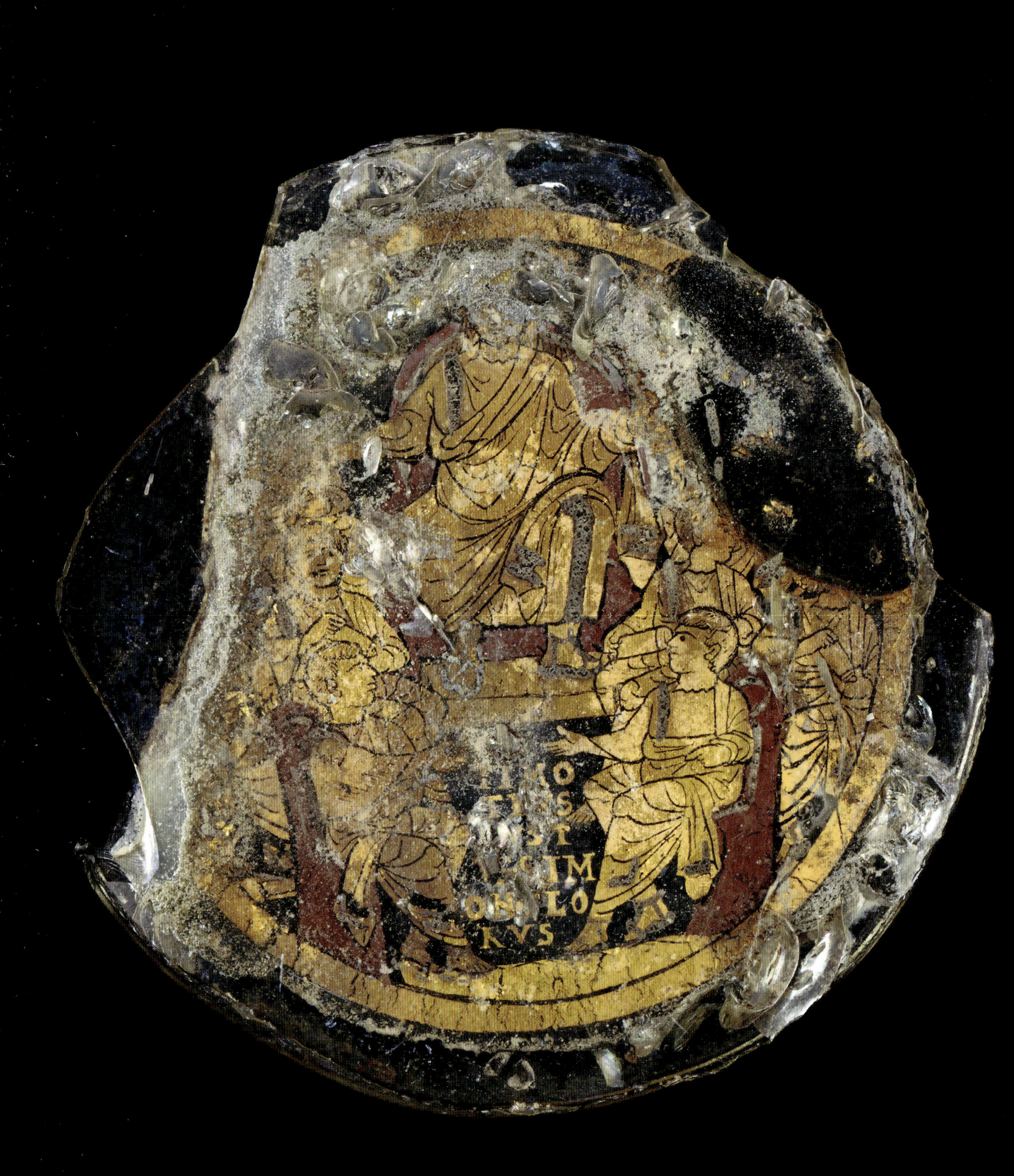

ROST
IST
CIM
LO
KVS

Chapter 4

Craft in context: the materials of the Wilshere Collection

What can be learned from the materials of the Wilshere Collection? In this chapter recent experimental work on making gold-glass, undertaken for the study of the British Museum collection (Howells 2015), is summarised; some key points are illustrated by individual gold-glasses in the Wilshere Collection. The results of XRF and other chemical analysis of the gold-glass in the Wilshere Collection (Appendices 4a, b), set alongside similar research undertaken for the British Museum's collection, help us to understand the complex manufacturing processes of the craft of making gold-glass and to develop a sequence of dates for late antique production. The use of gold-glass in the course of the fourth century AD is reviewed to explain that new social needs required new products, which led to changes in quality.

Marble sarcophagi, like gold-glass, had a similar two-stage production process. The practice of recycling materials is considered across the range of media in the collection: gold-glass, sarcophagi and inscriptions.

Gold-glass

Late antique gold-glass is not esteemed by modern historians of Roman art and society for its quality: it is, in the eyes of many scholars, nothing more than a clever craft (see Chapter 3, p.84). Nonetheless, the process of making gold-glass belies its apparent lack of aesthetic value. Crafting gold-glass required technical facility if not, in most cases, great artistry.

Making gold-glass

In a recent experiment to recapture the craft of making sandwich gold-glass, in which the gold leaf design is attached to a glass base and protected by a covering layer of clear glass, the late Daniel Howells combined the advice of modern British glass-makers Mark Taylor and David Hill, experts in experimental glass archaeology,

Christ as teacher, with saints Timotheus, Sixtus, Simon and Florus below. Detail of cat. 22

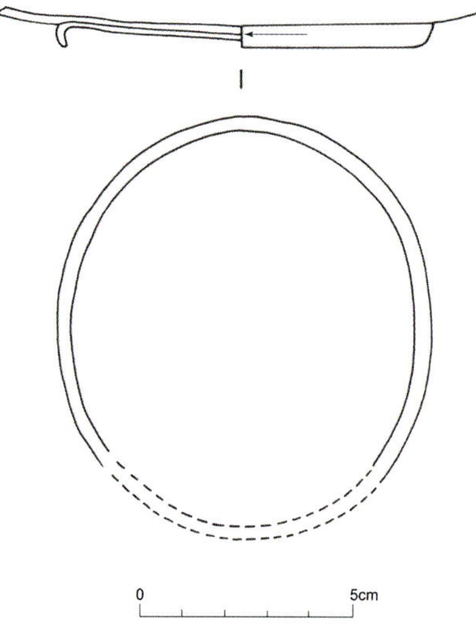

Fig. 41 The base of an oval, gold-glass dish (**cat. 3**). At upper left may be seen the simply bent foot-ring below the layer of gold leaf, which is marked with an arrow. Drawing by Yvonne Beadnell

with information from a tenth-century treatise by the Italian monk Eraclius.[1] Howells described how the base and foot-ring are formed by inflating transparent glass on a blowpipe, leaving a *parison* (constriction) between the pipe and the glass bubble.[2] The *parison* is then reheated to make the glass pliable, so the bubble of glass beyond it can be flattened and its sides made cylindrical against a flat, hand-held, metal or wooden surface. The *parison* is then cut from the blowpipe and slowly cooled. The flattened base may then be separated from it, with the base-pad's cylindrical walls forming a simple, downturned foot.

According to Eraclius, the circular sheet of gold leaf was attached to the base with gum (Fig. 41). In modern practice any water-soluble glue that evaporates in intense heat may be used. When dry, with the gold leaf adhering securely to the upper surface of the base, text and image may be cut: a Roman stylus would have sufficed. The letters of the text were mostly set within parallel guidelines; indeed the sometimes extravagant serifs may be seen as the remnants of such lines, whose position could also be marked with dots of gold leaf (Fig. 42). Such guide marks are to be distinguished from those marking the start and end of words and phrases; the latter are usually aligned with the centre of the adjacent letter (Fig. 39).

Over-painted enamelled decoration was sometimes added to the finished image, as in the green emerald settings of the jewels separating the saints in cat. **11** (Fig. 42). Excess gold leaf, once scraped off the base, could be collected for recycling. Howells noted that the process of removing excess gold leaf was often done sloppily in antiquity, and details of image and text were sometimes accidentally removed or retained. In cat. **11**, for example, the proper left foot of St Peter appears joined with, and indistinguishable from, the proper right foot of the adjacent saint (Fig. 42).

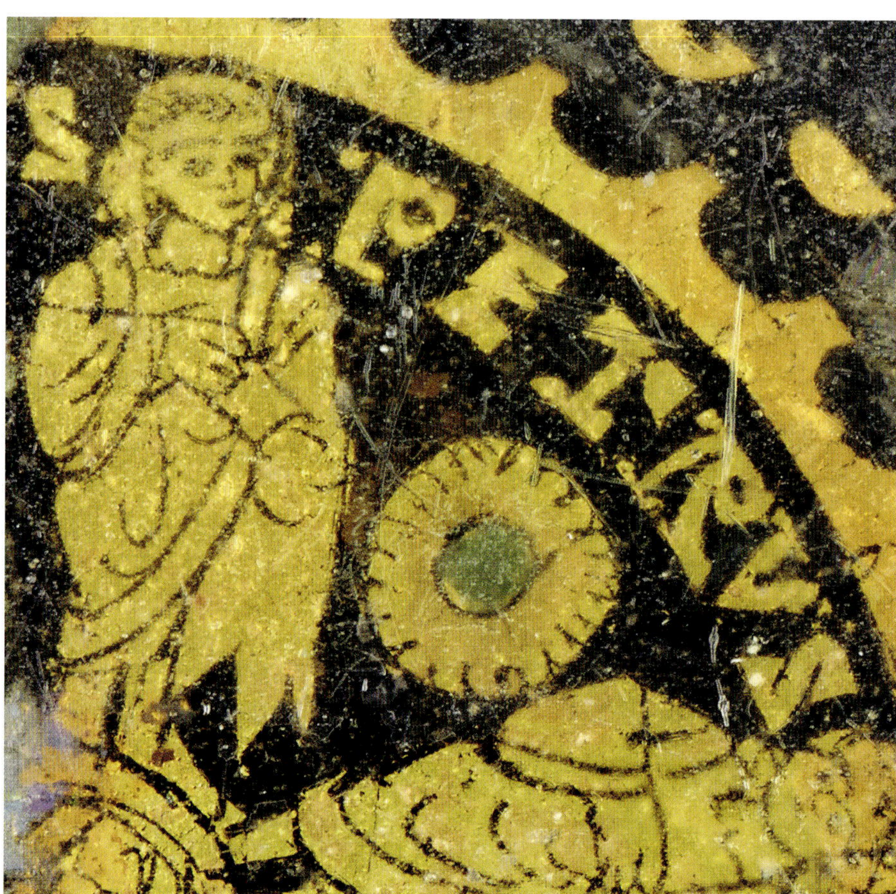

Fig. 42 Detail of cat. **11**, showing a dot and a triangle of gold leaf beside the letter 'P', used to mark the start of this section of text. The horizontally extended serifs retain the position of the guide lines.

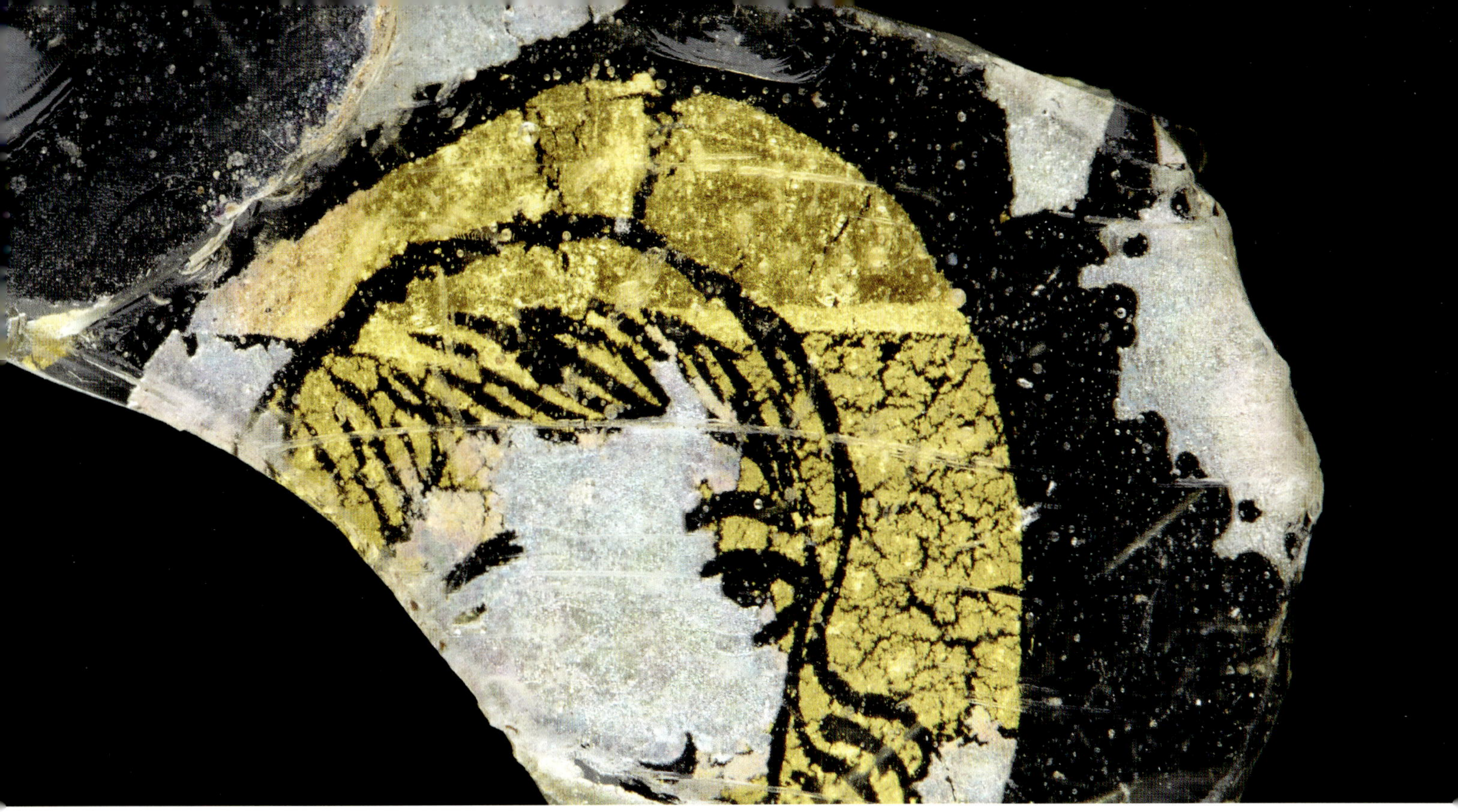

The decorated base may then be slowly reheated to a maximum temperature of 550° C. (Higher temperatures risk distortion of the foot-ring.) The reheated base is removed from the oven by pushing it on to a wooden paddle with a stick: slippage results in scoring the gilding, an error sometimes evident in ancient gold-glass (Fig. 43).[3]

The gilded base is then placed into an oven-like box on the floor, thereby retaining its heat. The glass-maker stands over the box to inflate a new *parison* of glass at a similar temperature to the disc below, fusing the gold leaf between the two glass elements. The fused vessel is removed from the blowpipe and slowly cooled overnight. Once cooled, the excess upper portion of the *parison* (known as the *moil*) may be removed and recycled. This leaves a vessel in the shape of an open, shallow bowl, the rim of which could be smoothed with stones. Howells notes the difficulty of applying handles to vessels formed in this way, which raises a question about the accuracy of Boldetti's well-known drawing of a gold-glass vessel prised from the plaster wall of a *loculus* in the catacombs.[4] The survival of multi-layered vessel bases such as cat. **13** suggests that the glass-maker was not always content with the shape of the finished vessel, in which case he simply blew a better shaped *parison* over the top of the discarded one. This results in an additional layer of glass covering the gold leaf (Fig. 44).

Fig. 43 Cracked nimbus to the right of the head of Christ on the fragment of gold-glass cat. **8**; this and the scored line above are the result of slippage in removal of the glass from the oven.

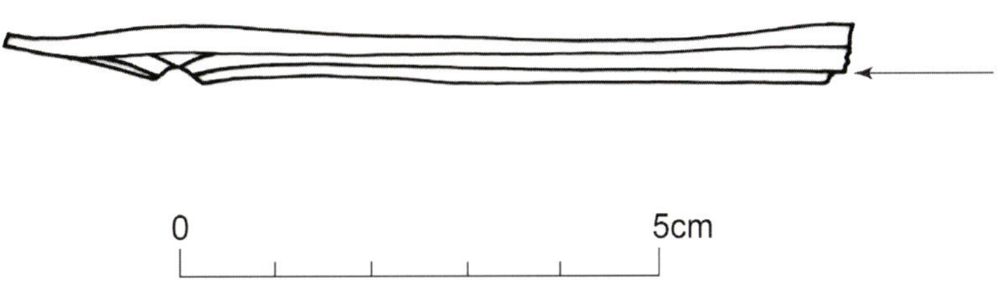

Fig. 44 Drawing of cat. **13** by Yvonne Beadnell. The arrow shows that the gold leaf was applied to the base layer, while the presence of two layers above suggests that the glass-maker was dissatisfied with his first attempt to blow the covering vessel wall, which has cracked through the base layer at the left, and simply blew another one over it.

Chemical analysis of Roman glass

In recent years significant advances have been made in the understanding of the chemistry of Roman glass. New analysis has changed our understanding of how glass in the Roman empire was produced. Though much effort is currently being invested in a search for sources of raw glass in the western Mediterranean basin, Roman glass appears chemically so homogeneous that, in its raw form, it is widely thought to originate from a single region – the arc of the southeast Mediterranean coast sweeping from Sinai to Syria.[5] Indeed, isotopic analysis of cat. **21** shows that the raw glass for this vessel base came from the Syria–Palestine region (Appendix 4b). Along this coastline the quality of sand blown east from the Nile Delta surpassed all others available, and the area possessed easily accessible natural deposits of natron, a sodium compound used as an alkaline flux in the making of glass. Huge raw glass factories, most but not all of very late antique date, have been excavated in the modern states of Egypt and Israel.[6]

However, the evidence of analysed glass vessels and excavated glass workshops suggests a much longer history. After the region came under Roman rule or influence following the defeat of Mark Antony and Cleopatra VII of Egypt at the battle of Actium in 31 BC, the Romans controlled access to the components of raw glass. They imported it to Europe where there were plentiful sources of timber and iron, especially in Alpine areas. Timber was felled to fire long-burning, high temperature kilns, and iron was used to make heavy-duty blowpipes, enabling the glass-maker to pick up substantial gobs of molten glass to turn into bottles and containers. Thus did glass move from a luxury craft, producing small perfume bottles and drinking cups for the few, to an industry supplying the masses – not only with vessels that imparted no taste to food or drink, but also with commodities such as oil, wine and fish sauce that could be transported and/or served in glass containers and vessels.[7]

Despite this revolution in glass production in the later first century AD, some glass-makers continued to make luxurious coloured products. This was particularly the case in Egypt, where Alexandrian glass-makers used a 'vitreous earth' they regarded as essential to the production of multi-coloured designs of glass; they also claimed to copy in glass the shape of every kind of pottery imported to Alexandria from all over the known world.[8] Indeed, the glass-makers of Egypt retained a reputation for making elaborately patterned coloured glass into the fourth century AD.[9]

Modern attempts to identify gold-glass workshops

Most research on the workshops of gold-glass makers has focused upon the iconographical details of the gold leaf, be it the style of the figures, the lettering of the text, the nature of the border surrounding the scene or a combination of all three.[10] However, as noted above, the form of the text may reflect the processes of positioning and cutting it rather than the stylistic quirks of a particular workshop. The gold leaf engravers must have worked in the glass-makers' workshops, as the application of the gold leaf is itself a stage of the vessel assembly. Nonetheless, until the publication of Howells' catalogue of the gold-glass in the British Museum in 2015, relatively little attention had been paid by modern scholars to the nature of the glass itself, though chemical analysis of the glass was recommended as the only way to resolve questions of workshop identity as long ago as 1899:

Hier kann nur die chemische Untersuchung des Glases weitere Resultate zu erzielen hoffen.

('Here only chemical research on the glass can bring hope of further results.')[11]

XRF [x-ray fluorescence] analysis of glass reveals its chemical composition by measuring the secondary, fluorescent x-ray emitted by a glass object when it is excited by a primary x-ray source from within the XRF analyser (see Appendix 4a). Sometimes this non-destructive process can reveal more details of the manufacturing process described above. XRF analysis of all accessible layers revealed the various decolouring agents used to make the gold-glass objects in the Wilshere Collection (Appendix 4a). The results fall into four main groups:

1. **The transparent base of a chalice and perhaps also the cover of a possible medallion, decoloured with antimony only**

2. **Clear glass bases of open vessels such as dishes and shallow bowls, vessel inlay and a perfume flask, decoloured with manganese only**

3. **Clear glass bases of dishes and shallow bowls decoloured with a consistent mixture of antimony and manganese (the glass in this group is presumed to have been recycled from groups 1 and 2). This group may also include some revival of the medallions and closed cups more typical of group 1.**

4. **Small medallions with outer layers of coloured glass, once set into vessel walls, and decoloured with a highly varied mixture of antimony and manganese that does not suggest recycling.**

The iconographic and textual content of the gold leaf was examined within the context of each group to develop a relative sequence of the development of the Wilshere gold-glasses. The results appear to be chronologically sensitive to what is known of changing attitudes to caring for the dead in the fourth-century Roman world (see further in Chapter 3).

The chemical categorisation of the Wilshere Collection is therefore used here to form the basis of the catalogue, in a new departure for the ordering of gold-glass. However, it must be admitted that effectively each modern catalogue of gold-glass has constituted a new departure, as no consistent system of reference to different types of gold-glass has emerged beyond the conventional use of numbers established by Morey along with some of his terminology; such usage reflects the wide scope of Morey's catalogue, which is ordered according to current museum location.[12] Thus Morey's proposed groups, such as '*Dignitas Amicorum*' or 'Peter and Paul', defined by iconographical or textual content, are frequently referenced in more recent scholarship, while his terminology for describing borders as 'reciprocal', for example, has also passed into the scholarly literature on gold-glass.[13]

The recently published catalogue of late antique gold-glass in the British Museum is arranged according to the iconography of the gold leaf, despite the inclusion of a preliminary chapter giving an account of XRF and other forms of chemical analysis of the glass, in which the gold-glasses are assigned to types equivalent to the groups described here. In addition, further distinction is made within each chemically determined type by observation of technical variation in gold leaf application.

Unfortunately, in the difficult circumstances of the posthumous editing of the catalogue, the lack of consistency has led to discrepancies in dating, with many of the objects assigned to Type 1 (equivalent to the Ashmolean's group 1) stylistically dated towards the end of the production sequence of gold-glass, instead of the start: the chronology varies by up to a century.[14]

With regard to the Wilshere Collection, it has proved difficult to find consistency in lettering style and border design within the chemically defined groups, perhaps for the technical reasons suggested above. Moreover, XRF analysis suggests that some glass-makers were associated with more than one engraver of gold leaf, the latter working in a distinctly individual manner on vessels made from the same batch of raw glass (see below, p.100).[15] Regrettably it was not possible to extract gold leaf for analysis, so we do not know its origin, nor indeed whether it came to Rome by a route that could have included the shipment of decoloured raw glass.

Primary workshops of gold-glass and the decolouring process

It is often asserted that gold-glass was made in Alexandria, even in late antiquity. Certainly the gold-glass in the Wilshere Collection conforms to what is widely understood as the 'Alexandrian' type of glass mentioned in the Edict on Maximum Prices issued on behalf of the emperor Diocletian in AD 301.[16] At 24 and 30 denarii per pound respectively in raw form and worked to a polished but undecorated state, the category of 'Alexandrian' glass was twice the price of 'Judaean', at 13 and 20 denarii. However, both sets of maximum prices seem unrealistically low with respect to the estimated cost of production.[17] Most modern specialists in ancient glass, noting that raw Judaean glass is described in the Edict 16.1.2 as *Iudaicis vir(i) dis* ('green Judaean glass'), take the term 'Alexandrian' to mean glass that has been deliberately decoloured in its raw state. However, even in late antiquity, the term Judaean may have retained geographical resonance – the more so if the Edict had been compiled in Antioch and published in Alexandria, with emphasis on, if not exclusive reference to, prices in that region of the empire.[18]

In the process of decolouring, the natural bluish-green tinge of Roman glass, arising from traces of iron elements in the sandy component of the raw form, was eliminated from the glass by adding to the flux manganese, antimony or both. All the Wilshere gold-glass has been treated in this way, and in that sense it may all be regarded as 'Alexandrian'.[19]

Decolouring was evidently part of the primary production of the glass. Only one of the Wilshere gold-glasses was suited to isotopic analysis, used to determine its origin: despite being made of recycled glass, a process that happened in Rome, analysis revealed the ultimate origin of the raw natron glass to be the Syria–Palestine region (see above and Appendix 4b). Indeed, additional distinctions between groups of glass identified by decolouring agent show that this primary process had some impact upon secondary workshop practice.

Secondary workshops: location and practice

Since the publication of Morey's museum-based catalogue, with its exclusive focus on Rome as the centre of production of gold-glass vessels, scholars have attempted to rebalance the picture, adding finds of gold-glass vessels from elsewhere in Europe. Complete and fragmentary vessels have been found in archaeological sites in Sicily, western Italy, Corsica and the south coast of France, and along much of the Rhine–Danube frontier and its hinterland.[20] Nonetheless, a count of the items listed by Howells gives to Rome 66 of the 106 examples of all types of gold-glass with known archaeological contexts; next comes Cologne with eight, followed by Ostia and Trier with only three each; a further five sites has produced two gold-glasses each, while the remaining 16 have just one. Rome's dominance thus remains overwhelming. Collection history also demonstrates a link with the *lipsanoteca* (see above, p.61), indicating that much gold-glass with no archaeological context, including five items in the Wilshere Collection, originated from Rome and its environs. Moreover, it has proved difficult to determine whether gold-glass found outside Rome was locally manufactured or imported from the capital. Sandwich gold-glass bowls decorated with small medallions excavated in graves in Cologne, for instance, were once believed to be local products, but are now regarded as metropolitan imports.[21] A further link between Rome and Cologne/Trier is offered by the coincidence of the Greek toast *pie zeses* ('Drink! Live!'), the text mostly written in Latin script and appearing in these two regions on a variety of media, always in a funerary context.[22]

The consistency of results from the XRF examination of gold-glass in the British Museum and the Wilshere Collection suggests that, with the exception of Type/Group 3, the raw glass used in gold-glass vessels was not recycled, although small amounts of cullet (recycled broken glass crushed for remelting) were sometimes added to the mix. The use of specific decolourants as described above may be linked to secondary workshop processes, as described below.

Some observations on manufacturing processes from XRF analysis of individual glasses in the Wilshere Collection

Dana Norris

Below we consider some observations on manufacturing processes that have emerged through XRF analysis of gold-glasses.[23] Where XRF analysis reveals a nearly identical composition of the inner and outer glasses, it may be assumed that they were made from the same batch of raw glass. Some variation in chemical composition would be expected if cullet or other raw materials were introduced into the furnace. Such practice could explain why the glass layers seen in cat. **23**, fragment a) are slightly varied: the layers were made a short time apart and the addition of cullet to the furnace altered the composition slightly.

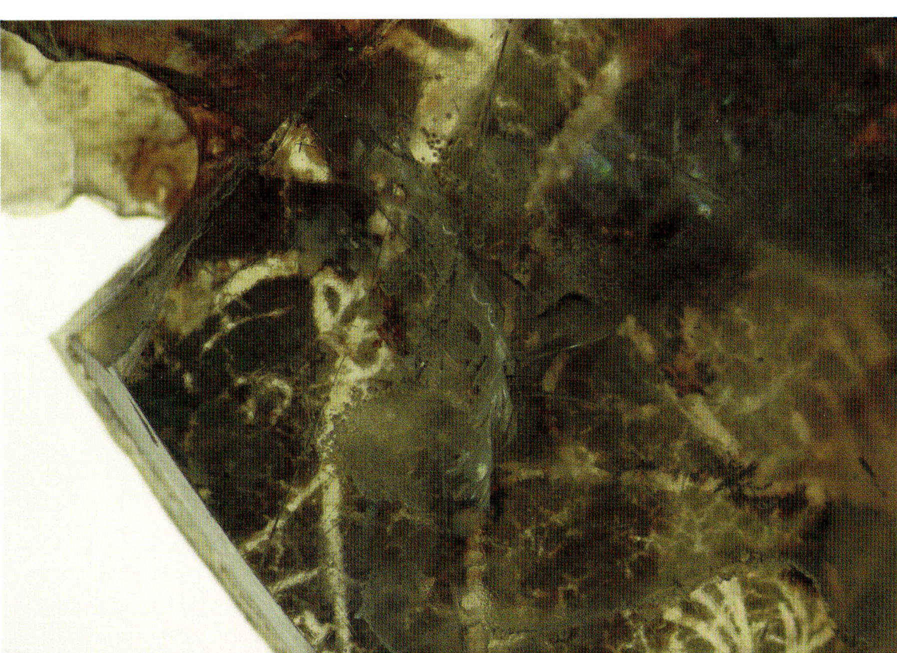

Fig. 45 Detail of part of cat. **23**, fragment a, showing the layers of glass at the left, with the gold leaf between them partially exposed. Photo: Dana Norris

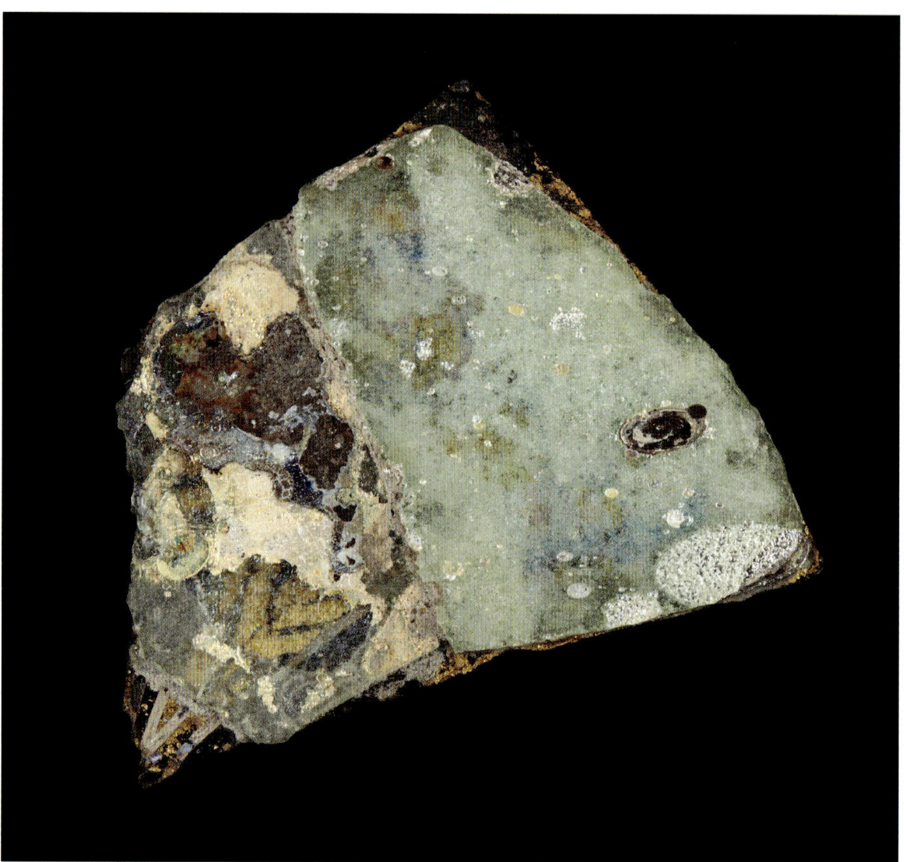

Fig. 46 The second layer (left) and third layer (right) of protective glass above the gold leaf decoration (cat. **16**)

Cat. **16** has no indication of a foot-ring or a curve. This object may have been manufactured in the kiln using the slumping technique, in which the sealing layer of glass was made at the same time as the layer decorated with gold leaf; both layers were annealed, polished and fused in the kiln. Such a process would give a flat surface suited to use as inlay or window-glass. Using this manufacturing method, it would be easy to assemble the layers from glass held in stock in the workshop, thus using glass of differing composition. In this example a third layer could have been attached with adhesive, most likely after a breakage of the second layer caused by a change of use of the glass (see catalogue entry below, p.149). A degraded layer visible between the latter and the decorated layer suggests that the adhesive withstood the elements, but water penetrated the join and began the process of degradation.

Decolorants and the use of coloured enamel

Within the Wilshere Collection, Dana Norris observed that glass vessels decoloured with manganese alone (group 2) were decorated with a wide range of enamel colours painted on to the engraved surface of the gold leaf, including green, red and blue. In contrast, glass vessels decoloured with a mixture of manganese and antimony (group 3) were decorated only with red and black enamel. If such consistency were observed across a wider range of glass, it may be argued that we see here evidence of changes in glass production over time. group 3, decorated with a limited range of colours, may be dated later than group 2: given the regular pattern of its chemical composition, the vessels in group 3 are most likely formed within the Rome workshops of glass recycled from groups 1 and 2.

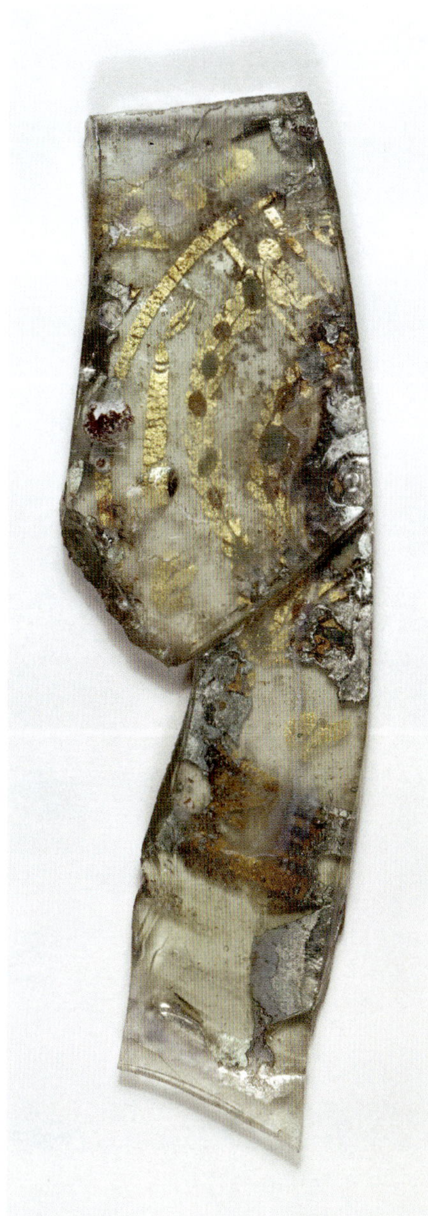

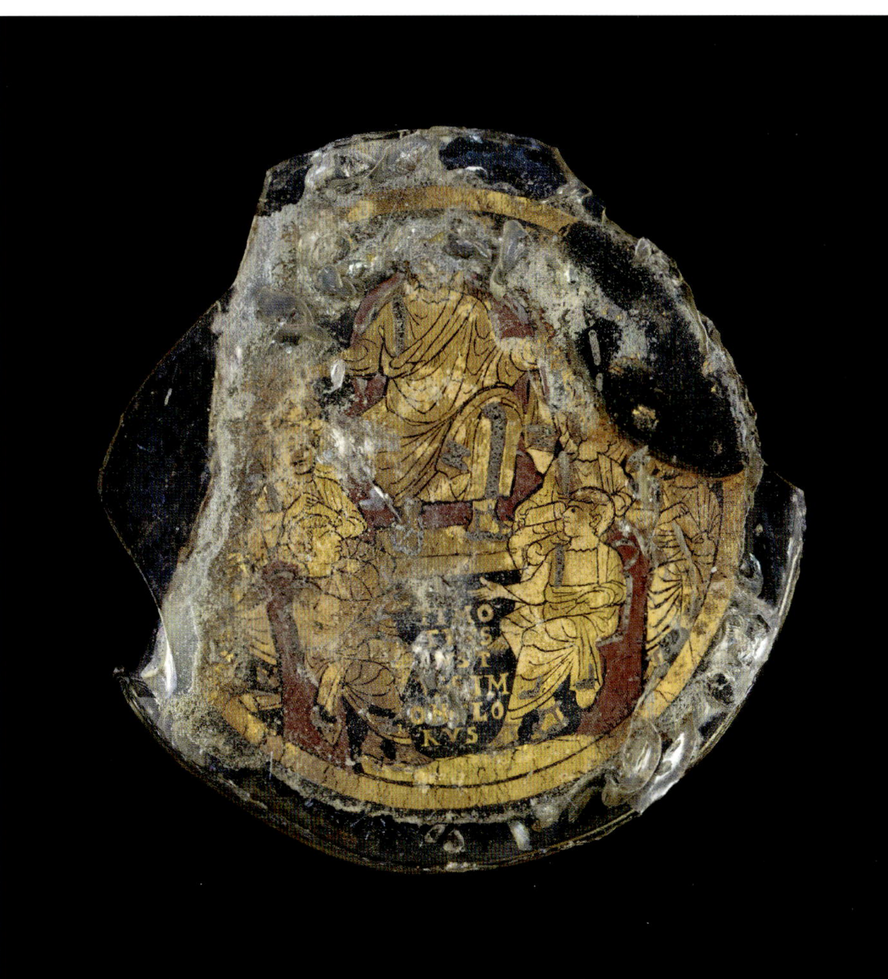

Fig. 47 Red and green enamel fruits on the branches of the menorah decorate the base of a dish (cat. **13**) decoloured with manganese only (group 2)

Fig. 48 Christ the teacher with Peter, Paul and four named saints, who sit on red chairs; their tunics, sandals and the floor bear their names painted in black. This gold-glass medallion (cat. **22**) decorates the base of a dish decoloured with a mixture of antimony and manganese (group 3).

Table 1

Gold-glasses in the Wilshere Collection decorated with enamel colours, grouped by decolouring agent

Ashmolean Museum accession and catalogue number	Enamels used	Decolouring agent/ Group number
AN2005.6/**13**	Red, green	Mn/2
AN2007.10/**11**	Green	Mn/2
AN2007.40/**6**	Blue	Mn/2
AN2007.11/**22**	Red, black	Mn + Sb/3
AN2007.14/**35**	Red	Mn + Sb/3
AN2007.26/**21**	Red, black	Mn + Sb/3
AN2007.35/**23**	Red, black	Mn + Sb/3

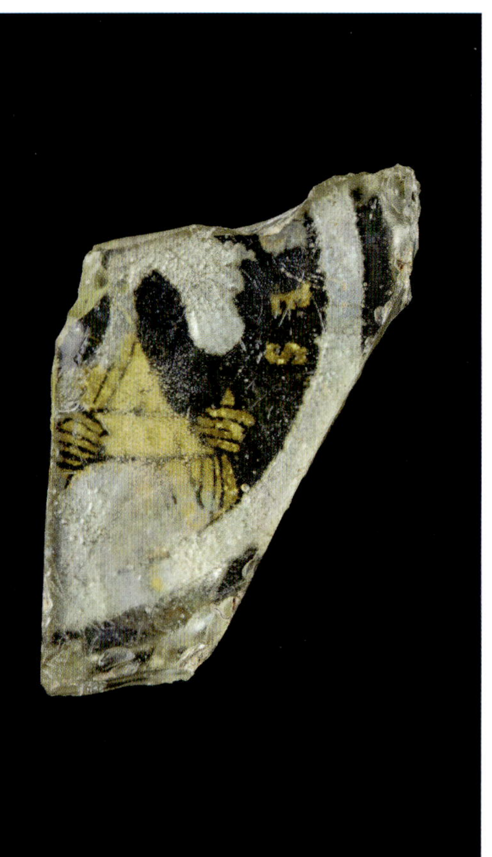

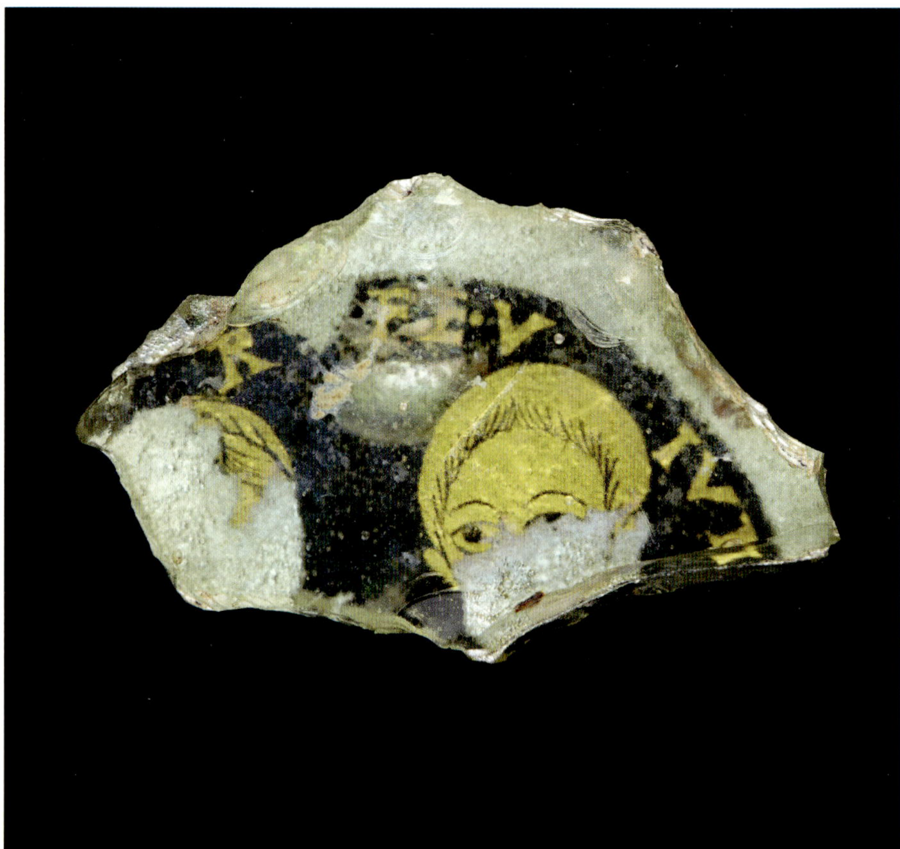

Fig. 49 The lettering on cat. **19** (right) and cat. **20** (left) appears to be the work of two different hands, but the gold leaf was used with the same batch of glass

Gold-leaf engravers and their workshops

It is possible that the cutters of the gold leaf specialised in vessel types, even within a single workshop. Both cats **19** and **20**, for example, are made of recycled glass and possess respectively an inner and an outer layer so similar that they must have been made from the same batch of glass flux. However, judging by the letter forms, the engraving of the gold leaf does not appear to be the work of the same craftsman. Indeed, the fragments come from two different products: a probable medallion (cat. **19**) and a small cup (cat. **20**), both apparently late fourth-century revivals of third-century products. The engraver of the medallion (cat. **19**) may have worked on a very similar object now in the Cabinet des Médailles, Paris, while the engraver of cat. **20** may have worked on a fragmentary vessel portraying Saints Sixtus and Timothy, now in the British Museum.[24] However, the latter vessel was apparently not made of recycled glass, but glass decoloured with manganese only.[25]

Generally the gold leaf decoration contains much narrative content that is specific to Rome, strengthening the impression given by the distribution of surviving late antique gold-glass that most of it was surely produced there. However, no secondary glass workshop specialising in gold-glass has been archaeologically identified in Rome. A likely zone of manufacture is the district of Trastevere, on the 'left bank' of the Tiber. The area had a long tradition of selling recycled cullet, among other disagreeable activities satirised by the first-century poet Martial. His surviving work contains 12 references to glass-making:[26]

... transtyberinus ambulator,
Qui pallentia sulphurata fractis
Permutat vitris.
('... such as one who ambles in Trastevere, selling sulphur matches
for broken glass')
Martial, *Epig.i*, 42.

In an epigram addressed to Priscus, Martial sneers:

Que sulphurato nolit empta ramento
Vatiniorum proxineta fractorum

('[Vulgarisms] such as even a dealer in broken Vatinian glass would not
purchase at the price of a sulphur match'
Martial X, III, *ad Priscum*

Vatinian cups were named after Vatinius, a cobbler from Beneventum who became a courtier of the emperor Nero. His grotesque features were recalled in the features of certain glass cups, none of which may be clearly identified in the archaeological record of glassware from the first century AD.[27]

The district of Trastevere had been occupied and inhabited by Jewish immigrants in the early empire (Philo, *Embassy to Gaius*, 155–6). Over the course of subsequent centuries Trastevere became multi-ethnic, attracting freedmen and slaves engaged in commercial activity using the adjacent River Tiber; its population spoke many languages and worshipped deities familiar in the eastern provinces of empire.[28] Close by was located the substantial Jewish cemetery at Monteverde: as any surviving occupational designation in the simple funerary texts is concerned with the community, no professions beyond synagogue officials and a supplier of (presumably Kosher) meat appear to have been recorded (see above, p.82 for similar material in the Wilshere Collection from Vigna Randanini). As a result no glass-makers are identifiable among the dead.[29]

Nonetheless, further indication of the manufacture of gold-glass vessels by immigrant craftsmen from the eastern Mediterranean comes from the form of the vessels. Where unusual forms of the gold-glass vessels from Rome may be reconstructed (for example cats **3**, **18**, **1**), they are comparable to glass vessels without gold leaf decoration found in the late antique cemeteries of Egypt, Syria and Cyprus (Fig. 50).

Indeed, despite the Roman relevance of much of the iconography, the *omorphorion* stoles worn by some of the saints are an eastern ecclesiastical feature, with some comparison in wall paintings of the sixth-seventh centuries from the basilica at Caesarea Maritima. Moreover, the story of Isaiah's martyrdom is itself of Syrian origin.[30] It is, then, not out of the question that glass-makers travelled with the raw glass from the region of primary production and settled in Rome to produce relatively expensive vessels – just as had occurred in the early first century AD. Then glass was still a luxury product, and some distinguished glass-makers based in Rome not only signed their work but also recorded their city of origin, such as Artas, Phillipos and Neikon of Sidon, or Aristeas the Cypriot; others such as Ennion claimed authorship in Greek.[31] Nonetheless the Latinised Greek and misspelled Latin texts, characteristic of much text on gold leaf, are typical of texts in other media found in fourth-century Rome. The formulaic toasts we read on late Roman gold-glass are now widely categorised as institutionalised code-switching – that is, the insertion of a ready-made phrase into the base language. Such a practice was encountered widely in antiquity and is today in the modern world.[32]

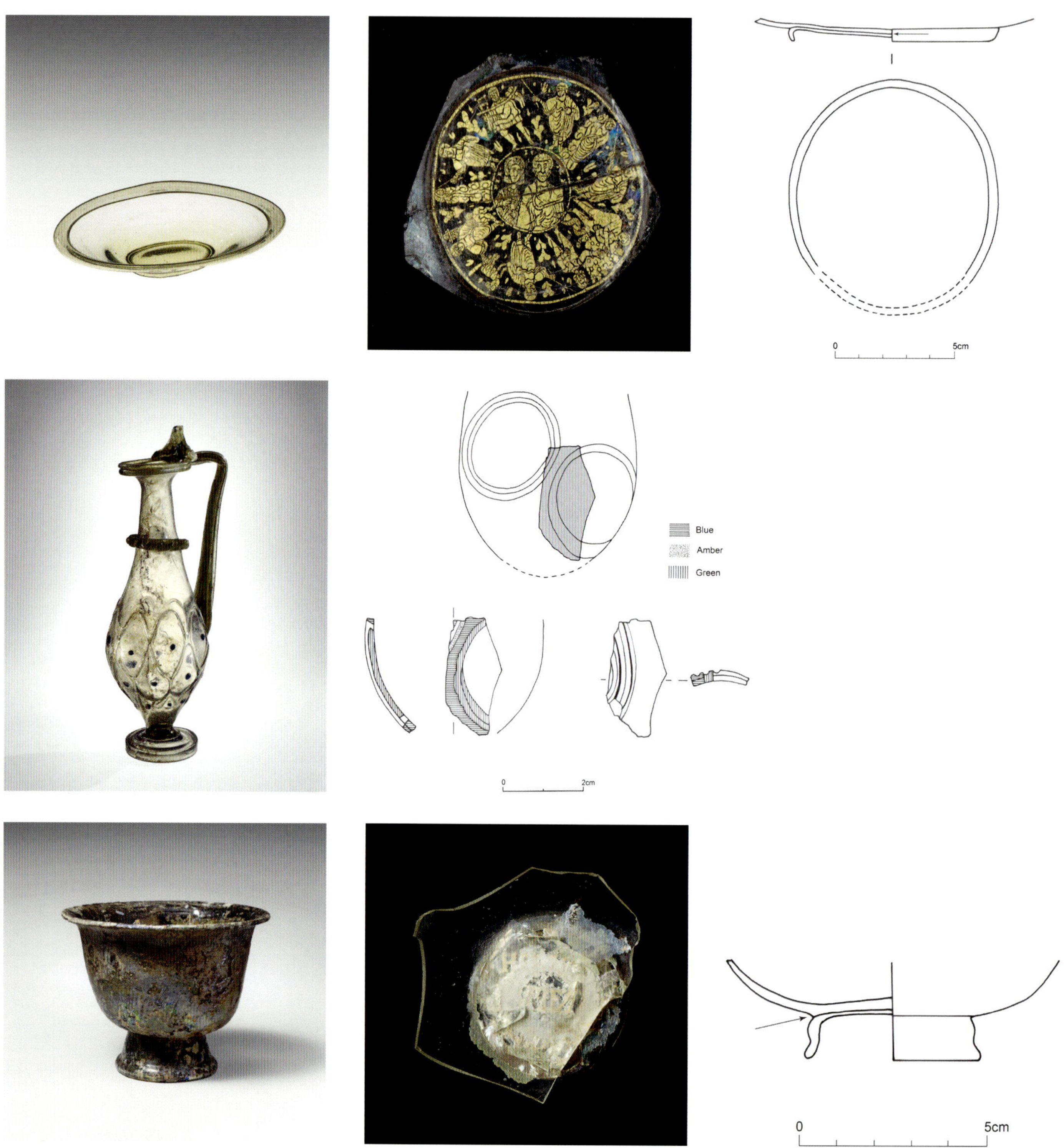

Fig. 50 Oval dish from Egypt, Corning Museum of Glass, *c.*AD 400, compared with oval medallion from a gold-glass dish (cat. 3); jar from Syria, Corning Museum of Glass, *c.*AD 300–400, compared with fragment of gold-glass perfume bottle, cat. 18; chalice from a tomb at Idalion, Cyprus, Metropolitan Museum of Art, New York, AD 300–400, compared to base of a gold-glass chalice (cat. 1). All drawings by Yvonne Beadnell

Dating gold-glass from decolouring agents

As group 3 glass was most likely recycled from glass products of groups 1 and 2, it may be concluded that group 3 is of later date. Indeed, earlier analysis of decolourants of glass from excavated contexts, mostly in northern Europe, suggests that primary glass producers first used antimony as a decolourant, then manganese became dominant, and finally the two agents were mixed.[33] Thus the associations tabled above between the chosen decolourant and the range of added colours may reflect changes in secondary workshop practice over time. We may also be seeing – and in the discussion of this point we should also include group 1, glass decoloured with antimony only – a growing lack of access to decolourants, antimony being replaced with the more widely available manganese. The glass of group 3, apparently recycled from groups 1 and 2 in the secondary workshops, may represent a diminution in the long-distance trade in raw glass from Syria–Palestine to Rome.

The interpretation of the results as reflecting ever-diminishing access to raw materials is not without its problems. Although we may be confident of the principal sources of raw glass, we do not know the precise origins of the decolouring agents. Anatolia was once regarded as a major source of antimony, which was principally refined for medical use, but recent research favours southeast Italy as a source for antimony used as a decolorant. Yet if either source were used in glass manufacture, access should not have become the problem that would have arisen had the agent been sourced in, say, the southern Caucasus or Persia, both of which became unstable and hostile to Rome in the later third century.[34] Moreover the interpretation of Group 4, small gold-glass medallions with coloured outer layers, which were set into the walls of shallow bowls, remains a puzzle. The clear glass was probably not recycled, as the results are so varied, with no clear relationship to Groups 1 and 2. The gold leaf medallions contain no added enamel, so cannot be subjected to the comparisons made above for Groups 2 and 3.

This type of gold-glass vessel may have been in use in the early–mid-fourth century. This is the date suggested by the context of the graves in Cologne, where some near-complete vessels have been recovered, and also by the iconography of the gold leaf, which consistently illustrates the *Commendatio Animae* prayer with stories of salvation from the Old and New Testaments, seen in many of the bowls in group 2, but rarely within group 3 (Fig. 51).[35] Thus mixed decolorants were evidently used for various reasons, and there may have been technological or functional factors

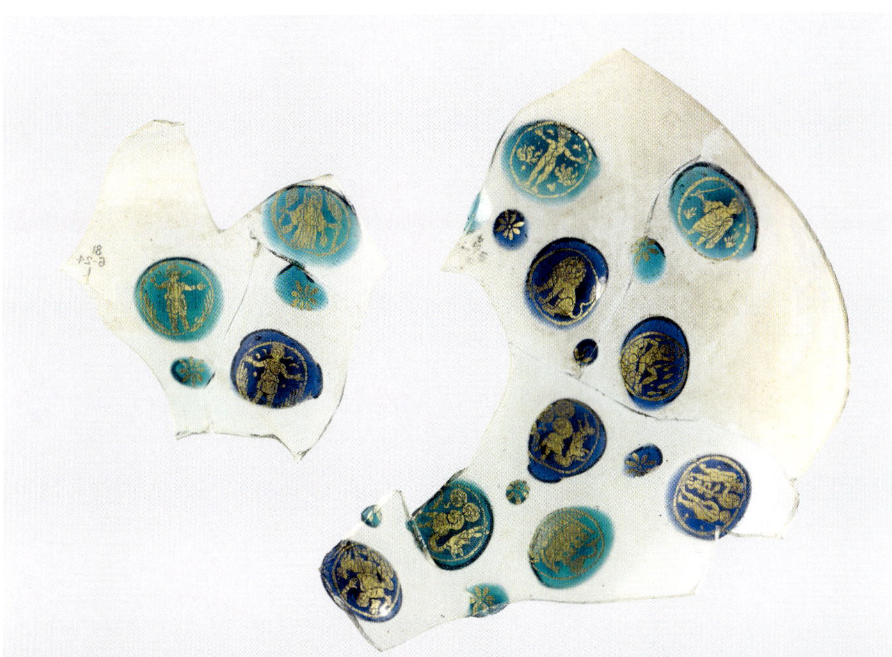

Fig. 51 Bowl decorated with swirls of gold-glass medallions set against glass coloured with copper and cobalt. From the cemetery of St Severin, Cologne, Germany. British Museum PE 1881.6.24–1

determining their use for the clear glass vessel walls covering gold leaf that had been pasted on to small, coloured glass medallions.

Applying this relative sequence to glass in the Wilshere Collection, the glass of group 1 – the chalice (cat. **1**), and perhaps also the partially coloured inscribed medallion (cat. **2**) – are most probably the earliest vessels, perhaps dating to the third or early fourth century AD. However, results from the medallion do not fall exactly on the antimony line, as a small amount of manganese is present. They might also be interpreted as mixed, in which case the medallion would correspond to the composition of group 4, otherwise comprising small, unlettered medallions from the walls of vessels with clear glass inner and coloured outer layers (see above). Nonetheless, in favour of an early date for these two objects is the unusual lettering, which in neither case matches any of the glass assigned to groups 2 and 3, nor any of the fourth-century workshops proposed by Faedo and Lega. The lettering of cat. **2** is indeed very close to that of a clear glass plaque in the Vatican collections decorated with an image of Apollo, which is dated to the third century.[36]

It appears that the secondary producers using glass decoloured with manganese alone were active in the early–mid-fourth century. Glass-makers using manganese as a decolourant produced the greatest number of funerary vessels within the Wilshere Collection (group 2) and also the greatest variety of products. These include other types of glass vessel, for example the probable perfume jar (cat. **18**) and the fragment of inlay (cat. **16**).

Although both group 2 and group 3 (clear glass vessels with mixed decolourants) share some aspects of iconography, the rise to dominance of saints Peter and Paul can be uniquely associated with this latest group of glass using both decolourants. There is a wide range of quality within this group, and more glasses were grozed (their edges carefully crushed with pliers). Such a process, if undertaken in antiquity, could have been used to make disc-shaped tomb markers, as opposed to irregularly broken vessels offered as gifts to the dead.[37]

Each of these main groups of secondary glass-makers made gold-glass vessels aimed at ensuring salvation for the deceased, and for venerating martyrs. Perhaps surprisingly, glasses of high quality are more prominent in group 3 than group 2. However, glass and engraving of varied quality appears in both groups. It is then likely that the factor that determined quality lay not in the date of the commission but in its nature. Glass of higher quality might be commissioned by families and dependents to mark the death of individuals (see the remarks on the gold-glass made for Orfitus and Constantia, Chapter 3, p.85–6), while the lower-quality work may be linked to the Church's enthusiasm for the commemoration of martyrs and for curbing extravagant private expenditure on funerals. The single piece of Jewish gold-glass falls within the larger group, using only manganese as a decolorant.

The changing uses of gold-glass in antiquity

Gold-glass has a long history, and the uses to which it has been put have had an effect on production techniques. In the tomb of Philip II, constructed in later fourth-century BC Macedonia, it was used to decorate the fronts of wooden funerary couches that were also inlaid with exquisitely carved ivory.[38] Nearly a century later, gold leaf was cut into elegant patterns of foliage within the layers of a pair of cast glass double cups found in a Hellenistic tomb at Canosa, southeast Italy (Fig. 52).[39]

These early uses are concerned with the care and commemoration of the dead, the combination of gold and glass selected for its economic and social value – and no

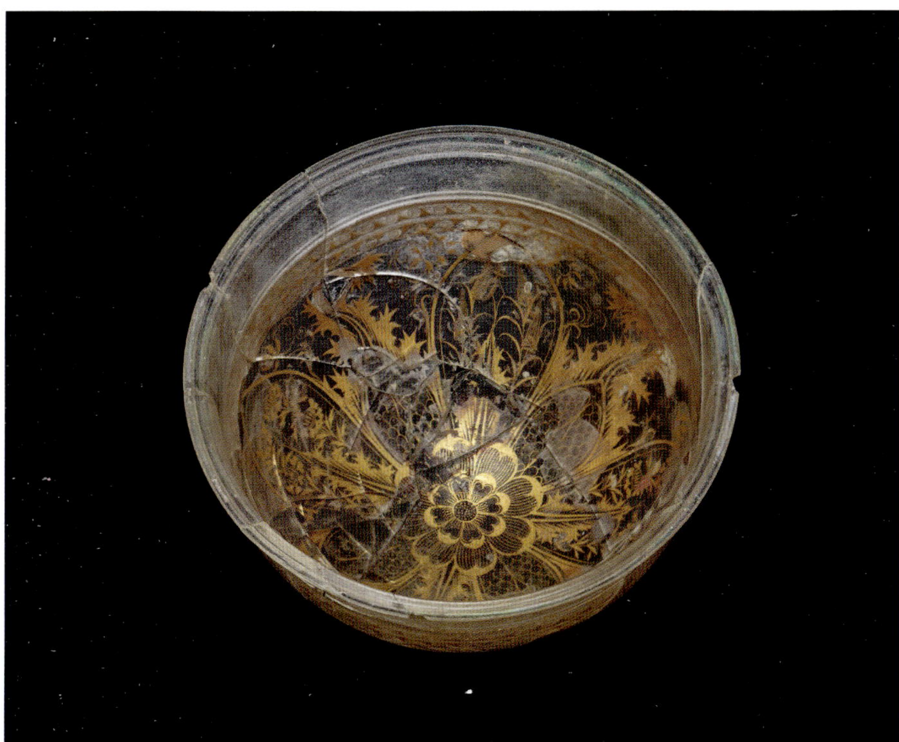

Fig. 52 Gold-glass cup from a tomb at Canosa, southeast Italy, 24.75 cm in diameter (max). Hellenistic Greek, perhaps made in Alexandria about 250 BC. British Museum GR 1871,0518.2

doubt also for its quality of glowing in the darkness of a tomb. The craft was revived for similar purposes, but with some significant technical modifications, in the second and third centuries AD. Further changes that occurred in the fourth century are described below.[40]

Howells' experiments and his observations of surviving ancient gold-glass led him to conclude that Cameron was correct in suggesting that late antique gold-glass was not an exclusive, high-quality product and that it was not usually made for an aristocratic market.[41] Here it is suggested that the clients were personally wealthy, professionally distinguished members of the *familiae* of the landowners of the catacombs, imperial or aristocratic (see above, p.77), many of whom converted to Christianity in the course of the fourth century. At about that time gold-glass portrait medallions, designed to fit into metal mounts as a professional badge of identity or personal memento, began to fall out of use. So, apparently, did plaques and small vessels, both with unprotected gold leaf decoration and made for immediate placement in the tomb, along with chalices and small cups, many bearing toasts to the deceased in text alone.

With the exception of a possible revival in the late fourth century (see above, p.100), all such products, when analysed, have been found to be made of glass decoloured with antimony only (here group 1).[42] All were commissioned for use by, or in commemoration of, a single individual. These products were replaced by a variety of apparently new forms, including perfume flasks and inlay; however, the dominant innovation of the mid-fourth century was the shallow, open bowl or dish of circular or ovoid form, intended for the service of food to a group rather than a drink to an individual. Gold-glass shallow bowls and dishes were produced as two distinct types. One had a gold leaf medallion incorporated into the base, protected by an undecorated vessel wall, while the other had a plain base but within the vessel wall incorporated small medallions, in which the gold leaf was applied to blobs of coloured glass (Figs 34, 35 and 51). Different decolorants were used to make these

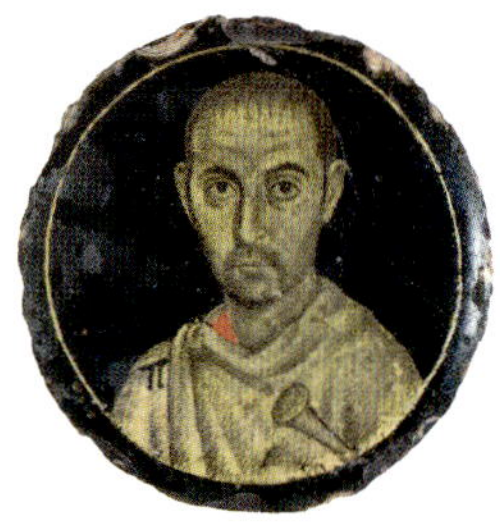

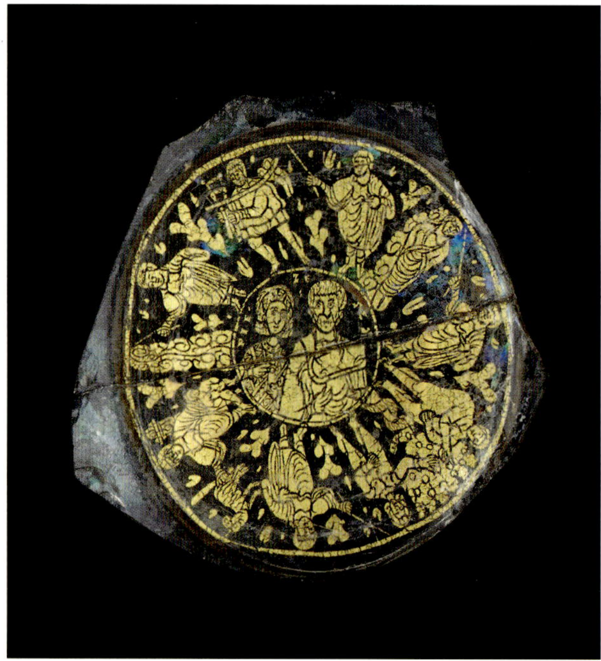

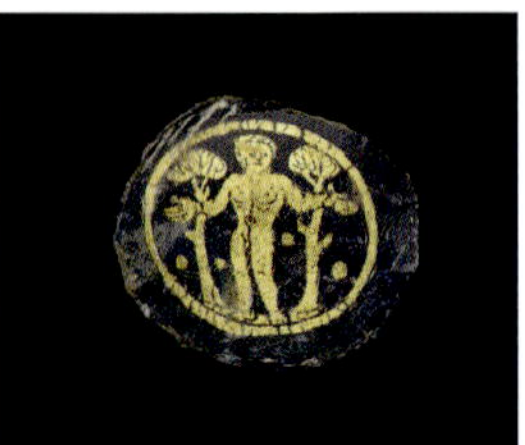

Figs 53, 54 and 55. The decline of quality of engraving results from a change in vessel shape: 53) a portrait medallion of a soldier–musician, AD 250–320, Victoria and Albert Museum Inv. No. 1052.1868; 54) the base of an oval dish with portraits of an elaborately dressed couple, group 2, about AD 350–70, cat. 3; 55) a small medallion from the wall of a shallow bowl, perhaps representing the martyrdom of the prophet Isaiah, group 4, about AD 330–60, cat. 30. All objects are shown approximately to scale relative to each other.

variant vessel types, here classed as Groups 2/3 and Group 4, whose makers were therefore drawing on different sources of raw and recycled glass.

However, the designs engraved on the gold leaf used in the vessels of Groups 2 and 4 are similar in content and quality. The distinction is rather one of scale: the small medallions are set into vessel walls bearing a single image rather than the series of images, often with identifying and celebratory text, seen on the vessel bases (Figs 54 and 55). The reduced format of the small medallions allowed the building of a narrative from a sequence, the latter so placed within the vessel wall as to produce swirls of colour in a style imitating earlier types of glass vessel without gold leaf (Fig. 51). These distinctions may well represent the products of different secondary workshops based in Rome, but the decolouring process was part of primary production taking place in the eastern Mediterranean, so it is not out of the question that a single metropolitan workshop produced both types of vessel. Though the gold leaf engravers had to work closely with the glass manufacturers in the secondary workshop in a time and temperature-sensitive production process, they may have circulated between workshops and appear to have specialised in vessel types, even within a single workshop (see above, p.100).

Gold-leaf designs on the open vessels commissioned for use by a group appear to the modern viewer markedly less well executed than those of the individually commissioned portrait medallions (Figs 53–55). However, the latter had not been forgotten, as the central area of the vessel base was often given over to a medallion portrait either of an individual, a couple or (increasingly) Christ or a saint. Given the likely social and temporal continuity of the production of gold-glass, it is probable that the noticeable drop in the quality of engraved gold leaf reflects that change of format from medallions, unprotected plaques or drinking vessels, each focused upon an individual client, to open vessels catering for a group. There may well have been changes of workshop, and there was certainly a change in the decolourant used to make the glass transparent (see above, p.104).

Late in the fourth century, there appears to have been some revival of interest in producing medallions and small, closed vessels for individual clients (see above, p.100, Fig. 49). As pagan, Christian and Jewish subjects in gold leaf decoration of the fourth century were similarly treated by the engravers, it seems preferable to attribute the decline in quality to the change in vessel type and social usage rather than to religious pressure, which became a significant factor in the development of later fourth-century Christian glass (see above, p.80). Nonetheless, despite the evident decline in quality of draughtsmanship, private individuals portrayed on fourth-century gold-glass vessels are often splendidly dressed (Fig. 54). It is therefore probable that some gold-glass was commissioned by dependents and clients of the personally wealthy, who saw to it that their patrons were depicted in attire reflecting their status and resources.

Marble sarcophagi and inscriptions

The two-stage manufacturing process described for gold-glass (see above, p.96) also applies to many Roman sarcophagi. These were roughly cut and hollowed out in the island quarries of Thasos and Proconnesus, then shipped to Rome where the front and short sides of the chest were carved with decoration specific to the metropolis.[43] The tombstone of Eutropius, a stonecarver shown drilling a lion's mane with an assistant, indicates the presence in Rome of Greek-speaking specialist craftsmen, engaged with carving motifs widely popular in the metropolis but not current in the areas immediately served by the quarries. However, it was necessary to order this particular motif at the quarry, as the lions' heads projected considerably from the chest. They were therefore left as bosses projecting from the roughly finished surface of the chest; sarcophagi in this form have been found in the quarries of Thasos and in the San Pietro wreck, near Taranto.[44] The latter site produced many such sarcophagi shipped as hollow chests, some in the shape of vats and some intended for multiple burial. The lids, often personalised with portraits and inscriptions, were made at Rome, often of Carrara marble from northern Italy.[45]

Evidence for the recycling of marble in late antiquity

The sarcophagi in the Wilshere Collection show no evidence of recycling. This is true both of the three fragments of lids (cats **37**, **38** and **39**) and of the complete chest (cat. **40**) – and even of the large front of a sarcophagus (cat. **41**), later in date than the rest. Apparently it was possible to order a freshly cut sarcophagus in Rome even in the last decade of the fourth century, though the choice of marble might have been restricted to Carrara, the long-distance trade in partially finished sarcophagi (especially chests) from the islands of Thasos and Proconnesus having apparently ceased. Cat. **41** is a work of exceptional quality, showing, like the contemporary gold-glass cat. **22**, that superior craftsmanship could be commissioned in Rome up to the end of the fourth century by individual clients of sufficient means. The front of the sarcophagus was most likely gilded, with traces of the preparatory bole still visible on the surface of the crisply, confidently carved stone.

Marble funerary inscriptions present a different story, with much evidence of recycling – especially of architectural decoration from buildings that presumably had fallen out of use. As with contemporary Christian funerary inscriptions from southern Italy (see pp.87–88), there is evidence from the Jewish burials in the Vigna Randanini for the reuse of marble in late antiquity. In 2012 six of the slate frames

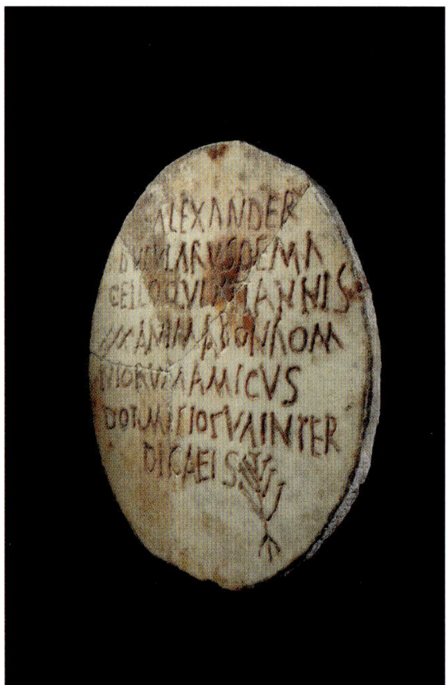

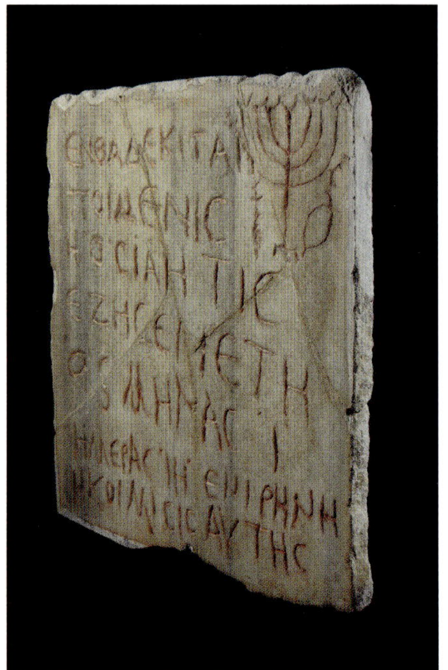

Fig. 56 Angled photos of inscriptions (cats **48** and **50**) show the thinness of the recycled slabs, most likely originally used as wall veneer

were removed to examine such evidence and look for traces of ancient mortar. The extreme thinness of the slab commemorating Alexander (cat. **48**) suggests that it was not cut from a column shaft, but from wall cladding. A similar source may be proposed for cat. **50**, the gravestone of Poimenis (Fig. 56).

The slab commemorating the infant Noumenis (cat. **49**) has a concave curvature to the back of the block which suggests it may have been reused from the short end of a pagan sarcophagus. Some of the iron stains on these blocks may recall earlier usage, for example, to pin revetment to a wall or to attach a lid to the sarcophagus chest. A void at the side of the slab commemorating Justus (cat. **43**) may be the result of casual damage. The two prominent sockets cut into the lower part of this slab once held iron clamps to secure the stone in place; the ancient lead seal survives in the left-hand socket. A hole is cut into the back of the slab commemorating Melition (cat. **46**); this is filled with mortar, with a further spread of mortar across the back of the slab. This thicker stone could have served as floor revetment in earlier use. Stains from iron nails appear towards the base of the slab. The Christian inscription of Sapis from Cumae (cat. **52**) was itself later recycled as a threshold block, in which role it was found by the nineteenth-century collector Abbate Giuseppe di Criscio of Pozzuoli, from whom Wilshere purchased the slab (see above, p.65).

Given the substantial evidence for reuse of these slabs, a range of marbles is represented within the funerary texts in the Wilshere Collection. Samples were removed for isotopic analysis of cats **49** and **50**; both appear Proconnesian to the naked eye, but the results suggest Carrara (Appendix 5). Cats **44** and **47**, whose slate frames were not removed, are of fine-grained marble, possibly from Carrara. This is probably also true of cat. **48**, though the iron dowels used to repair the slab have given it a rosy glow more characteristic of Pentelic marble from Athens. Cat. **46**, and most notably the veined slab cat. **45**, are of bluish tone, perhaps representing Carrara bardiglio; a sample of marble was taken from the latter. Indeed, the results overwhelmingly indicate the use of Carrara marble for all but cat. **53**, the tombstone of Victurina from Aeclanum, whose signature, offering higher values for ratios of oxygen, corresponds more closely to that of Proconnesian marble (Fig. 57).

Given that most slabs were recycled from architectural elements, the widespread

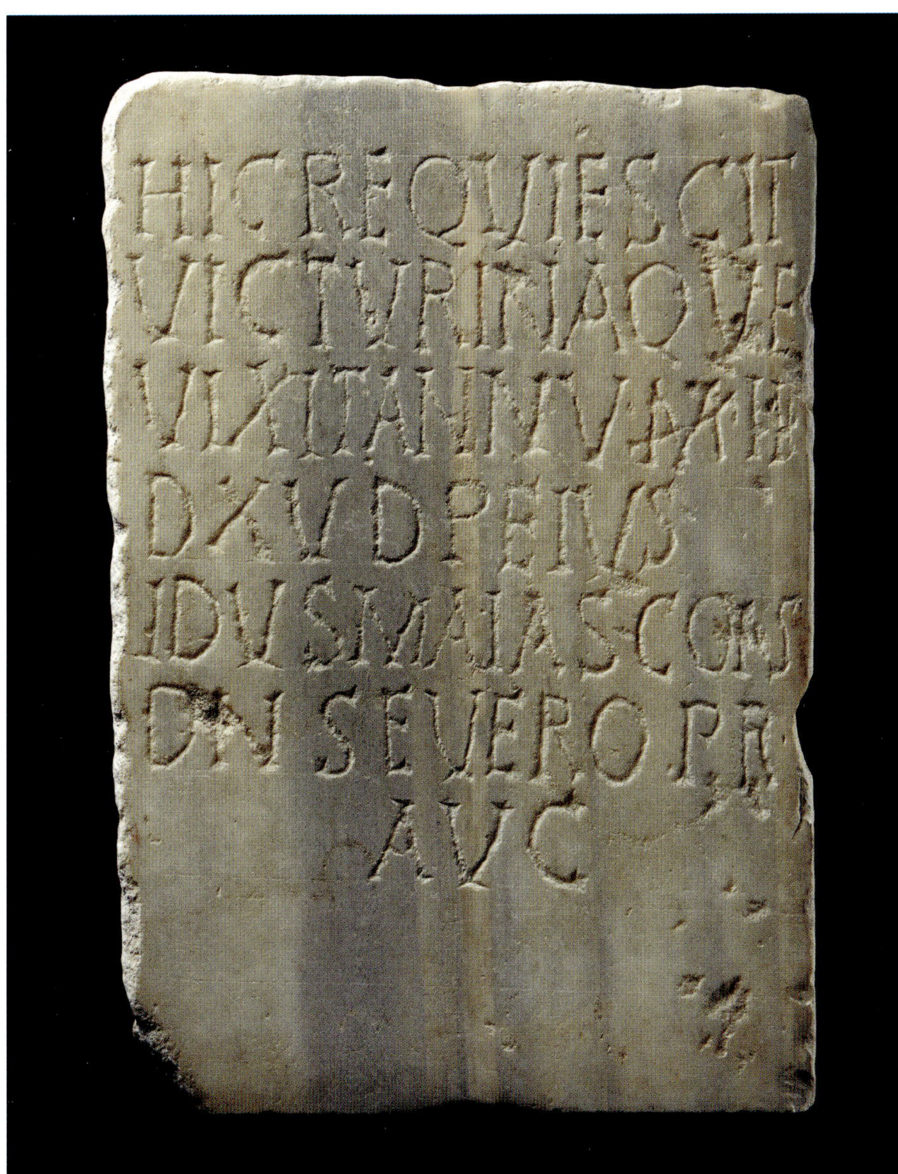

Fig. 57 Cat. **53**: Blue bands typical of Proconnesian marble appear on the slab re-used for the memorial of Victurina at Aeclanum, southern Italy (cat. **53**)

use of Carrara marble is not surprising. For much of the duration of the Roman empire, it was the building marble of choice in the city of Rome and across Italy.

Judging quality in late Roman texts and sarcophagi

Lettering and decorative/pictorial engraving and painting of funeral inscriptions is of varied quality, ranging from the elegant, drafted Latin script of the tombstone of Sapis from Cumae (cat. **52**) to the irregular, shallow Greek lettering of the tombstone of Venerosa (cat. **47**) from the Vigna Randanini. As with variable quality in gold-glass, it is preferable to explain such distinctions by the nature, and perhaps also the location, of the commissions, rather than by date. The latest text (cat. **55**), the memorial to Maria from Aeclanum, dated by Felle to AD 546, is of relatively poor quality compared to the others from Aeclanum, but much more regular, competent in Latin syntax and legible than several apparently late texts from the Vigna Randanini. However, it is unlikely that the latter are of later date than those from

Aeclanum, where the relatively high quality more probably reflects the ecclesiastical significance of the town, a literate elite population and a consequent ability to support the workshops of engravers. There appears to be no relationship between the quality of lettering and evidence for the reuse of stone.

Equally, sarcophagi tend to vary in quality according to the scale of the commission rather than the date. Thus the majestic front of a sarcophagus (cat. **41**) dates to the Theodosian period, though its superb sculptural quality might suggest an earlier date. In contrast, cat. **38** is most probably Constantinian work of poor quality. However, the latter fragment was valued and distinctively framed by Wilshere, as the poorly carved surface bears ample traces of paint and gilding.

Conclusion

In conclusion, material analysis has much to offer the student of late antique funerary art, notably in defining the detailed stages of production in glass and marble. Some general observations derived from material analysis undertaken for this study are summarised below, with the proviso that the observations drawn from objects in the Wilshere Collection are numerically insignificant.

Recycling

Some clear gold-glass vessels (Group 3) were made of glass recycled from earlier products in the later fourth century, when access to raw glass and/or decolourants seems to have become more difficult for Roman glass-makers.

Sarcophagi were not apparently made of recycled elements, though here, as in gold-glass production, we may see some diminution of access to raw materials in the course of the fourth century, as the choice of marble was much reduced.

Funerary inscriptions were frequently recycled, principally from the architectural decoration of buildings no longer in use.

Chronology

Distinguishing the elements used to decolour raw glass allows the development of a relative chronology of gold-glass, which is based upon a comparison with stratigraphically dated glass from excavations. Observation of painted enamel decoration on gold-glass further defines the proposed chronological groups.

Observation of the engraved decoration of the gold leaf layer gives further insights into the stages of production.

There is a clear distinction in the choice of decolorant between medallion portraits, plaques and chalices intended for use by individuals in the third and early fourth centuries, and vessels intended for use by a group of mourners in the mid–later fourth century.

Within the pictorial iconography of the later gold-glass plates and bowls and marble sarcophagi, we see a diminution of focus on individual salvation in favour of commemoration of saints and martyrs of the church. Among the latter, the inexorable rise of Peter and Paul as dominant patrons of Rome is clearly linked to vessels made of recycled glass, and may be related to Pope Damasus's promotion of their cult in the mid–later fourth century.

Funerary inscriptions are much more difficult to place in chronological sequence, apart from late Christian texts with consular dates.

Artistic quality

There is a distinct drop in quality between gold-glass medallions and plaques made for use by individuals, here dated to the third and early fourth centuries, and open vessels made for use by groups in the mid–later fourth century.

Quality in all media seems to have been determined by the resources of the individual commissioning the work, even at the end of the fourth century.

Variation in quality is therefore not a reliable indicator of date, except as indicated above.

Variation in quality in the lettering of inscriptions was apparently regionally influenced by the skills available in specific locations and/or to specific communities.

Notes

1. The better known twelfth-century writer Theophilus used Eraclius as a source, and both writers have been conflated in some later manuscripts: Howells 2013, 113.
2. See Howells 2013, 114–18 for the entire process, which is summarised here.
3. Howells 2015: 47, pl.28.
4. See Howells 2015: 48 for the problem of the handles. Boldetti's drawing is illustrated, see p.25, Pl.10.
5. Schibille et al. 2012 offer a good summary of recent research.
6. Weinberg 1988; Gorin-Rosen 2000; Nenna et al. 2000.
7. Stern 1999, 442–50.
8. Strabo, 16.758; Athenaeus, II.784c.
9. Nenna 2002.
10. Faedo 1978; Nüsse 2008; Lega 2012.
11. See Harden 1987; Smith 2000 for the forms of the vessels; Vopel 1899: 77 for early interest in chemical analysis.
12. Morey 1959.
13. Unfortunately Morey did not live to complete his intended study justifying his categorisation of gold-glass. See Morey 1959: ix.
14. Howells 2015.
15. See Lega 2012 for an analysis of dates based upon letter forms.
16. Stern 1999, 460–6; the relevant text of the Edict is given in Latin, Greek and English in Table 1, p.462. See also Barag 1989, 2005.
17. Stern 1999, 464 suggests that for this reason the Edict itself would have encouraged recycling.
18. Stern 1999, 461 for the origin of the Edict, drawing on Corcoran 1996, 205–33. Barag 1987, 2005 argued that the name Judaea was obsolete by the fourth century, and suggested a technical distinction, which has won wide acceptance. Jackson, Cool and Wager 1998: 60 and Whitehouse 2004: 190 reasonably argued that both geographical and processual interpretations were possible.
19. On decolouring see Jackson 2005 and Schibille et al. 2012.
20. Howells 2015: 54–5, Figure 14, and 153–62, Appendix A.
21. Howells 2015: 58.
22. Adams 2003: 407 with n.186; see also Biville 1989: 107. For the funerary context see Cooley 2012: 110–1.
23. For the process of XRF analysis, see p.95 above.
24. Morey 1959, no.400 for the medallion in the Cabinet des Médailles, Paris; Morey 1959, no.313 and Howells 2015: 77–9, no.9 for the cup now in the British Museum, BEP 1863,727.12.
25. Meek in Howells 2015: 37, Table 6.
26. Whitehouse 1999, retrieved from cmog.org/article/glass-epigrams-martial (accessed 27 October 2016).
27. Whitehouse 1999, retrieved from cmog.org/article/glass-epigrams-martial (accessed 5 November 2016).
28. Rossi and di Mento 2013: 152.
29. Rossi and de Mento 2013: 302–3, no.189 for the meat supplier (βουβλάρις). See below, p.00 for the memorial to Alexander, a similar meat supplier from Vigna Randanini (cat. **48**).
30. I am grateful to Efthymios Rizos for this observation; see also Howells 2015: 70 and, on the Caesarea paintings, Avner 1999: 110. I am grateful to Sean Leatherbury for this reference. For Isaiah see Rini 2006.
31. Harden 1987: 89; Lightfoot and Wight 2014.
32. Adams 2003: 407 for texts on gold-glass.
33. Jackson 2005.
34. Healy 1978: 42–3 for Anatolia, the Caucasus and Persia; Degryse and Schneider 2008 for southeast Italy.
35. Nüsse 2008: 254; see von Boeselager 2012 for a fragment of a clear gold-glass base buried after AD 340 beneath the head of a woman in Grave 91, Luxumbourgerstrasse, Cologne. For a later date within the fourth century see Painter in Harden 1987.
36. Similar lettering to that of cat. 1 appears on BM S 120, assigned to Type 1 by Meek 2013: 129, Table 6.
    Morey 13 = Vatican Museums Inv. No. 60697. For workshops of gold leaf engravers see Lega 2012.
37. On grozing and its date see Howells 2013: 117.
38. Kottaridi 2011: 82–3 and (more detail) 88–9.
39. Harden 1968; Tait 1991: pls.54–6; Tokyo National Museum 2003a, p.86, cat. 66.
40. Painter in Harden 1987: 262–8.
41. Howells 2015: 64; Cameron 1998: 298.
42. See Appendix 1 and Meek in Howells 2015: 30–40 for analysis of the British Museum gold-glass.
43. Walker 1985.
44. Wurch- Kozelj and Kozelj 1995; Ward-Perkins and Throckmorton 1965.
45. Walker 1990: 92.

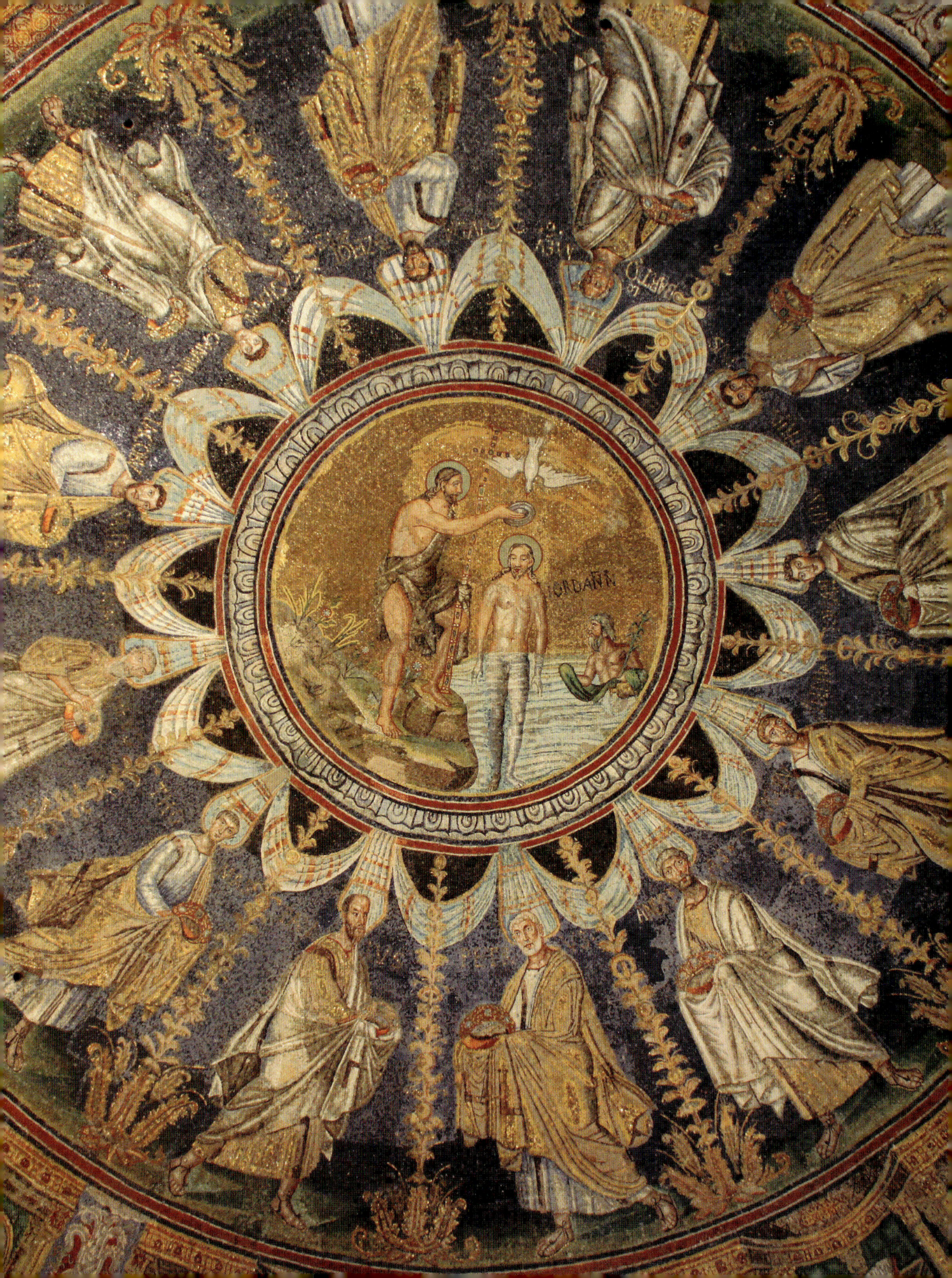

Chapter 5

Picturing prayers: the iconography of the Wilshere gold-glasses

Sean V. Leatherbury

The gold-glasses of the Wilshere Collection are extraordinary not only for their provenance history and object types, but also for the range of images with which they are decorated. While the collection includes glasses commissioned by Jewish and pagan patrons, the majority of the Wilshere glasses are decorated with Christian images of two types: narrative scenes derived from the Old and New Testaments, as well as the apocrypha, and non-narrative images which depict the saints, symbolic motifs such as the Good Shepherd or fish, or the Christian deceased whom the glasses were intended to celebrate. The images on the bases of these glasses, intimately connected to contemporaneous catacomb wall paintings, acted as visual representations of prayers for the deceased. They also prefigured the monumental mosaics of the churches of the city of Rome, and reveal the close artistic relationships between different religious groups in the city during the fourth century AD.

Christian images as prayers for salvation

Many of the Wilshere glasses present visual prayers on behalf of the Christian dead through their narrative and non-narrative images. While all such glasses were material representations of prayers for the deceased, their imagery changed over time. These iconographic changes not only mirror larger developments in the history of Christian worship in the city of Rome, but also appear to have directly participated in those developments.

Indeed, the imagery of two of the Wilshere glass bases (cats **3** and **23**) and many of the individual figures appearing in the small medallions set into the walls of vessels appears to have been directly connected to an early Christian prayer, the *Proficiscere*,

12 apostles depicted on the dome of the orthodox Baptistery, Ravenna. Detail of Fig. 64.

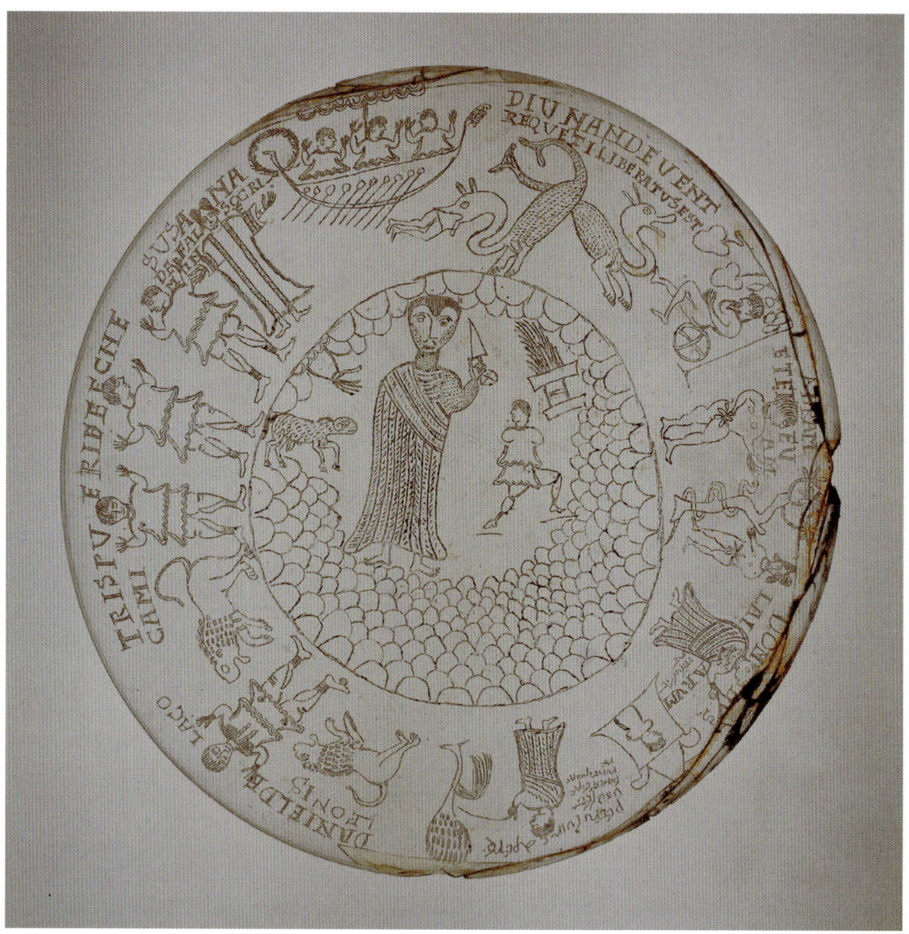

Fig. 58 Glass bowl with engraved Old Testament scenes, from Podgoritza, fourth or early fifth century AD, now in St Petersburg, State Hermitage Museum

used in the ritual for the committal of the soul of the deceased (the *Commendatio animae*).[1] The prayer begins with a general petition ('Deliver, Lord, his soul from all the dangers of Hell, and from the toils of punishment and from all tribulations') and continues with further petitions for God to save the deceased as he saved Elijah, Noah, Abraham, Job, Isaac and other prophets and saints of the Old and New Testaments.[2] In the centre of one of the glasses, cat. **3**, the narrative scenes around the edge frame the deceased couple's hope of salvation, expressed in their portrait, with the images of Old and New Testament miracles of deliverance featured in the *Proficiscere* prayer. Just as God had redeemed Adam and Eve and saved Isaac from Abraham's knife, and as Christ had healed the lame man and brought Lazarus back from the dead, so too will the heavenly Father and Son save this pair.[3]

While the two Wilshere glasses are not inscribed with the text of the *Proficiscere* prayer itself, a fourth- or early fifth-century engraved glass bowl from Podgoritza (Roman Doclea), now in the Hermitage Museum, St Petersburg, pairs a similar set of Old Testament scenes with verses in Latin from the text of the prayer. The scenes include Abraham and Isaac (in the centre), Jonah and the Whale, Adam and Eve, Moses striking the rock, Daniel in the Lion's Den, the Three Hebrews in the Fiery Furnace and Susannah and the Elders (Fig. 58).[4]

The miracles included in the prayer seem to have influenced the choice of the episodes depicted on the Wilshere glass, though the text was clearly not a strict guide for the artist. He included Christ's miracles as well, such as the raising of Lazarus, in order to construct links between the Old and New Testaments in which the figures and events of the Hebrew Bible are seen as prefigurations or 'types' of those of the

New Testament ('typology').[5] Viewed in its fourth-century context, the Wilshere glass seems to have functioned as a visualised prayer for the deceased couple, who hope to be 'delivered' as were Adam and Eve, Isaac and the other figures encircling the central medallion.[6]

The tender portrait of the couple in the centre of this glass also bears links to the realm of funerary art and ritual. Earlier third-century gold-glasses also bear bust-length portraits of wealthy individuals and families against a blue ground in what is known as the 'brushed' technique style,[7] executed with very fine incised dots, their cumulative appearance simulating fluid brushstrokes.[8] These glasses are generally smaller in size than later examples, and may have been mounted and worn on necklaces as portrait medallions.[9] One of the Wilshere glasses, cat. **2**, is most likely a small fragment of one of these glasses. The fourth-century portrait glasses, including cat. **3**, are larger in size as they are excised from complete vessels, and are decorated with images much more closely related to funerary portraiture. Several other glasses in the collection may include portraits of married couples, including cats **19** and **20**: these two are unfortunately fragmentary, but the former preserves an inscription that refers to the male figure pictured: 'RUFE VIVI[S]' ('Rufus, may you live!'). A more complete example is the central medallion of cat. **3**, where a richly- and fashionably-dressed couple is paired with a Greek inscription written in Latin characters, expressing a hope that the deceased may live eternally in heaven: 'PIE ZESES' ('Drink that you may live!').[10]

In format and arrangement the portrait resembles images of couples on Roman funerary stelai[11] and sarcophagi. An example is the sarcophagus of Adelphia and her husband, made in Rome between AD 325 and 350 (Fig. 59):[12] on the glass and the

Fig. 59 Sarcophagus of Adelphia, Rome, AD 325–50, now in Syracuse, Museo Archeologico Nazionale

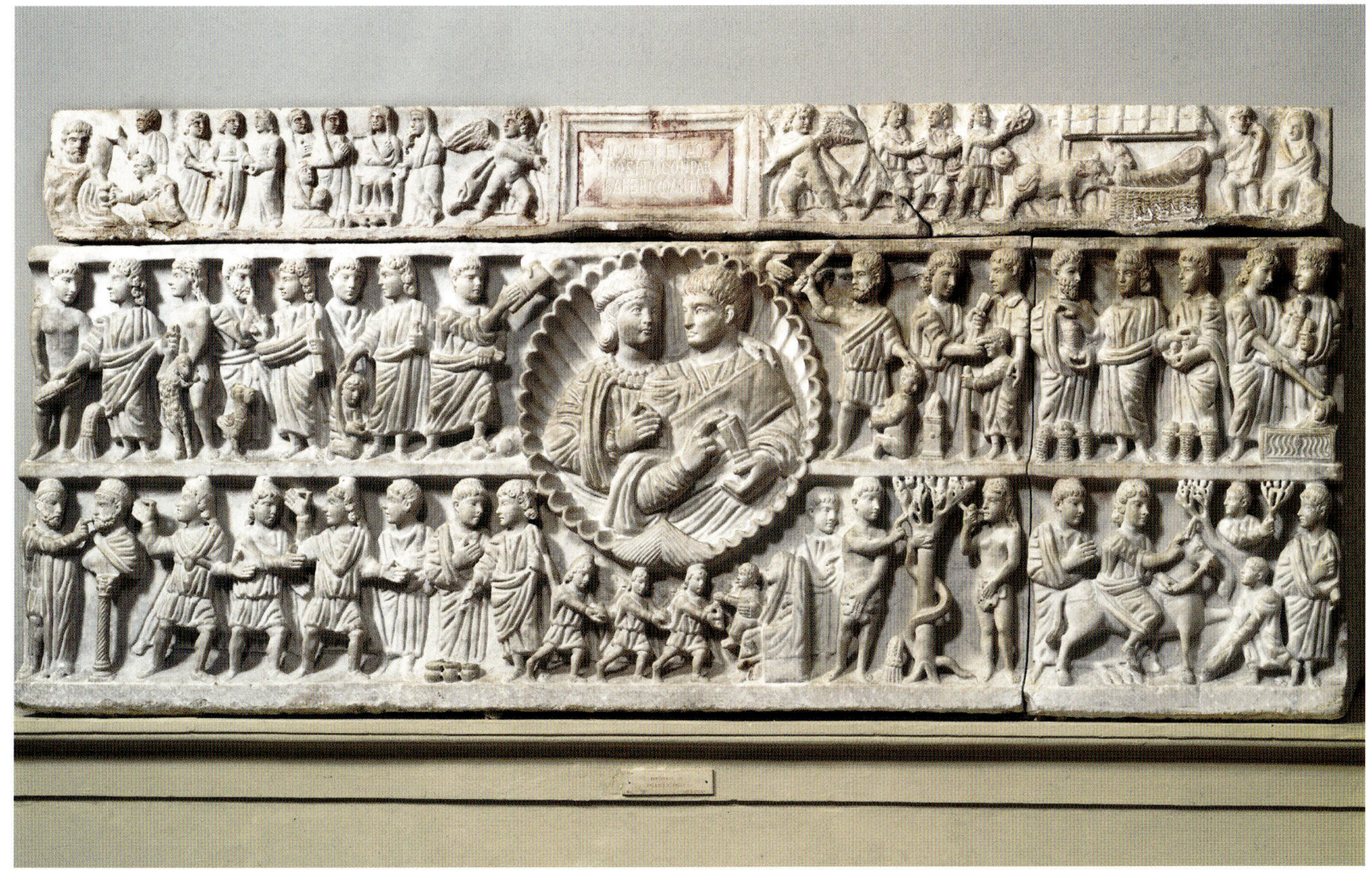

sarcophagus alike, the husband stands in front, his wife behind. While the husband gazes directly at the viewer and makes the typical gesture indicating speech with his right hand, the wife looks to him.

On the glass, however, she is not bereft of symbols of her elevated position: in addition to her elaborate hairstyle, jewelled necklace and embroidered clothes, she holds a scroll signifying her education or status – or possibly her role as manager of household accounts.[13]

Another glass in the collection, cat. **23**, also includes Old and New Testament scenes related to the *Proficiscere* prayer, though the centre of this glass depicts not a couple (as does cat. **3**), but Peter and Paul, those quintessentially Roman martyrs also invoked by the prayer.[14] The two princes of the Church, identifiable by their features as well as by their inscribed names, gaze at one another. Made of recycled glass, this vessel was most likely made later in the fourth century than cat. **3**. While the image of the married couple looked to popular types of Roman funerary images, the glass with Peter and Paul was witness instead to the increasing popularity of saints and their images in the period – a development that appears to have intensified in the later part of the fourth century (see above, p.104).

Constantine certainly gave the Christian religion a massive boost through his patronage of the church after his defeat of Maxentius in AD 312, building basilicas on imperial properties throughout Rome. Yet some of the growth of the cult of saints in particular, or at least the visual trappings of that cult, seems to have occurred later in the fourth century than had been previously thought.[15] The construction of the great martyrs' basilicas once attributed solely to Constantine, including the shrines of Peter (now the Vatican), Paul (on the Via Ostiense) and Agnes (on the Via Nomentana), recently has been found to have involved (or to have been executed entirely by) his children Constans (d.350) and Constantina (d.354) and his successors, after the emperor's death in 337.[16] In the catacombs, Pope Damasus and his successors took action in the second half of the fourth century to develop and monumentalise the cult of the martyrs. They set up large inscribed marble plaques at the burial sites of saints, including in the so-called Crypt of the Popes in the Catacomb of San Callisto, where the inscriptions praise the popes martyred in the first centuries of Christianity as models for the Christian faithful (Fig. 60).[17] The images of male saints depicted on other Wilshere glasses, probably produced after *c.*350 (for example, cats **10**, **11**, **26**), are additional testaments to the large-scale growth of the cult of saints and martyrs in the later fourth century.

The glasses contribute to the larger picture of religious and artistic developments in early Christian Rome, as the imperial and ecclesiastical hierarchies began to assert greater control over images and forms of representation.[18] Importantly, the glasses chart the replacement of images of the dead, perhaps primarily intended for their families and close friends, with the portraits of saints, testifying to the increasing importance of a corporate Christian identity influenced by changing practice – primarily the move of worship from the catacombs to the basilicas, richly adorned with monumental portraits of the same saints.[19] However, while the Christians of Rome seem to have developed a preference for images of saints in the course of the fourth century, older types of images, including portraits of the deceased (as on cat. **19**) did not die out entirely. Instead they co-existed for a time with newer images of saints. While their imagery changed to some extent, the functions of the gold-glasses remained substantially the same: to celebrate and commemorate the deceased, either through their own portraits or through images of the saints and martyrs of Rome, in whose spiritual care and physical proximity they were placed for eternity.[20]

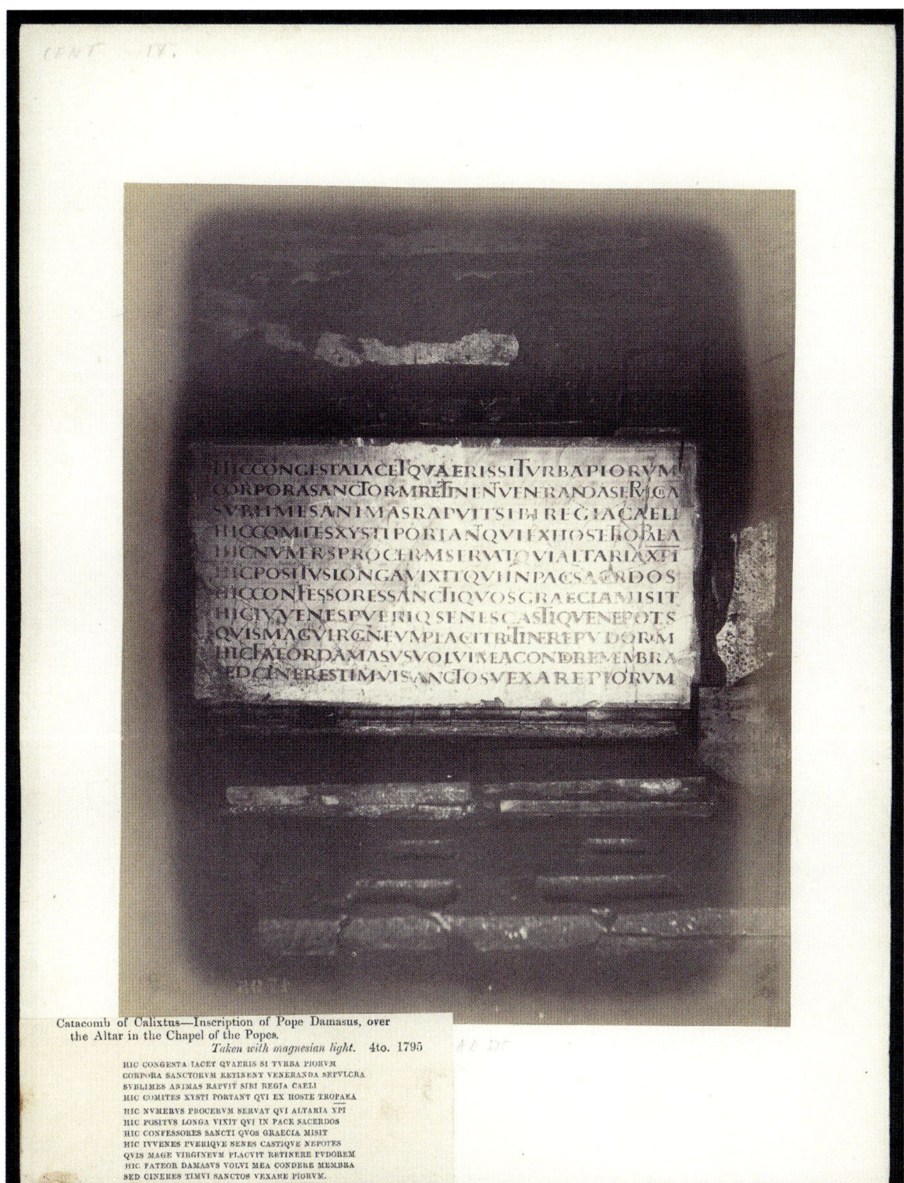

Fig. 60 Inscription of Pope Damasus, Chapel of the Popes, Catacomb of San Callisto, Rome, AD 366–84 (John Henry Parker Archive, The British School at Rome)

From miniature to monumental

In addition to marking the changing attitudes and aesthetic tastes of the period, the collection contains a number of glasses whose formats prefigure those of monumental images in late fourth- and early fifth-century churches and chapels in Rome and Ravenna.[21] Several of these vessels have been studied in detail, especially the portrait of Christ as philosopher-teacher, seated and surrounded by apostles and other saints (cat. **22**), which is unique among the corpus of extant gold-glasses. This particular format was adapted from representations of poets, doctors and sages – as seen in a mid-fourth-century mosaic of the Seven Sages at Apamea in Syria, where the sages are seated in a semicircle with the famous philosopher Socrates in the centre.[22] By depicting Christ as philosopher-teacher, artists were able to adapt a Graeco-Roman type to suit new Christian figures, immediately endowing Christ with visual legitimacy and emphasising his role as teacher of the apostles (and of all

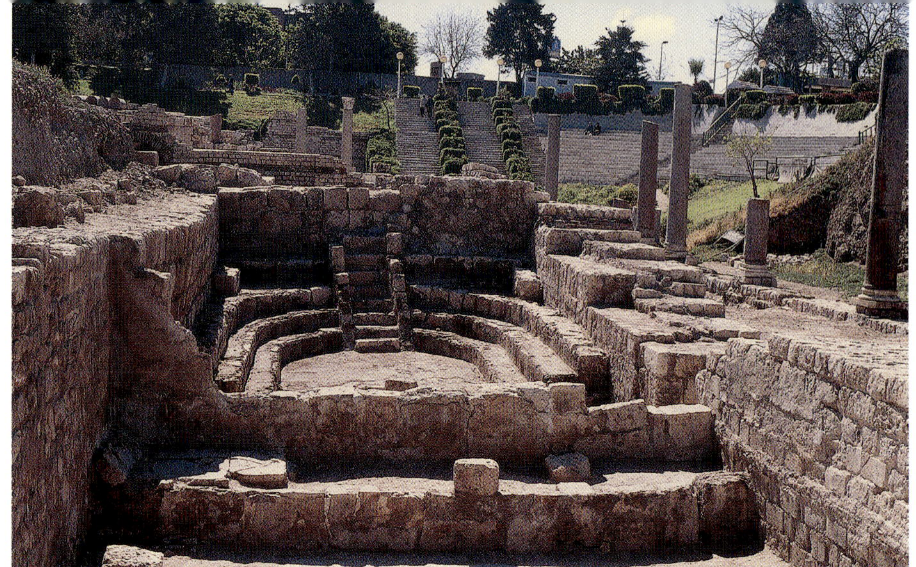

Fig. 61 Lecture room with *kathedra*, Kom el-Dikka, Alexandria, fifth-seventh century AD (Judith McKenzie/Manar al-Athar)

the faithful). However, recent excavations at Alexandria in Egypt have confirmed that artists derived the semicircular arrangement from the actual set-up of ancient schools. The late antique lecture rooms at Kom el-Dikka are apsidal in plan, and feature a central seat elevated on steps (*kathedra*, lit. 'throne') and semicircular benches along the walls (Fig. 61).[23] The format of seven figures seated in a semicircle had already been adapted for use in the painted decoration of the catacombs of Rome by the third century, as in the ceiling painting in the Catacomb of Peter and Marcellinus (also called the Catacomb 'Inter Duas Lauros'), where Christ is depicted in the centre with three apostles to either side.[24]

The Wilshere gold-glass includes more figures than does this earlier representation – in addition to Christ, at least eight saints, possibly ten – as well as two different types of chairs: Christ and the two figures at the bottom of the base sit in high-backed seats, with Christ's chair elevated on one step; the other saints are seated on backless chairs. Expanding the cast of characters on the glass, as well as experimenting with different types of seats, the creator of this glass seems to have worked in the tradition of fourth-century catacomb painters, and (later) fifth-century mosaicists, who installed images of Christ and his 12 apostles in key locations within churches and chapels. Notable results can be seen in the late fourth- or early fifth-century apse of the Cappello di Sant'Aquilino in Milan (Fig. 62) and the early fifth-century apse of Santa Pudenziana in Rome.[25]

The iconography of the gold-glasses is linked closely with that of contemporary catacomb paintings, though discerning the precise direction of influence is nearly impossible due to the difficulty of dating the works. However, while the corpus of catacomb paintings has been used to chart the evolution of later monumental painting and mosaic programmes, the gold-glasses are frequently absent from the discussion.[26] The images that decorate works of so-called 'minor' or 'decorative' art, such as ivories, silver and ceramic vessels, jewellery and the gold-glasses, were fully integrated into the artistic currents of the period.

Several glasses in the Wilshere Collection appear to be related to contemporaneous monumental painting and sculptural programmes in the catacombs. The two glasses with Old and New Testament scenes previously discussed (cats **3** and **23**) resonate with a number of catacomb paintings, among them a mid-fourth-century vault painting in the Catacomb of Domitilla with scenes divided into compartments as on the Wilshere glasses; both are influenced by the round, curving space of their respective settings.[27] As do the glasses, the painting seems to take its repertoire of scenes at least partially from the miraculous deliverances included in the *Proficiscere* prayer. A glass decorated with an architectural scheme featuring portraits of the saints Peter, Paul, Julius and Sixtus (cat. **25**) and an inscription listing their names echoes developments in the catacombs as well. The portraits, framed by medallions, derive from the Roman clipeate portrait image (*imago clipeata*), also used for portraits of saints on the vaulted ceiling of the Catacomb of Santa Tecla, executed in *c.*350–400.[28] The rectangular format of the inscription must relate to the monumental inscriptions set up in the catacombs around the same date by Pope Damasus (Figs 33, 60).[29]

Several Wilshere glasses also depict central bust portraits of Christ (cats. **8**, **10** and **11**), which are connected to similar (albeit rare) ceiling paintings of Christ in the catacombs, including in the Cubicolo di Santa Cecilia.[30] These glasses, at least two of them (cats **10** and **11**) laid out in the round as vault decorations in miniature, foreshadow the popularity of mosaics of Christ as All-Father (Pantocrator) in the domes of Middle Byzantine churches.[31] Their almost architectural scheme, probably conceived and made shortly after AD 350, also reveals the artistic processes by which the radial arrangement of Roman depictions of the Zodiac inspired round processions of Christian saints in monumental art of the period, for example in the domes of the two surviving early Christian baptisteries of Ravenna in Italy. On the glasses, saints stand in pairs around the central bust of Christ, a format which perfectly suits the circular shape of the vessel's base. Each saint,dressed in a tunic and mantle, holds a scroll (as did the female figure on cat. **3** and possibly a similar figure on cat. **20**), identifying them as learned men in the mode of classical philosophers.

While both glasses are fragmentary, they appear to have shown six saints when complete. The saints on both glasses are quintessentially Roman, a mix of apostles and local Roman saints. The more fragmentary glass (cat. **10**) features Pope Sixtus II, who was martyred in AD 258 under the persecutions of the emperor Valerian; he appears again on the second glass (cat. **11**), accompanied by the apostle Peter

Fig. 62 Mosaic of Christ Seated with the Apostles, Cappella di Sant'Aquilino, San Lorenzo Maggiore, Milan, fourth century AD (Jas' Elsner)

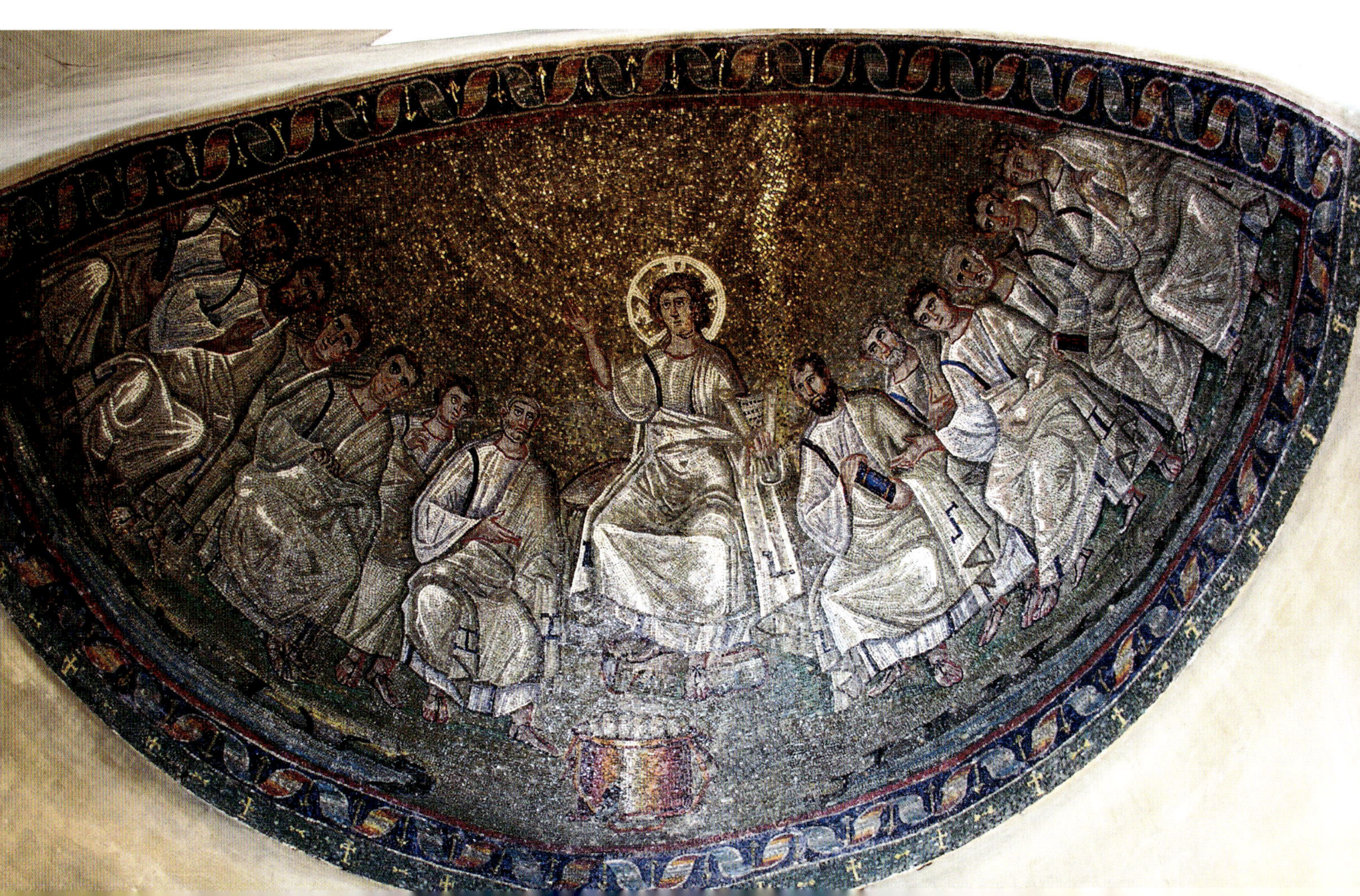

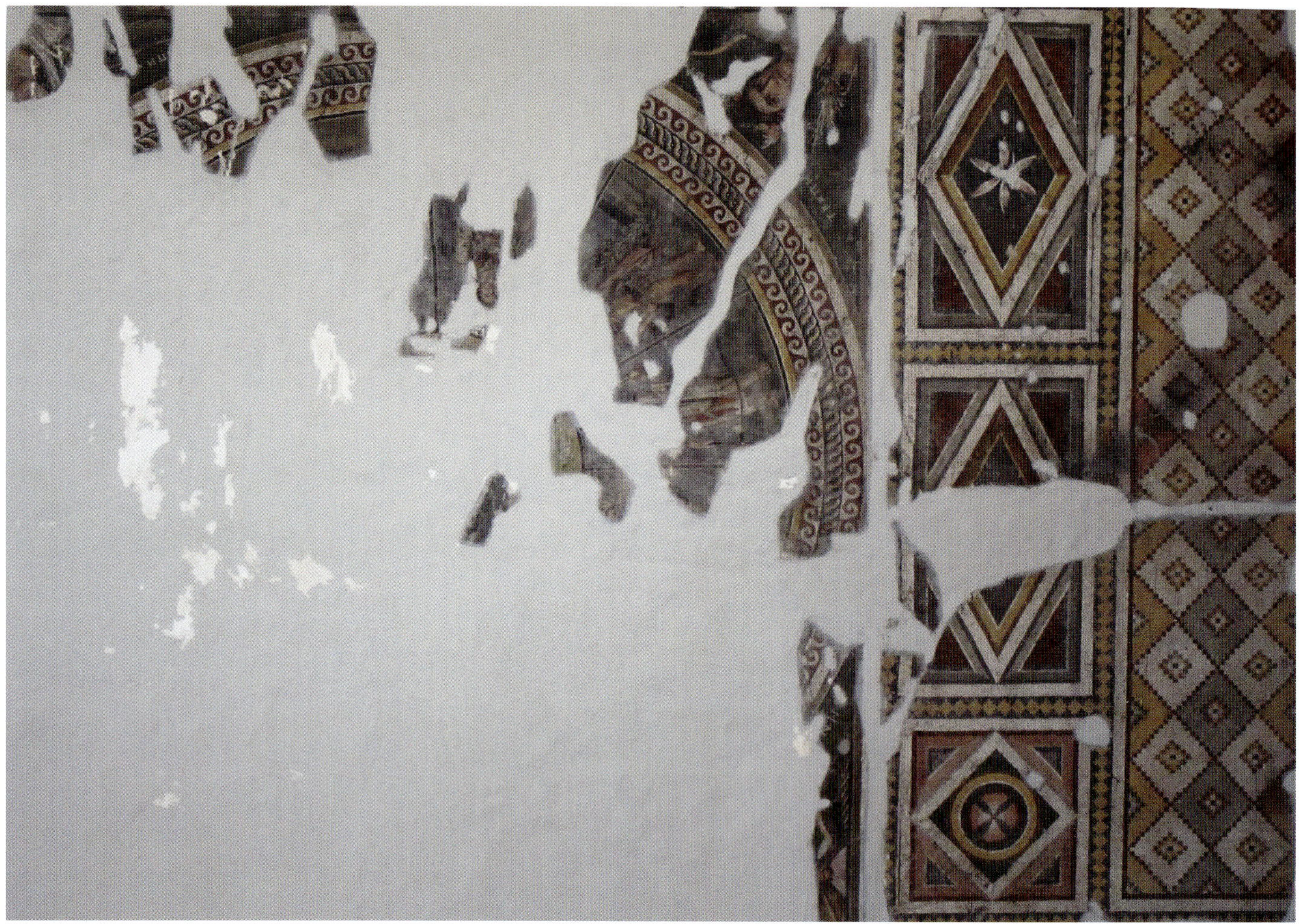

Fig. 63 Mosaic pavement of the House of the Calendar, Antioch, second century AD, now in Antakya, Hatay Archaeological Museum (Sean Leatherbury/Manar al-Athar)

('the rock' on which the church was built) and Luke the Evangelist (who, according to legend, came to Rome with the apostle Paul). In the fourth century Peter and Sixtus were buried in the catacombs themselves: Peter in the Basilica *ad catacumbas* on the Via Appia (now the church of San Sebastiano) and Sixtus in the Crypt of the Popes within the Catacomb of San Callisto.[32] The martyrdoms of all three saints also were celebrated as part of the calendar of liturgical feasts at their shrines in the catacombs: Peter (and Paul) on 29 June, Luke on 18 October and Sixtus on 6 August.[33]

The Wilshere glasses are among the first extant glasses to use this format for images of saints, and form a group with glasses in the Vatican Museum, the Museo Archeologico Nazionale in Florence, the Museo Archeologico Oliveriano in Pesaro and the British Museum.[34] The artists derived the radial format from Roman representations of the Zodiac or the cycle of the months. An instance of this occurs in the floor mosaic from the dining room (*triclinium*) of the House of the Calendar at Antioch, dated to the second century AD. The mosaic depicts full-length male and female personifications of the 12 months of the year radiating outwards from a central medallion (Fig. 63).[35] Strikingly, these figures face each other in pairs, as do the saints on the two Wilshere glasses.

Other similar mosaic representations appear closer to Rome, including a late Roman mosaic of the months found in a villa mosaic from Carthage, now in the British Museum.[36] The Zodiac and the cycle of the seasons continued to be popular images in the late antique period, used to evoke associations of time, the cosmos and the proper order of things, and they appear on the mosaic pavements of churches and synagogues in late antique Palestine.[37] Each of these representations has its subtle differences, such as the modes of dividing up the figures, directional orientations, etc. However, all share the striking radial format that forces an observer to walk around the floor mosaic to read the full image – creating a distinctly physical viewing experience as he or she contemplates the nature of secular and sacred time.

While the cycle of 'saints in the round' on the gold-glasses was not meant to be used as a strict calendar, the format nonetheless reminded a viewer of the calendar of liturgical feasts associated with each saint. The feasts were celebrated in the Roman catacombs themselves, requiring worshippers to travel to different catacombs of the city in order to pay homage to saints at their graves. Artists harnessed the radial format to create a dynamic procession or progression of saints. Some of them move, others face the spectator head-on and yet others seem to be turning, as if to converse with their brothers. On the more complete Wilshere glass (cat. **11**) the saints radiate outwards from the bust portrait of Christ, with their feet closest to his image – an appropriate visual device as they derived their holiness from their proximity to the Son of God. The saints are meant to be viewed as if they are processing, continually moving around the edge of the glass as the viewer turns the vessel in his or her hands before impressing it into the catacomb wall.[38]

Because of its suitability for round and/or curved spaces, the format seen on the Wilshere glass was used by mosaicists to represent the procession of the apostles, most famously in the late fourth- or early fifth-century mosaics of the dome of the Orthodox (Neonian) baptistery (Fig. 64) and of the Arian baptistery in Ravenna, built almost a century later.[39] Instead of six saints, as on the Wilshere glass, the

Fig. 64 Dome mosaic of the baptism of Christ and apostles, Orthodox Baptistery, Ravenna, late fourth or early fifth century AD (Sean Leatherbury)

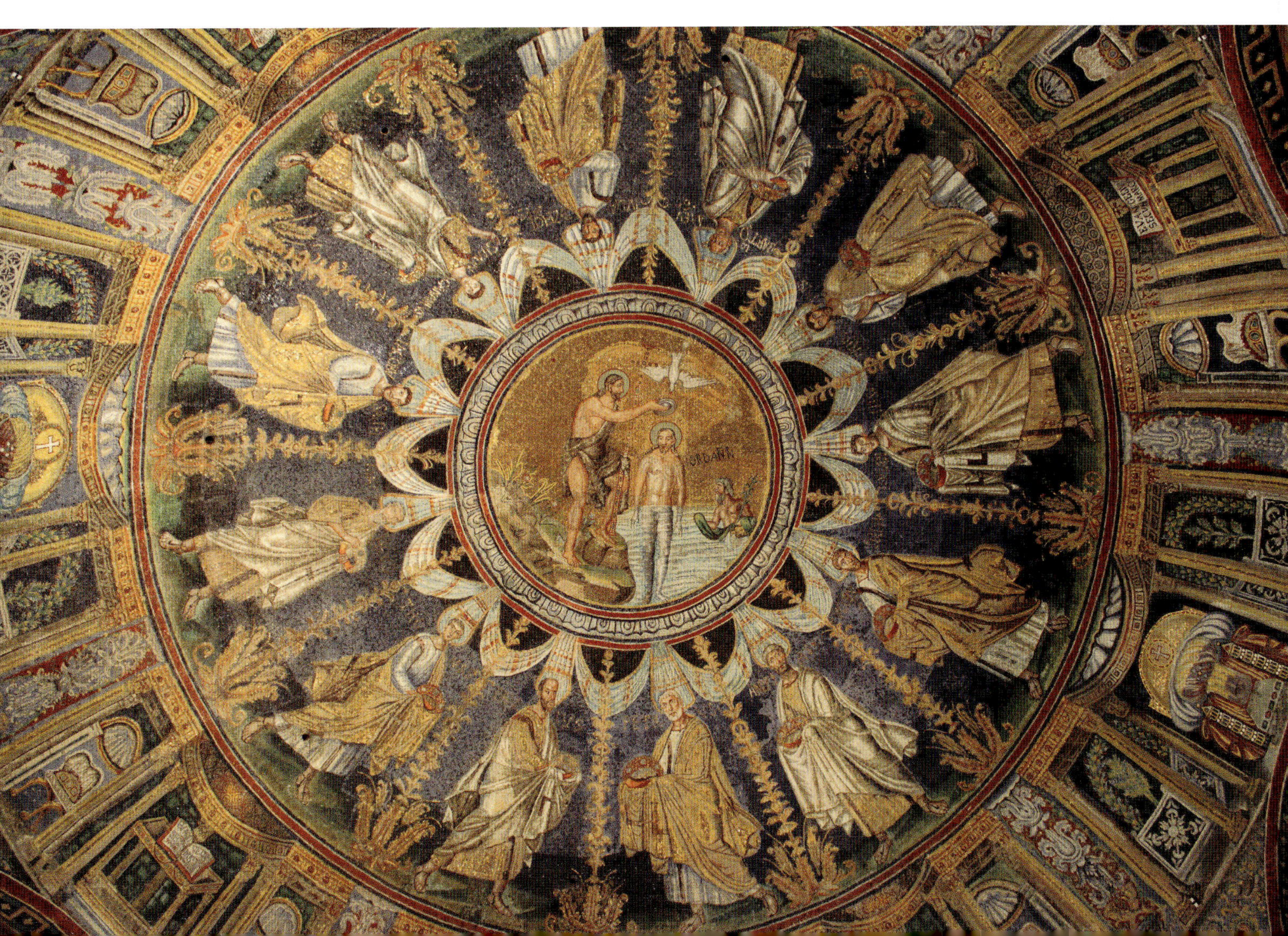

full complement of 12 apostles appears in the dome of the Orthodox baptistery, separated into 12 compartments by plant candelabra. Scholars previously have connected the mosaic to the Roman depictions of the Zodiac and the cycle of the seasons, which certainly influenced the format as well as the way in which viewers engaged with the work. In order to 'read' the procession fully, one must walk in a circle around the baptistery, replicating the circular motion of the procession.[40] However, a missing transitional stage between pagan Zodiac and Christian procession of apostles may have been the gold-glasses themselves, whose production in Rome spurred further experimentation with the radial format in the domes of Ravenna, the new imperial capital in the west. In the Orthodox baptistery, the group of saints becomes a more mobile procession than on the Wilshere glass, but it still contains a mix of static and moving figures who engage with each other and with the viewer.[41]

Iconography and religious affiliation

Most of the Wilshere glasses are decorated with imagery drawn from the evolving Christian artistic tradition. Among them are glasses decorated with symbols that strongly declare the religious affiliation of their patrons, such as the two Christograms (formed by the Greek letters *Chi-Rho*) inscribed on the glass with a man and a woman praying (cat. **21**). These symbols make it clear that the figures depicted are Christians, though their pose of prayer was common to both pagan and Christian traditions of worship.[42] However, the same glass workshops that made these objects also produced glasses with imagery drawn from Jewish and pagan traditions.[43] The collection includes one glass with an image of the Graeco-Roman hero and demigod Hercules (cat. **27**); another glass possibly decorated with the figure of the Good Shepherd (cat. **9**) – a pagan image adapted by Christians to represent Christ as the good shepherd of men who lays down his life for his sheep (John 10:1–21). There are also two flat pieces of glass of uncertain function, including inlay (?) glass (cat. **35**) and a fragment of a platter or tray (cat. **16**), both decorated with decorative motifs of vines emerging from a vase (*kantharos*) and an apparently secular scene of fishing.[44] Finally, one glass displays a Jewish motif, the menorah of the Second Temple in Jerusalem (cat. **13**).

Charles Wilshere was particularly interested in Judaism and its art. In addition to the glass with the menorah, he purchased a number of Jewish funerary inscriptions from the owners of the land on which one of the few Jewish catacombs of Rome, the Vigna Randanini catacomb, was located. Wilshere seems to have been most interested in inscriptions paired with images: while the majority of memorials in the catacombs appear to have been undecorated, many of the inscriptions acquired by Wilshere feature menorahs as well as liturgical implements such as the *shofar* (horn) and *lulab* (palm branch). These images, based on their arrangement, were incised before the text was. In addition to their function as epitaphs for individuals, such inscriptions and images would most probably have been seen by their Jewish commissioners and viewers as images of communal piety and personal salvation (see p.82).

The glass with the image of the 'pagan' demigod Hercules has a more complicated context. The glass, a small blue medallion, depicts a youthful Hercules capturing the Ceryneian Hind of the goddess Artemis (the third of the hero's Twelve Labours).[45] It would originally have been embedded into the walls of a clear glass bowl or cup resembling the bowl excavated from the St Severin cemetery in

Cologne, Germany, now in the collection of the British Museum (Fig. 51).[46] The iconography of the Wilshere medallion derives from earlier Roman models, such as the cycle of Hercules' labours on a sarcophagus made in Rome *c.*230–50; on this the hero is depicted in the same pose as he subdues the Hind, with one knee on top of the animal's back.[47] The medallion might have formed part of a more extensive programme on a glass commissioned by a patron who worshipped the demigod, perhaps featuring the full cycle of Hercules' labours.[48] At least one other extant gold-glass was intended to memorialise pagan patrons, a vessel base in the British Museum; it depicts a married couple flanking a small votive statuette of Hercules encircled by an inscription: 'ORFITUS ET CONSTANTIA.IN NOMINE HERCULIS ACERENTINO FELICES BIBATIS' ('Orfitus and Constantia, may you live happily in the name of Hercules of Acerentia'). The reference here may be to the small Italian town of Acerentia (modern Acerenza) in southern Italy.[49]

However, affection for the hero was not solely the province of pagan patrons in the fourth century AD. Hercules was in fact a popular hero among educated Christians; even some of the early Church Fathers, including Basil the Great, admired him for living a life of virtue and of honest work. In his 'Address to young men, on how they might derive benefit from Greek literature', Basil retells an allegorical tale (repeated from Prodicus of Ceos, a fifth-century BC sophist) that praises Hercules for choosing the path of Virtue over Vice through his commitment to completing his labours as punishment for the murder of his wife and children.[50] While the medallion was perhaps part of a 'pagan' programme featuring the cycle of the labours, this glass may instead have been incorporated into a programme commissioned by a Christian who appreciated classical literature and myth. It thus allowed Christian patrons to read the heroic accomplishments of Hercules against the miracles and deeds performed by Moses, Daniel (for example cats **31**, **32** and **33**), Jonah and Christ (cat. **34**), as well as against popular decorative images such as animals (for example cats **28** and **29**).[51]

Conclusion

A closer look at the iconography of the Wilshere Collection reveals the processes through which early Christian art developed out of Roman visual traditions in the city of Rome itself, shaped in large part by Christian funerary practices. Sacred prayers performed as part of Christian rites, such as the *Proficiscere* prayer, directly influenced the cycles of imagery depicted on the glasses. However, these texts did not constrain the imaginations of artists and their patrons. They drew instead upon the powers of typology to unite miracles of salvation from the Old and New Testaments in order to construct more potent visual prayers for the deceased. Images of the wealthy dead gradually gave way to depictions of martyrs, linked to the monumental painted and mosaic images then being installed in the catacombs and martyrial shrines of the city. While figures of Christ and the saints became ever more present in both miniature and monumental artworks, the visual and literary traditions of Greece and Rome persisted. Artists still alluded to the tastes and erudition of the deceased through traditional Roman costume, gesture and images of 'pagan' figures such as Hercules, whose appeal survived the coming of Christianity.

Notes

1. The text of the prayer was most recently edited in Dumas 1981: 461. Earlier editions include le Blant 1879: 229 and Leclercq 1923: 435–6, republished by Tkacz 2001: 113. On the prayer see Tkacz 1991; Tkacz 2001: 109–37, with further bibliography; Spier 2007: 8–10; on connections to the gold-glasses see Howells 2015: 93–101. On the date of the prayer, which remains controversial, see Tkacz 2001: 113ff, who summarises the debate. Scholars who prefer an earlier (second–third century) date include Leclerq 1923, le Blant 1879: 231, Morey 1941: 62 and Besserman 1979, 57. The most recent editor, Dumas, dates the assembly of the text to the Carolingian period: Dumas 1981: xxiii. However, even if the full text of the prayer was assembled later, its elements were in circulation earlier. For example, Augustine includes sections of the prayer in his *Commentaries on Psalm 21, Commentary* 2.6, written as early as 395: Tkacz 2001: 118–24.
2. Text from le Blant 1897: 229, trans. Tkacz 2001: 116.
3. le Blant 1897: 229, verse six of the prayer: *Libera, Domine, animam eius, sicut liberasti Isaac de hostia, et de manu patris suae Abrahae* ('Deliver, Lord, his soul, just as you delivered Isaac from sacrifice, and from the hand of his father Abraham').
4. Hermitage Museum, inv. no. 73; Bank 1977/8: 275–6, figs 26–9; Tkacz 2001: 124–7; Spier 2007: 9, fig. 4. Other similar works include the so-called Arras Cup, found in the grave of a woman in the cemetery at Homblières (Aisne) (Louvre inv. no. MNC 919), and a bronze medallion now in the Vatican. See Tkacz 2001: 127–8.
5. On early Christian imagery and typology see Jensen 2007.
6. This connection to the prayer is further evidence that the glasses did not have a primary use in domestic contexts, but rather were produced to commemorate deceased individuals, couples and families. For a recent summary of this debate see Meredith 2015 and above, p.76.
7. Howells 2015: 28–9, 68, 114.
8. For example, the famous Brescia Medallion, now in the Museo Civico Cristiano, Brescia and now embedded in the centre of a medieval Langobardic cross (the so-called 'Desiderius Cross'): de Mély 1926: 1–9; Morey 1959: no. 237. Other examples are in the Metropolitan Museum of Art, New York: Weitzmann 1979: cats 264–5 (= Morey 1959, nos 452 and 454). On portrait glasses in the collection of the British Museum see Howells 2015: 114–31; on the evolution of portrait types from glasses produced with the 'brushed' to the 'cut' or 'incised' technique see Meredith 2015.
9. Meredith 2015: 227–8.
10. On the formula, common on epitaphs as well as on glassware, see Ferrua 1974; Adams 2003: 407; Cooley 2012: 110–11.
11. For example, a carved Roman funerary portrait of a family, presumably once attached to a larger gravestone, now in the Sofia Museum, Bulgaria. Grabar 1968: fig. 178.
12. Now in the Museo Archeologico Regionale P. Orsi in Syracuse, Sicily: Dresken-Weiland 1998: no.20, pl. 9–10.
13. On the symbolism of the scroll in gold-glass portraits see Howells 2015, 125; on representations of learned women on sarcophagi see Huskinson 1999. On the role of women in the Roman family and in Roman society see Gardner 1986; Dixon 2001; D'Ambra 2006. On changes in the legal status and role of women in late antiquity see Clark 1993; Osiek 2006, 144ff; Cooper 2007.
14. Verse 12 of the prayer: 'Deliver, Lord, his [the deceased's] soul just as you delivered Peter and Paul from prison…', trans. Tkacz 2001: 116; Latin text in le Blant 1897: 229.
15. See Pietri 1976.
16. On the decorative programme of Old St. Peter's see Bowersock 2005; Bardill 2012: 243–5. Constantina's dedicatory inscription for Sant'Agnese is *ICUR* 2, 44; *ILCV* 1, 1768; her mausoleum, Santa Costanza, is located beside the church, which was rebuilt in the seventh century. Generally see Curran 2000.
17. Utro 2003; Grig 2004a:127–35. On Damasus generally see Reutter 2009; Löx 2013. His inscriptions are edited by Ferrua 1942; on the impact of Damasus's epigraphic programme on Christian life in the city see Pietri 1961; Trout 2003; Sághy 2012; Thunø 2015: 172–81; Sághy 2016. On the rise of the cult of saints in the period in Rome especially see Brown 1981; Howard-Johnston and Hayward 1999; Diefenbach 2007; Thacker 2007; Sághy 2010.
18. For example Grig 2004b.
19. On this development see recently Yasin 2009; Löx 2013.
20. On the Christian desire for burial in proximity to the saints (*ad sanctos*) see Brown 1981: 27, 34–5; Duval 1988; Yasin 2009: 46–100.
21. Scholars previously have attempted to connect several Vatican glasses with monumental images in Rome, for example Bisconti 2001–2.
22. Hanfmann 1951, who traces the format back to at least the second century; Grabar 1968: 72–3; Balty 1995: 42–6, 299–305.
23. McKenzie 2007: 206–19, figs 369–71.
24. Hanfmann 1951: fig. 4; Guyon 1987: 409–11; Deckers et al. 1987: 199–200; Thunø 2015: 190–1.
25. On Sant'Aquilino see Grabar 1968: 72–3; Mathews 1993: 118. On Santa Pudenziana see Ihm 1960: 130–2; Oakeshott 1967: 65–7; Matthiae 1967: vol. 1, 55–76; Mathews 1993: 98–109. Recently on the restoration of the mosaics see Tiberia 2003.
26. Bisconti 2001–2; Grig 2004a.
27. Kostof 1965: fig. 137. See also a ceiling in the Cubicolo di Santa Cecilia, which features Moses striking the rock, Noah' s ark, the Three Hebrews, Abraham and Isaac and the Multiplication of Loaves and Fishes, with Christ in the centre: Garrucci 1873: tav. 24. On other gold-glasses with central images of Christ in the collection of the British Museum see Howells 2015: 79–84.
28. Mazzei 2010: 39–40, tav. 40, 42.
29. *Supra* n.17.
30. Garrucci 1873: tav. 29.5, 33.2, 66.1.
31. Deckers 2007: 108.
32. Wilpert 1910. On Damasus's inscriptions in the Crypt of the Popes see *supra* n.17.
33. Peter's feast is recorded as being celebrated in the catacombs as early as AD 258 in the Codex-Calendar of 354. See Salzman 1990: 46–7.
34. Morey 1959: nos 105, 240, 291, 307 and 354; on the British Museum glass (Morey 1959: no.307; BM BEP 1863,07–27.13) see Howells 2015: 81–2, no.12. Another example, in the Museo delle antichità in Parma, illustrates all 12 apostles: Morey 1959: no.235. Later glass artisans used the same format on the walls of vessels, as on an engraved glass cup of the late fourth or early fifth century found in the Necropolis of Saint-Martin-de-Corléans at Aosta in the Italian Alps, which depicts Peter, Paul, Sixtus and other saints: Paolucci 1997: 175–8.
35. Levi 1947: 36–8; Hachlili 2009: 51–2, fig. III–14; more generally see Levi 1941.
36. BM inv. 1967,0405.1–2: Hinks 1933: 89ff.
37. Synagogues with Zodiac mosaics include the fourth-century synagogue at Hammath Tiberias, where the Zodiac decorates the central nave: Dothan 1983; Hachlili 1988: 301–9, fig. 39a; Hachlili 2009: 18–19, Figure II–1, 35–49; generally on the Zodiac in Jewish art see Hachlili 1977; Magness 2005. Christian buildings feature the Zodiac much more rarely; surviving examples include the sixth-century Monastery of the Lady Mary at Beth Shean, where a cycle of the months adorns a funerary chapel ('Hall A'): Ovadiah 1987: 26–30, no.26, pl.XXI.
38. On pairs of saints see Grig 2004a: 218.
39. See Deichmann 1969: 130–51 (on the Orthodox baptistery) and 209–12 (Arian baptistery); Deichmann 1974: 15–47, 251–8; also Jensen 2011: 198–204.
40. Kostof 1965: 112–7.
41. On the procession see Wharton 1995: 124–5, who corrects the misapprehension that the mix of figures is the result of a mistake committed by an incompetent artist, for example Wilpert 1916: vol.1, 70–1.
42. Jensen 2000: 35–7.
43. Grig 2004a: 205. Generally on pagan, Christian and Jewish co-existence in the catacombs of Rome see Elsner 2003; Lewis 2016.

44. Though these motifs may have been purely decorative, they may also have been interpreted as symbolic. For example, the *kantharos* with a vine may have been read by Christian viewers as a symbol of Christ's status as the 'true vine' (John 15:1): see Maguire 1987.
45. On the local cult of Hercules in Rome, whose centre was the so-called 'Ara Maxima' ('Greatest Altar') near the Forum Boarium, see Winter 1910; Bayet 1926; Palmer 1990; Schultz 2000.
46. BM BEP 1881,0624,1; Morey 1959: no.349; Harden 1987: no.154; Howells 2015: 90–101, no.16. On these medallions generally see Utro 2000.
47. Now in the Museo Nazionale delle Terme, inv. 8642: Palma and de Lachenal 1983: 38–41, no.17; Jongste 1992: cat. F.6, 84–6, fig. 47.
48. As proposed by Howells 2015: 134–5. Howells also discusses a similar medallion with Hercules and the Cretan bull in the British Museum, BM BEP OA 4309.
49. BM 1863,0727.3; Morey 1959: no.316; Howells 2015: 121–3, no.35, who presents several different translations and interpretations of the inscription. On the identity of 'Orfitus', who may have been Memmius Vitrasius Orfitus, a prefect of Rome in the 350s, see Cameron 1996. See also above, p.00.
50. Basil, *Address* 5.11–14, *PG* 31, cols 563–90; trans. Deferrari and Maguire 1934, 396–9.
51. On the continuing popularity of Hercules in late antique art see van den Hoek and Herrmann, Jr. 2007, reprinted in van den Hoek and Herrmann, Jr. 2013: 203–54; see also Nagy 2016.

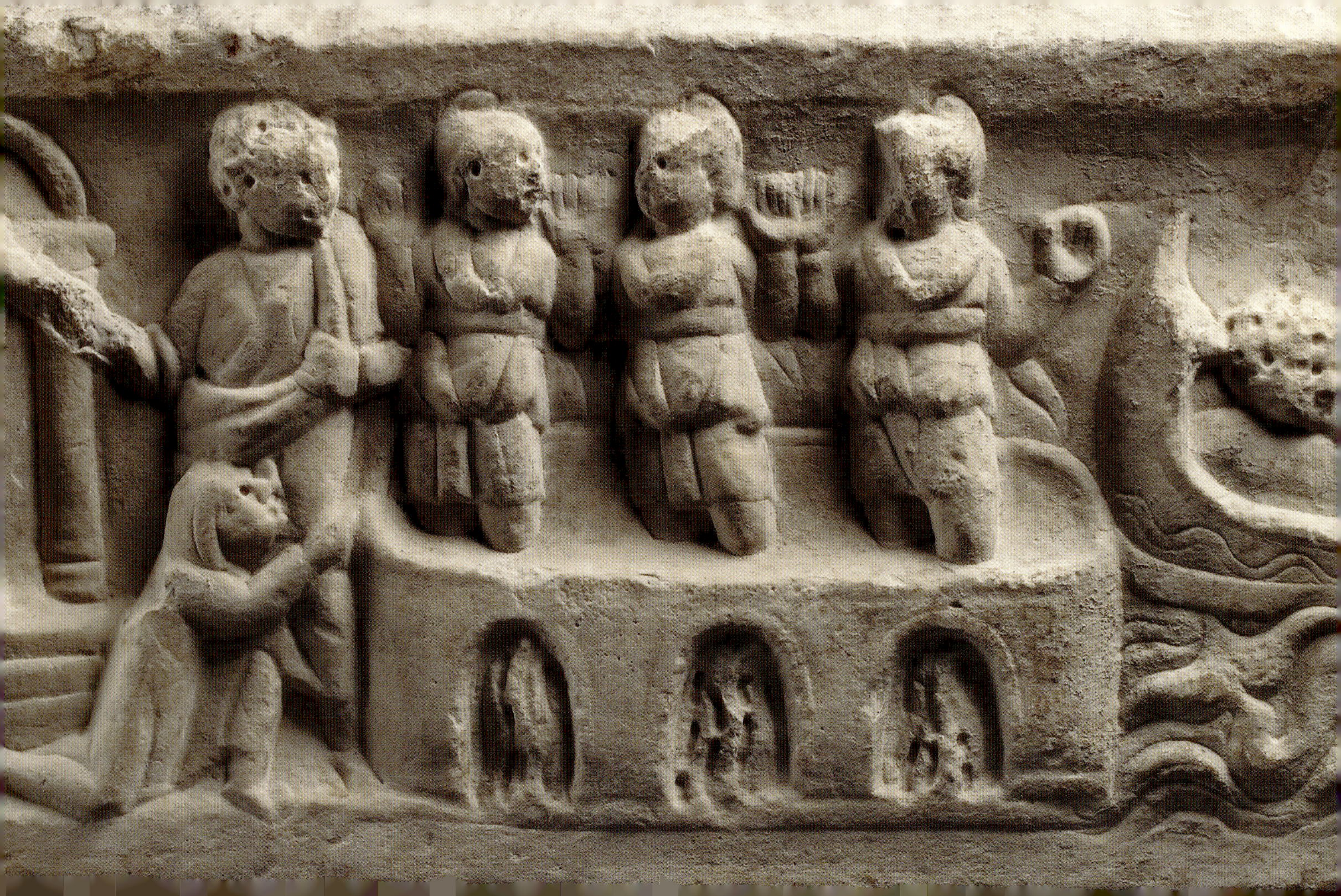

Catalogue of objects from the Wilshere Collection in the Ashmolean Museum

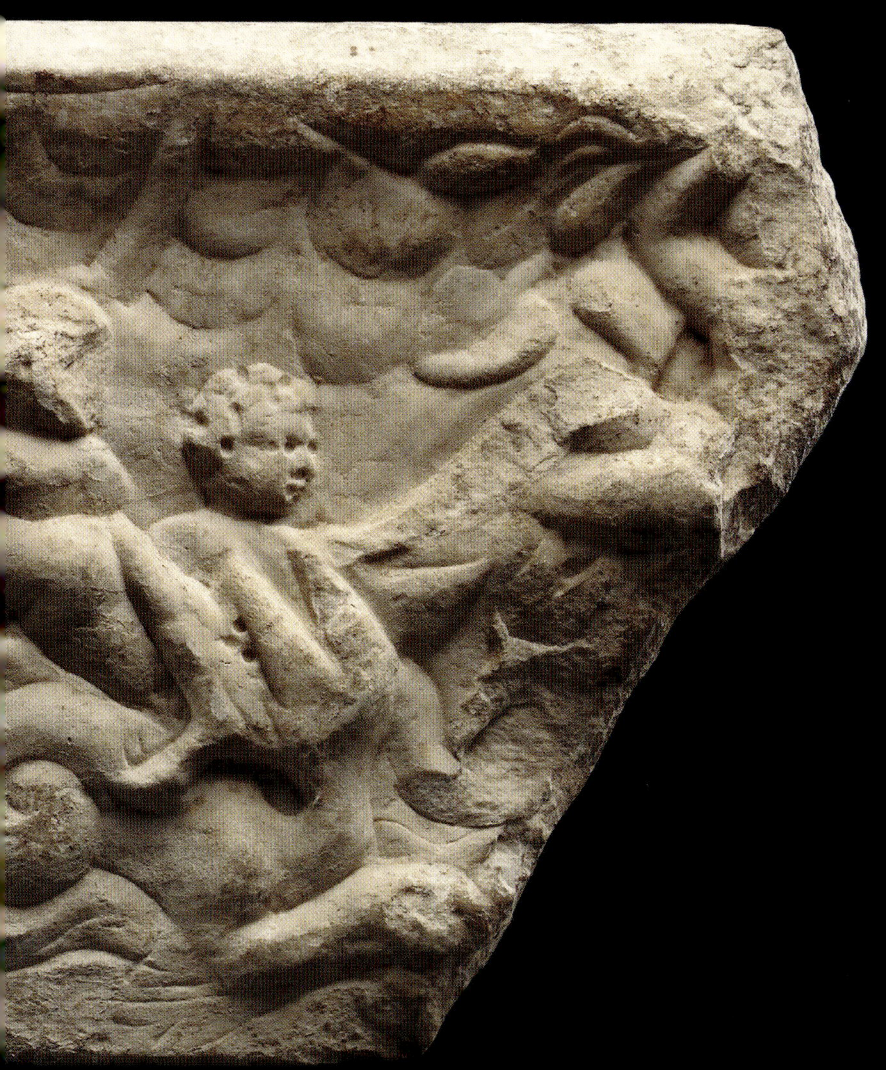

Note

Latin inscriptions in all media in the Wilshere Collection and other Ashmolean collections are the subject of a new, online corpus edited by Alison Cooley (Cooley 2017). Greek inscriptions follow the most recent published edition; unpublished texts follow the editorial conventions of McLean 2002.

Abbreviations

H. = height
W. = width
L. = length
TH. = thickness (measured from top to bottom or front to back)
DIAM. = diameter.

UL = upper layer of glass protecting gold leaf
LL = lower layer of glass, to which the gold leaf is adhered
ML = middle layer, where the first attempt at blowing a protective layer was unsuccessful and repeated to form the UL.

Max. = maximum
Min. = Minimum

Dimensions of gold-glass are given in millimetres (mm); the larger sarcophagi and inscriptions are measured in centimetres (cm).

Where possible, drawings of gold-glass by Yvonne Beadnell and images of the smaller gold-glasses are at 1:1 scale.

Gold-glass

Group 1

Gold-glass decoloured with antimony only

1 AN 2007.38

Base of a glass chalice, inscribed in gold leaf to Heraclides or Heracles

H. 27 mm; W. 72 mm (max.); pedestal: H. 12 mm; DIAM. 47 mm
UL. Colourless, transparent with slight yellowish tinge. TH. 4.5 mm
LL. Colourless, transparent with slight yellowish tinge. TH. 1.5 mm

The raw glass was decoloured with antimony only.

Present condition
The walls of the vessel, broken along a jagged edge, are thinner at the top than at the base, where the chalice rests on a pedestal with raised foot-ring, largely intact. The glass is lightly bubbled and has stress fractures. The base has iridescent opalescence, with flaky weathering at the interface. As a result the text is only legible when back-lit.

Gold leaf decoration
The gold leaf is cut with text only, as the vessel is a drinking chalice of restricted format. The text is set in three lines, in Greek transliterated into Latin. Letter heights are 5–6 mm. Unfortunately the lower part of the first letter of the second line is partially lost. It is therefore not clear whether a D or P is represented, though the loop of the P of 'Pie' in the same line appears different. Two alternative readings are offered here:

> HERACLIDA PIE ZE/SES. (To Heraclides! Drink! May you live!') or
> HERACLI / PA(CE) PIE ZE / SES ('Heracles, in peace, drink, may you live')[1]

The letters are large and confidently formed, with exaggerated serifs, in a distinctive script that prefigures modern stencilling.

Collection history
Purchased in Rome by Charles Wilshere in 1870.[2]

Bibliography
Morey 1959: no.391, pl.XXXII; Smith 2000: pl.XCIII, b; Cooley 2017: 264–5, no.405.

Comment
Many other gold-glasses contain the same toast. It is used in conjunction with the full range of pictorial iconography, whether Christian, Jewish or pagan.[3]

There are several other examples of gold-glasses with centrally placed text.[4] Of these, Morey nos. 20, 22–4 are the bases of chalices sufficiently similar in vessel form and in the style of the text to be considered with this glass the likely products of a single workshop, the text possibly engraved by the same hand.[5] Within that group, no.23 is the only other gold-glass with the 'pie zeses' inscription placed centrally, not in the outer border or as a supplement to portraits or scenes: 'Luci pie zeses cum tui(s)' ('Luke, drink, live with your [family, friends or associates]!').

Related gold leaf text appears on glasses now in Paris and New York. The glass in the latter is perhaps from the same workshop: though the text is in Greek, the font is very similar.[6] Similar styles of font are also seen on a glass plaque and a possible vessel base within the British Museum's collection, both lacking protective layers of glass and both decoloured with antimony only.[7] Many other gold leaf texts encourage the subject of the toast to live, eat and drink, including nos. 22 and 24 from the group posited as the products of a single workshop.[8] Nonetheless, if the first reading is correct, the name Heraclides appears unique within the repertoire of personal names on gold-glass.[9]

A complete glass chalice of exactly similar form was taken from a fourth-century AD tomb at Idalion, Cyprus by Luigi Palma di Cesnola; it is now in the collections of the Metropolitan Museum of Art, New York.[10] The Ashmolean's glass was commissioned for a person of Greek origin or a freedman who had been given a Greek name when enslaved.[11]

The decolouring of the Ashmolean's chalice with antimony only suggests that it belongs early in the series of gold-glass vessels. It is here proposed that this glass is one of a group of chalices bearing text only, with exhortations to the dead to live, drink and/or eat. In this respect we may note the denunciation of the cult of the dead by Zeno, Bishop of Verona from about 350–80:

> ...Displeasing to God are those who... have suddenly produced martyrs for their own purposes, with carafes and chalices...[12]

Indeed, though the use of the toast 'Pie! Zeses!' continued through the repertoire of gold-glass, the chalice does not appear to have survived as a widely used vessel form to the end of the sequence. However, cats **19** and **20** offer possible examples of a Theodosian revival of medallions and small drinking cups more typical of the late third–early fourth centuries.[13]

Endnotes

1. Cooley 2017: 264.
2. Vatican City, Biblioteca Apostolica Vaticana, Vat. lat. 14249, 1870.357, written by Wilshere in Rome to de Rossi and undated within the year. However, the year may be assigned by the details given of packing ancient inscriptions on stone for shipment to England, a process described in other correspondence of 1870.
3. For example Morey 1959: nos. 2,29, 39, 41, 44, 47, 48, 57(?), 78, 89, 90, 91, 92, 96, 99, 113, 114, 118, 193, 205, 223, 236, 239, 244, 259, 261, 266, 273, 300, 302, 314, 344, 346, 366, 391, 418, 420, 426, 441 and 451.
4. Morey 1959: nos. 19–24, 129 (small medallion with outer blue layer), 202–4, 208–9, 227, 231, 233, 275, 409, 419, 420 (with portraits and radiating scenes of biblical salvation within the outer border) and 445.
5. These are in the collections of the Vatican Museum. It is hoped that XRF analysis will be carried out to see whether the decolourant and chemical composition of the raw glass clusters are close to the results obtained for the glass discussed here.
6. Morey 1959: no.420 (Paris, Petit Palais): a fragmentary text '[...]URSI/[...]NAES/[...] MAXI/[...]PIE/[...]E'; Morey 1959: no.445 (New York, MMA): 'Arbakti pie', in Greek; the recipient was named Arbaktios.
7. Howells 2015: 141–3, nos. 50 and 52. For the results of SEM–EDX analysis see Meek in Howells 2015: 35, Table 5.
8. See also Morey 1959: nos. 204, 209, 227, 233, 275 and 419.
9. It is wrongly, though tentatively, read by Morey, p.78 as 'Heraclius?'.
10. MMA 74.51.258. See above, Fig.00, p.00.
11. See above, p.00 for possible users of late Roman gold-glass.
12. Zeno, *Tractatus* 1, 25, 6, 11, quoted by Rébillard 2009, 144–5.
13. See Appendix 4a for the results and p.103–4 for discussion of the sequential dating of decolorants.

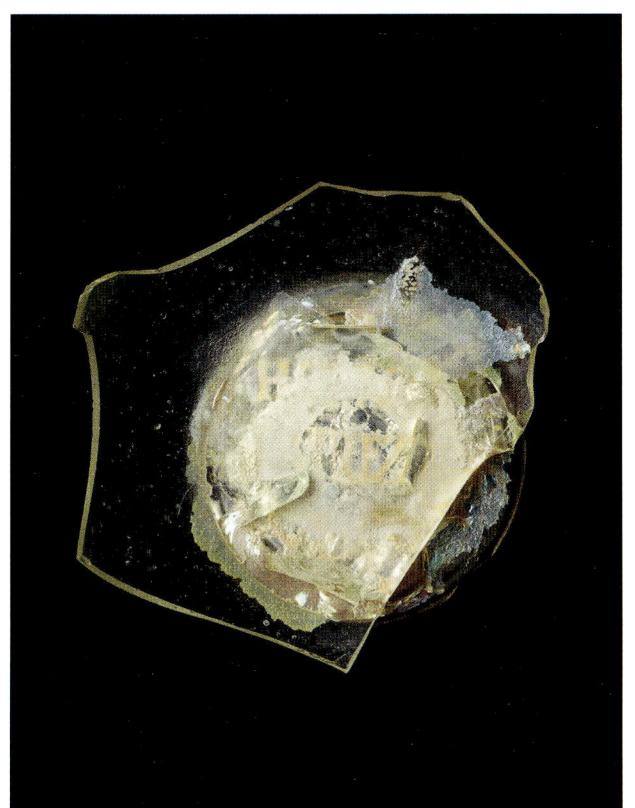

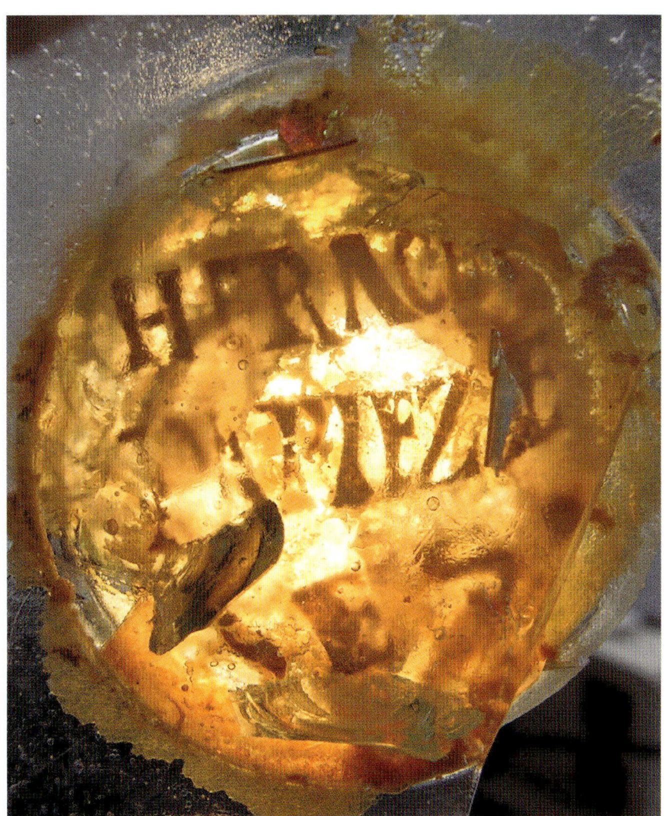

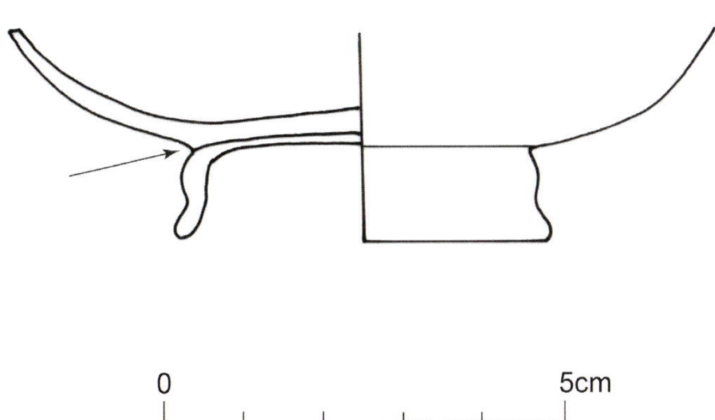

Photographs taken from above by David Gowers, 2013 (above, left) Dept of Conservation, Ashmolean Museum (above, right) Drawing by Yvonne Beadnell, 2012

2 AN 2007.17

Fragment of a glass medallion, inscribed in cut gold leaf [...] NOM [...]

Photograph: David Gowers, 2013

H. 22 mm (max.); W. 20 mm (max.)
UL. Colourless, transparent. TH. 1.5 mm
LL. Blue, transparent. TH. 1.2 mm

Decoloured with antimony and a small amount of manganese.

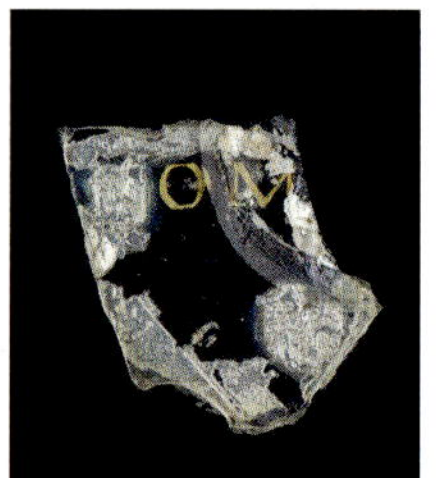

Present condition
Cast, ground and polished glass, bubble-free and of very high quality. The foil is intact. There is a hole in the lower layer of glass. The fragment is broken on all sides and the glass is chipped on the upper surface. Iridescent silver corrosion has occurred between the glass layers, due to hydration.

Gold leaf decoration
The fragment is inscribed near the broken edge '[...] N OM [...]' in elegantly formed letters 4 mm in height. Beneath the silver corrosion to the left of the letter O the ghost of the letter N is clear.[1] There is no trace of any border. Below the letter O are two flecks of gold leaf.

Collection history
Probably acquired in Rome by Charles Wilshere after 1865.

Bibliography
Morey 1959: no.370, pl.XXXII; Cooley 2017: 248–50, no.297.

Comment
The high quality of the glass and the gilded letters, combined with the ground, flat surface, suggest that this fragment comes from an inscribed medallion of third-century date. A gold-glass text containing the same sequence of letters is published by Morey no.40:

> (VI) CTO (R VIV) AS IN **NOM**INE LAURE[N]TI[I ('Victor [perhaps a personal name or denoting a victorious individual], may you live, in the name of Laurence')

The lettering style of the Ashmolean fragment corresponds very closely to Morey no.13 (Vatican Museums, Museo Sacro Cristiano Inv. No. 60697) – a clear glass plaque of which the protective layer has been almost entirely lost, if indeed it ever existed.[2] In this case the text following the broken line of the edge of the fragment, also without a border, reads '[VIV]AS MULTIS ANNIS (P)IE (*hedera*)' and, to the right of the figure, horizontally aligned, 'ZESES' ('May you live for many years. Drink! Live!'). In the field a sinuous, now headless figure turns to the left to step away from an elaborately decorated table. The table supports a celestial half-globe, decorated with stars and bound with bands; the latter are also decorated with stars and discs between bands, alternating with stars.

Furthermore the O has the same flattened upper and lower profile as the last letter of the name STRATO on the gold-glass base of a cup in the British Museum. This cup unusually honours a gladiator, shown in shaded, cut and engraved technique. It was also decoloured with antimony only.[3]

The low level of manganese present in the Ashmolean's fragment could permit an assignation to group 4: clear glass with coloured outer layers, where the clear glass was decoloured with a mix of antimony and manganese but in too random a pattern to indicate recycling. However, the fragment is here assigned to group 1, glass decoloured with antimony, as the level of manganese present coincides with the British Museum's range of glass assigned to that group, there named Type 1.[4] The high quality of the glass-making and engraving of the Ashmolean's fragment, along with the flat format and resemblance of the text to that of the evidently pagan glass in the Vatican, also indicate an early date for this piece, *c.*AD 250–330.

Endnotes
1. The letter N was not recorded by Cooley 2017: 248.
2. See also *CIL* XV, II, 1. *Instrumenta* 7048; Vopel 1899: 33, nos. 86, 81 and 84. See above, p.77 for plaques with no protective cover, intended for immediate placement in the grave.
3. Howells 2015: 135–6, no.42. For the analysis see Meek in Howells 2015: 37, Table 6.
4. Meek in Howells 2015: 30–40.

Group 2
Gold-glass decoloured with manganese only

The upper side of the base and a detail of the gold leaf scenes. Photographs by David Gowers, 2013. Drawing by Yvonne Beadnell, 2012

3 AN 2007.13
Base of an oval, gold-glass serving dish: a married couple surrounded by biblical scenes of salvation

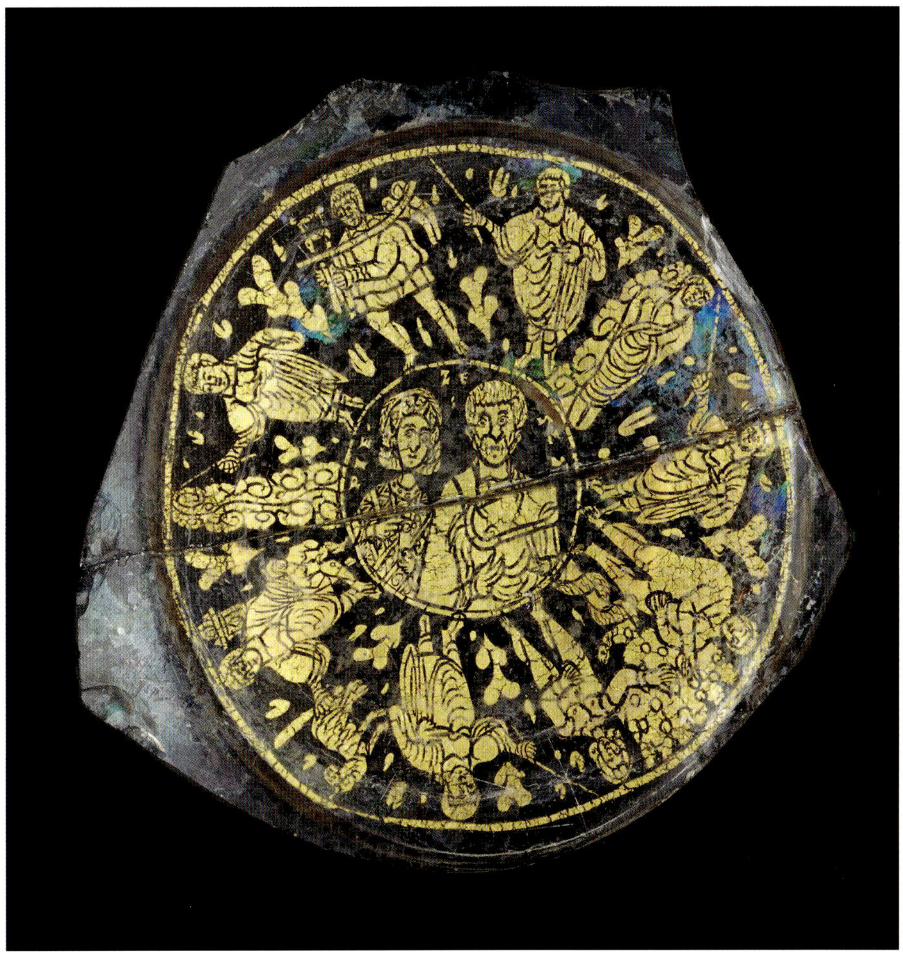

Dish: DIAM. 108 mm (max);
foot-ring: H. 50 mm; DIAM. 94 mm
UL. Colourless, transparent. TH. 1.8 mm
LL. Colourless, transparent. TH. 1.5 mm

The raw glass was decoloured with manganese only.

Present condition
The entire base survives, but has been broken in half and repaired. Even allowing for the repair, it is slightly oval in form, reflecting the shape of the vessel.[1] In one area the foot-ring has been cut back for a length of 5 cm, and in another it has been chipped away. The vessel walls of lightly bubbled, transparent glass survive to 1.5 cm (max.) around more than half of the perimeter of the base. The foil is fragmented but very legible.

Gold leaf decoration
A married couple is shown in the central medallion, the wife dressed in a stole of which one side is decorated unusually with zigzags separated by plain bands; the tunic is barely visible beneath a jewelled neck collar. Her hair is drawn back from her face and confined in radial bands, rolled back beside the chin to form a heavy plait at the crown of the head. She holds a vertical *rotulus* in both hands, and stands behind her husband, who holds out his hands in prayer. He wears a *toga contabulata* over a long-sleeved tunic.

Both faces are oval and schematic in form. The man's hair is combed down on the forehead, receding slightly at the temples. Inscribed around their heads in letters 1 mm in height is the Latinised Greek text: 'PIE ZESES' (Drink! May you live!'). The portraits and text are enclosed within a simple narrow band. Around it are depicted biblical scenes of salvation in radial arrangement. Above the couples' heads, Christ heals the paralysed man. Moving clockwise around the glass, Christ raises the mummified Lazarus from the dead. He redeems Adam and Eve, shown plucking apples from a tree, with the serpent entwined around its trunk. His Old Testament predecessors appear as well: Abraham makes preparations to sacrifice Isaac before the miraculous ram appears in front of him, the burning altar behind, and Moses strikes water from the rock. The field is filled with flowers evoking a paradisiacal landscape. Like the central medallion, the outer scenes are enclosed by a simple, narrow gold line.

Collection history
Purchased by Charles Wilshere from Tommaso and Vincenzo Capobianchi, 152 Via del Babuino, Rome between 1862 and 1865; acquired by Vincenzo Capobianchi at the 1862 public sale of the Museo del Barone Alessio Recupero, Catania, Sicily.

This glass does not appear in the papers of Gaetano Marini, Prefect of the Vatican Library and Keeper of the Vatican Archive in Castel Sant'Angelo. Garrucci 1876 notes that his sketch is taken from the original glass, once in the Museo Recupero, that he had given (i.e. published) the first time (in 1858) from a most imperfect sketch, left in the papers of Signor [Seroux] d'Agincourt.

Bibliography
Garrucci 1858: no. 3, 1–3, tav. I; Garrucci 1862/3: nos. 2, 5; Garrucci 1864: nos. 2, 4–6, tav. I; Chaffers 1866: 28, fig. 17; Garrucci 1876: 117, tav. 171, 2; Vopel 1899: nos. 126, 8, 16–7, 47, 60–1, 64, 73–6, 81 and 100; Leclercq 1923: no.470, col.1855; Webster 1929: nos. 71, 153, pl.V, 1; Bolten 1937: no.21, 60; Morey 1959: no.366, pl.XXXI; Faedo 1978: 1041–2, tav. XLIII, 2; Smith 2000: cat. 23, pl.XVIII.c; Vattuone 2000: 132, 135 unnumbered fig.; Nüsse 2008: 231, Abb. 7; Vickers 2011: 610–1, fig. 2; Howells 2015: 94, pl.64; Cooley 2017: 246–8, no.396.

Comment
The large, oval disc of gold leaf represents a married couple encircled by scenes of Christ and his Old Testament predecessors, Moses and Abraham, enacting or participating in scenes of salvation. Husband and wife appear on several glasses, leading some to see the vessels as wedding gifts.[2] However, married couples on gold-glasses are often shown with their children and the ceremony of marriage is not a feature of gold-glass decoration, as it is of sarcophagi depicting significant stages in life.[3] A funerary commemoration of married life, engaging the mourners, seems more appropriate here, combined as it is with scenes of personal salvation

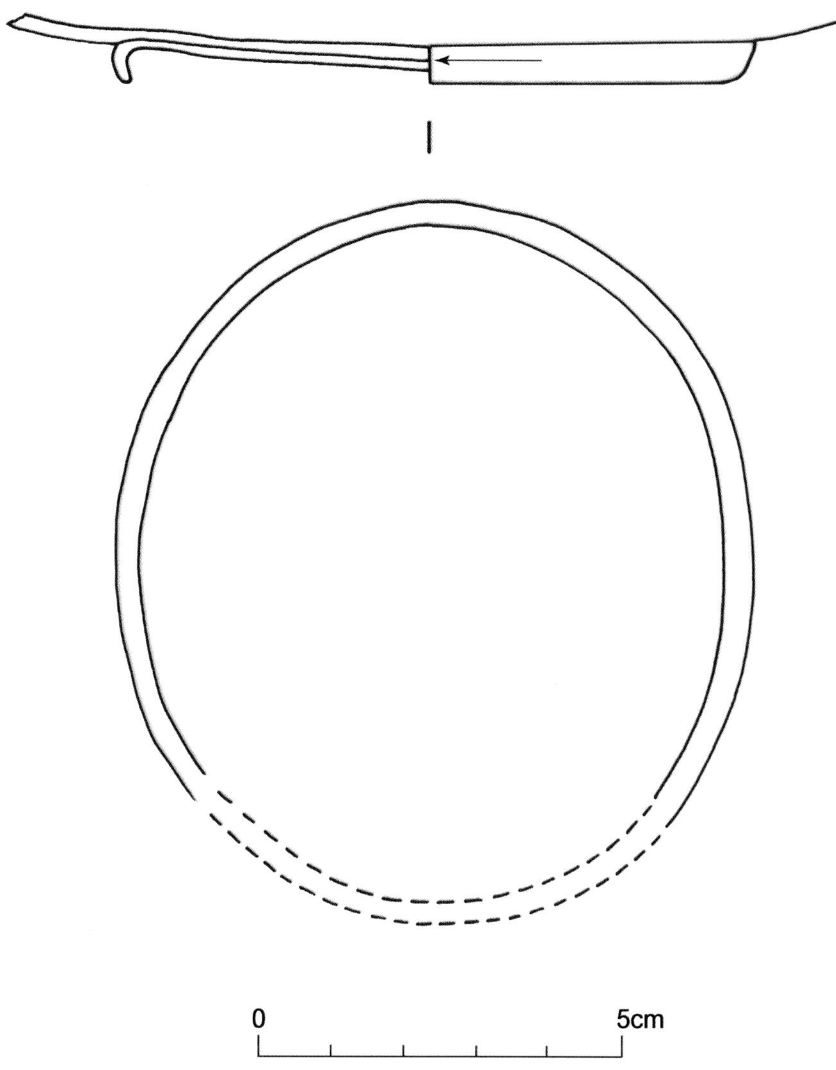

also widely known in funerary contexts, not least catacomb paintings (see further below).[4] Written within the central medallion, the inscription addressed to a single individual exhorts the deceased to celebrate his or her future eternal life in heaven.[5]

Several other gold-glasses preserve similar iconographic programmes, including another Wilshere glass, cat. **23**, and glasses in the Cimitero di Panfilo in Rome (Morey no.224), the St Ursula plaque in the British Museum, very like cat. **23** in composition (Morey no.347 = Howells 2015, no.17), the Petit Palais Collection Dutuit in Paris (Morey no.420) and the Metropolitan Museum of Art in New York (MMA inv. 16.174.2, Morey no.448, who reports that it was found in the catacomb of San Callisto). The Vatican and New York glasses are the closest in size to the Wilshere glass (respectively 10.5 cm and 10.2 cm in diameter). The New York glass is laid out in a similar fashion to the Wilshere glass and also features a married couple in the central medallion, although the Wilshere glass depicts more scenes.

However, when combined with the bust portraits in the centre, the sequence of scenes on this glass not only represents scenes of salvation. It also replicates the miracles of deliverance invoked by the prayer used in the ritual for the committal of the deceased's soul, the *Commendatio animae*.[6] Scholars have previously noticed the general correlation between the prayer and early Christian artworks, including the gold-glasses, but have not specifically connected this group of glasses with Old and New Testament scenes to the text of the prayer.[7] While the earliest textual evidence for the prayer does not appear to predate the fourth century, the Wilshere glass and related works must be taken as evidence for the use of a version of the prayer in practice in Rome in the fourth century. The glasses also offer proof of the prayer's flexibility, presenting different combinations of scenes of salvation in a different order than in the *Commendatio* prayer.

The biblical scenes around the edge are consistent with other early Christian narrative cycles in the catacombs, including catacomb paintings and sarcophagi,[8] as well as on other gold-glasses. At the bottom of the glass Christ appears as a magician, redeeming Adam and Eve, whose sin of eating from the Tree of Knowledge is represented (Genesis 3).[9] To the right, Christ resurrects Lazarus (John 11); he is wrapped in a shroud and rests against a rocky hill instead of his tomb – an iconography unique to the glasses and perhaps intended to balance the scene of Moses striking the rock.[10] Next Christ heals the paralysed man, who stands up and carries his bed on his back (Matthew 9: 1–8; Mark 2: 3–5; Luke 5: 18–20) as he does on the glass in New York (Morey no.448). The final two scenes illustrate Old Testament events: Moses, whose appearance is identical to that of Christ, strikes water from the rock (Numbers 20: 8–22),[11] and Abraham, about to sacrifice his son Isaac, hears God's voice and sees the sacrificial ram (Genesis 22: 1–19).[12]

While the scenes are not laid out in a specific order, their selection and relationship to one another are significant, and serve to connect the Old and New Testaments through typology. Moses' appearance as a prophetic, salvific figure prefigures the birth of Christ,[13] as Isaac's near-sacrifice prefigures his crucifixion,[14] while Christ appears three times as magician (echoed by Moses-as-magician), creating a visual rhythm that drives the exegesis of the images. Based upon the use of manganese alone as a decolorant, the choice of iconography and the slight roughness of its style, this oval glass dish was probably made in the middle years of the fourth century. Its shape and potential size suggest that the dish may have been designed for serving fish, though there is no reference to fish in the iconography of the gold leaf.

Endnotes

1. For a complete oval glass vessel from the Fayum, Egypt see above, Fig. 50: Corning Museum of Glass CMG 75.1.113.
2. For example Morey 1959: nos. 1, 7, 9, 39, 41, 43, 59, 91–4, 98–9, 113, 225, 259, 315–6, 337 etc. Wedding gifts: Painter in Harden 1987: 281, no.156, where Eros appears between a man and a woman. Howells 2015: 122–3, no.36 offers a cautious reading.
3. Cameron 1996: 298; Reinsburg 2006: 75–85 for the depiction of marriage on sarcophagi.
4. Meredith 2015.
5. Ferrua 1974 discusses the formula.
6. See above, p.oo.
7. For example Bisconti 1996, 92; Vanni 2003, 133.
8. For example the Sarcophagus of Adelphia. See above, chapter 5, fig. 2.2.2.
9. Also on Morey 1959: nos. 47, 420. On Christ as magician see Mathews 1993: 54–91; Jefferson 2014.
10. For example Morey 1959: nos. 44, 108, 157, 260; also Partyka 1993, 69.
11. Also on another Wilshere glass, AN2007.35, and Morey nos. 142–3, 312, 421.
12. Also on Morey 1959: nos. 71, 349, 395, 436; generally see Smith 1922; Jensen, in Spier 2007: 78–83.
13. Matthews 1993: 54–91.
14. Tertullian, *Adversus Iudaeos* 10.6 and 13.20–2; Paulinus, *Epistula* 29. For other examples see Jensen in Spier 2007: 85 n.20.

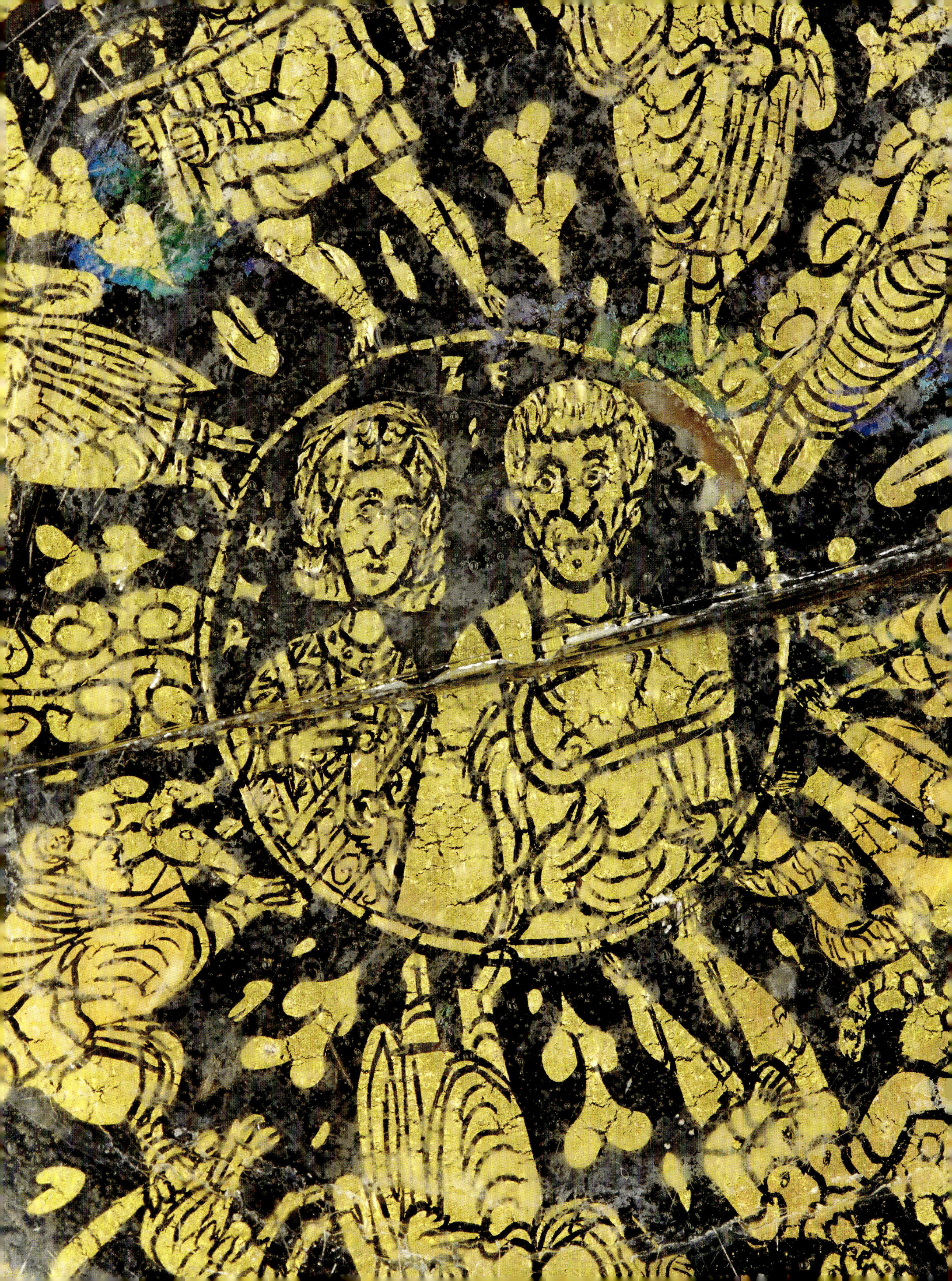

4 AN 2007.25

Fragment of a gold-glass bowl: the sleeved right arm of a woman, enclosed by an outer band inscribed in Latin

H. 43 mm (max.); W. 33 mm (max.)
UL. Colourless, transparent. TH. 4.0 mm
LL. Colourless, transparent. TH. 1.1 mm

Raw glass decoloured with manganese only.

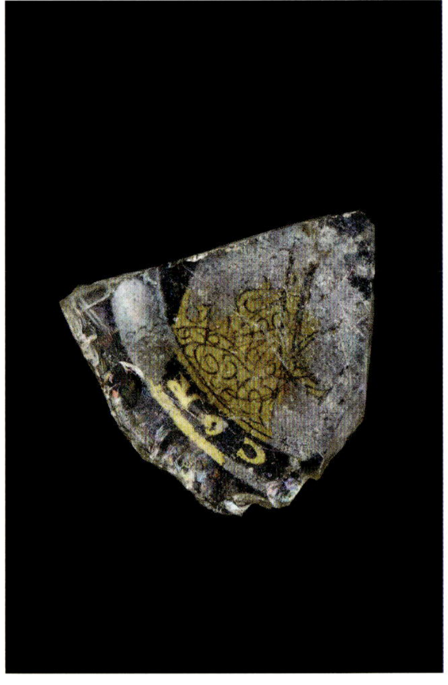

Photograph by David Gowers, 2013

Present condition
The fragment is broken on all sides. Only spurs remain of the cut-down foot-ring and the upwardly curving wall of the vessel. There is grey iridescent corrosion on both faces of the slightly fragmented foil, and an iridescent film on the upper glass surface.

Gold leaf decoration
On the fragment is preserved the lower part of the bust of a woman wearing an intricately embroidered mantle enfolding her right arm. Around the lower edge of the bust is a double-band border bearing the Latin inscription '[DIGNITAS AMI]CORV[M]' in letters 2 mm in height. The letters RV are ligatured.

Collection history
Purchased by Charles Wilshere from Tommaso and Vincenzo Capobianchi, 152 Via del Babuino, Rome; previously acquired by Vincenzo Capobianchi at the 1862 public sale of the Museo Recupero, Catania, Sicily. Acquired by Baron Alessandro Recupero in Rome from the brother and heir to the Vatican's curator of relics Abbot Severini between the latter's death in 1800 and 1803, when Recupero died.

Bibliography
Garrucci 1862: 8, no.XII; Morey 1959: no.378, pl.XXXII; Vattuone 2000: 135, unnumbered fig.; Cooley 2017: 255–7, no.401.

Comment
While a number of gold-glass vessels inscribed 'dignitas amicorum' within a double-band border have survived (Morey includes 17 in his corpus),[1] only one (cat. **21**, of later date) includes a figure of a woman wearing an embroidered mantle. In that example the figure is standing in prayer, rather than apparently portrayed as a bust, as here. Almost certainly the woman shown in this fragment would have appeared alongside her husband. The drapery has a very similar pattern to Morey 92– 4, especially to no.93, inscribed 'MAXIMA VIVAS CVM DEXTRO' ('Maxima, may you live with Dexter'). With her richly embroidered mantle the woman probably also wore an elaborate necklace or jewelled collar.

The phrase *dignitas amicorum* is difficult to translate. It may be intended to place both viewer and the commemorated individual within a community of friends of equal status (Cooley, 2017). In other examples (*ICUR* III no.8482a; *ILCV* 866b/d, 877), the phrase is combined with the exhortation 'drink, may you live', so we may understand it within a context of commensality. Mostly the phrase is associated with scenes of Christ crowning a pair of martyrs who appear facing each other, usually dressed in omophorion stoles. Morey 274, in the Museo di Castelvecchio, Verona, suggests a more complex image of drapery (not visible to Morey), possibly of seated or kneeling figures of saints or disciples, but not apparently representing an embroidered mantle or stole.[2] Often, however, the inscription includes an injunction, possibly directed to the deceased individual, to live happily in Christ, live with your family and to drink; the text could thus be associated with funeral feasts, if it did not actually form part of the toast. The text has sometimes been misunderstood as a reference to the dignity or value of friendship, and consequently seen as part of a toast, but *amicorum* evidently refers to a group of friends.[3] The identity of such a group is unclear. It may refer to the martyrs often portrayed with the text, but could also be a reference to a burial club.[4]

This base has been dated to AD 350–75, a range that would fit with the use of manganese alone as a decolourant.[5]

Endnotes
1. Morey 1959: nos. (cat.)**37**, 45, 47, (cat.)**49**, (cat.)**58**, 187, (cat.)**236**, (cat.)**241**, 271, 274, 285, 314, 329(?) 365 (cat. **26**), 379 (cat. **21**), 388 (cat. **23**), 390 (cat. **5**).
2. 'infiltration makes design illegible' (Morey 1959: 48).
3. More complete inscriptions run as follows:
-'DIGNITAS AMICORUM VIVAS CUM TUIS ZESES' (Morey 1959: 37)
-'DIGNTIAS AMICORUM VIVAS CUM TUIS FELICITER' (Morey 1959: 45)
-'DIG(nit)AS (a)MICORUM, PIE (zeses)' (Morey 1959: 47)
-'(Di)GNITAS AMICORUM PIE ZES(es cum tuis omni)BUS BIBAS' (Morey 1959: 49)
-'DIGNITAS AMICORUM VIVAS; CUM TUIS FELICITER' (Morey 1959: 187)
-'DIGNITAS AMICORUM VIVAS CUM TUIS FELICITER; PIE' (Morey 1959: 241)
-'DIGNITAS AMICORUM PIE ZESES VIVAS' (Morey 1959: 236)
-'(Digni)TAS AMICORUM, PIE' (Morey 1959: 274)
-'DIGNITAS AMICORM VIV[...]AS IM PACE DEI ZESES [...]' (Morey 1959: 285)
-'BICULIUS DIGN(itas a)MICORUM VIVAS, PIE ZESES' (Morey 1959: 314)
-'[..] DIGNITAS AMICORUM VIVAT(is) [...] (in pa)CE DEI ZE(ses)' (Morey 1959: 388, illegible now, recorded by Garrucci)
-'DENGNETAS AMICOROM ELARES EN CRISTO' (Morey 1959: 450).
4. Grig 2004 argues for grandees of the Church.
5. Faedo Group 3 = Morey 1959: 379 (cat. 21) and 59; see also Nüsse 2008: Abb. 11. For a commentary on the likely date of 350–75, drawn by Faedo from the iconography and the inscription, see Faedo 1978: 236.

5 AN 2007.37

Fragment of a gold-glass bowl or plate: part of a figure and a fragmentary Latin inscription

H. 30 mm (max.); W. 13 mm (max.)
UL. Pale green, transparent. TH. 5 mm
LL. Pale green, transparent. TH. 7 mm

Photograph by David Gowers, 2013.

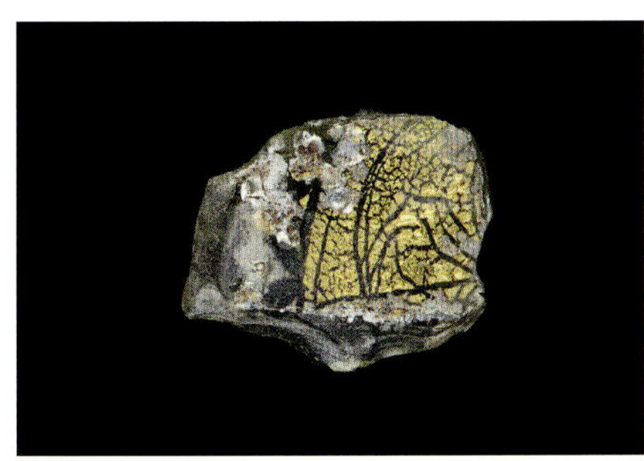

Present condition

The fragment is broken and chipped all around. Part of the cut-down foot-ring is preserved below the unusually thick base. The glass is bubbled; the upper surface is polished. The foil is fragmented with iridescent silvery corrosion on the interface, obscuring the inscription and part of the figure.

Gold leaf decoration

The fragment probably represents the proper right shoulder of a draped figure. It may possibly be seated in a chair with a curved back support or wearing a flowing shoulder-back mantle, like the figure of Christ raising Lazarus in the grozed base of a cup now in the Vatican Museums, Museo Sacro Cristiano.[1] On the outer edge are remains of the letters TA and the edge of a curved letter after A, perhaps S. The double line at the left of the figured gold leaf may represent the inside edge of the border.

Collection history

Probably acquired by Charles Wilshere in Rome after 1865.

Bibliography

Morey 1959: no.390, pl.XXXII.

Comment

From the position of the text, it is likely that the fragment belonged to the left side of the gold leaf scene. The figure portrayed in gold leaf is likely to be a saint or a martyr, or possibly a character from a biblical scene (compare cat. **3**). The clothing suggests a religious subject: the surviving folds do not match known gold-glass portraits of togate male figures, and females, who are usually placed on the left of the scene, are mostly dressed in elaborately decorated mantles. A religious subject is also suggested by the way in which the walls of the glass have been cut away to form a medallion, and by the thickness of the lower layer. In this context it is probable that the text, at least in part, may be reconstructed as '[DIGNI]TA(S)? [AMICORUM]' ('the dignity of friends'); for commentary on this phrase see above, cat. **4**.

Endnotes

1. Morey 1959: no.77, pl.XIII.

6 AN 2007.40

Fragment of a gold-glass plate or bowl: standing figures and fish swimming in turquoise water

H. 35 mm (max.); W. 33 mm (max.)
UL. Colourless, transparent. TH. 3–4 mm
LL. Colourless, transparent. TH. 1 mm

Raw glass decoloured with manganese only.

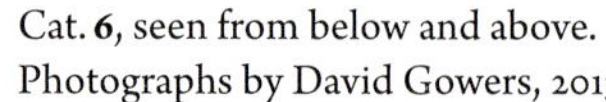

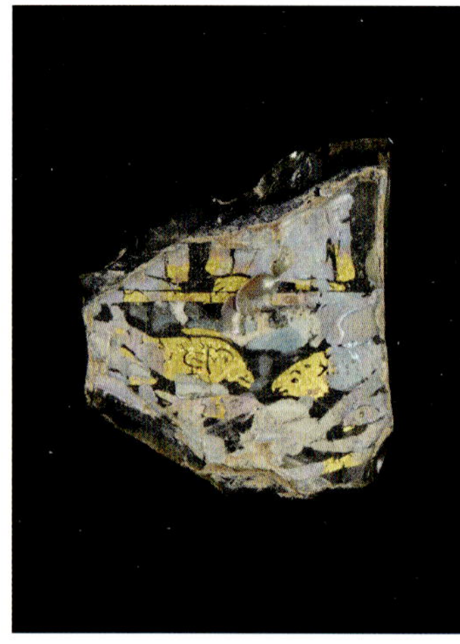

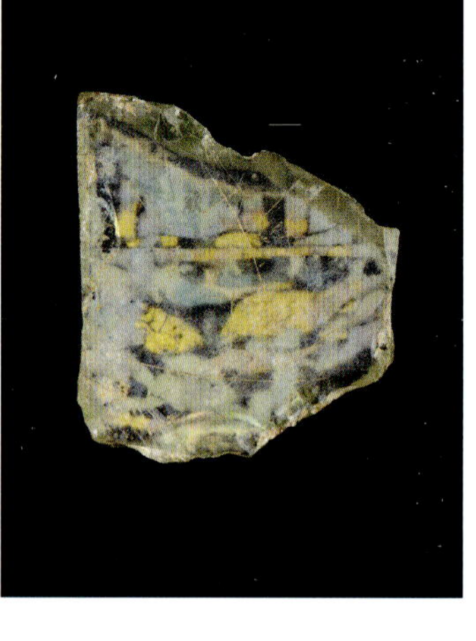

Cat. **6**, seen from below and above. Photographs by David Gowers, 2013

Present condition

The fragment is broken on all sides. Its surface is concave; a curved line of gold foil at the base of the fragment shows that it probably comes from the centre of a dish. The edge of the fragment shows a pronounced curvature. The lower layer has been chipped away beneath the upper, which has few bubbles; consequently there is no sign of a base-ring. Silvery iridescence on the interface obscures parts of the decoration, cut and incised in gold foil. The foil is intact except for the borders, which are fragmented.

Gold leaf and painted enamel decoration

The scene is divided into two zones by a narrow, horizontal line of foil. Above are the splayed feet of two standing figures, standing on the baseline. Both wear long cloaks which, together with their stance, suggest that they may have been shown at prayer. Below are two large fish, perhaps a tunafish or Nile perch on the left and a carp on the right. Two smaller fish swim below them. The water in which the fish swim is painted turquoise. The scene is enclosed with a single narrow band curving around the base of the fragment.

Collection history

Purchased by Charles Wilshere from Tommaso and Vincenzo Capobianchi, 152 Via del Babuino, Rome between 1862 and 1865; acquired by Vincenzo Capobianchi at the 1862 public sale of the Museo del Barone Alessio Recupero, Catania, Sicily.
This glass does not appear in the papers of Gaetano Marini, Prefect of the Vatican Library and Keeper of the Vatican Archive in Castel Sant'Angelo.

Bibliography

Garrucci 1862/3: no.12, 8; Garrucci 1864: no.10, 90–1, tav. X; Garrucci 1876: 146, no.10, tav. CLXXIX; Vopel 1899: no.441, 111; Leclercq 1923: no.281, col.1842; Morey 1959: no.393, tav. XXXII (pictured as 376, pl.XXXII, conflated with cat. **16**); Vattuone 2000: 135, unnumbered fig.

Comment

In the plates of his catalogue Morey confuses the description of cat. **16** with the image of this glass, which shows at least two pairs of confronted fish swimming in turquoise water and watched by human observers.[1] Based on their shapes, the larger fish on the right appears to be a carp, with a pronounced dorsal fin towards its tail, and the fish on the left a tunafish or Nile perch, with a distinctive mouth. Tunafish or Nile perch and carp were considered delicacies in the Roman world. The former are large sea and Nile river fish while the latter, native to the River Danube, were domesticated in that region by the Romans and transported around the Mediterranean – a practice that continued into the sixth century, as reported by Cassiodorus (*Variae*, 4).[2]

If the line at the base of the fragment is correctly interpreted as the bottom edge of a central medallion, then the fragment must have come from a large oval dish, perhaps used for serving fish. However, the line might represent the outer edge of a semicircular pond in which the fish were kept. Either way, the size of the complete image would have been substantial. It may be the case that the fragment was cut down to preserve and reuse the fish as a Christian symbol within the catacombs, as appears to have been the case with cat. **16**. The figures, then, even if restored as *orantes*, were not necessarily Christian. Other gold-glasses also preserve blue pigment for water, including a gold-glass bowl base in the Metropolitan Museum of Art, which represents the Roman god Oceanus pouring forth the blue waters of the ocean.[4]

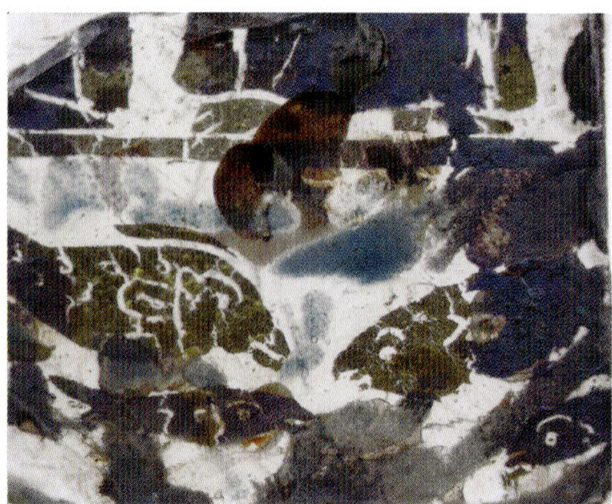

Detail of the feet of the figures and the fish. Photograph by Dana Norris, 2012

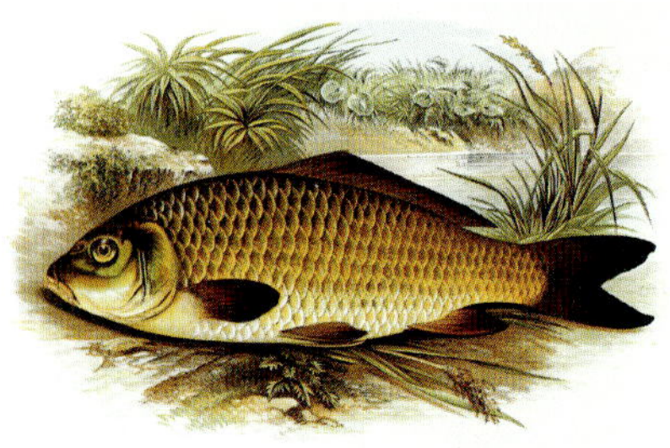

Cyprinus carpio (carp), engraving by Alexander Francis Lydon (1836–1917). Alexander Francis Lydon [Public domain], via Wikimedia Commons

Endnotes

1. Though both glasses are illustrated pl.XXXII, nos. 376 and 380, the description for no.380 corresponds to a third fragment, cat. **20**. The text entry for no.393, which correctly gives the dimensions , shape and lack of foot-ring for this fragment, is not illustrated, as Morey regarded the gold leaf as illegible due to iridescence.
2. Balon 1995: 28–34. On carp see further cat. **16**.
3. MMA 17.194.2343: Smith 2000: cat. 351, pl.LXXXVII.d.

Photograph by David Gowers, 2013

7 AN 2007.36

Fragment of a gold-glass medallion, plate or bowl: a head and raised left arm of two female figures, perhaps personifications of Rome, Constantinople or Ecclesia (the Church)

H. 28 mm (max.); W. 25 mm (max.)
UL. Colourless, transparent. TH. 3 mm
LL. Colourless, transparent. TH. 1.2 mm

The raw glass was decoloured with manganese only.

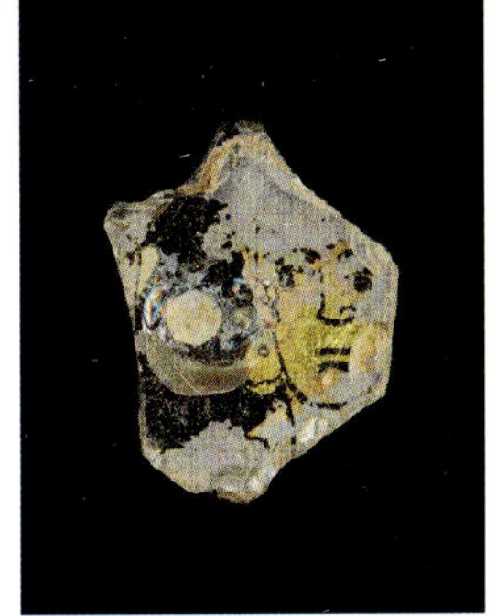

Present condition

The concave fragment of glass is broken on all sides, with visible stress fractures. The lightly bubbled glass is of high quality, with both surfaces polished. Purplish silver iridescence on the interface obscures part of the gold leaf decoration. There is no trace of a foot-ring.

Gold leaf decoration

The face of a woman is shown, her head slightly turned to gaze to her right. She has elaborately curled and wound hair, but is unveiled. The folds of a mantle appear beside the neck. Parts of the raised right and middle fingers of the proper left hand of a missing, adjacent figure are visible at the left edge of the fragment. In between the head and hand is a circular blob of gold leaf.

Collection history

Acquired by Charles Wilshere in Rome, probably after 1865.

Bibliography

Morey 1959: no.389, pl.XXXII.

Editor's Note: the shape of the fragment illustrated as 389, pl.XXXII does not correspond to this fragment, which is closer to the illustration of Morey 390. Both images are of very poor quality. However, the dimensions given in the text entry for 389 are correct. Morey did not see any gold leaf decoration on this fragment; perhaps he was working only from the photographs.

Comment

The partially turned pose and the presence of a proper left, not a right, raised arm indicate that a second figure was present, to the left of the preserved fragment. The glass appears similar to representations of Maria at prayer with Agnes.[1] One or more discs, some of which evidently represent fruit, also appear in the background of such scenes. However, there is no trace of an inscription, to be expected in the portrayal of a saint, nor is there any sign of a veil. These discrepancies, along with the turned gaze of the surviving figure, suggest that this was not a scene of prayer, as has been supposed. Instead it is likely that the fingers on the left of this fragment belong to the raised left hand of the missing second figure, raised not in prayer but to hold a staff or sceptre.

Compare the reconstructed base of a gold-glass plate in the Vatican (Morey 90):[2]

two female figures seated frontal on faldstools, with identical **coiffures of rectangular plait behind the head projecting at nape of neck**, wearing necklace or ornamental collar, sleeveless tunic girdled at waist, buttoned on shoulders, and striped with red, and palla, dotted to indicate embroidery or jewels, draped over the knees. **Each holds in left hand a staff resting on ground**, adorned with alternating red and green dots to indicate jewels, and in the right a green orb outlined and banded with gold. The diadem or mural crown discernible on the head of the figure to left may be assumed for the other, though obscured by film [This is not visible in Morey's photograph, pl.XV]. In front of, and between the seated figures, a woman kneels to right, wearing a similar necklage (*sic*) or collar over a dalmatic in deep red striped with gold; her hair is waved over the forehead and bound with a fillet. She extends with both hands a patera painted green. In field to left and right, a leaf-spray.

Editor's Note: Quoted text in **bold** describes features directly comparable with the Ashmolean fragment. The comment in square brackets is added.

Morey does not identify the figures, evidently intended either as pagan deities or personifications, perhaps of cities (Rome and Constantinople?) or of the Church and the Synagogue (Ecclesia and Synagoga).[3] Though Morey describes the figures as frontal, their heads are inclined towards the kneeling woman between them; the inclination of the figure to the right is identical to that of the surviving figure on this fragment. On the present fragment, the impassive gaze and shading below the mouth suggest a personification or deity, drawn in the Hellenistic Greek tradition.

The decolouration of this fragment with manganese alone suggests a date in the middle decades of the fourth century AD.

Endnotes

1. Garrucci 1876: pl.191.2 is especially close. See also images of Agnes alone, pl.191. 1 and 191. 3.
2. Morey 1959: 21–2, no.90. Ssee also de Rossi, *Inv*.293; Garrucci 1876: pl.CCI,4; *CIL* XV, II, I (*instrumentum*), 7051 for the funerary toast ANIMA/DULCI/SPIEZ(eses) – ('Sweet soul, drink! May you live!') and Vopel 1899: no.61, pp. 9, 27ff, 40, 80 and 83.
3. Female personifications of cities continued to be popular in the fourth century and beyond. These included in Rome the find spot of gilded silver statuettes representing Rome, Constantinople, Antioch and Alexandria as crowned women which apparently decorated a chair, forming part of the Esquiline Treasure, BM BEP 1866,1229.21–4; see Shelton 1981: pls.35–7; Bühl 1995: 107–42. On personifications of the Church (Ecclesia) as a female figure, most notably seen in the fifth-century wall mosaics of Santa Sabina on the Aventine in Rome, see Rowe 2011: 47–51.

8 AN 2007.33

Fragment from the centre of a gold-glass dish: head of Christ with nimbus

H. 15 mm (max.); DIAM. 24 mm
UL. Colourless, transparent. TH. 1.5 mm
LL. Colourless, transparent. TH. 1.0 mm

Raw glass decoloured with manganese only.

Photograph by David Gowers, 2013 (above). Detailed microscopic view showing differential cracking of the gold leaf by Dana Norris, 2012 (below).

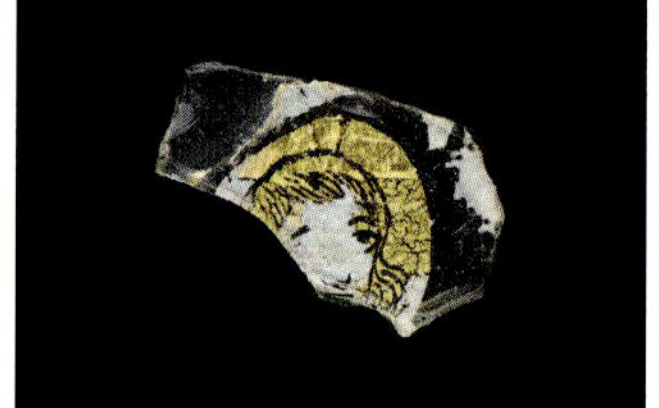

Present condition

The very thin glass is lightly bubbled, the upper surface polished. The foil is densely fragmented in the lower part of the image and more broadly so above, with a clear dividing line between the two (see detailed image above). This suggests that the foil was applied in two layers, probably after the vessel slipped as it was removed from the annealing oven (Chapter 4, p.93, fig. 43).

Gold leaf decoration

Christ is shown as a young man in three-quarters view, with large, rounded eyes and long hair falling to the surviving proper left side of the neck – a style described by Garrucci as Galilean. The strands of hair are carefully defined. Beyond the asymmetrical halo are the remains of the edge of the circular central medallion.

Collection history

Very likely purchased by Charles Wilshere from Vincenzo Capobianchi, Via del Babuino 152, Rome. According to Garrucci the fragment was still with Vincenzo Capobianchi when he was compiling volume III of *Storia dell'Arte Cristiana*, published in 1876.

Bibliography

Garrucci 1876: III, 161, no.7, with tav. CLXXXVII; Vopel 1899: no.448, p.111; Leclercq 1923: no.288, col.1842; Morey 1959: no.386, pl.XXXII; Vattuone 2000: p.136, unnumbered fig.

Comment

Most probably this fragment formed the centre of a shallow bowl decorated with radiating figures of saints: compare cats **10** and **11**, both fragmentary, with central busts of Christ. In these representations the figure of Christ varies, with or without nimbus, beard or long hair.[1] A date in the middle decades of the fourth century seems likely for this fragment, which was decoloured with manganese alone.

Endnotes

1. Other representations of figures of Christ centrally placed within a circular medallion include Morey 1959: nos. 190 (nimbus, hair unclear but not apparently falling on shoulders), 235 (beardless with long hair, no nimbus), 291 (beardless, details of hair unclear), 307 (= Howells 2015: 81, no.12, beardless with long hair but no nimbus), (cat. 11, fragmentary) and 363 (cat. 26, fragmentary).

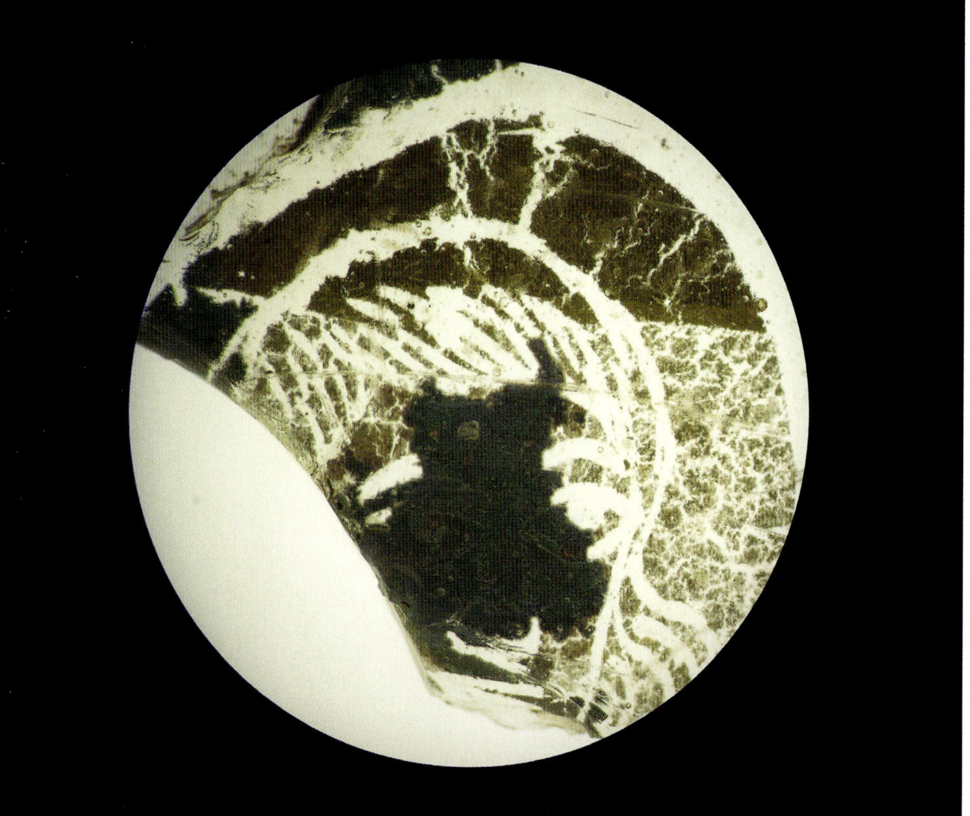

9 AN 2007.9

Base of a glass vessel with foot ring: standing male figure in tunic and fringed mantle, with sheep

Photograph from above by David Gowers, 2013. Drawing made for Dr Marlia Mango in 1987 by the late Rupert Cook (above). Scaled drawing by Yvonne Beadnell, 212 (below).

DIAM. 87 mm (max.)
UL. Pale green, transparent. TH. 1.7 mm
LL. Pale green, transparent. TH. 1.7 mm

The raw glass was decoloured with manganese only.

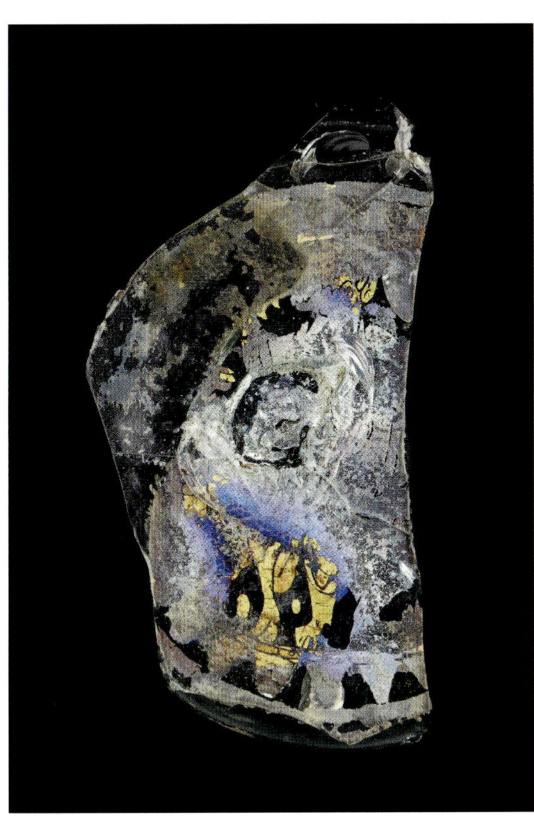

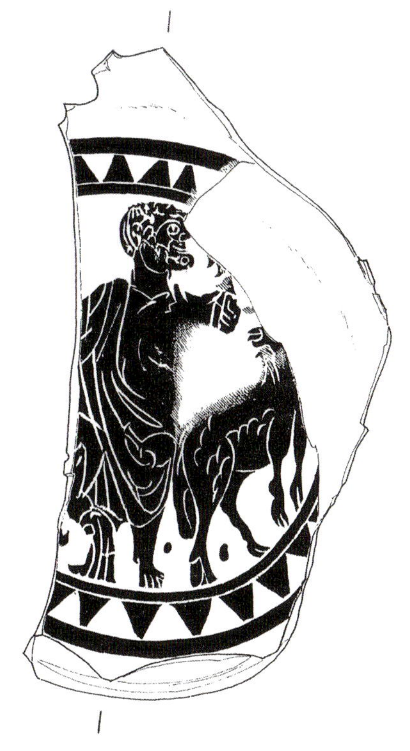

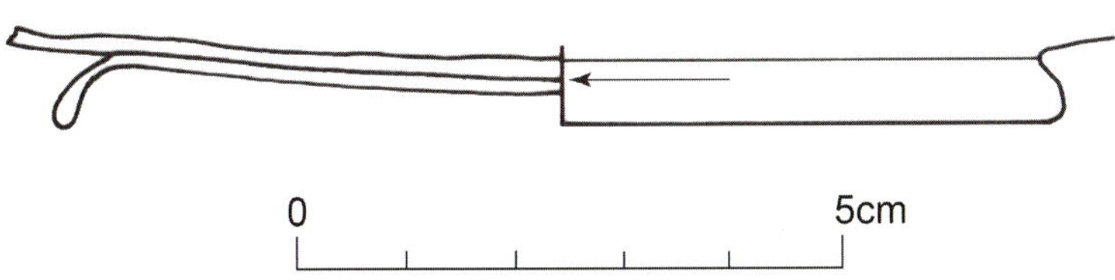

Present condition

The right half and part of the left half of the base and most of the walls are broken off. A 40 mm length of foot-ring remains on one side, along with a tiny spur of wall, 1 cm in height, on another. The surviving fragment of the vessel has horizontal cracks across the centre and the lower layer of glass on the base has a hole (10 x 15 mm) broken off from beneath the upper layer on the left side. The existing gold foil is weathered and slightly fragmented, and has formed a silvery-purple iridescence. The glass is relatively free from bubbles.

Gold leaf decoration

This piece preserves the image of a standing male figure with a jutting beard and curly hair, wearing a tunic and fringed mantle. The figure's head is turned to the left, where stands a fat-tailed ram in left profile with its head reversed (paraphrased from Morey, p.61). The image was drawn for Garrucci in the 1870s (1876: Tav. 169, 5) and (from the underside of the glass, so reversed) for Marlia Mango in 1987, when it was in much better condition than it is today (above). It is bordered with a double band enclosing serrations. There is no sign of any text.

Collection history

Garrucci states that he acquired the glass in Rome at an unspecified date, and it was by the time of writing (i.e. before the publication of volume III of *Storia dell'Arte Cristiana* in 1876) in the collection of Charles Wilshere.[1] A likely time for the sale is 1871–2, a period when Wilshere was actively helping Garrucci, then suffering hardship following the collapse of the papal states. However, there is no mention of the acquisition in the surviving letters of Wilshere to Garrucci, now kept in the Biblioteca di San Luigi, Posilippo.

Bibliography

Garrucci 1876: 113, no.5, tav. CLXIX; Vopel 1899: no.182, pp.9, 16, 61, 102; Leclercq 1923: no.16, col.1827; Morey 1959: no.362, p.61, pl.XXXI; Vattuone 2000: 135 (as no known provenance).

Comment

Garrucci interpreted the glass as representing Abraham's sacrifice of Isaac, with the former's head turned up and to his right to hear the command of God, while the ram to his right turns to look at him. Isaac's left leg appears in front of Abraham's left foot. By the time of compilation of Morey's catalogue, the glass had succumbed to 'heavy infiltration of iridescent film', and the unidentified figure was described as 'seated, frontal, in tunic and *pallium*, head with short beard turned left; to left a sheep standing in profile left, head reversed'. However, the drawing of 1987 clearly shows a standing figure, with jutting beard and tousled hair, looking up as if to hear a command from above, with a fat-tailed sheep beside him.The clothing recalls that of the biblical figures appearing in the scenes of salvation on cat. **3**.

The image of sheep and a shepherd appears on four other gold-glasses, with the shepherd either seated or standing.[2] On the gold-glasses, Christ as the Good Shepherd is usually shown standing, bearing a sheep on his shoulders.[3] A representation of Christ as the Good Shepherd may have been intended here, but Garrucci's interpretation of the scene as the moment of divine intervention in Abraham's sacrifice of Isaac cannot be discounted.

The 'double-band border inclosing serration', as Morey categorises this form of border, is an uncommon type. Another example is Morey 43 (Vatican Museum), which represents a couple and also lacks text. The decolouration of the raw glass with manganese only suggests a date in the middle decades of the fourth century.

Endnotes

1. Garrucci 1876: 113, pl.169, no.5: 'Frammento acquistato da me in Roma, ora del Signor Wilshere'.
2. Morey 1959: nos. 11 and 257: Vatican and Florence, Museo Archeologico Nazionale, shepherd seated facing right and frontal; 236 and 394: Rome, Galleria Sangiorgi and Ashmolean Museum, Oldfield 44, shepherd standing.
3. Morey 1959: nos. 14, 455, 57, 101, 118 (all Vatican Museum); 220, 224 (Rome, Cimitero di Panfilo); 239 (Catania, Museo di Castello Ursino); 245, 247 (Florence, Museo Archeologico Nazionale) and 273 (Verona, Museo di Castelvecchio). On the motif of the Good Shepherd, known from pagan and Christian contexts, see Taylor 2002; on the long history of the motif see Freeman 2015.

10 AN 2007.8

Segment of the base of a gold-glass vessel: a central head of Christ, surrounded by radially arranged figures of saints

DIAM. 66 mm (max.)
UL. Pale green, transparent. TH. 28 mm
ML. Pale yellowish-green, transparent. TH. 28 mm
LL. Pale green, transparent. TH. 0.9 mm

The gold leaf is set between the middle and lower layers of lightly bubbled glass.
The raw glass was decoloured with manganese only. It appears that the glass-maker was dissatisfied with the protective layer (here ML), and blew a second upper layer (UL) to cover it. The condition of this piece, with a chip lost from the lower surface before 1987, allowed characterisation of a chip of glass by ICP-MS analysis (see Appendix 4a).

Present condition

A small spur of foot-ring is preserved. The edge of the vessel has been broken away and chipped back along the perimeter of the base. The top layer of glass is broken away at the centre. Iridescence has formed on all three layers. The foil is intact, except for the single ring outer border, where it is fragmented.

Gold leaf decoration

The short-haired, beardless head of Christ appears in a central medallion, identified with the Latin inscription 'CRIS([TVS]' in letters 2 mm in height.

On the outer edge of the medallion's single ring border stand radially arranged saints, separated by large rolled scrolls (*rotuli*). Originally there were eight; the surviving figure of 'SVSTVS' (Pope Sixtus) is conventionally shown as a youthful philosopher in Greek dress, his face unshaven, his forearms outstretched. His name appears to his right above the *rotulus* in letters 3 mm in height, beyond which the right foot of the adjacent figure stands on the outer edge of the central medallion. The end of the name of the saint to his left is preserved as 'VS'; [Timothe]us was conjectured by Garrucci as a restored full name, as he often appears next to Sixtus.

Collection history

Acquired in Rome by Charles Wilshere before 1876. Its acquisition, but not the date of purchase by Wilshere, is noted by Garrucci.

Bibliography

Garrucci 1876: 113, no.3 with tav. 169; Vopel 1899: no.311, pp.8, 15, 59, 85, 107; Leclercq 1923: no.150, col.1834; Webster 1929: no.78, p.153; Ladner 1941: no.7, p.33; Morey 1959: no.361, pl.XXXI; Smith 2000: Pls.L, d; Vattuone 2000, p.132, 134–5, unnumbered fig.; Cooley 2017: 236–8, no.392.

Comment

This is one of a series of gold-glass vessels depicting Christ surrounded by saints, replicating the design of domes and semi-domes in churches.[1] Another inspiration for the design could have been calendar and season mosaics, the order of the saints perhaps reflecting that of their feast days (see above, p.121). For comparable designs in other gold-glass bases, see cat. **11**, where the bust of Christ is also beardless, but has long hair. Particularly close to the figure of Christ on this glass are Morey nos. 105 (Vatican Museum), 235 (Parma, Museo delle antichità), 240 (Florence, Museo Archeologico Nazionale), 291 (Pesaro, Museo Archeologico Oliveriano) and 307 (London, British Museum).[2] The full-length figures of saints alternate with *rotuli* (scrolls) or other devices, including columns. *Rotuli* also appear alone along the outer edges of gold-glass, or between/next to busts of figures: see Morey nos. 69, 72, 89 and 98. Of the figures, 'Sustus' (Sixtus / Xystus) appears frequently, on Morey nos. 55, 74, 102, 105? (Vatican Museum), 240, 250, 258 (Florence, Museo Archeologico Nazionale), 291? (Pesaro, Museo Archeologico Oliveriano), 313, 344 (London, British Museum), as well as on two of Wilshere's glasses, here cats **25** and **22**. Xystus (Sixtus) is either Sixtus I (117/9–126/8) or more likely II (257–8); both were Bishops of Rome (popes) and martyrs.[3] The date of this fragment, which is decoloured with manganese only, is likely to be in the middle decades of the fourth century AD.

Endnotes

1. Compare the dome mosaics of the Orthodox Baptistery, Ravenna (see above, p.121, Fig. 64).
2. On the early iconography of the beardless Christ see Grabar 1969: 119–21; Mathews 1993 and Levine 2012; Spieser 2015: 178–90.
3. See above, p.119–120.

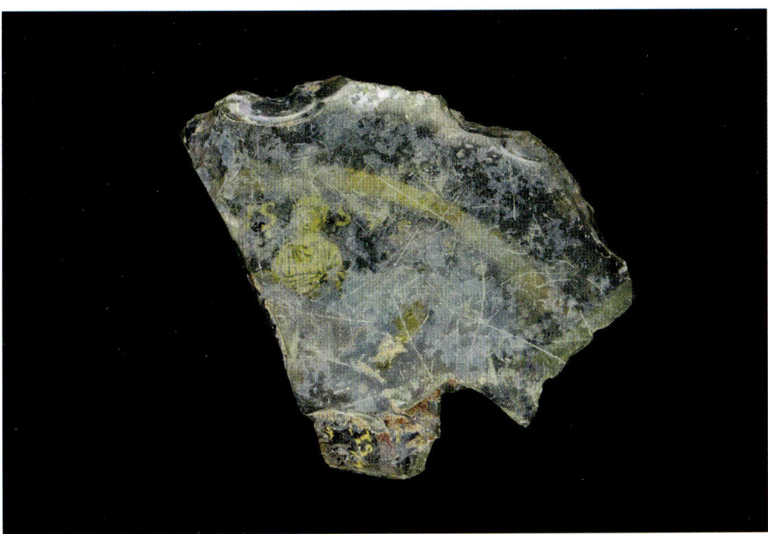

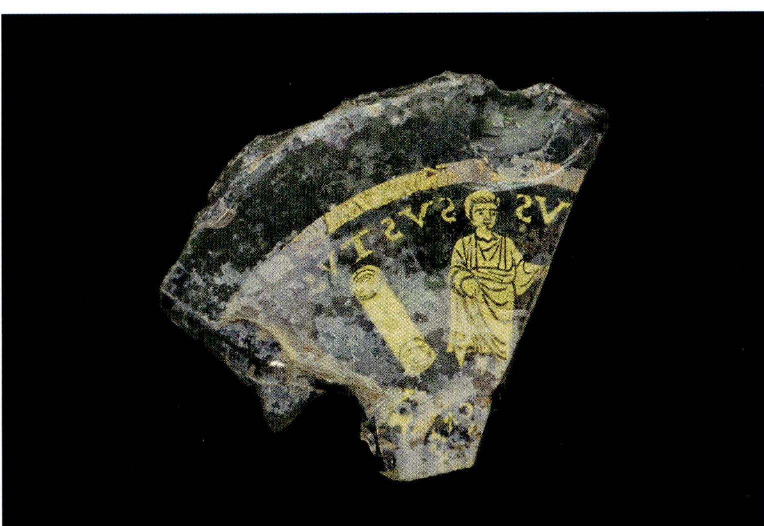

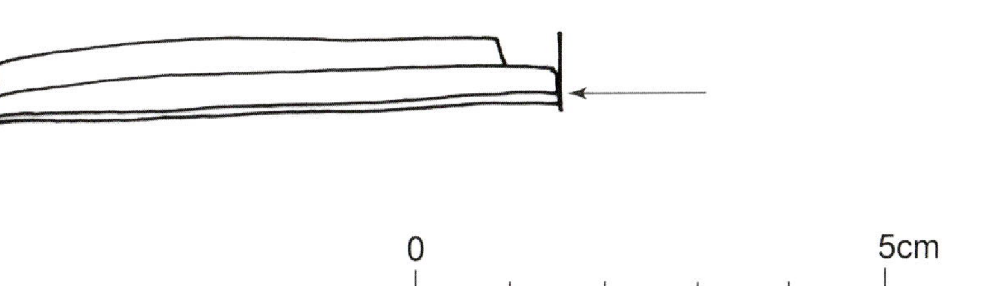

The occluded inner layer of glass and the more legible outer layer, with text reversed. Photographs by David Gowers, 2013. Drawing by Yvonne Beadnell, 2012

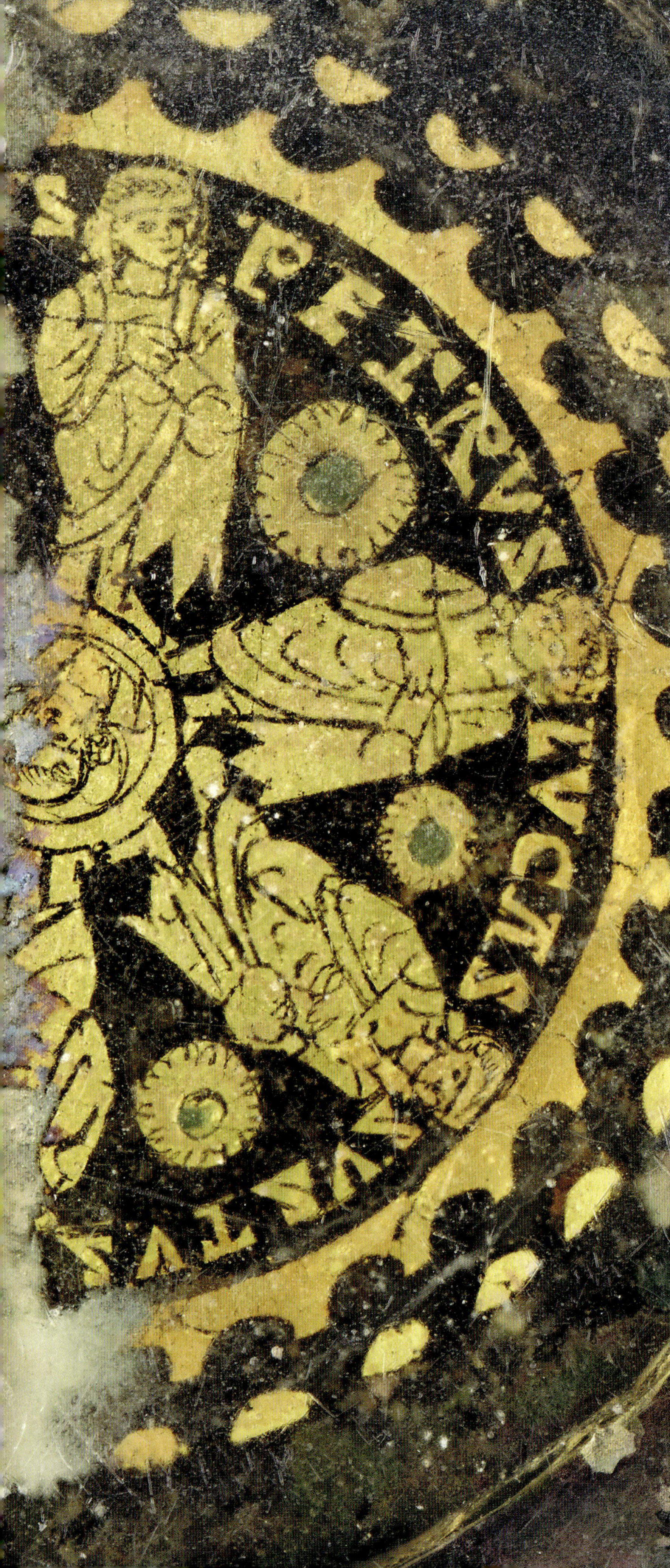

11 AN 2007.10

Segment of the base of a glass plate or shallow bowl: central medallion of Christ, surrounded by figures of St Peter, St Luke and the martyred Pope Sixtus

DIAM. 93 mm (max.)
UL. Pale green, transparent. TH. 3.1 mm
LL. Pale green, transparent. TH. 1.2 mm

The raw glass was decoloured with manganese alone.

Present condition

The upper surface of the base dips slightly at the outer perimeter. Just under half of the base has been deliberately cut away at an unknown date,[1] and most of the walls are broken off, leaving the scar of the 90-mm diameter foot-ring and (max.) 11 mm of the vessel wall intact. The foot-ring is iridescent, and the slightly bubbled glass wall is only slightly corroded. Some particles of iron-rich soil remain around the outer edge of the foot-ring. The gold leaf is barely fragmented. Originally six figures would have been engraved around the central gold leaf medallion, most of which is preserved.

Gold leaf and painted enamel decoration

The central medallion contains a haloed bust of a beardless, long-haired Christ. Around it radiate four figures, shown in frontal view, each dressed in tunic and mantle and holding a *rotulus* (scroll). The figures stand on the edge of the central medallion and are separated by jewels set with emeralds; the latter are represented in green enamel paint, applied to the upper surface only.[2] The figure of St Peter is larger than the others.

Inscribed in Latin within the field between the heads of the figures, reading from left to right in letters 3mm in height '[Iohann]ES/ PETRVS/ LVCAS/SVSTVS' ('John(?), Peter, Luke, Sixtus'). Probably Paul would have been included in the full cycle.[3] The named saints are enclosed by a reciprocal border with half-discs.

Collection history

Purchased by Charles Wilshere between 1862 and 1865 from Tommaso and Vincenzo Capobianchi, 152 Via del Babuino, Rome; acquired by Tommaso Capobianchi at the 1862 public sale of the Museo del Barone Alessio Recupero, Catania, Sicily. Garrucci simply notes that the glass was in the Museo Recupero.

Bibliography

Garrucci 1862: 6, no.V; Garrucci 1864: 143, no.4, tav. XXV; Garrucci 1876: 175 with tav. 194, 4; Vopel 1899: no.387, pp.9, 15, 51, 85, 109; Leclercq (1923), no.228, col.1839; Webster 1929: 153, no.74; Ladner 1941: 33, no.6; Morey 1959: no.363, pl.XXXI; Testini

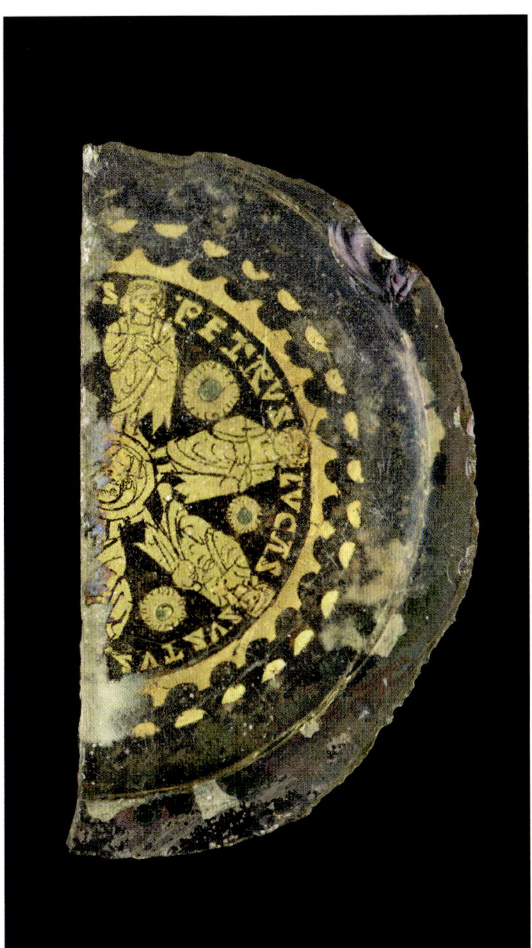

Photograph by David Gowers, 2013.
Drawing by Yvonne Beadnell, 2012

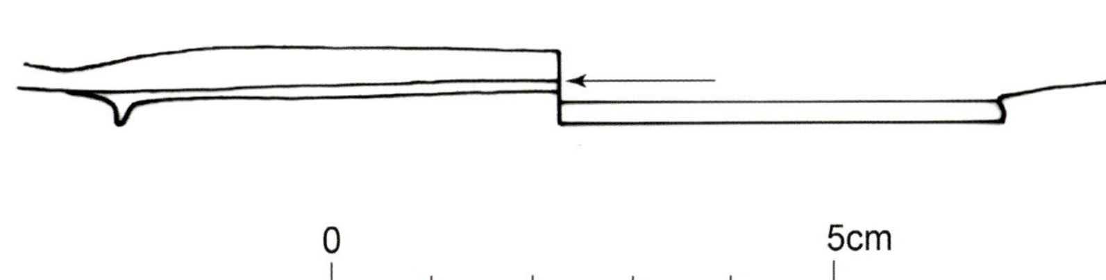

1969: no.151, pp.274, 314; Smith 2000: pl.LI, a; Vattuone 2000: 132, 134 unnumbered fig., 135; Vickers 2009–11:611, fig. 5; Cooley 2017: 238–41, no.393.

Comment

The design is comparable to cat. **10**, where Christ is short-haired, the border a solid gold band and the figures 20 per cent larger in scale. The closest parallels for the design are Morey 1959: nos. 105, 235, 291 and 307; these gold-glasses also portray Christ in similar fashion. For 'Sustus' (Sixtus or Xystus), see cat. **10**. 'Lucas' appears on Morey nos. 79 and 105 (Vatican Museum) as Saint Luke the Evangelist (with halo on Morey 79, without halo here and on Morey 105).

Peter appears as one of a series of saints on Morey nos. 38, 127(?) and 291. It is important to distinguish these representations of Peter, which do not particularly differentiate him from his fellow-saints, from the later scenes in which he dominates, often with Paul (see for example cat. **23**). The figures are neatly formed, if rather sketchy, and some of the gold leaf has been carelessly removed (see Chapter 4, p.92 with fig. 42).

'Serrated discs', as Morey has it, are rarely used to separate figures; dots are the usual 'filler' devices. Marlia Mango identified the discs as wreaths, but in close view they look more like jewels, with the rarely seen painted green setting representing a gem set in a gold mount. Comparable fillers appear on Morey nos. 72, 75, 98, 104, 117 (Vatican Museum); 288, 291 (Pesaro, Museo Archeologico Oliveriano), 313, 349 (London, British Museum: see Howells 2015 nos. 9,(?), 438 (Munich, Nationalmuseum), 446, 459 (New York, MMA). Some may have been intended as stylised stars, for example Morey 193 (Vatican Museum), 221 (Rome, Cimitero di Panfilo).

In contrast, the outer double-border motif is common; see for example cat. **12**. The use of manganese alone as a decolourant suggests a date in the mid-later fourth century, about AD 350–70.

Endnotes

1. The practice is known in glass vessels of late antique date (see for example the gold-glass base representing St Laurence, The Metropolitan Museum of Art, New York, inv.no. 18.145.3, illustrated by Howells 2015: 74, Plate 38), but it remains unexplained: see Price 2015.
2. For further details on the technique see Chapter 4, p.99.
3. Testini 1969: 314, no.151.

12 AN 2007.5

Base of a shallow gold-glass bowl with a foot-ring: busts of Ursus and Dion[ysius]

DIAM. 114 mm (max.)
UL. Colourless, transparent. TH. 2.5 mm, not examined with HH-XRF
LL. Colourless, transparent. TH. 3.5 mm

Decoloured with manganese only.

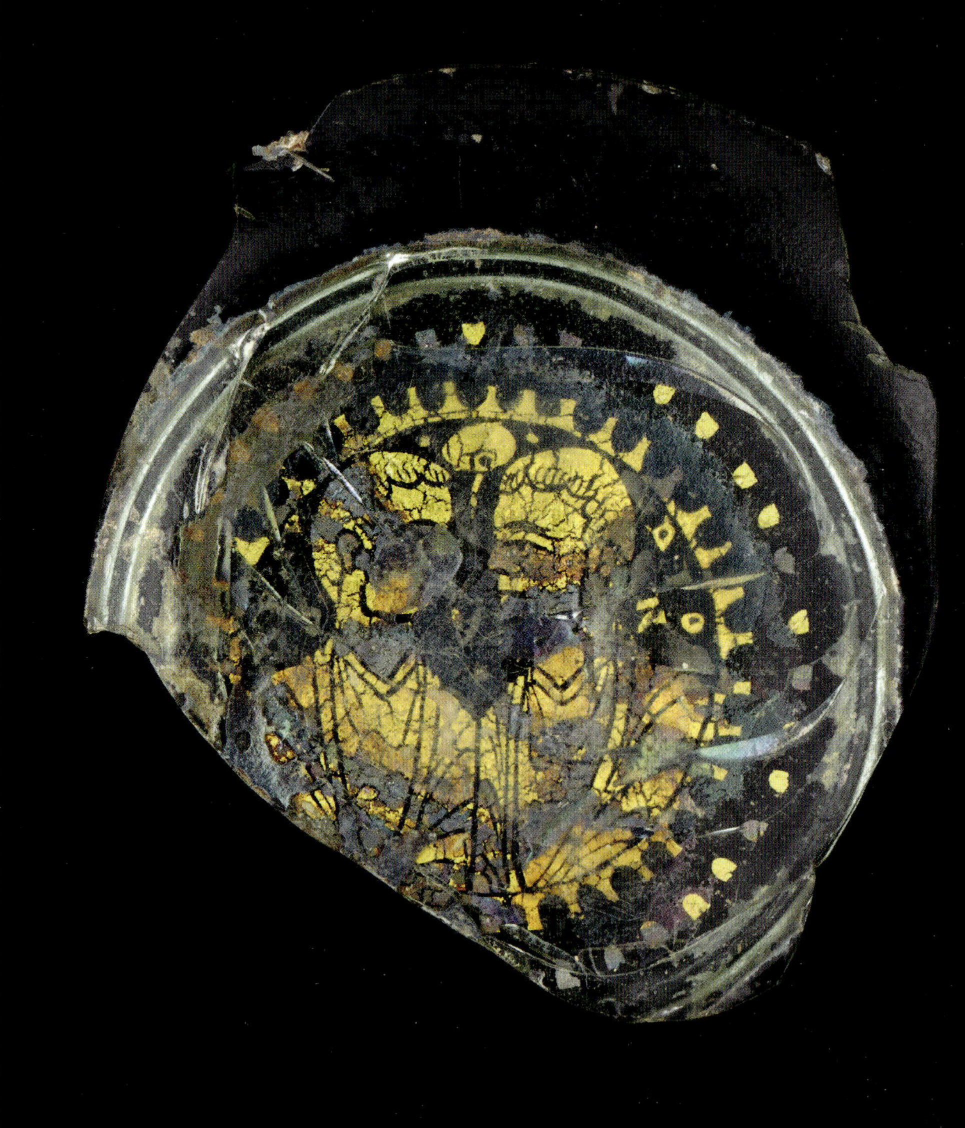

Present condition
The glass is lightly bubbled and the foil partly fragmented. Part of the base and most of the walls are broken off; most of the foot-ring and 20 mm of vessel wall survive. The double thickness of the base layer tails off at the edge. The lower layer of glass has extensive stress fractures with bluish black iridescent weathering; this is also present on the foot-ring. Mortar adheres to the inner and outer faces of the foot-ring and also extends across the broken edges of the glass. The raw glass used to make the base of the vessel was decoloured with manganese alone.

Gold leaf decoration
The two saints face each other, with a stylised crown with a trailing ribbon (*lemniscus*) set between their heads. Their names 'VRSV/S/' and 'DIO/N[ysius]' appear behind their heads, the letters irregularly spaced and varying between 2 and 3 mm in height. The young men are beardless; both wear tunics and wide, mantle-like stoles of *omorphorion* type, pinned below the breast with a brooch. The border is of the 'reciprocal type with half-discs' – a scalloped edge to the medallion containing the portraits, with spade-shaped pieces of gold-glass set in an outer ring, roughly corresponding to the gaps between the scallops.

Collection history
Purchased by Charles Wilshere from Tommaso and Vincenzo Capobianchi of Via del Babuino 152, Rome in 1865. Loaned by Wilshere to the South Kensington Museum 1865–93. Left to Pusey House, Oxford by Deed of Trust 1895. Loaned to the Ashmolean Museum Oxford, 1957–2007. Purchased by the Ashmolean Museum, 2007.

Formerly in the collection of the Baron Alessio Recupero of Catania, Sicily; sold to Vincenzo Capobianchi in Messina in 1862. In 1781 the glass was drawn for the Vatican librarian Gaetano Marini (see below and Chapter 2, p.56, fig. 24). Its location was then given as *R(omae) apud Ab. Severinium Lipsanophylacum*, the source of several of Recupero's purchases. The Abbot Giovanni Severini curated the sacred relics from the catacombs, which were kept in his home in the later years of the eighteenth century. He died in 1800 and his heir (his brother Andrea Severini) apparently sold the collection to private individuals. Among them was Recupero, who died in 1803, leaving his collection to his brother Giuseppe.[1]

Bibliography
Garrucci 1858: 38, no.8, tav. XVI; Garrucci [1862]: 7, no.IX; Garrucci 1864: 103–4, no.8, tav. XVI; Garrucci 1876: 156, no.8, tav. CLXXXV; Vopel 1899: no.420, pp.9, 12, 13, 54, 85, 110; Leclercq 1923: no.261, col.184; Diehl 1925: no.909; Webster 1929: 154, no.99; Morey 1959: 60, no.358, pl.XXXI; Smith 2000: pl.XXXI, a; Vattuone 2000: 132, 134, no.152; Cooley 2017: 230–2, no.389.

Comment
The unseen donor of the crown is Christ or an angel in this version of a well-known scene of martyrs or private individuals being crowned. The names Ursus and Dion[ysius] are not known from any other gold-glass. They may be the two beheaded martyrs Ursus the Theban, martyred c.AD 286, whose remains were later taken to Solothurn, Switzerland, and Dionysius (St Denis), Bishop of Paris, martyred c.AD 250.

Although the individuals appear unique, the scene is similar to Morey nos. 37 (Vatican, pl.VI); 50–1 (Vatican, pl.VIII); 53 (Vatican, pls IX); 60–7 (Vatican, pls X–XI); 241–2 (Florence, Museo Nazionale, pl.XXVI); 277 (Verona, Museo di Castelvecchio, pl.XXVII); 314 (London, British Museum, pl.XXIX); 459 (New York, Metropolitan Museum, pl.XXVI).

The border type is also common and is often associated with scenes of saints or private individuals being crowned. See Morey nos. 51, 53, 56, 62–4, 67, 83, 89–90, 92, 94–5, 99–104, etc. It was perhaps inspired by contemporary manuscript illumination.

The appearance of the figures and the border type suggest a date in the later fourth century, about AD 360–400 (= Faedo Group 1).[2] The use of manganese alone as a decolourant suggests a date at the earlier end of this spectrum.

Endnotes
1. See p.61 and Ferretto 1942: 205 for the sale of the relics curated by Severini.
2. Faedo 1978: 1032–49.

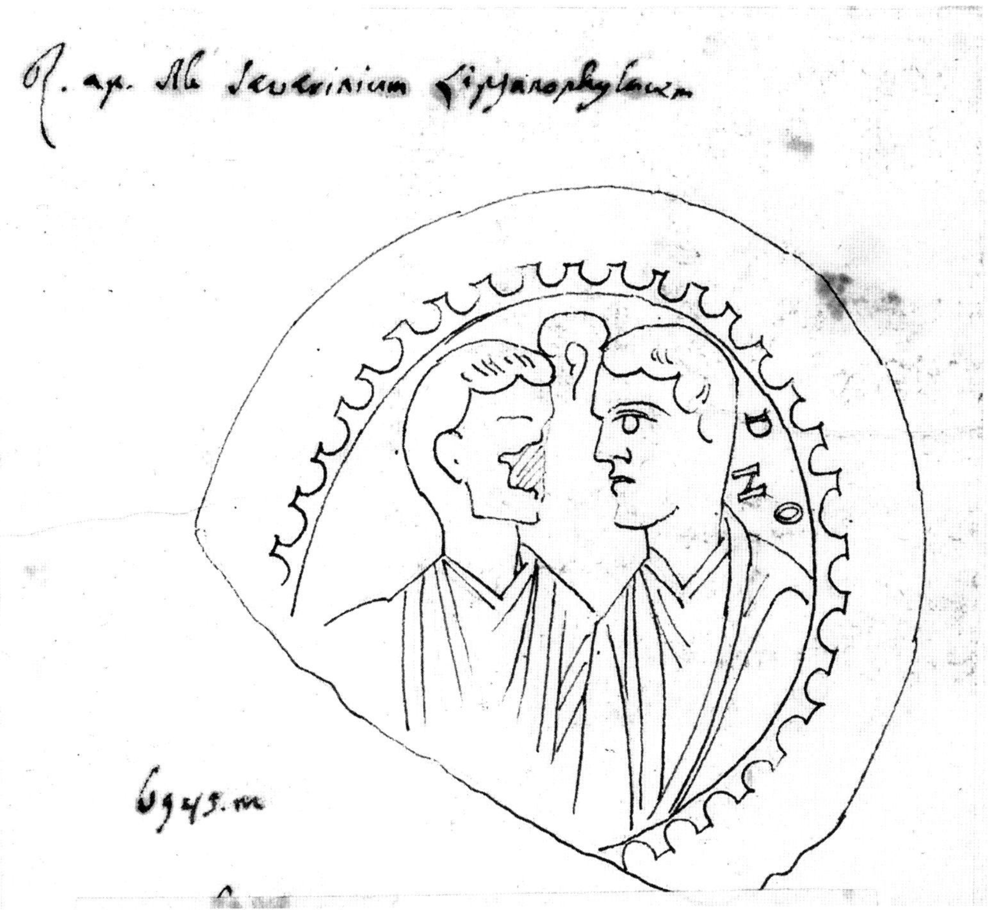

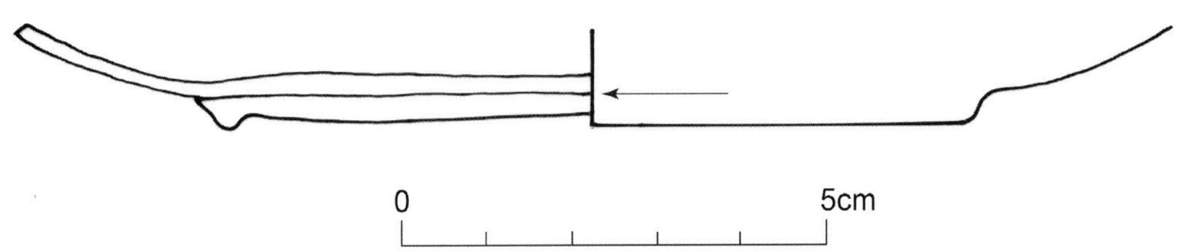

(opposite) Photograph by David Gowers, 2013. (above) A drawing of cat. **12**, made for Gaetano Marini when the vessel was in the care of the Abbot Severini, Vatican City, Biblioteca Apostolica Vaticana, Vat. lat. 9071, Card 9, p.120. Unfortunately the manuscript page referenced in the number below left did not yield any further information about the history of the glass (below) Drawing of the bowl by Yvonne Beadnell, 2012

13 AN 2007.6

Fragment of the base of a gold-glass and painted enamel vessel: menorah, taper and Greek inscription written in Latin script

W. 2.6 mm (max.); L. 88 mm (max.)
UL. Colourless, transparent. TH. 2.7 mm
ML. Colourless, transparent. TH. 1.1 mm
LL. Colourless, transparent. TH. 1.2 mm

The gold leaf is enclosed within three layers of naturally coloured, greenish glass, indicating that the glass-maker experienced difficulty with the blowing of the upper layer.[1] Visible in the drawing by Yvonne Beadnell is a crack through the middle and lower layers, the likely reason for the extra protective layer.

The raw glass was decoloured with manganese only.

Photographs taken by David Gowers, 2013 (left) and 2009 (right). The latter shows the coloured enamel representation of fruits on the branches of the gold leaf menorah.

(Facing page, above) Drawing by Yvonne Beadnell, 2012

(Facing page, below) Detail of the surviving lamp, showing the decorative gold disc behind it to the left. Photograph taken under the microscope by Dana Norris, 2012

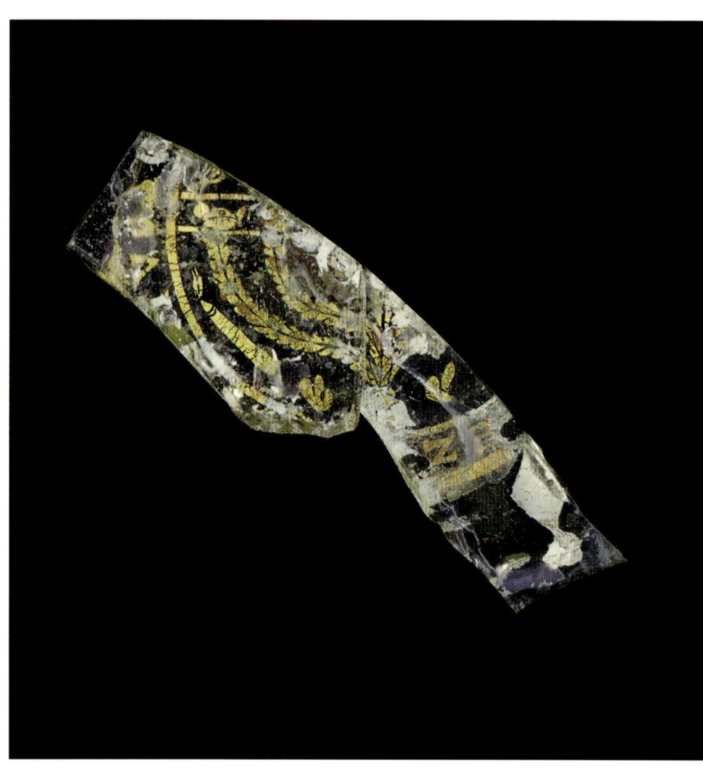

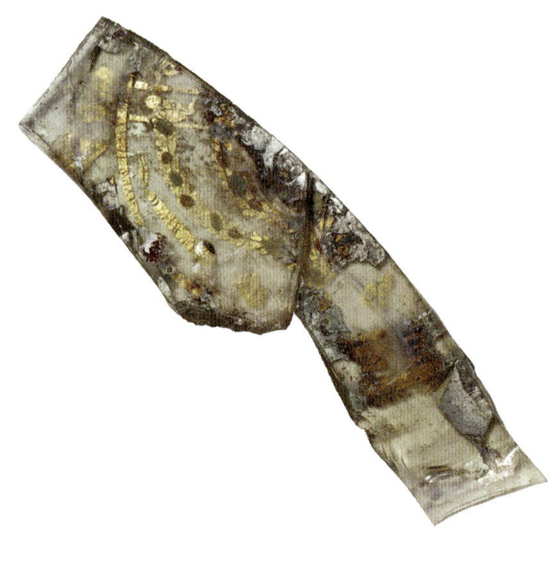

Present condition
The fragment was published by Morey (1959, no. 359) as 'cracked', probably a reference to the entire glass rather than the lower layers. By 1987 the fragment had broken into two pieces; it was mended before redisplay in 2009 after purchase by the Ashmolean. There is silvery iridescent weathering on the outer surface and on the surface bearing foil. The foil is slightly fragmented. The surface is slightly concave towards the centre of the vessel. Cut and incised gold foil decoration with green, reddish-brown and black painted details applied to the upper surface of the lowest layer of glass. The glass is slightly bubbled, its upper surface polished.

Gold leaf and painted enamel decoration
Menorah with arms rendered as leafy branches with red and green fruits alternating along their spines; seven fruits are visible on the outer branch and four on the inner. At the top of each arm is a lit lamp, of which only one survives intact on the outermost branch. The usual bar linking the arms is here turned into the lower line of a border framing the lamps. A brighter gold disc appears behind the handle of the lamp and a similarly bright vertical bar is to the right of the flame.

On each side of the menorah is a sprig and in the left field a lit taper decorated with black painted bands. At the broken edge of the glass is a partially preserved double-band border with inscription in letters 3 mm in height: 'TVOS [OMNES…PI]E Z(ESES)' ('… all your…Drink! May you live!').

Collection history
Wilshere Collection. Formerly in the collection of Vincenzo Capobianchi, 152 Via del Babuino, Rome. Only the evidence of omission supports Kraabel's argument that this fragment came from the Vigna Randanini.[2] In a publication of 2000 Hachlili suggested that most Jewish gold-glasses from Rome came from the cemetery of Monteverde. However, Hachlili earlier implied that only the Randanini catacomb was exposed during the nineteenth century.[3] Charles Wilshere

purchased stone funerary inscriptions from this catacomb directly from the family controlling the property, while according to Garrucci this glass was once in the collection of Vincenzo Capobianchi, son of Wilshere's principal Roman dealer Tommaso Capobianchi.

Bibliography

Garrucci 1881: VI, 164, no.1, tav. CDXCI; Webster, Ms.Catalogue, no.86 (not published in 1929); Frey 1936: II, 382, no.521; Goodenough, 1953–68, III, 111, no.972; Morey 1959: 60, no.359, pl.XXXI; Schüler 1966: (1966), 46–61, no.14; *Encyclopedia Judaica* 1972: Vol.7, pl.8; Kraabel 1979: 48–50, no.3; Noy 1995: no.594; Hachlili 1998: 298–300, no.10, figs VI–27 (diagram); Hachlili 2000: 430, 10.10, figs II–34; Smith 2000: pl.XCI, c; Vattuone 2000: 132, 134; Vickers 2009–11: 610, fig. 1; Cooley 2017: 232–4, no.390.

Comment

Of the 14 extant gold-glasses illustrating Jewish liturgical objects, this fragment is remarkably similar to a piece in the British Museum.[4] However, the latter includes other ritual objects and the leafy menorah appears not to have been decorated with coloured enamel. Other examples with coloured enamel fruit include a glass in the Israel Museum, Jerusalem.[5] On all three, similar glasses the toast *'PIE ZESES'* ('Drink! Live!'), in Greek transliterated as Latin, is exactly as found on Christian glass vessels and in pagan contexts (see Chapter 3, p.88).

The large-scale menorah is quite a rare type on Roman gold-glass. It may have been intended to evoke the menorah in the Second Temple removed to Rome by Titus.[6]

Though the gold leaf is fragmenting in this area, it is here assumed that the surviving lamp faces towards the centre of the menorah with raised flame, following a practice mentioned by a number of rabbinical sources.[7]

The leafy branches of the menorah suggest myrtle (*hadasin*), often bound with palm (*lulab* or *lulav*) and willow (*aravin*) and used in the *Sukkoth* (tabernacles) liturgy during the fall of Jerusalem, especially in the Temple. The coloured fruit seen on the Ashmolean glass is evoked in a sixth-century poem by the Rabbi Yannai, who imagined a lampstand where the cup-shaped calyces were formed in green gold, the bulbs in red and the flowers in white.[8] The lit taper appears unique within the Jewish gold-glass repertoire, and represents the act of lighting the lamps of the menorah.

The disc and bar beside the surviving lamp may represent part of a backdrop. More common on gold-glass is a dividing ground-line, on which is placed the tabernacle flanked by other ritual objects and/or doves.[9] If the lower edge of the ark of the scrolls had been intended, one would expect to see a series of horizontal lines representing steps to the right of the vertical bar.

Above the line to the left is perhaps a flower or possibly part of an *ethrog* or the base of a *lulab*. The base of the menorah appears to be a solid flaring cone, suggesting again that this might indeed be a representation of the Second Temple Menorah.[10]

Other examples of menorahs on gold-glass include Morey nos. 114 (Vatican, pl.XIX, two menorahs and a torah shrine flanked by lions); 346 (London, British Museum, pl.XXX); 426 (Cologne, Römisch-Germanisches Museum, pl.XXXIV, menorah flanked by two *lulab*); 433 (Würzburg, Universitätsmuseum, pl.XXXV, menorah in border flanked by two lions).

In a funerary context, the menorah may have been intended as a reflection of the Light of the Law by which a Jew hoped to be saved.[11] In this respect, the scene may be compared to Christian representations of the biblical narratives of salvation taken from the prayer for commendation of the soul. For further discussion of the significance of the iconography to members of the Jewish diaspora community in Rome, see Chapter 3, pp.82–84.

The form of the text contained within the border bands and the use of coloured blobs of enamel compares well with some glasses featuring portraits of individuals. These can be dated to the middle decades of the fourth century AD, a date further indicated by the use of manganese alone as a decolorant.

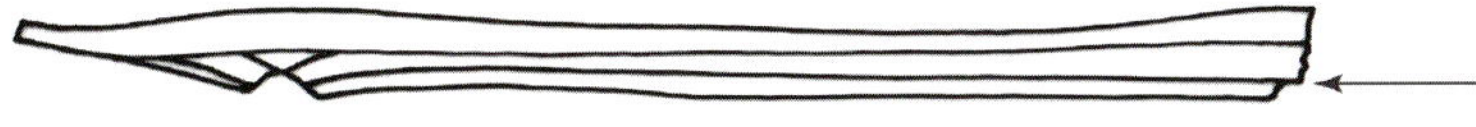

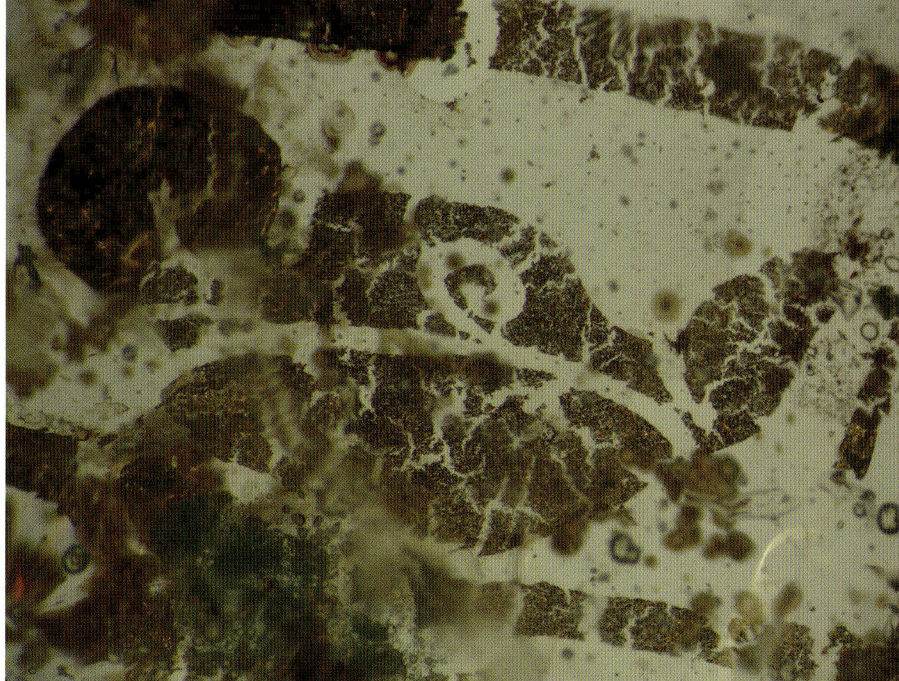

Endnotes

1. Howells 2015: 49. See also Chapter 4, p.93, Fig. 44.
2. Kraabel 1979: 49.
3. Hachlili 2000: 96; Hachlili 1988: 271, 273. On the Monteverde cemetery see recently Rossi and di Mento 2013.
4. BM BEP 1863.0727,10 = Morey no 346 = Howells 2015:132–3, no.40.
5. Inv. no.66.36.15; see Howells 2015: 134, Plate 113.
6. Josephus, *War* 7, 148–9, *Ant* 3, 144–6: 'and a lampstand, made of gold but constructed on a different pattern from those which we use in ordinary life. Affixed to a pedestal was a central shaft, from which there extended slender branches, a wrought lamp being attached to the extremity of each branch; of these there were seven, indicating the honour paid to that number amongst the Jews'. See Hachlili 2000: 23 and Fine 2016: 19.
7. Fine 2007: 35; 2016: 43.
8. Fine 2007: 34; 2016: 54-6.
9. Hachlili 2000: 97–103, Fig. II 33.
10. Hachlili 2000: 25, 49.
11. Hachlili 2000: 206.

Photographs by David Gowers, 2013

14 AN 2007.20

Fragment of a glass plate or shallow bowl with decorated gold leaf border

H. 5 mm (foot-ring); W. 25 mm (max.); L. 36 mm (max.)
UL. Pale green, transparent. TH. 2.2 mm
LL. Pale green, transparent. TH. 2.1 mm

The raw glass was decoloured with manganese only.

Present condition
The glass is of high quality. The surfaces have been ground and polished, and the glass is relatively bubble-free. Only a small section of glass survives along with part of the foot-ring and a tiny spur of wall. The foil is fragmented. There is iridescent weathering along the broken edge of the glass.

Gold leaf decoration
Only part of the reciprocal border survives. It is decorated with elongated half-discs.

Collection history
Probably acquired in Rome by Charles Wilshere after 1865.

Bibliography
Morey 1959: no.373, pl.XXXII.

Comment
Morey no.64 (Vatican Museum) illustrates a similar piece with parts of the border missing. However, this fragment cannot join it as the scale of the decoration differs.

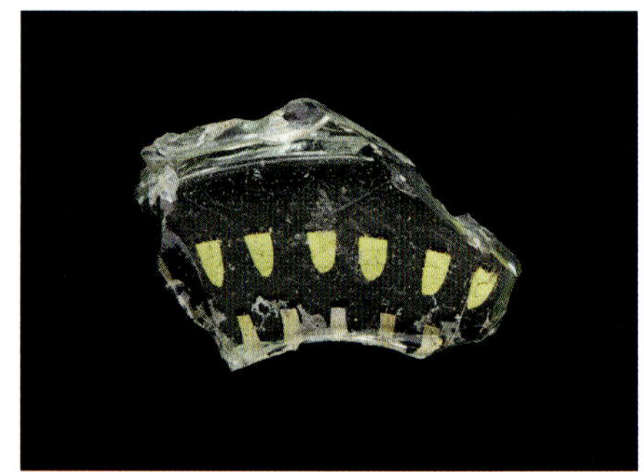

15 AN 2007.31

Part of a glass vessel inscribed in gold leaf SEM[PER?]

H. 23 mm (max.); W. 18 mm (max.)
UL Pale green, transparent. TH. 2.0–2.5 mm
LL. Pale green, transparent. TH. 1.0 mm

The raw glass was decoloured with manganese only.

Present condition
Only a small fragment survives, broken on all sides. From this it is not possible to reconstruct the form of the vessel. Above the text the upper layer of glass seems to taper downward, as if bending towards a rim. The lower layer of glass has broken away from the upper. There is iridescent silvery corrosion on the foil-bearing glass surface. The glass is bubbled and the foil fragmented.

Gold leaf decoration
The inner surface of the presumed vessel is decorated with an inscription in Latin in letters 6 mm in height, most likely to be restored as 'SEM(PER)'. The letters are large and confidently cut in thick script, with marked serifs at the top of the S and the middle bar of the E.

Collection history
Acquired by Charles Wilshere in Rome, probably after 1865.

Bibliography
Morey 1959: no.384, pl.XXXII; Cooley 2017: 259–61, no.403.

Comment
Morey interpreted the fragment as part of a disc, the front concave and the back flat, but there appears to be too much curvature to agree. The letters SEM probably represent the beginning of a word such as 'SEM[PER]' ('always') or, less likely, a name such as 'SEM[PRONIUS]'. The spacing between them is close, and there is too much space to the left of the S to suggest that it is anything other than the start of a word.

SEMPER does occur on the inscriptions of other bowl bases. See Morey nos. 36, a green glass medallion in the Vatican Museum, inscribed within the border 'HILARIS VIVAS CUM TUIS FELICITER. SEMPER REFRIGERIS IM PACE DEI', 'Hilaris may you live with your [family] in happiness. May you feast for ever in the peace of God', and 228, a white glass medallion still *in situ* in the plaster sealing of a tomb in the cemetery of Sant' Agnese, restored as '[SEMP]ER IM [PACE GAUDE](as)', 'always in [peace, rejoice]'. The letters given here in square brackets were not visible at the time of compilation of Morey's catalogue in 1958. In both cases, as is likely here, the word 'SEMPER' introduces not only a word but also a phrase, in the more complete texts inviting the deceased to feast or rejoice in peace.

As only manganese is used as a decolourant, the glass probably dates to the middle decades of the fourth century AD.

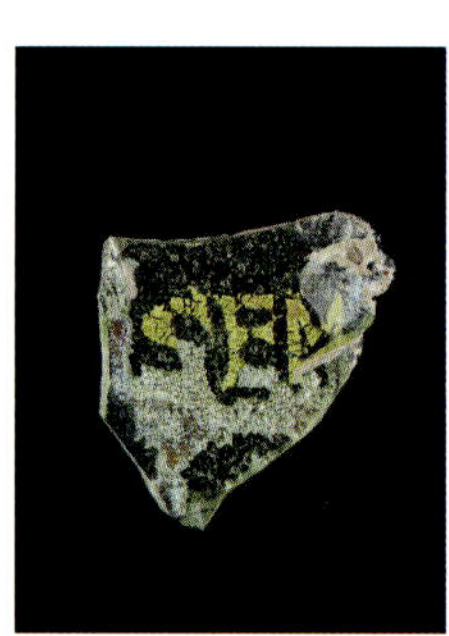

16 AN 2007.23

Fragment of a sheet of glass in two layers, decorated in gold leaf and brown pigment with a scene of fishing

H. 43 mm (max.); W. 55 mm (max.)
UL. (left) Colourless, transparent. TH. 1.65 mm
UL. (right) Colourless, transparent. TH. 1.7 mm
LL. Colourless, transparent. TH. 3 mm

The inner layer and its repair were decoloured in raw state with manganese only. The repair has a markedly higher level of antimony, more than twice the variation seen in cat. **23**, and four times the variation between the inner and outer layers of other vessels in the Wilshere Collection decoloured with manganese alone, rising from zero to 0.08 within the inner layer of glass (see further Appendix 4.1 and Chapter 4, p.98).

Present condition

The fragment is broken on all sides. The lower layer is a single sheet of glass; the upper is formed from two sheets of slightly different thickness and colour. The upper surface is heavily weathered, with the left half almost completely covered in iridescent colour and flaking. The lower surface is pitted, making the gold leaf image appear blurred. A silvery iridescence has formed around the folded foil.

Gold leaf and painted enamel decoration

This may only be seen in full from below. Two large, scaly fish swim in opposite directions. One is menaced by an S-shaped fish-hook fitted with a pointed barb, the other by a bag-shaped net with a painted brown frame on which crossed rods operate like a pair of tongs. Above the fish are two lines suggesting the edge of a basin or harbour. Below are the Latin letters PEV, read by Alison Cooley as PEX; she also reads the fish-hook as the letter S, but such a reading does not explain the barb. The letters are *c.*8 mm in height. To the right of the letters is a curved feature with a central fold, perhaps representing part of a rocky shore.

Collection history

Acquired by Charles Wilshere, probably in Rome, at an unknown date.

Bibliography

Garrucci 1862: 8, no.12; Garrucci 1864: 90–1, no.10, tav. X; Vopel 1899: 111, no.441; Leclercq 1923: no.281, col.1842; Morey 1959: no.376, pl.XXXII (labelled as no.380); Cooley 2017: 251–3, no.399;

Comment

Morey describes the fragment as: 'Broken all round. Front cracked; back heavily filmed and cracked across. Both surfaces flat. Two [or four, according to Garrucci's drawing] fish symmetrically arranged in profile facing inward; the design above them illegible.[1] Inscription [read by Morey as Greek] in unantique lettering:
'b E Λ.'

The omission of this piece from Garrucci's *Storia dell'Arte Cristiana* (*History of Christian art*, published from 1872–81) is perhaps significant, as the fragment is almost certainly of secular origin.

All scholars have confused the layers of glass, which has led to a misreading of the text and consequent misinterpretation of the scene. The join in the upper surface and the use of a different colour and thickness of glass suggests that this unusual piece was repaired at a later date. However, Marlia Mango is surely right in seeing this fragment as part of something other than the customary dish, plate or drinking cup.[2] She identified it as window-glass, on account of the two sheets making up the upper layer (which she believed to be the lower) and the latter's unusual pattern of weathering. However, no other sandwiched gold leaf window-glass has yet been recognised from fourth-century Rome. It is more likely that this fragment either belonged to a flat tray for serving large fish, similar to surviving fourth-century serving trays in silver and *terra sigillata*, or that it formed a decorative inlay for an

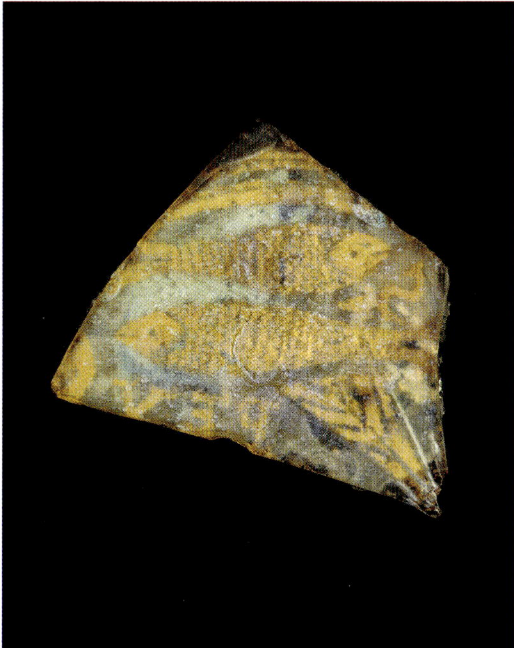

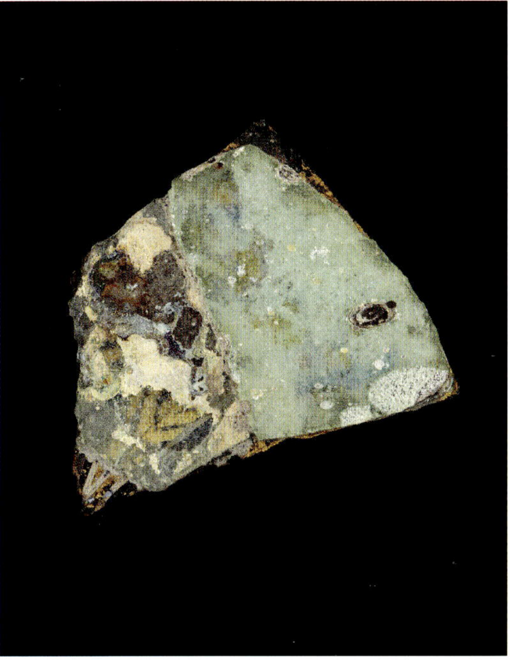

Photographs of cat. **16**: from below, with gold leaf image and text reversed, by David Gowers, 2009 (left); seen from above and showing the weathered and repaired glass by David Gowers, 2013.

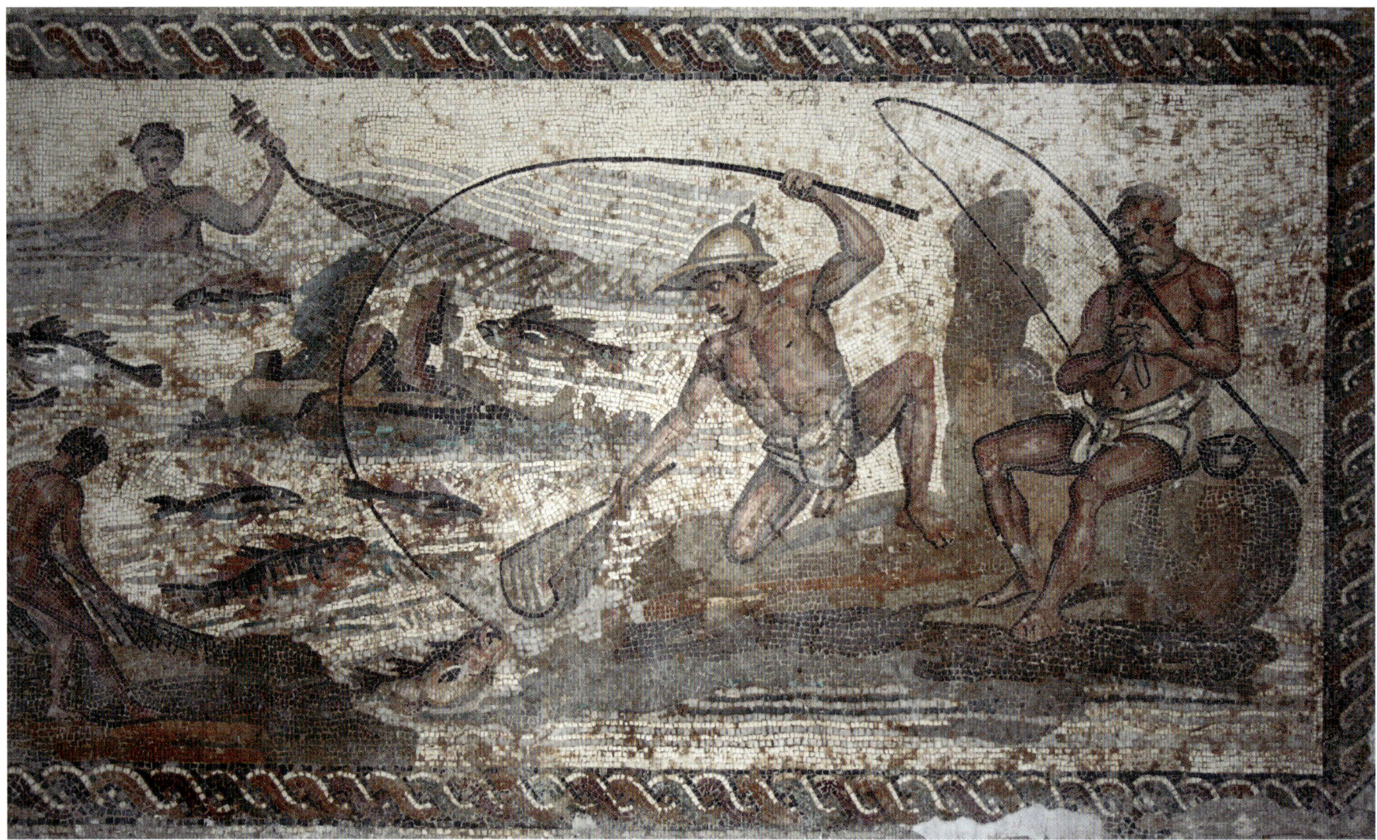

ornamental basin. Possibly, given the presence of the text, it was part of a pictorial map.

Morey did not offer a reconstructed reading of the assumed Greek text. However, with the layers of glass reversed, the gold leaf text might be read in Latin as PEV, though such a reading implies a small diminution in letter size (unfortunately the lower bars of the X read by Cooley are not preserved). Here too reconstruction is limited to the Latin equivalent of the Greek work for pine tree: '*peucus*', an improbable reading in this context. No personal names are likely contenders; however, the letters do coincide with PEV(CE), the name of the Peucic channel of the delta of the River Danube. In Roman times the Peucic channel was famous for its carp, almost certainly the identity of the large fish shown here. Despite lacking a dorsal fin, the shape of the fish's head, scale pattern and impression of relative scale are strikingly similar to ancient representations of carp, mostly confined to the region of the Danube and Thrace. By the fourth century AD the natural resources of the region were controlled by the Roman army.[3]

The fish is, of course, well known as a symbol of Christianity and, following the acrostic of his name in Greek, for Christ himself.[4] Other depictions of fish on gold-glass include Morey nos. 198 (only one fish, less detailed) and 392 (here cat. **36**: two fish, similar in the design of their scales and heads, curled around a central inscription).

Dölger demonstrated, the representation of a pair of fish swimming in opposite directions is commonly found in many media. However, other than in scenes of Jonah and the whale, no representation of the *act of fishing* may be associated with indisputably Christian artistic contexts – despite biblical references to Christ inviting the disciples to become fishers of men and the appearance of a single large fish as the main dish in scenes of funerary feasts.

Indeed it is likely that, in its original context, the scene on this fragment had a secular significance. It may be compared to scenes of fishing in Nilotic landscapes, notably one in a mosaic panel of the baths of the Villa of the Nile at Leptis Magna. The mosaic (above) features a complex series of fishing scenes, perhaps representing a competition or festival celebration, among them one of an agile young fisherman crouched on a rocky islet; he wields a rod and line and a net of exactly similar design to catch a large fish.[5] However, on the fragment of gold-glass the reading PEU and the probable identification of the fish as carp suggest a Danubian delta setting. The fragment was then cut out of its original setting for reuse, presumably in a Christian context. The paired fish thus became the main subject and the fishing tackle peripheral; any fisherman was eliminated with almost all of the landscape. It was at this point in the object's history that the repair to the upper layer of glass is likely to have been made.

The lettering corresponds to Group 8 of the styles identified in a study of gold-glass by Claudia Lega.[6] She dates the group to AD 380–400 on stylistic and iconographic grounds. However, given the admittedly variable use of a single decolourant, the dating requires reconsideration – this fragment could well be mid-fourth century.

Endnotes

1. This is surely a confusion with cat. **6**.
2. Unpublished catalogue entry, drafted in the 1980s.
3. Unpublished seminar given in Oxford on 29 October 2012 by John Wilkes. For control of fishing in the Danube delta see CIL III, no.781; Latyschev 1885: no.3; 1916, Vol.1, no.4; Oliver 1965: 143–56; *Inscripțile din Scythia Minor* I (Bucureşti 1983), no.67 (Text A), no.68 (Text B), no.69 (unattributed fragment).
4. Dölger 1922–43.
5. Aurigemma 1960.
6. Lega 2012: tab.1, 283; see also Nüsse 2008.

Mosaic panel with a scene of fishing. Villa of the Nile, Lepcis Magna, now Tripoli Museum. Photo: Philip Kenrick, 2010.

17 AN 2007.34

Fragment of the rim of a glass bowl, decorated internally with gold leaf and externally with a narrow band of turquoise blue glass

Photograph by David Gowers, 2013.
Drawing by Yvonne Beadnell, 2012

H. 13 mm (max.); L. 32 mm (max.) UL. Colourless, transparent. TH. 1 mm
LL. Colourless, transparent. TH. 1 mm

The raw glass was decoloured with manganese only.

Present condition
The rim of a vessel apparently cast in two layers with gold-foil decoration laid between them, the foil now badly fragmented. Around the edge of the rim is applied a narrow strip of turquoise blue glass, now with silver iridescence, visible on the outer face only. Embedded in the opposite, broken edge are tiny, dark flecks, perhaps of soil.

Collection history
Acquired by Charles Wilshere in Rome, probably after 1865.

Bibliography
Morey 1959: no.387, pl.XXXII.

Comment
Morey describes the fragment as follows: 'White glass fragment, in two thin layers, of a bowl or cup. Back has three listals across one end, evidently part of an external moulding. Gold leaf is apparently a stippled filling for a border, whose curve is visible below.'

Analysis of the glass in the 1980s suggests that the raw glass is high in calcium. It may come from Syria. Copper rather than cobalt was used to colour the external band.

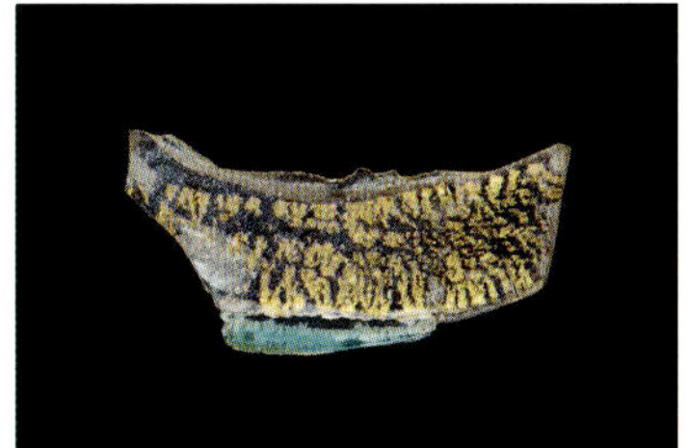

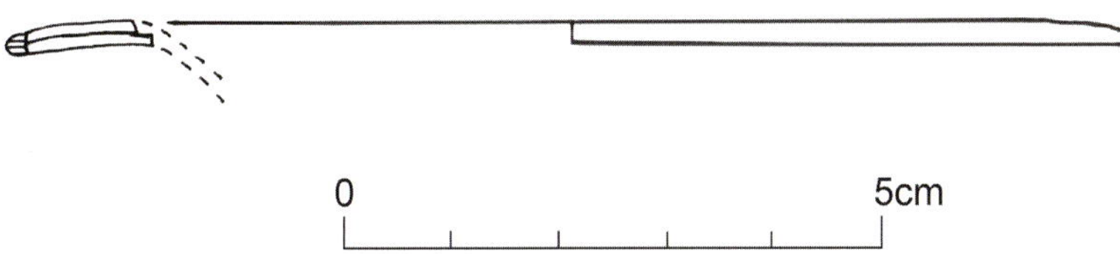

18 AN 2007.30

Fragment of a high-walled glass flask with inlaid discs of plain glass set in coloured glass rims, the discs filled with gold foil

Photograph by David Gowers, 2013.
Drawing by Yvonne Beadnell, 2012

H. 28 mm (max.); W. 13 mm (max.) Vessel: UL. Blue. TH. 1 mm
LL. Blue. TH. 2 mm
DISC: UL. Colourless, transparent. TH. 1 mm
LL. Colourless, transparent. TH. 2 mm
DISC BORDERS: Green, TH. 3 mm; amber, TH. 3 mm

The raw, clear glass used to make the discs was decoloured with manganese only.

Present condition

The convex cobalt blue glass vessel has been cast in two layers. Only a small fragment of the vessel, broken on all sides and probably coming from near the base of the vessel, survives (see shaded area of drawing). The surviving inlaid disc is pitted, with purple and silver iridescence. The upper surface of the glass is pitted.

Gold leaf decoration

The vase was decorated with inset discs of gold foil set between two discs of colourless glass, each disc held in place by single bands of green and amber glass. On the outer surface of the vessel, overlapping all the discs of inlaid glass and foil, are three inscribed concentric grooves.

Collection history

Purchased in Rome by Charles Wilshere, probably after 1865.

Bibliography

Morey 1959: no.383, pl.XXXII.

Comment

Morey offers no identification of the fragment of blue glass. Similarly shaped, larger pitchers from Syria, used to pour oils or liquids, are in the collections of the Corning Museum of Glass (see p.00, fig. 00).[1] A small, globular flask of blue glass with similar inscribed grooves but no inlaid discs, dated to the third or fourth century AD, is in the collections of the J. Paul Getty Museum.[2] Such vessels were probably used to anoint the dead with oil and/or perfume.

Endnotes

1. CMG 64.1.18, 68.1.2. See Whitehouse 2001: 178–9, no.718; 215–6, no.783.
2. JPGM 2003.350. Wight 2011: 90, figure 63.

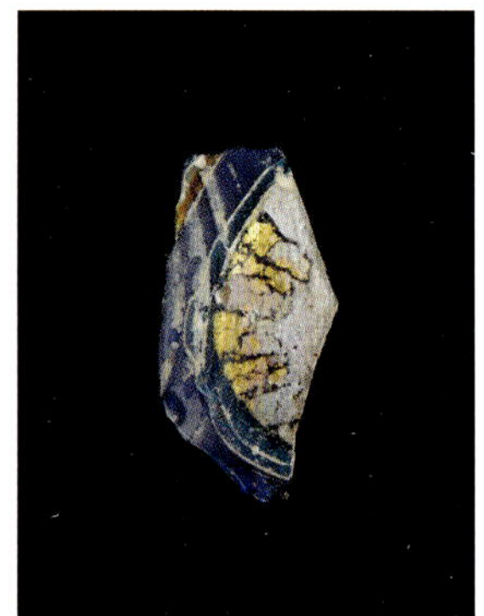

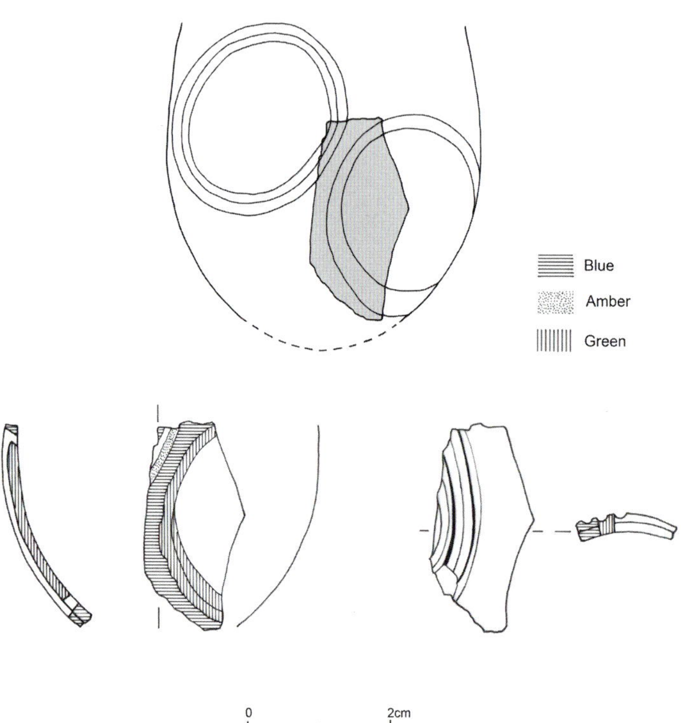

Group 3
Clear glass decoloured with a mixture of antimony and manganese

Photograph by David Gowers, 2013.
Drawing by Yvonne Beadnell, 2012

19 AN 2007.24

Fragment, perhaps of a medallion: portraits of a man named Rufus and an unnamed woman

H. 24 mm (max.); W. 39 mm (max.) UL. Very pale green, transparent. TH. 3.2 mm
LL. Very pale green, transparent. TH. 1.1 mm

The raw glass was decoloured with a mixture of antimony and manganese. In composition the outer layer of cat. **19** is so similar to the inner layer of cat. **20** that they are likely to have been made from the same batch of raw glass, most probably obtained from recycling glass in the Rome workshops.

Present condition

The fragment is broken on all sides and the lower surface is chipped. The glass is lightly bubbled, its surface polished. The finely cut and incised foil is fragmented and corroded. A silvery iridescence has formed on both surfaces and spread to the outer vertical edges of the glass. There is no foot-ring and the base is somewhat concave.

Gold leaf decoration

The upper parts of two heads, female (left) and male (right) are slightly inclined towards one another. The woman has centrally parted hair, with a large roll or plait at the crown of her head. The evidently youthful man has a high domed forehead and a cap of hair brushed towards it and around his face. He has large, almond-shaped eyes and fine, arched brows.

Between the figures the man is addressed in Latin RVFE, and to the left and right of his head 'VIVA[S]' ('… Rufus, may you live…'). There is an interpunct before the first letter of 'VIVA[S]'. The upper layer of glass is fractured above the letter A, which was read as I by Morey. Two strokes seem clear; however, if so, the letter A would have lacked a crossbar, as is sometimes the case with gold-glass text.

It is not known whether the woman was named; if so, nothing survives of her name. The silvered border was formed of a single band.

Collection History

Probably acquired in Rome by Charles Wilshere after 1865.

Bibliography

Garrucci 1876: 182, no.7 with tav. 197 lists this fragment as being in the Cabinet des Medailles, Paris;[1] Morey 1959: no.377, pl.XXXII; Cooley 2017: 253–5, no.400.

Comment

The name of the male figure, 'Rufus', is not otherwise attested in Morey's corpus. The portraits probably represent a married couple. The woman's hairstyle may be compared with Morey 89, 93–4, etc. In 1987 Marlia Mango noted a similar, unpublished piece in Zurich.

Both this object and Morey 400 – a very similar piece preserving the head of a young man with a comparable hairstyle set to right of centre of the glass, inscribed above '?G A IVIVA', now in the Cabinet des Médailles, Paris – are described by Morey as discs with concave bases and no sign of a foot-ring. It may thus be suggested that they represent a late fourth-century revival of the third-century portrait medallion. Both are of small scale and unusually distinctive quality, and do not appear to have been cut or broken from vessels.

Male figures rendered in similar style appear on the base of a cup now in the British Museum; two-thirds of its foot-ring has been preserved.[2] On the cup named images of the saints Sixtus and Timotheus are presented. This gold-glass has been ascribed to Faedo Group 8, as an example of Theodosian 'neo-classicism' dated to AD 380–400, with Morey 400. The use of recycled glass in the Ashmolean examples, at least, supports the late fourth-century date proposed for this group on iconographical grounds.[3]

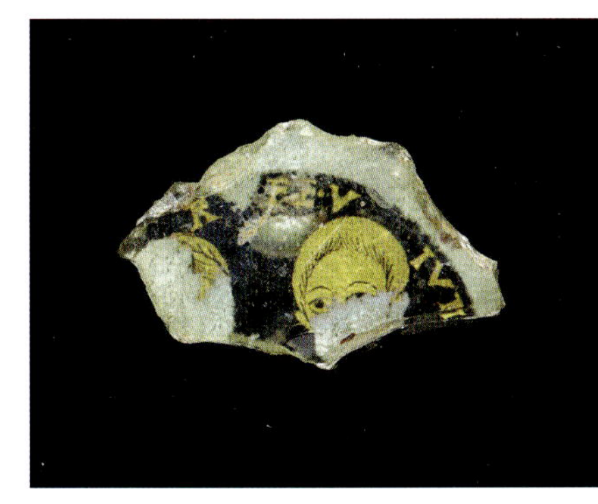

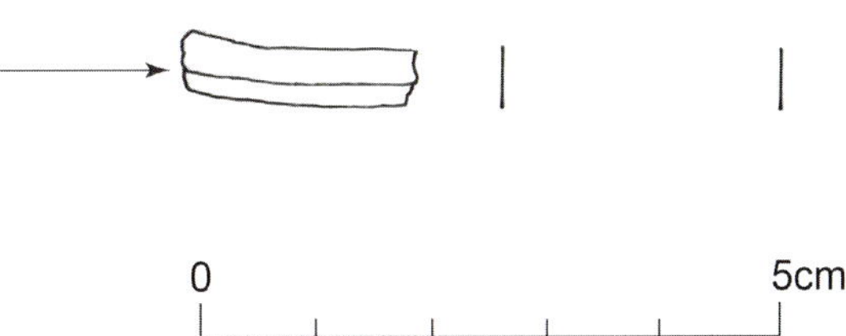

0 5cm

Endnotes

1. Most likely Garrucci confused the Wilshere fragment with tav. 197.8 = Morey 400.
2. Nüsse 2008 Abb.20 = Morey 313 with text p.238. See recently Howells 2015: 77–9, no.9. See also below, cat. 20.
3. See below, cat. 20 for discussion of the chemistry of the Ashmolean and British Museum pieces.

20 AN 2007.27

Fragment of the base of a small glass cup or bowl: part of a figure holding an open scroll, with part of an inscription

Photograph by David Gowers, 2013. Drawing by Yvonne Beadnell, 2012

H. 50 mm (max.); W. 23 mm (max.)
UL. Transparent, colourless. TH. 2.8 mm
LL. Transparent, colourless. TH. 2.0 mm

The glass was decoloured with a mixture of antimony and manganese. The composition of the inner layer of this vessel is so similar to that of the outer layer of cat. **19** that they were probably made from the same batch of recycled glass.

Present condition

The fragment comes from the right side of the vessel base. Two short stubs of foot-ring, 3 mm in height, are preserved. The lightly bubbled glass base is flat, with a slightly irregular surface containing stress fractures. There is silvery iridescence on the corroded foil, and some apparently free-floating on the glass. The upper surface is pitted so that the gold foil image appears blurred. The straight break at the left side of the fragment may have been a deliberate cut, as in cat. **11**. The angular break at the base is comparable with those of Morey 313, the base of a cup representing Sixtus and Timotheus (see above, cat. **19**).

Gold leaf decoration

All that survives is the proper left side of a figure, from shoulder to hip. The figure holds up with both hands an unrolled scroll (*rotulus*), as do the saints on cat. **22**. The mantle is decorated with scrolls along the broad band of cloth above and below the *rotulus*. More scroll-like decoration appears above the double lines drawn from upper right to lower left across the band of cloth. The double lines therefore form part of the textile decoration and do not indicate multiple folds of a toga (*contabulatio*). Inscribed to the right of the figure in Latinised Greek is the word '(ZE)SES' ('Live!'). Despite the similarity of the glass layers, the inscription is in a different hand to that of the probable medallion cat. **19** and must belong to a different object, in this case a vessel. Beyond the inscription is a simple band defining the edge of the scene; this too is very like that of cat. **19**.

Collection history

Purchased by Charles Wilshere at an unknown date from Tommaso and Vincenzo Capobianchi, 152 Via del Babuino, Rome. This fragment did not form part of the Museo Recupero.

Bibliography

Garrucci 1864: 168, no.7, tav. XXXII; Garrucci 1876: 186, no.7, tav. 200; Vopel 1899: 99, no.101; Leclercq 1923: no.445, col.1852; Morey 1959: no.380, pl.XXXII (not illustrated); Vattuone 2000: 136, unnumbered fig.

Comment

Due to confusion between this and another of the Wilshere glasses, cat. **3**, this glass was not illustrated in Morey's catalogue, nor was the text included in Cooley's 2017 publication. The vessel base displays a figure holding an unrolled scroll or *rotulus*, in a Christian context to be understood as symbolising the Old Testament.[1] While men, especially prophets, are usually associated with this symbol, the elaborately decorated mantle is more frequently worn by women.[2] However, in double portraits of husband and wife the woman is almost always placed on the left-hand side of the base (to her husband's right), rather than on the right-hand side as on this glass.[3] It is also unusual for a wife to hold an open scroll.[4] It is possible, then, that the figure represents either Christ or a prophet in unusually decorative clothing, or a female figure of authority, possibly a personification of the Church or a city (compare cat. **7**).

Above the figure, a damaged portion of the glass whose foil has silvered was unconvincingly identified by Garrucci as part of a dove. The inscription around the edge of the base would have originally read '[PIE ZE]SES', ('Drink! Live!'). This exhortation to the reader and user of the vessel, common on many of the gold-glasses as well as on other Roman drinking vessels, is found on two other glasses in the Wilshere Collection, cats **1** and **3**.

It is possible that this glass forms part of a contemporary, late fourth-century group comprising both medallions with portraits of individuals and vessels representing ecclesiastical subjects (see cat. **19** above). The similarity of the outer layer of recycled glass to the inner layer of cat. **19** suggests that both products were made in the same glass workshop, but that different engravers were used for the medallion and the vessel. Indeed the lettering of this example appears closer to that of a vessel, perhaps of similar form, now in the British Museum than it does to the medallion cat. **19**.[5] However, chemically the Ashmolean and the British Museum vessel bases do not appear to belong to the same group. This raises the question of whether a single, Rome-based workshop might have used both raw glass decoloured with manganese only (British Museum vessel) and recycled glass (Ashmolean vessel and medallion) at the same time.[6]

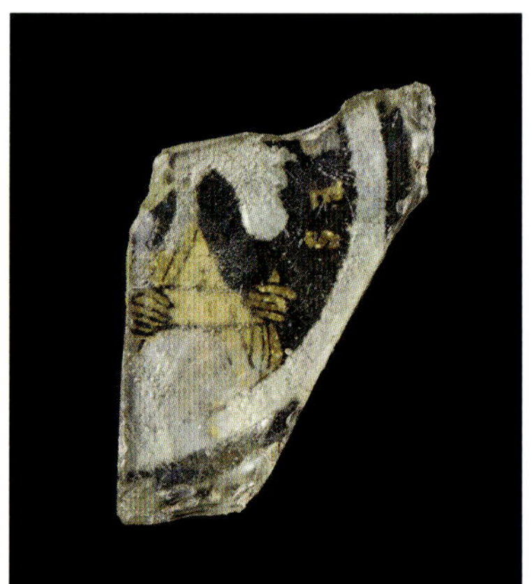

Endnotes

1. Tkacz 2002: 98–9 with Fig. 4 for the principal image of the Brescia casket: Christ opens the scriptures in the synagogue in a scene of revelation; Spier 2007a: 132, Fig. 97 for an image of the prophet Jeremiah holding an unrolled scroll from the presbytery of San Vitale, Ravenna.
2. Mantles with similar decoration are worn by a number of women on glasses in the Vatican Museum, Museo Sacro Cristiano, for example Morey nos. 59, 91, 93–4, etc.
3. As in the central roundel on cat. **3** (p.133), but see Morey 113.
4. Garrucci 1876: tav. 197.3 illustrates a woman named Praeiecta wearing a similarly decorated mantle, viewed to the right of her husband and holding a closed scroll.
5. British Museum BEP 1863, 0727.12: Morey 1959: no.313; Howells 2015: 77–9, no.9.
6. For semi-quantitative XRF analysis of the British Museum vessel see Meek in Howells 2015: 37, Table 6 (Type 2b).

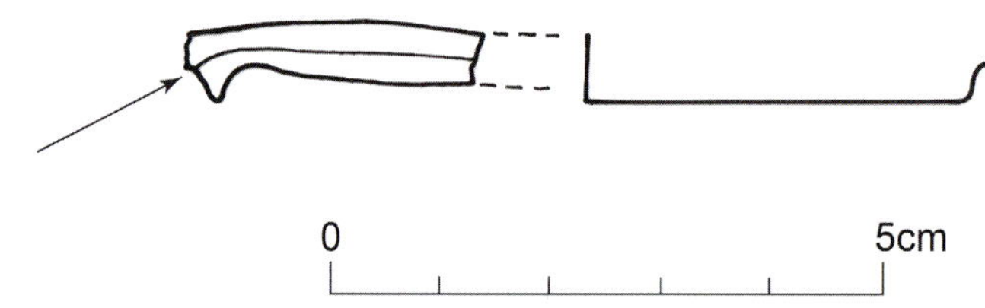

21 AN 2007.26

Base of a gold-glass plate or shallow bowl: a man and a woman at prayer beside a tree and a rock with flowing water

Photograph by David Gowers (2013).

DIAM. 114 mm; TH. 5.1 mm
UL. Pale greenish, transparent. TH. 4.0 mm
LL. Colourless, transparent. TH. 1.1 mm

The raw glass was decoloured with a mixture of antimony and manganese, most likely recycled. Isotopic analysis has revealed the raw glass to be of Syro–Palestinian origin (see Appendix 4b).

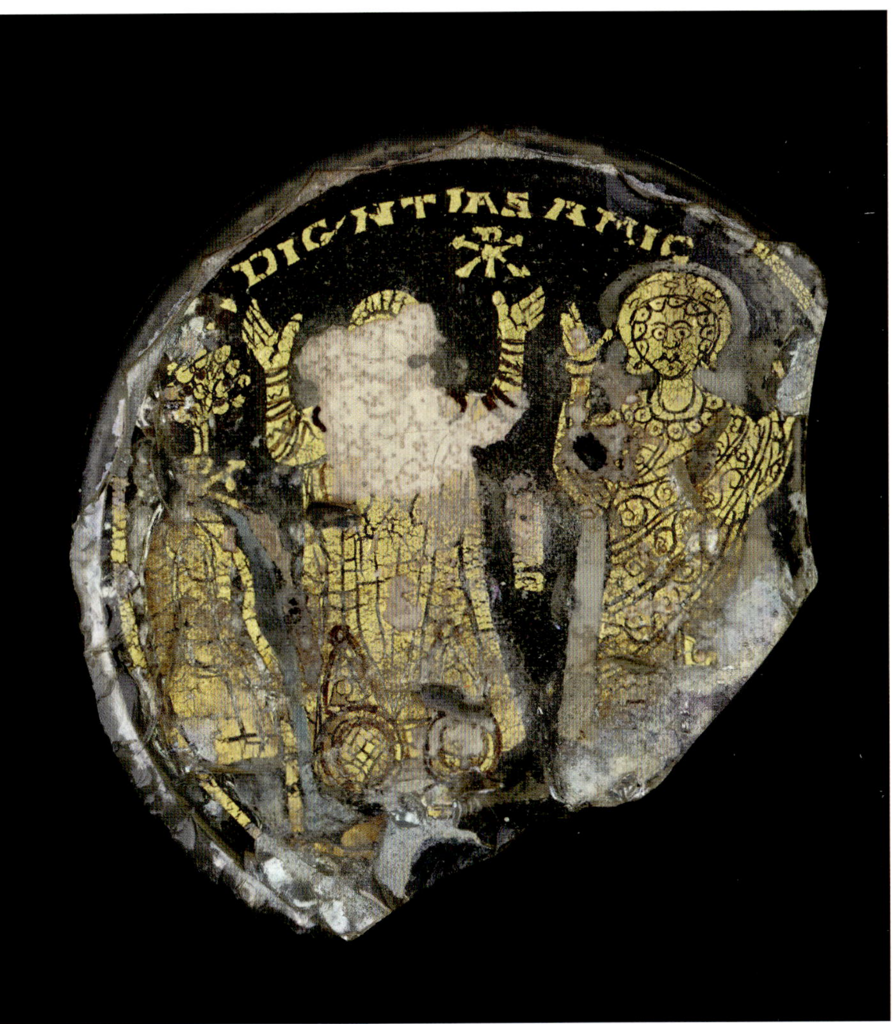

Present condition
Part of the base and all of the vessel wall are broken away. Over half of the foot-ring survives. There are stress fractures in the bubbled glass. Iridescent weathering appears beneath the upper layer of glass, especially over the upper part of the male figure. The bluish tinge following the outline of the female figure and the feature on the left is probably a bloom formed by weathering. There is a hole in the foil to the right of the centre, in which part of the proper right arm of the female figure has been lost. Generally the cut and incised foil is fragmented; surface details were rendered in red and black pigment, of which the red has faded to brown.

Gold leaf and painted enamel decoration
A man and a woman stand, their arms raised in prayer, separated by a rolled scroll (*rotulus*). Both are elaborately dressed in contemporary clothes. The medallions and hooped sleeves of the man's tunic are decorated in brownish-red enamel; the woman wears a heavy jewelled collar, an elaborately scrolled mantle and patterned dalmatic tunic beneath. Her hair appears in small, scalloped curls around a round face; the hair is apparently confined behind the curls in a jewelled snood. To the man's proper right is a tree bearing painted fruit; beneath it is a Christogram, and below that water flows over a rock. A second Christogram appears above the man's left hand. Between the figures floats a scroll, and above their heads is inscribed in Latin letters 3 mm in height 'DIGNTIAS (*sic*) AMIC [ORUM]'. The scene is confined within a narrow band of gold leaf, now much fragmented.

Collection history
Purchased by Charles Wilshere from Tommaso and Vincenzo Capobianchi, 152 Via del Babuino, Rome; acquired by Tommaso Capobianchi at the 1862 public sale of the Museo del Barone Alessio Recupero, Catania, Sicily. The glass was in Recupero's collection by 1797, when Seroux d'Agincourt was supplied with a *calco* (copy).[1]

Bibliography
Garrucci 1858: 52–3, no.4, tav. XXV; Garrucci [1862–3]: 6–7, no.8; Garrucci 1864: 142–3, no.3, tav. XXV; Garrucci 1876: 175, no.3, tav. CXCIV; Vopel 1899: no.139, pp. 8, 12–13, 23, 42, 44–5, 82, 101; Leclercq 1923: no.483, col.1856; Webster 1929: 153, no.80, pl.V, 2; Morey 1959: no.379, pl.XXXII; Faedo 1978: 1049–50, tav. L.1; Smith 2000: 116, cat. 299, pl.LXXIII.c (drawing); Vattuone 2000: 132, 135 unnumbered fig.; Nüsse 2008, 229, 235 Abb.11, 236; Vickers 2011, 612, figs 8–9; Cooley 2017, 257–9, no.402; Norris 2015: 6.

Comment
Portraits of a man and a woman at prayer decorate the gold-glass base of this large vessel, with the figures assuming the traditional 'orant' position, both arms raised to the heavens.[2] Garrucci misidentified the subject of this glass, taking the praying figures for the female saints Perpetua and Felicitas, while both Garrucci and Morey mistakenly saw a statue of a male figure on the hill to the left of the scene, which Garrucci believed to represent Saint Cyprian. However, the 'hill' supports only a tree laden with fruit and a rocky waterfall. Moreover, the two standing figures are most probably not saints; they are more likely to be the private (and wealthy) deceased individuals for whom the glass was commissioned in order to celebrate their faith and to express the hope that their belief would be rewarded in the afterlife.[3] Similar portraits appear in the catacombs, for example the orant woman (often called the *donna velata* or 'veiled woman') in the Catacomb of Priscilla,[4] as well as on early Christian sarcophagi.[5]

Drawings by Yvonne Beadnell (2012), left and the late Rupert Cook (1987), right

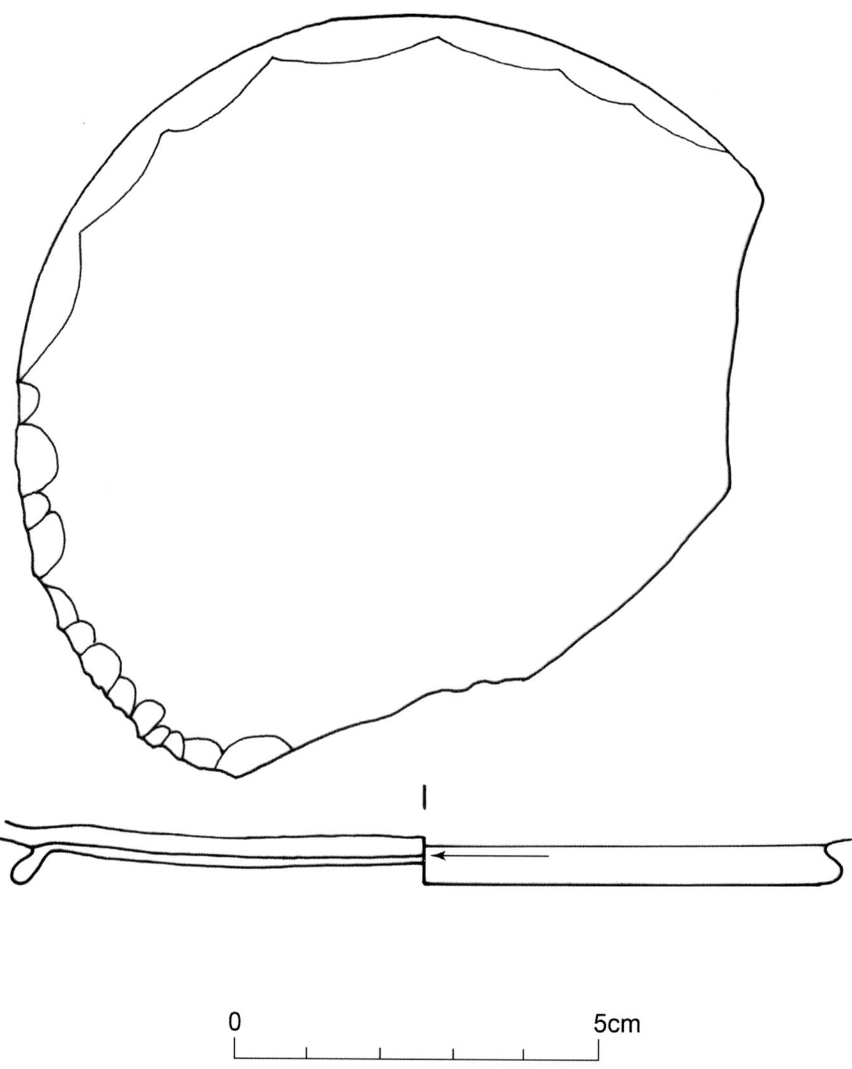

While images of the deceased and Old Testament figures as orants are common (for example Isaiah or Daniel on cat. **30**, Susanna or Agnes on cat. **23**), rarely are two orants depicted side by side, although a similar format is found on ivories and sarcophagi.[6] A painting of a male and a female orant standing next to a hill, identical in composition to the Wilshere glass, decorates the so-called 'Greek Chapel' of the Catacomb of Priscilla.[7] The painting has traditionally been thought to represent Daniel and Susanna praying for salvation (as part of a larger Susanna cycle), but this identification has been questioned by Nicola Denzey, who identifies the two as a deceased husband and wife.[8]

In addition to its funerary implications, the setting of the scene perhaps evokes the previous baptism of the deceased. While orants are often represented between trees, as is Susannah on cat. **23**, the fruit-bearing tree growing from the rocky hill with its flowing spring to the extreme left of the glass echoes the symbolic elements of baptism expressed by Tertullian: '...water is restored from its defect of "bitterness" to its native grace of "sweetness" by the tree of Moses. That tree was Christ'.[9] The Christogram (*Chi-Rho*) underneath the tree strengthens this association between the tree and Christ.[10]

Stylistically the work resembles glasses in the Vatican Museum (Morey no.59) and in Pesaro (Morey no.283). The former represents a family group, the latter St Agnes between Christ and Laurence.[11]

The placement of the inscription within the main field, framed by a single-band border, is uncommon. It only occurs on one other gold-glass, now in the Museo Archeologico Oliveriano in Pesaro, which also features a 'dignitas' inscription (Morey no.285).[12] The unusual iconography of the scene, combined with the clumsy execution of the figures in the landscape and the misspelled 'dignitas amicorum' inscription, along with the use of recycled glass, all suggest a date around 380–400, at the end of the spectrum proposed by Faedo (AD 350–400).[13] Nonetheless the quality falls far short of those glasses (here cats **19** and **20**) associated with 'Theodosian neo-classicism', possibly because this large dish was intended for use by a group rather than an individual.[14]

Endnotes

1. Garrucci 1858: 52–3.
2. On this pose see Jensen 2000: 35–7.
3. Orants appear in a paradisiacal setting in the paintings of the Cubicolo di Santa Cecilia in the Catacomb of San Callisto: Garrucci 1873: 19, tav. 15,2. A couple and their children appear on a gold-glass in the British Museum between two trees with a *Chi-Rho* in the centre: BM 1863,07.1863,0727.7 (= Morey nos. 308–9, pl.XXIX). See Howells 2015: 129–31, no.39. However, they are not at prayer.
4. Grabar 1967: 99–102, 116–7, figs 96, 115.
5. Examples from Rome include Bovini and Brandenburg 1967: cats 67 (Vatican Museum), 555 (Catacomb of Praetextatus), 747 (Santa Maria Antiqua), 771 (Museo Nazionale); on the sarcophagi see Koch 2000: 21–2.
6. Other exceptions include the male and female orants on the fifth-century Pola Casket: Donati 2000: 225–6, no.95, fig. 170; Deckers in Spier

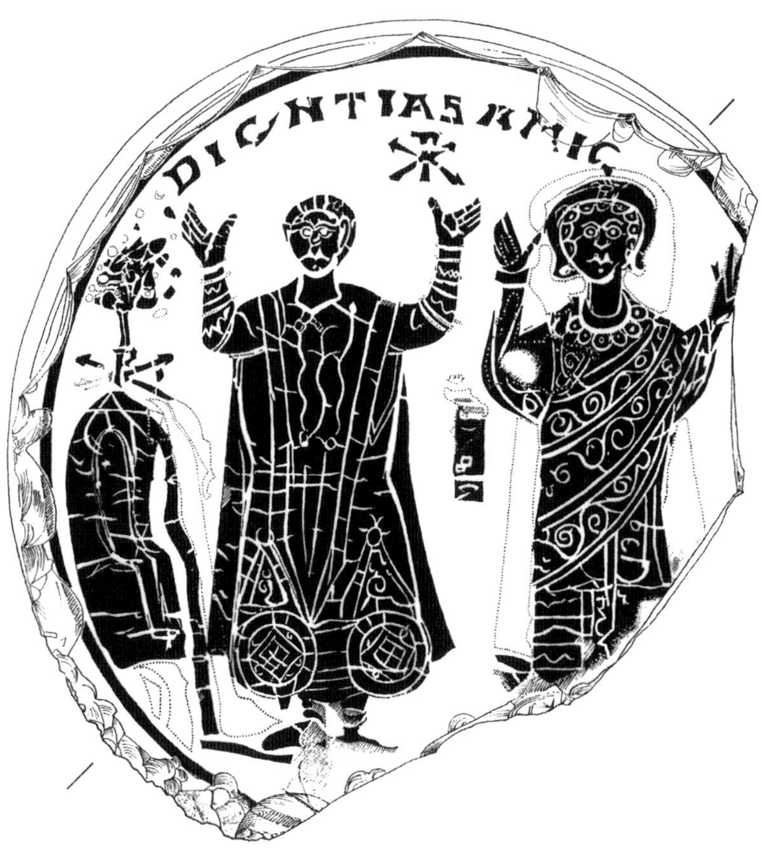

2007: 101; also a sarcophagus from Rome with an *imago clipeata* of two female orants, now in San Sebastiano, dated by inscription to 392: Bovini and Brandenburg 1967: cat. 240, pl.54.
7. Illustrated in Grabar 1967: 113–4, fig. 113.
8. Denzey 2007: 110–12, although her interpretation of the woman in the painting as a female deacon is highly controversial. For the traditional interpretation of the scene see Schlosser 1966; De Bruyn 1970.
9. Tertullian, *De baptismo* 9.1.
10. The *Chi-Rho* also appears on Morey nos. 36, 72, 76, 106, 112, 126, 250, etc.
11. Faedo's workshop 3: cf. Nüsse 2008: Abb.11.
12. On the 'dignitas' inscriptions see cat. **4**.
13. Faedo 1978: 1052. Nüsse 2008: 236 suggests an earlier fourth-century date on grounds of the inclusion within the group of some glasses portraying Christ as the Good Shepherd.
14. Chapter 3, p.104.

22 AN 2007.11

Base of a shallow glass bowl decorated with a scene of Christ teaching with Peter and Paul and eight (?) saints

Photograph by David Gowers, 2013. Drawings by Yvonne Beadnell , 2012 and by the late Rupert Cook, 1987

DIAM. 93 mm (max.)
UL. Very pale green, transparent. TH. 2.7 mm
LL. Very pale green, transparent. TH. 1 mm

The raw glass was decoloured with a mixture of antimony and manganese, probably recycled.

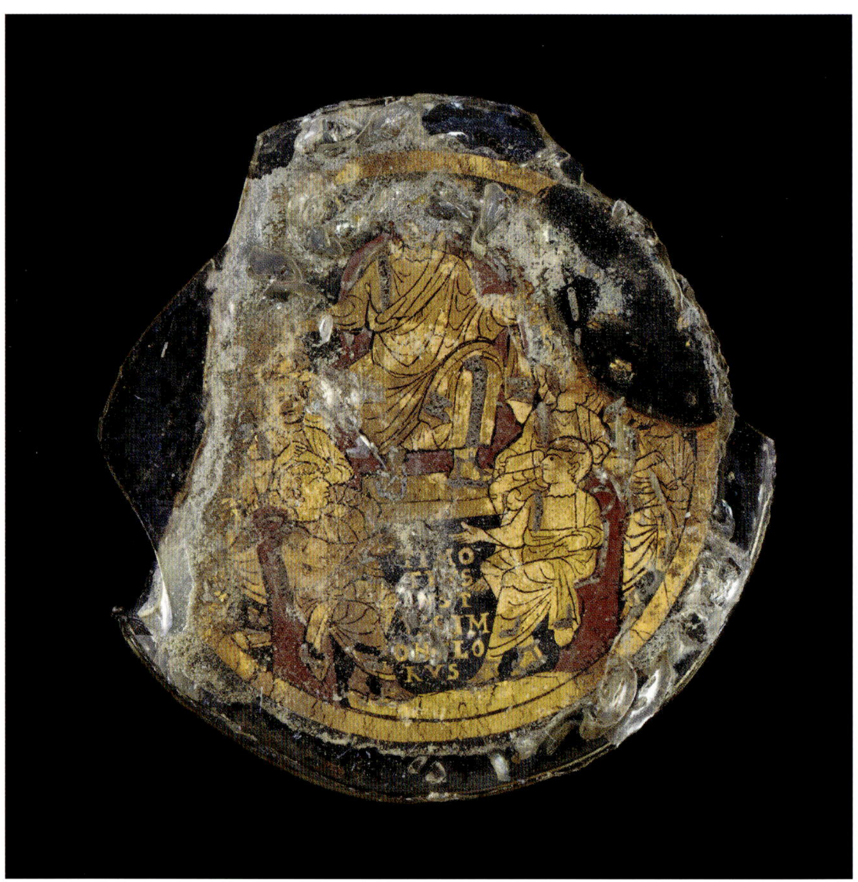

Present condition

The original diameter of the foot-ring was 9.4 cm. The outer layer is fractured on the upper left and right sides, with part of the inner layer missing on the left side. Elsewhere the inner layer has been clipped back to the edge of the medallion, but over half of the foot-ring remains intact on the outer layer. The underside of the base is concave. The two layers of slightly bubbled glass are nearly colourless, with a pale green tinge. The figured and inscribed foil is intact; the border is fragmented. Red and black pigment is applied directly to the glass to highlight features of furniture and clothing.

Gold leaf and painted enamel decoration

The beardless Christ is enthroned in a chair, painted in deep red enamel. He faces front with Peter and Paul flanking him and Timothy, Justin (so Morey, but better Sixtus, see further below), Simon and Florus seated below. Christ's tunic has black *clavi* and a scalloped neck, and his mantle is decorated with an H motif, the latter shown on its side. His feet rest on a footstool; the sandals are also shown in black. Apparently this colour application was not entirely successful; the surface has bubbled, most likely at the time of fusion. Christ gives a scroll to Peter (on his proper right, beardless and dressed in a mantle), and to Paul (to his left, the figure largely lost) a diptych, with seven lines of text clearly visible though never intentionally legible.

The junior saints are seated on red-painted chairs with high backs. Their names are inscribed in the centre field. Timothy and Sixtus hold open scrolls, very similar to that held by the figure in cat. 20, but here held at an angle so they remain visible over the heads of Simon and Florus. Simon reads from an open diptych; Florus listens to him. All the saints wear tunics with scalloped edges and mantles and black sandals. Florus has two L motifs woven into his mantle, which is also black. Two further saints are to the outermost right and left. At the back of the thrones two unidentified saints stand and receive scrolls from Timothy and Sixtus.

Inscribed in Latin letters 2 mm in height behind the head of Christ 'CRISTVS'; behind the heads of Peter and Paul 'PET[RV]S/[PAVL]V[S]' and, in the centre ground between the junior saints, 'TIMO/TEVS/IVST/VSSIM/ON FLO/RVS'. The text was correctly read by Cooley as 'CRISTVS PETRVS [PA]V[LVS]⊠TIMO/TEVS/SVSTVS/SIM/ON FLO/RVS' (see the drawing by Rupert Cook right).

The outer band enclosing this unusually complex scene is plain gold.

Collection history

Purchased by Charles Wilshere in 1862–5 from Tommaso and Vincenzo Capobianchi, 152 Via del Babuino, Rome; acquired by Tommaso Capobianchi in 1862 at the public sale of the Museo del Barone Alessio Recupero, Catania, Sicily. The glass was drawn for Gaetano Marini (Biblioteca Apostolica Vaticana, Vat. lat. 9071, p.206, no.7: the drawing was annotated *R(omae) apud Alexiam Recupero*, i.e. the glass was already in the collection of Alessio Recupero in Rome. The drawing (above, p.60, fig. 28) suggests that the condition of the glass has changed little since the late eighteenth century.

Bibliography

Garrucci 1858: 40–1, no.4, tav. XVIII; Garrucci 1862–3: 5, no.4; Garrucci 1864: 111–14, no.4, tav. XVIII; Garrucci 1876: 159–60, no.4, tav. CLXXXVII; Vopel 1899: no.306, pp.8, 16, 31, 53, 58, 85–6, 107; Leclercq 1923: no.144, col.1834; Webster 1929: 154, no.104, pl.VI,2; Ladner 1941: 33, no.5; Morey 1959: no.364, pl.XXXI; Grabar 1968: 72, fig. 171 (drawing); Testini 1969: no.152, pp.274, 314; Smith 2000: cat. 166, pl.XLIII.a; Vattuone 2000: 132, 135, unnumbered fig.; Vickers 2011: 611–12, fig. 7; Cooley 2017: 241–3, no.394.

Comment

The iconography of this vessel base is unique among extant gold-glasses. One small fragment of another gold-glass, now in the Victoria and Albert Museum, London, may have depicted a version of the same scene, although only the seated figure of Timothy is preserved.[1] The scene is set as if Christ were a professor seated in his *cathedra* in a late antique lecture room. It is depicted in the same arrangement as that of the apsidal lecture

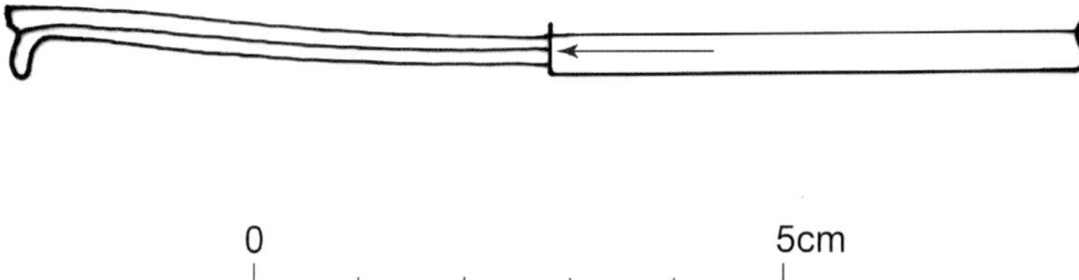

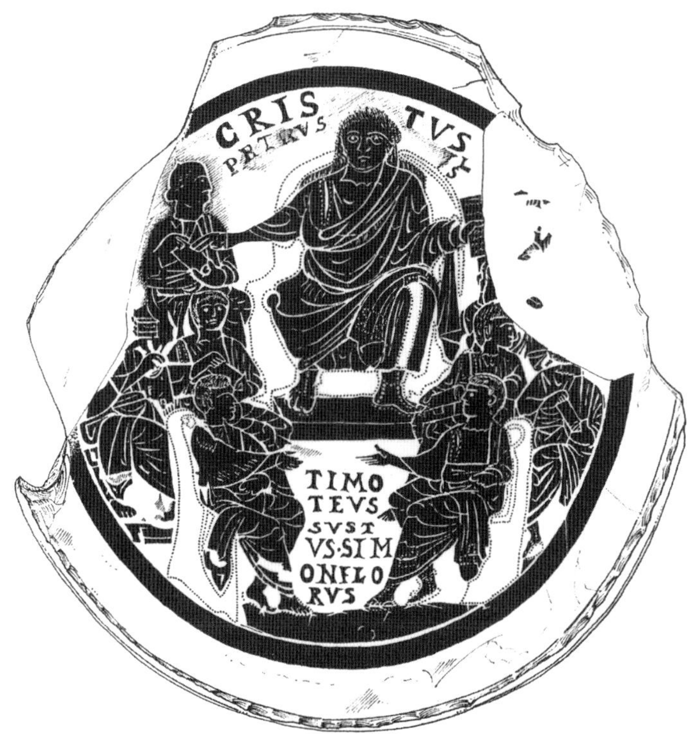

rooms at Kom el-Dikka in Alexandria, which feature a central *cathedra* flanked on either side by rows of semicircular benches.[2] Images of Christ as teacher of the apostles and other saints derived from classical depictions of the poets or philosophers composed in the same vein, which decorated the villas of wealthy Romans,[3] as well as the catacombs, including the fourth-century Via Latina Catacomb, where a central sage (possibly Aristotle), seated with his students in a circle, conducts a lesson on the nature of the soul.[4] On this glass Christ is instead represented as the true philosopher and the 'great doctor' (*medicus magnus*).[5]

While the semicircular arrangement of this glass is rarely found on gold-glass, similar scenes were popular in painted programmes of the catacombs in Rome.[6] This occurred most famously in the Catacomb of Domitilla,[7] but also appears in the cubiculum of Santa Cecilia within the Catacomb of San Callisto,[8] as well as in the Catacomb of Sant'Ermete, where Christ and the Apostles each sit in a *cathedra* with a high rounded back around the curve of an *arcosolium* (arched niche for a sarcophagus).[9] Christ and the two saints in the foreground sit on the same type of high-backed seats, painted in red enamel, while the other figures appear to sit on seats without backs, at least one of which (the seat to the far right of the glass) has feet in the shape of lions' paws.[10]

Peter and Simon ('the Zealot') (Luke 6:15, Acts 1:13) were among the original Twelve Apostles, and Paul described himself as an Apostle (Romans 1:1) and as the 'Apostle of the Gentiles' (Romans 11:13; Galatians 2:8). The most popular martyr to be depicted on gold-glasses, Timothy was a disciple of Paul (1–2 Timothy); he was martyred in Ephesus in the first century, and his feast was later to be celebrated at the Basilica of St Paul on the Via Ostiense.[11] Timothy appears here with Sixtus, in a pairing frequently seen in gold-glass.[12] Florus is to be identified either as St Florus, a stonemason martyred with his brother Laurus in Illyricum in the second century,[13] or possibly as a companion of the fourth-century pope Damasus.[14] He is rarely depicted on gold-glasses; only one other representation of him survives on a glass in the Vatican where he appears with Peter, Simon and Damasus.[15]

The heads of the figures are highly individualised and well drawn. In its overall execution this polychrome glass is of very high quality. It is likely to have been an individual commission. The use of recycled glass and the inclusion of figures who may be identified as associates of Damasus suggest a date in the late fourth century, possibly as late as the Theodosian era, when art of exceptional quality was produced in various media (see, for example, the gold-glass medallion and small cup, cats **19** and **20**, and the sarcophagus, cat. **41**). The plain gold band around the edge of the scene may also be compared to cats **19** and **20**. A similarly composed narrative in a more generous format appears on a near-contemporary apse mosaic, dated to c.AD 401–17, in the basilica of Santa Pudenziana on the Via Urbana, Rome.[16]

Endnotes

1. V&A, inv.C.13-1946a (= Morey 1959: no.352; also possibly an even more poorly preserved glass in the British Museum 1886.11-17.330 (= Morey no.303; Howells 2015: 76–7, no.7).
2. Grabar 1968:72–3; McKenzie 2007: 212–16, figs 370–1. See above, p.118, fig. 61.
3. Balty 1995: 42–6, 299–305.
4. Bargebuhr 1991: 83–6, Taf.44.
5. Augustine, Sermon 299.6 (*PL* 38, 1372).
6. On the development of the iconography see Hanfmann 1951.
7. Testini 1966: fig. 174.
8. Painted above a doorway: Garrucci 1873: 22, tav. 18.1.
9. Garrucci 1873: 89, tav. 82.1.
10. The drawing in Grabar 1968: fig. 171 identifies these stools as examples of the curule seat (*sella curulis*). Such stools with crossed legs were typically reserved for holders of public office, but no evidence of these seats survives, either on the glass as it is preserved or on the earlier drawings included in Garrucci's works.
11. *Depositio martyrum*, ed. Mommsen, *MGH* 9, vol.1, 72. While he is mentioned in the Calendar of 354, Timothy's hagiographical tradition seems to be later in date: Grig 2004b: 218–9.
12. See, for example, British Museum BEP 1863,0727.2, Howells 2015: 77–9, no.9.
13. For his life see *BHG* 1, 209–10; Delehaye 1904.
14. Grig 2004b: 210–12, who follows the suggestion of Vopel 1899: 87. See above, p.00.
15. Morey 1959: no.107.
16. Tiberia 2003.

23 AN 2007.35a,b; AN 2007.42
Fragments of a glass dish: Saints Peter and Paul surrounded by scenes of salvation

Photograph by David Gowers, 2014 (top). Photographs showing detail of painted blood of the martyred Isaiah by Dana Norris, 2012 (below)

DIAM. 110 mm; TH. 4.5 mm
UL. Colourless, transparent. TH. 2.5 mm
LL. Colourless, transparent. TH. 2.0 mm

The raw glass was decoloured with a mixture of antimony and manganese, probably recycled. There is considerable variation in the chemical composition of the fragments, suggesting a complex production process in which recycled cullet was added to the mix in the later stages of firing (above, pp. 97–8, fig. 45).

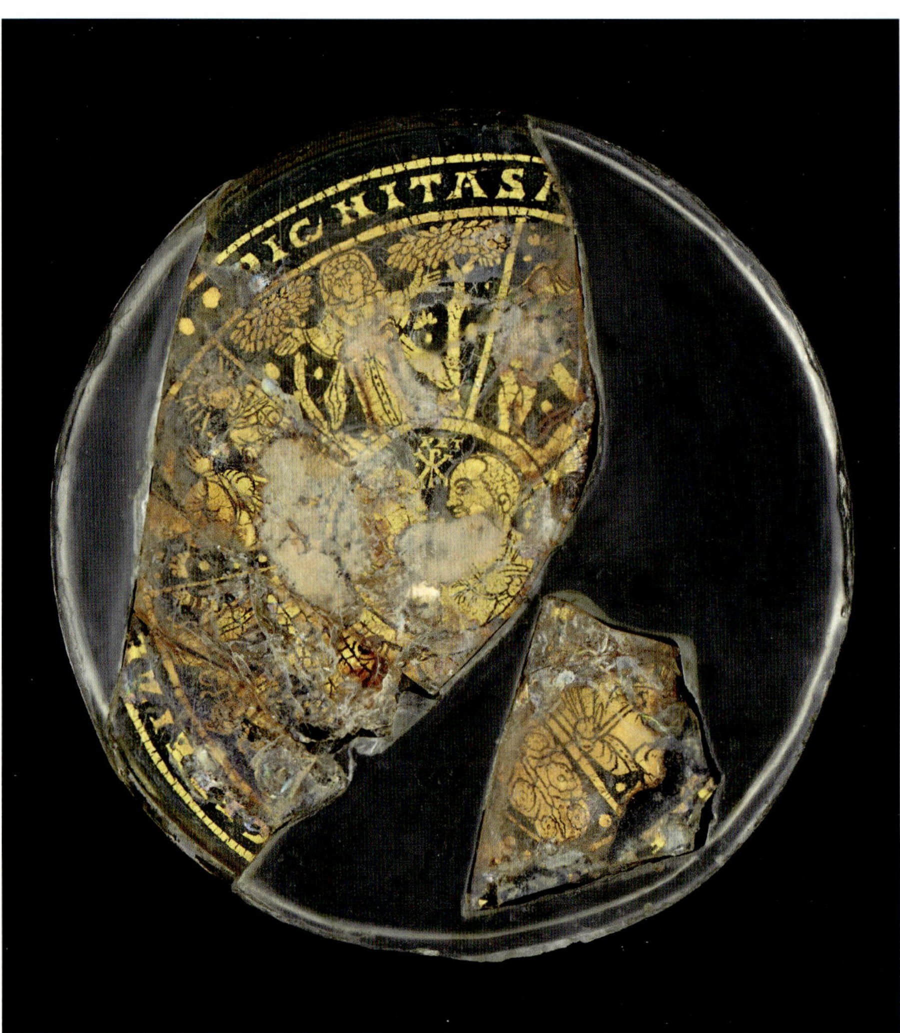

Present condition
The fragments form the base of a shallow plate or bowl with a foot-ring. The surface of the lightly bubbled glass is slightly concave. Cut and incised gold foil decoration, now largely fragmented, is laid between the two layers of glass. Part of the base and nearly all the vessel walls are broken away; tiny spurs of wall extend horizontally outwards above the surviving remains of the foot-ring, the angle suggesting that this was a plate. The glass has suffered stress fractures and appears opalescent due to weathering. There is surface iridescence on the upper layer and surface cracks on the lower, which has broken away on three of the fragments. In the 1980s this piece was in four fragments, two of which were joined. A third fragment, AN2007.42, the heads of the Hebrew boys in the fiery furnace, has been reattached to AN2007.35a. A fragment drawn for Garrucci (actually for Marini?) has now been lost.

Gold leaf and enamel paint decoration
Two busts facing one another, inscribed with the names PAVL/VS and PET/RVS, in letters 1 mm in height, are set in a central medallion defined by a single band. Between their brows is a *Chi-Rho*. The saints are dressed in simple, round-necked tunics, their right arms held in the sling of their mantles. Paul is clean-shaven with short hair and a large, square jaw. Peter is bearded, with receding, curly hair. Radiating around the medallion are scenes of salvation from the Old Testament and the Apocrypha. Moving clockwise, these represent the three Hebrew youths praying for deliverance from the fiery furnace, followed by the unjustly accused Susannah standing at prayer between two trees. She is elaborately dressed in rich, contemporary clothes and wears a veil. The next scene shows the martyrdom of Isaiah, red enamel blood flowing from his hips where he has been cut with a saw held by two men. Fragment AN2007.35b bears scenes of Moses driving away the serpent (?) and striking water from the rock. The next panel is missing, while in the last, now fragmentary, scene a standing man confronts a radiate male bust. This has been interpreted by Garrucci as Isaiah listening to God's will that King Hezekiah of Judah be healed (II Kings XX, I and Isaiah 38:1).

The double-band border is inscribed in Latin and transliterated Greek: 'DIGNITAS AMICORUM VIVAT [IS CVM TVI(S) FE(LICITER) IN PA]CE DEI ZE[SES]' ('The dignity of friends. You (pl.) live with your people with good fortune in the peace of God may you (sing.) live!'). The underlined text is now lost or illegible, but was recorded for Marini (see drawing) and published by Séroux d'Agincourt and Garrucci. Two stops mark the start and end of the text.

Collection history
Acquired by Charles Wilshere from Tommaso and Vincenzo Capobianchi, 152 Via del Babuino, Rome between 1862 and 1865; purchased by Tommaso Capobianchi in the 1862 public sale of the Museo del Barone Alessio Recupero, Catania, Sicily. Drawn for Gaetano Marini in the late eighteenth century, at which date it was still in the care of Abbot Giacomo Severini (p.57, fig. 26). It is likely that the glass was sold to Alessandro Recupero after Giacomo Severini's death in 1801, when his brother and heir Andrea is known to have sold off items in his care to private collectors.

From published drawings the nineteenth-century history of this vessel base appears somewhat chequered.[1] A drawing published by

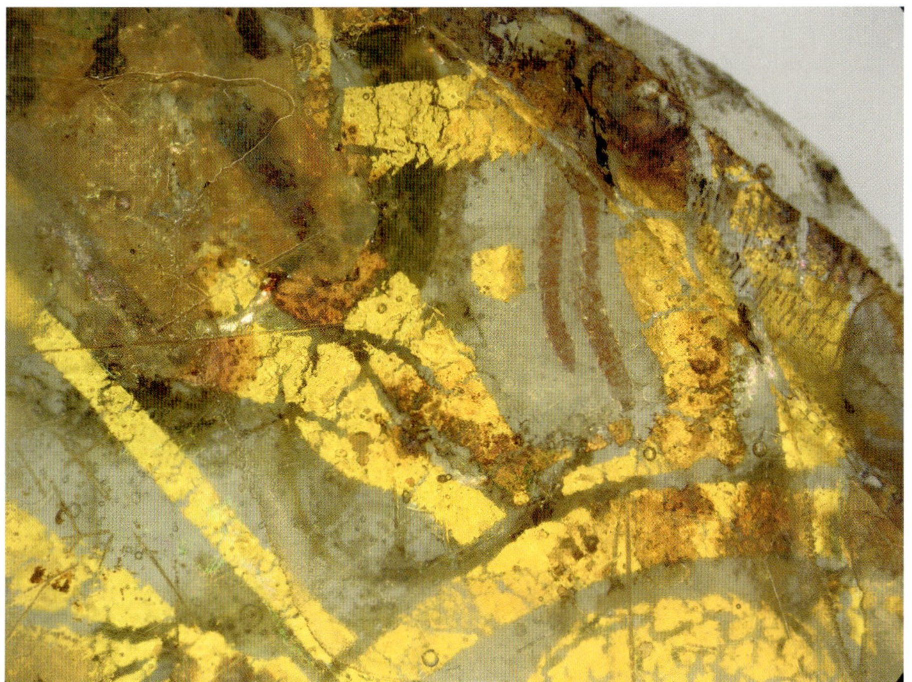

sun), with a sundial or gnomon beneath, is rare; it may perhaps be associated with Isaiah, though this would be out of sequence on the glass.[5] Also rare and unclear in interpretation is the figure of Moses slaying the serpent, alternatively to be seen as Aaron's rod.

Among a group of 16 gold-glasses bearing the 'Dignitas amicorum' legend, Morey no.37 is similar to the central medallion. In this case, however, the figures of the saints fill the whole field. Morey nos. 49, 58, 241, 274, 314 and 365 (cat. **26**) combine the text with facing busts of the saints. Paul's gesture, perhaps representing speech, is also common, for example Morey 50, 66, 70, 72 and 74. So is the *Chi-Rho*, which appears on Morey 36, 72, 76, 106, 112, 126, 250, 309 and 315.

For more complete 'Dignitas Amicorum' texts see cat. **4**, n.3. None of these combines both plural ('VIVATIS') and singular ('ZESES') in a single text. The appearance of Peter and Paul as dominant figures in the centre, the use of recycled glass indicated by the mixed decolourants and the style of the lettering, featuring a G with cedilla, suggest a late date in the sequence of gold-glass, in the last quarter of the fourth century.

Séroux d'Agincourt in 1829 offers the same text as appears on the drawing made for Marini in 1781, but the pictorial scenes are reversed, as if drawn from the underside of the glass. The joining fragment showing the Hebrew youths in the fiery furnace with the end of the inscription is missing – as it is in the drawing published by Garrucci in 1858. This simply shows the same text, with the scenes viewed from the interior of the glass, in the correct order.

In 1862 Garrucci published a catalogue of the 12 Recupero glasses, by then in Capobianchi's shop. The drawing published there (tav. 1) shows the glass in exactly the state it is in today, with the upper right fragment lost and the scene of Moses drawing water from the rock just touching the main preserved area; the Hebrew youths are here correctly joined to the main fragment. This important publication demonstrates that the damage we see today had occurred before Wilshere bought the glass. In 1876 Garrucci published a drawing that must have been a composite of his 1862 work. The lost portion shows most of the Isaiah scene and part of Moses and the serpent restored to the glass in the same, more detailed style than that of the eighteenth-century artist.

Bibliography

Séroux d'Agincourt 1829: 10, no.27, 19, tav. XII; Garrucci 1858: 1, no.2, tav. I; Garrucci 1862–3: 4, no.I; Garrucci 1864: 3, tav. I; Garrucci: 1864: 4, no.I; Garrucci 1876: III, 117–21, no.3, tav. CLXXI; Vopel 1899: no.293, pp.9, 16–17, 23, 51, 59, 61, 64–5, 68, 70, 76, 81–2, 106; Leclercq 1923: col.1833, no.131; Webster 1929: 154, no.103, pl.VI, 1; Morey 1959: no.388, pl.XXXII; Testini 1969: 314, no.153; Smith 2000: pl.LII, c; Vattuone 2000: 132, 136, unnumbered fig.; Rini 2006; Vickers 2009–11: 611, fig. 3; Cooley 2017: 261–4, no.404.

Comment

The series of scenes follows the prayer for the commendation of the soul, in which the Lord is asked to save the deceased as he saved the biblical characters listed in the prayer. The prayer is discussed in detail above (pp.113–5). This is an interesting and unusual example of salvation scenes combined with named figures of the senior saints of Rome, rather than individual portraits, as in cat. **3**. Here the saints reinforce the plea for salvation by offering protection to the deceased. Susannah is very similarly dressed and coiffed to the female figure shown at prayer on cat. **21**. Christ or Paul may stand in for Moses; the figure is similarly dressed and coiffed to the bust of Paul in the central medallion, and appears as a miracle worker with a wand in the scene of the serpent. Unlike cat. **3**, the scenes are taken only from the Old Testament. Among five other glass vessels with biblical scenes of salvation published by Morey no.347 – an unprotected gold-glass plaque found in Cologne and now in the British Museum – is particularly close in design to this example. However, this also includes New Testament scenes.[2]

Of the individual scenes, the most graphic and interesting is the martyrdom of Isaiah, perhaps drawn from apocryphal sources of Syrian origin.[3] A less graphic example may perhaps be seen on the small medallion cat. **30**; the subject is otherwise unknown in gold-glass. The depiction of the veiled Susannah in late antique dress has given rise to some confusion with Agnes, but the latter is usually named. Susannah, along with the Hebrew boys in the fiery furnace and Moses striking the rock, are also seen in other funerary imagery, including catacomb painting and sarcophagi.[4] The beardless figure raising a hand to a radiate bust of the moving sun (or possibly Christ as the

Endnotes

1. They are most conveniently published by Rini 2006: Pls 1–4.
2. 'The St Ursula bowl', BEP S 317, Howells 2015: 101–3, no.17. The others are Morey 1959, nos. 224, 366 (cat. 3), 421 and 448.
3. Rini 2006.
4. Susannah (?) orant between two trees: also Morey 349 (?); Susannah in catacombs of Domitilla 58; Gordiano, ed Epimaco 1; Maius 12; Pietro e Marcellino 51, 71; Praetextatus 5; Priscilla 39; Via Latina 1. Sarcophagus in Rome, Santa Maria Antiqua, central female orant (possibly the deceased?) in front of two trees: Bovini and Brandenurg 1967: 747 (Rome; Koch 2000: pl.14); sarcophagus in Rome, Museo Nazionale: Bovini and Brandenburg 1967: 777 (Rome; Koch 2000: pl.28). Moses striking the rock: gold-glass, see Morey nos. 142, 143, 224?, 312, 347?, 366 (cat. 3) and 421; in catacombs: cf. cat. **3**; Via Latina 2; on sarcophagi, cf. Koch 2000: 144 (with further bibliography); Bovini and Brandenburg 1967: nos. 1, 35, 987, 768, 145, 935b and 783 (all Rome); Dresken-Weiland 1998: nos. 2 and 20; also provincial examples. Three Hebrews in the fiery furnace: on gold-glass see Morey 347 and 448; in catacombs see Nestori 1993: Balbina 1; Callixtus 27; Domitilla 31, 33, 62, 69; Ermete 4, 10; Giordani 5; Maius 5, 12, 16, 19; Pietro e Marcellino 71; Ponziano 4; Priscilla 7, 39; Via Anapo 8; Via Latina 1, 13; Via Paisiello 1.
5. See also the mosaic of the Mausoleum of the Julii, St Peter's: Perler 1953; Bardill 2012: 326–37 for a wider discussion of the connection between images of Christ and the sun (Helios/Sol).

24 AN 2007.19

Photograph: David Gowers, 2013

Segment of the edge of the base of a clear glass vessel decorated in gold leaf with border motifs and a Latin inscription

DIAM. 29 mm (max.); L. 41mm (max.)
UL. Pale green, transparent. TH. 2.2 mm
LL. Pale green, transparent. TH. 1.0 mm

The raw glass was decoloured with a mixture of antimony and manganese, so was most likely recycled.

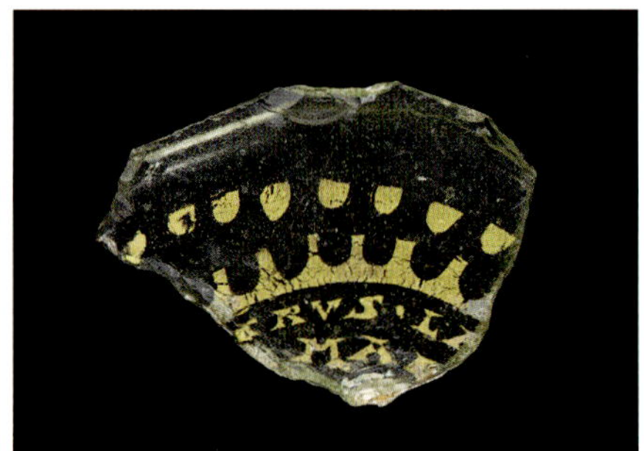

Present condition
The foot-ring and all but a tiny spur of the vessel wall are lost. The glass is lightly bubbled and the vessel has a slightly concave surface. There is iridescent weathering along the chipped edge of the fragment. The gold foil is fragmented.

Gold leaf decoration
Inside a reciprocal border with shield-shaped half-discs, two lines of Latin text are partially preserved: ;[PE]TRVS.LA[URENTIUS.]... / [ANI]M AI[N]...' ('Peter. Laurence(?)/....soul in(?)'). The text has been read by Cooley as '[---] TRVS LA[---]/[....]MAT[....]
Peter? Lazarus? ....mat...'.

Collection history
Probably acquired by Charles Wilshere in Rome after 1865.

Bibliography
Morey 1959: 62, no.372, pl.XXXII; Cooley 2017: 250–1, no.398.

Comment
In border design and stylised lettering style with diagonal S this fragment resembles Morey 1959: no.94, linked by him to the workshop of nos. 92 and 93. However, on the latter glasses families are represented and the text, as in other gold-glasses with similar lettering style, simply fills vacant space around the figures, without regard for ease of recovering the sense.

In contrast no.24 gives the impression of two ordered lines of lettering with a spacer dot between the saints' names, albeit disrupted by the irregular orientation of individual letters. As the location of the names usually corresponds to the position of the images, it may be the case that this glass was decorated with heads or busts of Saints Peter and Lawrence, along with a prayer for the soul of the deceased.

25 AN 2007.7
Base of a large plate, with images of Peter, Paul, Julius and Sixtus

DIAM. 105 mm; TH. 5.4 mm
UL. Pale green, transparent. TH. 3.9 mm
LL. Pale green, transparent. TH. 1.5 mm

The raw glass was decoloured with a mixture of antimony and manganese, so was probably recycled.

Present condition
The vessel, most likely a plate, was grozed, i.e. chipped away around the entire diameter of the base. The walls are thus entirely lost, but the foot-ring is nearly intact. The chipping process worked inwards on to the upper layer of glass (above, p.78, fig. 33). The glass is lightly bubbled.

Stress fractures appear in both glass layers; the surface of the upper layer is badly weathered and iridescent, thus almost totally obscuring the gold foil decoration. A milky opalescence, probably representing leaking manganese originally used to decolour the glass, appears on the lower layer. Only some of the foil has fragmented, along the borders, while the portraits have survived largely intact.

Gold leaf decoration
The design of the gold leaf is formally arranged, with four pediments framing a border decorated with widely spaced small blocks of gold leaf. Within a central, rectangular frame, busts of the senior saints Peter and Paul look down at two medallion portraits of the popes Julius and Sixtus. All four names are inscribed in the upper register in Latin, in letters 4 mm in height: 'PETRVS P/ AVLVS.IV/ LIVS.SV/STVS'. All four figures are similarly dressed in simple tunics and stoles of the *omorphorion* type, pinned below the breast. The gaze of each figure is slightly inclined inwards. The popes have a golden nimbus behind their heads, and their circular portraits, reminiscent in form of third-century gold-glass medallion portraits, are set within broad octagonal frames. The latter may perhaps recall the metal mounts in which the third-century medallions were originally set.

Collection history
Purchased by Charles Wilshere from Tommaso and Vincenzo Capobianchi of Via Babuino, 152, Rome between 1862 and 1865.[1] Purchased by Tommaso Capobianchi at the public sale of the museum of the Baron Alessio Recupero of Catania, Messina 1862.

Drawn for Gaetano Marini, librarian of the Vatican, in 1781, when it was recorded as being located *Roma, apud Ab. Severinium*

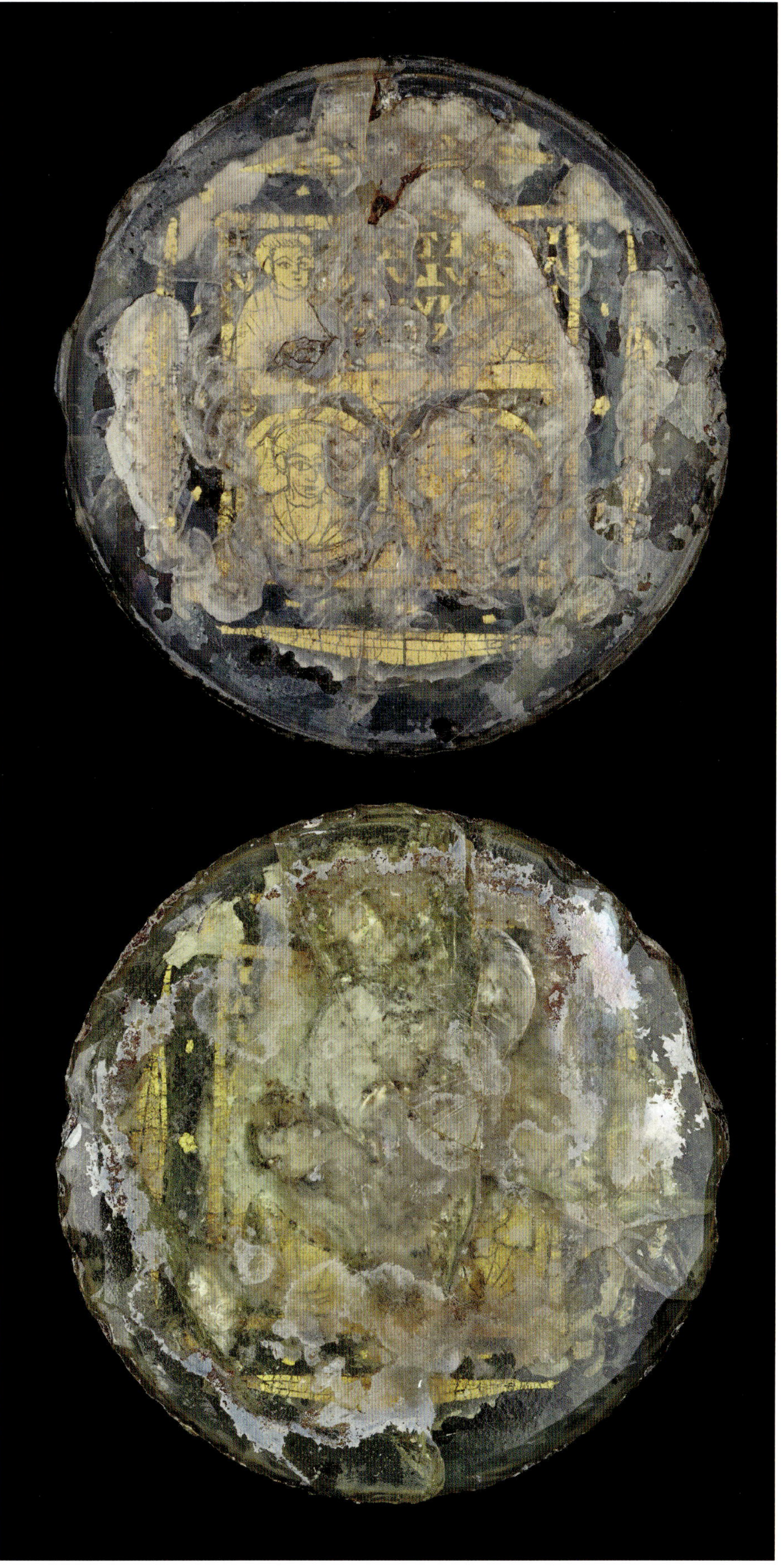

Photographs of the more legible outer layer of glass (top), with a detail of the reversed text (overleaf) and the occluded inner layer (below). David Gowers, 2012

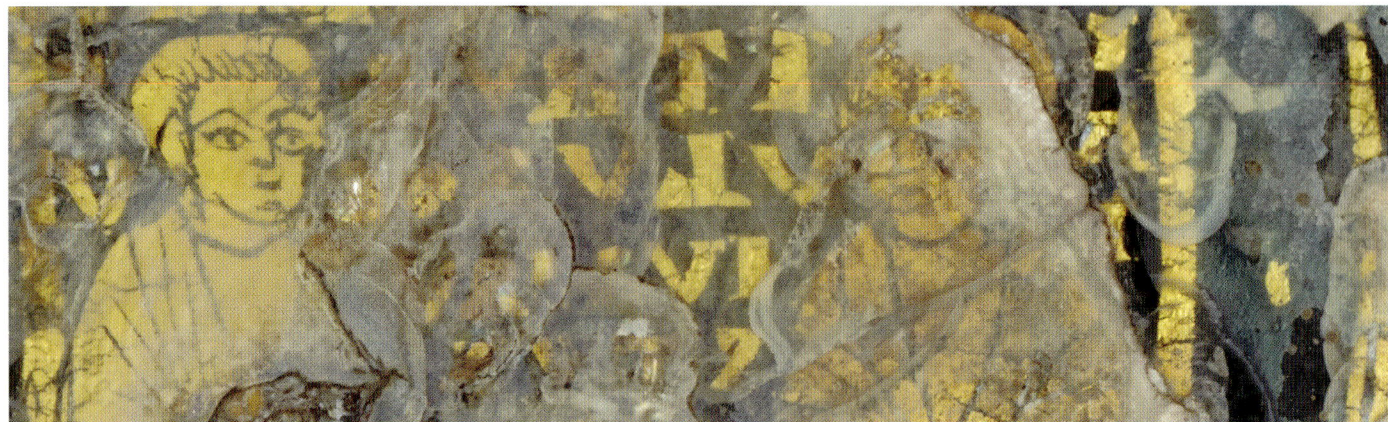

Gipsanophylacum (Vatican City, Biblioteca Apostolica Vaticana, Vat.lat. 9071, p.209, no.8). In his publications Garrucci used the sketch, badly drawn but with the text accurately transcribed, which had been supplied by the Abbot Severinus. The saints are here named Petrus, Paulus, Ju[l]ius and Sixtus.[2]

Bibliography

Garrucci 1858: 52, no.1, tav. XXV; Garrucci 1862: 6, no.VII; Garrucci 1864: 140–2, no.1, tav. XXV; Garrucci 1876: III, 174, no.1, tav. CXCIV; Vopel 1899: no.380, pp.10, 14, 25, 54, 55, 85 and 109; Leclercq 1923: no.221, col.1838; Webster 1929: 153, no.79; Ladner 1941: 35, no.19; Morey 1959: 60–1, no.360, pl.XXXI; Testini 1969: 276, 314, no.150; Smith 2000: pl.XXXV, c; Vattuone 2000: 132, 134 unnumbered fig.; Vickers 2009–2011: 611, fig. 6; Cooley 2017: 234–6, no.391.

Comment

The design of the gold leaf is unique, though four busts are also found on Morey no.106 (Vatican Museum) where the two pairs are separated by a horizontal line. The upper registers are occupied by busts set in medallions of Pastor and Damas(us) and Simon and Damas (us); on the latter piece Peter is shown with Florus. Busts of Peter and Paul are sometimes paired in the upper register of gold leaf medallions, for example Morey 254 (Florence, Museo Archeologico Nazionale), where the patron saints preside over full figures of saints set in a colonnade, and 287, of similar design (Pesaro, Museo Archeologico Oliveriano).

Peter and Paul are also paired on cats 22 and 23, although the iconography differs in both cases.[3] Peter and Paul normally appear on gold-glass as two large busts facing each other, sometimes with Christ in between them, crowning both (for example Morey 37 and 50) or with a wreath with *lemnisci* between them (for example Morey 61 and 67).

Much has been published on the iconography of Peter and Paul in fourth- and fifth-century Roman art as an expression of the *concordia apostolorum*.[4]

Julius and Sixtus (variously spelled Sustus or Xystus), portrayed in medallions in the lower register, were both Bishops of Rome (Popes): Julius from 337–52, Sixtus as either Sixtus I (117/9–126/8) or II (257–8). Both were martyred.

Julius only appears on gold-glass when Sixtus is present. Iulius (Julius) is portrayed on Morey nos. 102, 105 (Vatican Museum), 291? (Pesaro, Museo Archeologico Oliveriano, also paired with Peter). 'Sustus' (Sixtus/Xystus) appears more frequently, on Morey nos. 55, 74, 102, 105? (Vatican Museum), 240, 250, 258 (Florence, Museo Archeologico Nazionale), 278 (Verona, Museo di Castelvecchio), 291? (Pesaro, Museo Archeologico Oliveriano), 313 and 344 (London, British Museum), as well as on nos. 10 and 11.

The border, described by Morey as a 'square-band border surrounded by a row of irregular dots and flat triangles in exergues' is rare; other examples are Morey 79, with full figures of Genesius and Luke separated by a column supporting a *tabula* naming the saints (Vatican Museum, returned by Charles Wilshere to de Rossi in 1894, p.36, fig. 57; figs 14, 27), and 88, with full figures of Peter and Paul similarly arranged. It is clear from these examples that the flattened triangles represent architectural pediments.

The monumental size of this dish and the formality of its decoration suggest that it was probably intended as an offering to the saints and/or the martyred bishops depicted in the centre of the plate.

The architectural format suggests that the plate may evoke the monumental commemoration of the martyrs within the catacombs, undertaken by Pope Damasus in the 360s–380s.
Made about AD 370–90.

Endnotes

1. Vattuone 2000: 132.
2. Garrucci 1858, 1864: tav. XXV, no.1.
3. Other examples of Saints Peter and Paul paired include Morey nos. 37, 50, 51, 53, 56, 60–7, 69, 70, 75, 83, 88, 95, 100, 105–6, 112, 125?, 126?, 176?, 199?, 200? (all Vatican Museum), 212? (Vatican City, Camposanto Teutonico), 240–3, 250, 254 (Florence, Museo Archeologico Nazionale), 267, 269 (Bologna, Museo Civico Archeologico), 277 (Verona, Museo di Castelvecchio), 286–7 (Pesaro, Museo Archeologico Oliveriano), 314, 341 (London, British Museum), 396? (Tel Aviv, Museum Haaretz), 438 (Munich, Nationalmuseum), 449–50, 455 and 457 (New York, The Metropolitan Museum of Art).
4. Testini 1969: 241–323; Donati 2000: 85–90; Kessler 1987: 265–75; Huskinson 1982; Pietri 1961: 275–82; Grig 2004a: 217–19.

26 AN 2007.12

Segment of the base of a gold-glass plate or bowl: Christ crowns two confronted saints, one of them John

| Photograph by David Gowers, 2013

DIAM. 80 mm (max.)
UL. Pale green, transparent. TH. 2 mm
LL. Pale green, transparent. TH. 0.7 mm

The raw glass was decoloured with a mixture of antimony and manganese, so was probably recycled.

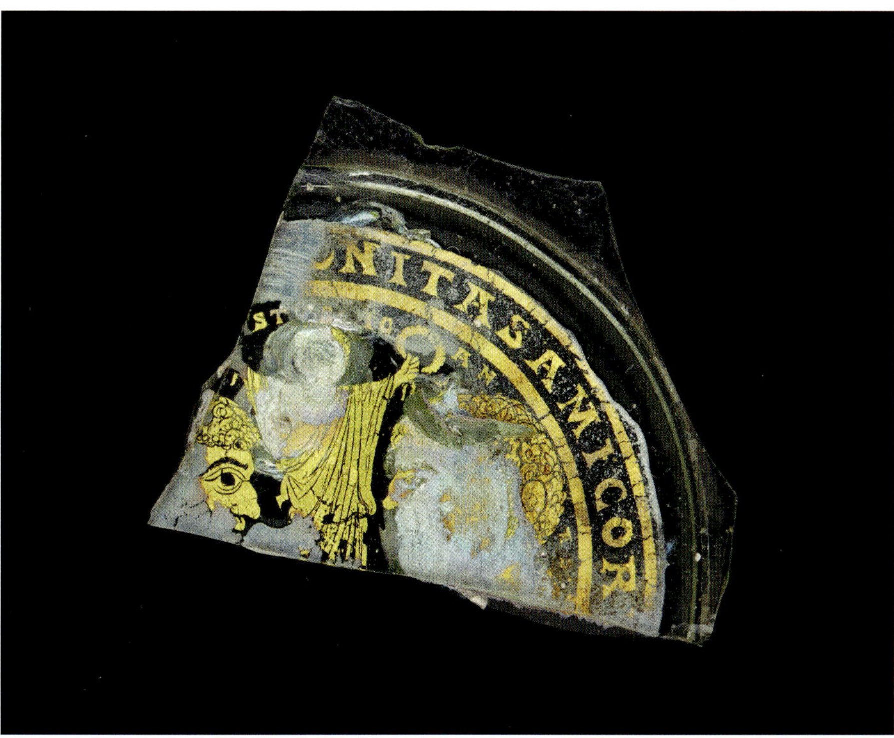

Present condition

The glass is lightly bubbled and the foil is fractured in some places (for example on the border bands and the face of the left figure), but not in others. Three-quarters of the base and most of the walls are broken away. On the surviving quadrant of the base the foot-ring and some of the wall remain, to a maximum length of 9 mm. There are stress fractures in the glass, and the foil surface has weathered to produce iridescent colour, thus obscuring parts of the figures in the top centre and on the right.

Gold leaf decoration

A small figure of Christ, beardless and with short hair, is shown frontally; he wears a tunic and pallium and holds a wreath in the left hand over one of two busts. The busts are shown with full, short hair, in profile and facing each other. The right hand of Christ, which would have also held a wreath, is lost in the break on the left. In letters 1 mm in height, Christ is named (CR)ISTVS, and the saint to his left is named IO AN ES (John). In the double outer ring is inscribed in Latin '[DI] GNITAS AMICORV[M]' ('the worthiness of friends'). This is part of a longer text, possibly including a transliterated Greek or Latin exhortation to drink and to live happily with one's family (see cat. **4**, n.3).

Collection history

In his publication of 1876 Garrucci records this fragment as 'trovato in Roma dal signor Wilshere' ('found in Rome by Mr Wilshere'.) This suggests that Wilshere did not buy the piece from one of the better known dealers such as Capobianchi or Depoletti; the exact source and date of acquisition remains unknown.

Bibliography

Garrucci 1876: III, 114, no.4, with tav. CLXX; Vopel 1899: no.411, pp.9, 52, 82, 85, 110; Leclercq 1923: n.252, col.1840; Webster 1929: 153, no.77; Morey 1959: 61–2, no.365, pl.XXXI; Smith 2000: pl.XXVII, a; Vattuone 2000: 132, 135; Vickers 2009–11: 611, fig. 4; Cooley 2017: 244–5, no.395.

Comment

The profile busts seen here are quite sophisticated, if stylised. The depiction of the figures' curly hair, bulbous noses and oversized eyes is similar to busts found on Morey nos. 49–52 (Vatican Museum). Of these, nos. 49 and 50, showing Christ crowning the more familiar combination of Peter and Paul, are particularly similar to this piece.

The image of Christ offering martyrs' crowns is paralleled in the apse mosaic of the sixth-century church of San Vitale, Ravenna. In this mosaic Christ is shown offering a crown to the martyr Saint Vitalis.[1]

Although only one other depiction of John in gold glass decoration is known (Morey no.86, here shown seated in conversation with Simon), the 'dignitas amicorum' type is common. While there is no absolute conjunction between the inscription and the image, more examples than not of the 'dignitas amicorum' inscription are combined with facing profile busts of figures crowned with wreaths (or martyrs' crowns) by Christ. For instance, Saints Peter and Paul are often depicted as facing profile busts (for example Morey nos. 50 and 53) and are paired with the 'dignitas amicorum' inscription. However, this is not always the case. Morey nos. 37, 49, 58, 236, 241, 274, 314, 379 (**21**) and 388 (**23**) preserve the inscription along with facing busts, while examples of facing figures minus the inscription include Morey nos. 45, 47, 187, 271, 285, 329? and 450.

Other examples of 'dignitas' inscriptions enclosed within a double-band outer border are Morey nos. 37, 45, 47, 49, 58, 187, 236, 241, 271, 274, 314, 378 (**4**),[2] 388 (**23**) and 450.

The use of recycled glass and the style of representation of the saints suggest a date late in the fourth century AD.

Endnotes

1. Deichmann 1974: 163–94; Deliyannis 2010: 171, 236–8.
2. See catalogue entry above for further discussion of the *dignitas amicorum* formula.

Group 4

Gold-glass with coloured outer layers and transparent inner layers, the latter decoloured with a variable mixture of antimony and manganese

27 AN 2007.16

Gold-glass diminutive medallion: Hercules tears the antlers from the Cerynian stag

DIAM. Varies between 27 and 28 mm
UL. Colourless, transparent. TH. 1.2 mm
LL. Pale blue, transparent. TH. 2.7 mm

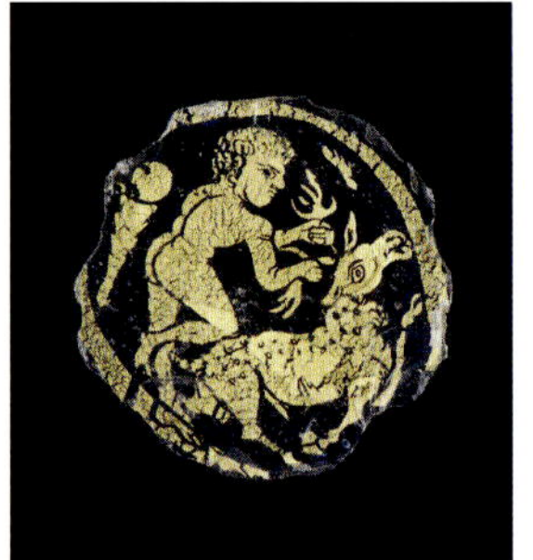

Present condition

The upper surface of the disc is irregular, with an off-centre depression corresponding to a shallow depression in the lower layer. The foil is fragmented. At the sides of the scene the oval border is lost where the disc has been trimmed from its bowl. The base is badly chipped and scratched; the upper surface is slightly chipped. The inner layer of transparent glass was decoloured with a mixture of antimony and manganese.

Gold leaf decoration

The beardless Hercules appears naked in three-quarter rear view, kneeling with his right knee bent on the stag's spotted back. Hercules' left foot and the stag's left hind leg protrude into the oval border of the medallion. The stag lies on the ground, its mouth open as if groaning with pain. The stag's legs have been broken by the club, which appears to the left of the scene, behind Hercules' back. With grim expression Hercules seizes the antlers and tears them off. A leaf spray (as Morey saw it) or possibly a fragment of antler falls in the upper field.

Collection history

Purchased by Charles Wilshere from Tommaso and Vincenzo Capobianchi, Via del Babuino 152, Rome; acquired by Vincenzo Capobianchi at the 1862 public sale of the Museo Recupero, Catania, Sicily.

Bibliography

Garrucci 1862: 7, no.X; Garrucci 1864: 191, no.3, tav. XXXV; Vopel 1899: no.44, pp.8, 33, 97; Leclercq 1923: no.386, col.1849; Webster 1929: 153, no.75; Morey 1959: 62, no.369, pl.XXXII; Smith 2000: 131, pl.LXXXIX, c; Vattuone, 2000: 132, 135, unnumbered fig.; Vickers 2009–2011: 612, fig. 10d.

Comment

The glass medallion was originally set into the wall of a transparent glass bowl, now lost (as above, p.103, fig. 51).

On the gold leaf disc, the protrusion into the borderline of the left foot of Hercules and the left hind leg of the stag is unusual. The violence of the scene is replicated in other media offering the same vignette.[1]

Representations of Hercules are rarely found in the gold-glass repertoire, and the repeated use of the epithet 'Acerentinus' (perhaps signifying 'god of the underworld') suggests that they were commissioned for the funeral feasts of pagan clients.[2] Among uninscribed images Morey no.12, now in the Vatican Museum, is a large medallion of fine, decoloured white glass illustrating Hercules fighting the Erymanthian boar, his lion skin floating behind him. Finally a small medallion in London most probably shows Hercules with the Cretan bull.[3]

Hercules is more commonly found on stone sarcophagi. A drawing of a sarcophagus (Uffizi 182) portrays him tearing the antlers from the Kerynian stag, and many show the complete 12 labours, also the subject of a series of paintings in the Via Latina catacomb.[4] The impressive range of Herculean iconography, despite the rarity of the subject in the catacombs, suggests that Hercules either remained an object of veneration by pagans or simply appeared in Christian contexts as a secular sign of familiarity with Greek mythology.

Endnotes

1. Weitzmann 1951: 152, pl.XLVIII, drawing of a sarcophagus, Florence, Uffizi no.182: Heracles kneels on hind to tear antlers; no.181, a rectangular ivory panel from a casket: Heracles kneels on the stag to club him.
2. See Chapter 3, p.85, fig. 39.
3. Smith 2000: 131–2, pl.LXXXIX, a–b; Howells 2015: 134–5, no.41.
4. On the role of Hercules in late antique iconography see further p.132–3, and Fasola and Mancinelli 2007: 70, figs 74 and 75 for the Via Latina cycle; more generally see Tronzo 1986.

Photograph: David Gowers 2013

28 AN 2007.29

Miniature gold-glass medallion, probably from a transparent glass bowl: the head of a roaring leopard

DIAM. Varies from 19 to 20 mm
UL. Colourless, transparent. TH. 1 mm
LL. Blue, transparent. TH. 5 mm

The inner layer of clear glass was decoloured with a mixture of antimony and manganese.

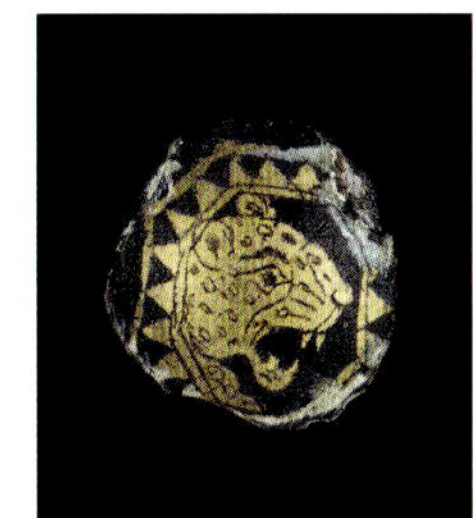

Present condition

The inner layer of glass is relatively bubble-free, while the outer contains bubbles. The lower surface is flat and the upper irregular. The foil is intact. The disc has been trimmed of the surrounding transparent glass, of which only a tiny spur may be seen along the lower edge. The lower layer retains a pronounced outer finished edge – perhaps, like the flattened base, intended for resetting the glass in a ring (compare cat. **29**). There is iridescent weathering at the right side of the upper surface, obscuring the gold foil border. The surface of the upper layer is pitted.

Gold leaf decoration

The leopard is shown in profile, turning to roar, its jaws open with four teeth exposed. The pelt and features are carefully engraved. The dramatic sensation of the roaring beast is magnified by the octagonal double border, decorated with tooth-like serrations. The latter is clumsily drawn freehand, overlapping the ear of the leopard.

Collection history

Purchased by Charles Wilshere from Tommaso and Vincenzo Capobianchi, Via del Babuino 152, Rome; acquired by Vincenzo Capobianchi at the 1862 public sale of the Museo Recupero, Catania, Sicily.

Bibliography

Garrucci 1862: 7, no.XI; Garrucci 1864: 210–11, no.9, tav. XXXVII; Garrucci 1876: III, 196, no.2, tav. CCIII; Vopel 1899: no.150, pp.11, 101; Leclercq 1923: no.495, col.1857; Morey 1959: no.382, pl.XXXII; Smith 2000: 129, pl.LXXXVI, a; Vattuone 2000: 136, unnumbered fig.; Vickers 2009–11: 612, fig. 10a.

Comment

A similar octagonal band frame with serration appears on a small blue glass medallion decorated with a male bust (Morey no.132). Morey 169, slightly larger at 2.5 cm diameter, shows a large-eared animal. It has been tentatively identified as a panther, but the pricked ears, segmented, patterned skin and truncated face shape possibly indicate a giraffe or, less exotically, a dog. The animal is set within a similar frame and counter-marked with a copper gilt B. Morey 396, a greenish glass base in Tel Aviv, illustrates St Peter and possibly St Paul with a wreath, *Chi-Rho* and plants between the figures and dots between the more regular serrations. Other instances of the serrated border appearing on larger gold-glass bases include two examples with marriage portraits, Morey nos. 43 and 225.

The head of a snarling, spotted leopard with bared teeth and prominent whiskers appears on the small medallion Morey no.171, with a plain border.

Divested of other medallions from the same vessel, the context of the motif of the wild animal head in gold-glass wall medallions remains unclear. Busts of wild animals appear as framed vignettes set into mosaic pavements, and are mostly associated with hunting or combat in a secular context.[1]

Endnotes

1. Smith 2000: 128–9; for an example in mosaic from the fourth-century villa at Piazza Armerina in Sicily. See Dunbabin 1999: 138.

29 AN 2007.15

Blue and transparent gold-glass medallion: roaring lion

DIAM. Glass (visible): 18 mm
UL. Colourless, transparent. TH. Not possible to measure
LL. Pale blue, transparent. TH. Not possible to measure

The inner layer of transparent glass was decoloured with a varied mix of antimony and manganese.

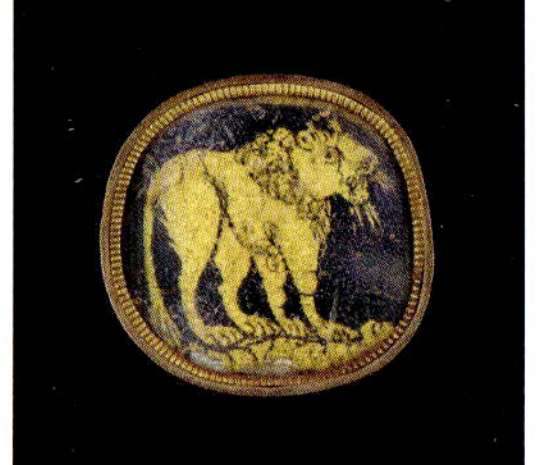

Present condition

The disc was originally set into a colourless glass bowl. It has been trimmed of its setting and most of the gold foil border, part of which is just visible in its eighteenth- or nineteenth-century setting of a gold ring. The lower layer of glass has retained a markedly convex lower surface, which must have made the ring uncomfortable to wear. The glass is lightly bubbled and has suffered a blow in the lower layer. The gold foil is intact.

Gold leaf decoration

The lion stands on uneven ground, facing to the right and roaring. The body is compressed to suggest a turn before pouncing, the tail swishing on the ground.

Collection history

Probably purchased by Charles Wilshere in Rome, after 1865. Morey states that the medallion was published by Vopel. However, the medallion listed by Vopel had been published with an illustration by Garrucci, and appears to be a different one.[1]

Bibliography

Morey 1959: 62, no.368, pl.XXXII; Smith 2000: pl.LXXXV, c; Vattuone 2000: 132; Vickers 2009–11: 612, fig. 10b.

Comment

The lion's aggressive stance suggests that it could have been one of a number of roundels illustrating the biblical story of Daniel. A similar lion, its body less compressed, stands on a ground line on an inscribed gold-glass fragment of a large plate bought in Egypt. The piece was formerly in the collection of Ray Winfield Smith and is now in the Corning Museum of Glass. This labelled lion has been interpreted as part of a much larger scene of the Zodiac.[2]

Endnotes

1. Morey 1959: 62; Vopel 1899: 8, no.152; Garrucci 1864: 210, tav. 37,3.
2. CMOG 59.1.280: Smith 1957: 222–3, no.447; Whitehouse 2001: 251, no.844.

30 AN 2007.32

Blue and transparent gold-glass medallion: naked man, his wrists apparently bound to two trees

Photograph by David Gowers, 2013.
Drawing by Yvonne Beadnell, 2012

H. 22 mm (max.); W. 25 mm (max)
UL. Colourless, transparent. TH. 2 mm
LL. Pale blue, transparent. TH. 3 mm

The inner layer of transparent glass has been decoloured with a varied mixture of antimony and manganese.

Present condition
The upper layer of glass is relatively bubble-free, while the lower has bubbles. The disc has a flattish base. The foil is intact apart from the fragmented border. The disc has been cut from its colourless glass setting in the wall of a bowl; crude chips from the cutting process appear at the edges. The top and base are scratched, and the surface of the foil is slightly corroded.

Gold leaf decoration
A naked, beardless man stands on the ground between two trees, his weight on his left leg. His wrists appear bound to the stumps of branches of each tree. His hands are held out, perhaps in a gesture of prayer; his eyes stare blankly and his mouth is clamped flat. His body is cut by a vertical line from the breastbone to the crotch. Four large gold leaf dots are set to the sides of each tree trunk.

Collection history
Acquired in Rome by Charles Wilshere from the collector and dealer Luigi Depoletti (Chapter 2, p.50, fig. 21).

Bibliography
Garrucci 1864: 18, no.7, tav. I; Garrucci 1876: 131, no.13, tav. CLXXIII; Vopel 1899: no.202, pp.8, 67, 103; Leclercq 1923: no.37, col.1828; Webster 1929: 154, no.91; Morey 1959: no.385, pl.XXXII; Smith 2000: pl.XXIV, d; Vattuone 2000: 132, 136.

Comment
If the dots represent fallen fruit, the figure might be identified as Adam. However, he usually appears with Eve, or alone and nude, his right arm raised and outstretched to pluck the fruit.[1] Moreover, dots are a common feature of gold-glass paradisiacal landscapes, see for example cat. **23**.

Trees are not normally included in landscape scenes with Daniel (see cats **32** and **33**). However, Daniel has been identified as a nude male orant of similar appearance to this figure, standing between two leafy plants or bushes.[2] He is frequently shown as an orant on marble sarcophagi.[3]

Given the exact symmetry of the trees, the vertical line through the man's torso, his fixed expression and the gesture more redolent of helplessness than prayer, the subject of cat. **30** might possibly be identified as the martyrdom of Isaiah, sawn in two at the order of King Manassah. The execution is achieved by the cleaving of the cedar tree in which the visionary prophet had taken refuge. A similar scene is depicted with the executioner present and the prophet's blood shown flowing in red enamel on cat. **23**. The story appears only in rabbinical sources.[4]

Endnotes
1. Morey nos. 138, 318 and 416.
2. Morey nos. 146, 349 and 319.
3. Bovini and Brandenburg 1967: 622 (Koch 2000: pl.22, Rome, Catacomb of Novatianus), 41 (Koch 2000: pl.42, Vatican), 364 (Koch 2000: pl.43, Rome, Catacomb of Callixtus), 43 (Koch 2000: pl.46, Vatican, 'Dogmatic Sarcophagus'), 241 (Koch 2000: pl.54, Rome, San Sebastiano), 45 (Koch 2000: pl.62, Vatican, 'Brother Sarcophagus'). Talmud Sanhedrin X and Targum to Isaiah. See for references to Isaiah's ascension Lange, Armin, Weigold and Matthias 2011: 244–5, and Bernheimer 1952: 19–34; Conti 1998: 149 for medieval versions of the story of Isaiah's martyrdom. My thanks to David Rini for these references.

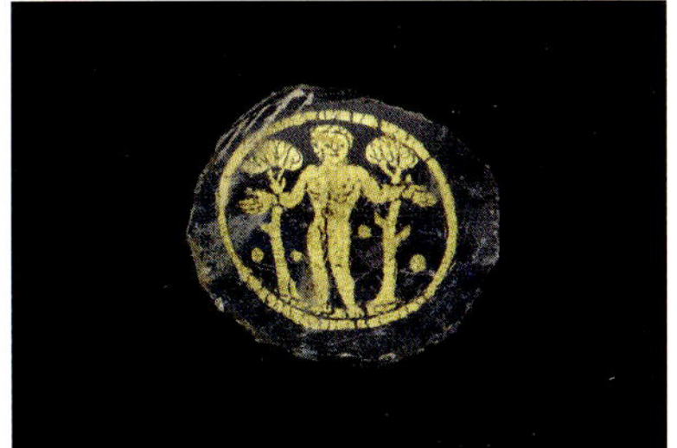

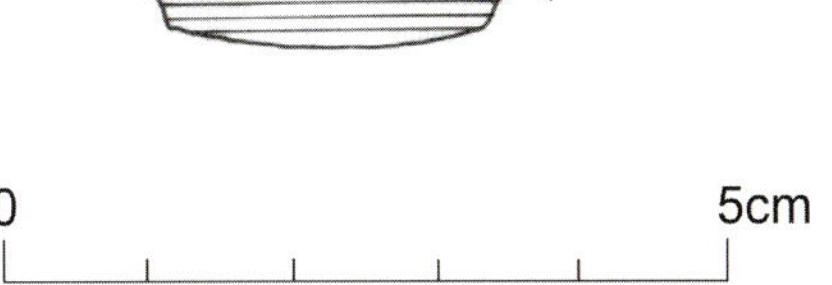

0 5cm

31 AN 2007.18

Photograph by David Gowers, 2013

Green gold-glass medallion: a serpent on a rocky hill

DIAM. 24 mm (max.)
UL. Colourless, transparent. TH. 1.2 mm
LL. Emerald green, transparent. TH. 4.2 mm

The clear glass covering layer was decoloured with a mixture of antimony and manganese.

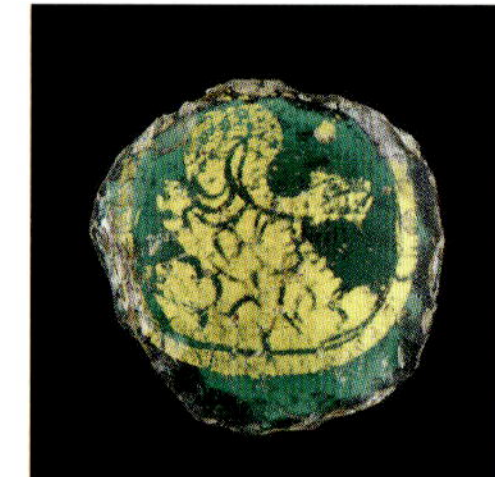

Present condition

The medallion has been trimmed of its setting in the wall of a transparent glass bowl. In the gold leaf, the upper left section of the single-ring border has also been trimmed away. The upper layer of glass is pitted, blurring the image; the bubbled surface of the lower, coloured layer is scratched.

Gold leaf decoration

The snake is coiled, alert with fangs bared ready for attack from a rocky or bushy hill. A dot of gold leaf appears above the serpent's head. The scene is enclosed with a single-ring border.

Collection history

Purchased by Charles Wilshere from Vincenzo Capobianchi, Via del Babuino 152, Rome. The piece was seen here by Garrucci prior to his publication of 1876.

Bibliography

Garrucci 1876: 132, no.15, with tav. 173; Vopel 1899: no.215, p.8, 67, 103; Leclercq 1923: no.50, col.1829; Webster 1929: 154, no.83; Morey 1959: 62, no.371, pl.XXXII; Smith 2000: 83–4, pl.XXV, b; Vattuone 2000: 132, 135; Vickers 2009–11: 612, fig. 10c.

Comment

Morey identifies the scene as the 'Snake of Babylon coiled on rocks with head right; in field, a dot'. Cat. **31** is the only depiction of a snake alone in Morey's corpus, although Morey no.345 shows a very similar snake uncoiling from a rocky mound to eat the poisoned cake offered by Daniel; he stands in the centre in military dress with a nimbate Christ behind.[1] Both the serpent and the poisoned cake are apocryphal figures in the narrative of Daniel, first appearing in the Septuagint of the second century BC.

This was probably one of a series of miniature medallions showing events in the story of Daniel, portrayed in cobalt blue and copper green swirls on the walls of a transparent glass bowl. It was probably made in the middle years of the fourth century AD(see above, p.00).

Endnotes

1. Smith 2000: 83–4.

32 AN 2007.21

Part of a gold-glass medallion: Daniel carries the poisoned cake

| Photograph by David Gowers, 2013

DIAM. 27 x 18 mm (max.)
UL. Colourless, transparent. TH. 1.0 mm
LL. Blue, transparent. TH. 3.mm

Present condition
Only half of the disc survives, with a tiny spur of wall from the transparent glass bowl in which it was originally set. The glass is lightly bubbled; the upper surface is slightly pitted, blurring the image. The lower surface is weathered, with iridescent weathering on the fractured edges. The surviving gold foil is intact except for the slightly fragmented border.

Gold leaf decoration
Moving to his right, Daniel carries the poisoned cake with both hands to the snake of Babylon. He wears a long-sleeved tunic, the lower sleeves decorated with black hoops in a style typical of the fourth century AD. He may also wear a short cloak (*chlamys*), just visible at the back of the neck. His hair is thick and held with a band; he has no beard. A tree or bush grows below his outstretched arms. The narrow, single-ring border closes with a disc and triangle beside the plant; this suggests that the fragmentation may have been intentional, giving the effect of a narrow necklace.

Collection history
Probably acquired in Rome by Charles Wilshere after 1865.

Bibliography
Morey 1959: no.374, pl.XXXII; Smith 2000: 82–3, pl.XXIV, h.

Comment
The story of Daniel poisoning the dragon is apocryphal and found only in the Greek version of the Book of Daniel. The scene of Daniel bringing barley cake to poison the snake of Babylon is common in gold-glass medallions and sarcophagi made in Rome.[1] There is some variation in the stance of the prophet (see also cat. **33**), who is also frequently depicted in catacomb paintings.[2] Daniel and the snake also appear on the back of a reliquary in Brescia.[3]

Endnotes
1. Gold-glass: Morey 1959: nos. 150, 151, 152, 322, 345 and 381 (the figure in cat. **33** runs in the opposite direction); see also Smith 2000: 82–3. Sarcophagi: Bovini and Brandenburg 1967: 674, 694, no. 60, 954, 146, 555, 189 and 804; Dresken-Weiland 1998: 40, 124, 151, 152. The scenes also feature on sarcophagi found in Gaul and on a sarcophagus found in Spain (Koch 2000: 153–4); see also Wischmeyer 1982 and Schrenk 1995.
2. Nestori 1993: 198–9.
3. Illustrated in Grabar 1967: fig. 337. See also Pillinger 1985: 285–95.

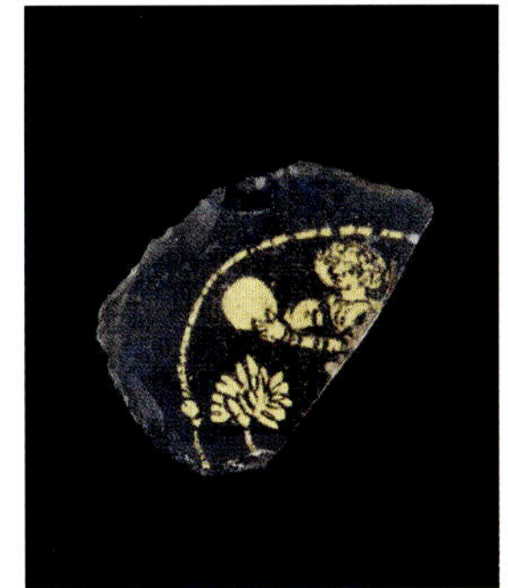

33 AN 2007.28

Miniature gold-glass medallion from a bowl: Daniel carries the poisoned cake

H. 26 mm (max.); W. 32 mm (max.)
UL. Colourless, transparent. TH. 2 mm
LL. Pale blue, transparent. TH. 3 mm

The clear glass was decoloured with a mixture of antimony and manganese.

Photograph by David Gowers, 2013

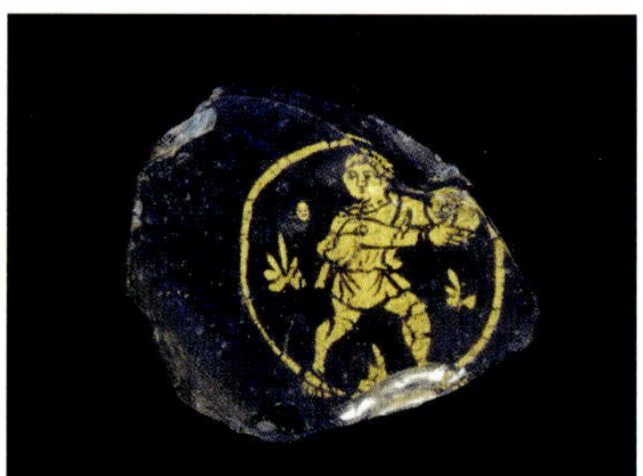

Present condition

Around 3 mm of the wall of the transparent glass vessel in which the medallion was inserted may be seen to the lower left of the figure. The upper layer of glass is relatively bubble-free and has a polished surface; the lower layer contains bubbles. The foil is intact apart from the border. At the upper right side of the disc the lens is broken, including the gold foil border. A small chip of glass is missing from the upper surface at the centre of the lower edge.

Gold leaf decoration

Daniel strides to his left through a paradisiacal landscape of flowers, holding out the poisoned cake at arms' length, his head turned away from it. He has short hair and no beard. Daniel wears a short, girdled, long-sleeved tunic decorated with bands (*clavi*) and narrow bands at the cuffs of the sleeves. He also wears a short cloak (*chlamys*). His bare feet overlap the border of the piece.

Collection history

Purchased by Charles Wilshere from Tommaso and Vincenzo Capobianchi, Via del Babuino 152, Rome, between 1862 and 1865; acquired by Tommaso Capobianchi at the 1862 public sale of the Museo del Barone Alessio Recupero, Catania, Sicily.

Bibliography

Garrucci 1862: 5, no.111; Garrucci 1876: III, 132, no.16, tav. CLXXIII; Vopel 1899: no.207, pp.8, 67,103; Leclercq 1923: no.42, col.1828; Webster 1929: 154, no.90; Morey 1959: no.381, pl.XXXII; Smith 2000: 82–3, pl.XXIV, i; Vattuone 2000: 132, 136, unnumbered fig.

Comment

See above cat. **32**. This is the only known example of Daniel depicted alone and running to his left. The circular-band border cuts across Daniel's foot, indicating that the border was executed after the figure had been cut.

34 AN 2007.22

Gold-glass medallion: Christ stands in a paradisiacal landscape holding up a wand

DIAM. 28 mm
UL. Colourless, transparent. TH. 1.1 mm
LL. Pale blue, transparent. TH. 4.1 mm

The clear glass layer was decoloured with a mixture of antimony and manganese.

Present condition

The upper layer of glass is relatively bubble-free, while the coloured glass contains bubbles. The disc has been trimmed of the surrounding vessel wall, of which only narrow edges remain. There is slight iridescence on the upper layer of glass and a whitish film on the base. The foil decoration is intact apart from the fragmented border. The reverse surface has glued to it a dealer's catalogue/sale ticket with the number 13 written in sepia ink; the paper is cut into facets recalling the gold leaf frame of the image on the other side. It seems unlikely that Wilshere affixed the label, as it does not appear on any other objects in his collection – nor does it match the numbering of his partial inventory of 1893, where the object is listed as no.2 of the medallions on page 9 (see Appendix 1).

Decoration

A full-length figure of Christ stands in three-quarter view, turned slightly to his right with his weight on his right foot. He is beardless, with a pudding-basin haircut falling straight across the brow. Christ is dressed as a philosopher in tunic, mantle and sandals. His right arm is outstretched to hold up a wand, the sign of his role as worker of miracles; the tip of the wand breaks into the border. In the field are leaf sprays and flowers, indicating a paradisiacal landscape. The border is a single, octagonal band.

Collection history

This medallion was in Charles Wilshere's collection by 1893 (Appendix 1). Vopel recorded a small gold-glass medallion designed for insertion into a vessel wall, decorated with a full-length male figure with a wand, as having been found in a tomb on the Via Portuensis in Rome and sold in England. However, Vopel describes a medallion set in a metal ring with a loop.[1]

Bibliography

Morey 1959: no.375, pl.XXXII; Smith 2000: pl.XIX, e; Vickers 2009–11: 612, fig.10e.

Comment

The figure of Christ as a miracle-worker holding a wand is frequently found in small gold-glass medallions.[2] The octagonal frame is common to most examples, as are the decorative vegetal elements.[3] Christ's wand is superimposed in front of border, here perhaps cut before the figure, in contrast to cat.**32**. The notion of Christ as magician equipped with a wand also applies to the raising of Lazarus (see for example cat.**3** and the sarcophagus cat.**40**).

Endnotes

1. Vopel 1899: 105, no.281, reported by Smith 2000: 274, 'Appendix A'. See also de Rossi 1891: 124, 128.
2. Morey 1959: nos. 161, 162, 163, 164, 214, 216, 218, 255, 317, 335, 349, 355, 404, 408, 414, 430 and 456 (see Smith 2000: 79–80).
3. Except Morey 1959: nos. 404, 408, 414, 430 and 456. All, perhaps significantly, are in French, German and American museum collections.

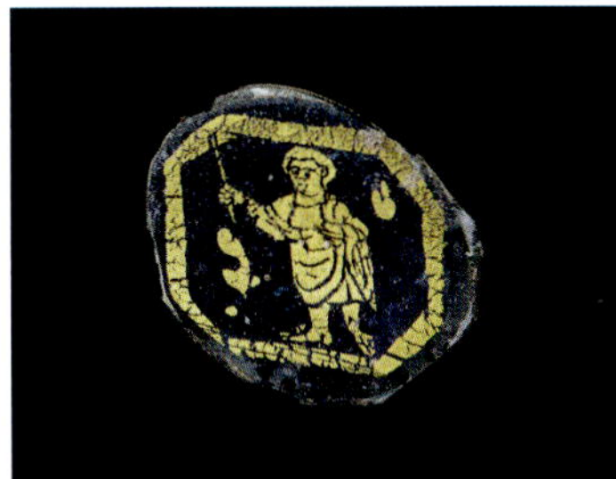

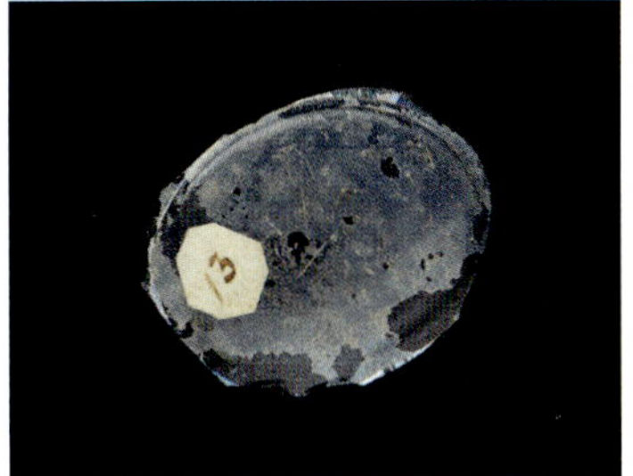

35 AN 2007. 14

Fragment of glass inlay: goldleaf flowers in a calyx crater with a dot of red enamel painted between the flowers

Photograph by David Gowers, 2013. Drawing by Yvonne Beadnell, 2012

Max. H. 27 mm, max. W. 35 mm
UL. Transparent, colourless. TH 1.0 mm
ML. Transparent, colourless. TH. 0.5 mm
LL. Multiple layers of blue glass. TH. 3.5 mm in total

The clear glass upper layer was decoloured with a mixture of antimony and manganese.

Present condition
Three edges of the piece are broken and the upper layer of glass is pitted. Silvery iridescent corrosion has formed on the middle layer and the bottom surface of the lower layer has weathered. The gilding is intact. The glass inlay was possibly intended as wall, floor or furniture decoration.

Collection history
Probably acquired in Rome by Charles Wilshere after 1865.

Bibliography
Morey 1959: 62, no.367, pl.XXXII; Smith 2000: pl.LIV, d; Vattuone 2000: 132.

Comment
This thick, flat fragment is likely to come from a piece of inlaid gold-glass rather than a vessel. The attractive image of flowers overflowing from a calyx crater represents a more organised, possibly paradisiacal landscape than the irregularly spaced buds and sprigs commonly used as background to figural narratives in gold-glass (for example cat. **3**). The motif is known from late antique paintings and mosaics.[1] For the use of coloured enamel as a decorative spacer on gold-glass see cat. **11**.

Endnotes
1. For example, the inscribed panel of a fourth-century pavement from Poreć, Croatia illustrated by Brown 2012: pl.7.

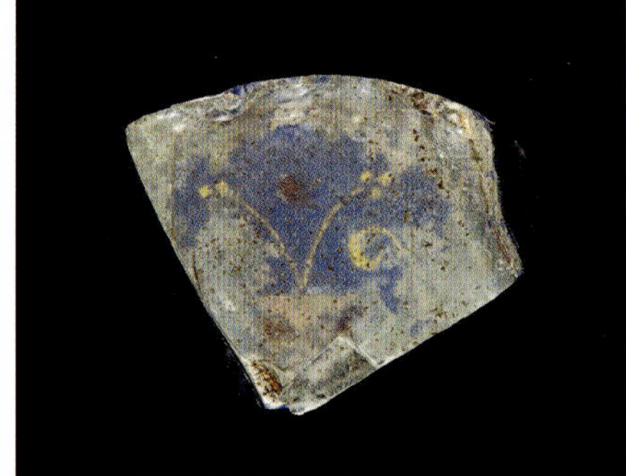

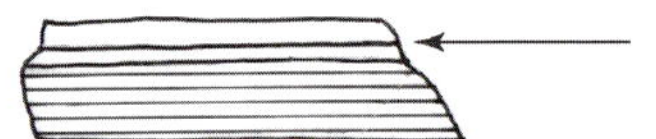

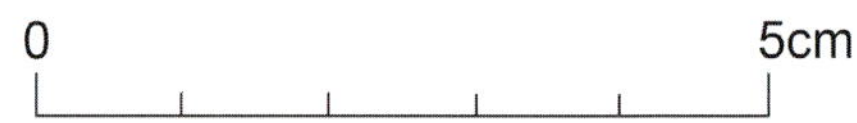

36 AN 2007.39

The base of a glass cup: two fish swim around a Latin text, set in a fish-shaped frame

H. 80 mm (max.); DIAM. 45 mm (max.)
Colourless transparent glass. TH. *c*.2 mm

This glass was not examined in 2012, as it was not possible to access a surface of certain ancient date. However, in 1987 a fragment of this glass was analysed for Dr Marlia Mango by Professor Julian Henderson. It was found to be a mixture of antimony and manganese in a ratio of 2:1.

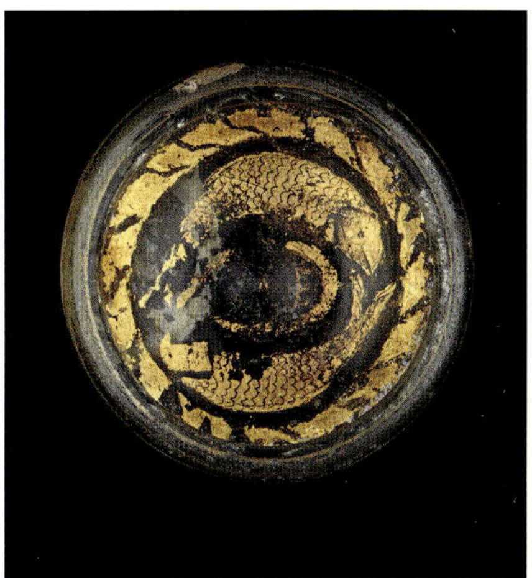

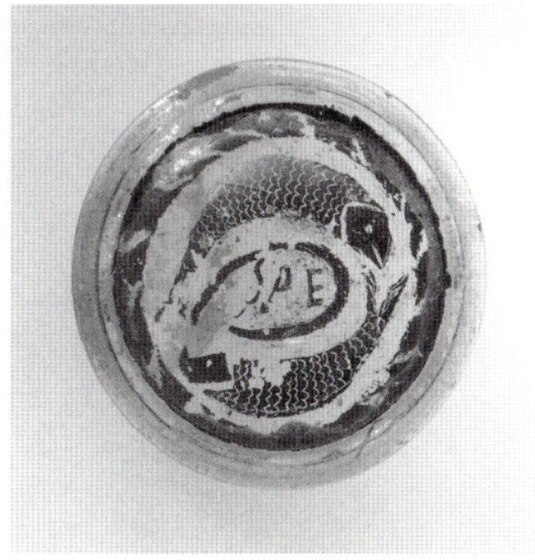

Photographs taken from above by David Gowers, 2013 (above) and an unknown photographer, possibly Dr Donald Harden or a photographer commissioned by him when he studied the glass in 1958 (below). Drawing by Yvonne Beadnell.

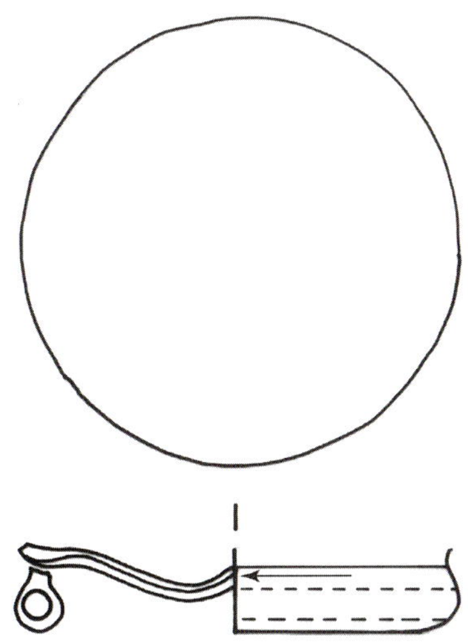

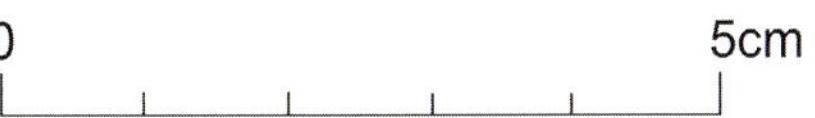

Present condition

The walls of the cup are entirely broken off, but the base is complete. The upper surface of the base is deeply concave, with a slightly raised centre. The glass is lightly bubbled, with some iridescence on the upper surface. The foil was most unusually applied to the lower surface of the base, originally unprotected by a second layer of glass and with the inscription reading backwards. A modern piece of glass has been inserted into the base to protect the exposed gold leaf, which has suffered some small losses. Two letters of the text have been lost since the glass was loaned to the Ashmolean in 1957. The original base had a complex, moulded profile.

Gold leaf decoration

Two plump fish swim in opposite directions around a fish-shaped frame drawn with a single line of gold leaf and enclosing the (now illegible) Latin inscription '[--]E'. From a photograph taken at the time the glass was loaned to the Ashmolean in 1958, the text is evidently to be reconstructed as 'SPE', ('in hope'). The fish appear within an outer frame of cabled form.

Collection history

Probably purchased in Rome by Charles Wilshere after 1865.

Bibliography

Morey 1959: no.392, pl.XXXII.

Comment

The two fish which swim around the edge of this glass are probably carp, and their appearance resembles that of the fish cut down from a larger, secular scene in gold-glass inlay (cat. **16**). Fish were eaten in the traditional Roman *agape* banquet.[1] They were also depicted in representations of Christian banquets on sarcophagi and in catacomb paintings,[2] many of which probably possessed eschatological symbolism as images of future meals to be enjoyed in paradise.[3]

While the fish was a symbol with many different meanings for early Christians, this gold-glass image and its frame are reminiscent of *ichthus* inscriptions and images on early Christian gravestones.[4] Two similarly confronted fish frame the Greek word for fish, '*ichthus*', on a late-third or early fourth-century engraved gem from Syria or Asia Minor. In this piece both image and inscription stand for the person of Christ (with *ichthus* as an acrostic for Christ's title in Greek, '*Iesous Christos Theos Huios Soter*' ('Jesus Christ, Son of God, Saviour').[5] The Latin inscription on the glass is now mostly illegible, with only two letters surviving, 'S[.]E'. However, it but should probably be read as the invocation 'in hope' rather than as a personal name.

The glass base features a cabled circular border, misidentified by Morey as a 'circle of leaves'. Its applied, unprotected decoration is of an unusual form typically associated with gold-glass plaques intended for immediate burial (see above, p.77). A glass discovered by Müller in the Monteverde catacomb in Rome featured similar unprotected decoration, but disintegrated upon discovery.[6]

Meek classed unprotected cut and shaded gold leaf within his type 1 (= Ashmolean group 1), glass, decoloured with antimony only.[7] Indeed, the likely chalice or cup form and the apparent lack of protection for the gold leaf might suggest an early date, along with the high proportion of antimony in the raw glass. However, the base and its gold leaf decoration are of more complex design and less accomplished execution than that of cat. 1. This piece is therefore included here with the gold-glass made from raw glass, decoloured with a mixture of antimony and manganese.

Endnotes

1. Ben-Sasson 2009; Spier 2007a: 5; Jensen 2000: 56; Rébillard 2009: 140–53.
2. As in San Callisto: Jensen 2000: 52, fig. 14.
3. On the symbolism of these scenes see Jensen 2000: 46–59.
4. For example the gravestone of Licinia Amias, now in the Vatican Museum: Dölger 1928: 159ff.
5. In the University of Pennsylvania Museum of Archaeology and Anthropology, Philadelphia, inv.29-128-2269; Spier 2007b: 196, cat. 26a. On the acrostic generally see Dölger 1928.
6. Müller 1912: 59; Schüler 1966: 58.
7. Meek in Howells 2015: 30.

Early Christian sarcophagi and a cinerary urn

37 AN 2007.44

The left end of a panel from the front of a sarcophagus lid: three biblical scenes of salvation

H. 29.2 cm, L. 80 cm, TH. 7cm

Fine-grained marble, probably from Carrara.

Present condition

The sarcophagus lid-panel is irregularly broken at the right end.

Decoration

The various scenes of salvation unfold with no visually signalled distinction between them. At the left end Christ raises Lazarus, with Mary Magdalene at his feet. Next in the sequence are the Hebrew boys, who raise their arms in prayer for salvation from the fiery furnace. The vignette is here ingeniously adapted from scenes familiar on pagan sarcophagi of cupids treading grapes in an oval tub. To the right Jonah is saved from the whale, and the broken right end of the fragment partially reveals him recovering from his ordeal beneath the gourd. The stone is lightly chiselled with little undercutting. The drill is used for dramatic effect in the eyes and hair of the figures and the flames of the furnace.

Bibliography

Webster 1929: 152–3, no.22; Vermeule and Von Bothmer 1959: 341–2, no.5; Sotomayor 1963: 225ff, no.4, fig. 20b; Carletti 1975: 125, no.23; Dresken-Weiland 1998: 75–6, no.213, Taf.76, 1; Koch 2000: 247, 616, no.138.

Comment

Webster dates the sarcophagus to the fourth century and Vermeule and von Bothmer to the late third. Meanwhile Koch combines the two with a date of AD 270/80–312/3, including the relief within his Group 9.4: small lid fragments with images of Jonah and other scenes, no.138. Dresken-Weiland compares this lid with another found in 1955 lying in an *arcosolium* in the Cimitero Maggiore. The latter combines a figure of the Good Shepherd with a woman at prayer, a scene of Adam and Eve and the awakening of the dead.[1] Of similar workmanship, this slab is of the same thickness but is 2 cm higher than the Wilshere fragment. Both could indeed be products of a single, metropolitan Roman workshop active in the early years of the fourth century AD.

Scenes of salvation drawn from the Old and New Testaments are often combined in sarcophagi of early fourth-century date. This is also the case with gold-glass: compare cat. 3. Both apparently draw upon the call for salvation of the deceased in the early Christian prayer for the commendation of the soul (see above, p.00).

Endnotes

1. Dresken-Weiland 1998: 65–6, no.164, Taf.67.1.

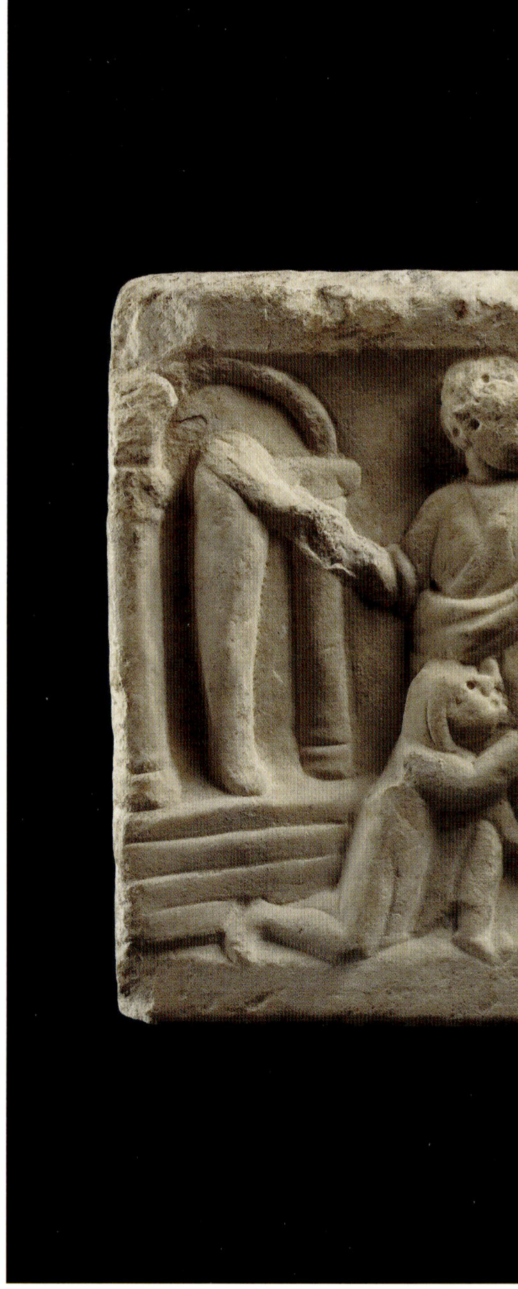

Photograph by David Gowers, 2013

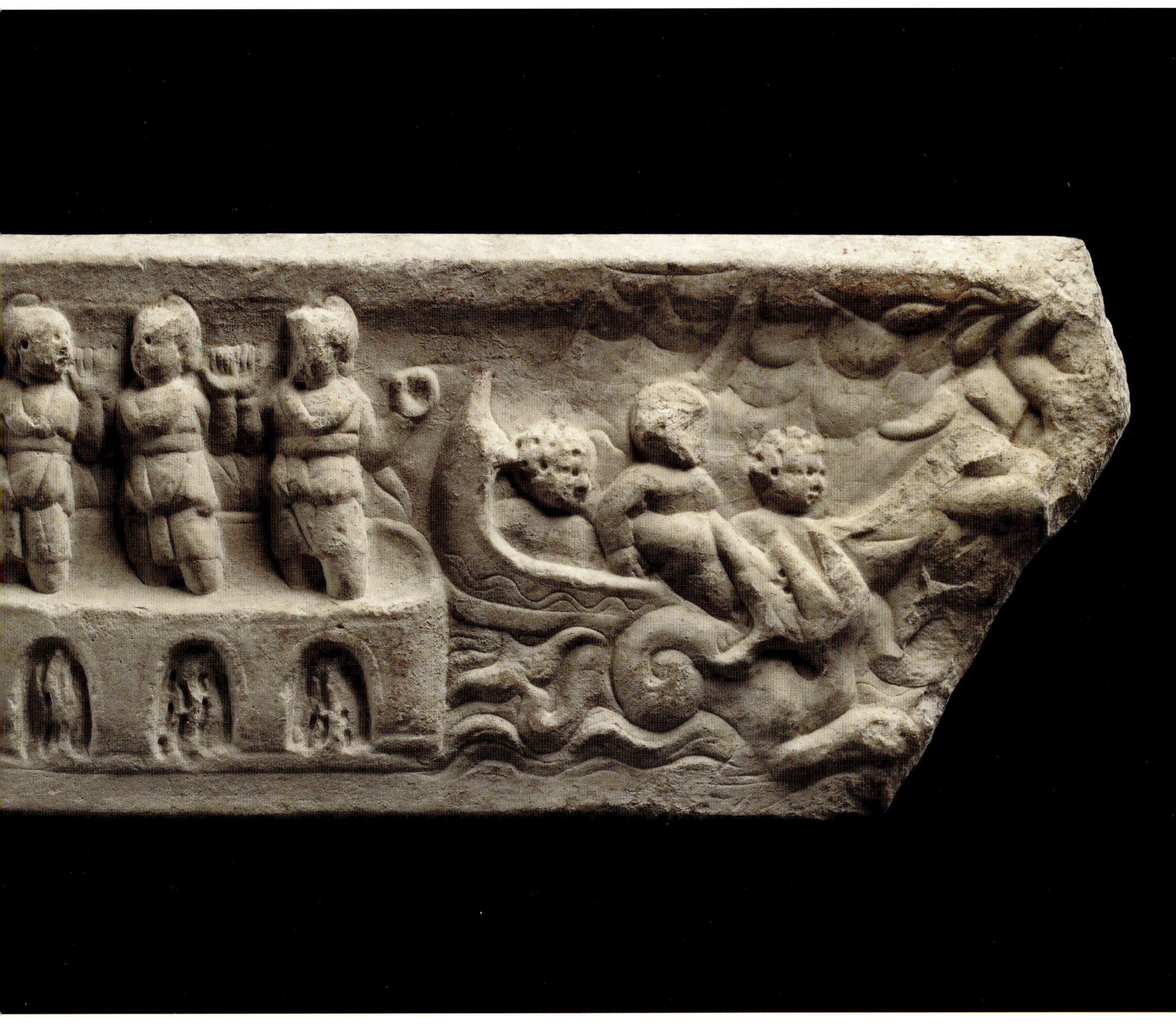

38 AN 2007.45

Fragment of the right side of a panel from the front of a sarcophagus lid, showing a meal at a *stibadium*

H. 27.2 cm; L. 43.5 cm. TH. not possible to measure in this mounted and framed piece. The measurements given here exclude the frame.

Fine-grained white marble, probably from Carrara.

Photograph by David Gowers, 2013

Detail showing surviving gilding on the tunic of the second servant, protected by the first servant's outstretched arm. Photograph by Jevon Thistlewood, 2013

Present condition

The relief is irregularly broken at the sides and base. The partially preserved cupid to the left of the scene once supported the right edge of a centrally placed shield or panel, showing that the fragment comes from the centre-right section of the lid-panel. There is also a break in the centre of the upper margin. The relief was mounted on Caen limestone and set on a purplish slate mount, the stone itself edged with brass. The reason for this unusual treatment is that the relief is gilded. Even today the gilding is well preserved in several places; a bole apparently formed of cinnabar red and black pigment survives beneath some patches of gilding, and in places on the white marble surface where the gilding has been lost. Despite the complex ancient and recent history of some painted and gilded sarcophagi from fourth-century Rome, it appears that the treatment of this fragment is ancient.[1]

Decoration

To the right of the cupid, whose head bends to watch the scene, two figures lean on a *stibadium* (a sigma-shaped rolled pillow). The figure at the left reaches out towards a fish set on a table top, just preserved at the lower right edge of the relief. The diners are served by a long-haired servant dressed in a long-sleeved tunic. He or she holds in the right hand a jug and in the left a *phiale*, a shallow bowl used to pour liquids, usually in a religious context. Here wine or water will be tipped from the *phiale* into the diners' beakers, if wine, or over their hands, if water intended for cleansing. A second standing figure with a topknot at the crown of the head, also dressed in a long-sleeved tunic, raises aloft an arm to light the scene with a torch; its flame runs along the upper margin of the relief. The first diner helps himself to fish while the second holds an upturned beaker to his lips. Above his head to the right is a large, clenched right fist, belonging to another figure beyond the broken edge. Above the figures is a plainly moulded rebate.

Bibliography

Webster 1929: 153, no.25; Vermeule and Von Bothmer 1959: 341–2, fig. 40; Amedick 1991: 139, no.109, with p.29.

Comment

The poorly preserved surface gives the figures a crude appearance. This may have led Webster to date the fragment to the late fourth century. However, as is clear from many other examples, including cat. **39**, the slash-like cutting of channels in the drapery of the figures is typical of Constantinian work (see cat. **37**).

Vermeule and Von Bothmer date the work to the fourth century, comparing the fragment to Lateran no.150. However, the closest comparison is offered by a walled-up sarcophagus front in Sesto Fiorentino, dated to the Constantinian period.[2]

Endnotes

1. Compare Sargent 2011, discussing a gilded garland sarcophagus now in Copenhagen.
2. Lateran no.150: Wilpert, 1929: pl.58. Sesto Fiorentino: Amedick 1991: no.244.

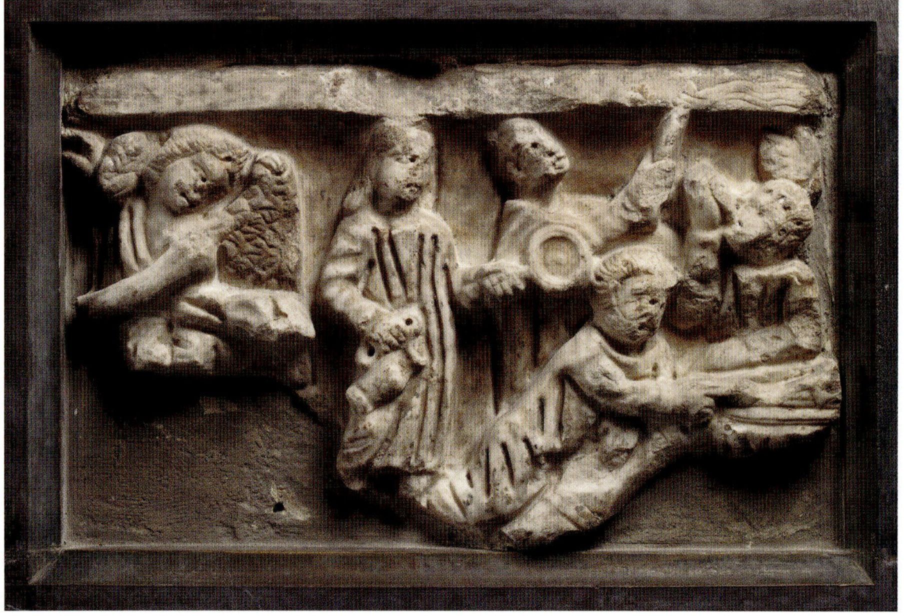

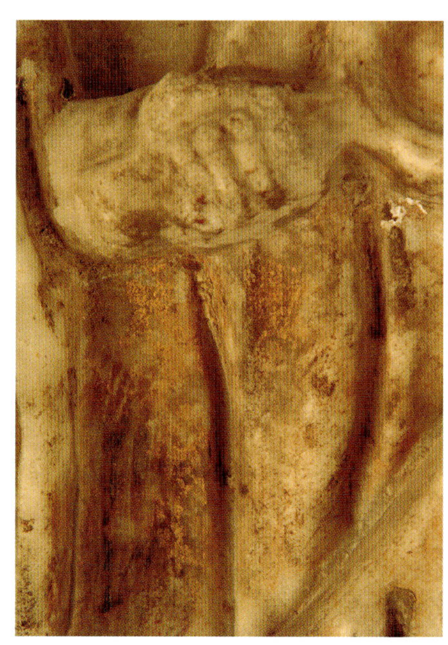

39 AN 2007.46

Part of a panel from the lid of a sarcophagus: a feast at the grave of a youth

H. 30 cm; L. 68 cm; TH. 6 cm

Medium-grained greyish-blue marble, probably Proconnesian.

Photograph by David Gowers, 2013

Present condition

The fragment is broken at both sides. It is clear from the surviving mouldings of a panel preserved at the right side that the piece came from the left central part of the lid of a sarcophagus.

There are brownish-yellow stains in places on the figured surface, but no clear traces of paint, bole or gilding. A rectangular dowel hole in the upper rear surface, 2 cm wide by 3.7 cm long and set 15.5 cm from the broken left edge, served either for mounting or moving the fragment or for attaching another element to the carefully chiselled, slightly curved surface. The cutting may be relatively recent, since the lid of the sarcophagus would have been attached at the base of the rear surface.

Decoration

Five men in short, belted tunics lean on a *stibadium* – a rolled, sigma or c-shaped pillow used for informal outdoor meals. The pillow is arranged around a small, circular serving table with feet in the shape of lion's paws. A plump fish is laid on the table, and two servants respond to calls for more wine. On the right of the group the fifth diner, a clean-shaven youth, is distracted, apparently by an open window in a building with a tiled roof to the right.[1]

Collection history

Acquired by Charles Wilshere between 1860 and 1890. Probably from Rome.

Bibliography

Webster 1929: 152, no.19; Vermeule and von Bothmer 1959: 341–2; Sotomayor 1963: 225, no.3, pl.20A; Himmelmann 1973: 66, no.56, pl.44b; Jastrebowska 1979: 48, no.39; Amedick 1991: 139, no.108, pl.36.9, p.29; Hartley 2006: 160, fig. 113.

Comment

The building shown to the right of the feast is most likely the distracted youth's tomb. Indeed he may be contemplating his fate, to lie in the tomb, and perhaps too the content of the central panel, lost beyond the left side of its frame and designed to take a personal funerary inscription. The missing left end of the lid would probably have shown young male servants mixing and heating wine in a crater perched over a fire.

Though there is no overtly Christian content, nor any sense of a lakeside setting, this scene is often identified as the meal shared by Christ and his apostles on the shore of the Sea of Galilee (John: 21) or as another meal scene recorded in the Gospel of Luke (Luke: 24).[2] However, though extremely popular in the late third and very early fourth centuries AD, outdoor meals were not seen as characteristic of Christianity after the legalisation of the faith by Constantine.[3] They are more likely to represent the *refrigerium* (funerary banquet) or *parentalia* (commemorative feasts for the dead), which the deceased was believed to attend. These festivals, with their reputation for drunkenness and louche behaviour, were not encouraged by the established Church.[4] Jastrzebowska notes the derivation of such scenes from earlier and contemporary representations of banquets after the hunt, attended only by men; she also observes that the serving of wine, bread and fish is typical of the funerary cult, whether consumed on couches or at the *stibadium*.[5]

The lid is probably early fourth century in date, to judge from its craftsmanship.[6] This features the apparently slashed drapery folds typical of the Constantinian era, also seen on the less well-preserved fragment cat. **38**. Here the drill is used to emphasise key elements of the narrative, for instance the table and the window in the building to the right). Drill-work also appears in the hair and hands of the figures; like the slashed drapery folds, this is a typical feature of the Constantinian period.[7] Conversely features of no importance to the narrative, such as the edge of the central panel, are left roughly worked with a claw or flat chisel.

Endnotes

1. Jastrzebowska 1981: 182–3 offers a description and typology of such scenes on sarcophagi.
2. Against the biblical setting see Jastrzebowska 1979: 47. Her classification of this fragment falls within a section titled 'Banquet habituel sans aucune indication permettant une interpretation', located within a wider group described as 'Scènes de banquet sculptées non chrétiennes'.
3. Koch 2000: 25.
4. Rébillard 2009: cover picture and 142–53.
5. Jastrzebowska 1979: 77.
6. AD 300–325 is suggested by Amedick, 1991: 139, no.108; Vermeule and Bothmer 1959 suggest the late third century.
7. Compare the Constantinian reliefs on the Arch of Constantine in Rome: Hartley 2006: 26–7, fig. 5; 45, fig. 16; 63, fig. 25.

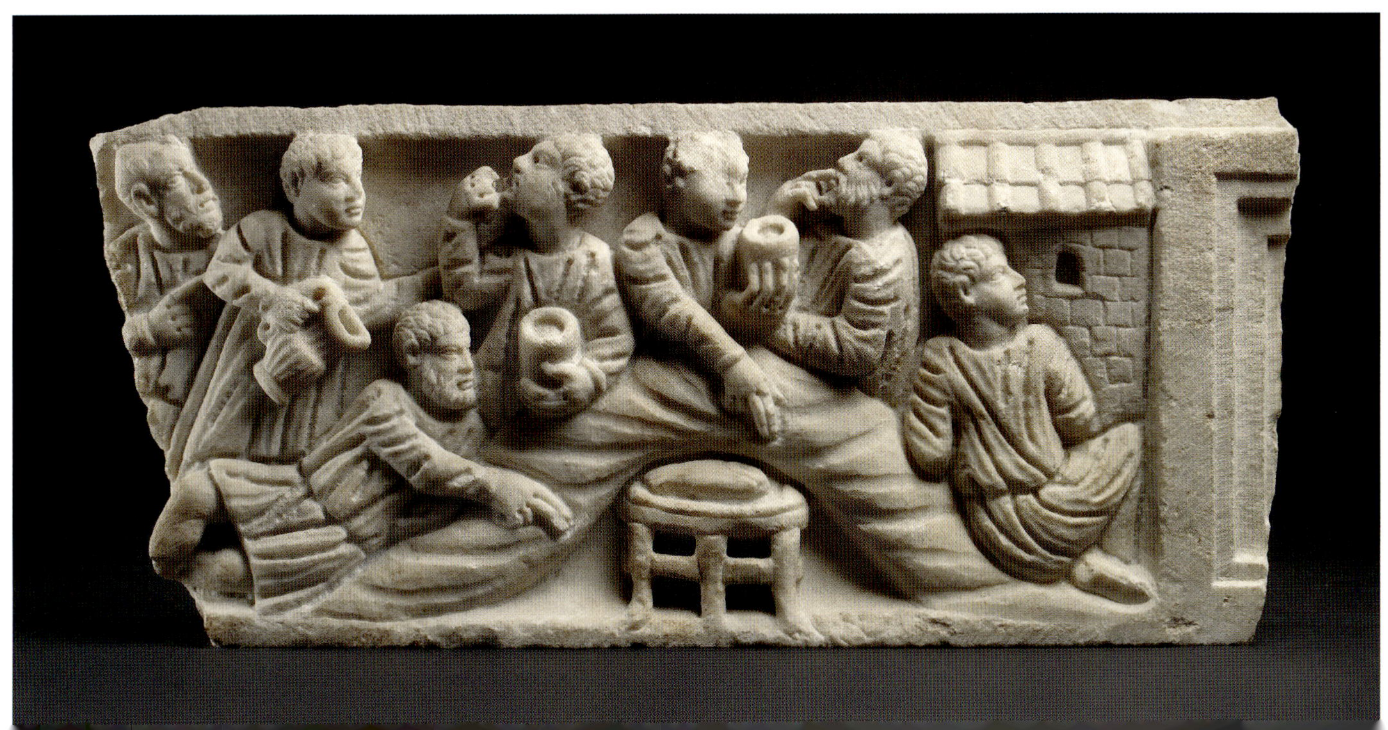

40 AN 2007.48

Child's sarcophagus chest: Christ's journey to Jerusalem; the feeding of the five thousand and the raising of Lazarus from the dead

H. 43 cm; L. 1.22 m; W. 46.7 cm

The chest is made of fine-grained white marble, probably from Carrara.

Present condition

The sides, back and interior surfaces of the chest are roughly finished with a point. Four dowel channels are cut into the upper edges of the short sides. These cuttings, *c.*10 cm long by 2 cm wide and located 6–8 cm from the carved/unworked front and back surfaces, once held iron clamps to fasten the lid (now lost) to the chest. The front channel on the right end still has lead preserved in the lower socket. Inside the chest the floor and walls are worked roughly flat; there is no sign of any ledge for the head.

The carved outer front surface is extremely weathered, with part of the ground line broken. To the right of the scene is a vertical break, while in the lower right half of the chest is an irregular line of breakage, which reaches up to the *aedicula* showing Lazarus. The chest was reused as a fountain basin, with lines of water wear clearly visible along the front edge. A hole to drain the water was cut in the lower back wall of the chest at the right end.

Decoration

The scenes on the front of the chest unfold as follows, from left to right: 1) Peter is arrested and betrays Christ; 2) Christ enters Jerusalem: to the left, a male figure; Christ rides a donkey; under the donkey its foal (unfinished and left as a boss, see Dinkler p.20); in front of the donkey a kneeling figure spreads his mantle (not fully finished, see Dinkler p.20); behind him a man views the scene from a tree; 3) the feeding of the five thousand: Christ distributes the loaves and fishes in baskets of different design; 4) Christ resurrects Lazarus, whose small, shrouded body stands before an *aedicula* on a podium in front of an elaborate architectural frame, including a Corinthian order and a pediment with *acroteria* and a wreath; the tomb is accessed by a flight of steps. On the ground in front of the tomb is a mourning woman.

Collection history

Acquired by Charles Wilshere, probably in Rome, between 1860 and 1890.

Bibliography

Webster 1929: 152, no.1; Wilpert 1929: Vol.2, pls.212, 235; Wilpert 1932: 109ff; Vermeule and von Bothmer 1959: 342, no.11, Pl.86, fig. 40; Sotomayor 1962: 80; Sotomayor 1963: 225, no.2, Taf.19a; Vermeule 1966: 69, no.8113, Fig. 270a; Dinkler 1970: 17, no.4, 19–20, Abb.5; Sotomayor 1975: 80; Dresken-Weiland 1998: 13, no.31, Taf.13.4; Koch 2000: 267, Group 1.3: children's sarcophagi, no.107.

Comment

The scenes are distinguished from each other only by the stance and gaze of the figures. The carving is competent, but not distinguished.

Webster dates the sarcophagus to the early fourth century; Vermeule and von Bothmer to the late third; Sotomayor (1962) to the 320s (1963) Constantinian; Dinkler to about 330; Dresken-Weiland to the 320s; Koch to the Constantinian period.

Dresken-Weiland compares this piece to a rather more static version of the scene in the Campo Santo Teutonico, Rome.[1] However, she also illustrates a more similar piece: a restored sarcophagus from the Villa de Felice (formerly the Villa Carpegna), Rome.[2] This has the same sequence of scenes, though more ambitiously designed and scaled for an adult: it is dated no later than 330.[3] On the short sides of this chest are scenes of the Hebrew boys in the fiery furnace and Adam and Eve, carved in low relief and very

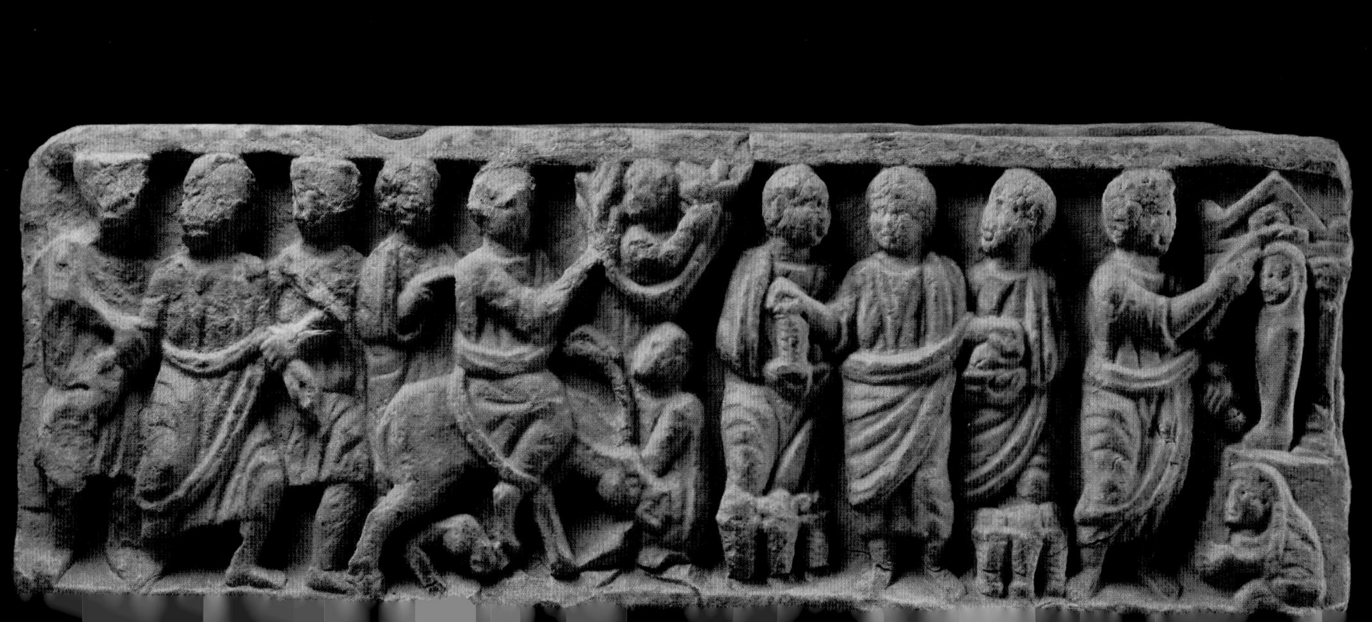

Photographs of front, back, interior and one short side by David Gowers, 2015

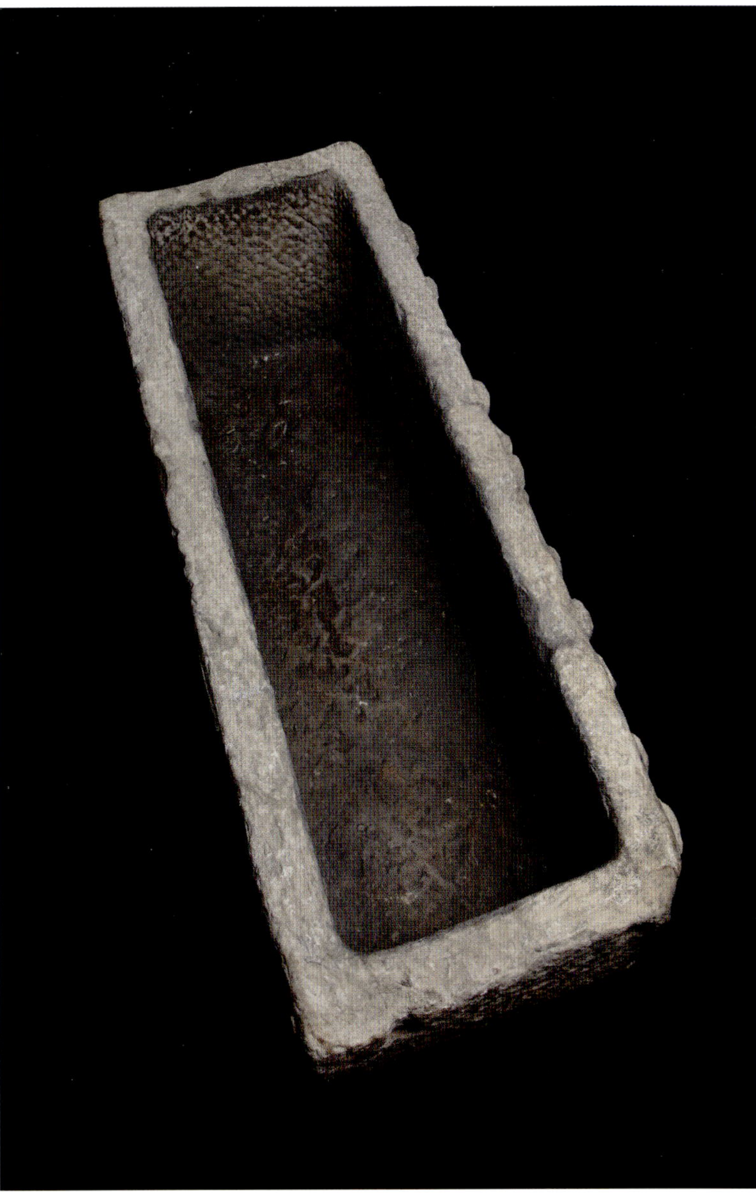

close to renditions of the same themes on gold-glass (for example cat. **23**). Dinkler notes that the composition falls within his earlier group as it is lacking a central orant figure.[4]

Generally Huskinson notes a lack of distinction in the decoration of Christian sarcophagi between those intended for adults and those intended for children. This forms a notable contrast to the pagan repertoire, where themes intended for children are clearly differentiated.[5]

Endnotes

1. Bovini and Brandenburg 1967: 345, no.841, pl.136.
2. Dresken-Weiland 1998: 13, no.30, Taf.13, 1–3, now displayed in The Metropolitan Museum of Art, Inv. No.1991.366, www.metmuseum.org/art/collection/search/466220, accessed 23 February 2017.
3. Evans 1993: 77–84, pls.1–3.
4. Dinkler 1970: 19.
5. Huskinson 1996: 69.

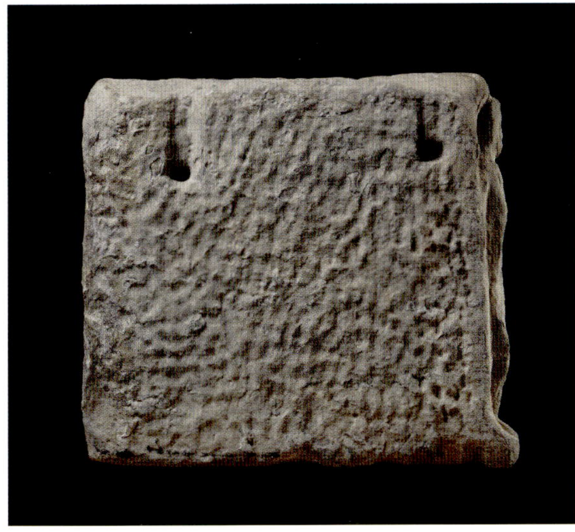

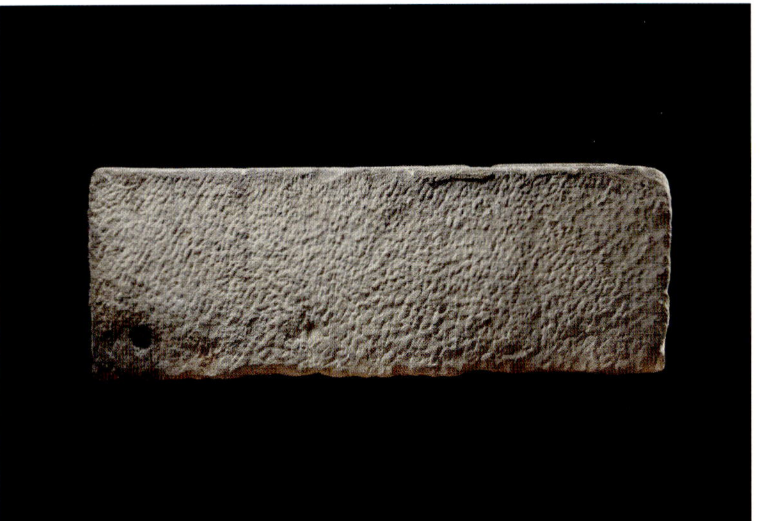

41 AN 2007.47a and b

The front of a sarcophagus chest: Christ (centre) with two saints, probably Peter (left) and Paul (right)

Photographs by David Gowers, 2013. The front of the sarcophagus (below); details of the surviving short left side, with carved lattice decoration, and of St Peter (opposite)

Present condition

The sarcophagus chest is broken at both ends. Only the front and stubs of both short sides survive. The front of the chest is broken into two pieces through the central figure of Christ (A, B). The back has been sawn through and the surface smoothed, probably for transportation to England in the 1860s.

A (left end): H. 55 cm; L. 116 cm; TH. 9.3 cm
B (right end): H. 55 cm; L. 103 cm; TH. 12.5 cm

The sarcophagus is made of fine-grained marble, probably from Carrara. The upper edge is cut to receive two horizontal dowels more than 25 cm in length which once joined the separated slabs. Two vertical cuttings with pour channels are preserved at the left and right ends of the strigillated panels. These probably held clamps attaching the lid to the chest. The left cutting has the Greek letters MAK incised vertically into the channel. The upper right corner of the sarcophagus front has been roughly repointed. The figure at the left end bears traces of a bole for painting and/or gilding.

Decoration

In a central panel Christ stands, turned to his left. He holds an open codex in his left hand and a stylus in his right. On the ground beside his left foot is a bundle of scrolls. In panels at the left and right ends of the sarcophagus two holy men, probably Saints Peter and Paul, hold scrolls. The figures are separated by two strigillated panels, each strigil decorated at the ends with small spheres. The right side of the chest was originally worked only with a fine point. In contrast, the left end was carefully carved with a lattice pattern.

Collection history

Rome, recorded by de Rossi as found in the vineyard of the Marchese Ricci Paracciani, behind the pyramid of Cestius near the destroyed oratory of the Church of San Salvatore. Bought by Charles Wilshere about 1866.[1]

Bibliography

De Rossi 1866: 33-6; Garrucci 1872–81: V, 162, no.56; Wilpert 1929: I, 52, no.16; Webster 1929: 152, no.7; Vermeule and von Bothmer 1959: 341–2; Sotomayor 1962: 178 no.102, fig. 20; Sotomayor 1963: 224, no.1, Taf.18; Sotomayor, 1975: 230; Dresken-Weiland 1998: 36, no.111, Taf.41,1; Koch 2000: 318, no.67; 493, n.146.

Comment

The carving of this exceptionally large sarcophagus is of very high quality, crisply finished with a chisel and no sign of drill-work. A bole to support paint or gilding is preserved on the figure at the left end. The discrepancy between the short left side, expertly carved with a lattice pattern, and the right, roughly finished with a point, suggests that the sarcophagus was set in the tomb against a wall on the right side but that the chest was visible at, and approached from, the left end.

Koch identifies this as one of a group of 36 sarcophagi of single figures set between and at the ends of strigillated panels. These are mostly from Rome, but are also known in northern Italy, Dalmatia and notably in southern France. The group is of variable quality, but includes some very fine work of the period of Valentinian and Theodosius; the chests were evidently commissioned individually in significant numbers. The repertoire of figures appearing in the panels includes apostles, worshippers, the Good Shepherd and Christ.[2] Here, given that all the figures hold scrolls or a codex, the scene is to be interpreted as the *traditio legis* – the compilation of new, holy law by Christ and its transmission to the apostles and patron saints of Rome, Peter and Paul.[3]

Vermeule and von Bothmer, followed by Dresken-Weiland, compared the iconography of this relief to a sarcophagus from a rural necropolis near Apt,[4] but a closer comparison is to be found nearer Rome in a sarcophagus front. Once built into the wall of a private house in Viterbo and now lost, this is dated to the late fourth century AD; Fiocchi Nicolai notes its typically Theodosian style.[5] The decoration of the ends of the strigil-shaped channels with small spheres is echoed in the Viterbo example. It also features in a large sarcophagus dated to 392, discussed in the entry for cat. **58**, and in a fragmentary Good Shepherd sarcophagus dated to the 390s; both were found at San Sebastiano on the Via Appia near Rome.[6]

Other, smaller examples are to be found in the Musei Capitolini: a very weathered chest from Campo Verano, dated to the turn of the fourth and fifth centuries, and an early fifth-century chest in SS Quattro Coronati, Rome, with a central Christogram set in a roundel balanced on a cross.[7] A comparable lattice pattern (here just seen on the surviving left side of the chest) is found in the front field of a sarcophagus from San Sebastiano, dated by the inscription above the latticed panel to AD 375.[8] The iconography and style of the relief is also closely comparable to the limestone votive relief from Amiternum (cat. **58**).

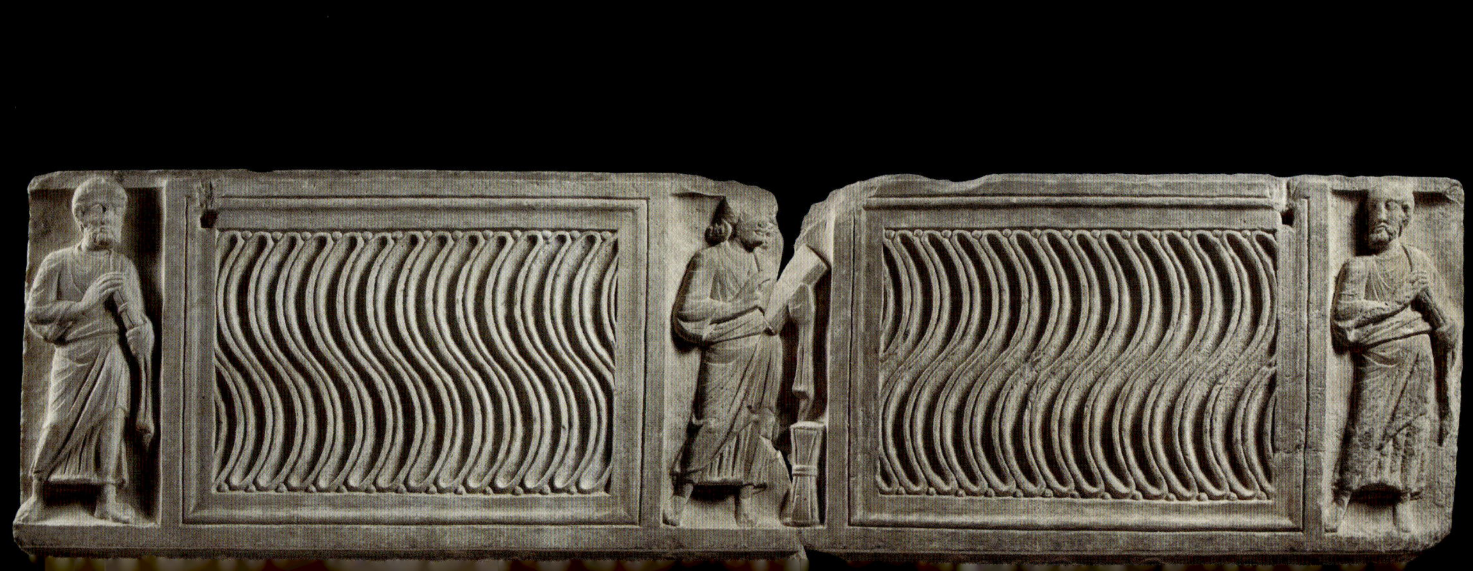

The letters MAK would not have been visible when the lid was in position. Most likely they represent the abbreviated name, hence the signature of the Greek sculptor.

Endnotes

1. De Rossi 1866: 33.
2. Koch 2000: 317–8, Group 2, no.67 for this example.
3. Huskinson 2015: 220–2 cautions against precise identification of the 'holy men' in such scenes, but does not discuss this example.
4. Christern-Briesenick 2003: no.30 (bibl.).
5. Dresken-Weiland 1998: no.112; Fiocchi Nicolai 1988: 132.
6. SEB 347 = Bovini and Brandenburg 1967: no.240, pl.54; SEB 267 = Bovini and Brandenburg 1967: no.235, pl.53.
7. Bovini and Brandenburg 1967: nos. 822 and 758, pls 132 and 119.
8. Koch 2000: pl.84 = Bovini and Brandenburg 1967: no.219.

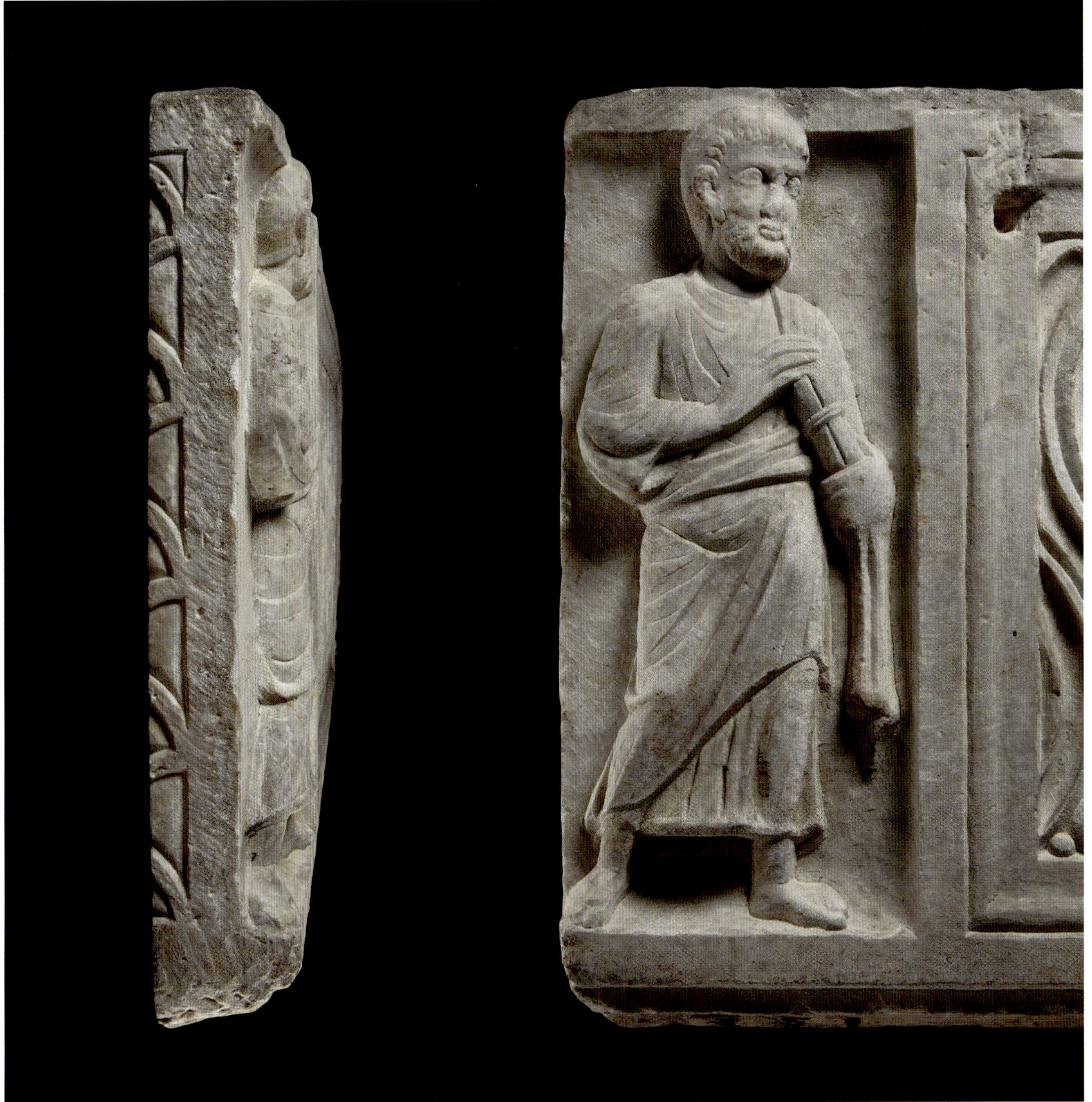

42 AN 2007.63

Photograph by David Gowers, 2013

Marble cinerary urn with lid of Cornelia Thalia

H. 22.2 cm; W. 39.3 cm; TH. 25.9 cm

Fine-grained, white marble, possibly Pentelic. No sample was taken in 2012.

Present condition

Intact, with no restorations. Ancient mortar survives, mainly on the left short side and lid of the urn.

Text and decoration

The centrally placed *tabula ansata* on the front of the chest is inscribed in Latin: 'diis ° manib(us) / Corneliae / Thaliae' ('To the departed spirits of Cornelia Thalia').

Faint traces of guidelines are visible in line 3.

The lower edge of the lid and the frame and wings of the inscribed tablet are simply moulded with a double rebate. The upper and lower edges of the chest add a curved *cyma reversa* moulding. The lid has a low, central pediment decorated with three rosettes, the central flower larger than the lateral. Double palmettes form corner *acroteria*. More palmettes appear within the handles of the tablet, and the spaces above and below are filled with rosettes. The lid is roofed with miniature marble tiles. On its right side is a hole for making offerings to the dead.

Collection history

From Rome, acquired by Wilshere from Luigi Depoletti. The exact provenance is unknown. Wilshere also bought a gold-glass miniature medallion from Depoletti (cat. **30**; on Depoletti see p.50, fig. 21).

Bibliography

N. Helbig 1886: CIL VI.3 no.16462; Vermeule and von Bothmer 1959: 342, Pusey House Oxford, no.7; Cooley 2017: 303–4, no.164.
Online: EDCS–12001357.

Comment

The effect of the design of the urn is of a miniature monument. It references grander architecture within the Etruscan tradition of visualising the container of ashes as a house for the dead. Within this grandiose setting individual modesty is preserved; no image or any further biographical details of the deceased are offered. The chest was apparently placed in a tomb in which it was intended to be seen and accessed only from the front and above. The sides are left plain and are still encrusted with mortar.

Made about AD 50–100, this piece is comparable with the urn *CIL* VI 3582. This also has ansate handles with palmettes, rosettes at the four corners of the inscribed panel and fairly restrained décor overall.[1]

Endnotes

1. Sinn 1987: Taf.53 no.303, AD 50–100; Cooley 2017: 304.

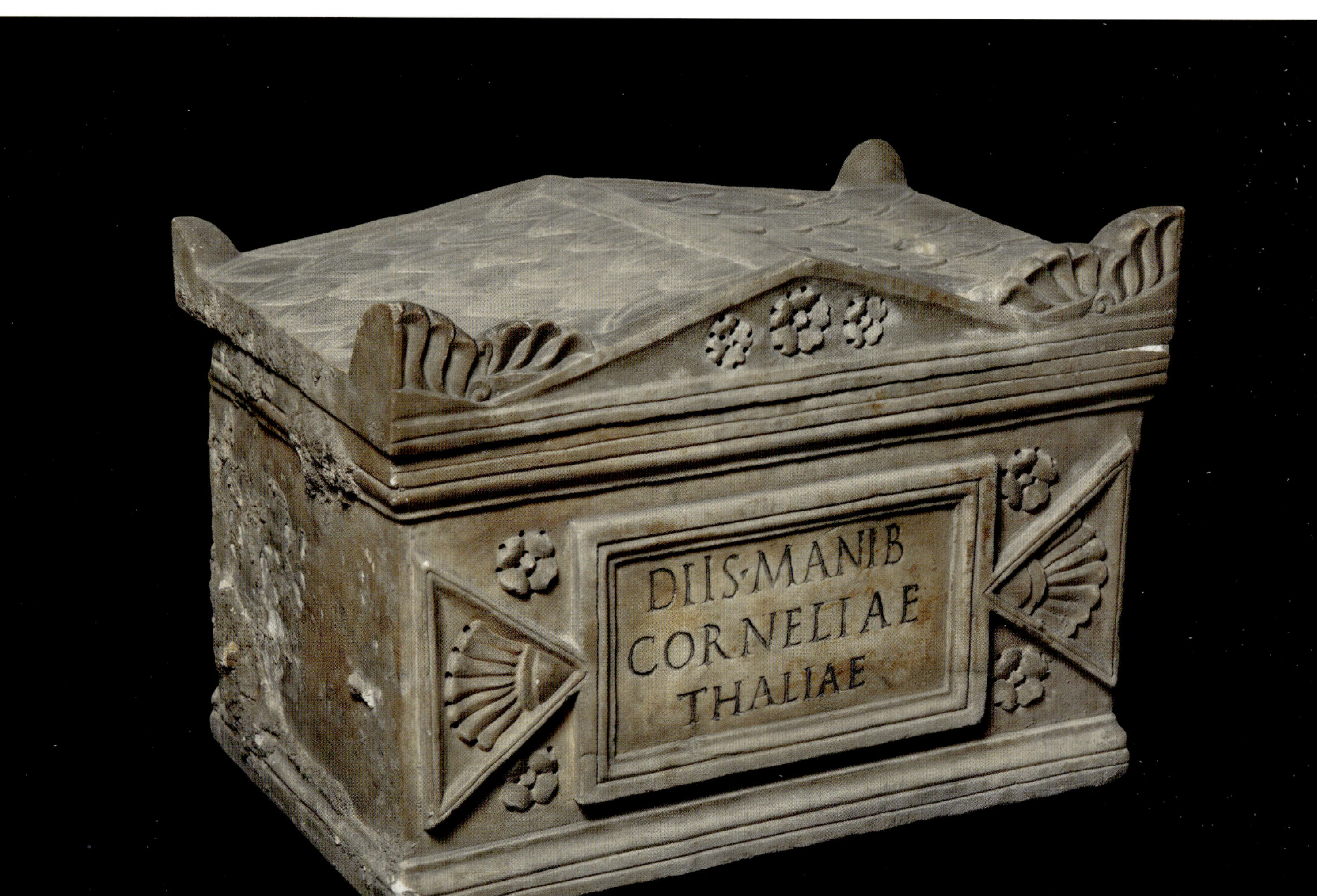

Funerary inscriptions

Photograph by David Gowers, 2013

A From Rome and environs

Jewish inscriptions from the Vigna Randanini catacomb, Via Appia Pignatelli

43 AN 2007.52
Funerary inscription of Justus

H. 21 cm; W. 39.2 cm; TH. 4 cm

Fine-grained white marble, probably from Carrara, central Italy.

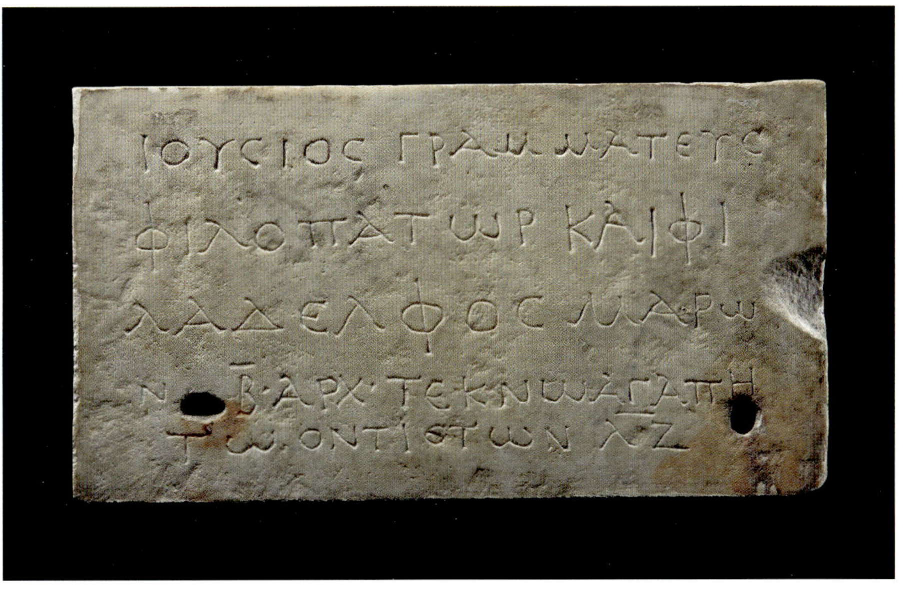

Present condition
The slab was removed from its modern slate backing in December 2012. Two holes are cut into the stone at the left end of line 4 and the right end of line 5 of the text. These once held iron clamps to secure the stone in place; the ancient lead seal survives in the left-hand socket. Half-way up the right side of the slab is a void – possibly the left edge of a cutting used to pour libations to the pagan dead, thus suggesting that the slab could have been recycled (compare cat. **52**, a former threshold block).

Text
The text is incised in five lines in near-cursive Greek in a neat hand.

> Ἰούσ<τ>ος γραμματεὺς
> φιλοπάτωρ καὶ φι
> λάδελφος. Μαρῶ
> ν β ἄρχ(ων) τέκνῳ ἀγαπη
> τῷ ὄντι ἐτῶν λ.ζ.

> ('Justus the secretary [of the synagogue], father-loving and brother/sister-loving. Maron, archon for the second time, for his beloved child, aged 37 years.')

H. 19 descending to 11 mm (letters), with serifs and cursive α, δ, λ, μ. Spaces between words, bars above numerals, points before and after abbreviation. In the name of the deceased, ι is written for τ. Though there is some variation in letter size, the line and letter spacing is reasonably regular as there was no need to navigate around pre-incised images of liturgical objects.

Collection history
Excavated in the Vigna Randanini catacomb, Via Appia Pignatelli, Rome in April 1862.[1] The text was copied by C. L. Visconti in 1863.[2] Acquired by Charles Wilshere in 1870 from Ignace Randanini, son of the proprietor of the land. Bequeathed by Wilshere by Deed of Trust to Pusey House, Oxford in 1895. Loaned to the Ashmolean Museum, Oxford in 1984. Purchased by the Ashmolean Museum, 2007.

Bibliography
Garrucci 1862: 47; Webster 1929: 151–2, no.20; Frey, 1936: CIJ 1, no.25; Leon 1960: 98, 129, 186 and 282, no.125; Kraabel 1979: 46–4, no.2, Pl.II; Robert and Robert 1979: 539–40, no.671; Vismara 1986: 383–4, 387; Van der Horst 1991: 89, 91; Noy, 1995: 290–1, no.344.

Comment
The text commemorates Justus as γραμματεὺς (secretary) of the synagogue where his father Maron held the post of ἄρχων (archon, a senior leader) for the second time. Both posts reflect the organisation around the synagogue of the Jewish diaspora community in Rome, using recognisable titles from civic society in the Greek cities of the eastern Mediterranean, where the community originated.[3] The inscription itself probably dates from the fourth century AD.

Garrucci records another five archons from the Vigna Randanini catacomb, one of whom was aged only six, suggesting that the post was, in some cases at least, hereditary.[4] In this case there seems to have been a sense of career progression; the 37-year-old Justus appears in a subordinate, clerical role, keeping membership lists up to date, conserving archives and preparing marriage contracts.[5] There are no symbols on this stone, and consequently no visual indication of Jewish faith. Furthermore, while Maron's name is Greek, his son Justus has a Roman name, indicative of social integration.

Probably fourth century AD.

Endnotes
1. PIAC: de Rossi archive no.16324. The text also appears in a folder entitled *Scavi del 1862 Marzo-Maggio*, no.16304. Rubbings of the texts of cats **43**, **47** and **50**, sent by Wilshere to de Rossi, are featured in no.16325.
2. PIAC: *iscrizioni del cimitero giudaico a Vigna Randanini copiate nel 1863 da C. L. Visconti* : 16271, no.50.
3. Leon 1960: 173–80 (*archon*) and 183–6 (*grammateus*).
4. Garrucci 1862: 54, 55, 59 and 61.
5. Van der Horst 1991: 92.

44 AN 2007.55
Funerary inscription of the archon Zotikos

Photograph by David Gowers, 2012

H. 54.3 cm; W. 97 cm (both to the edge of the frame)

Fine-grained greyish marble, perhaps from Carrara.

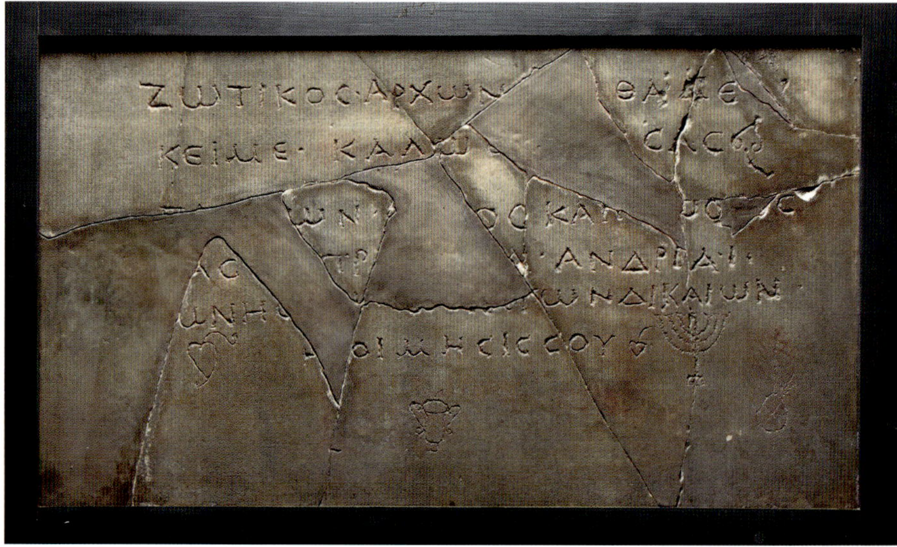

Present condition

This very substantial slab is partially preserved in 12 large fragments. A number of letters in the partially preserved six lines of Greek text read by Garrucci are no longer extant. Gaps in the slab have been filled in red cement and the whole is set within a slate frame.
It was not possible to remove the frame in 2012.

Text

The text reproduced here is taken from Noy (1995, no.342), as the stone is currently only partially accessible.

> Ζωτικὸς ἄρχων ἐνθάδε
> κειμε, καλῶς βειώσας (inverted *hedera*)
> πά[ντ]ων φ[ίλ]ος καί γνωστὸς
> [π]ᾶσ[ι ..]πρ[....]α ἀνδρὶ ἀϊ
> μνήσ[τῳ · μετ]ὰ τῶν δικαίων (*hedera*)
> ἡ κοίμησίς σου
> (*hedera,* ivy leaf, commonly used to mark breaks in the text) (menorah, seven-branched candlestick) (*lulab*, frond of the date palm tree) (vase)
>
> ('I Zotikos, archon, lie here, having lived a good life, friend of all and known to all ..pr….a for her husband, always remembered. Your sleep with the just.')

The letters, about 28 mm in height, are painted red. At the right end of the second line is an inverted *hedera*, 62 mm in height. The sixth and last line of the Greek text is edged by two *hederae*, 75 cm high x 34 mm wide and 45 mm high. A menorah, 85 mm high x 90 mm wide, and a *lulab*, 150 mm in length, appear at the end of the text, the menorah standing on a three-footed base. Goodenough noted that the *lulab* was balanced by traces of red paint, which probably represented the Hebrew letters of *shalom*.[1] There remain today traces of (now illegible) paint. At the base of the slab, centred below the text, is a *cantharus*, 60 mm high x 60 mm wide and perhaps with a lid. As with other funerary monuments from the Vigna Randanini catacomb, the text respects the incised symbols of Jewish faith, suggesting that the latter were carved first.

Collection history

Rome, Vigna Randanini catacomb, excavated before 1863. A rubbing of the text was taken by Visconti in 1863.[2] A second was sent to de Rossi, presumably after 1870 (the date is not specified) by Wilshere.[3] Acquired by Charles Wilshere in 1870 from Ignace Randanini, son of the proprietor of the land. Bequeathed by Wilshere by Deed of Trust to Pusey House, Oxford in 1895. Loaned to the Ashmolean Museum, Oxford in 1984. Purchased by the Ashmolean Museum, 2007.

Bibliography

Garrucci 164, no.15; Webster 1929: 151, no.9; Frey 1936: CIJ 1, 118; Ferrua 1941: 33; Robert 1946: 97; Goodenough 1953–68: vol.2, 22, no.126; vol.3, fig. 767; Stuiber 1957: 19, no.45; Leon 1960: 84, no.1 for the correct reading of ανδρί; 104, 125, 128, 281, no.118; Vismara 1986: 383; Reynolds and Tannenbaum 1987: 100; van der Horst 1991: 117; Noy 1995: 286–8, no.342, Pl.XV; Vickers 2009–11: 609.

Comment

This is the only inscription from the Randanini catacomb to have the deceased speak in the first person, a reflection of his leading role as *archon* of the community. [Eu]pra[xi]a is a possible name for the wife who set up the monument. Van der Horst notes the lack of prayer for peace accompanying the desire of Zotikos's wife for her late husband to share the post-mortal company of the righteous ones – that is, the biblical patriarchs Abraham, Isaac and Jacob, who were believed to receive the dead in their bosom and provide them with a celestial banquet.[4]

Noy notes the difficulty of interpreting the symbols below the text:[5]

> A long *lulab* with very short branches was inscribed, with a circle of 3 cm diameter at its base containing a cross. A short stem which seems to be another *lulab* protrudes from the circle to the right of the main *lulab*; Webster interpreted this as an amphora. Much longer branches for the main *lulab* were painted on the stone but not inscribed.

With no visible evidence of nail holes, this slab probably covered a stone sarcophagus set within an *arcosolium* (arched niche with low platform designed to support a sarcophagus) in a *cubiculum* (chamber) of the catacomb.

Endnotes

1. Goodenough 1953–68: 2, 22, reporting the observations of the Reverend Thomas M. Parker of Pusey House.
2. PIAC, de Rossi archive: 16281.
3. PIAC, de Rossi archive: 16282.
4. Van der Horst 1991: 117, with notes 10 and 11.
5. Noy 1995: 288.

45 AN 2007.53
Funerary epitaph of Sabeina

Photograph by David Gowers, 2013

H. 28.5 cm; W. 43.5 cm; TH. 3.7 cm

Blue marble with a strong diagonal vein, perhaps Carrara bardiglio. A sample was taken for stable isotope analysis in December 2012; the results matched the readings for the Carrara quarries (see Appendix 6 and p.00 above).

Present condition
The slab was removed from its modern slate frame in December 2012.

The slab is cracked vertically through the centre. It had been repaired with plaster and set in a slate frame. A sketch made by, and a rubbing made for, C. L. Visconti show the break repaired soon after discovery, as does the photograph taken for John Parker (p.63, fig. 29).[1] It has been repaired again with stainless steel dowels since removal of the frame, as the earlier restorations had dried. An iron stain from a nail, probably ancient, appears in the margin of the slab at the bottom right.

Text
The Greek inscription in six gently undulating lines, incised without guidelines, is set within a regular, grooved, rectangular frame worked with a flat chisel. The text begins and ends with a representation of a menorah set on a stand. The text and the menorahs are coloured in red.

Menorah: Πάρδος Σαβείν/αι θυγατρι τίς ἔζησεν ἔτη (*hedera*) δέκαεσζ. ἐν ἐι/ρήνη ἡ κοίμη/σις ἀυτῆς (*menorah*)

('Pardos to Sabeina his daughter, who lived 16 years. In peace is her sleep.')

Collection history
Excavated in May 1862 in the Vigna Randanini catacombs, Via Appia Pignatelli, Rome. Photographed among other funerary slabs exhibited at the entrance to the catacomb for J. H. Parker, 1865–70. Acquired by Charles Wilshere in 1870 from Ignace Randanini, son of the proprietor of the land. Bequeathed by Wilshere by Deed of Trust to Pusey House, Oxford in 1895. Loaned to the Ashmolean Museum, Oxford in 1984. Purchased by the Ashmolean Museum, 2007.

Bibliography
Garrucci (1865), 182, no.24; J. H. Parker archive, Ashmolean Museum, photo no.776; Webster 1929: 152, no.23; Frey 1936: *CIJ* I, 114, no.159 (from Garrucci and a copy by Visconti); I^{2} (1975), 30–1; Goodenough 1953–68: Vol.3, no.764; Leon 1960: 289; Kraabel 1979: 42–58; Noy 1995: 286–7, no.348.

Comment
Noy notes that the lower menorah was carved before the text, which is displaced to avoid it, and that the mason had difficulty in maintaining even spacing in line 2. In fact it is likely that both menorahs were carved before the text, resulting in the exaggerated left-hand margin and some crowding of the layout. The spelling of the numeral 6 is odd. Like Justus, son of Maron (cat. **43**), Sabina, daughter of Pardos has been given a Roman name.[2] The piece probably dates from the fourth century AD.

Endnotes
1. PIAC, de Rossi archive, 16273, no.35; Parker no.776.
2. Here, as elsewhere in the book, the Latin spelling Sabina is used.

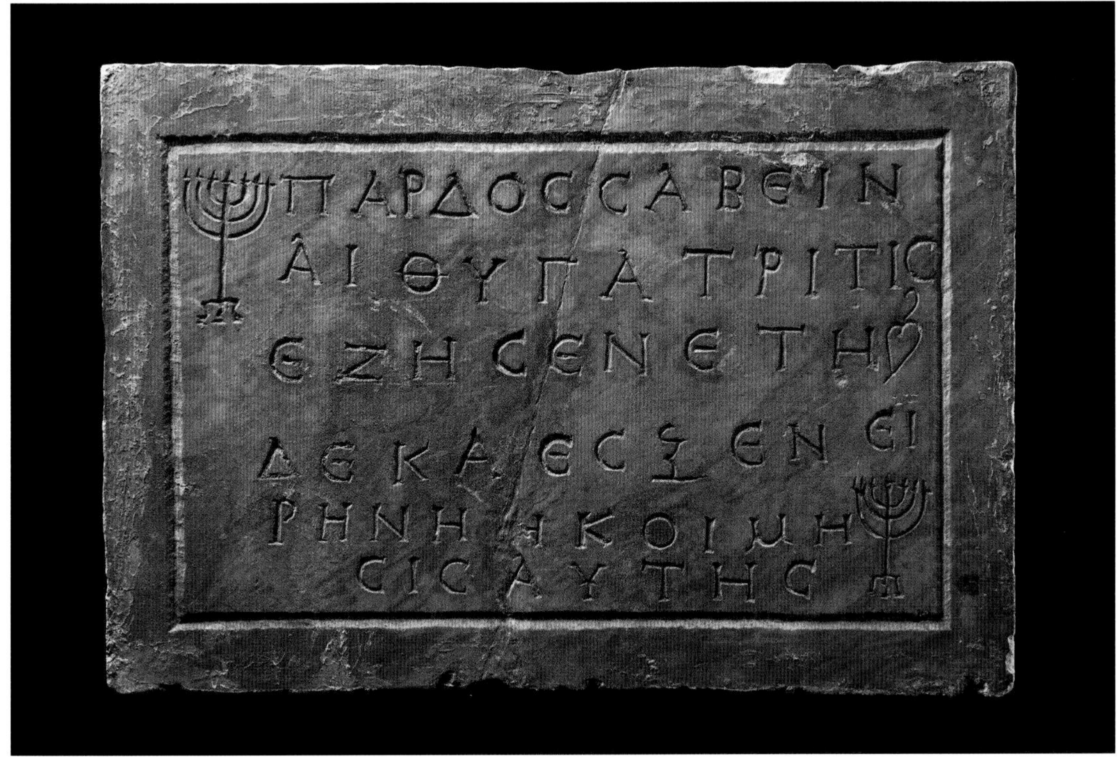

46 AN 2007.57
Marble epitaph of Melition

Photograph by David Gowers, 2013

H. 20.2 cm ; W. 46.7 cm; TH. 3.4 cm

Fine-grained, bluish marble, probably from Carrara.

Present condition

The slate frame was removed in 2012. The break at the lower left corner is antique, if not ancient, and the corner has been lost. A hole is cut into the back of the slab; this is filled with mortar, and there is a large spread of mortar surviving on the back of the slab. The left side has been cut. Stains from iron nails appear towards the base of the slab (compare cat. **43**). There is no trace of colour in the letters of the Greek inscription, the inscribed menorah or the *hederae*.

Three samples of mortar were removed for analysis in 2012 (see Appendix 6).

Text

As in the case of other inscriptions from Vigna Randanini, the Greek text is set around the engraved motifs in five lines:

Με.λι.τί.ω. μη.τρὶ. γλυκυ
τά τη
Δουλ.κι.τί.α. θυ.γά.τηρ
(*hedera*) .ἀ.νέ (menorah) θη.κα. (*hedera*)
ἥ.τις. ἔζη. (menorah) σεν. ἔ.τη. κ.θ΄

('For her dearest mother Melition, Dulcitia her daughter set (this) up. She lived 29 years.')

Letters 32 diminishing to 18 mm in height, with serifs. Menorah 63 x 68 mm; *hederae* 85 and 104 mm high. Triangular interpuncts between nearly every syllable of the words and each digit of the numeral. Drop-bar alpha, cursive-style delta and mu.

Collection history

Excavated in May 1862 from the Randanini catacomb, Via Appia Pignatelli, Rome and drawn for C. L. Visconti.[1] Acquired by Charles Wilshere in 1870 from Ignace Randanini, son of the proprietor of the land. Bequeathed by Wilshere by Deed of Trust to Pusey House, Oxford in 1895. Loaned to the Ashmolean Museum, Oxford in 1984. Purchased by the Ashmolean Museum, 2007.

Bibliography

Garrucci 1862: 58-9; Webster 1929: 152, no.27; Frey 1936, 1975: *CIJ* I, 100, no.141 (follows Garrucci and copy by de Rossi); I², 30; Ferrua 1936a: 131; Ferrua 1941: 33; Goodenough 1953–68: II, 21; III, pl.763; Leon 1960: 285, no.141; Solin 1982: 1290; Kraemer 1986: 89; Noy 1995: 291, no.345; dello Russo 2012: 34 confuses this inscription with *CII* 152 = *JIWE* 245.

Comment

The layout is decorative, with elegant interpuncts between each syllable and large symbols. Though Garrucci thought the symbols at the ends of line 4 were *ethrogin*, Noy is more likely right to see them as exaggerated *hederae*.[2] As in other funerary texts from the catacombs of Vigna Randanini, the symbols were incised before the text, thereby prohibiting the use of guidelines and determining the layout of lines 4–5. Melition is a Greek name, but, as in other instances of texts collected by Wilshere from the Vigna Randanini catacombs, her daughter has a Roman name, Dulcitia. The sweet natures of both women are reflected in their personal names and the epithet of Melition 'γλυκυ'.

The epitaph probably dates from the fourth century AD.

Endnotes

1. PIAC, de Rossi archive: 16327.
2. Dello Russo 2012: 35; Noy 1995: 291.

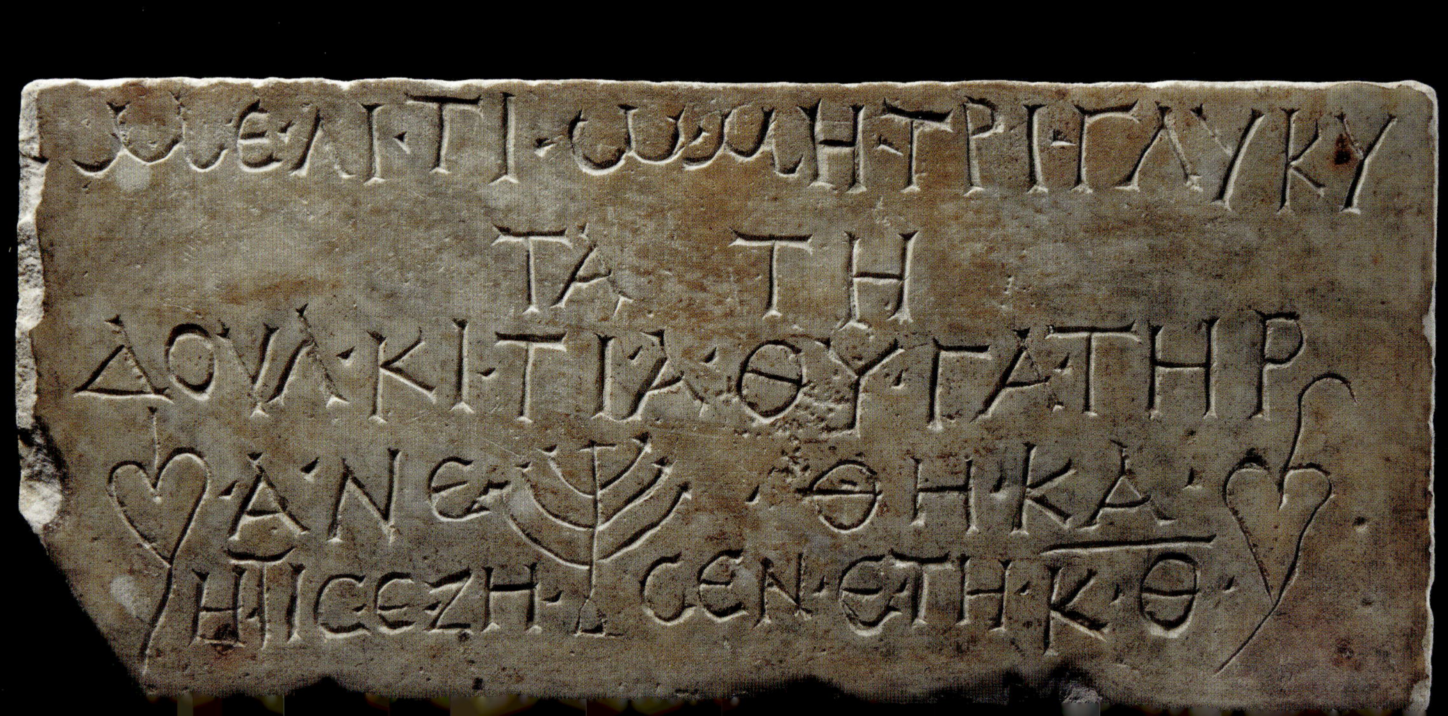

47 AN 2007.62
Funerary inscription of Venerosa

Photograph by David Gowers, 2013

H. 17.2 cm; W. 29.5 cm

Fine-grained, probably Carrara marble.

Present condition
The slate frame was not removed in 2012. The slab is chipped at the lower, left-hand corner and is broken along the right edge. The breaks were filled with plaster before the stone was set in the slate frame.

Text
Lightly incised around a large, roughly incised, centrally placed menorah, the four lines of Latin text are written in Greek script except for the numerals.

Βενερωσα
ἀνρων XVII
ἐ[τ] κου[μ] μαριτους
μησις XV

('Venerosa aged 17, and (she lived) with her husband 15 months')

Collection history
Rome, found in the Vigna Randanini catacomb before 1861.[1] The text was copied by Visconti in 1863.[2] Acquired by Charles Wilshere in 1870 from Ignace Randanini, son of the proprietor of the land. Bequeathed by Wilshere by Deed of Trust to Pusey House, Oxford in 1895. Loaned to the Ashmolean Museum, Oxford in 1984. Purchased by the Ashmolean Museum, 2007.

Bibliography
Herzog 1861: 102; Garrucci 1862: 32–3; Diehl 1927: *ILCV*, no.4954; Webster 1925–9: ms. no.28, as 'Jewish inscription of doubtful meaning' (not published); Frey 936: *CIJ* 268; Leon 1960: 99, 304 no.268, listed as not extant; Kraabel 1979: 43–6, no.1; Noy 1995: 294–5, no.349 (add.bibl.); dello Russo 2012: 33.

Comment
Kraabel translates as 'Venerosa, seventeen years, and with her husband fifteen months.'[3] However, though the sense is surely correct, Noy notes that Kraabel's reading of *marito s(uo)* is probably wrong.[4]

Compare the similarly shaped and inscribed gravestone of Marcella from the Vigna Randanini catacomb.[5] A Latin text of remarkably similar content was recorded by Bosio in the catacomb of Domitilla on the Via Ardeatina.[6]

ueNEROSA QVAE VEXIT
anNOS. XXX. ET.MENSES. II
CUM. MARITO. FECIT
ANNOS. (*hedera*) XIIII. M. V ET
D.XXVIII

('Venerosa who lived 30 years and 2 months. With her husband she made 14 years 5 months and 28 days.')

These texts are particularly notable for the attention given to the length of the marriages of the women in question, in addition to the deceased's exact age at death. No sentiment appears in the text, nor any reference to motherhood.

Endnotes
1. Herzog 1861: 102.
2. PIAC, de Rossi archive: 16270, no.12; 16295 includes a drawing with reference to readings by Herzog and Garrucci. Another appears on the back of 16330. Folder 16325 contains a rubbing probably sent to de Rossi by Wilshere.
3. Kraabel 1979: 45.
4. Diehl 1927: no.ILCV 4954
5. *CI*: 177, no.249 (photograph) = *JIWE* 229, no.261). PIAC, de Rossi archive: 16273, no.40.
6. Bosio 1632–4: Cap.XXIII, 296 = *ICUR* III N.S. 307, no.8585 (bibl.).

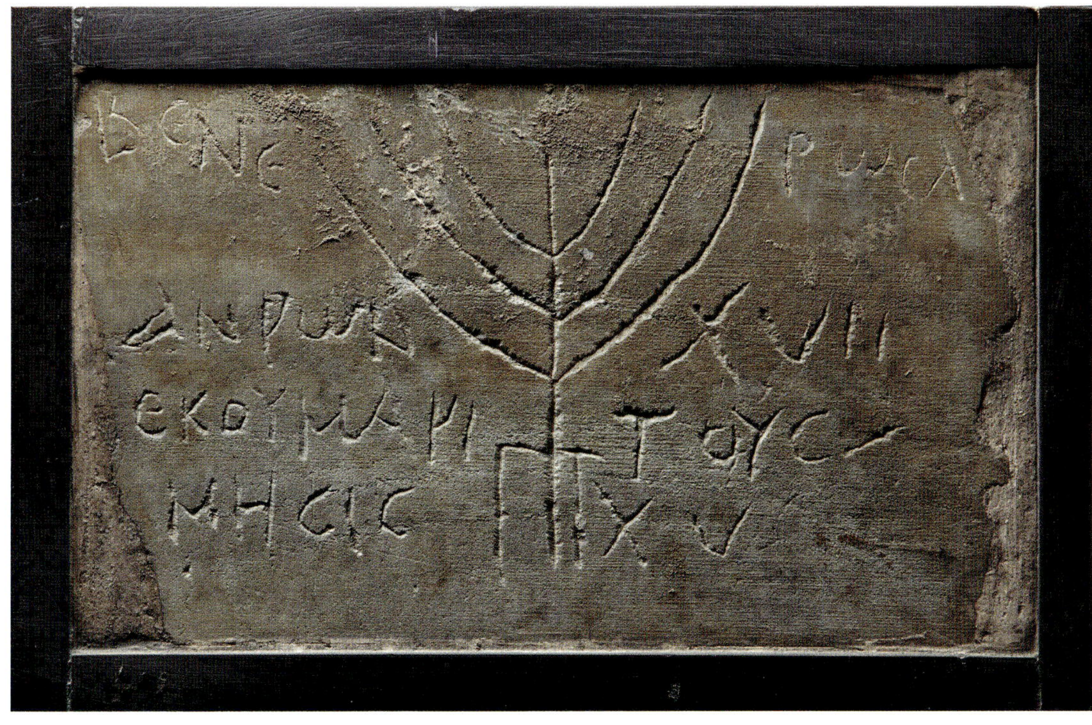

48 AN 2007.51
Funerary inscription of Alexander

DIAM. 32.1 cm; TH. 0.8 cm

Probably grey-toned Carrara marble from central Italy.

Photograph by David Gowers, 2013

Present condition

The Latin text is cut into a circular slab of fine white marble. It has been suggested that the slab was recycled from a column shaft,[1] but the removal of the inscribed slab from its modern slate backing in December 2012 revealed it to be very thin. It may thus have more probably been used as wall revetment – though the revetment itself may have been recycled from a column shaft. The back of the slab was scored with scratched lines; it was subsequently pitted with the marks of a drill-tip, carelessly used within the modern slate mount. The slab is joined from four fragments, probably using iron dowels which have stained the stone. Iron stains also appear at the edge of the slab, at the centre of the top, at the right side and below. These were probably made by ancient nails or dowels used to secure the marble in place, possibly in its first use. The stains have given the marble a somewhat rosy appearance, belying its likely source.

Text

The text is irregularly inscribed in seven undulating lines with no use of guidelines. The menorah at the end of the text is squashed into the circular slab at an awkward angle.

> Alexander / bucular(i)us de ma/cello q(ui) vixit annis / XXX anima bona om/[5]niorum amicus / dormitio tua inter / dicaeis ⊂ menorah ⊃
>
> ('Alexander, beef butcher [or seller of steers and heifers] from the market, who lived 30 years, a good soul, a friend to all, your sleep [is] among the just.')

Letters 22–30 mm in height and painted red.

Collection history

Rome, Vigna Randanini catacombs, found April 1862 in separate pieces. The right-hand fragment was found first, but the rest was quickly recovered, and the whole text was published by Garrucci in the same year. Two sketches by Visconti show the right side only and the full text.[2]

Purchased by Charles Wilshere in 1870 from Ignace Randanini. Dello Russo describes the fragment as coming from a sarcophagus.[3] The breakage of the slab is similar to that of some of the other texts from the Vigna Randanini in the Wilshere Collection (such as cats **49** and **50**). It is likely that they all came from the same, presumably vandalised area of the catacomb.

Bibliography

Garrucci 1862: 44–5; Armellini 1880: 430; Dessau 1913: *ILS* iii, 2, CXLII, no.9432 (from Garrucci); Diehl 1927: *ILCV* ii, 488, no.4856 (from Garrucci and Armellini); Webster 1929: 151, no.5; *CIJ*, I,(1936), 148–9, no.210 (follows Garrucci and copies by Visconti made in 1863); *CIJ*, I² (1975), 31; Robert 1937: 121; Collon 1940: 91; Ferrua 1941: 35; Goodenough 1953: Vol.2, 22, 3, pl.765; Stűber 1957: 119, no.45; Leon 1960: 90, 101, 130, 132, 138, 233, 293–4, no.10; Kraabel 1979: 42–58; Palmer 1980: 225; Mazzoleni 1980b: 31; Ferrua 1981: 192; De Ruyt 1983: 363; Vismara 1986: 356; Dietz 1987: 387 (from earlier editions); Priuli 1991: 295 (from Goodenough's photograph); Van der Horst 1991: 99, 117; Vickers 1992: 47–8, fig. 51; Noy 1995: 286–7, no.343, pl.XVI; Chioffi 1999: 48–9, no.37; AE 2002, no.198; 2005, no.16; Williams 2002: 122–33; Solin 2003: I, 198; Angerstorfer 2012: 277–386; dello Russo 2012: 27, n.105 (from a sarcophagus); Cooley 2017: 295–9, no.161 (full edition).

Comment

The text is the only example from the Randanini catacomb in the Wilshere Collection to be written in Latin, though the use of Latin is common enough at this catacomb.[4] The script is irregular: not all As have a crossbar, M appears for M and Γ for T occurs twice in line 6, suggesting an engraver more familiar with Greek. In line 6, RM is ligatured. The B of Bucularus is lower case and there are no interpuncts or spaces between the words. *Omniorum amicus* is a Latin version of the Greek πασιφίλος, common in Christian epitaphs, while *anima bona* is a Christian term that does not occur on any other Jewish inscriptions from Rome.[5] The use of the word *dicaeis* in the ablative at the end of the text suggests a translation of the Greek μετα των δικαίων ή κοίμησίς σου. A menorah is engraved in the stone at the lower right; its position next to *dicaeis* may signify that the latter refers to pious or righteous Jews.

The reading of Alexander's profession in line 2 has proved especially problematic. Priuli, following Webster, suggested that he was a sausage-seller, seeing a corruption of *botularius*, a term used by Seneca to describe a form of black pudding. However, as Noy notes, this is an unlikely product for a Jew to sell. From my reading of the stone, the most likely reading is *bucular(i)us*, deriving from *buculus*, meaning a steer or heifer. However, Cooley reads *butularus*, and it is indeed the case that reading of the third letter varies according to the position of the reader and the source of light. The same reading suggested to Chioffi that Alexander sold dried meat.[6]

The suggestion of Williams that Alexander sold ritually pure meat to the Jewish community is attractive, for the last line of the text states that his sleep is among the just or righteous.[7] Moreover no professions other than beef-seller appear to have been recorded among the Jewish communities buried in the Vigna Randanini, nor indeed in the Monteverde cemeteries of Rome. Generally the naming of individual roles in Jewish funerary texts from Rome appears confined to officials of the synagogue (see above, p.82). This and the Monteverde epitaph would then emphasise the importance of the supply of ritually pure meat to an observant community.

It is not specified where Alexander worked. The *Macellum Liviae* near Santa Maria Maggiore was restored in AD 367–75 by the emperors Valentinian, Valens and Gratian, at a time of new, restrictive laws on meat-selling; it thus seems a likely workplace.[8] However, it has also been suggested that Alexander worked at Nero's *Macellum Magnum* on the Caelian hill.[9]

The text is usually dated to the third or fourth century AD on onomastic or comparative grounds.[10] Nonetheless the use of Latin may indicate a date late in this range (see the preceding paragraph and p.82 above).

Endnotes

1. Noy 1995: 289, recording a suggestion made by Professor Michael Vickers.
2. PIAC, de Rossi archive: 16274, no.61 (right side only); 16272, no.25, and 16324 (whole text).
3. Dello Russo 2012: 27, n.105.
4. Garrucci 1862: 63 states that of the 43 legible inscriptions known by 20 May 1862, 30 were Greek and 13 Latin.
5. Noy 1995: 289.
6. Chioffi 1999: 47, n.235.
7. Williams 2002: 131, discussed in greater detail by Cooley 2017: 297.
8. Chioffi 1999: 48, n.243.
9. Collon 1940: 91 postulates a local Jewish community from this suggestion, dismissed by Leon 1960: 138.
10. Solin 2003: I, 198 suggests a third-century date on onomastic grounds.

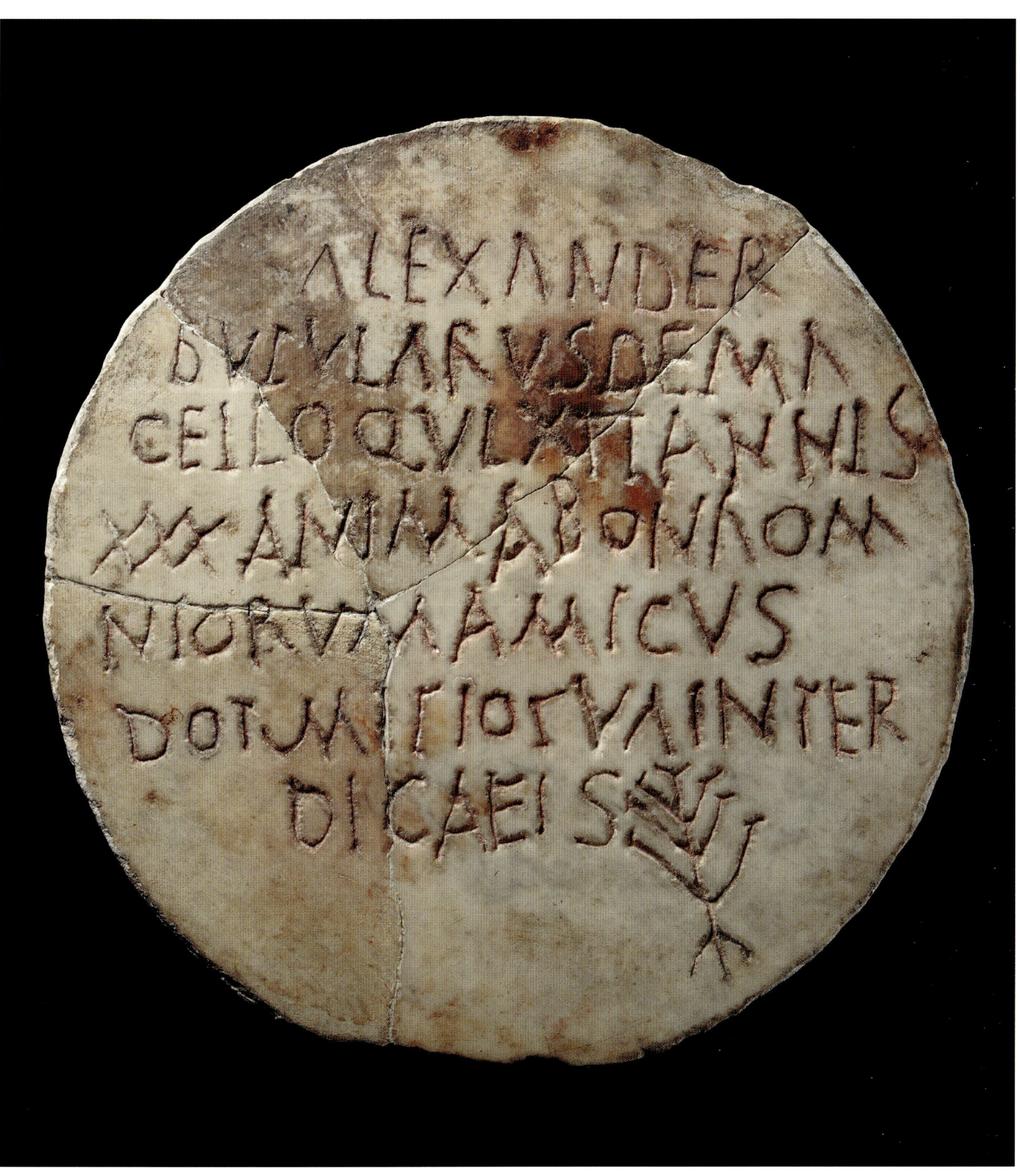
ALEXANDER

49 AN 2007.54
Marble epitaph of Noumenis

Photograph by David Gowers, 2013

H. 33.6 cm; W. 34.6 cm; TH. 2.5–3.2 cm (there is a concave curvature at the rear of the slab).

Polished medium-grained white marble with vertical blue bands. A sample of marble was taken for isotopic analysis in December 2012, which confirmed the source of the marble as Proconnesian (see Appendix 5).

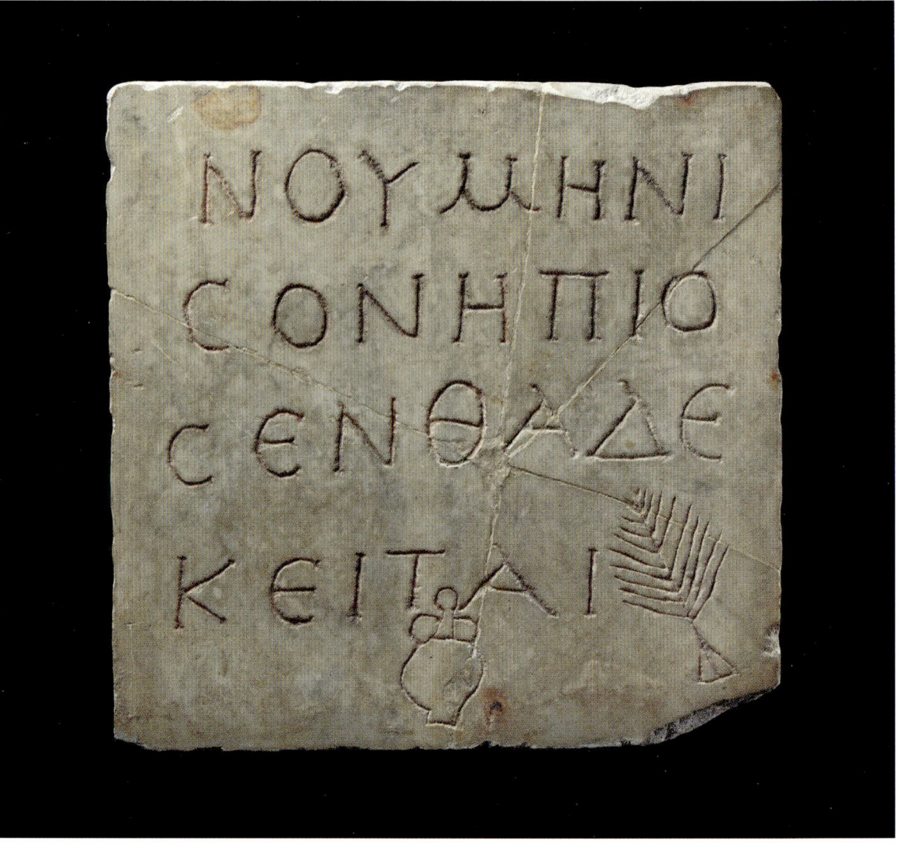

Present condition
The modern slate frame was removed in December 2012. The filled hole in the centre and the breaks across the slab were caused by a stabbing action, which also caused a percussion injury to the rear surface. An ancient iron nail is still in situ towards the centre of the lower edge. Iron stains to the right and left at the top may have been caused by earlier use of the stone to fix the sarcophagus lid to the chest.

A sample of mortar was removed for characterisation (see Appendix 6).

Text
The Greek inscription is incised in four lines. The third and fourth lines are less regular than lines 1–2, suggesting that the images of ritual objects were incised beforehand. Some letters have serifs, and cursive-style script is used for alpha, delta and mu. In height the letters are 3.6 cm (lines 1–2); 4.2 cm (line 3) and 3.4 cm (line 4). Letters and symbols are painted red.

Νουμήνι
ς ὁ νήπιο
ς ἐνθάδε
κέιται

('Numenius the infant lies here')

Incised at the centre of the stone intruding into the last line of text is an amphora, 7 x 4 cm; its handles and stopper are carefully detailed. Shown at an angle in the lower right-hand corner is a menorah or *lulab*, 10.7 cm high x 6.2 cm wide, with ten branches on either side.

Collection history
Excavated in the Vigna Randanini catacomb, Via Appia Pignatelli, Rome in May 1862.[1] Copied in 1863 by Visconti.[2] Acquired by Charles Wilshere in 1870 from Ignace Randanini, son of the proprietor of the land. Bequeathed by Wilshere by Deed of Trust to Pusey House, Oxford in 1895. Loaned to the Ashmolean Museum, Oxford in 1984. Purchased by the Ashmolean Museum, 2007.

Bibliography

Garrucci 1865: 182, no.20; Webster 1929: 151, no.4; Frey 1936: CIJ i, 101, no.143 (follows Garrucci and a copy by Visconti); 1975: i², 30; Ferrua 1941: 33; Goodenough 1953: ii, 23; iii, fig. 770; Leon 1960: 285; Noy 1995: 292 no.346.

Comment
The amphora probably held oil to anoint the deceased infant, who was given a Latin name. The slab was perhaps reused from the short end of a sarcophagus, the curve at the back of the slab reflecting the interior curve of the chest. The date is probably later fourth century AD. Compare cat. **50**, the memorial to Poimenis, and cat. **48**, the Latin memorial to the butcher Alexander, with a similarly placed menorah.

Endnotes
1. PIAC, de Rossi archive: 16329.
2. PIAC, de Rossi archive: 16273, no.36.

50 AN 2007.59

Marble epitaph of Poimenis

Photograph by David Gowers, 2013

H. 33.3 cm; W. 36.8 cm; TH. 1.6 cm

Medium-grained white marble with blue, vertical bands. A sample was removed for isotopic analysis, and found to be compatible with Carrara marble from central Italy (see Appendix 5).

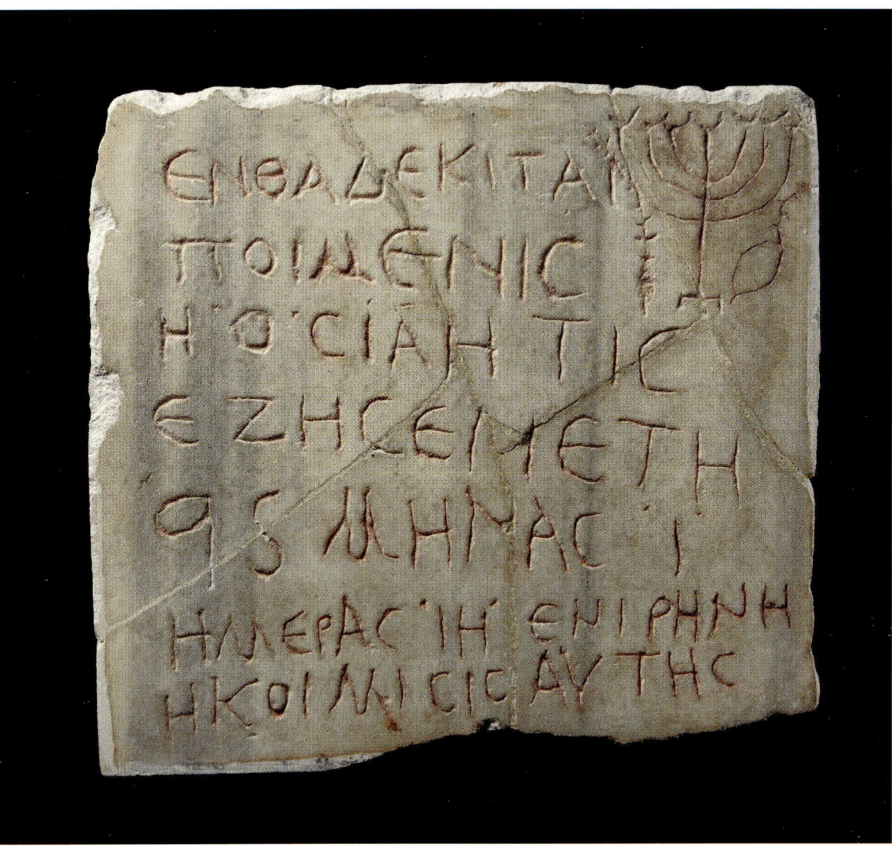

Present condition
The inscription was broken into five fragments before discovery in 1862. The modern slate frame was removed in 2012. The plaster in three of the four joins had dried out, causing the joins to fracture. They were repaired with resin and two stainless steel dowels.

Text

> ἐνθάδε κῖται
> Ποιμένις
> ἡ ὁσία ἥτις
> ἔζησεν ἔτη
> ϙϛ΄ μῆνας ι΄
> ἡμέρας ιη΄ ἐν ἰρήνῃ
> ἡ κοίμησις αὐτῆς
>
> ('Here lies Poimenis, the pious woman, she who lived 96 years 10 months 8 days. In peace her sleep.')

The Greek text is written in seven lines with poor alignment; the script has no serifs and letter heights vary between 18 and 42 mm (line 5). In the upper right corner is incised a seven-branched menorah, 96 mm high x 98 mm wide, with a *lulab* (palm branch) 97 mm in height and an *ethrog* (citron) 70 mm in length beside it. Though the position of the ritual objects determines the first two–three lines of text, the irregularity extends throughout. The last two lines even appear to respect the curved line of the break at the bottom right of the slab. Both the ritual objects and the letters of the text are filled with red pigment.

Collection history
Excavated in May 1862 in the Randanini catacomb, Via Appia Pignatelli, Rome. The text was copied by C. L. Visconti in 1863.[1] Acquired by Charles Wilshere in 1870 from Ignace Randanini, son of the proprietor of the land. A rubbing of the text was sent by Wilshere to de Rossi.[2] Bequeathed by Wilshere by Deed of Trust to Pusey House, Oxford in 1895. Loaned to the Ashmolean Museum, Oxford in 1984. Purchased by the Ashmolean Museum, 2007.

Bibliography
Garrucci 1862: 43; Webster 1929: 150, no.3; Frey 1936, 1975: CIJ i, 108–9, no.151 (follows Garrucci and a copy by Visconti); i^2, 30; Goodenough 1953–68: ii, 22, iii, pl.766; Leon 1960: 85, 103, 287 no.151; Noy 1995: 292–3, no.347; dello Russo 2012: 35.

Comment
The unusual thinness of this slab suggests that it was reused from a piece of wall revetment.

The reuse of a panel that was apparently already damaged, together with the extremely irregular lettering, indicate a lack of resources and skills. Though these features may reflect a late date, the panel and the form of its subsequent damage are comparable to cats **48** and **49** within the Wilshere Collection. All three epitaphs were discovered in May 1862, and therefore are likely to reflect contemporary use of the cemetery as it developed, probably in the later decades of the fourth century AD.

The name Poimenis, which can be read as masculine or feminine, is rarely used for a woman.[3]

Endnotes
1. PIAC, de Rossi archive, 16274, no.55.
2. PIAC, de Rossi archive, 16325.
3. Noy 1995: 293.

A Christian inscription, most likely from Rome or environs

Photograph by David Gowers, 2013

51 AN 2007.50

Moulded fragment of marble with a Latin inscription marking the grave of Decentius or Decentia, a Christian

H. 18.6 cm; W. 25.2 cm; TH. 2.8 cm (max.)

Fine-grained greyish marble, perhaps Carrara from central Italy.

Present condition

The fragment is broken at the lower edge and sides. The back is worked smooth, with some ancient mortar containing ground brick and tile adhering to the surface. This suggests that the fragment was at some time incorporated within a water basin. There is some trace of plaster or a base for paint or gilding on the front surface. The letters are filled with red pigment. More recent surface interventions include white plaster on the upper moulding and a splash of red paint to the right of the Christogram. The fragment was not conserved or mounted for Wilshere.

Description

The stone would have topped the facade of the tomb.

A *hedera* appears in the upper rebate of the moulded edge of the monument. Below the straight rebate is a doubly curved *cyma reversa* moulding, and below that is a fascia on which the text is inscribed. Beneath the fascia is a simple singly curved *cyma*.

Text

The Latin text on the fascia is in two lines:

(Christogram to left, occupying both lines)
LOCVS DECE
DECENTIVS

The letter heights are 2.6 cm in line 1, 4 cm (max.) in line 2.

Collection history

According to C. L. Visconti, this monument was owned by the internationally renowned sculptor Ferdinand Pettrich of Dresden, who died in Rome in 1872.[1] It is likely to have been acquired by Charles Wilshere in Rome, perhaps shortly after Pettrich's death in the city after an extraordinary career in North and South America. However, no evidence for any dispersal of Pettrich's collection after his death has yet emerged.

Bibliography

ICUR 1.3423 (1922); Cooley 2017: 293–5, no.160. Online: EDCS-40300506; EDB 33333 [Filippo Piazzolla, 27/06/2013: last updated Carlo Carletti 10/11/15].

Comment

The text marks the formal acquisition of a plot of land for burial by inhumation by Decentius on behalf of himself or Decentia. There are several instances of the name among the Christian funerary inscriptions of Rome, and a comparable text recording a similar act of purchase.[2] The transaction was made in the later fourth or fifth century AD. It is likely that this moulded block was reused from an earlier monument, perhaps a door jamb or even a statue base, and it may have been upended in second use.

Endnotes

1. Cooley 2017: 294.
2. Cooley 2017: 294–5.

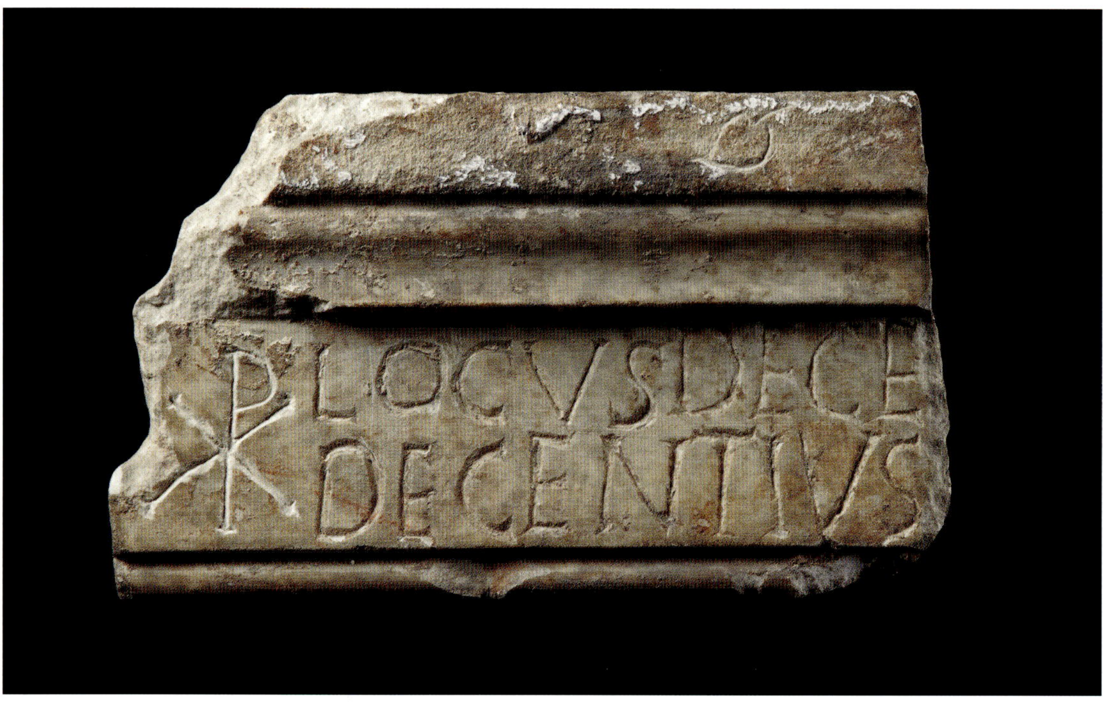

Photograph by David Gowers, 2012

52 AN 2007.49

Latin funerary inscription of Sapis

H. 22.5 cm; W. 46 cm; TH. 3 cm

Medium-grained marble with glittering crystals, perhaps from Proconnesus or Thasos.

Present condition

The left half of a circular cutting 39 mm in diameter and 10 mm in depth is preserved in the lower right edge of the relief. Below this a rectangular slot is cut horizontally, of which 70 mm of its length survives; the slot is 3 mm deep. The text is cut into the roughened surface of an otherwise smoothed block. The roughened surface bears later scratches.

The edges of the stone were sawn down prior to mounting in a slate frame. In December 2012 the slate frame was removed to reveal more of the cuttings from the stone's earlier use, along with some ancient mortar along the upper edge. A sample of this mortar was removed for analysis (Appendix 6).

Text

The text, preceded by a cross, reads:

> Hic requiescit/.in pace. Sapis (*hedera*)/. qui legis. ora pro me. ('Sapis rests in peace here (*ivy leaf*). Who(ever) reads this, pray for me.')

Letter heights are 37–30 mm, dropping to the lower measurement in the third line of the text. Within the letters are traces of brownish-red paint. The letters are cut within guidelines, with an evident attempt at monumental quality, not entirely successful. However some letters, notably Q and G, do achieve a stylish, calligraphic quality.

Collection history

Found at Cumae and purchased by Charles Wilshere from the noted antiquarian Abbot Giuseppe di Criscio of Pozzuoli (1826–1911) in 1868.[1] Wilshere noted that the block had been found recycled as a threshold. This may explain the cuttings in the right side of the block, which could be associated with the installation of a door.[2]

Bibliography

CIL X.1 no.3312 (1883); Diehl 1925, vol.1, no.2353; Webster 1929: 150, no.8; Cooley 2017: 292–3, no.159.
Online: EDCS–15400741; EDR–128960 (last updated 19/11/13, G. Camodeca)

Comment

This is a Christian epitaph cut into a former threshold block, most likely in the fourth century AD. Solin notes that the name Sapis may derive from an Italian toponym or an ethnic designation.[3] The gender of the deceased is uncertain. The injunction to the passer-by to pray indicates that the grave was sited in a publicly accessible location, perhaps beside a road.

Endnotes

1. On de Criscio see above, p.65 and Tuck 2005.
2. Letter to de Rossi of 3 November 1868 (Vatican City, Biblioteca Apostolica Vaticana, Vat. lat. 14247, 1868/270).
3. Solin 2006: 308–12.

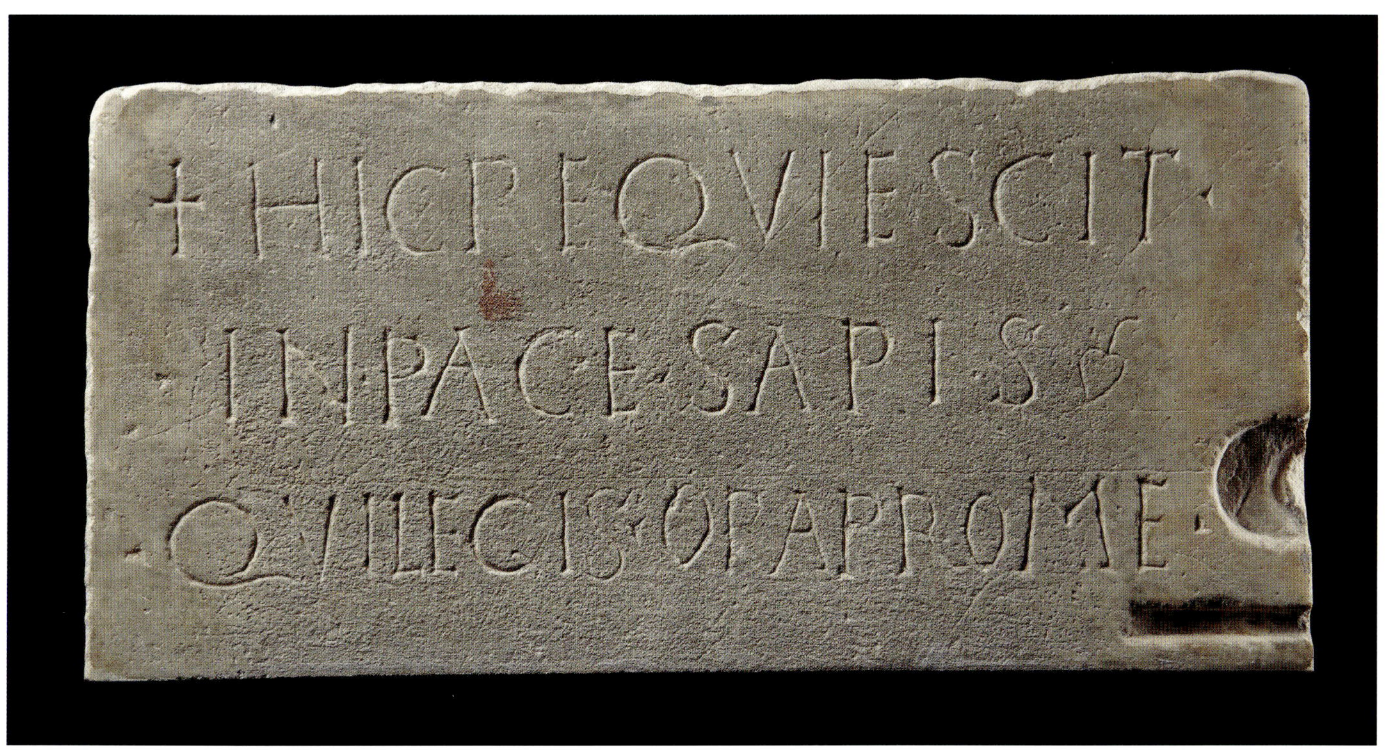

53 AN 2007.56
Funerary inscription of Victurina

H. 38.3 cm; W. 26.5 cm; TH. 3.5 cm

Creamy white marble with blue bands. A sample was taken in 2012 for Stable Isotope analysis, which revealed the marble to be Proconnesian (see above, p.00 and Appendix 5).

Present condition
The modern slate mount was removed in 2012, revealing on the right side of the slab a double moulding, most likely evidence of earlier architectural use. There is a break in the centre of the moulded edge. The upper edge of the slab is roughly finished at the top and left sides, with small traces of mortar; the lower is smoothly worked at the front, becoming rougher at the rear. The back of the slab is sawn smooth. There are traces of red pigment on the upper surface at each long side. There is some black pigment (or possibly dirt) in the letters. A mortar sample was removed for characterisation in 2012 (see Appendix 6).

Text
The seven lines of Latin text are set within guidelines, with an unused set at the base of the slab.

The text is incised in a rather feathery, serifed style, but is nonetheless fully legible.

There are no crosses or other Christian symbols.

hic requiescit / Victurina qu(a)e / vixit
ann(os) ° V ° m(enses) ° III ° / d(ies) XV
d(e)p(ositio) eius ° / 5 id(ib)us Maias °
cons(ule) / d(omino) n(ostro) Severo
pr(imo) / Au⸢g⸣(usto)

('Here rests Victurina, who lived five years, three months and fifteen days. Her burial on the ides of May in the consulship of our lord Severus, first Augustus.')

Collection history
From Aeclanum (Mirabella Eclana), near Avellino, Campania and kept in the museum formed by Romualdo Cassittiano at Bonito, near Avellino. Here it was seen and copied by Mommsen in 1852. Purchased by Charles Wilshere in Naples in 1868.

Bibliography
Guarini 1812, 1814: 118; 170, VII; Mommsen 1852: *IRNL* 1297; *CIL* IX.1373; de Rossi, f.55 (Vatican City, Biblioteca Apostolica Vaticana, Vat. lat. 10527) = *ILCV* 3028A; Webster 1925–9: ms. list no.6; Gambino 1982: no.17; Felle 1993: 100, no.41; Cooley 2017: 299–301, no.162 (recent edition, reproduced here).
Online: EDCS-12400877; EDR-135045 (last updated 15 January 2014, F. Lorusso) http://db.edcs.eu/epigr/bilder.php?bild=$ICI_08_00041.jpg (see above p.64) [image of ms sketch sent by Wilshere to de Rossi].

Comment
Felle reproduces the transcription of the text made by Wilshere, which is superimposed on the manuscript text of a note by de Rossi.[1]
Guarini read DEP, MAIOS and COS, and separated each word with a point. CON appears in *IRNL* and a ligatured NS in *CIL* IX, 6. Webster corrected the *CIL* transcription to 'two months'. Victurina is a local name. Felle suggests she was the daughter of a Victurinus, commemorated on a similar slab with a simple upper moulding and comparable lettering from the cemetery at Passo di Mirabella (*CIL* IX, 1370 = MANN 115405 = Felle no.36). *Idus* is a corrupted version of *idibus*, and the consul's name is Libius Severus, normally referred to as *primo consule*. The year is AD 462.

For the style of the lettering, compare the earlier inscription published by Lambert, inscription of the *innocens Dianensis*, dated to AD 397.[2]

Endnotes
1. Wilshere's transcript, sent to de Rossi from Welwyn, is now kept in the library of the Pontificio Istituto di Archeologia Cristiana (PIAC), Rome. See Fig. 30, p.64 above and Cooley 2017, also for the following observations on the text.
2. Lambert 2008: figs 34, 34a.

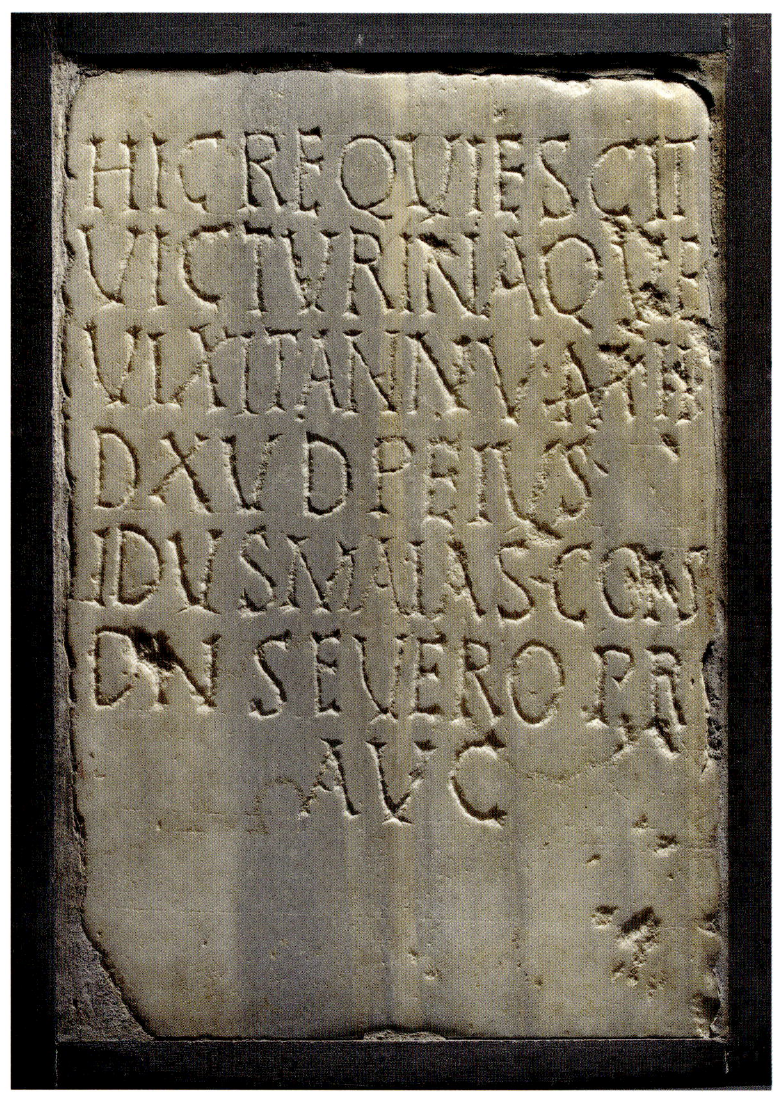

Photograph by David Gowers, 2013

54 AN 2007.58

Photograph by David Gowers, 2013

Funerary inscription of Veronilia

W. 45.5 cm; H. 28cm.
This inscription was not removed from its slate frame in 2012, so the thickness could not be measured.

Fine-grained, white marble, perhaps from Carrara in central Italy.

Present condition

The upper right and lower left corners of the slab had broken and were restored before framing.

Text

The six lines of Latin text read:

> Hic requiescit in [som]/no pacis
> Veronil<l=I>a s[p(ectabilis) f(emina)?] /
> quae vixit annos LXXX m[ens(es)] / sex
> depositio eius sub / di<e=I> VI Nonas
> No<v=B>emb[res] / Agapi<t=I>o v(iro)
> c(larissimo) cons(ule

('Here rests in the sleep of peace Veronilia, a woman of distinguished family, who lived 80 years and six months. Her burial was registered on the sixth day before the nones of November in the consulship of the *vir clarissimus* Agapitus, *in Christ*.')

Collection history

From 'Le Grotte proper Mirabellum', Mirabella Eclano, ancient Aeclanum
Bought by Wilshere in 1868, probably in Naples, from the sale of antiquities from the Museo Cassittiano, Bonito, near Avellino.

Bibliography

De Rossi f.53, from which CIL IX.1383, from which *ICLV* 3185D, from which Gambino 1982: n.27; Webster 1929: 151, no.10; Felle 1993:112, no.52 reproduces an ms transcription made by Wilshere for de Rossi.
On-line: EDCS-12400888

Comment

The letters and ligatures are deeply incised in the stone, which may have been reused.
Webster notes, p.151: '... Professor Beazley suggests *P.M. (Sancta Pia Modesta)* to supply the lacuna following the *S* after *Veronilia*.'[1] However, Felle restores S(pectabilis Femina), a woman of (according to him, moral) distinction, which seems more likely. For the date Webster notes 'it is perhaps easiest to suppose the *vi. Nonas* should be *iv.Nonas*', thus a consular date of 4 November AD 517'. He is supported by Felle, who gives the name of the consul as Flavius Agapitus.[2]

Veronilia is an unusual, perhaps local name, and the only instance attested in Diehl's Sylloge.[3] Kajanto suggests the form Veronilla.[4]

Endnotes

1. In CIL IX, 1383.
2. Degrassi 1952: 98.
3. Diehl 1927: 3185 .
4. Kajanto 1965: 14, 270.

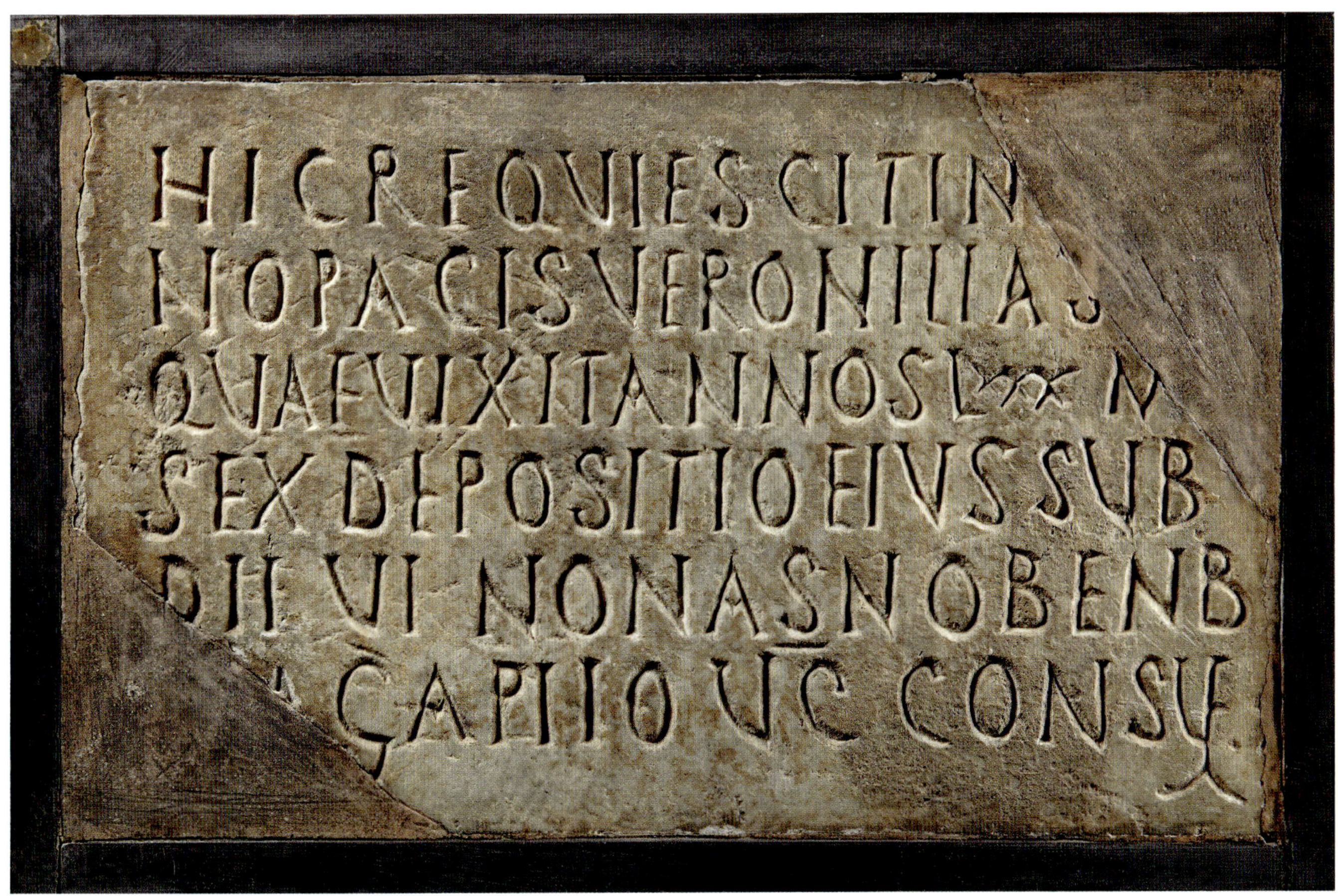

55 AN 2007.60

Latin funerary inscription of Maria

Photograph by David Gowers, 2012

H. 29.5 cm; W. 24 cm; TH. 4 cm

The stone is a banded blue and cream marble. A sample removed for Stable Isotope analysis indicates that it was quarried at Carrara in central Italy (see Appendix 5).

Present condition

The inscribed slab, which is in excellent condition, was removed from its slate frame in 2012. Some mortar adhered to the smooth back of the stone, and a sample was removed for analysis (see Appendix 6). The edges of the stone are carefully finished, with traces of red paint on the upper surface. There are possible traces of yellow paint in the lettering.

Text

Irregularly carved beneath two crosses, and starting and ending with crosses, the Latin text reads:

> ⊂ crux ⊃ ⊂ crux ⊃ / ⊂ crux ⊃ hic requi⌜e⌝s/cit i⌜n⌝ somno pa/cis Maria qu(a)e vi/xit ann⌜o⌝s pl(us) m(inus)/ [5]⌜X⌝XV depositio eius / IIII non(as) Ianuarias / ⌜q⌝uinquies p(ost) c(onsulatum) Basili / v(iri) c(larissimi) ind(ictione) X

> (‘Here reposes in the sleep of peace Maria, who lived more or less 25 years. Her burial on the fourth day before the nones of January, five years after the appointment of Basil to the consulship in the tenth indiction.’)

The irregularly cut letters are mostly 20 mm in height, but can vary from 15 to 39 mm. Some letter forms are unusual, for example N resembling H (lines 2, 4, 6 and 7). Guarini mistakenly noted interpuncts between every word; he also omitted description of the crosses marking the upper margin and the start and finish of the text. De Rossi drew on Wilshere's transcription.

Collection history

From Aeclanum (Mirabella Eclano), near Avellino, Campania. Purchased by Charles Wilshere in 1868 in Naples. Formerly in the Museo Cassittiano at Bonito, near Avellino.

Bibliography

Guarini 1833: p.73, n.18 (according to CIL); de Rossi, Biblioteca Apostolica Vaticana Vat. lat. 10528 f.54, (two *schedae*, one taken from Guarini 1833, the second from Wilshere); Mommsen 1852: IRNL no.1306; Mommsen 1883: CIL IX 1388; Diehl 1927: ILCV 3186b (following CIL); Webster 1929: 150, no.29; Salvatore 1982: 166–7, no.88; Felle 1993: 116, no.56, from CIL IX; Cooley 2017: 301–3, no.163 (recent edition, reproduced here).
Online: EDCS–12400893 [accessed 05/02/15]; EDR–133893 (last updated 19/05/14, F. Lorusso).

Comment

This text is one of 56 recorded funerary inscriptions from the cemetery at Mirabella of early Christian Aeclanum. It is possible that this slab, which measures almost exactly one Roman foot high, was recycled from a paving stone.

According to Webster: '…the year may be 487 or 546 according to the interpretation of the indistinct VH before "*quies*"'. In his corpus Felle opts for the later date, noting that it should be the ninth year of Basil's consulship. Basilius was the last named consul in the Roman West, AD 541; a system of counting after his consulship continued for 44 years.[1] The fourth day before the *nones* of January is equivalent to 2 January.

Endnotes

1. Marucchi 1912: 283.

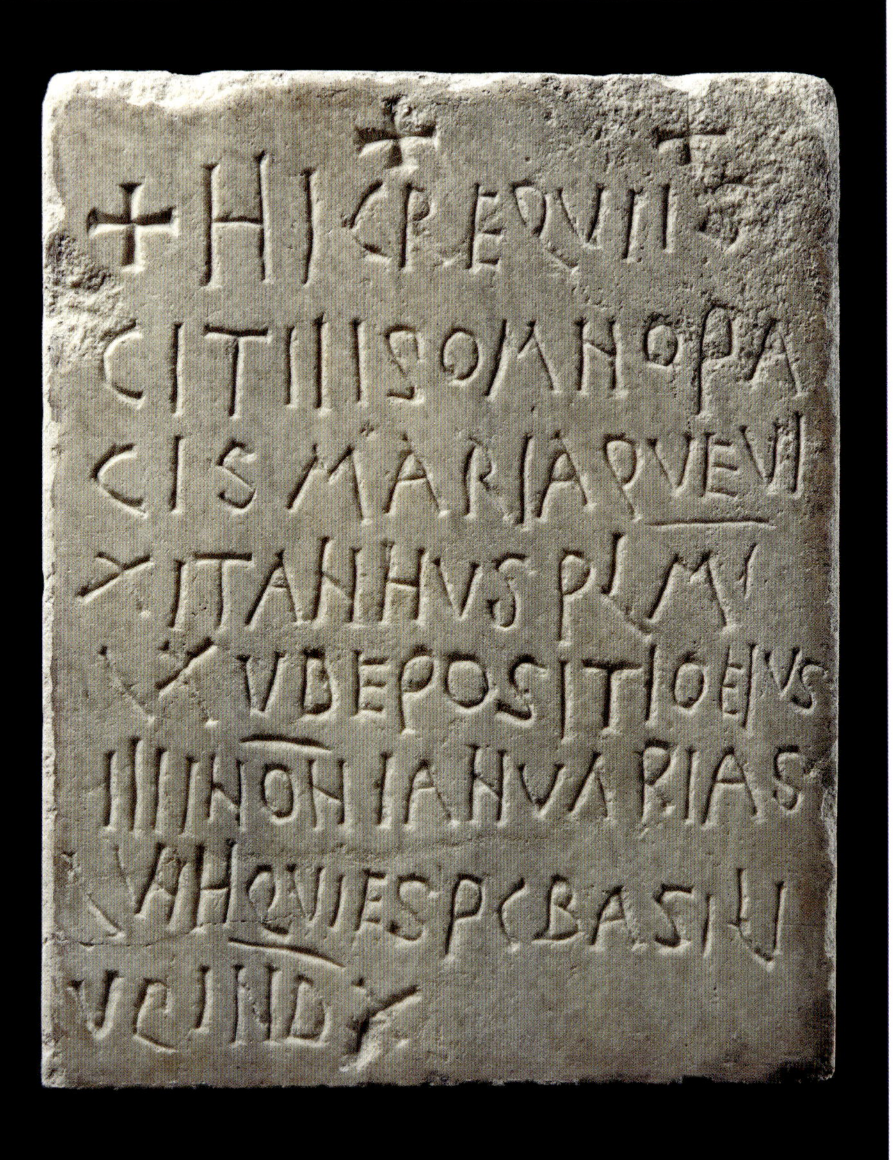

| Photograph by David Gowers, 2013

56 AN 2007.61
Funerary inscription of Claudia Soteris

H. 18.6 cm; W. 25.2 cm (within modern slate frame)

Limestone.

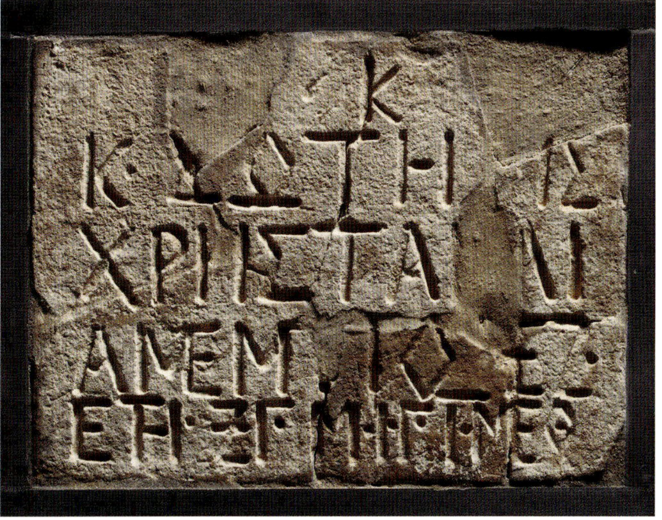

Present condition

The stone is reconstructed from six fragments. The upper right corner is lost, as is a piece left of centre of the upper edge and reaching down into the second line of text. Smaller chips are also missing from the left edge and the lower right corner. The stone is filled with plaster, extending from the lower left corner of the upper right break to the fourth line of text. The fragment below is stained red. The stone was not removed from its slate frame in 2012.

Text

The Greek inscription reads:

> [Θ(εοῖς)] · Κ(αταχθονίοις)
> Κ(λαυδία) · Σωτή[ρ]ις
> χρηστὰ κ̣α̣ὶ
> ἄμ̣ˆεμ̣ˆπτοˆς ἔ̈ζ(ησεν)
> ἔ̈τˆη · ξγ’ · μˆῆ(νας) · γ’ · ἡ̔ˆμˆέ(ρας) θ’

(‘To the nether gods, Claudia Soteris, good and blameless, lived 63 years, 3 months, 9 days.’)

The name Claudia is restored in *IG* IX, no.36, a publication unknown to Webster, who tentatively restored the name as Quinta(?). However, the former expansion is the more probable. The form of the opening sigma of Soteris is distorted by a vertical break in the stone.

The letters are very deeply cut with a bull-nosed chisel, and are painted in red.

Bibliography

IG XIV: 10, no.36; Webster 1929: 152, no.21.
Online: http://sicily.classics.ox.ac.uk/inscription/ISic0853.

Collection history

This funerary text was reported by Salvatore Politi to Georg Kaibel, editor of the Corpus of Greek Inscriptions from Sicily (*IG* XIV). Politi stated that it had been found in 1880 beside the tomb of Archimedes in Syracuse.[1] The reported findspot could well refer to the Necropoli Grotticelli, a Syracusan cemetery once thought to contain Archimedes' imposing tomb, but the grandiose, pedimented rock-cut structure is now identified as Roman.[2] According to Politi, the stone was moved to Syracuse Museum; it may have been regarded as too fragmentary for inclusion in the permanent collection, for the text does not appear in early inventories. Indeed the collection was not formally catalogued until after the museum had been inaugurated with national status in 1886.[3] In May of the previous year the stone was purchased by Wilshere while visiting Syracuse; no mention is made of the vendor.[4] However, in a subsequent letter to de Rossi, Wilshere gives a precise provenience as 'da un fosso sulle confine di Caradicia [? illegible] ed Epipoli' ('from a cut grave in the area of Caradicia [? Illegible] and Epipoli').[5]

Epipoli is located to the northwest of Syracuse. In a publication of 1941 Ferrua noted a tracing sent to de Rossi by Wilshere, on which the findspot was noted as a cut grave between Agradina and Tyche.[6]

Comment

Webster, following de Rossi and Wilshere, dated the inscription to the Byzantine period on grounds of palaeography, but it is surely pagan and of pre-Christian, Roman date. The distinctive letter forms (for example, rhomboid omega) were especially prevalent locally, while the formulaic epithet and the precise indication of age at death are typical of Greek epitaphs of modest quality made for people of relatively low social standing in early imperial Sicily.[7] Indeed, similar epitaphs were found in situ by Orsi in the Grotticelli cemetery above cremation burials packed in ceramic jars. One such epitaph of a certain Valeria was associated with a large bronze coin of Trajan.[8] However, late nineteenth-century exploration of the same cemetery had demonstrated that burials continued to take place there into the eighth century AD. Some indubitably fourth–sixth-century finds of bronze jewellery and lamps were associated with fragmentary epitaphs of this type, which were surely residual.[9] Possibly Wilshere's text was found broken in a late antique context of this sort.

Endnotes

1. *IG* XIV: 10, no.36.
2. The location of Archimedes' tomb, which was rediscovered and cleaned by Cicero (*Tusc. Disp.*5, 64–5), is currently unknown.
3. Jonathan Prag, *pers. comm.*, March 2017. Vatican City, Biblioteca Apostolica Vaticana, Vat.lat. 14273, 1885.339: letter from Wilshere to de Rossi of 20 May 1885.
4. Vatican City, Biblioteca Apostolica Vaticana, Vat.lat. 14273, 1885.509, dated 13 August 1885.
5. Ferrua 1941: 197–8 with fig. 34, p.198. I have not seen the tracing. De Rossi ms, Vatican City, Biblioteca Apostolica Vaticana, Vat.lat.10529, f.4.
6. Korhonen 2011:13, Tab.2.2; 18. I am grateful to Jonathan Prag for advice on this point.
7. Orsi 1913: 269, with fig. 11.
8. Orsi 1896: 346 for a fragment from the epitaph of Claudius, with rhomboid letter forms.

(below and opposite) Photograph by David Gowers, 2013

57 AN 2007.64

Fragment of a marble tombstone with text incised in Latin

H. 11.4 cm; L. 32.2 cm; TH. 4 cm

Fine-grained greyish marble, perhaps Carrara from central Italy.

Present condition

Broken on left and right sides and sawn through below. The front surface is broken at the upper left. The right side of the surface has been in contact with a deposit, perhaps soil, containing iron.

The front and upper surfaces of the stone are smoothly worked. The rear is roughly picked and more severely weathered, suggesting that the text was protected in subsequent reuse.

The fragment was not conserved or mounted for Wilshere.

Text

The two- line Latin text reads:

[--- VI]RGINIB[VS ---] / [---] ANNOS [---]

('? ... virgins......years....')

The first letter of the upper line has a splayed lower right diagonal stroke and possibly another similarly splayed at the lower left, where the surface is broken. There is no trace of the rounded upper R, but the splay is too wide for an A as preserved in line 2. To the right of the B is the left upper serif of the next letter, aligned with the rest. In line 2 the A has a dropped bar and the S is not lunate. In line 1 the letters are 34 mm in height; in line 2 they are 29 mm.

Collection history

Wilshere Collection. It is not known how Wilshere acquired this inscription.

Bibliography

Cooley 2017: 305, no.165.

Comment

The text is presumably funerary, with the second line giving the age of the deceased, of which only the term 'years' is preserved. A comparable text is known from Aquileia:

'vir]ginibu[s] [---] / et Mar[--- qui vixit] / ann(os) XXX [---] / depositus [--- Sep]/ tembris [---] / in pace'.[1]

'To, by or from the virgins [---] and Mar[--- who lived] thirty years [---] recorded [---Sep] tember [---] in peace.'

From this better preserved text a date in the fourth or fifth century AD may be suggested.

Endnotes

1. Brusin 1993: vol.3, no.3121, noted by Cooley 2017.

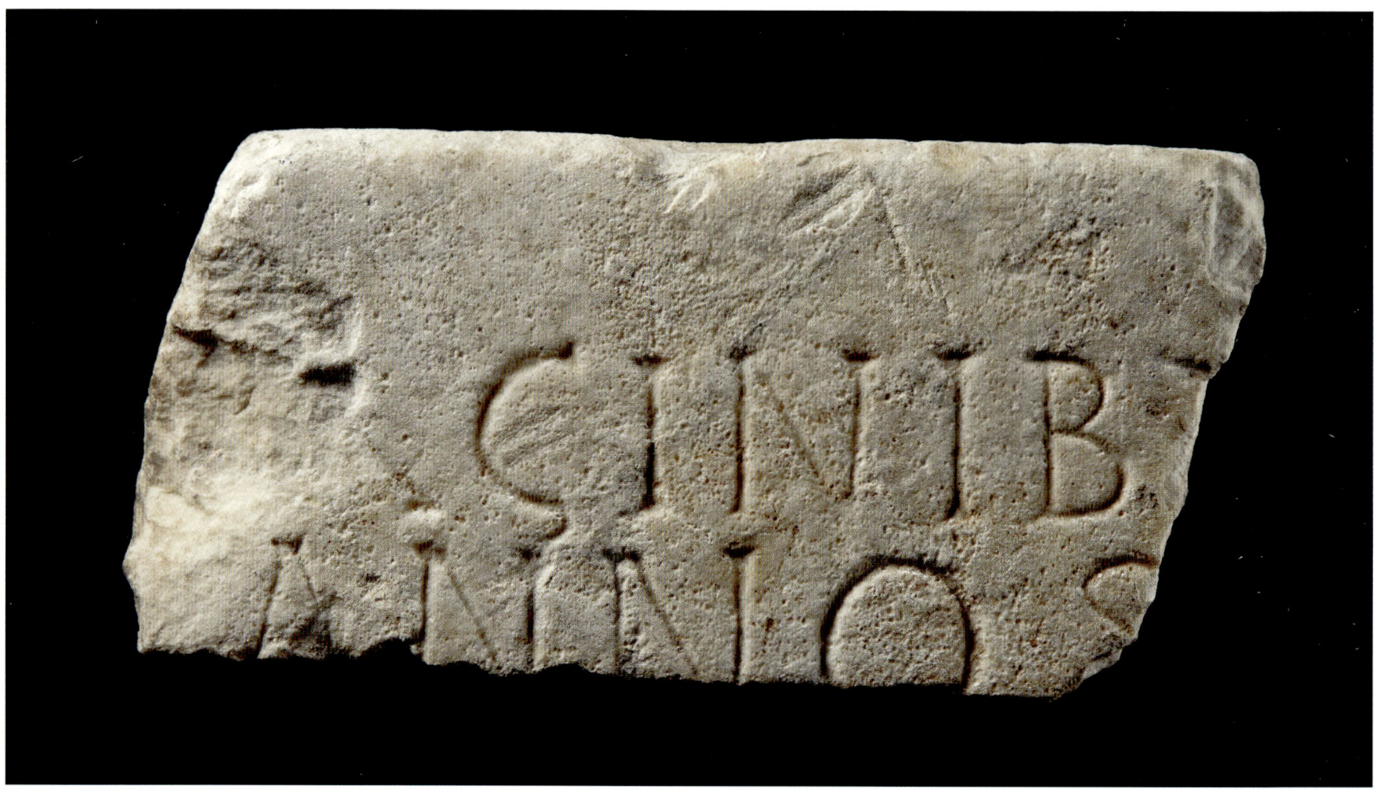

Christian votive relief and silver spoon

58 AN 2007.43

Limestone votive relief: a woman displays an open book to two men

H. 29 cm; W. 56 cm; TH. The thickness of the stone cannot be measured in its current frame.

Present condition

The relief, made of limestone, is now set in a slate frame which was added after 1880; it is not visible in the photograph published by de Rossi (1872) or the drawing in Garrucci VI (1880). The lower right corner has been broken off. Another crack runs diagonally from the upper frame through the neck and left shoulder of the central figure and the lower torso of the figure to the right. Both crack and break were repaired with plaster before the relief was set in its frame.

Decoration

A woman stands in the centre, holding an open book in her left hand and making a gesture of speech with her right hand. She wears a tunic and *palla*, with which she is veiled. On either side stand two bearded male figures clad in tunics and mantles, both of whom face the central figure. The man on the left extends his right hand towards the woman, while the man on the right holds up his right hand in acclamation and grasps his mantle with his left. A rectangular frame runs around the relief, broken by the heads of the three figures. Two cylindrical containers for scrolls (*capsae*) border the scene, and a third bunch of scrolls is tied together next to the feet of the left-hand male figure.

Text

Lygyrius (vac.) vot (vac.) um / sol (vac.) vit

('Lygyrius fulfilled his vow')

The first line of Latin text, in letters 10–22 mm in height, appears to either side of the central figure. The name *Lygyrius* falls between the male figure on the left and the female, with the noun *votum* set to her right, broken by the raised hand of the male on the right. The first three letters of the verb *solvit* appear below the name Lygyrius, while the last three are incised at approximately the same level to the right of the figure on the right. The height of the letters varies between 17 and 23 mm. Clearly the text was added after the figures had been carved; it was not designed into the relief.

Collection History

The relief was purchased by Wilshere in Rome in 1869/1870. Wilshere later believed the relief to have been found in the vicinity of the Roman Forum in 1870, and early epigraphic corpora (CIL, ICUR) recorded the relief as being in the possession of a *marmorarius* (a dealer in marbles) specialising in palombino marble, at the Mamertine Prison in March of 1869. However, Ernst Diehl (ILCV) reported that the relief was said to have been discovered either in Rome, at Sant'Agnese fuori le mura, or at Amiternum, 90 km northeast of the city. The latter provenance is supported by Garrucci (1880), who reported that he knew for certain that the relief was excavated at Amiternum.

The ancient settlement of Amiternum, by the late fifth century AD the seat of a bishop, includes Christian catacombs at S. Vittorino

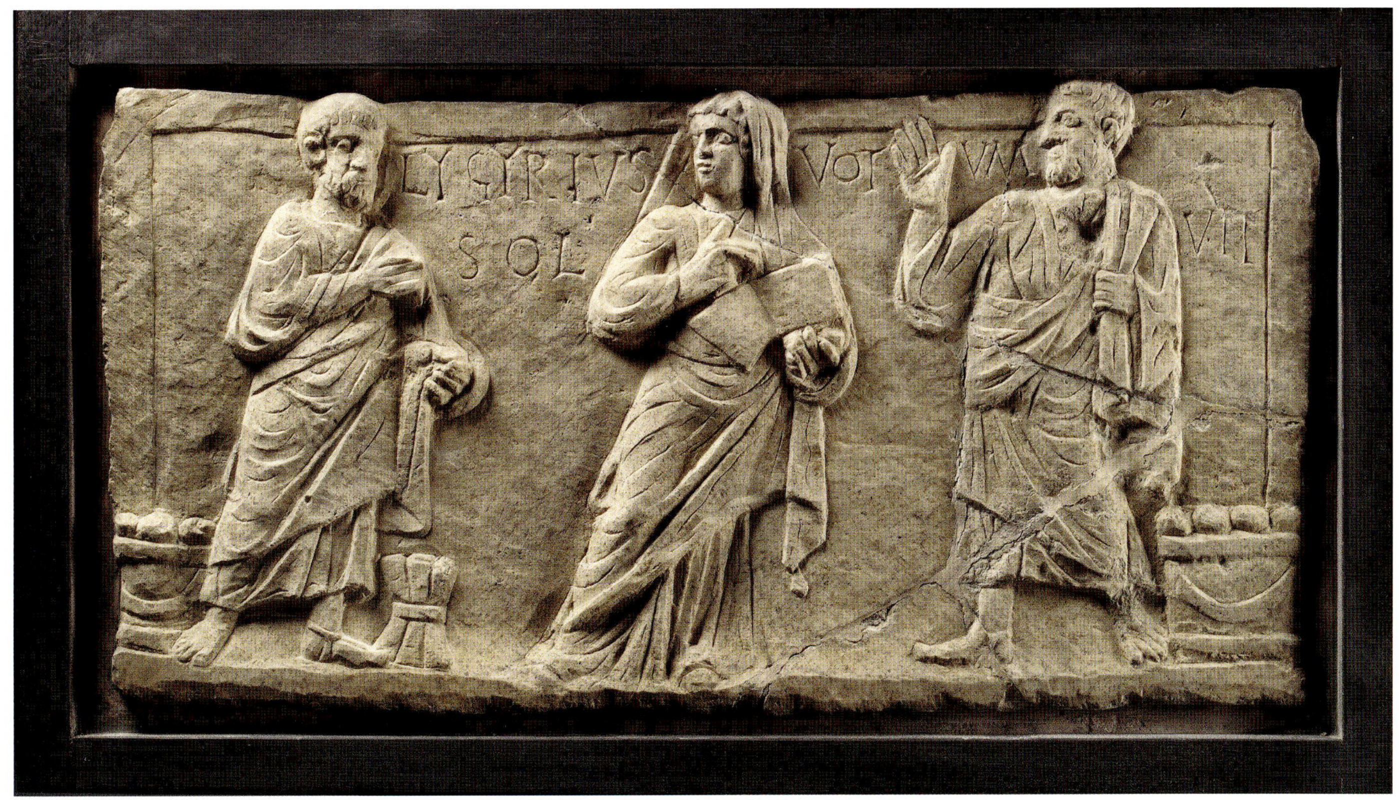

Bibliography

De Rossi 1872: 36–40, tav. 1; *CIL* VI, 1, no.843+ p.839 (1876), (as a 'marble relief'); Garrucci 1880: 11, tav. 411, no.4 (drawing); *ICUR* n.s. 1 (1922): no.3267; *ILCV* 1, no.1906B (1925); Vermeule and von Bothmer 1959: 341–2, Oxford, Pusey House, no.10; Schraudolph 1993: 247, cat. no.L220; Cooley 2017: 290–2, no.158.
Online: EDCS-17300981 (accessed 30 June 2015)
EDR149756 [last updated 5 August 2016, Benedetti] (accessed 16 June 2016)]
EDB33204 [Filippo Piazzolla, 21 June 2013; last updated by Antonio Enrico Felle 15 October 2015] (accessed 30 June 2015)

Comment

The central figure appears to be a personification of the Church or, more generally, of the Christian faith, by analogy with the personification of the Church of the Gentiles (*Ecclesia ex gentibus*) that appears in a fifth-century mosaic decorating the rear nave wall of the basilica of Santa Sabina in Rome.[1]

The composition of a central female personification of the Church, or a portrait of the deceased holding a scroll or a book and flanked by male apostles or saints, is common on sarcophagi produced in Rome in the fourth century.[2] Many of these examples, including a sarcophagus now in the Cimitero di San Callisto, also feature *capsae* filled with scrolls – intended to emphasise the authority of the male figures to either side.[3] The men are not named or differentiated by appearance, but they would seem to be apostles, most likely Saints Peter and Paul.[4] Both men raise their hands in gestures that echo those made by Peter and Paul in the apse mosaic of Santa Pudenziana in Rome, dated to *c.*AD 400.[5] In fact representations of Peter and Paul, whose poses match those of the two men on the Wilshere relief, were also present in the Santa Sabina mosaics, above the two female personifications.[6]

While the iconography of the relief resembles that found on sarcophagi of the same date, its inscription '*Lygyrius votum solvit*' endows the work with a different character and function. The Christian character of the iconography supports an identification of the relief as a Christian votive plaque, donated by a 'Lygyrius' (possibly to be read as 'Lygurius' misspelled) – either in fulfilment of, or to record the previous fulfilment of, his vow to God and to the Church.[7] 'Lygyrius', probably related to the tribe of the Ligures (associated with the modern region of Liguria), does not appear to have been a common name in the period. Only one other variant, 'Ligurius', is attested in a Christian funerary inscription from Rome.[8]

Interestingly, while the phrase '*...votum solvit*' is common in both pagan and Christian contexts in the period, this relief is unique among the corpus of late Roman votive reliefs in its combination of Christian iconography and votive formula.[9] The relief should be dated to the later fourth or early fifth century AD.

Endnotes

1. De Rossi proposed this as one possible identification: de Rossi 1872. On the Santa Sabina mosaics see Wilpert 1916: vol.3, pl.47; De Bruyne 1936: 265ff; Ihm 1960: 151–3; Darsy 1961: 96; Matthiae 1967: vol.1, 77–81, vol. 2, figs 49–50; Oakeshott 1967: 89–90; Wilpert and Schumacher 1976: 13; Steen 2002: 1943ff; Brandenburg 2004: 174–5; Thunø 2007, especially 21–2.
2. For example Bovini and Brandenburg 1967: cats 11 and 80 (Vatican Museum), 396 (Rome, Cimitero di San Callisto), 682 (Rome, St Peter's).
3. Bovini and Brandenburg 1967: cat. no.396.
4. As identified by de Rossi 1872.
5. Ihm 1960: 130–2; Oakeshott 1967: 65–7; Matthiae 1967: vol.1, 55–76; Dassman 1970: 67–81; Feld 1992: 253–62; Mathews 1993: 98–109. Hellemo 1989: 39–46.
6. The two Apostles are not extant, but are recorded by Ciampini 1699: vol.1, pl.48; see also Thunø 2007: 23, 22 fig. 5.
7. See de Rossi 1872 who relates the name to the Greek word for 'hyacinth', which was also imported into Latin (*lyncurius*).
8. '*Ligurio Suceso in pace*': *ICUR* n.s., 1, 3608. Other examples include *CIL* 1.1092, 1.449, 5.8988b, 5.3936, 13.1921, 14.1639, 14.2877.
9. On the formula '*votum solvit*' see de Rossi 1872; Schraudolph 1993: 66; Cooley 2017: 291.

59 AN 2007.41

| Photograph by David Gowers, 2014

Cochlear silver spoon

L. 17.8 cm; WT. 24.67 g; W. 3.1 cm (bowl); L. 6.3 cm (bowl); H. 1.6 cm (joining element); W. 0.3 cm (joining element/handle); L. 1.2 cm (joining element); L. 11.5 cm (handle); The spoon is thinly beaten to shape and apparently made of solid silver.

Present condition

Cracks radiate out towards the outer end of the bowl, where the spoon has been broken and glued back together. Silver corrosion appears on the rear surface behind the damaged area, which was evidently cleaned after conservation. Within the corrosion layer are tiny inclusions, perhaps of greenish glass or stone from the ancient burial environment. Blobs of corrosion appear on the handle, which has been broken in two places and repaired.

Description

The pear-shaped bowl terminates with an elegant offset in the form of an open scroll, to which the handle has been soldered. Offsets in the form of scrolls are found on spoons from the hoards at Thetford and Kaiseraugst, Switzerland.[1] The offset is worn smooth, most likely from use in antiquity. The handle, with no visible decoration, takes the form of a rod of square section, sharply tapering to a point. Some filing marks survive on the upper surface, by the offset. The inner surface of the bowl is engraved with a motif of a peacock facing left, holding in its beak a fish on a line. The style of the engraving is naturalistic and detailed. There are no visible inscriptions.

Collection history

Acquired by Wilshere in Rome in 1868.[2] A pencilled note in Wilshere's hand on the inside of the lid of the box in which he kept the spoon records that it was said to have been found at Porto (Portus) or Ostia, the ports of Rome (see p.50, fig. 22). However, this may have been inspired by de Rossi's publication of nine spoons from Portus and other areas around Rome, in which Wilshere's spoon is briefly described with no further indication of provenance.[3]

Bibliography

Unpublished.

Comment

This is a cochlear spoon, in which the point of the handle was used to open shells or spear food in the absence of forks; it was possibly also used as a toothpick.[4] The bowl of the cochlear spoon changed dramatically in shape, moving from small and round to large and pear-shaped in the course of Roman use from early to late empire, but the form of the utilitarian handle remained constant. It is likely that the diner used the offset, an innovation of the fourth century AD, to grasp the spoon at the point of balance.

This was surely a personal possession, rather than a liturgical piece. A close comparison is offered by MMA 17.191.211, found in northern France in the early twentieth century and formerly in the collection of J. Pierpoint Morgan.[5] Here the bowl is decorated with an engraved shell. The joining element is similar, as is the shape of the handle. Spoons nos. 79 and 80 from the Thetford hoard are also of similar form; these are dated to the second half of the fourth century AD.[6] Three spoons from the Hoxne hoard show birds pecking at plants or worms; these are dated to the late fourth or early fifth century AD, and are made of 95 per cent silver with an alloy of copper.[7]

At 24.67 g in weight and 17.8 cm in length, the spoon is closely comparable to two bearing similar incised decoration from Thetford, Norfolk (Johns and Potter 1983: 119): a spoon decorated with a fish weighing 24.3 g and 17.8 cm in length; another decorated with a panther weighing 22.3 grams and 17.7 cm long.[8]

The spoon may be dated to AD 350–400. The dominance of northwest Europe among similar examples reflects the preponderance of late Roman deposits of silver plate in the region. Nonetheless, it is clear that there was little regional variation in late antique cochlear spoons.

Endnotes

1. Johns and Potter 1983: 128–9; Kaufmann-Heinimann 1984: 20–1, Abb.21–2.
2. De Rossi 1868: 81. See p.00.
3. De Rossi 1868: 79–84, esp. pp.79 and 81.
4. Johns 1983: 100; 2010: 97-–132.
5. De Ricci 1911: 33,.no.211, pl.XI; Folting 1974: 265, pl.21; Neumeyer 2016: 104, fig. 16 (9). http://www.metmuseum.org/art/collection/search.46, accessed 30/6/2017.
6. Johns 1983: 128–9.
7. Johns 2010: 112–13, figs 5.21–3.
8. Johns and Potter 1983: 119.

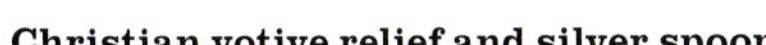

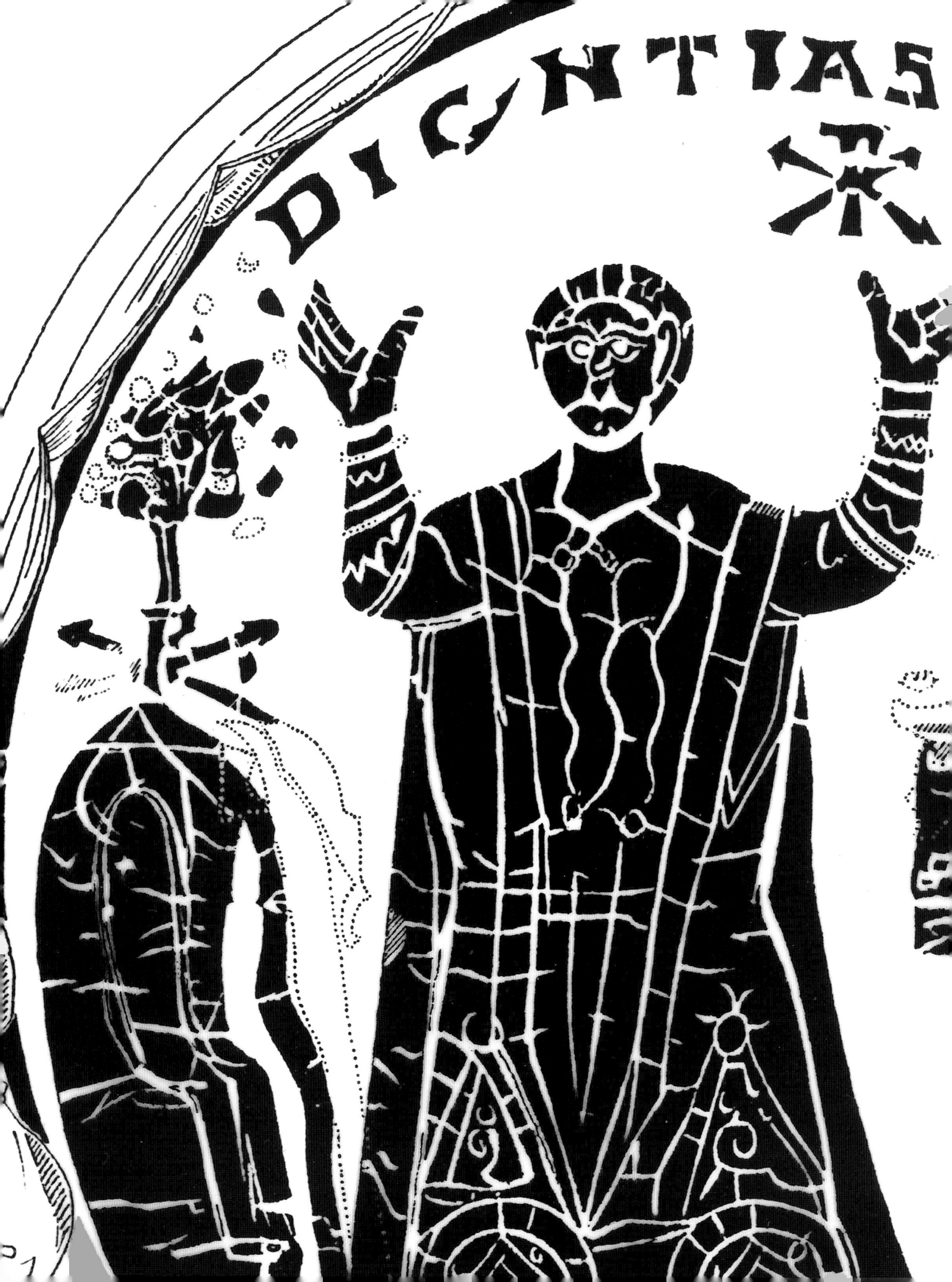
DIGNTIAS

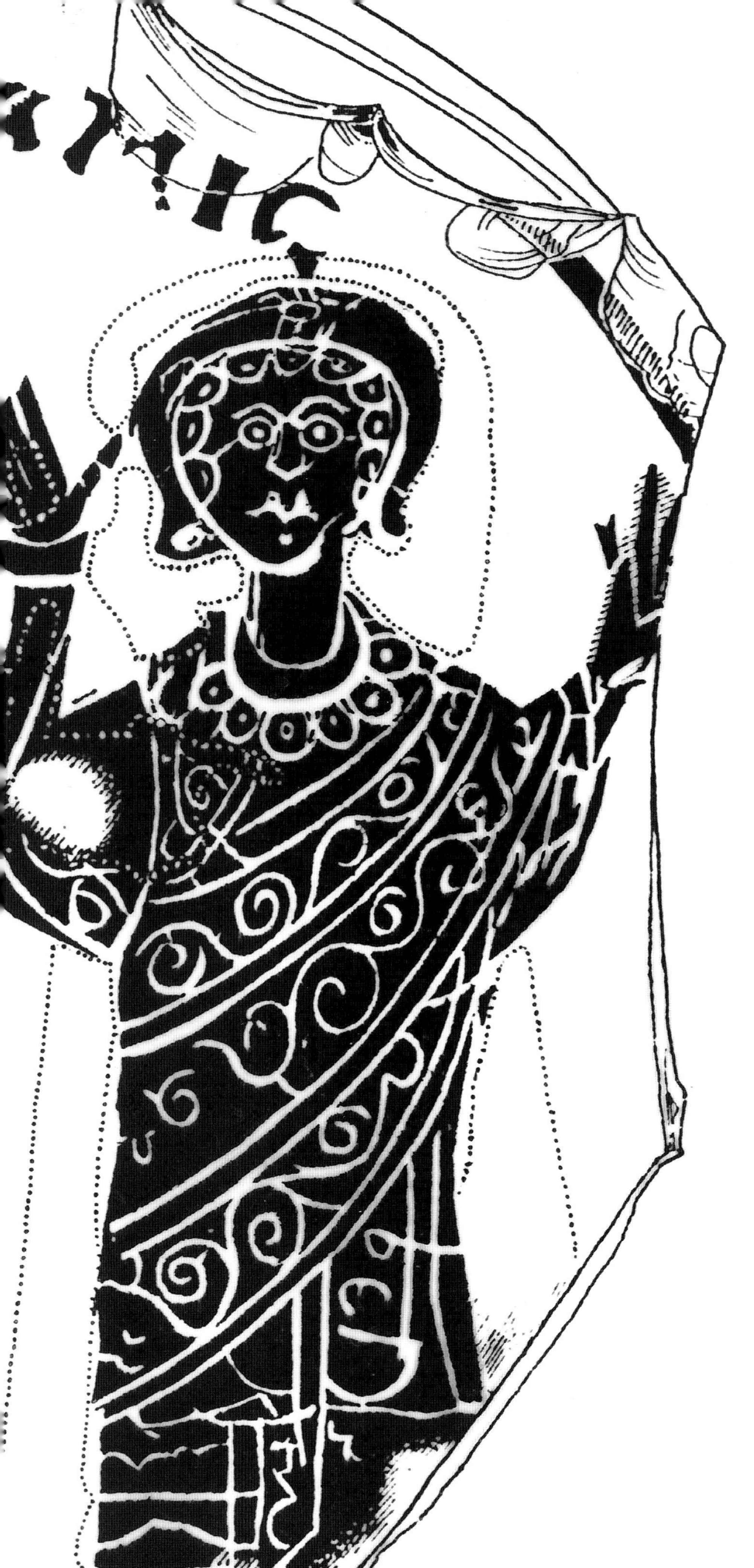

Appendices

Appendix 1

Concordance of objects from the Wilshere Collection

The table is arranged chronologically from left to right, providing in columns 6 and 8 a concordance of Ashmolean accession and present catalogue numbers. The numerical order is taken from Webster's manuscript list (column 3).

Colour codes

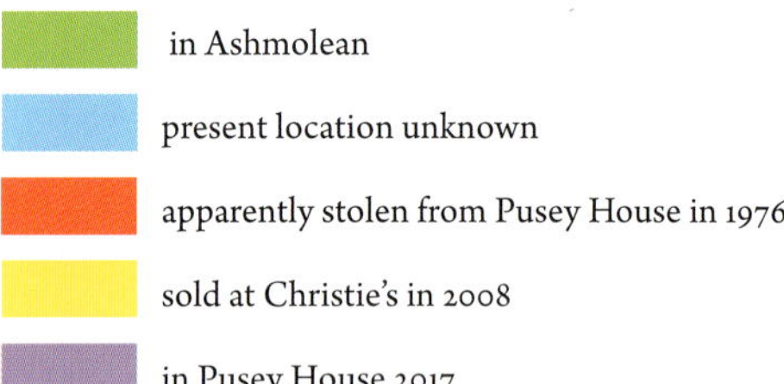

Wilshere 4/9/1893 (unspecified, but includes only small objects – probably the contents of the wooden box mentioned in Declaration of Trust, by 1895 at Keble College, Oxford)	Declaration of Trust 1895 in favour of Pusey House as heir; only large stone objects are itemised	Webster 1926–8 Typed ms. list of all objects then collected at Pusey House. Objects published in JRS 19 (1929) are marked *	Handwritten ms list compiled by John Boardman of objects transferred from Pusey House to the Ashmolean Museum as Loan 65. 8 February 1957 (gold-glass and one silver spoon)	Typed list compiled by David Brown of objects transferred from Pusey House to the Ashmolean Museum as Loan 65. May 1984 (stone inscriptions, sculpture and misc. ceramics).	Ashmolean acquisition 2007 registered by Michael Vickers; current locations elsewhere where known	Christie's sale no.7659, 13/10/2008, Lot 55	Catalogue 2017/ scheduled for online publication
N/A	19	1. Child's sarcophagus: entry of Christ to Jerusalem; miracles*	N/A	6	AN2007.48	N/A	40
N/A	5	2. Votive relief of Lygyrius	N/A	1	AN2007.43	N/A	58
N/A	13	3. Inscription of Poimenis*	N/A	17	AN2007.59	N/A	50
N/A	16	4. Inscription of Noumenis*	N/A	12	AN2007.54	N/A	49
N/A	9	5. Inscription of Alexander*	N/A	9	AN2007.51	N/A	48
N/A	2	6. Inscription of Victurina	N/A	14	AN2007.56	N/A	53
N/A	18	7. Front of sarcophagus with Christ, Saints Peter and Paul	N/A	5	AN2007.47a,b	N/A	41
N/A	1	8. Inscription of Sapis	N/A	7	AN2007.49	N/A	52
N/A	12	9. Inscription of Zotikos*	N/A	13	AN2007.55	N/A	44
N/A	3	10. Inscription of Veronilla	N/A	16	AN2007.58	N/A	54
N/A	N/A	11. Campanian oinochoe	N/A	Stolen from Pusey House 1976	N/A	N/A	N/A
N/A	N/A	12. Plate of *terra sigillata*	N/A	Stolen from Pusey House 1976	N/A	N/A	N/A
N/A	N/A	13. Terracotta (?) Etruscan ash chest: warriors; woman reclining on lid	N/A	Stolen from Pusey House 1976	N/A	N/A	N/A
N/A	N/A	14. Terracotta (?) Etruscan ash chest, same mould as 13	N/A	Stolen from Pusey House 1976	N/A	N/A	N/A
N/A	N/A	15. Animal lampstand, probably bronze	N/A	Stolen from Pusey House 1976	N/A	N/A	N/A
N/A	-	16. Marble cinerary chest of Cornelia Thalia	N/A	21	AN2007.63	N/A	42
N/A	N/A	17. Hellenistic ceramic urn; varnished black, with laurel wreath on shoulder.	N/A	Stolen from Pusey House 1976	N/A	N/A	N/A
N/A	N/A	18. Urn, Hellenistic or Roman	N/A	24?	AN2007.67	N/A	Online
N/A	7A	19. Fragment of sarcophagus lid: meal by the tomb*	N/A	4	AN2007.46	N/A	39
N/A	14	20. Inscription of Iousios.*	N/A	10	AN2007.52	N/A	43
N/A	10	21. Inscription of Quinta Soteris	N/A	19	AN2007.61	N/A	56
N/A	8	22. Fragment of sarcophagus lid: Raising of Lazarus, Hebrew boys in the furnace, Jonah and the whale*	N/A	2	AN2007.44	N/A	37

N/A	11	23. Inscription of Sabeina.*	N/A	11	AN2007.53	N/A	45
N/A	6	24. Fragment of sarcophagus: cupids gathering grapes	N/A	Stolen from Pusey House 1976	N/A	N/A	N/A
N/A	7	25. Fragment of sarcophagus lid: meal by the tomb, traces of gilding	N/A	3	AN2007.45	N/A	38
N/A	-	26. Loutrophoros, probably Pentelic marble.	N/A	23	AN2007.65	N/A	On-line
N/A	15	27. Inscription of Melition	N/A	15	AN2007.57	N/A	46
N/A	-	28. Inscription of Venerosa	N/A	20	AN2007.62	N/A	47
N/A	4	29. Inscription of Maria	N/A	18	AN2007.60	N/A	55
N/A	-	30. Roman glass urn with lid	N/A	Stolen from Pusey House in 1976	N/A	N/A	N/A
N/A	-	31. Piece of ancient marble	N/A	22? But Webster's entry does not mention inscribed text	AN2007.64?	N/A	57
-	-	32. Wooden painted panel of St Peter and St Francis. Italian, probably fifteenth century	N/A	N/A	N/A	?	N/A
Sheet 7, within unnumbered list of intaglios: Cornelian – SECU/NDU	N/A	33. Oval sard inscribed Secunda, with sealing	N/A	N/A	Purchased London 13/10/2008. Sold on to Brussels 2009. Located in Brussels 30/10/2016	Not published	N/A
Sheet 7, within unnumbered list of intaglios, expanded to VALE MODESTA	N/A	34. Round sard with a fish and inscription Val(eria) Mod(estina) and sealing	N/A	N/A	Purchased ondon13/10/2008. Sold on to Brussels 2009. Located in Brussels 30/10/2016	Published	N/A
Sheet 6, Cameo, large emerald – Head of a man in a tunic – high relief – toga fastened over shoulder by a cruciform fibula	N/A	35. Green glass paste: bust of boy in relief with cross over left shoulder	N/A	N/A	Not in Ashmolean	Unpublished	N/A
Sheet 7, within unnumbered list of intaglios, on a blood stone – EIRHNH below a palm branch	N/A	36. Oval agate with palm branch and inscription Eirene	N/A	N/A	Purchased 13/10/2008 and seen in London 17/4/2017. 1.1 x 0.9cm	Published	N/A
–	N/A	37. Oval plaque: the birth of Christ. Red stone seal with sealing wax, perhaps used by Wilshere for Christmas greetings. 3.2 x 2.7 x 0.3cm	N/A	N/A	In Pusey House	N/A	N/A
Sheet 7, within unnumbered list of amulets: yellow glass amulet; a cock standing; an upright fish (?)	N/A	38. Glass sealing with a cock and a snake	N/A	N/A	Not in Ashmolean	Unpublished	N/A

–	N/A	39. Glass sealing with a flower between two birds	N/A	N/A	Purchased 13/10/2008 and seen in London 19/4/2017.Glass paste looped pendant 2.2 x 2.1 cm x 2mm thick.	Included in the sale but not described in the catalogue.	N/A
–	N/A	40. Clay sealing with Hebrew characters	N/A	N/A	Not in Ashmolean	Unpublished	N/A
–	N/A	41. Sealing with portrait of woman	N/A	N/A	Not in Ashmolean	Unpublished	N/A
–	N/A	42. Black octagonal ring with gnostic charm Kraabel 1979	N/A	N/A	Sold on by purchaser; details not recorded	Illustrated and described as Roman magical gem in dark green speckled jasper	N/A
-	N/A	43. Paste with gnostic sign	N/A	N/A	Not in Ashmolean	Possibly the magical gem described as cornelian?	N/A
Sheet 6. Intaglio in red cornelian mounted as a ring; on one side the good Shepherd bearing the sheep; 2 lambs, one springing against him the other feeding; a sheep lying down turned from him; on the left a tree with a bird sitting on the top, perhaps the olive and dove	N/A	44. Red jasper of the Good Shepherd, set in modern ring	N/A	N/A	Not in Ashmolean	Unpublished	N/A
–	N/A	45. Piece of glass vessel with marks	Not in original loan list but received on loan 19/2/1958 at the request of Dr Donald Harden and described in a receipt signed by John Boardman as two fragments of a glass bowl with incised decoration.	N/A	Purchased 13/10/2008 and located in London, 30/10/2016; seen in London 19/4/2017. The fragment described right is from a bowl; the second incised fragment measures 4.5 x 3.4 cm x 2.5 mm thick, and is from a flat tray or inlay	Illustrated and described as a Roman pale green glass bowl fragment, with wheel-cut linear and abraded decoration, part showing a dancing maenad with fillet hanging over right arm and holding a thyrsus in the other, first half of fourth century AD, 7.6 cm (3 in) across max. x 2 cm x 1.1 mm thick	N/A
–	N/A	46. Clay plaque with reclining figure on the obverse and reverse	N/A	N/A	Not in Ashmolean	Unpublished	N/A
–	N/A	47. Piece of onyx with inscription of Sennacherib	N/A	N/A	Not in Ashmolean	Unpublished	N/A

–	N/A	48. Piece of glass bottle	N/A	N/A	Not in Ashmolean	Could be one of the four fragmentary Roman glass shards mentioned in the description	N/A
N/A	–	49. Fragment of marble tombstone from the Aventine. Greek inscription- 'lived 24 years, 7 months, 19 days.' At the bottom, a grasshopper	N/A	–	Probably consigned to the sale; seen at Christie's but not included with other objects acquired by the purchaser.	Greek inscribed stone tablet is mentioned in the description but with no details given.	N/A
–	N/A	50. Fragment of open glass bowl	N/A	N/A	Not in Ashmolean	Could be one of the four fragmentary Roman glass shards mentioned in the description	N/A
–	N/A	51. Bottom of glass cup	N/A	N/A	Not in Ashmolean	Could be one of four fragmentary Roman glass shards mentioned in the description	N/A
–	N/A	52. Bone label inscribed in Greek Dipsaichos	N/A	N/A	Purchased London 13/10/2008. Located in London, 30/10/2016, seen 19/4/2017. Stone, 4 x 3 cm x 4 mm thick. Name is retrograde Dapsaikos = personal name derived from/or substantive word for abundance. Similar personal name known from Syracuse	Unpublished	N/A
	N/A	53. Fragment of bronze plaque with the *agnus dei* embossed	N/A	N/A	Not in Ashmolean	Unpublished	N/A
–	N/A	54. Wooden fish	N/A	N/A	Purchased London 13/10/2008. Located in London, 30/10/2016	Illustrated and described: a Roman wood fish token inscribed 'IX', pierced at tail, circa first–second century AD 5.6 cm (2¼ in)	N/A

–	N/A	55. Chalcedony with Arabic inscription	N/A	N/A	Not in Ashmolean	Unpublished	N/A
–	N/A	56. Piece of wood from the Mount of Olives	N/A	N/A	Not in Ashmolean, but Wilshere's note of its identity, written for Pusey House on the back of a message penned to his late wife, is in the archive transferred from Pusey House in 2008	Unpublished	N/A
–	N/A	57. Bronze ring with cruciform monogram and letters	N/A	N/A	Purchased 13/10/2008 and seen in London 19/4/2017. 2.3 cm x 1.7 cm at bezel, 1.3 cm at hoop, x 1.8 cm thick	Could be one of two bronze rings, Roman to Byzantine period, mentioned in the description of the group	N/A
–	N/A	58. Bronze ring with sacred monogram and letters and stars in the field	N/A	N/A	Purchased 13/10/2008 and probably sold on without record	See above, no.57	N/A
–	N/A	59. Bronze ring	N/A	N/A	Not in Ashmolean	See above, no.57. The description also lists another bronze ring, sixteenth century AD	N/A
–	N/A	60. Silver spoon engraved with peacock	Top of page 3, unnumbered	N/A	AN2007.41	N/A	59
–	N/A	61. Plaque in silver setting, possibly representing the Ascension. Perhaps wrongly identified by Webster, the scene engraved on a red stone, perhaps jasper, surrounded by medieval Latin script, represents the seven sleepers of Ephesus.Total height 9.7cm, w.6.4cm, th. Ca. 0.6cm. H. stone ca. 4.8cm; w.ca.4.2cm.	N/A	N/A	In Pusey House March 2017	N/A	N/A
–	N/A	62. Bronze pendant cross with embossed Madonna, above her the monogram A.M. on the left arm HIS and cross, on the right IOZEE. On the post, IAOSANTISSIMOSACRAMENTO. H. 14cm. W. 8cm. T.1cm.	N/A	N/A	In Pusey House March 2017	N/A	N/A

Sheet 7. Rings: 1. Gold. KYPIA (Kupia) – The P being on the bezel	N/A	63. Gold ring with inscription KYPIA, the P on the bezel	N/A	N/A	Purchased London 13/10/2008 and sold on to Brussels 22/1/2009; resold at Daguerre Auctions, Paris, 5/5/2009. Current location unknown	Illustrated and described as '… one [of two Roman gold rings] inscribed with "KYRIA (Lady)" across the shoulders and raised circular bezel, 3rd century AD'	N/A
Sheet 7. Rings: 3. Gold, a palm branch	N/A	64. Gold ring with palm branch	N/A	N/A	Purchased 13/10/2008 and probably sold on without record	Illustrated and described as 'the other [Roman gold] ring with palm branch on flattened lentoid-shaped bezel'	N/A
Sheet 7. Rings: 2. Gold. (ST)ERCORI VIVA(S) on a bezil (*sic*), between them a dove in intaglio	N/A	65. Gold ring with inscription, *(St) ercori viva(s)*, and on the bezel a bird with a branch in its mouth	N/A	N/A	Not in Ashmolean	Unpublished	N/A
Sheet 6. Cameo. Red and white onyx – part of a red fish on a white ground	N/A	66. Sardonyx cameo with fish	N/A	N/A	Purchased London 13/10/2008 and sold on to Brussels 22/1/2009, set in gold ring 3/2009; sold Christie's New York 11/12/2009, lot 464. Present location unknown	Illustrated and described as 'a fragmentary late Roman cornelian cameo with fish (red mullet), circa 4th century AD.'	N/A
Sheet 8. Rings: 4 Silver; a palm branch issuing from X	N/A	67. Silver ring with palm branch, c.f. no.64	N/A	N/A	Purchased 13/10/2008 and probably sold on without record	Described as 'a silver ring, similar [to the Roman gold rings] with palm branch'	N/A
Sheet 7. Intaglio – Cornelian FELI CITAS	N/A	68. Red jasper, inscribed Felicitas	N/A	N/A	Not in Ashmolean	Unpublished	N/A

–	N/A	69. Gold medal of Leo XIII, 1890	N/A	N/A	Not in Ashmolean, though Pusey House's label for the medal, a feature of correspondence between Wilshere and de Rossi, was transferred with the archive in 2008	Unpublished	N/A
–	N/A	70. Medal of Cardinal. Obverse, head; legend, Petrus Sarbus Venetus Cardinalis S. Marci. Reverse, coat of arms; legend, Has aedes condidit anno Christi MCCCCLV. D. 3.5cm. Th.0.4cm.	N/A	N/A	In Pusey House March 2017	N/A	N/A
-	N/A	**Gold-glass (Fondi d'oro).** 71. Bottom of cup. Wilshere, Description no.2. (Bibl.) In the centre, busts of woman clad in mantel (*sic*) with a roll in her hand, and of man clad in toga contabulata; behind, inscription PIE ZHCHC, 'Drink and live'. Round the outside small scenes, the healing of the paralytic, the raising of Lazarus, Adam and Eve, Abraham and Isaac, Moses and the rock*	Top of page 2, unnumbered first entry. Busts of man and wife; biblical scenes: Adam & Eve & serpent; Abraham and Isaac, Moses and rock, healing of lame man, Lazarus. Ins. PIE ZHSHS. L. 10.5. (bibl.)	N/A	AN2007.13	N/A	3
Sheet 1. Glass [Second entry] Fragment of the base of Chalice – white glass; small part of foot remaining; Abraham with the knife in his hand almost entire; the foot and tail of the ram and part of the body. Isaac is totally absent.-	N/A	72. Fragment in very bad condition, possibly the Good Shepherd. (bibl.)	Page 4 1st entry(?) Male figure; radiate border. L. 8.8	N/A	AN2007.9	N/A	9
–	N/A	73. Fragment of sheep, round the edge Dignitas) ami)COR(um)	Drapery (?) Ins. COR. L. 4.2	N/A	AN2007.25	N/A	4
–	N/A	74. Semicircular fragment of the bottom of a cup. Wilshere, Description, no.5. (bibl.). In the centre, head of Christ with nimbus. Round the outside, saints inscribed Johann)ES. PETRUS. LUCAS. SUSTUS (the murdered pope Sixtus), divided from each other by a rosette. The whole surrounded by a scalloped gold band	4 figures, bust in centre disc. Ins. ES PETRUS LVCAS SVSTVS. L.9.3 (bibl.)	N/A	AN2007.10	N/A	11

–	N/A	75. Fragmentary medallion with Herakles and the stag (bibl.)	Page 3. Headings: Gilt glass fragments Medallions on blue background seventh entry Heracles and the Stag. L. 3.0. (bibl.) Marginal note: In a case with lion's head on radiate border	N/A	AN2007.16	N/A	27
–	N/A	76. Medallion of panther's head surrounded by dog-tooth ornament (bibl.)	Page 3 as above Webster no.75, eighth entry. L. 2.0	N/A	AN2007.29	N/A	28
Sheet 2. 1 Fragment of thin glass, doubtless the base of a Chalice, probably of the fourth century. Subject – Our Lord crowning two apostles; he has the nimbus; he holds in either hand a wreath over their heads. The letters ISTVS (the initials CR being missing) are above His head. Above that of one saint are the letters IOANES (Ioannes), doubtless the apostle St John, the other St Peter or some other apostle; round the margin of the design are the letters …NITAS AMICOR… (Dignitas amicorum) 'Honour of thy friends' – a common but rather enigmatical acclamation. There are many glasses extant with this type of decoration, as may be seen in Garrucci's 'Vetri ornati di oro' –	N/A	77. Fragmentary bottom of cup (bibl.) A small figure of Christ wearing the nimbus, crowning two saints; inscriptions behind Cr) ISTUS IOANES (the other saint on the analogy of Garrucci, pl. 193.3 will probably be St. Peter.) Round the margin, dig(NITAS AMICORUM	Page 3. Fragments (not in cases) Entry no. 9 figure with wreath between 2 heads. Ins. GNITASAMICOR IST IO AN L.6.9 Webster no.77 (bibl.)	N/A	AN2007.12	N/A	26
2 Fragment of base of chalice – 3 layers of glass. Design of the wheel type. In the middle CHR CRIS. A small portion of the Head only, of our Lord. On the other side of which were of course the missing letters TVS. Round the Christus, divided from it by a Circle and within an outer circle, were doubtless standing figures of saints divided by a roll (of the Gospel); one figure only and the feet of a second remain. The name of the martyred Pope SYSTVS and the final VS of another name. From the absence of the nimbus and the character of the letters and vesting, this may be of early fourth century date	N/A	78. Fragmentary bottom of cup. In centre, head of Christ without nimbus. Inscription CRIS)tus. Outside saints inscribed SUSTUS, Timothe)US; divided from one another by the gospel roll. (bibl.)	Page 1. Gilt glass fragments (in cases) [First entry] Male figure and scroll. Ins. CRIS VS SVSTVS. (no.3). L.7.0 Webster no.78 (bibl.)	N/A	AN2007.8	N/A	10

–	N/A	79. Bottom of cup. (bibl.) Four heads set in a square frame divided horizontally by gold line, the bottom two each with a nimbus, the top two without nimbus but separated by inscriptions, PETRUS.PAULUS. IULIUS.SUSTUS. The whole is surrounded by a framework of gold lines whose inner contour is square and outer octagonal. Compare for style no.74	Page 1. Gilt glass fragments (in cases) [fourth entry] Four heads in square frame. Ins. VS,PAVLVS,IVLIVS,SVSTVS. L.11.0. Webster no.79 (bibl.)	N/A	AN2007.7	N/A	25
–	N/A	80. Bottom of cup. (bibl.). Man and woman praying, between them a roll; they wear, the man the paenula and the dalmatica with an ornament consisting of a triangle surmounted by a circle over each knee, the woman a mantel (*sic*) and a jewelled diadem (bibl.) Garrucci interprets them as St. Laurence and St.Agnes. To their left, a rock, above it the sacred monogram, above that a tree, probably the eternal rock of the church, surmounted by the vine of life. Added red and green*	Page 1. Gilt glass fragments (in cases). [seventh entry] Man and woman praying. Ins. DIGNITAS AMIC. L. 11.0. Webster no.80, pl.5.2 (bibl.)	N/A	AN2007.26	N/A	21
–	N/A	81. Fragmentary medallion of leopard's head Repeat of entry no.76	Page 3. Gilt glass fragments Medallions on blue background [eighth entry] Lion's head (*sic*) in a radiate border. L.2.0. In a case with Heracles and the Stag	N/A	AN2007.29	N/A	28
Sheet 4. 8 Fragment of Chalice – a horizontal line divides the lower part of 2 figures from fishes apparently swimming in water below them; one fish is complete. Of the two figures the drapery of both is visible but the feet of one only	N/A	82. Fragmentary bottom of cup. Two men standing. Fish in the margin	Page 3 Fragments (not in cases) [5th entry] Legs of two figures; fish in exergue. L. 3.7	N/A	AN2007.40	N/A	6
Sheet 6. Medallions [Cont'd] Green under white glass, apparently, a dragon on a mound. Query from history of Bel and the Dragon?	N/A	83. Medallion. (bibl.) Snake on rock. Vopel interprets this as the snake of Babylon which Daniel poisoned. (bibl.)	Page 3 Gilt glass fragments Medallions on blue background [fifth entry] Dragon. L.2.2 (green). Webster no.83. (bibl.)	N/A	AN2007.18	N/A	31

–	N/A	84. Fragmentary bottom of a cup. Two fish and net (?).In the field, letters Z and PEV	Page 4 Fragments (not in cases) [Cont'd} [13th entry] Fish. Ins. bEΛ S. L. 5.5	N/A	AN2007.23	N/A	16
–	N/A	85. Fragmentary bottom of a cup. Part of male bust. Inscription, seSES	Page 3 Fragments (not in cases) [sixth entry] Shoulder of figure with scroll (?). Ins. ES. L.5.1	N/A	AN2007.27	N/A	20
Sheet 9. Fragment of base of Chalice; white glass; part of 7 branched Candlestick in gold; divided by two lines from upper part wanting – (PI)EZ(ESES and apparently TVOS	N/A	86. Fragmentary centre of cup. Single candle, and the foliated branches of the seven branched candlestick. Inscriptions ZE)ses, and LOUI [bibl.]	Page 3 Fragments (not in cases) [7th entry] Wreath. Ins. .Z IVO>O. L. 8.7 (2 frs.)	N/A	AN2007.6	N/A	13
–	N/A	87. Small fragment of drapery	? Drapery. L. 3.1	N/A	AN2007.37?	N/A	5?
–	N/A	88. Bottom of small cup. Two fish and monogram; inscription SPE, ?spes	Page 3. Fragments (not in cases) [third entry] Complete base. Ins. SPE. D. 4.7	N/A	AN2007.39	N/A	36
–	N/A	89. Medallion of lion set in a ring	Page 3. Gilt glass fragments Medallions on blue background first entry Lion – mounted in a gold finger ring (no. 301).	N/A	AN2007.15	N/A	29
?Sheet 5. Medallions 4. ⅔ds gone. ⅓rd left. [Lack of description suggests a repeat of the preceding entry no.3. Magi bearing gifts]	N/A	90. Fragmentary medallion. [bibl.] Daniel with the poisoned cake. [bibl.]	Page 3. Gilt glass fragments Medallions on blue background sixth entry Fr., youth with ball. L.2.8 [3rd entry is listed as Webster no 90 but this is the more complete of the two versions of this scene.]	N/A	AN2007.21	N/A	32
Sheet 5. Medallions 1 Blue glass under clear glass; a standing figure between 2 trees	N/A	91. Medallion. [bibl.] Daniel delivered to the lions, [bibl.]	Page 3 Gilt glass fragments Medallions on blue background [fourth entry] Man bound to two trees. L.2.6. Daniel. Webster no.91. [bibl.]	N/A	AN2007.32	N/A	30

–	N/A	92. Fragment of medallion with sheep (?)	Page 4 Fragments (not in cases) With blue background first entry Disc on wall of bowl. L. 3.0?	N/A	AN2007.30	N/A	18
–	N/A	93. Fragment of broad gold band round the edge of cup	Page 4 Fragments (not in cases) [Cont'd. 11th entry.] ? Border. L. 3.3	N/A	AN2007.34		17
–	N/A	94. Fragment of double dot pattern round the edge of cup	Page 3 Fragments (not in cases) [fourth entry] Indented border. L. 3.6	N/A	AN2007.20	N/A	14
Sheet 4. 7 Another small fragment of clear and blue glass with the letters OM well designed		95. Small fragment inscribed NOM(ine.	Page 4 Fragments (not in cases) With blue background [second entry] Ins. OM. L. 2.9	N/A	AN2007.17	N/A	2
Sheet 4. 6 Small fragment on which are the letters SEM, apparently of late date	N/A	96. Small fragment inscribed SEM(per	Page 3 Fragments (not in cases) [second entry] Ins. SEM. L. 2.2	N/A	AN2007.31	N/A	15
–	N/A	97. Indecipherable fragment	?	N/A	?	?Possibly the piece of gold-glass mentioned in the lot entry	?
Sheet 3. 3 Fragment of base of small Chalice, probably not for Eucharistic use. Portions of the heads of 2 figures with the lettering R F E VIVI, part of some acclamation regarding a certain Rufus	N/A	98. Fragmentary bottom of cup. Two male busts. Inscription, sempe] R RF[eliciter VIVI(te c.f. for style no.79	Page 3. Fragments (not in cases) [eighth entry] Two heads. Ins. R FE.V IVT. L.3.9	N/A	AN2007.24	N/A	19
–	N/A	99. Fragmentary bottom of cup. [Bibl.] Two male busts with monogram between them. Inscription; URSUS DION	Page 1. Gilt glass fragments (in cases) [fifth entry] Male busts. Ins. VRSVS DION. L.11.4. Webster no. 99 [bibl.]	N/A	AN2007.5	N/A	12
Sheet 5. 9 Fragment of Chalice, doubtless originally showing the Blessed Virgin between S. Peter and Laurencius as indicated by the letters MAR in the middle with (PE)TROS on one side and LA(VRENTIVS) on the other	N/A	100. Fragment of cup. Only the scalloped edge and the names remain. Pe)TRUS MARIA LA(urentius. The representation was the Virgin between St. Peter and St. Lawrence	Page 3 Fragments (not in cases) [first entry] Indented border. Ins. TRVS. LA MAI	N/A	AN2007.19	N/A	24

Sheet 5. Medallions 3. Magi bearing gifts – very complete	N/A	101. Fragmentary medallion. Man with crown carrying round object. It might be Daniel with the poisoned cake, but the crown makes in more likely that it is one of the Magi bringing a gift	Page 3 Gilt glass fragments Medallions on blue background Boy with ball. L.3.2 'Daniel & poisoned cake.' Webster no.90 (*sic*). [bibl.]	N/A	AN2007.28	N/A	33
Sheet 5. 9 Small fragment. Part of a head apparently with nimbus	N/A	102. Fragment with male head and nimbus; c.f. for style no.79	Page 4 Fragments (not in cases) [Cont'd. fourteenth entry] Head. L. 2.4	N/A	AN2007.33	N/A	8
–	N/A	103. Fragmentary bottom of cup. [bibl.] In the centre busts of S.S. Peter and Paul with the sacred monogram between them. Paul is unbearded. Round the outside small scenes, the three children in the fire, Zedekiah making the sundial go backwards, Susanna between two trees, the martyrdom of Isaiah, Moses and the serpent, Moses and the rock. Round the margin inscription, DIGNITAS A(micorum vivatis felic)ITE (r in pa)CE DE ZE(ses. A fragment has been lost since Garrucci saw the cup, containing the half of the martyrdom of Isaiah and the serpent of the next scene, and on the margin the letters MICORUM VIVAT*	Page 2. Gilt glass fragments (in cases). [Cont'd. seventh entry] [Marginal note] ? fragments SS. Peter and Paul, Ins. PET; biblical scenes: Hezekiah and sundial, Moses and serpent, Moses and rock. Ins. DIGNITAS A ITE CE DEI ZE. 2 fragments, L. 11.0 and 4.5. One fr. Missing since Garrucci. Webster no.103 (*sic*), pl.6.1. [bibl.]	N/A	AN2007.35, 42 (now joined)	N/A	23
–	N/A	104. Large fragment of the bottom of cup. [bibl.] Christ enthroned with four saints sitting at his feet on either side. Christ wears the Dalmatica and Pallium, he points with the right hand to the roll held by Peter and with the left gives a tablet to Paul. Inscription, CRISTUS PETRUS Paulus TIMOTHEUS SUSTUS SIMON FLORUS, two other names are missing*	Page 1 Gilt glass fragments (in cases) [fourth entry] Christ enthroned with 4 saints. Ins. CRISTVS PETRVS,TIMOTEVS SVSTVS SIMON FLORUS. L. 9.3. Webster no. 104, pl.6.2	N/A	AN2007.11	N/A	22
–	N/A	105. Four Roman coins of the fourth century	-	N/A	Not in the Ashmolean	? Not mentioned in selective description of the group	N/A

Sheet 1. Glass, part of Chalice. The foot entire. Sufficient of the cup to show its curve. Inscribed HERACLI TA PIEZE SES gold letters; all glass white	N/A	Not identifiable in Webster's list	Not identifiable on loan list	N/A	AN2007.38	N/A	1
Sheets 3–4. 4 Fragment of glass of the same character Treble thickness, of clear glass, light blue and dark blue glass. The small remains of gilding seem to indicate some ornamental design	N/A	Not identifiable in Webster's list	Page 4 Fragments (not in cases) With blue background [third entry] Floral. L.3.5	N/A	AN2007.14	N/A	35
–	N/A	Not identifiable in Webster's list	Page 4 Fragments (not in cases) [Cont'd. fourteenth entry] Head. L. 2.4	N/A	AN2007.36	N/A	7
N/A	–	Not identifiable in Webster's list	N/A	–	AN2007.50	N/A	51
–	N/A	Not identifiable in Webster's list	N/A	25. Shallow dish (pottery) part of rim broken. Diameter 0.115m	AN2007.66	N/A	Online
–	N/A	Not identifiable in Webster's list	N/A	24. Pot with handles. H. 0293m, circumference 0.89m, diameter of rim 0.152m	AN2007.67	N/A	On-line
–	N/A	Not identifiable in Webster's list	N/A	26 Mummified cat in 2 parts	?	N/A	?
Page 9 Medallions no.2. Standing figure of Our Lord bearing rod blue glass	N/A	Not identifiable in Webster's list	Page 3 Gilt glass fragments Medallions on blue background second entry Male figure. L. 2.9	–	AN2007.22 On the reverse is glued a paper sales ticket inscribed in pencil no.13 and cut to match the gold leaf border	N/A	34

Appendix 2

Transcript of the list of entries to the National Exhibition of Works of Art, Leeds, 1868 Museum of Ornamental Art

Contributed by C. W. Wilshere Esq., Brighton

[Undated and unsigned. Wilshere's name is misspelled Wiltshire and corrected at the top of each page, in the same hand, presumably that of the borrowing curator who compiled the descriptions.]

Notes:
Editorial additions are given in square brackets.
Catalogue and museum numbers are given in bold font at the end of each entry.
The gold-glasses are all from the sale of the Museo Recupero in 1862 (see above, pp. 48–49. fig. 20).
The ecclesiastical embroideries, presumably *opus anglicanum*, have not been traced.

Fol[io] I

DESCRIPTION

/ Specimens of early Christian glass found in the cemetries [*sic*] of the primitive Christians near Rome. – They consist of circular medallions which have originally formed the bases of patera [*sic*] or bowls, & being double folds of glass, have been preserved while the more fragile sides of the vessels have perished, They are ornamented with figures, animals etc cut out in gold leaf the outlines of features & draperies being etched with a steel point & in some instances filled in with a red back-ground and protected from injury by a covering of glass. They are figured & described in "Vetri Ornati di figure in oro" by Garrucci; The Greek monogram of Christ is displayed on the labarum of Constantine & the coins of the lower Empire fixes the date of these extremely rare & interesting objects at about the commencement of the fourth Century No 1 Portion of a glass patera representing in the centre the busts of St Peter and St Paul between them the sacred monogram, surrounded

Fol[io] 2

DESCRIPTION. continued

1 by 6 compartments of scriptural subjects & round the border an imperfect legend, beginning Dignitas Amicorum etc. Three of the subjects are perfect, the rest wanting. Diam.3½ in
[No.**23**. **AN2007.35**]

2 Glass patera, in the centre the bust of a man and his wife, above is written "Pie Zeses" may you live happily, around is a series of scriptural subjects – Diam 3½ in –
[No.**3**. **AN2007.13**]

3 Centre portion of a small beaker with a man holding out a circular object, perhaps one of the Magi
[No.**33**. **AN2007.28**]

4 The centre of a glass patera representing Christ seated on a throne surrounded by Apostles and Martyrs, Inscribed above "Cristus Paulus Petrus and below Timoteus, Justus, Simon, Florus. The names of others and a portion of the subject are deficient Diam 3 in
[No.**22**. **AN2007.11**]

5 The half of a Patera, with a bust of Christ in the centre and three saints, inscribed. Petrus Lucas Sustus ~
[No.**11**. **AN2007.10**]

Fol[io] 3

DESCRIPTION. continued

6 – The centre of a Patera representing two youthful figures in the tunic and pallium with a column between the supporting a tablet inscribed "Genesius Lucas" in a square border –
[Returned to Vatican, 1894. Museo Sacro Cristiano, Inv. **60775**]

7 The centre of a Patera, the subject divided into two compartments each with two busts. In the upper, Peter and Paul, in the lower Julius and Sustus, in a square border –
[No.**25**, AN2007.7]

8 The centre of a Patera representing a priest in prayer vested in an alb, Chasuble and Stole on his right a veiled throne surmounted by the sacred monogram and on his left a female also in prayer. Round the border is an imperfect legend . "Digntias Amic " (sic)
[No.**21**, AN2007.26]

9 The centre of a Patera with two male busts, bare-headed, face to face, clad in tunic and pallium & the names Ursus & Dion – in a circular border
[No.**12**, AN2007.5]

11 The base of a glass beaker, in an Octagonal border is the head of a Leopard with open jaws –
[No.**28**, AN2007.29]

Transposed
10 The base of a glass beaker with circular medallion of Hercules overcoming the Arcadian Stag, behind in the field is his Club
[No.**27**, AN2007.16]

Fol[io] 4

DESCRIPTION. Continued

12 Fragment of glass, representing four fish swimming & above the lower part of a man, perhaps the miraculous draught
[No.**6**, AN2007.40]

13 Fragment of glass with a slight sketch of some uncertain object & a portion of the sentence "Dignitas amicorum etc"
[No.**5**, AN2007.37]

14 Ecclesiastical Embroidery of the 15 Cent[ur]y representing St Lawrence under a canopy holding a gridiron – (framed and glazed)
[Not traced]

15 Ecclesiastical Embroidery of the 15 Cent[ur]y representing St Augustine holding in his right hand a pastoral staff
[Not traced]

Appendix 3

Transcript of Charles Willes Wilshere's Declaration of Trust

Dated 3rd May 1895
Declaration of Trust
of a collection of Christian
Antiquities

Hazel & Baines
Oxford

10/- stamp This Indenture made the 3rd day of May
1895 between Charles Willes Wilshere of The
Frythe Welwyn in the county of Herts Esq of the
first part and The Right Honourable Charles Lindley
Viscount Halifax of Stickleton Hall in the County of
York John Archibald Shaw Stewart of no 71 Eaton Place
In the county of Middlesex Esq The Reverend William
Inge D D Provost of Worcester College in the University
of Oxford and Sir Offley Wakeman of Greater Peverey
in the County of Salop Baronet of the second part
Whereas the said Charles Willes Wilshere being possessed
Of the collection of early Christian antiquities (short
particulars whereof are specified in the Schedule hereto)
and being desirous of making provision for the permanent
care and preservation thereof recently delivered such
collection to the several persons parties hereto of the
second part being the Trustees of the Pusey House
(as they hereby acknowledge) to be held by them and
their successors as such Trustees upon and for the
trusts and purposes hereinafter declared concerning the
same Now this Indenture witnessed that it is hereby
agreed and declared that the said several persons
parties hereto of the second part and the persons or
person lawfully appointed from time to time in
succession to them as Trustees of Pusey House
(all which persons both those now parties and those
to be hereafter appointed as aforesaid are hereinafter
referred to as "the said Trustee or Trustees) shall
henceforth stand possessed of the said Collection
Upon trust that the said Trustees or Trustee shall
at such times as they think fit arrange for
and provide a proper and suitable place at Pusey
House in Oxford for the reception and preservation
of the said Collection The place wherever the same
may be deposited being rendered so far as practicable
exempt from damage by fire and shall subject new page
to reasonable and proper regulation to be made from time
to time by the said Trustees or Trustee permit the
said collection to be open for the inspection and
examination of Students at Pusey House aforesaid and
of such other persons as the said Trustees or Trustee
shall be at liberty to permit the inscribed stones and
bas reliefs mentioned in the first part of the schedule
or any of them to remain at The Frythe near Welwyn
where they now are or to remove them or any of them
to any place or places in Oxford but not elsewhere
which they shall in their uncontrolled discretion
think suitable for the proper exhibition and security
of the said collection, and to permit the contents of
the wooden box mentioned in the second part of the
Schedule to remain at Keble College, where it now is
or to remove it to any other place in Oxford but
not elsewhere as before provided with regard to the
inscribed stones and bas reliefs Provided always
that the said Trustees or Trustee shall not be at
liberty to deal in any way with the said Collection
except in accordance with the written instructions of
the Governors of the Pusey House In witness whereof
the said parties to those present have hereunto set
their hands and seals the day and year first above
written

The Schedule before referred to

First Part
Inscribed stones and bas reliefs (at present at
The Frythe Welwyn in charge of the said
Charles Willes Wilshere new page

No.	Description	Dimensions
1.	Inscribed stone † HIC REQUIESCIT IN PACE SAPIS QUI LEGIS ORA PRO ME	8¾ in x 13½ in
2.	" VICTVRINA (Tombstone)	15 in x 10½ in
3.	" VERONILLA (do)	11½ in x 18¾ in
4.	" MARIA (do)	11¾ in x 9½ in
5.	Bas relief. LYGYRIVS	10½ in x 21½ in
6.	" VINTAGE	20 in x 17 in
7.	" The Breakfast at Tiberias (fragment)	8¾ in x 14¼ in
7A.	" ditto	11½ in x 26½ in
8.	" The Raising of Lazarus fra[?] (do)	11¾ in x 32 in
9.	Inscribed stone "Alexander" (circular)	12½ in
10.	" ΒΕΝΕΡΩCΑ	11¾ in x 6¾ in
11.	" ΠΑΡΔΟCCΑΒΕΙΝ	17½ in x 11¾ in
12.	" ΖΩΤΙΚΟC ΑΡΧΩΝ	33¾ in x 22½ in
13.	" ΠΟΙΜΕΝΙC	14 in x 12¾ in
14.	" ΙΟΥCΙΟC	15 in x 8½ in
15.	" ΜΕΛΙΤΙΩ	24 in x 7¾ in
16.	" ΝΟΥΜΗΝΙC	13¼ in x 13 in
17.	" Chi-rho LOCUS DEC DECENTIVS (fragment)	11¾ x 7 in
18.	Front of Sarcophagus: centre, our Lord with book At side, S. Peter and S. Paul	68½ in x 20 in
19.	Sarcophagus: Our Lord entering Jerusalem	40 in x 16½ in
	Second Part A wooden box containing seven leather cases, the latter containing fragments of ancient Christian glass (at present at Keble College, Oxford)	

Signed, sealed and delivered by	Charles Willes Wilshere	(seal)
the before named Charles Willes Wilshere		
in the presence of	Halifax	(seal)
Frederic Preedy		
Caldecote. St Neots. Herts.		
Land Agent		
	J. G. Shaw Stewart	(seal)
Signed, sealed and delivered by		
The before named Charles Lindley	William Inge	(seal)
Viscount Halifax in the presence of	Offley Wakemann	(seal)

Butler to Viscount Halifax
79 Eaton Square

(Back cover)
Signed sealed and delivered by the before named
John Archibald Shaw Stewart in the presence of
Charles Shadbolt
71 Eaton Place
Butler to J. G. Shaw Stewart Esq.
Signed sealed and delivered by the before named
William Inge in the presence of
Henry Baines
Solr . Oxford
Signed sealed and delivered by the before named
Sir Offley Wakeman in the presence of
Philip R. Cobb
Greater Peverey Shrewsbury
Butler to Sir Offley Wakeman

Appendix 4a

Scientific examination of the gold-glass in the Wilshere Collection

Andrew Shortland, Kelly Domoney and Julian Henderson

Scientific examination of the sandwich gold-glass vessel bases and wall medallions in the Ashmolean's collections was undertaken by Andrew Shortland and Kelly Domoney of the University of Cranfield, using portable, hand-held X-ray fluorescence (HH-XRF) analysis. The examinations were carried out on an Oxford Instruments X-Met 5100, running quantitative empirical calibration. Elements analysed in this process are aluminium, silicon, calcium, titanium, iron, cobalt, nickel, copper, zinc, antimony and lead, although it should be noted that only antimony and manganese were used to group the glasses as described in this paper. The other results are included here for their value as a comparison to other published work.

It should be noted that glass of this type could be expected to contain around 20 per cent soda and 0.5–1.0 per cent magnesium. However, the portable XRF used is an air path device and low energy X-rays are attenuated in this air gap. This means that low atomic number elements (such as sodium and magnesium) cannot be detected. The methodology followed was identical to that in Scott et al. 2012a and 2012b, where an empirical calibration was developed and tested specifically for the analysis of soda lime silicate glasses.

In all 35 pieces of gold-glass were examined, with readings or samples taken from the inner and outer layers of glass (Table 1, Figure A). Here the inner layer refers to the vessel wall, which also served to protect the gold leaf decoration applied to the outer layer, the latter comprising the separately blown base of the vessel or medallion. For the purposes of the examination, the group of gold-glasses with colourless inner layers and coloured outer layers is numbered 3, colourless inners and 3x, coloured outers, as a combination of decolorants was used. However, in the catalogue text this group is numbered 4 to strengthen clarity in the narrative, for the results show that this group is very different from Group 3, the colourless vessel bases using a mix of decolourants. One gold-glass (AN2007.39, cat. **36**) did not have an accessible, definitively ancient surface to apply HH-XRF.

Further analyses were carried out on these glasses by laser ablation-inductively coupled plasma mass spectrometry (LA-ICP-MS) (AN2007.8, cat **10** and AN2007.37, cat. **5**) and Patrick Degryse analysed a sample from one base, AN2007.26, cat. **21**, by isotopic analysis (see Appendix 4b). In 1987 ten clear inner layers of small gold-glass medallions with coloured outer layers from the same collection were analysed by Julian Henderson for Dr Marlia Mango of the University of Oxford (now numbered as AN2007.17, cat. **2**; AN2007.18, cat. **10**; AN2007.21, cat. **32**; AN2007.22, cat. **34**; AN2007.28, cat. **33**; AN2007.29, cat. **28**; AN2007.30, cat. **18**; AN2007.32, cat. **30**; AN2007.34, cat. **17**; AN2007.39, cat. **36**). These results remain unpublished, but they, and the mounted samples, were kindly provided for the present programme of research. The electron microprobe-wavelength dispersive X-ray spectrometry analyses were repeated by LA-ICP-MS, and showed excellent agreement with the 1987 results, adding the greater detail possible with the low detection limits of the ICP-MS technique.

In this appendix only the results of the HH-XRF analysis are discussed, the other analyses being the subject of further scientific papers (Walker et al., 2017).

Results

Table 1 HH-XRF results

(wt% oxide, BDL = below detection limit, * foot ring of the vessel, picked out with an attached ring of glass)

Sample	Colour	Al_2O_3	SiO_2	CaO	TiO_2	MnO	Fe_2O_3	CoO	NiO	CuO	ZnO	Sb_2O_5	PbO
Group 1: Natron glass, Sb decoloured													
2007.38 (inner)		4.3	65	6.2	0.04	0	0.38	BDL	BDL	BDL	BDL	0.32	0.04
2007.38 (outer)		4.1	67	6.5	0.04	0	0.37	BDL	BDL	BDL	BDL	0.33	0.04
Group 2: Natron glass, Mn decoloured													
2007.5 (outer)		3.2	63	8.2	0.04	0.6	0.4	BDL	BDL	BDL	BDL	BDL	BDL
2007.20 (inner)		3.3	66	8.2	0.04	0.9	0.43	BDL	BDL	BDL	BDL	BDL	BDL
2007.20 (outer)		2.4	57	7.9	0.04	0.9	0.41	BDL	BDL	BDL	BDL	BDL	BDL
2007.25 (inner)		3.8	61	8	0.04	1.4	0.45	BDL	BDL	BDL	BDL	BDL	BDL
2007.25 (outer)		3.6	58	7.8	0.04	1.3	0.44	BDL	BDL	BDL	BDL	BDL	BDL
2007.36 (inner)		4.4	63	8.5	0.05	1	0.48	BDL	BDL	BDL	BDL	BDL	BDL
2007.36 (outer)		4.5	62	8.3	0.05	1.4	0.5	BDL	BDL	BDL	BDL	BDL	BDL
2007.9 (inner)		2.6	60	7.7	0.04	0.7	0.38	BDL	BDL	BDL	BDL	BDL	BDL
2007.9 (outer)		2.1	53	7.4	0.04	1	0.36	BDL	BDL	BDL	BDL	BDL	BDL
2007.40 (inner)		4.7	48	7.6	0.06	1	0.48	BDL	BDL	BDL	BDL	BDL	BDL
2007.40 (outer)		4.6	55	8.1	0.06	1.2	0.44	BDL	BDL	BDL	BDL	BDL	BDL

2007.33 (inner)		2.9	63	8.8	0.05	1.1	0.44	BDL	BDL	BDL	BDL	BDL	BDL
2007.33 (outer)		3.1	64	9.1	0.05	1.1	0.47	BDL	BDL	BDL	BDL	BDL	BDL
2007.6 (inner)		4	58	7.8	0.05	1.1	0.44	BDL	BDL	BDL	BDL	BDL	BDL
2007.6 (outer)		3.6	62	8.4	0.05	1.1	0.43	BDL	BDL	BDL	BDL	BDL	BDL
oldfield.44 (inner)		2.6	58	9.3	0.05	1.4	0.45	BDL	BDL	BDL	BDL	BDL	BDL
oldfield.44 (outer)		3.3	63	9.3	0.05	1.5	0.44	BDL	BDL	BDL	BDL	BDL	BDL
2007.10 (inner)		3	61	9.7	0.05	1.5	0.48	BDL	BDL	BDL	BDL	BDL	BDL
2007.10 (outer)		3	66	9.6	0.05	1.7	0.52	BDL	BDL	BDL	BDL	BDL	BDL
2007.13 (inner)		3	63	8.1	0.04	1.3	0.49	BDL	BDL	BDL	BDL	BDL	BDL
2007.13 (outer)		3	55	7.7	0.05	1.6	0.45	BDL	BDL	BDL	BDL	BDL	BDL
2007.30 outer		2.2	43	5.9	0.02	0.64	0.31	BDL	BDL	BDL	BDL	BDL	BDL
2007.34 inner		4.8	43	5.6	0.04	0.79	0.34	BDL	BDL	BDL	BDL	BDL	BDL
2007.31 (inner)		4	61	6.7	0.13	1.4	0.95	BDL	BDL	BDL	BDL	BDL	BDL
2007.31 (outer)		3.7	63	6.8	0.11	1.3	0.98	BDL	BDL	BDL	BDL	BDL	BDL
2007.23 (inner)		3.4	63	6.6	0.07	1	0.75	BDL	BDL	BDL	BDL	0.08	BDL
2007.23 (outer)		4.5	59	8.9	0.03	0.9	0.54	BDL	BDL	BDL	BDL	BDL	BDL
2007.23.repair		3	61	6.9	0.14	1.4	1	BDL	BDL	BDL	BDL	BDL	BDL
Group 3: Natron glass, Mn+Sb decoloured													
2007.24 (inner)		4	53	6.4	0.06	0.9	0.54	BDL	BDL	BDL	BDL	0.15	BDL
2007.24 (outer)		3.6	65	7.2	0.05	0.9	0.67	BDL	BDL	BDL	BDL	0.15	BDL
2007.27 (outer)		2.7	60	6.8	0.06	1	0.59	BDL	BDL	BDL	BDL	0.13	BDL
2007.27 (inner)		3.4	62	7.1	0.07	1	0.66	BDL	BDL	BDL	BDL	0.14	BDL
2007.7 (inner)		2.7	62	6.6	0.06	1	0.68	BDL	BDL	BDL	BDL	0.12	BDL
2007.7 (outer)		4.5	60	6.1	0.04	0.7	0.59	BDL	BDL	BDL	BDL	0.16	BDL
2007.11 (inner)		6.1	58	6	0.05	0.7	0.68	BDL	BDL	BDL	BDL	0.16	BDL
2007.11 (outer)		2.3	64	6.6	0.06	0.8	0.65	BDL	BDL	BDL	BDL	0.19	BDL
2007.19 (inner)		2	56	7.3	0.09	0.8	0.71	BDL	BDL	0.02	BDL	0.24	0.04
2007.19 (outer)		2.4	62	7.3	0.07	0.7	0.71	BDL	BDL	0.03	BDL	0.26	0.04
2007.15 (ring)*		5.5	58	6	0.04	0.36	0.55	BDL	BDL	0.04	BDL	0.4	0.07
2007.35b (inner)		5.9	62	5.4	0.06	0.44	0.74	BDL	BDL	0.03	BDL	0.29	0.05
2007.35b (outer)		6.8	56	5.2	0.05	0.48	0.83	BDL	BDL	0.11	BDL	0.28	0.11
2007.35a (inner)		4.1	64	6.6	0.06	0.54	0.7	BDL	BDL	0.03	BDL	0.28	0.05
2007.35a (outer)		5	57	5.6	0.07	0.6	0.88	BDL	BDL	0.11	BDL	0.27	0.11
2007.42 (inner)		5.1	59	5.6	0.05	0.46	0.74	BDL	BDL	0.03	BDL	0.27	0.05
2007.42 (outer)		6	54	5.7	0.07	0.6	0.79	BDL	BDL	0.12	BDL	0.26	0.11
Group 3X: Natron glass, Mn+Sb decoloured inners, coloured outers													
2007.14 (inner)		4.9	54	8.1	0.04	0.9	0.46	BDL	BDL	BDL	BDL	0.94	BDL
2007.16 (inner)		3	65	7	0.04	0.4	0.57	BDL	BDL	BDL	BDL	0.73	0.08
2007.21 (inner)		2.9	66	7.2	0.05	0.4	0.6	BDL	BDL	0.04	BDL	0.47	0.08
2007.22 (inner)		3.3	68	6.9	0.05	0.7	0.58	BDL	BDL	BDL	BDL	0.7	0.04
2007.18 (inner)		3.9	60	7	0.07	0.99	0.66	BDL	BDL	0.02	BDL	0.11	0.04
2007.28 (inner)		2.9	72	7	0.05	0.4	0.56	BDL	BDL	BDL	BDL	0.44	0.07
2007.29 (inner)		3.8	75	7.3	0.05	0.43	0.59	BDL	BDL	BDL	BDL	0.82	0.08
2007.32 (inner)		3.3	67	7.3	0.07	0.78	0.85	BDL	BDL	0.04	BDL	0.58	0.05
2007.17 (inner)		2.7	64	6.4	0.04	0.15	0.4	BDL	BDL	BDL	BDL	0.44	0.1
2007.16 (outer)	blue	2.8	67	7.3	0.09	1	1.1	0.12	BDL	0.16	BDL	1.5	0.28
2007.21 (outer)	blue	7	56	5.9	0.06	0.03	2.16	0.13	BDL	0.31	BDL	0.66	0.07
2007.22 (outer)	blue	11.7	54	4.9	0.03	0.25	0.86	BDL	BDL	0.14	BDL	1.65	0.16
2007.18 (outer)	green	4	64	7	0.07	0.59	2.47	BDL	BDL	0.82	0.07	0.1	0.21
2007.28 (outer)	blue	2.6	74	7.3	0.05	0.4	1.36	0.09	BDL	0.2	BDL	0.67	0.17
2007.29 (outer)	blue	3.9	62	6.5	0.08	0.8	1.1	0.12	BDL	0.16	BDL	1.33	0.26
2007.32 (outer)	blue	4	63	7.2	0.07	0.52	1.13	0.08	BDL	0.16	BDL	1.7	0.43
2007.17 (outer)	blue	3.8	50	6.1	0.12	0.05	1.56	0.1	BDL	0.28	BDL	0.55	0.05

On the graph the colourless inner layers and coloured outer layers of group 3x are shown separately. AN2007.35 and 42 (cat. **23**) is also shown separately, to indicate the possible range of variation within fragments of a single vessel.

Table 1 tabulates the results of all the HH-XRF examinations; Figure A shows the same results as a graph. The results show that the composition of all the clear gold-glass examined was consistent with being made from soda-lime-silica glass, although sodium could not be detected. This is what would be expected from Roman glass that uses natron as a flux. This was the standard means of producing glass in the Roman and late antique world.

Gold-glass in both the Ashmolean and the British Museum collections was intentionally decoloured, thereby counteracting the iron in the sand used in the primary production of glass, which imparts a bluish-green hue; the resulting raw glass is more or less colourless. The results of HH-XRF examination shows that the Ashmolean's collection of gold-glass falls within known compositional groups defined by the use of specific decolouring strategies: the use of antimony alone, manganese alone or a mixture of the two, the last most likely reflecting the use of recycled glass (Meek in Howells 2015: 31 and Foster and Jackson 2010).

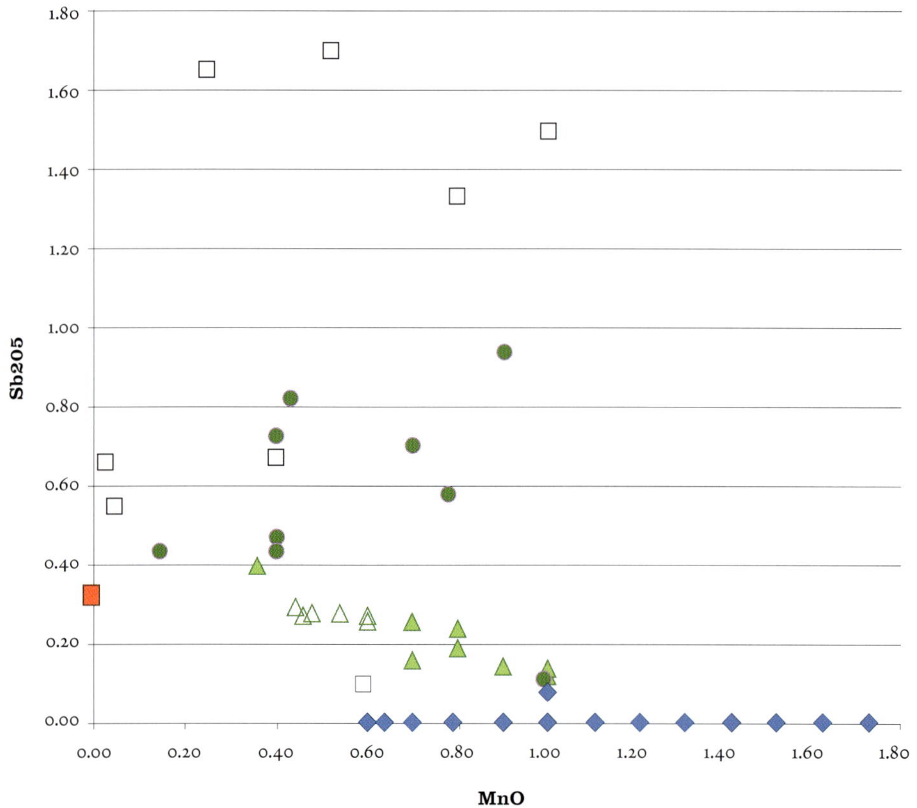

Fig. A HH-XRF results, where the groups of gold-glass are plotted on a graph. Group 3, colourless inners and Group 3x, coloured outers, form the gold-glass medallions catalogued as Group 4.

Appendix 4b

Sr-Nd isotopic characterisation of a Roman gold-glass sample

Ashmolean Museum, entry AN 2007.26, Catalogue 21

Patrick Degryse and Annelore Blomme

Earth and Environmental Sciences
Geology Division • Centre for Archaeological Sciences
KU Leuven (Belgium)

Patrick.Degryse@kuleuven.be

Introduction

In the past decade a growing number of studies have focused on the provenance determination of Roman glass production (glass making or *primary production*) through the use of isotopic analysis (e.g. Wedepohl and Baumann 2000, Freestone *et al.* 2003, Degryse and Schneider 2008, Degryse *et al.* 2006, 2009). In particular Sr-Nd isotopic ratios appear to be good tracers for the silica raw materials used in Roman glass production. These ratios show systematic variation between different possible sand sources in the empire as a consequence of a differing geological environment (Brems et al. 2012a, 2012b, Degryse 2014).

The application of strontium isotopes in ancient glass studies depends primarily on the assumption that the strontium in the glass is incorporated with the lime-bearing constituents (Wedepohl and Baumann 2000). It has been assumed that the contribution of a natron flux to the strontium balance of ancient glass is negligible (Freestone *et al.* 2003). Minor contributions may be attributed to feldspars or heavy minerals in the silica raw material (Freestone *et al.* 2003, Degryse *et al.* 2006). Where the lime in a natron glass was derived from Holocene beach shell, the strontium isotopic composition of the glass is that of modern seawater (Wedepohl and Baumann 2000; Freestone *et al.* 2003). Where the lime was derived from 'geologically aged' limestone, the Sr signature in the glass is a reflection of seawater at the time this limestone was deposited, possibly modified by diagentic alteration (Freestone *et al.* 2003).

The introduction of neodymium isotopes in glass studies is even more recent. The Nd in glass is likely to have originated from the heavy or non-quartz mineral content of the sand used as raw material. Nd isotopes are used as an indicator of the provenance of siliciclastic sediments in a range of sedimentary basin types. This offers great potential in tracing the origins of primary glass production. Degryse and Schneider (2008) have shown that samples of glass dating from the first to third century AD could not originate from the known region of primary glass production in Syro-Palestine and Egypt. Instead the Nd signature of the glass corresponded to a western Mediterranean or north-western European signature. Since then several studies have used Sr-Nd isotopic signatures to trace the source materials of ancient glass-making (e.g. Ganio *et al.* 2012), in particular in the Roman world (Degryse 2014).

Aims

In this study, a colourless Roman 'gold-glass' sample was analysed for its Sr-Nd isotopic composition.

The aim was to see whether the isotopic composition of this sample was consistent with standard Roman glass (e.g. as analysed by Degryse *et al.* 2009, Degryse 2014) and whether a primary origin for the colourless base glass used could be given. The analysis protocol and measurement conditions used were those of Ganio *et al.* (2012).

Result

Sample AN2007.26 had the following isotopic composition:

$^{87}Sr/^{86}Sr$	$^{143}Nd/^{144}Nd$	ε Nd
0,70905 ± 0.00008	0,512393 ± 0.00010	-4,8

Discussion

The Sr isotopic composition of the glass sample reflects a near Holocene signature, indicating the use of a lime stabiliser in the form of sea shell. The Nd signature of the glass is consistent with an origin of the silica raw materials for the production of this glass in the eastern Mediterranean (Brems *et al.* 2012b, Degryse, 2014). Therefore the Sr-Nd signature of the gold-glass studied corresponds well to what is assumed to be the typical composition of a colourless base glass with a primary origin in Roman Syro-Palestine.

References

Brems, D., Ganio, M., Latruwe, K., Balcaen, L., Carremans, M., Gimeno, D., Silvestri, A., Vanhaecke, F., Muchez, P., Degryse, P., 2012a. 'Isotopes on the beach Part 1 – Strontium isotope ratios as a provenance indicator for lime raw materials used in Roman glassmaking.' *Archaeometry* 55 (2), 214–34, doi: 10.1111/j.1475-4754.2012.00702.x.

Brems, D., Ganio, M., Latruwe, K., Balcaen, L., Carremans, M., Gimeno, D., Silvestri, A., Vanhaecke, F., Muchez, P., Degryse, P., 2012b. 'Isotopes on the beach Part 2 – Neodymium isotopic analysis for provenancing Roman glassmaking.' *Archaeometry* 55 (3), 449–64, doi: 10.1111/j.1475-4754.2012.00701.x.

Degryse, P., ed., 2014. *Glass making in the Greco-Roman World*. University Press: Leuven.

Degryse, P., Schneider, J., Haack, U., Lauwers, V., Poblome, J., Waelkens, M., Muchez, Ph., 2006. 'Evidence for glass "recycling" using Pb and Sr isotopic ratios and Sr-mixing lines: the case of early Byzantine Sagalassos.' *Journal of Archaeological Science* 33, 494–501.

Degryse, P. and Schneider, J., 2008. 'Pliny the Elder and Sr-Nd isotopes: tracing the provenance of raw materials for Roman glass production.' *Journal of Archaeological Science* 35, 1993–2000.

Degryse, P., Henderson, J., Hodgins, G., 2009. *Isotopes in Vitreous Materials*. University Press: Leuven.

Ganio, M., Boyen S., Brems D., Scott R., Foy D., Latruwe K., Molin G., Silvestri A., Vanhaecke F., Degryse P., 2012. 'Roman glass across the Empire: an elemental and isotopic characterization.' *Journal of Analytical Atomic Spectroscopy* 27 (5), 743–53, DOI: 10.1039/c2ja10355a.

Wedepohl, K. H. and Baumann, A., 2000. 'The use of marine molluskan shells for Roman glass and local raw glass production in the Eifel area (Western Germany).' *Naturwissenschaften* 87, 129–32.

Appendix 5

Table showing the results of stable isotope analysis of four marble epitaphs

Peter Ditchfield

Samples were removed in 2012 by specialist conservator Elspeth Morgan. Stable isotope analysis was undertaken by Peter Ditchfield of the Research Laboratory for Art and Archaeology, University of Oxford. In the table, the epitaphs are listed by accession numbers AN2007.54, 53, 56 and 59, respectively cats **49, 45, 53** and **50**. The epitaphs originate respectively from the Jewish catacomb at Vigna Randanini (cats **49** and **45**); the Christian cemetery at Aeclanum (cat. **53**) and Rome or environs (cat. **50**). All results are consistent with the isotopic signature of Carrara marble, with the exception of AN2007.56, cat. **53**, which falls within the signature of Proconnesian marble. For further discussion see above, pp. 108–9, fig. 57.

Lab number	Owner	Sample	Raw d13C	Raw d18O	*Corrected Raw d13C*	*Corrected Raw d18O*	Cold finger used	Beam pressure	Craig corrected d13C	Craig corrected d18O
A13/1659	08-May-13	NOCZ	2.211	-1.695	*2.111*	*-1.830*	no	7.74E-09	2.315	-1.836
A13/1660	08-May-13	NOCZ	2.297	-1.553	*2.196*	*-1.692*	no	6.94E-09	2.402	-1.699
A13/1661	08-May-13	NOCZ	2.132	-1.783	*2.034*	*-1.887*	yes	1.59E-08	2.235	-1.893
A13/1662	08-May-13	NOCZ	2.123	-1.891	*2.025*	*-1.997*	yes	1.51E-08	2.229	-2.004
A13/1663	Peter Ditchfield	AN2007-54 A	2.149	-1.423	*2.049*	*-1.557*	no	7.78E-09	2.240	-1.564
A13/1664	Peter Ditchfield	AN2007-54 B	2.167	-1.334	*2.067*	*-1.469*	no	7.74E-09	2.256	-1.475
A13/1665	Peter Ditchfield	AN2007-54 C	1.814	-1.391	*1.714*	*-1.526*	no	7.71E-09	1.881	-1.531
A13/1666	Peter Ditchfield	AN2007-53	2.512	-1.967	*2.412*	*-2.102*	no	7.71E-09	2.646	-2.109
A13/1667	Peter Ditchfield	AN2007-56	2.910	-3.997	*2.809*	*-4.133*	no	7.52E-09	3.139	-4.143
A13/1668	Peter Ditchfield	AN2007-59	2.621	-1.449	*2.521*	*-1.583*	no	7.74E-09	2.745	-1.591
A13/1669	08-May-13	NOCZ	2.298	-1.603	*2.198*	*-1.738*	no	7.72E-09	2.405	-1.744
A13/1670	08-May-13	NOCZ	2.039	-1.901	*1.937*	*-2.064*	no	3.94E-09	2.137	-2.071
A13/1671	08-May-13	NOCZ	2.232	-1.670	*2.131*	*-1.813*	no	6.42E-09	2.337	-1.819

Standards

x mean	2.19	-1.73	2.09	-1.86
sigma	0.10	0.14	0.10	0.13
diff	-0.10	-0.13		

Appendix 6

Mortar samples from funerary inscriptions in the Wilshere Collection

Graham Morgan

Mortar samples were removed from the rear surfaces of five marble funerary slabs by the consultant stone conservator Elspeth Morgan in December 2012. All samples were examined microscopically and analysed where enough sample was present.

1. AN 2007.49 (**52**) top edge
   Pale grey with white lime, charcoal, angular to sub-angular quartz grains and black mica flakes – analysed

2. AN 2007.54 (**49**) bottom edge
   Brown to grey with black mica, quartz grains, white lime and charcoal

3. AN 2007.56 (**53**) top edge
   Buff with quartz and charcoal

4. AN 2007.57 (**46**) back
   Buff with quartz, white lime and black mica

5. AN 2007.57 (**46**) bottom edge
   Brown to buff with white lime, angular to sub-angular quartz, black mica and charcoal – analysed

6. AN 2007.57 (**46**) top edge
   Buff-grey-red with quartz, red 'brick' dust and white lime

7. AN 2007.60 (**55**) back
   Pale grey with angular to sub-angular quartz, white lime, black and white mica, charcoal and traces of red 'brick' dust – analysed

All the samples were tested for sulphates using the barium chloride method. Only no.4 showed definite traces, while no.6 was sulphate-free and the rest showed just traces. This results suggest contamination from the 'recent' plaster backing rather than the addition of gypsum in the original lime mortar mix.

Micro-carbonate determination

Three samples were large enough for carbonate determination using the Jedrzejewska method, giving values approximating to the lime content. The percentage of other soluble material relates to anything else which dissolved in the acid, such as iron and alumina (Jedrzejewska 1960).

no	wt	mls	carbonate	%	residue	%	% other sol.
1	0.3823	21	0.08569	22.4	0.23	60	17.6
5	0.2125	19	0.07753	36.5	0.0951	45	18.5
7	0.5217	62	0.253	48.5	0.211	40.5	11
standard	0.3387	83	0.0040989/ml	100			

Discussion

The analysed samples are fairly typical lime plaster mixes. They tend to a rather lime-rich mixture, as might be expected when they were used to bond the plaques on to a wall. Most lime plasters have about 20–30 per cent lime. The aggregate residues seem to be mostly quartz sand with silt and traces of mica. This should relate to the local geology. Nos 1 and 5 come from the Vigna Randanini catacomb, located on the Via Appia near Rome, while no.7, richer in lime, comes from Aeclanum near Avellino, in central southern Italy. The fine grey silt, particularly with the red 'brick-like' material, may be derived from the lime kiln residues, but it also resembles the volcanic ash found in Roman mortars. The deliberate addition of volcanic ash, which greatly improved the strength and water-resisting properties of the lime mixture, was commonly used in Rome in the first century BC, a fact noted by Vitruvius, who called the substance 'pit sand'. Various types of volcanic ash can be found around Rome including black, red and grey types (Morgan 1960).
The use of these various materials is discussed at length in my work on Romano-British Mortars and Plasters (Morgan 1992).

Graham Morgan
Leicester, 2013
Updated June 2017

Bibliography

Jedrzejewska, H., 1960. 'Old mortars in Poland: A new method of investigation.' *Studies in Conservation* vol. 5, pp 132–8

Morgan, M. H., 1960. *Vitruvius: The Ten Books on Architecture*. Dover: New York

Morgan, G. C., 1992. 'Romano-British Mortars and Plasters.' Leicester Research Archive, http://hdl.handle.net/2381/27695; British Library EThOS Service at http://ethos.bl.uk.

Abbreviations

Full references are given in the endnotes and/or bibliographical entries.

AE	*L'Année Epigraphique*
CCSL	*Corpus Christianorum Series Latina*
CIJ	*Corpus Inscriptionum Iudaicarum*
CIL	*Corpus Inscriptionum Latinarum*
CSEL	*Corpus Scriptorum Ecclesiasticorum Latinorum*
EDB	Epigraphic Database Bari (3rd–8th century Christian epigraphy)
EDCS	Epigraphik Datenbank Clauss/Selby, Frankfurt
EDR	Epigraphic Database Roma (Latin)
ICUR	*Inscriptiones Christianae Urbis Romae septimo saeculo anteriores*
IG	*Inscriptiones Graecae*
ILCV	*Inscriptiones Latinae Christianae Veteres*
ILS	*Inscriptiones Latinae selectae*
IRNL	*Inscriptiones Regni Neapolitani Latinae*
JIWE	Jewish Inscriptions of Western Europe
MANN	Museo Archeologico Nazionale, Napoli
MGH AA	*Monumenta Germaniae Historiae inde ab anno Christi quingentesimo usque ad annum millesimum et quingentesimum auctores antiquissimi.*
PIAC	*Pontificium Institutum Archaeologiae Christianae, Rome*

Bibliography

Primary sources

Ambrose, *De Helia et ieiunio*. In K. Schenkl, ed., 1897, *Sancti Ambrosi Opera,* vol.2, *CSEL* 32, no.2; English translation by M. J. A. Buck, 1929. *Patristic Studies* 19.

Athenaeus, *Deipnosophistae* II. C. B. Gulick, ed., 1971. London.

Augustine, *Confessions* 6, 2, 2. J. J. O'Donnell and A. E. Mahoney, eds, *c.*1999 (electronic edition). Stoa Consortium Perseus Project. Medford, Massachusetts.

Augustine, *Epistles and Sermons.* In G. Partzen and S. Lössi, eds, 2008, *Sancti Aurelii Augustinii Sermoones in epistolas apostolicas.* Turnhout.

Augustine, *Commentary on Psalm 21.* In E. Dekkers and J. Fraipont, eds, 1956, *Enarationes in Psalmos I-L, CCSL* 38.

Basil, *Address to young men, on how they might derive benefit from Greek literature. PG* 31: 563–90. English translation by R. J. Deferrari and M. R. P. McGuire, 1934. *St Basil: the Letters IV*: 378–435. Cambridge, Massachusetts. 5. 11–14.

Cassiodorus, *Variae.* T. Mommsen, ed., 1894. *Cassiodori Senatoris Variae, MGH AA* 12.

Cicero, *Tusculanae Disputationes.* J. E. King, ed., 2014 (electronic edition). Cambridge, Massachusetts.

Flavius Josephus, *Judaean Antiquities* 3: 144–6. L. H. Feldman, ed., 2004. Boston.

Flavius Josephus, *De bello iudaico.* G. A. Williamson and E. M. Smallwood, eds., 1981. New York.

Jerome, *Epistles.* 2010 (electronic resource). Turnhout.

Paulinus of Nola, *Epistulae* 29. In G. de Hartel, ed., 1999, *CSEL* 29, second edition: v.1. Vienna.

Paulinus of Nola, *Poemae.* 2010 (electronic resource). Turnhout.

Strabo, *Geographia.* H. L. Jones and J. R. Sitlington Sterret, eds, 2004. Cambridge, Massachusetts.

Talmud, *Sanhedrin x. Targum to Isaiah.* J. Schlachter, H. Freedman and I. Epstein, eds, 1990. New York.

Tertullian, *Adversus Iudaeos.* E. Kroymann, ed., 1954, *CCSL* 2: 1337–98. Turnhout.

Tertullian, *De baptism.* J. W. Borleffs, ed., 1954, *CCSL* 1: 275–96.

Zeno, *Tractatus.* B. Lofstedt, ed., 1971, *CCSL* 22: 107–19.

Secondary sources

Acerbi, A., 1989. *L'Ascensione di Isaia: cristologia e profetismo in Siria nei primi decennia del II secolo*. Milan.

Adams, J. N., 2003. *Bilingualism and the Latin Language*. Cambridge.

Agnello, G., 1957. Il Museo Biscari di Catania nella storia della cultura illuministica italiana del settecento. *Archivio storico per la Sicilia orientale* X: 142–59.

Alföldi, A., 1943. *Die Kontorniaten*. Magyar Numizmatiki Társulat. Budapest.

Amedick, R., 1991. ASR *I*, 4, *Vita Privata auf Sarkophagen*. Berlin.

Angerstorfer, A., 2012. 'Antike jüdische Grabinschriften aus christlicher Zeit (ca. 100–500 n.Chr.). Spuren von Hoffnung auf eine Auferstehung der Toten und die "kommende Welt"'. In J. Dresken-Weiland, A. Angerstorfer and A. Merkt, eds, *Himmel-Paradies-Schalom: Tod und Jenseits in christlichen und jüdischem Grabinschriften der Antike*. Regensburg.

Armellini, M., 1880. *Il cimitero di S. Agnese sulla via Nomentana*. Rome.

Arringhi, P., 1651. *Roma subterranea novissima*. Rome.

Aurigemma, S., 1960. *I Mosaici della Tripolitania. L'Italia in Africa: Le scoperte archeologiche (a. 1911– a.1943): Tripolitania*, vol.1: *Monumenti d'arte decorative*. Parte Prima: *I mosaici*. Rome.

Balon, E. K., 1995. 'Origin and domestication of the wild carp, *Cyprinus Carpio*: from Roman gourmets to the swimming flowers.' *Aquaculture* 129: 3–48.

Balsamo, P. and Wright Vaughan, T., 1810. *A view of the present state of Sicily: its rural economy, population and produce, particularly in the county of Modica*. London.

Balty, J., 1995. *Mösaiques antiques du Proche-Orient: chronologie, iconographie, interpretation*. Paris.

Bank, A. V., 1977–8. *Byzantine art in the collections of Soviet museums*. Leningrad.

Barag, D., 1971. 'Gold-Glass', in *Encyclopedia Judaica*, vol.7: cols 606–8. Jerusalem.

Barag, D., 1987. 'Recent Important Epigraphic Discoveries related to the History of Glassmaking in the Roman Period.' *Annales de l'Association Internationale pour l'Histoire du Verre* 10: 109–16. Madrid-Segovia 1985; Amsterdam 1987.

Barag, D., 2005. 'Alexandrian and Judaean Glass in the Price Edict of Diocletian.' *Journal of Glass Studies* 47: 184–6.

Bardill, J., 2012. *Constantine: Divine Emperor of the Christian Golden Age*. Cambridge.

Bargebuhr, F. P., 1991. *The paintings of the "new" catacomb of the Via Latina and the struggle of Christianity against paganism*. Heidelberg.

Bayet, J., 1926. *Les origines de l'Hercule romain*. Paris.

Benoit, F., 1954. *Sarcophages paléochrétiens d'Arles et de Marseille*. Paris.

Ben-Sasson, R., 2009. 'Fish-ta(i)les: Jewish gold-glasses revisited.' In K. Kogman-Appel and M. Meyer, eds, *Between Judaism and Christianity: art historical essays in honour of Elisheva (Elisabeth) Revel-Neher*: 25–38. Leiden.

Bernheimer, R., 1952. 'The Martyrdom of Isaiah.' *The Art Bulletin* 34: 19–34.

Bertini Calosso, A., 1907. 'Gli affreschi della grotta del Salvatore presso Vallerano.' *Archivio della Regia Società Romana di Storia Patria* XXX: 189–241.

Besserman, L., 1979. *The Legend of Job in the Middle Ages*. Cambridge, Massachusetts.

Bettiolo, P. and Norelli, E., 1995. *Ascensio Isaiae*. Series Apocryphorum, 7. Turnhout.

Bielefeld, D., 1997. *Stadtrömische Eroten-Sarkophage. Faszikel 2: Weinlese und Ernteszenen*. Berlin.

Bignami Odier, J., (1973). 'La Bibliothèque Vaticane de Sixte IV è Pie XI. Recherches sur l'histoire des collections de manuscrits avec la collaboration de José Ruysschaert.' *Studi e Testi* 272: 185–90. Vatican City.

Bisconti, F., 1983. 'Martirio (iconografia).' *Dizionario Patristico e di Antichità Cristiane II*: cols 2152–4.

Bisconti, F., 1992. 'Altre note di iconografia paradisiaca.' *Bessarione* 9: 89–117.

Bisconti, F., 1996. 'Genesi e primi sviluppi dell'arte cristiana: i luoghi, i modi, i temi.' In *Dalla terra alle genti. La diffusione del Cristianesimo nei primi secoli*: 71–93. Milan.

Bisconti, F., 2001–2. 'Vetri dorati ed arte monumentale.' *Rendiconti. Atti della Pontificia Accademia Romana* 74: 177–93.

Biville, F., 1989. 'Les héllenismes dans les inscriptions latines paiennes de la Gaule (1e–4e siècles après J.-C.).' *Actes de la table ronde tenue au CERGR les 5 et 7 octobre 1988 (Université de Lyon)*: 99–115. Paris.

Bodel, J. 2008. From *Columbaria* to Catacombs. In L. Brink, O. P. and Deborah Green, eds, *Commemorating the Dead. Texts and Artifacts in Context*: 177–242. Berlin, New York.

von Boeselager, D., 2012. 'Römische Gläser an der Luxemburger Straße in Köln.' *Kölner Jahrbucher* 45: 7–526.

Boldetti, M. A., 1720. *Osservazioni sopra i cimiteri dei SS. Martiri ed antichi cristiani di Roma*. Rome.

Bolten, J., 1937. *Die Imago Clipeata, ein Beitrag zur Porträt- und Typengeschichte*. Paderborn.

Borg, B. E., 2013. *Crisis and ambition: tombs and burial customs in third century CE Rome*. Oxford.

Borg, B. E. and Witschel, C., eds, 2001. 'Veränderungen in Repräsentationsverhalten der römischen Eliten während des 3. Jhr. n. Chr.' In G. Alföldy and S. Panciera, eds, *Inschriftliche Denkmäler als medien der Selbstdarstellung in der römischen Welt*: 47–120. Stuttgart.

Bosio, A., 1632. *Roma Sotterranea*. Opera postuma compita, disposta & accresciuta dal M. R. P. G. Severani. Rome.

Boutry, P., 2002. 'Gaetano Marini (1740–1815), s.v. Souverain et pontife.' *Recherches prosoprographiques sur la curie romaine à l'âge de la restauration (1814–1846)*: 583–5. École Française de Rome, Rome.

Bovini, G. and Brandenburg, H., 1967. *Repertorium der christlich-antiken Sarkophage*. Band 1: *Rom und Ostia*. 2 vols. Mainz.

Bowersock, G., 2005. 'Peter and Constantine.' In W. Tronzo, ed., *St Peter's in the Vatican*: 5–15. Cambridge.

Brandenburg, H. and Vescovo, A., 2005. *Ancient Churches of Rome from the fourth to the seventh century: the dawn of Christian architecture in the west*. Turnhout.

Brown, P., 1981. *The cult of the saints: its rise and function in Latin Christianity*. Chicago.

Brown, P., 2012. *Through the eye of a needle: wealth, the fall of Rome, and the making of Christianity in the West, 350–550 AD*. Princeton.

Brusin, G., 1993. *Inscriptiones Aquileiae III*. Udine.

Brydone, P., 1840. *A Tour through Sicily and Malta*. Edinburgh.

Bühl, G., 1995. *Constantinopolis und Roma: Stadtpersonifikationen der Spätantike*. Zurich.

Buonocore, M., 1989. 'Corrispondenze epigrafiche nei codici vaticani latini 9042–9060 di Gaetano Marini.' *Miscellanea Bibliothecae Apostolicae Vaticanae III*: 107–20. Biblioteca Apostolica Vaticana, Vatican City.

Buonocore, M., 1991. 'Miscellanea epigrafica e codicibus Bibliothecae Vaticanae.' *Epigrafica. Rivista Italiana d'Epigrafia LII*: 215–34.

Buonocore, M., 1997. *Appunti di topografia romana nei Codici Lanciani della BAV*. Biblioteca Apostolica Vaticana, Vatican City.

Buonocore, M., 1999. 'Ida Calabi Limentani e la storia degli studi epigrafici. Riflessioni su un metodo da seguire.' *Acme. Annali della Facoltà di Lettere e Filosofia dell'Università degli Studi di Milano* 52, 3: 80–1.

Buonocore, M., 2000. 'Miscellanea epigraphica e codicibus Bibliothecae Vaticanae, XIV.' *Epigraphica* 62: 213–38.

Buonocore, M., 2001. 'Per un'edizione dei codici vaticani latini 9071–9074 di Gaetano Marini: l'epigrafia cristiana dalle origini fino all'anno mille.' *Miscellanea Bibliothecae Apostolicae*

Vaticanae, VIII. Biblioteca Apostolica Vaticana: 45–71. Vatican City.

Buonocore, M., 2007. 'Gaetano Marini e la genesi del primo corpus delle iscrizioni cristiane latine e greche.' *Acta XII Congressus Internationalis Epigraphiae Grecae et Latinae, Barcelona*: 203–9.

Buonocore, M., ed., 2015. *Gaetano Marini (1742–1815) protagonista della cultura europea. Scritti per il bicentenario della morte*, vols.I–II. Biblioteca Apostolica Vaticana ST 492–3. Vatican City.

Buonocore, M., 2015. 'Gaetano Marini e i suoi corrispondenti: i codici Vat. Lat. 9042–9060.' In M. Buonocore, ed., 1: 105–226.

Calabi Limentani, I., 1987. 'Note su classificazione ed indici epigrafici dallo Smezio al Morcelli: antichità, retorica, critica?' *Epigraphica* 49: 177–202.

Cameron, A., 1996. 'Orfitus and Constantia: a note on Roman gold-glasses.' *Journal of Roman Archaeology* 9: 295–301.

Cardi, G. 1909. *Iano Planco medico riminese e la sua scuola: comunicazione letta alla 1a riunione annuale della Società italiana di storia critica delle scienze mediche e naturali, Faenza*. October 1908. Faenza.

Carletti, C., 1975. 'I tre giovani ebrei di Babilonia nell'arte cristiana.' *Quaderni di Vet.Chr. 12*.

Carusi, E., ed., 1916–40. *Lettere inedite di Gaetano Marini*: vol.1, *Lettere a Guid'Antonio Zanetti*; vol.2, *Lettere a Giovanni Fantuzzi*; vol.3, *Appendici: due lettere a G. A. Zanetti; lettere di Giovanni Fantuzzi a Gaetano Marini*. Rome.

Cavallari, F. S. and Holm, A., 1883. *Topografia archeologia di Siracusa*. Palermo.

Chaffers, W., 1866. 'Glass: its manufacture and examples.' *The Art Journal*, n.s.5: 278–80.

Charles, R. H., 1919. *The Ascension of Isaiah*. London.

Christern-Briesenick, B., 2003. *Repertorium der christlich-antiken Sarkophage III. Frankreich, Algerien, Tunisien*. Mainz.

Chioffi, L., 1999. *Caro: il mercato della carne nell'Occidente romano: reflessi epigafici ed iconografici*. Rome.

Ciampini, G., 1699. *Vetera Monimenta*, 2 vols. Rome.

Clark, G., 1993. *Women in late antiquity: pagan and Christian lifestyles*. New York and Oxford.

Collon , S., 1940. 'Remarques sur les quartiers juifs de la Rome antique.' *Mélanges de l'École française de Rome* 57: 72–94.

Conti, M., 1998. *The life and works of Potamius of Lisbon: a biographical and literary study with English translation and a complete commentary on the extant works of Potamius*. Turnhout.

Cooley, A. E., 2012. *The Cambridge Manual of Latin Inscriptions*. Cambridge.

Cooley, A. E., 2017. *Ashmolean Latin Inscriptions Catalogue*. Ashmolean Museum, Oxford: Online Catalogue.

Cooper, K., 2007. *The Fall of the Roman Household*. Cambridge.

Curran, J. R., 2000, 2002 (second edition). *Pagan City and Christian Capital. Rome in the Fourth Century*. Oxford.

Curran, J. R., 2010. *Pagan City and Christian Capital. Rome in the Fourth Century*. Oxford scholarship online.

Cussans, J. E., 1870–81. *A History of Hertfordshire*. London.

D'Ambra, E., 2006. *Roman Women*. Cambridge Introduction to Roman Civilisation. Cambridge.

D'Ambrosio, A. and Giammellini, R., 2001. 'Giuseppe de Criscio a novant'anni dalla morte.' *Bollettino Flegreo* ser.3, 14: 7–13.

Darsy, F., 1961. *Santa Sabina (le chiese di Roma illustrate)*. Rome.

Dassman, E., 1970. 'Das Apsismosaik von S. Pudenziana in Rom. Philosophische, imperiale und theologische Aspekte in einem Christusbild am Beginn des 5 Jhr.' *Römische Quartalschrift* 65.1: 67–81.

De Benedictis, C., 1991. *Per la storia del collezionismo italiano. Fonti e documenti*. Florence.

De Bruyne, L., 1936. 'Nuove ricerche iconografiche sui mosaici dell'arco trionfale di S. Maria Maggiore.' *Rivista di archeologia cristiana* 13: 239–69.

De Bruyne, L., 1970. 'La cappella greca di Priscilla.' *Rivista di archeologia cristiana* 46: 291–330.

De Callatäy, F., 2016. 'Il venditore d'antichità by Vincenzo Capobianchi, 1880; possibly the most scholarly work of the neo-Pompeian painting (*sic*)'. *Anabases* 23.2: 47–73.

Deckers, J. et al., 1987. 'Die Katakombe "Santi Marcellino e Pietro"'. *Repertorium der Malareien*. Vatican City and Münster.

Deferrari, R. J. and Maguire, M. R. P., eds and trans., 1934. *Saint Basil. The Letters*, vol.4. London and Cambridge.

Degryse, P. and Schneider, J., 2008. 'Pliny the Elder and Sr-Nd isotopes: tracing the provenance of raw materials for Roman glass.' *Journal of Archaeological Science* 35 (7): 1993–2000.

Deichmann, F. W., 1969. *Ravenna. Haupstadt des spätantiken Abendlandes. Geschichte und Monumente*, 1. Teil. Wiesbaden.

Deichmann, F. W., 1974. *Ravenna. Hauptstadt des spätantiken Abendlandes. Kommentar*, 2. Teil. Wiesbaden.

Deichmann, F. W., 1993. *Archeologia Cristiana*. Rome.

Delehaye, H., 1904. 'Castor et Pollux dans les legends hagiographiques.' *Analecta Bollandiana*: 427–32.

Delehaye, H., 1907. *The Legends of the Saints: an introduction to hagiography*, V. M. Crawford, trans. London.

Deliyannis, D. M., 2010. *Ravenna in late antiquity*. Cambridge.

Dello Russo, J., 2011. 'The Discovery and Exploration of the Jewish Catacomb of the Vigna Randanini in Rome: Records, Research and Excavations through 1895.' *Roma Subterranea Judaica* 5. International Catacomb Society. Boston.

Dello Russo, J., 2012. 'Raffaele Garrucci and the Jewish Catacombs of Rome.' *Roma Subterranea Judaica* 6. International Catacomb Society. Boston.

De Mély, F., 1926. 'Le medallion de la croix du musée chrétien de Brescia.' *Arethuse* 10 (Jan.): 1–9.

Denzey, N., 2007. *The bone gatherers: the lost worlds of early Christian women*. Boston.

De Rossi, G. B., ed., 1857–61, 1888, 1915. *Inscriptiones Christianae Urbis Romae septimo saeculo antiquiores*, with *Supplementum*. Rome.

De Rossi, G. B., 1872. 'Un singolare marmo votivo cristiano scritto e figurato.' *Bullettino di archeologia Cristiana*, second series, anno 3: 36–40.

De Rossi, G. B., 1864, 1866, 1868, 1870. Various mentions of Wilshere and his collection in the *Bullettino di Archeologia Cristiana*, vols ii, iv, vi, vii and x. [Page numbers are given in the footnotes to the text.]

De Rossi, G. B., 1877. *La Roma sotterranea Cristiana*, vol.3. Rome.

De Ruyt, C., 1983. *Macellum: marché alimentaire des Romains*. Louvain-la-Neuve.

De Santis, P., 1994. 'Elementi di corredo nei sepolcri delle catacomb romane: l'esempio della regione di Leone e della galleria Bb nella catacomba di Commodilla.' *Vetera Christianorum* 31: 23–51.

Dessau, H., 1892–1916. *Inscriptiones Latinae selectae*. Berlin.

Diefenbach, S., 2007. *Römische Erinnerungsräume: Heiligenmemoria und kollektive Identitäten im Rom des 3. bis 5. Jahrhunderts n. Chr.* Millennium-Studien 11. Berlin and New York.

Diehl, E., ed., 1925–67. *Inscriptiones Latinae Christianae veteres*. Berlin.

Dietz, K., 1987. 'Passauer Viehhändler. Ein *collegium bubulariorum* auf einer Inschrift aus Passau.' *Chiron* 17: 383–93.

Dinkler, F. and Brandenburg, H., 1970. *Der Einzug in Jerusalem: ikonographische Untersuchungen im Anschluss an ein bisher unbekanntes Sarkophagfragment*. Opladen, Leverkusen.

Dixon, S., 2001. *Reading Roman women: sources, genres and real life*. London.

Dölger, F. J., 1922–43. *Ichthus: das Fisch-Symbol in frühchristlicher Zeit*. Münster.

Donati, A., ed., 2000. *Pietro e Paolo. La storia, il culto, la memoria nei primi secoli*. Milan.

Donato, M. P., 2000. *Accademie romane: una storia sociale, 1671–1824*. Naples.

Doni, G. B., 1731. *Inscriptiones antiquae nunc primae editae*. Florence.

Dothan, M., 1983. *Hammath Tiberias: early synagogues and the Hellenistic and Roman remains*. Jerusalem.

Dresken-Weiland, J., 1998. *Repertorium der christlich-antiken Sarkophage, Band 2. Italien mit einem Nachtrag Rom und Ostia*. Wiesbaden.

Dufresne, C., ed., 1884–7. *Glossarium mediae et infimae latinitatis*. London.

Dumas, A., ed., 1981. *Liber sacramentorum Gellonensis*. Corpus Christianorum. Series Latina 159A. Turnhout.

Dunbabin, K. M. D., 1999. *Mosaics of the Greek and Roman World*. Cambridge.

Duppa, R., 1829, second edition. *Travels on the Continent, Sicily and the Lipari Islands*. London.

Duval, Y., 1988. *Auprès des saints corps et âme: l'inhumation "ad sanctos" dans la chrétienté d'Orient et d'Occident du IIIe au VIIe siècle*. Paris.

Elsner, J., 2003. 'Archaeologies and Agendas: Reflections on Late Ancient Jewish Art and Early Christian Art.' *Journal of Roman Studies* XCIII: 114–28.

Entwistle, C. and James, L., 2013. *New Light on Old Glass: Recent Research on Byzantine Glass and Mosaics.* British Museum Research Publication 179. London.

Entwistle, C. and Finney, P. C., 2013. Late antique glass pendants in the British Museum.' In Entwistle and James, 2013: 131–77.

Engemann, J., 1968–9. 'Bermerkungen zu spätrömischen Glasern mit Goldfoliendekor.' *Jarhbuch für Antike und Christentum* 11–12: 7–25.

Evans, H., 1993. 'An early Christian sarcophagus from Rome Lost and Found.' *Journal of the Metropolitan Musuem of Art, New York* 28: 77–84.

Faedo, L., 1978. 'Per una classificazione preliminare del vetri dorati tardoromani.' *Annali della Scuola Normale Superiore di Pisa*, Serie III, 8, 3: 1025–70.

Fantuzzi, G., 1789. *Notizie degli scrittori bolognesi.* Bologna.

Fasola, U. M. and Mancinelli, F., 2007. *Guide to the catacombs of Rome.* Florence.

Feld, O., 1992. 'Das apsismosaik in S. Pudenziana als Bild der Gemeinschaft mit Christus.' In G. Casper, B. Müller and J. Biemer, eds, *Gemeinsem Kirche sein. Theorie und Praxis der Communio. Festschrift der Theologischen Fakultät der Universität Freiburg i. Br. für Erzbischof Oskar Saier*: 253–62. Freiburg.

Felle, A. E., 1993. *Inscriptiones Christianae Italiae Septimo Saeculo Antiquiores VIII. Regio II Hirpini.* Bari.

Ferrara F., 1829. *Storia di Catania sino alla fine del secolo XVIII.* Catania.

Ferretto, G., 1942. *Note storico-bibliografiche di archeologia Cristiana*. Rome.

Ferrua, A., 1936. Epigraphica Ebraica. *Civ.Cattolica* 87.3: 461–73; 87.4: 127–37.

Ferrua, A., 1941. Addenda et corrigenda al CIJ. *Epigraphica* 3: 30–88.

Ferrua, A., 1941. Epigrafia sicula pagana e Cristiana. *Rivista di Archeologia Cristiana* 18: 151–243.

Ferrua, A., 1942. *Epigrammata Damasiana.* Vatican City.

Ferrua, A., 1974. ZESES è ZHCHIC o ZHCAIC? *Aevum* 48: 329–34.

Ferrua, A., 1981. *Nuove correzioni alla silloge del Diehl ILCV.* Vatican City.

Ferrua, A. and Carletti, C., 1985. *Damaso e I martiri di Rome: anno Damasi saeculari XVI.* Vatican City.

Fine, S., 2005. 'The Temple Menorah: –Where is It?' *Biblical Archaeology Review* 31: 4, 18–25, 62–3.

Fine, S. 2007. 'Jewish art and biblical exegesis in the Greco-Roman world.' In J. Spier, ed., *Picturing the Bible*: 25–49. Kimball Art Museum, Fort Worth, Texas.

Fine, S., 2016. *The Menorah: from the Bible to modern Israel.* Cambridge, Massachusetts.

Fiocchi Nicolai, V., 1988. 'I cimiteri paleocristiani del Lazio, 1. Etruria meridionale.' *Monumenti di antichità Cristiana* 10.

Fiocchi Nicolai, V., 1998. 'Premessa, in memoria di Enrico Stevenson nel 1. centennaio delle morte.' *Rivista di Archeologia Cristiana* 74: 7–13.

Fiocchi Nicolai, V., 2001. *Strutture funerarie ed edifice di culto paleocristiani di Roma dal IV al VI secolo.* Vatican City.

Fiocchi Nicolai, V., Bisconti, F. and Mazzoleni, D. 2009. *The Christian Catacombs of Rome. History, Decoration, Inscriptions.* Third edition in English, Cristina Carla Stella and Lori-Ann Touchette, trans. Regensburg.

Foltiny, S., 1974. 'Spätrömische und völkerwanderungszeitliche Silberlöffel aus der alten Welt im Metropolitan Museum of Art in New York.' In *Opuscula Iosepho Kastelic sexagenario dicata.* Situla, vols 14–15. National Museum of Slovenia, Ljubljana.

Freeman, J. A., 2015. 'The Good Shepherd and the Enthroned Ruler: a Reconsideration of Imperial Iconography in the Early Church.' In L. M. Jefferon and R. M. Jensen, eds., *The Art of Empire. Christian Art in its Imperial Context*: 159–96. Minneapolis.

Freestone, I., Gorin-Rosen, Y. and Hughes, M. J., 2000. 'Primary Glass from Israel and the Production of Glass in Late Antiquity.' In M.- D. Nenna, ed., *La Route du Verre. Ateliers primaires et secondaires du second millénaire av. J-C. au Moyen Âge*, 2000: 65–83. Lyon.

Frey, J.-B., 1936 (second edition, B. Lifshitz, ed., 1975). *Corpus Inscriptionum Iudaicarum. Receuil des inscriptions juives qui vont du IIIe siècle av. J.-C. au VIIe siècle de notre ère, I: Europe.* Sussidi allo studio delle antichità cristiane, I. Vatican City.

Fusco, M. A., 1981. 'La formazione della società promotrice di belle arti di Napoli 1860–1866.' In F. Haskell, ed., *Saloni, gallerie, musei e la loro influenza sullo sviluppo dell'arte dei secoli XIX e XX. Atti del Congresso Internazionale di Storia dell'Arte* 7: 157–62. Bologna.

Gambino, N., 1982. *Aeclanum cristiana.* Lioni.

Gardner, J. F., 1986. *Women in Roman law and society.* London.

Garrucci, R., 1858, 1864 (second edition). *Vetri ornati di figure in oro trovati nei cimiteri dei cristiani primitivi di Roma e raccolti e spiegati da Raffaele Garrucci.* Rome.

Garrucci, R., 1861. *Nuova interpretazione di un vetro cimiteriale ornato di figure d'oro.* Tipografia Civiltà Cattolica I, fasc. 288: 692–703. Rome.

Garrucci, R., 1862. *Cimitero degli antichi Ebrei scoperto recentemente in Vigna Randanini.* Rome.

Garrucci, R., 1862–3. *Descrizione dei vetri ornati di figure in oro appartenenti al sig. Tommaso Capobianchi negoziante d'antichità in via del Babuino n. 152.* Rome. Undated, but catalogues glasses from the Recupero Collection sold in Catania in 1862; a copy is registered in the Italian State Archive in July 1863.

Garrucci, R., 1865. *Dissertazioni archeologiche di vario argomento* ii. Rome.

Garrucci, R., 1872–81. *Storia dell'arte cristiana nei primi otto secoli della chiesa e corredata della collezione di tutti i monumenti di pittura e scultura incisi in rame su cinquecento tavole ed illustrati.* Six volumes; see especially vol.III (1876). Prato.

Gasperoni, G., 1942. 'Il contributo di Gaetano Marini al movimento erudito e storico del Settecento.' *Accademie e Biblioteche d'Italia* XVII: 78–90.

Giacomelli, A., 1944. 'Fantuzzi, Giovanni.' In *Dizionario Biografico degli Italiani* 44: 713–23. Istituto della Enciclopedia Italiana, Rome.

Goodenough, E. R., 1953–68. *Jewish symbols in the Graeco-Roman period.* Bollingen Series XXXVII, 13 vols. Princeton.

Gori, A. F., 1727–43. *Inscriptiones antiquae in Etruriae urbibus extantes.* Florence.

Gorin-Rosen, Y., 2000. 'The Ancient Glass Industry in Israel: Summary of the finds and new discoveries.' In M.-D. Nenna, ed., *La Route du Verre. Ateliers primaires et secondaires du second millénaire av. J-C. au Moyen Âge*, 2000:: 49–63. Lyon.

Gottschalk, R., 2015. *Spätrömische Gräber im Umland von Köln.* Mainz.

Grabar, A., 1967. *The beginnings of Christian art, 200–395.* S. Gilbert and J. Emmons, trans. London.

Grabar, A., 1968. *Christian Iconography, a study of its origins.* Princeton.

Grabar, A., 1969 (revised UK edition). *Christian Iconography, a study of its origins.* London.

Grig, L., 2004a. *Making Martyrs in Late Antiquity. London.*

Grig, L., 2004b. 'Portraits, pontiffs and the Christianisation of fourth-century Rome.' PBSR 72: 203–30.

Gruter, Jan (Gruterus), 1602–3. *Inscriptiones antiquae totius orbis romani.* Heidelberg.

Guarini, R., 1812. *Richerche sull'antica città di Eclano.* Naples.

Guarini, R., 1834. *Alcuni suggelli antici.* Naples.

Gude, M., 1731. *Antiquae inscriptiones quum Graecae, tum Latinae, olim a Marquado Gudio collectae; nuper a Ioanne Koolio digestae hortatu consilioque Ioannis Georgii Graevii; tunc a Francisco Hesselio editae cum adnotationibus eorum.* Leuven.

Guerrini, L., 1982. *Palazzo Mattei di Giove: le antichità.* Rome.

Guidetti, P. and Micheli, F., 2007. 'Ancient art serving marine conservation.' *Frontiers in Ecology and the Environment* 9, 7: 374–5.

Guyon, J., 1974. 'La vente des tombes à travers l'épigraphie de la Rome chrétienne (IIIe – VIIe siècles): le role des *fossores, mansionarii, praepositi* et prêtres.' *Mélanges de l'École Française de Rome* 86: 549–96.

Guyon, J., 1987. *La cimitière aux deux lauriers.* École Française de Rome. Rome.

Hachlili, R., 1977. 'The zodiac in ancient Jewish art: representation and significance.' *Bulletin of the American Schools of Oriental Research* 228: 61–77.

Hachlili, R., 1988. *Ancient Jewish art and archaeology in the land of Israel.* Leiden.

Hachlili, R., 1998. *Ancient Jewish Art and Archaeology in the Diaspora.* Leiden.

Hachlili, R., 2000. *The Menorah, the ancient seven-armed candelabrum. Origin, form and significance.* Leiden, Boston and Cologne.

Hachlili, R., 2001. *The menorah, the ancient seven-branched candelabrum: origin, form and significance.* Leiden.

Hanfmann, G. M. A., 1951. 'Socrates and Christ.' *Harvard Studies in Classical Philology* 60: 205–33.

Hansen, J., 1820. *Route of Lieutenant-General Sir Miles Nightingall, K.C.B., overland from India, in a series of letters from Captain Hansen, late Assistant Quarter-Master-General with the Field Army of the Madras Establishment.* London.

Harden, D. B., 1968. 'The Canosa Group of Hellenistic Glasses in the British Museum.' *Journal of Glass Studies* X: 21–47.

Harden, D. B., 1987. *Glass of the Caesars.* London.

Healy, J., 1978. *Mining and Metallurgy in the Greek and Roman World.* London.

Heddon, H. Parry, 1893. *Life of E. B. Pusey,* 4 vols. London.

Heid, S. and Dennert, M., 2012. *Personenlexikon zur Christlichen Archäologie: Forscher und Persönlichkeiten vom 16 bis 21 Jahrhundert*: (s.v.) 868–70. Regensburg.

Hellemo, G. and Waaler, E. R., 1989. *Adventus Domini: eschatological thought in 4th century apses and catacheses.* Leiden.

Herzog, E., 1861. 'Le catacombe degli Ebrei in Vigna Randanini.' *Bullettino dell'Instituto di Corrispondenza Archeologica* XXXIII: 91–104.

Hinks, R. P., 1933. *Catalogue of the Greek, Etruscan and Roman paintings and mosaics in the British Museum.* London.

Van der Hoek, A. and Herrmann Jr., John J., 2013. *Pottery, Pavements and Paradise: Iconographic and Textual Studies on Late Antiquity*. Supplement to *Vigiliae Christianae*, vol.122. Leiden and Boston.

Hollander, H., 1970. Isaiah, s.v. Isaias. In Kirschbaum, E., ed., *Lexikon der Christlichen Ikonographie* II: cols. 354–9. Rome.

Hopkins, Keith, 1983. *Death and Renewal.* Cambridge.

Howard-Johnston, J. and Hayward, P. A., eds., 1999. *The Cults of the Saints in Late Antiquity and the Middle Ages: Essay on the Contribution of Peter Brown.* New York and Oxford.

Howells, D. T., 2013. 'Making Late Antique Gold-glass.' In Entwistle and James, eds, 2013: 112–20.

Howells, D. T., 2015. *A Catalogue of the Late Antique Gold-Glass in the British Museum.* British Museum Research Publication 198. London.

Huskinson, J., 1982. *Concordia Apostolorum: Christian Propaganda in Rome in the Fourth and Fifth Centuries: a Study of Early Christian Iconography and Iconology.* Oxford.

Huskinson, J., 1999. 'Women and learning: gender and identity in scenes of intellectual life on late Roman sarcophagi.' In R. Miles, ed., *Constructing identities in late antiquity*: 190–213. London and New York.

Huskinson, J., 2015. *Roman Strigillated Sarcophagi. Art and Social History.* Oxford.

Ihm, C., 1960. *Die Programme der christlichen Apsismalerei vom vierten Jahrhundert bis zur Mitte des achten Jahrhunderts.* Wiesbaden.

Ilardi, K., 2015. 'Il codice Vat. lat. 9073: note preliminare.' In M. Buonocore, ed., 2000, II: 1314–38.

Jackson, C., 2005. 'Making colourless glass in the Roman period.' *Archaeometry* 47: 763–80.

Jackson, C. M., Cool, H. E. M. and Wager, E. C. W., 1998. 'The Manufacture of Glass in Roman York.' *Journal of Glass Studies* 40: 55–61.

Jaeger, M., 2008. *Archimedes and the Roman Imagination.* Ann Arbor, Michigan.

Jastrzebowska, E., 1979. 'Les scènes de banquet en peintre et en sculpture chrétienne du IIIe et du IVe siècles.' *Recherches Augustiniennes* 14: 3–90.

Jefferson, L. M., 2014. *Christ the Miracle Worker in Early Christian Art.* Minneapolis.

Jensen, R. M., 2000. *Understanding early Christian art.* London.

Jensen, R. M., 2007. Early Christian Images and exegesis. In J. Spier, ed.: 65–85.

Jensen, R. M., 2008. 'Dining with the Dead.' In L. Brink, O. P. and Deborah Green, eds, *Commemorating the Dead. Texts and Artifacts in Context*: 107–43. Berlin and New York.

Jensen, R. M., 2011. *Living Water: Images, Symbols and Settings of Early Christian Baptism.* Supplements to *Vigiliae Christianae* 105. Leiden.

Johns, C. M., 2010. *The Hoxne Late Roman Silver Treasure: gold jewellery and silver plate.* British Museum, London.

Johns, C. M. and Potter, T. W., 1983. *The Thetford Treasure: Roman jewellery and silver.* British Museum, London.

Jongste, P. F. B., 1992. *The twelve labours of Hercules on Roman sarcophagi.* London.

Kajanto, I., 1965. *The Latin Cognomina.* Helsinki.

Kaufmann-Heinimann, A., 1984. *Der Silberschatz von Kaiseraugst.* Römermuseum, Augst.

Kemp P., 1996. *Underwater warriors.* London.

Kessler, H. L., 1987. 'The Meeting of Peter and Paul in Rome: an Emblematic Narrative of Spiritual Brotherhood.' *Dumbarton Oaks Papers* 41: 265–75.

Koch, G., 2000. *Frühchristliche Sarkophage.* Munich.

Korhonen, K., 2001. 'Osservazioni sul collezionismo epigrafico siciliano.' *Arctus* 35: 85–102.

Korhonen, K., 2011. 'Language and identity in the Roman colonies of Sicily.' In R. Sweetman, ed., *Roman colonies in the first century of their formation*: 8–18. Oxford.

Kostof, S., 1965. *The Orthodox Baptistery of Ravenna.* New Haven.

Kottaridi, A., 2011. *Macedonian Treasures: a tour through the Museum of the Royal Tombs at Aigai* Athens.

Kraabel, A., 1979. 'Jews in Imperial Rome: More Archaeological Evidence from an Oxford Collection.' *Journal of Jewish Studies* 30: 41–58.

Kraemer, R., 1986. 'Non-literary evidence for Jewish women in Rome and Egypt. *Helios* 13: 85–101.

Ladner, G. B., 1941. *Die Papstbildnisse des Altertums und Mittelalters*, 3 vols. Vatican City.

Lambert, C. M., 2005. 'De tre epigrafi paleocristiane eclanesi ritrovate e di due recentemente scoperte.' *Vetera Christianorum* 42, 2: 289–305.

Lambert, C. M., 2008. *Studi di epigrafia tardoantica e medievale in Campania, vol.I. Secoli IV–VII.* Florence.

Lanciani, R., Malvezzi Campeggi, L. and Buzzetti, C., 2000. *Storia degli scavi di Roma e notizie intorno le collezioni romani di antichità* 6. Rome.

Lange, A. and Weigold, M., 2011. *Biblical quotations and allusions in second temple Jewish literature*, Göttingen.

Latyschev, B., ed., 1885. *Inscriptiones antiquae orae septentrionalis Ponti Euxini Graecae et Latinae*, 4 vols. St Petersburg.

Latyschev, B., ed., second edition, 1916. *Inscriptiones antiquae orae septentrionalis Ponti Euxini Graecae et Latinae.* St Petersburg.

Le Blant, E., 1879. 'Les bas-reliefs des sarcophages chrétiens et les liturgies funéraires.' *Revue Archéologique* n.s. 38: 223–41, 276–92.

Leclercq, H., 1932. 'Fonds de coupes.' In F. Cabrol and H. Leclercq, eds, *Dictionnaire d'Archéologie Chrétienne et de Liturgie*, VI: cols 2145–63.

Lega, C., 2003. 'Il cosidetto Tesoro della *Domus dei Valeri* al Museo Sacro Vaticano. Alcune osservazioni critiche', *Bollettino dei Monumenti Musei e Gallerie Pontificie* XXIII: 77–105.

Lega, C., 2012. 'Il corredo epigrafico dei vetri dorati: novità e considerazioni.' *Sylloge Epigrafica Barcinonensis* X: 263–86.

Lega, C., 2015. 'I vetri raccolti nel corpus delle iscrizioni cristiani di Gaetano Marini (codice Vat. lat. 9071).' In M. Buonocore, ed., II: 1211–53.

Leon, H. J., 1960. *The Jews of Ancient Rome.* Philadelphia.

Levi, D., 1941. 'The allegories of the months in classical art.' *Art Bulletin* 23: 251–91.

Levi, D., 1947. *Antioch Mosaic Pavements*, 2 vols. Princeton.

Levine, A., 2012. *The image of Christ in late antiquity: a case study of religious interaction.* D.Phil thesis, University of Oxford. https://ora.ox.ac.uk/object/uuid:bf650377-9f51-4e53-bb6f-d60d750745d3.

Lietzmann, H., 1923, 1993. 'The Tomb of the Apostles *ad catacumbas*.' *Harvard Theological Review* 16: 147–8, republished in E. Ferguson, D. M. Scholer and P. C. Finney, eds, 1993. *Studies in Early Christianity: A Collection of Scholarly Essays.* New York and London.

Lightfoot, C. S., ed., 2014. *Ennion. Master of Roman Glass.* New York, New Haven and London.

Ligorio, P., 1553. *Libro di M. Pyrrho Ligori Napolitano delle antichità di Roma, nel quale si tratta de' circi, theatri e anfiteatri, con le Paradosse del medesimo auttore, quai confutano la commune opinione sopra varii luoghi della città di Roma.* Venice.

Lipsius, S., 1588. *Inscriptiones antiquarum quae passim per Europam liber.* Leiden.

Longmead, G., 2006. *Memories of Welwyn Town and Village.* Welwyn, Hertfordshire.

Löx, M., 2013. *Monumenta Sanctorum. Rom und Mailand als Zentren des frühen Christentums. Märtyrkult und Kirchenbau unter den Bischöfen Damasus und Ambrosius.* Spätantike-frühes Christentum-Byzanz. Kunst im ersten Jahrtausend. Reihe B: Studien und Perspektiven, Bd. 39 Wiesbaden.

Lutraan, K. L., 2006. *Late Roman Gold-glass: Images and Inscriptions.* Unpublished Master's degree thesis, McMaster University.

Maffei, S., 1765. *Clarissimi viri Scipionis Maffei Marchionis Artis criticae lapidariae quae extant ex ejusdem autographo ab ... Ioh. Francisco Seguierio... et a Sebastiano Donato Presbytero Lucensi*. Lucca.

Magness, J., 2005. 'Heaven on Earth: Helios and the Zodiac Cycle in Ancient Palestinian Synagogues.' *Dumbarton Oaks Papers* 59: 1–52.

Maguire, H., 1987. *Earth and Ocean. The Terrestrial World in Early Byzantine Art*. University Park, Pennsylvania.

Mai, A., 1831. *Scriptorum veterum nova collectio e Vaticanis codicibus edita*, v.1. Rome.

Mariani, I. Miarelli and Moretti, S., 2015. 'Seroux D'Agincourt e l'<amico carissimo>.' In M. Buonocore, ed., 2015, II: 1568–93.

Marini, G., 1795. *Gli atti a monumenti de'Fratelli Arvali scolpiti già in tavole di marmo ed ora raccolti, dicifera*. Rome.

Marini, M., 1822. *Degli aneddoti di Gaetano Marini, commentario di Marino Marini. Catalogo de' manoscritti che furono di monsignor Gaetano Marini*. Rome.

Martiniello, L., 1996. *Aeclanum tra archeologia e storia*. S. Pietro di Montoro Superiore (Avellino).

Marrucchi, O., 1912. *Christian Epigraphy. An Elementary Treatise*. J. Armine Willis, trans. Cambridge.

Mathews, T., 1993. *The clash of gods: a reinterpretation of early Christian art*. Princeton.

Matthiae, G., 1967. *Mosaici medioevale delle chiese di Roma*, 2 vols. Rome.

Mazzei, B., ed., 2010. *Il cubicolo degli Apostoli nelle catacombe romane di Santa Tecla: Cronaca di una scoperta*. Vatican City.

Mazzoleni, D., 1980. 'Iscrizioni giudaiche nell'antica Roma.' *Mondo Archeologico* 49: 28–31.

Mazzoleni, D., 2011. 'Le iscrizioni musive della Grado basilica di S. Eufemia nel "Vat. Lat. 9071 di Gaetano Marini".' *Marmoribus Vestita* 2 (Studi di Antichità Cristiana, 63): 923–44. Vatican City.

Mazzoleni, D., 2015. 'I codici Vat. lat. 9071–9074 di Gaetano Marini.' In M. Buonocore, ed., 2015, II: 1254–1261.

McKenzie, J., 2007. *The art and architecture of Alexandria and Egypt, c.300 B.C. to A.D. 700*. New Haven.

Mecenate, R., 1823. *Osservazioni sugli aneddoti di Monsignor Gaetano Marini. Pubblicati nel commentario da suo nipote monsignor Marino Marini*. Rome.

Meek, A., 2013. *Gold-Glass in Late Antiquity: Scientific Analysis of the British Museum Collection*. In Entwistle and James, eds: 121–30.

Meek, A., 2015. 'The scientific analysis of the British Museum's gold glass collection.' In Howells, ed., 2015: 30–40.

Meredith, H. G., 2015. 'Engaging Mourners and Maintaining Unity: Third and Fourth Century Gold-Glass Roundels from Roman Catacombs.' *Religion in the Roman Empire* 1: 219–41.

Meredith, H. G., 2015b. *Word becomes image. Openwork vessels as a reflection of late antique transformation*. Oxford.

Milojčić, V., 1970. 'Zu den spätkaiserzeitlichen und merovingischen Silberlöffeln.' *49. Bericht der Römisch-Germanischen Kommission 1968*: 111–48.

Minoccheri, L., 1894. *Cenni storici sulla lipsanoteca del vicariato in Roma e sua annua esposizione delle sante reliquie*. Rome.

Momigliano, A., 1950. 'Ancient history and the antiquarian.' *Journal of the Warburg and Courtauld Institutes* 13, nos 3/4: 285–315.

Mommsen, T., ed., 1852. *Inscriptiones Regni Neapolitani Latinae*. Leipzig.

Mommsen, T., ed., 1883. *Corpus Inscriptionum Latinarum X: Inscriptiones Bruttiorum, Lucaniae, Campaniae, Siciliae, Sardiniae Latinae*. Berlin.

Morcelli, S. A., 1781. *Steph. Antonii Morcelli De stilo inscriptionum Latinarum libri* 3. Rome.

Morey, C. R., 1942. *Early Christian Art*. Princeton.

Morey, C. R., 1959. *The Gold-Glass Collection of the Vatican Library with additional catalogues of other gold-glass collections*G. Ferrari, ed. Vatican City.

Morris, I., 1992. *Death-Ritual and Social Structure in Classical Antiquity*. Cambridge.

Müller, N., 1912. *Die jüdische Katakombe am Monteverde zu Rom. Der älteste bisher bekannt gewordene jüdische Friedhof des Abendlandes*. Leipzig.

Musumarra, C., 1958–9. 'La cultura a Catania tra la fine del sec. XVIII e la prima metà del XIX.' *Archivio Storico per la Sicilia Orientale* XI–XII: 65–122.

Nagy, L., 2016. 'Myth and Salvation in the Fourth Century: Representations of Hercules in Christian Contexts.' In M. R. Salzmann, M. Sághy and R. L. Testa, eds, *Pagans and Christians in Late Antique Rome: Conflict, Competition and Coexistence in the Fourth Century*: 377–398. Cambridge.

Negroni, A., 2015. 'Il codice Vat. Lat. 9074: composizione e caratteristiche.' In M. Buonocore, ed., 2013, II: 1339–78.

Nenna, M.-D., ed., 2000. *La Route du Verre. Ateliers primaires et secondaires du second millénaire av. J-C. au Moyen Âge*. Colloque organisé en 1989 par l'Association Française pour l'Archéologie du Verre. Travaux de la Maison de l'Orient et de la Méditerranée Jean Pouilloux 33. Lyon.

Nestori, A., 1993. *Repertorio topografico delle pitture delle catacombe Romane. II edizione reveduta ed aggiornata*. Roma Sotterranea Cristiana, per cura del PIAC V. Vatican City.

Nestori, A., 1998. 'G. B. de Rossi e la Pontificia Commissione di Archeologia Sacra.' *Acta XIII Congressus Internationalis Archaeologiae Christianae*: 185–204. Vatican City–Split.

Nieddu, A. M., 1998. 'Bibliografia di Enrico Stevenson.' *In memoria di Enrico Stevenson nel 1. centennaio della morte. Rivista di Archeologia Cristiana* 74: 15–26.

Norris, D. E., 2015. 'Illuminating late Roman Gold Glass.' *Ashmolean Magazine* 66: 6–7. http://www.glassreflections.sgt.org/eP/eP004.pdf

Northcote, J. S. and Brownlow, W. R., 1868, 1879. *Roma Sotterranea or an account of the Roman catacombs especially of the cemetery at San Callixtus; compiled from the works of Commendatore de Rossi with the consent of the author*. London.

Noy, D., 1995. *Jewish Inscriptions of Western Europe, vol.2. The city of Rome*. Cambridge.

Nüsse. H.-G., 2008. 'Römische Goldgläser – alte und neue Ansätze zu Werkstattfrage.' *Prähistorische Zeitschrift* 83: 222–56.

Oakeshott, W., 1967. *The mosaics of Rome from the third to the fourteenth centuries*. London.

Oliver, J. H., 1965. 'Texts A and B of the Horosthesia Dossier at Istros.' *Greek, Roman and Byzantine Studies* 6: 143–56.

Olivier-Poli, G., 1825. *Continuazione al nuovo dizionario istorico degli uomini che si sono renduti piu' celebri per talenti, virtù, sceleratazze, errori, ecc., la quale abbraccia il periodo gli ultimi 40 anni dell'era volgare*, tomo VII. Naples.

Orsi, P., 1896. 'Siracusa. Di una necropoli dei bassi tempi riconosciuta nalla contrada "Grotticelli".' *Notizie degli Scavi*: 334–56.

Orsi, P., 1913. 'Di alcuni ipogei recentemente scoperti a Siracusa.' *Notizie degli scavi*: 257–75.

Osiek, C., 2006. *A Woman's Place: House Churches in Earliest Christianity*. Minneapolis.

Osiek, C., 2008. 'Roman and Christian Burial Practices and the Patronage of Women.' In L. Brink, O. P. and Deborah Green, eds, *Commemorating the Dead. Texts and Artifacts in Context*: 243–70. Berlin and New York.

Ovadiah, R. and A., 1987. *Hellenistic, Roman and early Byzantine mosaic pavements in Israel*. Rome.

Palma, B. and de Lachenal, L., 1983. *Museo Nazionale Romano, vol.1. Le sculture. 5. I Marmi Ludovisi nel Museo Nazionale Romano*. Rome.

Palmer, R. E. A., 1990. 'Cults of Hercules, Apollo Caelispex and Fortuna in and around the Roman cattle market.' *Journal of Roman Archaeology* 3: 234–44.

Paolucci, F., 1997. *I vetri incise dall'Italia settentrionale e dalla Rezia nel periodo medio e tardo imperiale*. Florence.

Paolucci, F., 2002. *L'arte del vetro inciso*. Florence.

Parisi, N., 1971. *Dizionario Biografico degli Italiani* 13: 257–9, s.v. BOSIO, Antonio. Rome.

Partyka, J. S., 1993. *La resurrection de Lazare dans les monuments funéraires des necropoles chrétiennes à Rome*. Warsaw.

Pentland, J. B., 1867. *A Handbook of Rome and its Environs*. Eighth edition. London.

Pepe, L., 1996. 'L'Istituto nazionale della Repubblica romana.' *Mélanges de l'École Française de Rome* 108: 703–20.

Perler, O., 1953. *Die Mosaiken in der Juliergruft im Vatikan*. Freiburg.

Physick, J. F., 1982. *The Victoria and Albert Museum: the History of its Building*. London.

Pietri, C., 1961. 'Concordia Apostolorum e renovatio Urbis.' *Mélanges de l'École Française de Rome* 73: 275–322.

Pietri, C., 1976. *Roma Cristiana: recherches sur l'Église de Rome, son organisation, sa politique, son idéologie de Miltiade à Sixte III (311–440)*. Rome.

Pillinger, R., 1985. 'Notizien zur "Drachentötung des Daniel" auf dem Elfenbeinkästen von Brescia.' *Pro Arte Antiqua: Festschrift für Hedwig Kenner*. Sonderschriften. Österreichisches

Archäologisches Institut, Band 18: 285–95. Vienna.

Poddi, M., 2015. 'Considerazioni di carattere generale sul codice Vat. lat. 9071 di Gaetano Marini.' In M. Buonocore, ed., 2015, II: 1262–78.

Policastro, G., 1950. *Catania nel Settecento; costume, architettura, scultura, pittura, musica*. Turin.

Polverini Fossi, I., 1992. '"Siam sempre sosopra ed in gran moto per I francesi." Gli echi della rivoluzione nelle lettere di Gaetano Marini a Carlo Eugenio Duca di Würtemberg (1789–1793).' *Archivio della Società Romana di Storia Patria* 115: 181–215.

Price, J., 2015. 'Bowls in two halves, a curious feature of some late Roman tableware.' *JGS* 57: 41–6.

Priuli, S., 1991. 'Inscriptiones Latinae Liberae Rei Publicae'. In *Epigrafia: Actes du colloque en mémoire de A. Degrassi*. Coll.EFR 143: Università de Roma-La Sapienza and École Française de Rome: 288–99. Rome.

Provoost, A., 1995. '*Les representations de martyrs à la fin de l'Antiquité.' Martyrium in multidisciplinary perspective: memorial Louis Reekmans*. Leuven.

Ramieri, A. M., 1998. 'E. Stevenson: cenni biografici ed inediti documenti.' In memoria di *Enrico Stevenson nel 1.centennaio della morte. Rivista di Archeologia Cristiana* 74: 329–51.

Rébillard, E., 2009. *The Care of the Dead in Late Antiquity*. Elizabeth Trapnell Rawlings and Jeanine Routier-Pucci, trans. Cornell, New York.

Recupero, A., 1797. 'Lettera a Signor Saint-Vincent su le collezioni di medaglie.' *Magazzino Enciclopedico di Millin* 1: 340–63.page nos?

Recupero, A., 1815. *Storia Naturale e Generale dell'Etna, del Canonico Giuseppe Recupero. Opera Postuma*, 2 vols. Palermo.

Recupero, Giacinto, 1834. 'Alessandro Recupero.' *Giornale di scienze, letteratura ed arti per la Sicilia*; Tomo 47, Anno 12, Luglio, Agosto e Settembre: 158–63. Palermo.

Recupero, Giacomo, 1834. *Per lo stabilmento di un Istituto archeologico nella R. Università degli Studi di Catania*. Catania.

Recupero, Giuseppe, 1808. *Monumenti antichi inediti della collezione Recuperiana*. Palermo.

Reinsburg, C., 2006. *Die Sarkophage mit Darstellungen aus dem Menschenleben. Dritter Teil. Vita Romana*. Antike Sarkophagreliefs I.3. Berlin.

Reutter, U., 2009. *Damasus, Bischof von Rom (366–384): Leben und Werk*. Tübingen.

Reynolds, J. and Tannenbaum, R., 1983. *Jews and Godfearers at Aphrodisias*. Cambridge Philological Society, Supplementary Volume 12. Cambridge.

Rini, D., 2006. '"Serra lignea" alle origini dell'iconografia martiriale del profeta Isaia.' *Annali della Pontificia Insigne Accademia di Belle Arti e Lettere dei Virtuosi al Pantheon* 6: 257–76.

Rini, D., 2015. 'Gaetano Marini e l'antiquaria a Roma tra Settecento e Ottocento.' In M. Buonocore, ed., vol.II: 1488–1515.

Ristow, S., 2007. *Frühes Christentum im Rheinland. Die Zeugnisse der archäologischen und historischen Quellen an Rhein, Maas und Mosel*. Cologne, Münster.

Robert, L., 1937. 'Inscriptions juives, grecques et latines à Oxford.' *Revue des Études Juives* 102: 121.

Robert, L., 1946. 'Un corpus des inscriptions juives.' *Hellenica* iii: 90–8. Paris.

Robert, J. and Robet, L., 1979. 'Bulletin épigraphique.' *Revue des Études Grecques* 92, no.438: 413–541.

Rocciolo, D., 2008. 'Marini, Gaetano.' *Dizionario biografico degli italiani*, vol.70: 451–4. Rome.

Rossi, D. and di Mento, M., eds., 2013. *La catacomba ebraica di Monteverde: vecchi dati e nuove scoperte*. Rome.

Rowe, N., 2011. *The Jew, the Cathedral and the Medieval City: Synagoga and Ecclesia in the thirteenth Century*. Cambridge.

Russell, G., 1819. *A Tour through Sicily in the year 1815*. London.

Rutgers, L. V., 1988. 'Ein *in situ* erhaltenes Sarkophagfragment in der jüdischen Katakombe an der Via Appia.' *Jewish Art* 14: 16–27.

Rutgers, L. V., 1995. *The Jews of Late Ancient Rome: Evidence of Cultural interaction in the Roman Diaspora*. Religions of the Greek and Roman World 12. New York and Leiden.

Sághy, M., 2010. 'Martyr Cult and collective Identity in fourth-century Rome.' In A. Marinković and T. Vedriš, eds, *Identity and Alterity in hagiography and the Cult of Saints*: 17–35. Zagreb.

Sághy, M., 2012. *Renovatio memoriae*: Pope Damasus and the Martyrs of Rome. In R. Behrwald and C. Witschel, eds., *Rom in der Spätantike: historische Erinnerung im städtischen Raum*: 251–67. Stuttgart.

Sághy, M., 2016. '*Romanae gloria plebis*: Bishop Damasus and the Traditions of Rome.' In M. Salzmann, M. Sághy and R. L. Testa, eds, *Pagans and Christians in Late Antique Rome: Conflict, Competition and Co-existence in the Fourth Century*: 314–27. Cambridge.

Salzmann, M. R., 1990. *On Roman time: the codex-calendar of 354 and the rhythms of urban life in late antiquity*. Berkeley.

Salvatore, A., 1982. *Aeclanum*. Avellino.

Schermann, T., 1907. *Prophetarum Vitae Fabulosae*. Leipzig.

Schermann, T., 1907b. *Propheten und Apostellegenden nebst Jüngerkatalogen des dorotheus und verwandter Texte*. Leipzig.

Schibille, N., Degryse, P., O'Hea, M., Izmer, A., Vanhaecke, F. and McKenzie, J., 2012. 'Late Roman Glass from the "Great Temple" at Petra and Khirbet et-Tannur, Jordan – Technology and Provenance.' *Archaeometry* 54, 6: 997–1022.

Schlosser, H., 1966. 'Die Daniel-Susanna-Erzählung in Bild und Literatur der christlichen Frühzeit.' In W. N. Schumacher, ed., *Tortulae: Studien zu altchristlichen und byzantinischen Monumenten. Römische Quartalschrift für christliche Altertumskunde und Kirchengeschichte* 30. Supplementheft: 243–9. Rome.

Schultz, C. E., 2000. 'Modern Prejudice and Ancient Praxis: Female Worship of Hercules at Rome.' *Zeitschrift für Papyrologie und Epigrafik* 133: 291–7.

Schmidt, T. M., 1980. 'Ein jüdisches Goldglas in der frühchristlich-byzantinischen Sammlung.' *Staatliche Museen zu Berlin, Forschungen und Berichte* 20, 1: 273–80.

Scott, R., Braekmans, D., Brems, D. and Degryse, P. 2012a. 'Danger: High Voltage! The Application of Handheld X-ray flourescence (HH-XRF) to Experimental Glass: Pitfalls and Potentials.' In R. B. Scott, D. Braekmans, M. Carremans and P. Degryse, eds, *Proceedings of the 39th International Symposium for Archaeometry*, Leuven: 268–273.

Scott, R. B., Shortland, A. J., Degryse, P., Power, M., Domoney, K., Bryen, S. and Braekmans, D., 'The analysis of in-situ 17th-century painted glass from Christ Church Cathedral, Oxford.' *Glass-Technol. Part A*. 53: 65–73.

Schraudolph, E., 1993. *Römische Götterwiehungen mit Reliefschmuck aus Italien. Altäre, Basen und Reliefs. Archäologie und Geschichte herausgegeben von Tonio Hölscher* Band 2. Heidelberg.

Schrenk, S., 1995. *Typus und Antitypus in der frühchristlichen Kunst*. Münster.

Schüler, I.,1966. 'A Note on Jewish Gold Glasses.' *Journal of Glass Studies* 8: 46–61.

Seroux d'Agincourt, J. B., 1823. *Histoire de l'art par les monuments depuis decadence su IVe siècle jusqu'à son renouvellement au XVIe, III: Peinture*. Paris.

Shelton, K. J., 1981. *The Esquiline Treasure*. London.

Sherlock, D., 1973. 'Zu einer Fundliste antiker Silberlöffel.' *Bericht der Römisch-Germanischen Kommission* 54: 203–11.

Smith, S. L., 2000. *Gold-glass vessels of the late Roman empire: production, context and function*. Unpublished doctoral dissertation, Rutgers State University of New Jersey, New Brunswick, N.J.

Solin, H., 1982. *Die griechische Personennamen in Rom. Ein Namenbuch*. Berlin and New York.

Solin, H., 2003. *Die griechische personennamen in Rom. Ein Namenbuch*. Second edition. Berlin and New York.

Sotomayor, M., 1963. 'Una importante y mal conocida colección de objetos paleocristianos.' *Römische Quartalschrift* 58: 223–9.

Spier, J., 2007a: *Picturing the Bible*, exh. cat., Kimbell Art Museum. Fort Worth, Texas.

Spier, J., 2007b. *Late Antique and Early Christian Gems* (vol title). Spätantike, frühes Christentum, Byzanz (series). Kunst im ersten Jahrtausend, Reihe B, 20. Wiesbaden.

Spieser, J.-M., 2015. *Images du Christ des catacombs aux lendemains de l'iconoclasme*. Geneva.

Spinazzè, S., 2010. 'Artisti antiquari a Roma tra la fine dell'Ottocento de l'inizio del Novecento: lo studio e la galleria di Attilio Simonetti.' *Studiolo* 8: 103–22.

Steen, O., 2002. 'The Apse Mosaic of S. Pudenziana and its Relation to the Fifth century Mosaics of S. Sabina and S. Maria Maggiore.' In F. Guidobaldi and A. Guiglia Guidobaldi, eds, *Ecclesiae Urbis. Atti del Congresso Internazionale di Studi sulle chiese di Roma*, vol.3: 1939–48. Vatican City.

Stern, E. M., 1999. 'Roman Glassblowing in a Cultural Context.' *American Journal of Archaeology* 103: 441–84.

Stuiber, A., 1957. *Refrigerium Interim*. Bonn.

Tait, H., 1991. *Five Thousand Years of Glass*. British Museum, London.

Taylor, A., 2002. 'The Problem of Labels: Three Marble Shepherds in Nineteenth-Century Rome.' In E. K. Gazda, ed., *The Ancient Art of Emulation: Studies in Artistic Originality and Tradition from the Present to Classical Antiquity*. Ann Arbor, Michigan.

Tellini, B. and Manodoro, A., 1995. *Messer Filippo Nero, santo: l'apostolo di Roma*. Exh. cat., Valicelliana Library. Rome.

Testini, P., 1969. 'L'iconografia degli apostoli Pietro e Paolo nelle cosiddette 'arti minori'.' *Saecularia Pietro e Paolo*: 241–323. Vatican City.

Thacker, A., 2007. 'Rome of the Martyrs: Saints, Cults and Relics. Fourth to Seventh Centuries.' In E. Ó'Carragain and C. Neuman de Vegvar, eds, *Roma Felix: Formation and Reflexions of Medieval Rome*: 13–49. Aldershot.

Thümmel, H. G., 1994. 'Tertullians Hirtenbecher, die Goldgläser und die Frühgeschichte der christlichen Bestattung.' *Boreas* 17: 257–65.

Thunø, E., 2015. *The Apse Mosiac in Early Medieval Rome: Time, Network and Repetition*. New York and Cambridge.

Tiberia, V., 2003. *Il mosaico di Santa Pudenziana a Roma. Il Restauro*. Todi.

Tisserant, E., 1909. *L'Ascension d'Isaie*. Paris.

Tkacz, C. B., 1991. 'Commendatio animae.' *Oxford Dictionary of the Bible* 1: 488. Oxford.

Tkacz, C. B., 2002. *The key to the Brescia Casket: typology and the early Christian imagination*. Notre Dame, Indiana.

Tognini, C., 1884. *La coltura letteraria e scientifica in Rimini*. Rimini.

Tomlin, R., 2005. 'The sociolinguistics of address in Latin.' *Journal of Roman Archaeology* 18: 648–9.

Torrey, C. C., 1946. *The Lives of the Prophets*. Philadelphia.

Toynbee, J. M. C., 1971. *Death and Burial in the Roman World*. London.

Tronzo, W., 1986. *The Via Latina catacomb: imitation and discontinuity in fourth-century Roman painting*. London.

Trout, D. E., 2003. 'Damasus and the Invention of Early Christian Rome.' *Journal of Medieval and Early Modern Studies* 33.3: 517–36.

Tyskiewicz, M., 1898. *Memories of an Old Collector*. London.

Tuck, S. L., 2005. *Latin inscriptions in the Kelsey Museum: the Denuison and De Criscio collections*. AnnArbor, Michigan.

Utro, U., 1997. 'Médaille en bronze représentant les Apôtres Pierre et Paul.' *Pierre et Rome: vingt siècles d'élan créateur*. 98–9, no.22. Paris.

Utro, U., 2003. 'Le immagini e il culto dei santi sui vetri dorati durante il pontificato di Damaso e Siricio (366-399) in 387 d.c.' In R. Pasini, ed., *Ambrogio e Agostino: le sorgenti dell'Europa. Catalogo della mostra, Milano, Museo Diocesano 7 dicembre 2003–2 maggio 2004*: 136–41. Milan.

Van der Horst, P. W., 1991. *Ancient Jewish epitaphs: an introductory survey of a millennium of Jewish funerary epigraphy (300 BCE–700 CE)*. Kampen.

Vanni, F. M., 2003. 'Bibbia e Vangelo nei vetri.' In P. Pasini, ed., *387 d.c.: Ambrogio e Agostino: le sorgenti dell'Europa*. Catalogo della mostra, Milano, Museo Diocesano 7 dicembre 2003 – 2 maggio 2004: 135–8. Milan.

Vattuone, L., 2000. 'I vetri dorati della collezione Wilshere nella Pusey House di Oxford.' *Annales du 14e congrès de l'Association Internationale pour l'Histoire du Verre*: 132–6.

Vermeule, C. C. and von Bothmer, D., 1959. 'Notes on a new edition of *Michaelis: Ancient Marbles in Great Britain*, Part Three: 2.' *American Journal of Archaeology* 63: 341–2.

Vickers, M. J., 1992. *The Ancient Romans*. Ashmolean Museum, Oxford.

Vickers, M. J., 2009–11. 'The Wilshere Collection of early Christian antiquities in the Ashmolean Museum, Oxford.' In *Miscellanea Emilio Marin, sexagenario dicata. Kačić, Acta provinciae SS. Redemptris Ordinis Fratrum Minorum in Croatia* 42: 605–14. Split.

Visconti, E. Q., 1798. *Lettera su due monumenti nel quale è memoria di Antonia Augusta*. Letta nella seduta della classe di filosofia, lettere e arti dell'Istituto Nazionale della Republica Romana Il dì 13 Pratile Anno VI. Rome.

Vopel, H., 1899. *Die altchristlicehn Goldgläser: ein Beitrag zur altchristlichen Kunst und Kulturgeschichte*. Freiburg.

Walker, S., 1985. 'The marble quarries of Proconnesus: isotopic evidence for the age of the quarries and for *lenos*-sarcophagi carved at Rome.' In P. Pensabene, ed., *Marmi Antichi. Problemi d'impiego, di restauro e d'identificazione. Studi Miscellanei* 26: 57–65. Rome.

Walker, S., 1990. 'The sarcophagus of Maconiana Severiana.' In G. Koch, ed., *Roman Funerary Monuments in the J. Paul Getty Museum*, vol.1: 83–94. Malibu, California.

Walker, S., Shortland, A. J. and Henderson, J., 2017 forthcoming: 'Patterns in Production: the Wilshere Collection of Gold-Glass Examined.' In D. Rosenow, I. Freestone, M. Phelps and A. Meek, eds, *Things that Travelled – Mediterranean Glass in the First Millenium AD. Conference held at University College, London, the British Museum and the Wallace Collection, in co-operation with the Association for the History of Glass, London 27th – 29th November 2014*. University College London Publishing.

Wallis, F. W., 1993. *Popular Anti-Catholicism in Mid-Victorian Britain*. Lampeter.

Ward-Perkins, J. B. and Throckmorton, P., 1965. 'The San Pietro Shipwreck.' *Archaeology* 18: 201–9.

Webb, M., 2010. *The Churches and Catacombs of Early Christian Rome* (second edition). Brighton.

Webster, T. B. L., 1929. 'The Wilshere Collection at Pusey House in Oxford.' *Journal of Roman Studies* 19: 150–4.

Weinberg, G. D., 1988. *Excavations at Jalame: site of a glass factory in late Roman Palestine*. Columbia, Missouri.

Weitzmann, K., 1951. *Greek Mythology in Byzantine Art*. Princeton.

Weitzmann, K., ed., 1979. *Age of Spirituality: Late Antique and Early Christian art, third to seventh Century*. New York.

Wharton, A. J., 1995. *Refiguring the post-classical city: Dura-Europos, Jerash, Jerusalem and Ravenna*. Cambridge and New York.

Whitehouse, D. B., 1999. 'Glass in the epigrams of Martial.' *Journal of Glass Studies* 41: 73–81.

Whitehouse, D. B., 2001. *Roman Glass in the Corning Museum of Glass* II. New York.

Whitehouse, D. B., 2004: 'Glass in the Price Edict of Diocletian.' *Journal of Glass Studies* 46: 189–91.

Wight, K., 2011. *Molten Color. Glassmaking in Antiquity*. The J. Paul Getty Museum, Malibu, California.

Williams, M., 2002. '*Alexander, bubularus de macello*: humble sausage-seller or Europe's first identifiable purveyor of kosher beef?' *Latomus* 61: 122–33.

Wilpert, J., 1909. *Die Papstgräber und die Cäciliengruft in der Katakombe des hl. Kallistus*. Freiburg im Breisgau.

Wilpert, J., 1910. *La cripta dei papi e la cappella di Santa Cecilia nel Cimitero de Callisto*. Rome.

Wilpert, J., 1916. *Die römischer Mosaiken der kirchlichen Bauten vom IV. –XIII. Jahrhundert*. Freiburg im Briesgau.

Wilpert, J., 1929. *I sarcofagi cristiani antichi*, vol.I. Vatican City.

Winter, J., 1910. *The Myth of Hercules at Rome*. New York.

Wischmeyer, W., 1982. *Die Tafeldeckel der christlichen Sarkophage konstantinischer Zeit in Rom: Studien zur Struktur, Ikongraphie und Epigraphik*. Rome.

Wurch-Kozelj, M. and Kozelji, T., 1995. 'Roman quarries of apse-sarcophagi in Thassos of the second and third centuries.' In Y. Maniatis, N. Herz and Y. Basiakos, eds, *The study of marble and other stones used in antiquity*: 39–50. London.

Yasin, A. M., 2009. *Saints and Church Spaces in the Late Antique Mediterranean: architecture, cult and community*. Cambridge.

Index

This index is in alphabetical, word by word order. It does not cover the Contents List, Preface, Acknowledgements or Bibliography. Location references are to page number (Roman numerals), figure number (italic) and catalogue number (bold) and appear in that order.